Deciphering the City

William A. Schwab
The University of Arkansas

PEARSON
Prentice
Hall

Upper Saddle River, New Jersey 07458

Library of Congress Cataloging-in-Publication Data

Schwab, William A.
   Deciphering the city/William A. Schwab.
      p. cm.
   Includes bibliographical references and index.
   ISBN 0-13-113495-7
      1. Cities and towns.   2. Sociology, Urban.   I. Title.

HT151.S3215 2005
307.76—dc22

2004003246

Publisher: Nancy Roberts
Executive Editor: Chris DeJohn
Assistant Editor: Sharon Chambliss
Editorial Assistant: Kristin Haegele
Full Service Production Liaison: Joanne Hakim
Senior Marketing Manager: Marissa Feliberty
Marketing Assistant: Adam Laitman
Assistant Manufacturing Manager: Mary Ann Gloriande
Cover Art Director: Jayne Conte
Cover Design: Koala Bear Design
Manager, Cover Visual Research & Permissions: Karen Sanatar
Cover Illustration/Photo: Lowell Boileau, "Dawn" © Lowell Boileau, http://atDetroit.net
Composition/Full-Service Project Management: Brenda Averkamp/Carlisle Communications
Printer/Binder: Phoenix Book Tech Park

Credits and acknowledgments borrowed from other sources and reproduced, with permission, in this textbook appear on appropriate page within text.

Pearson Education LTD., London
Pearson Education Singapore, Pte. Ltd
Pearson Education Canada, Ltd
Pearson Education—Japan
Pearson Education Australia PTY, Limited

Pearson Education North Asia Ltd
Pearson Educacíon de Mexico, S.A. de C.V.
Pearson Education Malaysia, Pte. Ltd.
Pearson Education, Upper Saddle River, New Jersey

10 9 8 7 6 5 4 3 2 1
ISBN: 0-13-113495-7

For my children Jennifer, Mark, and Judd
In hope of a peaceful future in the global era

Brief Contents

Contents

Preface

Cities have always fascinated me. I remember as a young boy driving through the neighborhoods of Cincinnati on family outings wondering to myself why the people and buildings were located where they were. Although I pursued a degree in urban planning before choosing urban sociology for my doctoral work, it was the depth and scope of urban sociology that attracted me to the field. Where else can one study the historical development of cities, compare urban patterns across cultures, explore the behaviors associated with urban life, describe the contribution cities make to the global economy, examine the internal structure of cities, and study neighborhoods with the same techniques used by anthropologists to study preliterate tribes?

Although forty years have passed since those family outings, I am still fascinated with the city. I have been a sociologist for thirty years and have worked on international development projects for the past decade in Bolivia and Jordan. The urban sociological lens has served me well. Whether I am in Cairo, Damascus, Amman, or Irbid, Jordan, or La Paz, Santa Cruz, Sucre, or Cochabamba, Bolivia, the cultures are different, but the underlying physical and social patterns of these cities are the same. In fact, my work in the developing world motivated me to write this text. First, through my work in the Middle East and Latin America, I am convinced that we are in the midst of a revolution called *globalization* that is transforming our lives and cities. This is a theme I weave throughout the book. Second, my work abroad proves that the lens of sociology makes known the city's patterns and processes. And third, I want to share my sheer delight of applying this knowledge to deciphering the city. The book examines not only many of the central issues in urban sociology, but provides practical tools for the real world. For example, I apply this knowledge to everyday problems like reading the patterns of the city, making strangers known and safe, finding an apartment or buying a house, and not becoming a victim.

Following the introductory chapter "Why Study the City?," the first section of the book consists of two chapters designed to introduce you to the revolution of globalization. The global era began with the fall of the Berlin Wall on November 9, 1989. Before the wall's fall, there were two competing ideologies in the world—one socialist and one capitalist. In the first years following the fall, many theorists thought that the competition had ended, and free-market capitalism and liberal democracy had become the dominant ideology shaping the world's societies and economies. Since September 11, 2001, thinking has changed. Many theorists now think that economic competition has been replaced by competition between civilizations. Chapter 2 explores globalization and its consequences for cities in the more-developed world. We will examine what forces made globalization possible; how these changes affect the social, political, and economic institutions of these societies; how globalization has changed the role of cities in the global economy;

and who has won and who has lost in this new world order. Chapter 3 shifts this discussion to the less-developed world. In this chapter, we explore issues surrounding development, population change, and urbanization in these societies. We will see why population growth is the critical issue facing the world, the theories used to describe population change, the effects of rapid population growth on these societies, and how rapid growth shapes urban patterns—primacy and spontaneous settlements—in the less-developed world. We end the chapter by exploring theories of development, and why sociologists have trouble explaining development.

Section two consists of three chapters that introduce you to the psychology of the city and the community building process. In chapter 4 we explore the world of strangers and the techniques we use to make strangers known and less threatening. We all create and use mental maps of the city. We explore how we use these maps to add to our sense of community, safety, and well-being. We apply what we have learned to reduce your chances of becoming a crime victim, and I share some survival strategies that have kept my students and me safe all over the world.

Chapters 5 and 6 explore community—the social aspects of urban life. What is community? Are the images of the community of the past correct? Do members of modern societies have shallow and superficial relationships? Do we still have ties to kin and neighbors? These are some of the important questions facing sociologists. To answer them, I present the evolution of the concept of community over the past two centuries. In chapter 5, we explore the ideas and theories of community in the modern world. Chapter 6 addresses these same questions for the postmodern world in which we now live. I think you will find these chapters helpful in understanding how we cope in today's world and why we live our lives the way we do within our communities.

The third section of the book consists of five chapters that introduce you to the city's structure and the forces that shape it. In chapter 7, we learn how to read the patterns of the city. I present the early attempts by sociologists, economists, and geographers to develop urban models. We see how the assumptions of these models have changed and examine an alternative model developed by Michael White that provides a template for reading North American cities. We then turn to the work of social scientists who see the city through very different lenses. The first is the work of the political economist and geographer David Harvey. Harvey uses a Marxist lens to describe a group of powerful and influential actors who shape the cityscape for their own ends—profit. Next, we see the city through a lens provided by a group of social scientists from southern California known as the Los Angeles School. They use a postmodern lens to describe a decentered, decentralized, and randomly patterned cityscape made up of a series of new urban elements like edge cities and privatopias. They describe a city shaped by the forces of globalization.

Purchasing a new home is the largest investment most Americans make in their lifetimes. And most buyers know that if they make a bad home purchase, it will haunt them for decades. In chapter 8, we explore the how, why, when, and where of housing. We discuss how people make the decision to move and what factors enter into this decision. We explore how, why, and where people search for a new home and where they eventually locate. And we see the consequences of these decisions on neighborhoods, communities, and society. Chapter 9 applies the principles learned in the previous chapter to a problem that I hope each of you will face—buying a home. I call chapter 9 a house-buying primer. We walk through the home-buying experiences of two young couples, my former students. We follow them through the home-buying process, uncover tips on being a good consumer, and discover how to get information on houses, neighborhoods, and communities using the Internet and other sources.

Sociologists study many urban patterns. In chapter 10, we look at the changing relationship between the central city and fringe. Are suburbs a new phenomenon, or do they represent the normal fringe development of a city? Are the images of the suburb as the bastion of the well-educated, white, affluent middle class, and the central city as the home of the poor, uneducated, and minorities correct? Are suburbs all alike or are there different suburban types? Does suburban growth intensify the political, social, and economic problems of the central cities, or is this a myth? Are the needs of women, the elderly, and minorities met in the suburbs? These questions are important to sociologists, and we use data from Census 2000 to answer them. We will also examine the problem of urban sprawl in this chapter.

Segregation is another important pattern of the city. Social scientists recognize that income, race, and ethnicity not only divide the nation, but also shape the residential structure of our cities. In chapter 11 we use data from Census 2000 to describe changes in the socioeconomic, ethnic, and racial segregation in this society. We discuss how segregation is measured; which theories attempt to describe it; which ecological, voluntary, and involuntary factors are responsible for segregation; and what the spatial outcomes of this process are. Segregation has its costs and benefits, and we end the chapter by looking at the consequence of this process for the most highly segregated group in our society—African Americans.

The final section consists of two chapters that explore urban problems and potential solutions. Most social problems are national in scope but play out in our cities. An entire book could be devoted to urban problems, but I have chosen three—inequality, homelessness, and crime. Nations no longer shape their economies, global forces do. The well-being of our citizens is no longer determined by economic changes within our national borders but by what economic groups in our society contribute to the global economy. The rules have changed and there are winners and losers. What happens to the losers? What are the consequences of downward social mobility for millions of Americans trapped in the margins of this revolution? How are these economic changes mirrored in our cities? The first section of chapter 12 explores one of the most important problems facing this society—what do we do for those left behind?

For some reason the plight of the homeless has slipped out of our national consciousness. What we do hear is that rates of homeownership are at record highs, and thirty year mortgage rates are at historic lows. But millions of Americans live in substandard dwellings, and somewhere between 350,000 and 2 million Americans are homeless. In this section, we ask, Where are the homeless? Who are they? Why are they homeless? Are the numbers changing?

Public safety is one of the most intractable problems facing city governments, and the fear of crime is one of the factors that motivated millions of Americans to leave central cities for the fringe. The interesting thing is that crime rates declined throughout the 1990s. We live in a far safer society than a generation ago. But most Americans are unaware of this trend, and the fear of crime has become a national obsession. Are police departments doing a better job, or are other forces at work? Who is responsible for our, at times, irrational fear of crime? Urban crime and our attempts to control comprise the third urban problem explored in chapter 12.

We have built 70 percent of all the structures that have ever existed in our nation in the past half-century. But what have we built? How have we built it? How has it shaped us? The answers to these questions are not always positive. In the final chapter of the book, we explore the work of a group of planners, researchers, and developers known as the *new urbanists,* and their attempts to address the problems of urban sprawl. The new urbanists apply the principles of the small town, village, and traditional neighborhood to new developments, whether they are in the central city or the suburban fringe. In the opening section of chapter 13, we describe urban sprawl, the social and environmental costs associated with it, and the economic and technological forces that shaped it. We will then turn to types of community planning in the United States. We describe the pragmatic character of American planning in its attempt to address the health, housing, social, and transportation problems of U.S. cities. We then examine society's most recent attempts to deal with urban problems, smart growth and the new urbanism. We outline the history of this movement, the forces that created it, the principles that guide it, and solutions it proposes for our urban problems. We provide a portrait of Kentlands and other new urbanist developments. We ask, Have these communities met their promise? Are consumers willing to pay more for them? Do they increase social interaction and create community? We end the chapter with a peek at the city of the future, and ask, What can we expect to see in the city of 2050?

I have decided to pursue a distinctively different perspective from many other texts. This book is decidedly applied and student oriented in its general outlook. I believe the knowledge conveyed here about cities can be used to the reader's benefit, not just as an urban scholar, but also as an urban resident. That is, knowledge provides a unique benefit. While ignorance may be said to create bliss, knowledge provides the reader with practical tools. Knowledge can be a useful resource if it can be applied to real-world problems. I hope that this book helps readers do just that. Cities are, in one sense, neutral media, providing potential opportunities as well as risks and problems for the resident. While clearly not everyone has the same access to these opportunities, knowledge of cities as opportunity spaces, as well as risk spaces, is especially useful in a changing urban world.

While I cover much of the same material commonly found in contemporary urban textbooks, I am influenced by a basic assumption in urban ecology. Urban ecology focuses on the growth and development of cities as unique social spaces. This assumption is that cities are a unique class of places, and that understanding their uniqueness is important to understanding how everyday life is structured in them. I believe that residence in these places matters to the everyday lives of people. Urban life is best understood by first defining what is unique about cities themselves. That idea is not without some controversy, and I discuss it in the first chapter.

Acknowledgments

For the last decade, my research interests have shifted from neighborhood change and health care to cultural resource management and international development. I now spend much of my time working on development projects in Jordan. But urban sociology is my first love, and writing a text is my way of getting back into the literature of my field. This is my third book. I began *Deciphering the City* in the spring of 1999, thinking I could complete it in two years. Like so many things in life, chairing a department, my work in Jordan, raising a teenager, appreciating my wife and friends, and dealing with the vagaries of life intervened. Now that my work is at a close, I would like to acknowledge those people who aided me along the way.

First, I would like to thank Mark LaGory, my colleague at the University of Alabama at Birmingham. Mark and I are old friends, and we began the project together. Mark left the project in 2000, but our discussions helped frame the book. Closer to home, I owe a special thanks to my colleague and mentor, Dan Ferritor. Dan, the former department chair and chancellor emeritus, hired me in 1976, and has been my colleague, friend, and mentor these many years. Thanks, Dan, for sharing your sociological insight. Thanks also for your criticism, suggestions, support, and willingness to listen.

Chris DeJohn, my editor at Prentice Hall, saw the value of my work and gave the project leadership and direction. Thank you, Chris, I will always be grateful. And, thank you to the reviewers: Mark Weigand (Metropolitan State College), William Egelman (Iona College), and Joong Hwan-Oh (Hunter College). On the production side, I would like to thank Brenda Averkamp of Carlisle Publishers Services for her fine job producing the book, as well as my copy editor, Karen Bankston, for her thorough and sensitive editing of my manuscript.

I circulated the book manuscript among the doctoral students in my contemporary community course this spring. I asked them to take it apart. God help those who get their wish. Your remarks in the margins in red, green, purple, blue, and black helped make this a better book. My research assistant, Nick Santos, deserves special thanks for the library research, photocopying, and running down obscure citations. A special thanks also to my former administrative assistant, Sharon McFarland, and my secretary, Dolores Rice, for their help with all those tasks in writing a book.

Writing has always been difficult for me, and I have spent years of my life staring at the blank page. My wife, Judy, a gifted writer and a former teacher of writing, helped me in my journey in becoming a writer. I will always be your most grateful student. Voice, unity, and coherence, and all the words of your craft now have meaning to me. Thank you for your passion for the written word, and your support of my work these past twenty years. Not every author is as fortunate as I having a loving and supportive spouse.

A text is a collaborative enterprise. Peruse the bibliography and you will find the hundreds of researchers who contributed to this book. Thank you all for expanding our knowledge of human's most fascinating invention—the city. I have tried to faithfully represent your research. If I have not, I alone am responsible. I welcome your comments and suggestions at bschwab@uark.edu.

Bill Schwab
Fayetteville

1

WHY STUDY THE CITY?

Introduction

Flying over a great city at night is an unforgettable experience. From the plane, the city appears dazzlingly jewel-like, a majestic living thing, with clear pattern and order. The intense activity seen at the city's heart pulses rhythmically, spilling over into rivers of light radiating outward in all directions. Farther away from the city's center, these streams diminish into shallow pools of diffused light. As the plane comes closer to earth, various districts and neighborhoods become apparent and distinguish themselves from one another in form and grain. As the plane nears the airport, the city's cellular structure is visible, with separate buildings, natural features, highways, and other constructed forms (see Photo 1.1).

Once the plane lands, however, the city seems less orderly, as the sights, sounds, and general bustle of the airport rush like floodwaters over the weary traveler. Deplaning, passengers race down crowded corridors, alongside motorized carts with horns blaring. Those leaving the airport jostle for positions nearest the conveyer belts carrying their luggage. Buzzers sound, red lights flash, nerves fray from too long a wait for stray suitcases. Once all possessions are retrieved, travelers cram into taxis and shuttle buses for the ride to the city center. Leaving the airport, the chaotic pace continues. Drivers weave in and out of traffic, frantically careening to their destinations. Horns blare, tempers flare. Welcome to the city.

These places called cities demand our attention. They engage us viscerally, evoking strong emotions ranging from joy to disgust over what is seen and experienced there. It is hard not to have feelings about them. Thomas Jefferson, one of the principal architects of American government, viewed cities as a corrupting force: "I view great cities as pestilential to the morals, health and the liberties of man," while agricultural pursuits "are the best preservative of morals." He is, of course, not alone in his distaste for cities and city life. Although his words seem a little naive and old-fashioned, more contemporary writers, such as Mike Davis, see Jefferson's negative vision of urban America as having come to fruition in urban southern California.

> Is there any need to explain why fear eats the soul of Los Angeles? Only the middle-class dread of progressive taxation exceeds the current obsession with personal safety and social insulation. . . . The rhetoric of urban reform persists, but the substance is extinct. "Rebuilding L.A." simply means padding the bunker. (1998, pp. 363–364)

1

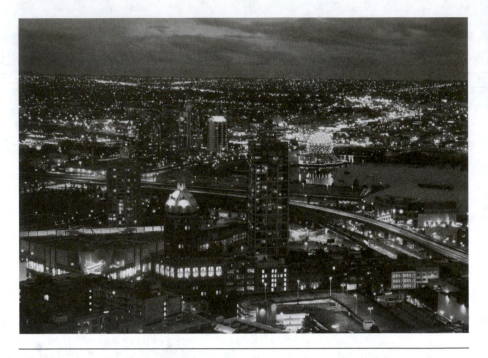

Photo 1.1   *The miracle of the twenty-first century city is best appreciated at night. Above is Vancouver, B.C., one of the world's most beautiful cities, day or night. (Source: © CORBIS Royalty Free.)*

The carefully manicured lawns of Los Angeles's Westside sprout forests of ominous little signs warning: "Armed response!" . . . Welcome to post-liberal Los Angeles, where the defense of luxury lifestyles is translated into a proliferation of new repressions in space and movement, undergirded by the ubiquitous "armed response." (1992, p. 230)

On the other hand, others staunchly defend the city and its offerings. "A big dirty city is better than a technicolor sunrise out in the sticks, no matter how many songbirds are tweeting. In the city you may feel lost, but you also figure you are not missing anything" (Bissell, 1950, p. 33). Among the most frequently mentioned virtues of the city is the freedom it affords its residents. "City air makes men free" (Weber, 1958, p. 94). "The freedom of the city is the freedom of the mind and the freedom of expression" (Lapham, 1976, p. 13). The great diversity of activities and cultures contained in cities provides the potential for liberty unknown in other community forms. Besides the autonomy afforded by the city, urban communities are places with a great deal of activity and action, and writers note the energy characteristic of cities. The poet Carl Sandburg, for example, describes Chicago, as the city of "big shoulders," "stormy," "husky," "brawling," and "youthful."

Cities are distinctively human environments, products of inventiveness, cooperation, competitiveness, and greed. Indeed, the city can be described as the most human of environments, for the city more so than any other ecosystem bears a distinct human imprint. Its character reflects its creators and residents. No other type of residential environment contains as many human-created elements.

Historically, cities served as both *magnets* and *containers*, drawing large numbers of people to them in search of opportunity and freedom, while at the same time dividing and separating residents from the outside world. These unique places have the potential to magnify and intensify both the best and worst aspects of human capacities—serving as centers of invention and civility, while at the same time promoting divisiveness and dramatic inequities. Their birth coincides with the emergence of great human achievements: the first states, the world's great spiritual traditions, and the arts and sciences. Developing at the same time, however, were notably negative features such as sophisticated techniques of warfare, slavery, economic exploitation, and dramatic differences in wealth.

Cities have the capacity to bring us together or tear us apart. While they offer opportunities for some, they can also suppress opportunities for others. They inspire certain people, while degrading others. To understand the city requires you to recognize its capacity for both good and ill at the same time (Krupat, 1985). For just as Sandburg praised Chicago's energy and industry in his poetry, he also acknowledged it as "wicked," "crooked," and "brutal"—capable of producing and maintaining hunger and poverty under the shadow of great prosperity.

It is interesting to note that we Americans generally reflect this love-hate relationship with cities. A recent national survey showed that 36 percent of adults think of cities as centers of business, culture, and progress, while a roughly equal percentage view cities as centers of crime, poverty, and other social problems (*American Demographics*, 1998). When it comes to large cities, however, the view is more certain and negative, with fewer than 10 percent preferring to live in a large city.

What Is the City?

To this point, I have used the words *city* and *urban* loosely without providing any clear definition of these terms. In fact, authors often use many different terms to refer to urban phenomena: *metropolis, metropolitan statistical area, urbanized area, urban, urbanism,* and *urbanization.* These terms can be confusing because different writers use different terms to mean the same things, yet each term has a more specific meaning. Before I go on to discuss the plan of the book, it is important to clarify these terms.

City scholars have long tried to distill the essence of the city into a concise definition. Some have focused on the distinctive physical appearance of cities. For the historian Lewis Mumford, the city is a unique physical entity. It is a "permanent container and an institutional structure, capable of storing and handing on the contents of civilization" (Mumford, 1961, p. 90). Most early cities were identifiable by their outer walls and gate, a pattern of streets, a house block, and a market. They were compact areas that *contained* the population and its activities. While it is generally believed that places with many of these physical features could be found as early as 8000 B.C.E. at Jericho and 7000 B.C.E. at Catal Huyuk in what is now Turkey, urban development actually did not spread through the Middle East until around 3500 B.C.E. It was not until then, however, that the first walled settlements bore all the distinctive marks of what could clearly be called cities. The physical appearance of the city has changed dramatically over time. Ancient and medieval cities actually functioned as containers and were usually walled and crowded. Spaces in these cities often contained a mixture of residential and commercial uses, with people living and working in the same buildings, and public and private spaces ill defined.

Industrial cities, on the other hand, do not have this container-like appearance. More recent cities, characteristic of the last few centuries, are noted by one or more heavy concentrations of economic activity with high-rise office buildings and by the densely populated residential areas surrounding these activity nodes. Public and private spaces are more clearly defined. In many areas, cities over the last few decades appear to be growing together, swiftly consuming the once green rural spaces that separated them and losing the clearly defined spaces that characterized cities in the last few centuries. William Whyte refers to this recent phenomenon as *urban sprawl* (1958) and bemoans the numbing sameness and lack of spatial uniqueness emerging in the urban landscape.

> *Flying from Los Angeles to San Bernardino—an unnerving lesson in man's infinite capacity to mess up his environment—the traveler can see a legion of bulldozers gnawing into the last remaining tract of green between the two cities, and from San Bernardino another legion of bulldozers gnawing westward.* (Whyte, 1958, p. 302)

In short, the visual distinctiveness of urban spaces has not only changed over time, it actually seems to be blurring in recent decades. Cities have gone from "walled" to "sprawled" spaces.

While not all urban areas share the same physical appearance, they do have some common characteristics. One common feature is a particular economic institution—the market. For Max Weber, the city is a place "where the local inhabitants satisfy an economically substantial part of their daily wants in the local market" (Weber, 1958, p. 67). People no longer live off the land; instead, what they need for daily life is found in the market located and organized in cities. The presence of a permanent marketplace not only affects the economic character of the place, it seems to influence the culture of inhabitants. It promotes a rational, less-traditional culture, and attracts diverse populations. Thus, the market's presence makes for a meaningfully different way of life in cities.

The market-oriented nature of the city is a matter of degree. In some societies the urban community organizes economic relations and becomes the place for the free exchange of goods between city center and hinterland. Many of the ancient city centers weren't true market centers, but rather religious and military centers (Keyfitz, 1967). They gained the food necessary to sustain an urban population of nonfood producers by religious traditions and often by sheer force. The old slogan, "All roads lead to Rome," suggests the vital role the city played in the ancient world, but it does not tell the whole story. These roads were military routes built primarily for the army rather than for the easy flow of market goods. The goods that flowed into ancient Rome were more likely to be in the form of tribute and taxation than products intended for the market.

Perhaps the most commonly used definition of cities focuses on its population characteristics. Wirth (1938) defines the city as a relatively large, dense, and permanent settlement of socially heterogeneous individuals. He believes that the *scale* and *diversity* of social life is dramatically different in cities and is affected by these demographic factors. Indeed, these factors produce what he believes is a unique way of life offered in the city. The sheer immensity of the urban setting encourages unique experiences. Philip Hauser describes the importance of scale for the urban experience by exploring the impact of population density.

> Let us consider the differences in potential social interaction in a community with a fixed land area but varying population density. Let the land area be that which lies within a circle with a 10-mile radius, namely 314 square miles. In such an area the size of the population under different density conditions is shown below.

Population density (Population/square mile)	Number of persons (Circle of 10-mile radius)
1	314
50	15,700
8,000	2,512,000
17,000	5,338,000
25,000	7,850,000

> The density of one person per square mile is not too far from the density of the United States when occupied by Indians. The density of 50 is approximately that of the United States today, and also that of the world as a whole. The density of 8,000 in round numbers, was that of central cities in metropolitan areas in 1950, and the 25,000 density figure that of New York.

> Thus, in aboriginal America the person moving about within a circle of 10-mile radius could potentially make only 313 different contacts. In contrast the density of the U.S. as a whole today would make possible over 15,000 contacts in the same land area; the density of central cities in the U.S., in 1950, would permit over 2.5 million contacts; the density of Chicago over 5.3 million contacts; and the density of New York City about 7.9 million contacts. These differences in density and therefore in potential social interaction necessarily affect the nature of collective activity and social organization. (Hauser, 1963, p. 4)

While definitions such as Wirth's are helpful in identifying important urban characteristics (density, size, and heterogeneity), they are not specific enough to make real-world distinctions between urban and nonurban places. Two basic issues present themselves when differentiating urban areas from other places. First, how great a population concentration is actually necessary to be considered urban? Is the minimum scale necessary for urbanism 2,000, 10,000, or 100,000 people? Once an appropriate size has been chosen, how do you decide where the city's boundaries are? Do you use political boundaries or boundaries based on population density or social and economic activity?

Many different, often arbitrary, definitions of *urban* are used throughout the world. Approximately one-third of the countries providing data on urbanization to the United Nations employ a population-size-only definition. Unfortunately, the official minimum sizes range from as low as 250 to as high as 40,000, making comparisons between countries difficult. Size-only criteria can be misleading. For example, in Japan a number of "cities" in the 100,000 to 500,000 range have more than half of their lands devoted to agricultural use (Hawley, 1971). That is why some nations combine size with other criteria such as the number of inhabitants employed in nonagricultural pursuits. Other nations, however, use criteria based on legal or governmental requirements that are even more arbitrary than size, such as whether a place is an administrative center (such as a county seat or regional center).

This variation in criteria makes it difficult to determine the level of urbanization present in a place, yet I believe as urban sociologists that knowing the amount of urbanization will tell us a lot about the quality of life in such places. An urbanized country reflects a distinctively "urban" influence, in which the population resides predominantly in places that are socially and economically differentiated and of significant scale. If I rely merely on the standards of the countries themselves to assess urbanization levels, however, the comparisons run the risk of being rather capricious. Hence, the most typically used measure of urbanization is the percentage of residents in cities of 100,000 or more. While this statistic does not favor countries with small populations, where there may only be one city of this size, it is easy to calculate and widely used by students of the city.

The other issue in measuring a country's degree of urbanization is deciding on where urban places begin and end; that is, what are their boundaries? The easiest solution is to accept the political boundaries of the city, but these do not always capture the real urban community in which people carry out their daily lives. In the United States, for example, larger urban places have a central city or several such central cities, surrounded by densely populated suburbs that stretch out for many miles. People living in these places participate in a social and economic space stretching beyond the boundaries of the political unit in which they reside. For example, many residents in suburban towns work in the central city, while residents of the central city often work outside in one of these suburbs. To deal with this problem of boundary definitions, the U.S. Census Bureau has established a number of terms, the best known of which are *metropolitan area* (MA) and *urbanized area* (UA). The general concept of the metropolitan area is "that of a core area containing a large population nucleus, together with adjacent communities having a high degree of economic and social integration with that core" (U.S. Census Bureau, 2000). This term became effective with the 1990 census and is used as a general concept to refer to more specific units such as the metropolitan statistical areas (MSA), the consolidated statistical area (CSA), and the primary metropolitan statistical area (PMSA). Generally speaking, when we talk about cities or urban areas, we are referring to metropolitan areas. Within these areas, however, there are distinctively different community spaces—central cities, suburbs of various ages and types, and rural-urban fringe areas that make up the urban mosaic we call the *metropolitan area*. Sometimes metropolitan statistical areas blend together, or spatially consolidate, as urban sprawl obliterates the distinctions between areas. These are referred to as *consolidated statistical areas*.

The Importance of Understanding Cities

These nitty-gritty definitional distinctions aside, it is essential to understand the city's potential to affect your life. After all, over three-fourths of Americans now live in urban areas, and the world's urban population has increased twentyfold in this century from 150 million urban residents to nearly 3 billion. Cities are, in one sense, a basic machine used for living. Without the city's infrastructure or the products and services produced by urban economies, you could not get by on a daily basis. We have grown dependent on this machine, yet cities are more than mere devices built to supply residents' needs. Cities are living things with a life and character all their own. Like other living things, each city has a distinctive personality ranging from positive characteristics such as youthful, hip, inviting, sophisticated, diverse, and stimulating to senescent, staid, exclusive, unimaginative, and depressing. Also like us, they display multiple personalities and show different faces to differing groups of peoples. The "machine" works differently for each of the groups and signifies different things.

While each city can be said to be *distinctive*, urban areas clearly share *common traits*, and they all possess a *potential for dualism* that must be understood and harnessed by its residents. To get by in an urban world requires that we appreciate all three of these aforementioned aspects of cities—their individuality, their commonality, and their constructive and destructive potential. Whether you live in a city or not, you are likely to be influenced by them. Like it or not, cities, and the changes taking place within them, affect you. You cannot afford to ignore them, even if you choose not to live in them. These places matter greatly.

In a literal sense, history began with the first cities. Yet urbanization is a recent development in human evolution. Although our species has lived on earth for more than 40,000 years, the first city-like settlement did not emerge until around 10,000 years ago. This is only the last one-fourth of human existence, and most of this fraction of time involved just a tiny percentage of the world's population. Indeed, urban residence was rare until the twentieth century. As late as 1920 only 14 percent of global population was urban. Even now, slightly less than half of the world's population (45 percent) lives in cities. In spite of those numbers, we clearly live in an urban world. In advanced nations, urban areas are the place of residence for the vast majority. In all countries they are the centers of wealth, innovation, and social change. Indeed, the degree to which a nation is urbanized is one of the clearest indications of its level of development. Before the Industrial Revolution no society had achieved even a moderate level of urban growth. Since then, no society has experienced development without becoming highly urbanized.

Cities are where modern life is organized and where the future is being forged. In economically developed countries, most everybody lives in cities, while in developing countries the fastest rates of community growth are occurring in cities. Historically, people have turned to the city to seek new opportunities and experiences. Rural migrants come to them, sometimes in desperation, but always with hope. Their vitality is alluring, their diversity intoxicating and exciting. Cities concentrate the great range of humanity, our virtues and vices, our wide range of experiences and beliefs, into a small amount of shared space. More happens in these places than in other community forms not simply because the scale of life is bigger, but because these places condense a variety of cultures and personalities in one place. It is not surprising, therefore, that these places of great promise are also places of great trouble. Indeed, most contemporary social and economic problems can be said to be "urban" problems.

Urban Problems

Although less than half of the earth's population lives in cities, the world is experiencing an urban crisis of immense proportions. Cities are, by definition, large concentrations of diverse peoples living on small amounts of land (Wirth, 1938). Because of their physical, social, and economic complexity they are difficult to manage. This management problem is made more difficult because the city's political boundaries don't fit the actual boundaries of the metropolitan community area, yet these areas are the actual spaces most of us use for daily living. Each metropolis is effectively composed of many different decision-making units—central cities, suburban cities, counties, townships, police and fire districts, sewer and water districts, and so forth—all with separate voice and vote over the area's future. It is, thus, more an agglomeration of places than an autonomous, self-governing unit.

Management problems are further accentuated by the emergence of the global economy. Each city's destiny is controlled increasingly by global economic and political forces often outside of local urban residents' sphere of influence. Extra-local economic forces determine the future health and development of cities, yet cannot be adequately planned for or controlled. Older cities and suburbs with a heavy concentration in manufacturing activity have been particularly hard hit. In the global economy businesses have greater flexibility than ever before. Producers can pull up stakes and move with ease. Capital is portable. Labor costs vary greatly internationally. Attracting business, and then keeping it, is of great concern to local leaders. Cities place great emphasis on their ability to stay afloat and grow in the new economic circumstances of the high-technology, postindustrial global economy. They are "growth machines" (Logan & Molotch, 1987), living or dying on their ability to expand.

Growth-related issues are often at the forefront of current urban crises. While growth is a basic goal of many cities, it produces its own problems. In the United States, urban sprawl and the deterioration of inner-city areas are major issues. These represent problems of "uneven development" that dramatically distinguish the social topography of the new urban landscape. The very poor are concentrated more and more in inner-city areas with no jobs. The isolation deepens the cycle of poverty and violence found in such places. But sprawl also touches suburbia and rural urban fringe areas. The governor of Maryland, Parris Glendening, describes the problems associated with sprawl:

> In its path sprawl consumes thousands of acres of forests and farmland, woodlands and wetlands. It requires government to spend millions extra to build new schools, streets and water and sewer lines. In its wake, sprawl leaves boarded-up houses, vacant storefronts, closed businesses, abandoned and often contaminated industrial sites, and traffic congestion stretching miles from urban centers. (Planning Commissioners Journal, 1999)

Sprawl also eats away at a sense of community. The uncontrolled growth that is spawned leaves in its wake vast unbounded stretches of residential and commercial development with no visual cues that allow us to identify it. The numbing sameness of such spaces creates a kind of visual placelessness that fails to promote a sense of community identity.

While urban sprawl is not a problem in lesser-developed countries, urbanization there often far exceeds the ability of local institutions and infrastructures to handle it. In many cases the pace of urban population growth far outstrips the city's ability to absorb that growth, creating megacities with severe growing pains and tolerating the emergence of illegal settlements of migrant poor. Such settlements outside the city lack the infrastructure necessary to maintain even minimum health standards for the impoverished masses living in dangerously crowded, inadequate makeshift housing.

These rapidly expanding cities experience a range of problems, including high rates of unemployment and underemployment, inadequate sanitation and water supplies, homelessness and severe housing shortages, overloaded transportation systems, various forms of pollution, health and nutrition problems, rising crime rates, and municipal budget crises (Dogan & Kasarda, 1988). In spite of the huge problems associated with these places, migrants continue to flood into them at an unprecedented rate. In the next twenty-five years it is estimated that 114 of the 134 urban areas in the world with more than 4 million residents will be in developing countries. These 114 places will account for 88 percent of the world's total population living in large metropolitan areas (Dogan & Kasarda, 1988). It is in this context that the developing world is sometimes said to be overurbanized.

Urban Promises and the Importance of the City

In spite of all the problems associated with cities, they hold great promise for the future. The new global economy is reshaping world geography. A small number of global cities are becoming decision-making centers in which the world's economic future is being shaped. Indeed, cities are where the work of globalization gets done. It is here that communication and management functions are concentrated. While many cities have suffered precisely because of the emergence of the global economy, others have gained renewed importance; these so-called *global cities* have become the command and control points for the world economy (Sassen, 1994). This underlines the theme of dualism mentioned earlier concerning the urban scene. It is clear that while some cities hold great promise and opportunity for residents, others do not. In addition, within even the most promising of urban areas, there is great variation across the cityscape: Some places weaken and endanger those who live there, while others energize and provide opportunity for residents.

In addition to the emergence of a global economy, a new information technology has swept the world like a great tidal wave, transforming the ways in which we get information and share it with others. This technological revolution, characterized by a host of microelectronic devices, computer hardware, and software innovations, is thought to be as socially and economically significant as any class of technological achievements in human history, including the agricultural revolution that began 10,000 years ago in the Near East and the Industrial Revolution that started just 200 years ago in Western Europe. While we now live in a world so technologically advanced that whole communities have emerged in cyberspace through chat rooms and web pages that unite people of like interests into virtual communities, humans have not been liberated from spatially bounded places of residence. In spite of predictions to the contrary, place of residence still matters greatly for everyday life. And urban places are particularly significant forces globally and locally. Where you live matters greatly. It influences the friends you have, the health and psychological hazards to which you are exposed, and the resources and services at your disposal (Fitzpatrick & LaGory, 2000).

Since cities represent the most often used and influential places in the world, it stands to reason that your success and survival in that world depends on the knowledge you have about such places. How are these places different from other living arrangements? How do they structure our lives? What dangers and opportunities can we encounter in such places? How do different groups of people experience the city? How are cities being affected by global economics? Do cities really vary much in what they offer residents? How can we get to know a city and what it has to offer? What things should we look for before we move between and within cities? How are cities changing, and what effects might these changes have on us?

The Book's Perspective

These questions are critical for each of us to answer, and an urban studies textbook is the appropriate place to find answers. In short, this book can be viewed as a survival manual for your future. Deciphering the city—that is, understanding its meaning for your life and work, understanding its structure and this structure's impact on everyday life—is essential knowledge. It can help you negotiate the challenges of a world experiencing great flux. Indeed, the world is very different from that of just a few generations ago. It is a world that has been transformed by a global economy and by significant technological changes. Not only is this world more complicated than any previously known, the city is a particularly challenging entity to understand. Cities are characterized by their great complexity: they have multiple personalities, they often offer very different faces to differing groups of people, and they are constantly evolving in form. Because they are relevant to our everyday lives and because they are quite complicated, it is critical for each of us to understand their impact on our lives and the lives of others. These places matter, and understanding how they matter is essential to our success in an increasingly urban world.

In this text I decipher the city by reviewing the research and writings of urban sociologists. My approach to the city is distinctly sociological. I do, however, take a slightly different perspective from that of standard urban sociology texts. Although many of the usual topics included in urban sociology texts will be covered here, the emphasis will be on providing knowledge for urban users rather than budding urban scholars. As already noted, cities are machines for living. At one level, this book represents something akin to the manual available to a mechanic. It describes how the urban machine works and how it can be used effectively when you have the right resources. Not everyone who lives in cities, of course, has these resources. Indeed, many people have, at best, access to only part of the machine. Knowing this is also critical to understand the experiences and problems facing countless urban others and to avoid the tendency we all have to place blame for group troubles on individuals. This knowledge can lead not only to greater tolerance, but also to an informed view of the social injustices inherent in city structures.

In reality, cities are much more complicated than machines—they are living things, with distinct personalities. One key to deciphering city life is understanding that places have distinctive characteristics and character. Knowing this, and using this knowledge, can help give each of us the opportunity to establish a richer sense of the places in which we live. Cities do not function uniformly but operate rather differently for different people. "Reading the city" and assessing its opportunities, as well as its pitfalls, is somewhat of an art and so this survival manual is clearly more than a *Popular Mechanics* of cities and city life.

Since most of you reading this text live in metropolitan areas, why is it necessary for you to study something with which you are already acquainted? What can you possibly learn that you don't already know? After all, you've spent a good part of your time living and working in these places already. In fact, however, being familiar with something does not mean that you are aware of everything important to know about that thing. Indeed, sometimes a sense of familiarity with something can breed ignorance. Persons who feel familiarity with something or someone often have no desire to know anything more. More to the point, however, this kind of knowledge is highly personal—reflective of a unique set of personal experiences. Certainly *knowledge by acquaintance* or familiarity is valuable. It gives you a "feel" for a place that can be extremely useful. It is a form of knowledge that is evocative and emotional. This knowledge also tends to be haphazard. Geographers note, for example, the dramatically incomplete and idiosyncratic quality of urban images and mental maps (Gould & White, 1974). Yet these incomplete and inadequate maps often color and affect your use of urban space and thus your urban experience. The *systematic knowledge* offered by analysis of a particular thing is quite different from personal knowledge or acquaintance. Social science offers a more analytical and systematic form of knowing that can be highly useful for you in understanding the city.

Because cities are complex entities, varying one from another, this form of information can be particularly valuable to residents. While it is certainly important to be acquainted with the individual city in which you live, it is also essential to understand how cities work as machines for daily living. This requires systematic understanding of how cities are organized, of the resources they offer residents, and of the variation in resources available due to location within the city. To know anything well involves both forms of knowledge—personal and systematic. This book prepares you to acquire both forms of understanding of the city and city life. In terms of systematic knowledge, it presents a great deal of information from social science research and theoretical writing about cities. Much of this is similar to what can be found in other urban sociological texts. In addition, however, this book is quite different from others in that it aims to prepare you to become familiar with cities as well. That is, I intend to provide you with useful information that can improve your understanding of the possibilities and problems that city structures generally pose for residents and with information to help you decipher the character of a particular city. Here, I review a variety of information sources that can help you negotiate the twists and turns of daily living within specific areas.

Throughout this book I hope to promote an appreciation of the fact that cities are more than just the contexts in which you live your lives. These places shape social and economic opportunities and affect your overall health and well-being. Where you live is important, and in the pages that follow I hope to provide an understanding of why and how that is true. Cities are fascinating places. They seem to have an underlying order, but at the same time they border on the chaotic.

I have titled this text *Deciphering the City*. The original meaning of the word *decipher*, according to *Webster's Unabridged Dictionary*, is "to translate from secret characters into intelligible form; . . . to read as words, to detect, reveal or unfold." My intent is to take this complex thing we call the city and provide the information necessary for you to make sense of it and use it. At the same time it can also promote an understanding of how other persons' lives are affected by residing in it. The first step is understanding the revolution called *globalization* that is changing our societies, cities, and lives. This journey begins in the next chapter, "Globalization and Urbanization in the More-Developed World."

2

GLOBALIZATION AND URBANIZATION IN THE MORE-DEVELOPED WORLD

Introduction

A historical event will often define a generation. This event occurs during its formative years, their late teens or early twenties, and forever marks their psyche. I am a member of the baby boom generation, and the date, November 22, 1963, is indelibly printed in my memory. John F. Kennedy was assassinated on this date, and every member of my generation can tell you where they were, and who they were with, when the news from Dallas reached them. For many of us, the murder of JFK was the end of our idealism and the hope that our generation could build a better society. For many of us, that fateful day in Dallas seemed to usher in a long national nightmare of riots and burning cities, the Vietnam War, and the assassinations of Robert Kennedy and Martin Luther King. It was a decade in which social movements redefined the roles of women and minorities in this society. It was a decade that redefined citizenship. It was a decade that changed American society forever.

The defining moment for my children's generation was a single traumatic event that happened on January 28, 1986. After an exhaustive national search of 11,000 applicants, NASA chose the first private citizen to fly in space. Christine McAuliffe was a pretty, likable mom and a high school teacher from Concord, New Hampshire. She may have been chosen to fly in space, but she was down to earth. She was not one of them; she was one of us. NASA developed curriculum guides for teachers of millions of primary and secondary students. Schools across the country competed to see whose science experiments would fly on the shuttle. NASA promoted the mission as the first classroom in space, and Christine was scheduled to give two 15-minute lessons from space on the fourth day of the flight. PBS planned to carry the broadcast nationwide. That morning, millions of primary school students huddled around classroom TVs and watched in horror as the shuttle was engulfed in flames seventy-three seconds after liftoff (Sieler & King, 1986). Dumbstruck, teachers and parents asked, "How could this have happened? What do we say to our children? How do we say it?" Children of the 80s generation learned a lesson that morning. It was not about the promise of space, but the truth of violent death, the fallibility of humans, and the vulnerability of our technology.

For the generation of my students born in the early 1970s, the fall of the Berlin Wall on November 9, 1989, defines their generation (See Photo 2.1). Most of them have vivid memories of the crowds tearing down that hated symbol of division. They remember the euphoria. They remember their teachers, parents, and even

Photo 2.1　*The Fall of the Berlin Wall, the Event that Marks the Beginning of the Global Era* (*Source:* © David Turnley/CORBIS.)

clergy remarking that this was the end of something called the Cold War. They remember hearing from our president that an evil empire had fallen. They remember the feelings of hope and optimism for a new, peaceful, and better world in their future.

The first plane hit the north tower of the World Trade Center at 8:48 A.M. I had arrived late to the office that morning and found more than a dozen students crammed into Debbie Hall's office watching the events unfold on a six-inch black-and-white TV. I asked, "What's going on?" And as someone was just about to tell me, the second plane struck the south tower at 9:03 A.M. We watched the events unfold over the next two hours like a billion other people worldwide connected by the Internet, fiber-optic cable, television, and twenty-four-hour independent news organizations. We watched in horror as, first, the north and, then, the south tower pancaked, taking 3,000 lives with them. By then, millions of Americans, and millions of people worldwide, had already begun to speak of these events as the defining moment of their lives. This is the defining event of your generation, and like mine in 1963, you will be able to tell your children where you were, who you were with, and when you saw the horrific events of September 11, 2001.

Each of these events is an important marker in our nation's rich historical tapestry. But the fall of the Berlin Wall and the attack on the World Trade Center are the most important because they transcend our nation. The fall of the Berlin Wall marked a new era in history. Before November 9, 1989, there were two competing ideologies in the world and two armed camps poised to annihilate each other. The first was an ideology based on the writings of Marx and Lenin. This ideology provided the underpinnings for totalitarian states that governed half the world's population through centrally controlled command economies. The other was an ideology based on the writings of John Locke, Adam Smith, and others who promoted free-market capitalism and liberal democracy. These thinkers profoundly influenced the founders of our democracy (Dahrendorf, 1997).

With the fall of the wall, the competition had ended and we thought free-market capitalism and liberal democracy had won. And with this victory, a new world order had emerged. One school of thought held that before the wall fell, we lived in a world of division. After the fall, we lived in a world of integration. Words like *globalization, global web,* and *global economy* entered the English language to describe this new integration of the world's economy. Many social scientists felt that globalization had revolutionized not only our economic relationships, but our political and social ones as well. Simply, globalization had ushered in a new era of peace and prosperity. This view ended with the collapse of the Twin Towers.

The events of September 11 did not happen in a vacuum. They happened in the context of the new international system called *globalization,* a system that came together in the 1980s and replaced the previous international system called *the Cold War.* Other eras were marked by the rise and fall of other international systems. The end of the First World War led to the rise of fascism and eventually to a Second World War that pitted Germany, Italy, and Japan against Britain, the United States, and the other democracies. The end of the Second World War led to the rise of communism and a Cold War between the Soviet Union and the United States and their client states. The end of the Cold War led to the rise of globalization and, we are now discovering, new divisions among the world's 196 nation-states, cleavages that a second school of thought contends are grounded in the history and culture of the world's major civilizations. From their perspective, September 11 not only breeched the wall of civilization but represented the first clash of civilizations in the global era.

I am an urban ecologist, and one of the tenets of my discipline is that changes taking place in society are reflected first and most clearly in our cities. I believe that globalization has not only changed societies but also the role, structure, and character of our cities. In this chapter, we will explore globalization and its consequences for cities. In exploring this relationship, we will address the following questions. What forces made globalization possible? How did these changes contribute to the fall of the Soviet Union and other command economies? How has globalization affected the social, political, and economic institutions of societies? How did these changes contribute to the rise of global terrorism? How has globalization affected the role of cities in our nation's economy? How has globalization affected the relationship between cities and regions of North America and the world? How has it affected Americans and the areas of cities in which they live? Finally, what have we gained and what have we lost in the globalization process?

This chapter focuses on the effects of globalization on North American cities. In the next chapter, we will continue this discussion by exploring urban patterns in other regions of the world.

A Revolution

When people hear the word *revolution,* they conjure up images of armed conflict. They think of historical events like the American Revolution or the French Revolution. These are certainly examples of revolutions, but there are other types of revolutions, such as the agricultural revolution and the Industrial Revolution. Social scientists define the term *revolution* as any rapid change in the institutions of a society. In the history of humankind, the most profound revolutions, those that have changed the course of human development, have been peaceful. Therefore, if we use the broad social science definition of revolution, globalization is a revolution. It is bringing about rapid and basic changes in the social, political, and economic institutions of societies around the world.

Globalization is the process that replaced the Cold War. Since the end of the Cold War, social scientists have been in a quandary on how to explain this new world order. Numerous competing theories have emerged, but I have chosen two because they represent the ends of a theoretical spectrum. Francis Fukuyama sees a new, peaceful, and prosperous world based in free-market capitalism and liberal democracy. At the other end is Samuel P. Huntington, who sees a more dangerous world divided along the fault lines of civilizations.

Fukuyama (1992) and others view globalization as a second American Revolution writ large. We won the Cold War. The Soviet Union, and the ideology upon which it was based, no longer exists (see Figure 2.1). There is only one pure Marxist state left in the world, North Korea, and it may be able to develop nuclear weapons and ballistic missiles, but it can't feed its own people. Members of this school note that authoritarian dictatorships of the right still exist in a dozen or so nations in the world, but most nations are moving toward democracy (Fukuyama, 1992). They look to our own hemisphere for examples of this global trend. All the nations in our hemisphere with one exception, Cuba, are now democracies with market economies. Even the People's Republic of China is in the midst of its second revolution this century. Although a communist party controls Mainland China, its government has abandoned most of its centrally controlled economy and has instituted market reforms. Over half of China's economy operates in a free market. Can political reforms be far behind (Oster, 1999)? They argue that the truth is no matter where one looks in the world today, there is one dominant political ideology, liberal democracy based on free-market capitalism.[1]

Huntington (1996) presents a compelling counterargument. He agrees that the technologies like the Internet and the end of the Cold War have led to the economic changes we call globalization. And he cites examples of regional and international organizations that have emerged to integrate the world's economy based in free-market capitalism and liberal democracy as envisioned by Fukuyama. The European Union (EU), North American Free Trade Agreement (NAFTA), International Monetary Fund (IMF), World Trade Organization (WTO), and World Bank are regional and international examples.[2] He also agrees that states will continue to be the major players in the world's political and economic system. But Huntington feels that with the end of the Cold War and the breakup of the Soviet Union, the international system of nations is no longer based on ideology but on culture. Rather than a world moving from integration to interdependency, Huntington and others see the emergence of a multicultural-, multipolar-, multiconflict-oriented world. In their minds, a far more dangerous world now exists because conditions may lead to a clash of civilizations. The recent war with Iraq is a potent example— the clash between Western and Islamic civilizations.

Culture is to society as DNA is to our bodies. Culture is the blueprint for living, and it pervades our societies and our souls. Accordingly, a society's culture, beliefs, values, institutions, and history pervasively affect how states view their self-interests. Freed from the ideology of the two superpowers, states similar in culture, language,

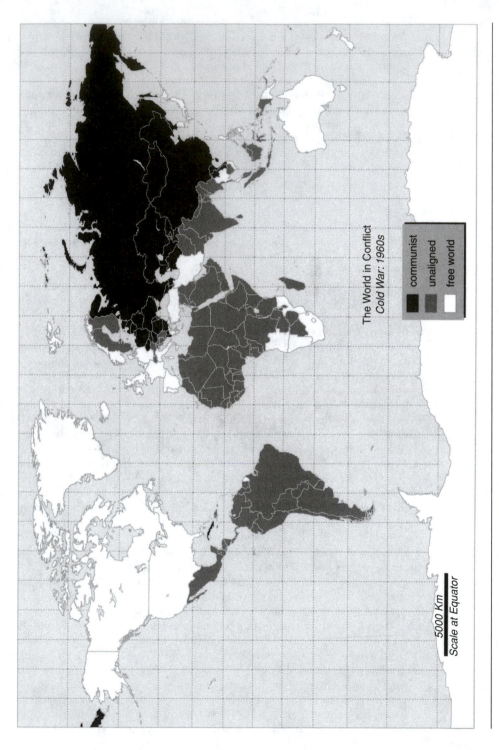

Figure 2.1 *The World in Conflict: Cold War: 1960s (Source:* Adapted from "The Clash of Civilizations" by Samuel P. Huntington.)

The World in Conflict
Cold War: 1960s

communist
unaligned
free world

5000 Km
Scale at Equator

and history are banding together against those that are different. Thus, Huntington sees a world order based in nine major civilizations (see Figure 2.2). And as our recent history shows, countries throughout the world are developing new and reinvigorating old antagonism and alliances based in their common culture and civilization. Some of these groupings transcend national borders. For example, the Kurds, who have gained so much attention during the Iraq War, are an ethnic group living in Turkey, Iraq, and Iran. Is Greater Kurdistan in our future? Huntington believes the major conflicts that grab the headlines—Russia's war in Chechnya, the bloody civil war in the former Yugoslavia, the rise of fundamentalism in the Islamic World and India, and the cultural clefs within Turkey and Mexico—are powerful examples of the reordering of nations in a new international system based on culture.

Globalization may mean that nation-states have lost control over the movement of ideas, images, capital, technology, and people across their borders. Improvements in transportation and communication technology have produced more frequent and more intense interactions among people of different civilizations than at any time in history. But this movement of people, ideas, and capital has also created the potential for more frequent and more dangerous conflicts among nations. Why? Because, according to Huntington and his followers, they are on the fault lines of civilizations.

Huntington acknowledges an emerging global economic system based in free-market capitalism, but not a global political system based in the ideology of liberal democracy. He certainly does not see an emerging globalized, homogenized culture or a new era of world peace and prosperity. Huntington contends Western civilization will continue to sustain its preeminent position by defining its interests as the interests of the "world community." This was the very language Secretary Powell used in the United Nations in the weeks leading up to the war with Iraq. And the West will continue to use its military reach when it deems it necessary, as we did in Kosovo and Iraq. The West will continue to integrate the economies of non-Western nations into a global economic system through the institutions it dominates, like the International Monetary Fund and the World Bank. But as Huntington puts it, the finance ministers of non-Western societies may support our economic efforts, but there is little support from anyone else in these societies. We may control their economies, but not their hearts and minds. Herein lies a very different and a far more pessimistic vision of the human condition in the twenty-first century.

We are presented with starkly different visions of a post–Cold War world. Fukuyama sees a safer, more prosperous world moving from interdependence to integration through the promise of free-market capitalism and liberal democracy. The failed diplomacy leading up to the war in Iraq seems to call his vision into question. Huntington sees a more divided, more complex, and, in many respects, more dangerous world brought on by the specter of a clash of civilizations. Although Fukuyama and Huntington have starkly different visions of the future, they agree on one thing—the revolution called globalization. They acknowledge that in the 1980s political changes along with breakthroughs in computer, communication, and transportation technology created a global economy. To understand this new world order and the role of cities in it, we must understand how this revolution occurred. For this analysis, we turn to Thomas Friedman, the Pulitzer Prize–winning correspondent for the *New York Times*, and his book, *The Lexus and the Olive Tree* (1999).

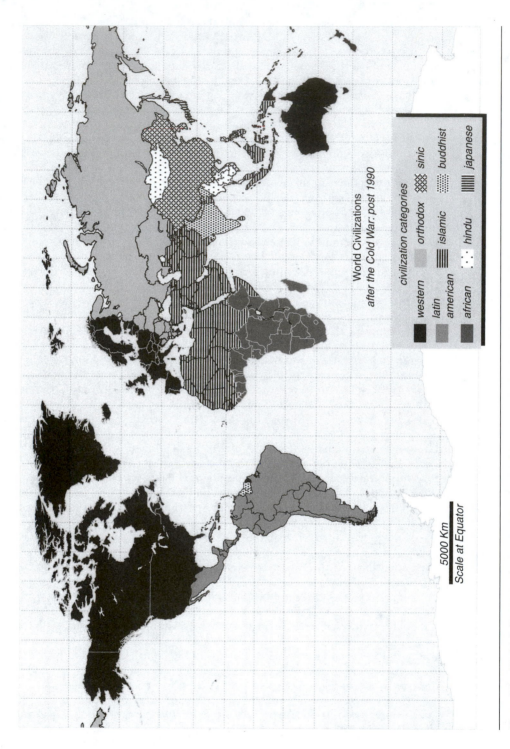

Figure 2.2 *World Civilizations: After the Cold War: post 1990 (Source: Adapted from "The Clash of Civilizations" by Samuel P. Huntington.)*

Thomas Friedman, *The Lexus and the Olive Tree*

Friedman argues that all societies in the world have two wants. People want and need roots—family, home, neighborhood, and culture. Those things that are lasting and satisfying Friedman represents with the olive tree, a tree that is deep rooted and long lived (Huntington's position). People also want things represented by the Japanese luxury automobile, the Lexus. They want a higher standard of living made possible by the promise of a global economy (Fukuyama's position). The new conflict in the world, according to Friedman, is not between competing ideologies; rather, it is between the human needs represented by the olive tree and the Lexus. The dilemma is that societies must embrace the social and economic changes necessary to compete in a global economy, while at the same time preserving the uniqueness of their culture and the quality of their environment. The goals of world terrorist organizations like Al Qaeda and the demonstrations and riots outside the meetings of the WTO, the IMF, and the World Bank are stark reminders of the inherent conflict between these often contradictory goals (Berman, 2003).

The Revolution Came in Four Installments

How did this revolution come about? According to Friedman (1999), four profound, independent social and technological changes converged in the 1980s to make the globalization of the world economy possible. They were the democratization of technology, finance, information, and decision making.

The Democratization of Technology

A company can build anything anyplace in the world today. Innovations in computers, telecommunications, digitization, and miniaturization allow millions of people in the world to be connected and to exchange information and knowledge. Prior to globalization, the world was divided into developed and developing nations. Developed nations, like the United States, Japan, and Western European countries, had industrial economies. Developing nations, the rest of the world, had fledgling industrial economies and depended heavily on exports of raw materials. In the old system, developing nations shipped raw materials to the developed world, and, if developed nations could find markets, they shipped high-value goods back to them.

With the democratization of technology, most countries of the world no longer ship just raw materials to the more-developed world. They have the technology to produce highly finished goods on their own. If a nation has a core of well-educated and highly skilled workers, they can import the technology they need. They can find funding from investors in one nation, subcontractors of components in another, and shippers, accountants, and marketers in still other nations. These new relationships span the globe and are made possible by the master technology—telecommunications and the Internet.

Examples of the democratization of technology are endless. Who would have guessed twenty years ago that Thailand would have an automobile industry that could rival Japan in the Asian market? Or who would have guessed twenty years ago that Taiwan would be the world's leading manufacturer of computer memory chips? Or that Malaysia would be the world's leading supplier of disk drives and flat-panel computer screens? Or that India would have the largest concentration of computer engineers in the world and would become one of the world's leading software developers? Or that Israel and China and dozens of other nations around the world would have their own Silicon Valleys (Allbritton, 1999)? This change in technology has given corporations an enormous advantage in scouring the world for the lowest costs of their basic inputs—raw materials, components, labor, finance, and buildings. Equally important is their ability to find the lowest costs of these inputs with a click on the Internet (see freemarket.com). Friedman suggests the democratization of technology is one of the important factors knitting the global web together, making it smaller and faster.

The Democratization of Finance

If you were a businessperson a generation ago and you needed a loan to start or expand a business, you really had only one choice. You would visit your friendly commercial banker. The term *good old boy* was invented to describe commercial bankers. Most commercial lending took place in New York City, and these staid, old banking firms were adverse to risk. The old saying, "A bank will only give you a loan when you don't need it," described commercial banks. As a result, it was often difficult to find the capital to start a new company. In those days, an AOL or an Amazon.com would probably not exist for a lack of capital.

Have things changed in the past twenty years! Starting in the 1980s, laws changed, and new actors entered financial markets using a dizzying array of new financing instruments to raise investment capital. Today brokerage firms, banks, risk capital firms, commercial banks, insurance companies, mutual funds, hedge funds, retirement funds, and others provide capital for businesses from the smallest start-ups to giant multinationals. The Federal Reserve finds one indication of this revolution in finance in a 1999 report estimating that more than $1 trillion is electronically transferred around the globe each day (Nason & Rogers, 1999). To put things in perspective, in 1900 the amount was $20 million to $30 million per day. These funds finance every conceivable activity in the global economy, and groups who have never had access to capital have a global financial market to tap into using the Internet.

There was a parallel revolution in investing. In the old days, if you wanted to buy stocks or bonds, you used a stockbroker. As a result, few Americans invested directly in these markets. You only have to turn on your television and see an ad for e-trade.com or schwab.com to know that there is a revolution underway in online investing. The old-style broker is a dying breed because online trading has lowered the transaction costs of buying and selling stocks to a low flat fee. AmeriTrade.com charges a flat $8 fee for stock trades for up to $5,000. As a result of these changes, stock ownership reached a historic high in 2002. Fifty-two percent of all Americans now own stocks directly, through mutual funds or in retirement programs (Hagenbaugh, 2003). Because of these changes, during the first decade of globalization, more wealth has been created in a shorter period of time than at any other time in human history. Sadly since 2001, these same investors have lost trillions. Friedman thinks the democratization of finance is the second key to globalization (Crutsinger, 1999, 2000).

The Democratization of Information

The democratization of information was made possible by the digitization of data, high-speed computers, electronic data storage, and the Internet. With a computer and a modem or high-speed Internet connection, anyone has access to information and knowledge anyplace in the world. You can just as easily peruse the card catalog in the Library of Congress or the Kremlin as in your local university library. You can find most government data through the federal government's information clearinghouse. In fact, you can search the public documents of most nations on the Internet.

Likewise, you are no longer at the mercy of your local bank. If you need a loan, you can check the interest rates of seventy banks at e-loan.com. If you are planning a trip to say, Bolivia, and are concerned about the health risks there, you can click on the web site of the Centers for Disease Control at www.cdc.gov. While you are online, you might as well make your airline, car rental, and hotel reservations for La Paz. In writing this book, I used the online archives of newsweeklies like *Time* and *Newsweek* and the newspaper archives of the *New York Times*, the *Washington Post*, and the *Christian Science Monitor*. I also used the e-journals in my university's library. In seconds, I had the full-length articles I needed delivered to my desktop computer via the Internet.

Friedman (1999) contends that the democratization of information has made another important contribution to globalization. Nothing keeps a government or a corporation honest better than someone looking over its shoulder. The information revolution means that governments and corporations are more transparent. People can keep an eye on what governments and corporations are doing and question their activities. The democratization of information is important in another way. How do you know where to invest your capital for the highest return at the lowest risk? Without the Internet and the democratization of information the global economy would be impossible. According to Friedman, this is the third piece of the globalization puzzle.

The Democratization of Decision Making

Prior to globalization, most decisions made in government or corporations occurred at the top. These organizations had hierarchical, pyramid structures, and only those at the top had the whole picture. Information worked its way from the bottom of the organization, and once a decision was made at the top, it would work its way down the layers of bureaucracy. In that era, most information was shuttled from office to office on paper, the volume was small, and it moved at a snail's pace.

Not anymore. Because of the democratization of technology, the person at the top is quickly overwhelmed by information. In today's world, financial information is outdated in minutes, not days or weeks. As a result, the role of top managers has changed. Corporate executives no longer make the day-to-day decisions they once did; they are paid to develop corporate strategies and to broker deals. The other decisions have been decentralized to people with the technical expertise to make them. Information is power, and with the decentralization of decision making has come the democratization of decision making.

Another change has led to the democratization of decision making. In the past generation, a new breed, symbolic analysts, has come on the corporate scene.

Symbolic analysts identify problems, come up with solutions, and then broker them into new goods and services. Their skills are in incredible demand, and they have little corporate loyalty. If you don't treat them right, they'll be working for your competitor next week. As a group, they have demanded and received greater say in running companies. As a result, organizations have become flatter, with far fewer layers. If you draw their organizational chart, you have a squat rectangle, not a pyramid. Why? In a faster, smaller world, decisions have to be made quickly and correctly. A CEO can't wait on a multilayered bureaucracy for information. The decision has to be made now! As a consequence, in many high-tech companies, the person at the top is just another colleague (Greenfield, 2000).

This revolution doesn't just stop at corporations. At the level of nations, the democratization of decision making is important. A democracy makes every citizen a stakeholder. As stakeholders, citizens have an interest in creating a stable and just society. But the most unappreciated aspect of a democracy is that it provides a means to peacefully remove an inefficient or corrupt government and to replace it with another. The global economy likes nothing better than predictability and stability, and this is what the democratization of decision making provides corporations and nations.

Fitting the Jigsaw Together

Why has the democratization of technology, finance, information, and decision making made globalization possible? These revolutions have made the cost of entry into any business much lower. Regardless of the field you are in, if you have a personal computer, credit card, phone line, modem, printer, and link to the Internet, you are in business. You don't even need computer skills because you can choose from thousands of companies to handle your web development and hosting. You don't need inventory because another web firm will do that for you. You don't need a delivery truck because FedEx, UPS, or the U.S. Postal Service will deliver your products for you. As the barriers of entry into markets have fallen, the potential for competition has increased. Why? Because you are no longer competing with the company down the street or in the next city, but with a company in Israel or South Africa or Japan or in all three. Competition is global.

Consumers are empowered too. Comparison shopping is effortless. Yahoo, Google, and Excite have evolved from search engines into portals and will search the web for the lowest price on any goods or service. On priceline.com and ebay.com, you can even bid on goods and services. The consequence of lower barriers to entry, an empowered consumer, and global competition is razor-thin profit margins. Only well-managed and efficient businesses survive.

Global competition also means that products move through the product cycle much faster. Prior to globalization, it took years for an innovative product to become a mass-produced appliance. Today, many consumer items are obsolete the day they reach the market. There is no better example than the computer. The computer has become an appliance. More than half of American households own one. Today, the product cycle for a computer is around three months. You can buy a low-end computer for around $600.

Competition in the PC market is ferocious, and only the fastest and smartest companies have stayed in business. The creator of the PC, IBM, lost $1 billion on its personal computer business in 2000. The inventor of the first home computer,

Apple, even with the astounding success of the iMac, is condemned to a niche market with around 8 percent market share. Three companies dominate the rest of the PC market: Dell, Gateway, and Hewlett Packard (HP). At this writing, Gateway is in trouble, and its future is in question. Dell and HP make so little profit on their computers, they have moved into Internet and business services to preserve their revenue streams. What if Dell, HP, Gateway, or Apple goes bankrupt? Will less competition mean higher prices? No. Within the global economy, someone somewhere will create a company to provide low-cost computers within a few months. And although the economy has slipped into recession, recent economic data suggest that the new economy endures (Francis, 2002a).

Between 1992 and 2000, the United States experienced unprecedented economic expansion with high growth, low unemployment, and low inflation. Alan Greenspan, the head of the Federal Reserve, was given much of the credit for the robust U.S. economy. Economists argue that the Fed has kept inflation in check by raising and lowering short-term interest rates. There's another explanation. We have low inflation and modest wage growth in the United States because of intense global competition. Regardless of the product or service there is a competitor willing to offer it faster and cheaper somewhere in the world (Scherer, 2000a, 2000b).[3]

There's No One at the Wheel!

To this point, Friedman (1999) has argued that changes in technology, finance, information, and decision making have made the global economy possible. These changes have lowered the costs of entering a market, empowered consumers, shortened the product cycle, and kept prices low. It has unleashed the power of capitalism to create new products and new wealth. It has unleashed capitalism's process of creative destruction, whereby inefficient companies are quickly forced out of business and replaced by another that takes over its buildings and employees. It is capitalism at its best and nastiest. It is a Darwinian struggle of the fittest. It is a system that takes no prisoners. But there is a big payoff. Since the fall of the Berlin Wall in 1989 and the events of September 11, the first decade of this new world order of globalization has witnessed an unprecedented rise in the standard of living of the world's population (Brandon, 2000). It's a mixed blessing. The floor under the billions of the world's population living in absolute poverty has risen, but, at the same time, the income disparity between the rich and the poor within countries (relative poverty) has grown. The same is true among nations (Francis, 2000). Nations that have the infrastructure and human capital to take advantage of the system have experienced unprecedented growth, and the average income of their citizens has grown relative to those nations ill equipped for globalization. We will explore these trends in the next chapter.

According to Friedman (1999), the fascinating thing is that no one is running the global market. There are supranational organizations like the World Trade Organization, International Monetary Fund, World Bank, European Union, and several United Nations agencies. But as we saw in the U.N. debate leading up to the Iraqi War, these organizations have no real police powers. According to Friedman, the invisible hand of the market is the real power in the operation of the global economy. What does this market do? When we speak of free-market capitalism, we are referring to the free competition in open and fair markets that determines the value of a good or

Photo 2.2   *The New York Stock Exchange, the home of the world's largest equity market, makes New York City the epicenter of the global economy. (Source:* © James Leynse/CORBIS.)

service. Humankind has never invented a more efficient system for distributing goods and services. And what are people buying and selling in these global markets? Anything. All kinds of goods and services move around the globe cheaper and faster today. But the most important commodity is investment capital.

The democratization of technology, finance, information, and decision making has created a global supermarket of investment instruments, but stocks and bonds are still king. New York City is the world's largest equity market, and the New York Stock Exchange (NYSE) is the largest stock exchange in the world (see Photo 2.2). Before 1989, a big trading day on the exchange was 100 million shares. In 2003, the NYSE regularly traded a billion shares a day. The directors of the exchange, terrified of lowering market share, began the twenty-four-hour trading day in 2000. With organizations like the NYSE, capital is literally moving in and out of countries and markets at the speed of light via the Internet.

There are two types of players in the market, short- and long-term investors. Short-term investors operate in both the stock and bond markets, and they move most of the money around the world. They are the army of analysts, brokers, and investors who scour the world for opportunities, determine risk, and make short-term investments. They can pour or pull billions of dollars, pounds, or yen in or out of a nation's economy in hours. The meltdowns of the Asian economies of Thailand and South Korea in 2000 are good examples. It only took a few hours for short-term investors to bring these economies to their knees. At this writing, Thailand and South Korea are making painful reforms to clean up their economies and woo back investors.

Long-term investors are corporations like Ford, GM, IBM, and Proctor and Gamble. They are making long-term international investments in things like factories, offices, and warehouses, so they can exploit the resources, labor, and markets of nations and regions around the world.

Regardless of type of investor, all want a few changes in your society before they invest—just a few. They want you to control corruption, permit a free press especially in economic reporting, create a free and fair stock and bond market, and create a free, open, and democratic society. Why? Because they know that countries that do these things are a good risk. They also want you to invest in your nation's infrastructure, especially communications and transportation. But more important than infrastructure, they want you to invest in the skills, talents, and knowledge of your people because the global economy is information and knowledge driven. So your most important asset is no longer those oil reserves, but the skills, talents, and knowledge of your citizens—your human capital. If you are willing to make these changes, pay the dues to join the club, then your citizens can expect a higher standard of living. If you aren't, well, have you taken a look at life in Albania lately?

The problem is that joining the club can exact some terrible costs. Societies want to preserve their cultures, but many demands of the global economy go against beliefs and values of many cultures. And from the experiences of the West, we know that unbridled capitalism destroys the environment. The most important questions for the global community are, "Can a society protect its environment and maintain its quality of life?" or "Can a society choose not to participate?"

Historical forces over which a single society has no control are pushing the rules of globalization forward. If you don't embrace the system, then your people will experience a declining standard of living. If you embrace change, then your society and its culture may begin to look like all the other societies in the world. There is no more intrusive and powerfully norming process in the world than globalization. As a result, political agendas that attempt to preserve a society's way of life are becoming secondary to economic ones. And who is to blame? The truth is that the rules of the global economy are not being enforced by governments, but by the invisible hand of the market.

How Things Can Change in a Faster, Smaller World

I wrote the first draft of this chapter in February and March 2000. In rereading it, I am struck by how quickly the world has changed. While I was writing in 2000, the stock market was at record highs, unemployment was at record lows, and per capita income was rising for all Americans. The nation's economy had grown in eight years by roughly the size of the gross national product of Germany, the world's third-largest economy, $1.8 trillion. We were at peace.

It's now March 2003. The value of stocks has been halved; investors in NASDAQ's technology stocks have lost $2.8 trillion in equity. Dozens of firms have already failed this year, and the nation's economy is in recession. In addition, the federal government is rolling up the largest deficit in history, state and city governments are facing their worst financial crisis in a half a century, and we are at war. The Bush administration, ignoring the United Nations, our NATO allies, and centuries of international law, has invaded Iraq, defying the very organizations that make globalization possible. So did Thomas Friedman get it all wrong?

Friedman foresaw globalization and the technology upon which it is based integrating world markets, transportation, and communications systems to a degree never witnessed before. It has enabled corporations, countries, and individuals to reach around the world farther, faster. And approximately half the world's nations are now active participants in the global economy because of this technology. But as we will see in the next chapter, the majority of nations in what Huntington labels the Islamic, African, and Latin civilizations have been bypassed. And, as our recent history proves, the resentment that this inequality creates makes us all vulnerable.

The technology that makes it possible to manage markets worldwide also permits individuals, what Friedman now calls *super-empowered individuals*, to do unimaginable harm. Osama Bin Laden used this technology to transfer people, money, and weapons worldwide. And it was all done from the relative safety of the Internet connection and satellite phone from his bases in Afghanistan. So Osama, a super-empowered angry man with geopolitical aspirations, didn't use cruise missiles or smart bombs to deliver his destruction on September 11, 2001. He used our transportation and communication technology, our open society, and nineteen angry young men.

Open Networks, Closed Regimes, by Shanthi Kalathil and Taylor Boas, calls into question Friedman's euphoria about electronically liberating the world. The authors look at eight regimes from Cuba to China to Saudi Arabia and find that, if carefully managed, the Internet can reinforce their power. In socially conservative Saudi Arabia, for example, the ruling royals delayed introduction of the Internet until sophisticated, Western-developed censorship software could be used to keep unwanted sites out. The Chinese government does much the same thing by controlling the servers, routers, and IP addresses upon which their nation's Internet operates (Leach, 2003).

More disturbing have been this nation's corporate scandals. Five companies—Enron, WorldCom, Tyco, Qwest, and Global Crossing—have squandered $460 billion in shareholder value since 2001 (Stevenson & Gerth, 2002). Investors lost trillions of dollars in the resulting plunge in the world's stock markets. What went wrong with the democratization of information and decision making? How could the toxic CEOs of these and other companies steal hundreds of millions of shareholder wealth in an era of transparency? Investigations of the Securities and Exchange Commission (SEC) and the New York State Attorney General's Office are giving us some answers.

It appears that the nation's largest brokerage and accounting firms, commercial banks, and their law firms colluded with CEOs and their corporate boards to deceive the world's investors by filing fraudulent earnings statements. Many of these parties are now paying the consequences. In 2002 the SEC had fined or were in settlement talks with Wall Street brokerage firms over conflicts of interests that could result in fines totaling more than $1 billion. Some individual brokerages could pay as much as $500 million. One of the nation's largest accounting firms, Arthur Andersen, was forced out of business after being found guilty of criminal charges in the Enron affair. And many of the nation's other large accounting firms are under criminal investigation, have paid multimillion-dollar fines, or are being sued by shareholders. Rounding out this sordid affair is that lawyers are suing other lawyers in some of the nation's largest and most powerful law firms for their unethical behavior (Luhby, 2002).

Probably the most telling of all the investigations were the findings of the nation's most aggressive attorney general, New York State's Eliot Spitzer. In his investigations, the attorney general discovered e-mail that showed that former high-flyer stock analysts had publicly lauded stocks while sending messages to insiders that derided the same companies. Merrill Lynch ended up paying $100 million to settle charges that it issued overly positive stock tips to investors (Luhby, 2002). Salomon is negotiating a settlement. They were not alone—the mixing of brokerage and consulting serious was endemic on Wall Street, and it is now illegal. The irony is that many of these analysts were caught with the same technology they used to manipulate markets—e-mail and the Internet.

Have we improved transparency in information, finance, and decision making? The Sarbanes-Oxley Act of 2002 is the most far-reaching series of changes to the laws of corporate governance, disclosure, and accounting oversight since the federal securities laws were enacted seventy years ago. The urgency of the legislation was reflected by the way it rolled through Congress and the unanimity of the vote—a 99–0 in the Senate and 423–3 in the House. "Throw the miscreants in jail" seems to have guided the writing of the bill. The law creates new crimes, including securities fraud, false certifications of quarterly and annual reports filed with the SEC, three new obstruction of justice crimes, whistle-blower protection, and across-the-board increases in fines and prison terms (Falvey & Wolfman, 2002). One provision makes CEOs personally responsible for the accuracy of their corporation's financial reports. Nearly 500 major U.S. corporations restated current and past corporate earnings statements in 2002 as a result of the law. As the Nobel Prize–winning economist Kenneth Arrow has concluded, "Virtually every commercial transaction has within itself an element of trust, certainly any transaction conducted over a period of time" (Arrow, 1972, p. 357). Have we restored trust and transparency in our markets? Time will tell. The jury is still out, or, more accurately, the investors are still on the sidelines.

What have we learned in the first decade and a half of globalization? I think there is no better insight into the operation of the global economy than our first foray of the dot-coms into the new economy—the center of greatest excesses in the 1990s bull market. The few dot-coms that have succeeded have strong, experienced management, sound business plans, excellent customer service, outstanding reputations, customer-friendly web sites, and loyal customers. They are market leaders. Many of these winners—such as E*trade, Ebay, Schwab.com, and DLJ Direct—have increased their profits in spite of the economic downturn (Shama, 2001). "Brick and click" describes other companies, like Wal-Mart, Lands' End, and Barnes and Noble, with existing customer bases and mature distribution systems that are also winners in e-commerce.

So what lessons do these dot-coms tell us about the global economy? First, it may be a new economy, but the basic rules of the market still apply. A good product, a sound business plan, experienced management, lean operations, and excellent customer service count. If you don't have these things, then you will go out of business. Second, the historic contradictions of capitalism still apply. Capitalism tends toward overproduction, and the oversupply of goods and services leads to economic booms and busts. Recession wrings the excess out of the system. And many early dot-coms, flush with the venture capital, were built on excess. Their CEOs told us that the old rules didn't apply to the new economy, and firms like Pets.com, a spectacular failure, spent $185 on every new customer to sell $35 worth of pet food! Where are the majority of the twenty-something dot-com millionaires now? Probably asking, "Would you like fries with that sandwich?"

We now know that the Internet allows companies to manage inventory, suppliers, labor, and capital far more efficiently than in the past.[4] As a result, companies make corrections faster, layoffs come sooner, and the economy sinks faster. Corrections are as brutal as ever, and they happen a lot faster. Friedman is right; we live in a faster, smaller world. And he accurately described the draconic role of the markets in correcting economic excess. Our current recession is wringing out the excess in our markets and our corporations. But I don't think Friedman could have anticipated the level of fraud, manipulation, and abuse made possible by globalization.

History repeats itself. The forces that created and destroyed the fortunes of millions of Americans in the 1920s are still at work in the 2000s. Like the 1920s the mess we are in happened inadvertently through our investing in things like fiber optics, semiconductor manufacturing plants, computer servers, dot-coms, and the Internet. We invested more than we should have, and in some cases we invested because we were lied to. And we borrowed to invest from creditors in a global financial place that Friedman so aptly describes. Since we had invested more than we should have to expand productive capacity, output soared, competition intensified, and profit margins slid. Because the law of supply and demand still applies, the market—a bear market this time—ended the excess (Grant, 2003). And like the Crash of 1929 that led to the creation of the SEC and the passage of our nation's first security laws, the Crash of 2001 led to the Sarbanes-Oxley Act of 2002 and a new set of laws to curb the excesses of a new economy. So maybe Friedman was wrong after all: Someone has to be at the wheel, and it's going to be government (Francis, 2002b).

Robert Reich and *The Work of Nations*

In 1991, Robert B. Reich published *The Work of Nations*. Reich was a political economist at Harvard at the time. He later became the secretary of labor during the first Clinton administration, and he used his office to prepare the nation for the global economy. Reich anticipated many of the changes described by Friedman a decade later. Note the themes Reich raises in the opening paragraph of his book.

> *We are living through a transformation that will rearrange the politics and economics of the coming century. There will be no national products or technologies, no national corporations, no national industries. There will no longer be national economies, at least as we understand that concept. All that will remain rooted within national borders are the people who comprise a nation. Each nation's primary assets will be its citizens' skills and insights. Each nation's primary political task will be to cope with the centrifugal forces of the global economy, which tear at the ties binding citizens together—bestowing ever-greater wealth on the most skilled and insightful, while consigning the less skilled to a declining standard of living. As borders become ever more meaningless in economic terms, those citizens best positioned to thrive in the world market are tempted to slip the bonds of national allegiance, and by so doing disengage themselves from their less favored fellows. (Reich, 1991, p. 1)*

So many of these themes are familiar. Robert Reich's contribution to debate, however, is his description of the changes taking place in American society. The most important changes are the shift from high-volume to high-value manufacturing, the rise of the global corporation, and the rise of the symbolic analyst.

From High-Volume to High-Value-Added Production

No nation in the world does high-volume manufacturing better than the United States. The Germans and the Japanese learned this in World War II. After the war, the United States had the only intact industrial economy in the world, and in the years following the war, American corporations shifted their industrial might to the production of consumer goods. All they needed were consumers.

Structural changes in the postwar economy provided those consumers. When these economic changes were combined with innovative social programs like the GI Bill and VA and FHA housing programs, millions of Americans were raised from poverty into the middle class. By 1955, no industrial society in history had a more equitable distribution of wealth than the United States (Halberstan, 1993). For the first time, a large and prosperous middle class allowed corporations to mass-produce goods for mass consumption. Corporations like General Motors had become vertically and horizontally integrated. They didn't just make cars; they owned subsidiaries that produced all the components that went into their cars. And virtually all these components were made in the United States. Anyone who owned an American-built car between 1950 and 1980 knows that quality wasn't a corporate concern. They could sell anything because they had a captive market. Mass production, mass consumption, and mass obsolescence were the market strategies of that era.

Things change. By the 1960s, the war-ravaged economies of Europe and Asia had recovered, and they had adopted American technology in their rebuilding efforts. By the 1970s, many of these nations were exporting cars and other consumer products to the United States that were not only cheaper, but of much higher quality. By the 1980s, many nations in the world had modern production technology, a critical mass of highly skilled and highly educated citizens, and a market strategy of competing in world markets on the quality of their products. American corporations hadn't sat idly by during the decades following the war. They had invested heavily in the emerging economies of the world. They were American corporations with global operations. After a long evolutionary process, two important changes occurred in the U.S. economy by the fall of the Berlin Wall in 1989. First, American corporations had become global corporations that were headquartered in the United States. Second, corporations' strategy had shifted from high-volume to high-value-added production. This type of production emphasizes quality and customer satisfaction.

Probably no other corporation epitomizes this transformation better than Ford Motor Company. Ford is still headquartered in Detroit, but at its world headquarters. Through most of the 1980s, Ford lost money on its North American operations, but remained profitable because of its production facilities and sales in Europe. In a massive shake-up in the early 1990s, Ford consolidated the management, design, parts inventory, and production of its cars worldwide. It began producing the same car, a world car, with only minor regional variations. So when you buy a Ford Escort, Ford's first world car, are you buying an American car? We know you are buying a car from a corporation headquartered in the United States, but . . . you decide.

The Ford Escort had a pedigree that looks something like this. It was contrived in France by a Ford subsidiary that designs cars and components for cars built and sold by Ford around the world. The Escorts built for the U. S. market had components fabricated by suppliers in Canada, the United States, and several

Asian countries. A consortium of investors brokered by a bank in London financed the car. Production insurance was underwritten by a Hong Kong company. A firm in New York did marketing, and the data processing was done through a company headquartered in Ireland. The Escort was assembled in Canada and the United States. After the car was sold, for around $20,000, and all the suppliers are paid, Ford's world headquarters receives around $4,000.

So who benefits, the economy of the United States or the economies of the nations making the components and providing the services? Or is this the right question? Is a national economy relevant at all? The answer is that the rewards go to the people whose skills, talents, and intellectual capital added value to the product, regardless of where they live. The amount of their reward was determined by the value they added to the product, and a global market determined this value. This process is repeated for every product and service in world commerce. The revolutions in technology, information, finance, and decision making mean products, services, and finance flow effortlessly across borders. A world without borders means that corporations have no borders, and American corporations are no longer American corporations, they are global corporations.[5]

We have already written about Ford. Let's take another American icon, IBM. Is IBM an American corporation? IBM has a twenty-one-member board of directors, and fifteen board members are not American citizens. If you ask an IBM executive, "Is IBM an American corporation?"—and I have—they will say something like this, "IBM is a corporation with operations that are competitive in markets around the world." You can ask the same question to a McDonalds or Hewlett Packard or GM or Merrill Lynch executive, and you'll get the same answer. But the truth is that the corporation may be headquartered in the United States, but most of their income from the value added to their products goes to people living outside the United States.

This change from high-volume to high-value-added production is one of the most important changes occurring in the global economy. Likewise, the change of corporations from national to global has fundamentally changed the nature of our nation's economy.

In the old world order, the welfare of all of us, rich and poor alike, rose and fell with the health of the national economy. But Reich argues that in a global economy this isn't the case anymore. Today, different groups of Americans have different experiences in the global economy. They rise and fall independent of each other, and their standard of living is not determined by the health of the American economy, but by what they add to the global economy. Those who are highly skilled and well educated will thrive, and their standard of living will improve. Those who have few skills and little education will sink. The reason is simple: Each economic group in the United States and everywhere else in the world competes with others in a global economy. The value of a group's labor is determined by a global, not a national economy.

New Economic Groups in the Global Economy

Who are these groups? Robert Reich focuses on three groups that make up 85 percent of the American workforce. They are workers in routine production services, in-person services, and symbolic-analytic services.

Routine Production Services

Routine production services are the kind of work we normally associate with old high-volume production. We used to call these workers blue-collar or factory workers. Their work is low-skilled, repetitive assembly-line work, and they are usually paid hourly or by the amount of work they do—piecework. This category also includes supervisors who routinely check the quality of the work of the line workers. Increasingly, this category includes workers who do routine data entry and filing in offices. These jobs are still very much in demand in the global economy. Companies still need things like cars, appliances, and computers assembled, data entered, and reports filed, but these workers are vulnerable because the value of their skills is determined on a world market. With the Internet, data entry, for example, can be done as well and more cheaply in Ireland or the Bahamas or thousands of other places in the world. In 2000, approximately a quarter of the American workforce could be classified as routine production services workers, but their numbers are dropping (Scherer & Eviatar, 2000).

In-Person Services

In-person services share much in common with routine production services. These jobs are repetitive and low skill, and usually these workers need only a high school education. Like routine production workers, these workers are paid by the hour or by the work they do. They differ from routine production workers in that their services are in person and cannot be sold worldwide. In-person servers include telephone operators, airline reservationists, retail clerks, waiters, janitors, telemarketers, hospital and nursing-home workers, and workers in the hospitality industry. In-person servers have one other quality not shared by routine service workers. They must be nice to people, even when verbally abused. This category of workers is one of the fastest growing in the nation, and they make up approximately 30 percent of our workforce.

Symbolic-Analytic Services

Symbolic-analytic services are the third job category, and it includes problem-solving, problem-identifying, and strategic-brokering activities. These workers compete for jobs in a global economy, but they don't do routine, standardized tasks. Traded instead are their skills, talents, and intellectual property. They are not paid by the hour or for the amount of work they do, but by the value they add to the things they help produce. They are engineers, bankers, lawyers, developers, and those involved in the financial services industry. They are that constellation of consultants—media consultants, tax consultants, marketing consultants, and production consultants—who work for companies like Ernst and Young and KPMG Pete Marwick. More often than not, they work for themselves as freelancers (see Monster.com). According to Reich, symbolic analysts solve, identify, and broker problems by manipulating symbols, not things. These symbols include innovative computer programming, mathematical algorithms, new financial instruments, innovative computer hardware, logistics, and schemes to deceive regulators and cheat investors. Their jobs are exciting, varied, and fun. They are not supervised; they are self-directed in their work. They don't have bosses; they have colleagues. Most symbolic analysts have college degrees, and unlike the other two categories, experience counts. Symbolic analysts hone their skills by doing, and the value of a symbolic analyst goes up over time.

Reich estimated that approximately 20 percent of the American workforce can be classified as symbolic analysts. Their numbers have grown dramatically in the past half century, but this growth seems to have slowed.

The future of each of these groups is determined by three factors: (1) replace-ability, (2) the value they add to a product or service; and (3) the value of their services to the global economy. This is why Reich argues that the futures of these three groups in a global economy will vary widely.

According to Reich, the future of the routine service worker is bleak. The reality is that these workers are easily replaced, they add little to the value of a product, and their work can be done by a worker in China or India for a fraction of what it costs in the United States. Unions have stalled the inevitable for some routine service workers, but these are workers in older industries like steel, autos, and glass. Union membership, however, is on the decline: Only about 10 percent of the American workforce is unionized. Tragically, the economic future of these workers is being determined by the lowest common denominator—what routine labor costs anywhere in the world. These were the workers who made up the majority of the protesters in Seattle at the World Trade Organization meetings (Kilborn & Nichols, 2000).

You might think in-service workers would be safe, but are they? Reich thinks this group will experience slow downward social mobility. Although they are not easily replaced because they provide services in person, they really don't add a great deal of value to a product. But does this mean they can't be replaced? The banking industry seems to think so. The banking industry has been able to slash the number of in-person servers with ATM machines and online banking. Computers are beginning to replace telephone operators. Offices have replaced tele-phone receptionists with interactive voice-activated computer systems, but you can't replace janitors or hospital and nursing-home operators.

Another challenge for in-service workers is competition for their jobs. We allow 800,000 legal immigrants into the United States each year, and more than 1 million illegal immigrants cross our borders annually. Most find their way to in-person ser-vice jobs, so technology and the untapped pool of English-speaking people around the world threaten the future of this group.

Until the beginning of the recession in 2001, symbolic analysts had a wonder-ful future. They are not easily replaced. There was a shortage of them worldwide, and their skills were in high demand. Their value doesn't decline with age; it increases with experience. Their skills are bought and sold in a global economy, but unlike the other two groups, their skills were in short supply, and high demand meant high incomes. Symbolic analysts give higher value to products, and they are in a position to demand a higher standard of living. This is why Reich calls symbolic analysts the "fortunate fifth." In the twenty-first century, most of the wealth created in the world will go to this group. But where? In 2003 more than 700,000 of their jobs were exported to nations like China and India.

The major consequence of a rising standard of living of the fortunate fifth and a declining standard of living for everyone else is a two-tier economy (Francis, 2000). In the coming century, many Americans will live in third-world poverty in the wealthiest nation in the world. Evidence shows that a two-tier economy is already emerging in the United States. In January 2000, two Washington-based think tanks reported that earnings for the poorest one-fifth of American families rose less than 1 percent between 1988 and 1998. During this same period the income of the richest fifth jumped 15 percent. Among other factors, the Center on Budget and Policy Priorities and the Economic Policy Institute attributed the widening income gap to a booming stock market favoring wealthier investors and on lower-paying service work replacing manufacturing jobs.[6] This shift is mirrored in other social indicators. For example, the number of homeless is growing, even in a booming economy. The Urban Institute estimates that 10 percent of the working poor in the United States was homeless in 1999.[7]

What are the social costs of a two-tier economy? With these statistics as a backdrop, the riots at the 135-member World Trade Organization can be seen as a reaction to the social costs of globalization. Environmentalists and union members took to the streets to protest declining standards of living for working Americans and an environmental degradation brought on by globalization. In the following year, these events were repeated in Switzerland, Italy, and Canada.

A New World Geography

To this point, we have argued that we are in the midst of a revolution that is creating a global economy. This revolution was made possible by the democratization of technology, finance, information, and decision making. These changes lowered the barrier of entry into markets, empowered consumers, shortened the product cycle, and unleashed the creative power of people through free-market capitalism. In the first decade of this revolution, it created more wealth than at any other time in history. It also has created enormous inequality within and among nations and threatened the integrity of cultures and the environment.

In the United States, corporations have been transformed from national to global entities, the economy has shifted from high-volume to high-value-added production, and human capital has become the nation's most important asset. As part of the global economy it helped to create, the well-being of our citizens is tied to the value they add to products through their talents, skills, and know-how. As the nation ended its longest economic expansion in history in 2001, this transformation had created an unprecedented amount of national wealth, but not all Americans have shared in it. Those who contribute most to the global economy, our nation's symbolic analysts, have watched their standard of living soar, while most Americans, trapped at the margins of the revolution, have watched theirs stagnate and decline.

Continents as Economic Units

This economic and social revolution has been accompanied by a revolution in the world's geography. A borderless world has changed the geographical units upon which economic competition takes place. The most sweeping change is that continents are replacing nations as a basic geographic unit in the global economy. The adoption of the euro as the common currency of Europe marks the creation of an economy as large as that of the United States. People, goods, and services now move freely across the national borders within the European Union, which expanded to twenty-five nations in 2004 when ten predominantly Eastern European nations were added to the EU. A supranational organization, the EU Central Bank now sets economic policies for the continent, not nation-states.

Continental-based economic competition was the basis for the Clinton administration's push for freer trade. The Bush administration shares these same policies. During the Clinton administration, the North American Free Trade Agreement was ratified. It is accomplishing the same thing in North America as the EU is in Europe. Goods and services now move freely from Mexico's southern border with Guatemala to the Arctic Circle. In 1999, Chile requested entry into NAFTA. Can a borderless Western Hemisphere be far behind? There are similar movements in Asia and the Middle East, and the General Agreement on Tariffs and Trade (GATT) aims to accomplish the same goals worldwide.

These changes have led to organized, sometimes violent, opposition to globalization. Demonstrators in major cities in the United States and Europe have spotlighted the social, cultural, and personal costs of globalization. Much of the opposition is organized by nongovernmental organizations (NGOs), and their number has exploded in size since the onset of globalization. Lester Salamon, a political scientist at the Johns Hopkins University, calls this phenomenon, "a global association revolution that may prove to be as significant . . . as the rise of the nation-state" (Knickerbocker, 2000, p.13). Two reasons behind this explosive growth of NGOs are that governments around the world are becoming more democratic and less authoritarian and that advancing means of communication allow citizens and activists around the world to share information and strategies (Knickerbocker, 2000).

Evidence of the growing strength and influence of these organizations was seen during the recent protests at the 2000 World Trade Organization meeting in Seattle. Aside from the handful of anarchists who trashed some buildings and got most of the media coverage, most protesters were from a large network of environmentalists, human rights activists, labor organizations, and others concerned with the economic and social impact of the secretive, government-sponsored WTO. While it may have looked to TV viewers as if spontaneous protests caught local officials by surprise, NGOs around the world had spent months developing strategies for expressing their concerns in Seattle. The spread of global communications in recent years has made it possible for activists like those in Seattle to quickly find out about one another's work and to join forces for maximum impact—often in a way that lessens the traditional power of governments (Knickerbocker, 2000). More recently, hundreds of NGOs on five continents used the Internet to coordinate their worldwide demonstrations against the war in Iraq.

There are many other examples of NGOs at work. NGOs pressured Nike to improve working conditions for its overseas employees, Home Depot to buy lumber harvested from sustainable forests, and Chevron to ensure that its operations would not harm the environment (Knickerbocker, 2000). We are witnessing a revolution in civic participation in government decision making on a global stage.

New Regional Economies

Within continents, regional economies are becoming more important than national ones. The average resident of Washington State has far more in common with Canadians living in British Columbia than with Americans living in New England. With the ratification of NAFTA, the integration of these regional economies has been accelerated. The best example is our Pacific Northwest, or as Canadians see it, their Southwest. Twelve million people are squeezed into a fifty-mile corridor between Vancouver and Eugene, Oregon. There is even a name for it—Cascadia. Growing numbers of Canadian and American symbolic analysts ply their trade in both countries. University students frequently cross the border for their educations. Two-nation tourism is popular. High-speed train service has linked Seattle and Vancouver since 1994. And intergovernmental problems are tackled by the joint British Columbia and Washington Governmental Cooperation Council founded in 1992. Cascadia has emerged without the help of the federal governments in either nation. And this same process is occurring along our entire 4,000 mile shared border. With a large pool of symbolic analysts, these regional economies are specializing in high-value goods and services. These regional economies, with their embedded metropolitan areas, will be important economic engines in the global economy in the twenty-first century (Porterfield, 1999).

The same thing is happening in other parts of the country. NAFTA has accelerated the integration of regional economies along our southern border with Mexico. The region's cities from San Diego to Phoenix to Houston have a long shared history with Mexico. They are now being integrated socially, economically, and culturally into vibrant regional economies. With a large pool of routine production workers and in-person servers, however, these economies will have a different future than those to the north. The same thing is happening in southern Florida—Miami has become our commercial gateway to the Caribbean and South America.

The Growth of the City-State

Remember Athens and Sparta from your history class. These powerful city-states, not nations, formed the cradle of Western civilization. According to Peirce, Johnson, and Hall (1993) and other social scientists, city-states are the cradle of globalization. These social scientists coined the term *city-state* to describe the sprawling metropolises like Vancouver, Seattle, and Portland at the core of regional economies like Cascadia. According to Peirce and his colleagues, a city-state contains a traditional central city, adjoining newer cities (sometimes called *edge cities*), suburbs, bedroom communities, and even rural areas. They become city-states when their region offers a meaningful degree of coordination of services. If they didn't, the city-state would lack control over the quality of services that are the key to spawning and luring new business. Around the nation, you find metroplans, regional planning and transportation authorities, coordinating boards, and special districts that plan and coordinate services across state, county, and local government lines. They tackle an array of problems: water, waste treatment, solid-waste disposal, transportation, policing, and planning—any regional activity that requires coordination. This process is well underway in the United States. More than half our population, around 140 million people, lived in thirty-nine metropolitan areas in 2000.

Globalization has simultaneously pushed power up to the international level and down to the local level. As city-states have risen in importance, state governments have become less important in economic development. Although states are delegated enormous powers by our Constitution, the global economy may reduce their role to collecting taxes for schools, roads, and human services. The economic engines in the global economy are city-states and their regional economies, not state government.

For the past fifty years, most central cities in the United States have experienced population decline and economic stagnation. Not anymore. The central cities of many of the nation's metropolises are experiencing a renaissance. Modern city-state thinkers believe a vibrant central core is essential to the health of the entire city-state. The city-state's core must provide an exciting and attractive central gathering place for conventioneers and tourists. It must also provide world-class business and telecommunication services, colleges and universities, medical centers, national sports franchises, shopping, restaurants, and cultural facilities if the city-state is going to lure business (Brummett, 2000).

Atlanta, the city, the core of the Atlanta city-state, is a wonderful example of this new trend. Look at a map and you'll see that the Atlanta metropolis takes up most of the center of the state of Georgia. Not only does Atlanta dominate the state and regional economy, but it has a global presence as well. The Atlanta city-state is emerging as a unified economic unit. It is tackling the problems of traffic and mass transportation with regional transportation and planning authorities. At its core, the city of Atlanta provides global corporate services, a world-class medical center, major professional sports teams, and a dizzying array of entertainment, restaurants, and shopping. Little wonder it is a major tourist and convention destination, and Atlanta's Hartsfield-Jackson Airport is the busiest in the world. This form of urbanization is repeating itself around the globe, and when a global corporation is looking for a new location for a plant or an office, it finds a city on the edge of an Atlanta, Dallas, Los Angeles, London, Berlin, Tokyo, or Hong Kong city-state.

A recent study commissioned by the United States Conference of Mayors supports the position that city-states are becoming the world's dominant geographic unit within which economic activity takes place (DRI-WEFA, 2001). Using Census 2000 data, the report shows that metro areas generated more than 80 percent of the nation's employment, income, and goods and services in the 1990s. The most interesting part of the report, however, is a comparison of the economic output of city-states and nations.

The gross domestic product (GDP) is a measure of the total output of goods and services by a nation's economy. The Conference of Mayors raised an interesting question. What if we calculated the total dollars of goods and services produced by a metro area, a *gross metropolitan product* (GMP), and then compared it to the nations of the world? GDPs and GMPs for nations and city-states are presented in Table 2.1. The United States has the world's largest economy with a GDP of nearly $10 trillion, followed by Japan's $4 trillion and Germany's $2 trillion economy. If New York were a nation rather than a city-state, it would be ranked as the fourteenth-largest economy in the world. Los Angeles would be ranked sixteenth, and Chicago would be ranked eighteenth.

I live in northwest Arkansas, which has the 259th largest economy in the world. (Wal-Mart's corporate headquarters in the metro area helps our rankings.) I work in Jordan, which has the 278th largest economy in the world. The 361,000 people living in the two-county metro area in northwest Arkansas generated $9 billion of goods and services in 2002. Jordan, a nation three-quarters the size of Arkansas, with a population of more than 5.5 million people, had a GDP of only $8 billion. City-states have become the economic engines of the global economy. Find the GMP of your city-state at the U.S. Conference of Mayors' web site at *http://www.usmayors.org/metroecono3/*.

Table 2.1   *World Rankings on GDP and GMP**

Rank	Country or Metro Area	GMP	Rank	Country or Metro Area	GMP
1	United States	10,446.0	51	**Oakland, CA**	105.5
2	Japan	3,996.0	52	South Africa	104.3
3	Germany	1,993.0	53	Venezuela	103.3
4	United Kingdom	1,568.9	54	**Newark, NJ**	103.0
5	France	1,436.8	55	Israel	102.7
6	China	1,237.0	56	**Baltimore, MD**	102.6
7	Italy	1,188.0	57	Argentina	101.1
8	Canada	727.0	58	**Denver, CO**	100.9
9	Spain	655.0	59	**Riverside-San Bernadino, CA**	100.4
10	Mexico	636.0	60	Iran	99.1
11	India	484.0	61	Malaysia	95.2
12	Korea, South	470.3	62	**St. Louis, MO-IL**	92.2
13	Brazil	452.0	63	**San Jose, CA**	88.3
14	**New York, NY**	448.9	64	**Tampa-St. Petersburg-Clearwater, FL**	87.5
15	Netherlands	419.0	65	Singapore	87.0
16	**Los Angeles-Long Beach, CA**	411.0	66	Egypt	85.4
17	Australia	398.0	67	**Pittsburgh, PA**	84.0
18	**Chicago, IL**	349.5	68	**Cleveland-Lorain-Elyria, OH**	82.3
19	Russia	347.0	69	Colombia	81.5
20	Taiwan	282.2	70	**New Haven, CT**	80.6
21	Switzerland	267.2	71	Philippines	77.1
22	**Boston, MA**	266.9	72	**Portland-Vancouver, OR-WA**	76.9
23	Belgium	247.0	73	**Miami, FL**	75.7
24	Sweden	240.9	74	**Charlotte-Gastonia-Rock Hill, NC-SC**	73.6
25	**Washington, DC-MD-VA-WV**	236.5	75	**Sacramento, CA**	71.9
26	Austria	203.6	76	Puerto Rico	71.8
27	**Philadelphia, PA-NJ**	192.4	77	Czech Republic	69.5
28	Norway	191.4	78	**Harford, CT**	69.1
29	Saudi Arabia	191.0	79	**Middlesex-Somerset-Hunterdon, NJ**	67.2
30	Poland	190.2	80	**Kansas City, MO-KS**	67.1
31	**Houston, TX**	185.4	81	**Fort Worth-Arlington, TX**	66.2
32	**Atlanta, GA**	177.9	82	Chile	65.4
33	Indonesia	172.8	83	**Columbus, OH**	64.0
34	Denmark	172.7	84	United Arab Emirates	63.1
35	**Dallas, TX**	166.9	85	**Cincinnati, OH-KY-IN**	63.1
36	Turkey	165.9	86	**Bergen-Passaic, NJ**	63.0
37	Hong Kong	163.0	87	**Norfolk-Virginia Beach-Newport News, VA-NC**	62.9
38	**Detroit, MI**	161.7	88	**Orlando, FL**	62.1
39	**Orange County, CA**	150.7	89	**Indianapolis, IN**	61.3
40	Finland	132.1	90	**Las Vegas, NV-AZ**	60.9
41	Greece	131.1	91	Hungary	60.5
42	**Minneapolis-St. Paul, MN-WI**	128.9	92	Pakistan	59.7
43	Thailand	126.4	93	New Zealand	58.3
44	**San Diego, CA**	125.0	94	**San Antonio, TX**	58.1
45	**Phoenix, AZ**	124.9	95	Peru	57.9
46	Ireland	122.4	96	Algeria	55.7
47	Portugal	121.3	97	**Milwaukee-Waukesha, WI**	55.4
48	**Seattle-Bellevue-Everett, WA**	120.9	98	**Greenboro–Winston-Salem–High Point, NC**	51.8
49	**Nassau-Suffolk, NY**	113.7	99	**Salt Lake City-Ogden, UT**	51.4
50	**San Francisco, CA**	110.6	100	**Buffalo-Niagara Falls, NY**	50.9

Source: DRI-WEFA Inc (2003) Metro Economies Report July, 2003. Retrieved February 22, 2004 from U.S. Conference of Mayors site: *http://www.usmayors.org.*

*City/Country Metros are the 319 metropolitan areas defined by U.S. OMB.

Clusters of Symbolic Analysts

Thus, city-states are the places where the global revolution is being played out. City-states are also the places where innovative goods and services are created, produced, and distributed. In the United States, as in no other nation in the world, symbolic analysts are concentrated in specialized geographic pockets within city-states where they live, work, and learn with other symbolic analysts. We all know about Silicon Valley, a pocket of symbolic analysts working in the computer hardware and software industry, in the San Francisco city-state. The Seattle city-state, with Microsoft and Nintendo at its economic core, constitutes another silicon center. Media is the message of Silicon Alley, centered on Manhattan's Flatiron District but stretching from New Jersey to Connecticut in the nation's largest city-state, New York. The Alley is home to many of the world's major media companies— AOL/Time-Warner, the *New York Times*, Viacom—as well as the highest concentration of the Internet's new power players in publishing and advertising. Route 128, in the Boston city-state, is the high-tech beltway surrounding the city of Boston. This stretch of highway is home to Lotus, Lycos, Data General, and more than 3,600 computer and electronic companies. There are the Silicon Hills of Austin, Texas, the home of Dell Computer and major facilities for IBM, Advanced Micro Devices, Motorola, and other programming and software companies (Allbritton, 1999). These pockets of symbolic analysts in every field imaginable are found across the nation and the world. Even smaller communities are developing symbolic analysts clusters like my home, Fayetteville, Arkansas. Fayetteville has become a world center for geographical information systems, high-temperature superconductivity, and large-scale integrated chip technology. As this new geography evolves, new political, social, and cultural forms will emerge to create and nurture these pockets of symbolic analysts. With the economies of these city-states dependent on global corporations and networks, they have developed new strategies for competing in a global economy.

New Strategies for Growing a City's Economy

Susan Clarke and Gary Gaile (1998) describe strategies for growing a city's economy in their book, *The Work of Cities*. According to the authors, the goals of all city governments are the same. They want an economic development strategy that (1) increases city revenues and the stability of their revenue streams, (2) decreases the city's vulnerability to external shocks by diversifying their local economies, and (3) provides good jobs and services to their citizens while protecting the community's quality of life.

For most of the twentieth century, cities tried to do this by attracting business by lowering the costs of doing business within their borders. You still see ads in business weeklies that tout a city's good business climate. And cities created good business climates with a variety of tools—tax abatement, subsidized job training, free land with subsidized site development. There are problems with this strategy, however. One is the prisoner's dilemma—you don't know what other communities are offering. And large corporations are masterful at playing one community against another. The other, more serious problem arises when community problems can't be addressed because tax abatements have robbed the city of needed revenues.

In the last decade, a new growth strategy has emerged that recognizes the policy approach championed by Robert Reich—investments in human capital. This strategy recognizes that the strength of a city's economy is a function of the value its citizens contribute to the global economy. The most progressive cities try to attract and keep businesses that hire large numbers of symbolic analysts. And when the fortunate fifth moves to town, large numbers of in-service workers are needed to serve them. This new strategy moves beyond the traditional place wars to grow the local economy by linking it to the global one.

Cities have different histories and economic bases, and the past determines how well cities can compete in the global economy. For example, the location of large land-grant universities in Columbus, Ohio; Madison, Wisconsin; and Berkeley, California, give these cities an enormous pool of symbolic analysts. This asset makes them competitive in a knowledge-driven global economy. But older industrial cities like Newark, New Jersey, and Akron, Ohio, are saddled with a pool of routine production workers. How do they compete in a knowledge-driven global economy? They are having a difficult time, and thousands of workers are being left behind.

Regardless of a community's assets, Clarke and Gaile (1998) describe the new roles of cities in growing their economies. The most important is their new role as strategic brokers. City leaders are pooling public and private money to create and expand businesses. In a break with the past, cities are assuming greater financial risks as entrepreneurs, and they are sharing risks and rewards with their partners. Other new roles identified by Clarke and Gaile include promoting global trade ties and encouraging the growth of symbolic analysts and in-person service sectors within their borders. But according to the authors, the most important strategy is investing in the city's infrastructure. Cities recognize that to attract and keep symbolic analysts and the businesses that employ them, they must provide a high quality of life. They are investing in high-technology industrial parks, fiber-optic services, new airports, revitalized recreation and entertainment centers, better schools, expanded libraries, and new cultural centers. Many of these investments are made on a regional basis for the benefit of the entire city-state. Cities are making these commitments because they recognize that the global economy is knowledge driven and a community's human capital is its most important asset.

Cities face unseen dangers hitching their future to the new economy. Seattle and the cities embedded in Cascadia offer no better example. Seattle was held up as a new economy role model for the rest of the country. Home of Microsoft, Starbucks, Boeing, and hundreds of new economy businesses, it held many of the nation's best factory and technology jobs. For much of the 1990s, national magazines touted Seattle as the best place for business and Portland as the most livable city in the United States. The Cascadia area economy was growing at twice the national rate, and per capita income was 20 percent above the national average. But now the attributes that made the Cascadia look like the vanguard of the new-century economy have come back to haunt this region. A staggering Asian economy, the worldwide downturn in the airline industry, and the dot-com bust dealt a triple blow to the area. Over the last year, no place in the country has had higher unemployment than this region. The Seattle area alone has lost almost 80,000 jobs, and Oregon and Washington state governments face the worst budget crisis in fifty years (Egan, 2003).

Although the importance of state governments in the global economy may be diminishing, power is granted to states, not cities, in our federal system. If a city wants to try a new investment strategy, state or federal law may ban it. In addition, state and federal governments make decisions over which cities have no control. For example, changes in federal tax laws may hurt a local business and force it to look overseas for relief. A punitive tariff against a foreign country for unfair trade practices may spoil a multimillion-dollar expansion in a city. A multibillion-dollar merger prevented by antitrust action by the Justice Department may close a city's corporate headquarters (Debre, 2000).

Regardless of these problems, the research by Clarke and Gaile suggests that cities are increasingly using entrepreneurial strategies that entail some risk of their own revenues to grow their local economy. These strategies are keyed on making local-global economic linkages, developing human-capital resources, developing telecommunication infrastructure, and improving the city's quality of life. In the process, public and private roles have blurred; local citizenship has been eroded; and in keeping the fortunate fifth happy, other groups are being ignored. One of the most serious by-products of this process has been the segregation and isolation of the unfortunate classes from the rest of the community.

A Tale of Two Cities

A theme woven throughout this chapter is that a fundamental change has occurred in the fortunes of labor. Well-educated and highly skilled workers who identify and solve problems and broker their production and marketing are flourishing in the global economy. Poorly educated and unskilled workers who provide routine production and in-person services are foundering. In 1991, Robert Reich predicted the emergence of a two-tier economy in the United States. He was right.

In this opening decade of a new century, many of America's working poor find themselves almost no better off than they were in the early 1990s and worse off than they were twenty years ago. Low unemployment rates have not boosted their incomes. Even middle-income Americans have made only marginal gains since 1980. Meanwhile, the wealthy get wealthier, and income disparity grows toward levels not seen since the Great Depression (McCaffrey, 2000).

Nationally, families in the bottom fifth of the income ladder earned an average of $14,021 in 2001. This is down an average of 6 percent from the late 1970s when inflation is taken into account. These figures come from a report cosponsored by the Economic Policy Institute and the Center on Budget and Policy Priorities and a 2003 U.S. Census report, which also suggests that middle-income families haven't exactly flourished either. Since the late 1970s, their inflation-adjusted incomes rose a small 5 percent to an average $51,538. The big winners in the '80s and '90s were the wealthiest one-fifth of U.S. families. Their income soared 30 percent during the same period to an average $159,644. The new economy has brought more job opportunities, but not everyone can share in them equally (Harris, 2000; U.S. Census, Bureau, 2003). The group that has fared the worst is high-school dropouts. According to a new report from the Federal Reserve, families headed by someone without a high-school diploma saw their inflation-adjusted income fall an average of $2,000 from 1989 to 1998.[8]

The pattern is clear. The major reason for the disparity in the growth of the working poor in this and other industrial societies is a lack of education. Millions of impoverished working Americans hold routine and in-person service jobs that do not provide a living wage. And as the income trends show, the widening gap is tied to the relationship between education and income. If these trends continue, by 2020, the top fifth of American earners will account for more than 60 percent of all income earned by Americans, and the bottom fifth 2 percent (Reich, 1991). Millions of citizens of the most prosperous nation in history will be living in third-world poverty.

These societal changes are working themselves out in space. The new urban geography in a two-tier economy is the creation of two cities in the same city-state. One city houses the symbolic analysts whose services are linked to the world economy. The other city houses in-person servers and routine production workers whose jobs are dependent on the symbolic analysts.

According to Robert Kaplan (1998), globalization and the emergence of a two-tier economy means a change in nation building and in the way we construct communities. He even suggests that we may be seeing the end of citizenship. In the future, cities, and even nations, will compete for citizens. The community with the highest quality of life wins. This seems to be borne out by the experience of many symbolic analysts. Symbolic analysts often have far more in common with a colleague half a world away than they do with their next-door neighbor. In a computer-driven, information- and knowledge-based economy, an economy tied together by the Internet, people can maintain close friendships with their colleagues around the nation and the world. Cheap and efficient air travel means they can visit them often.

Kaplan shows that symbolic analysts prefer self-contained engineered communities, rich in services and removed from the problems of society. He calls these new, insulated communities *urban pods*. According to Kaplan, they are emerging as a vast conglomeration of minifortresses linked by the Internet to other pods across the region and the world. The county is emerging as the political unit of urban pods. Examples include Johnson County (Kansas City), Dade County (Miami), Montgomery County (Washington, D.C.), and Orange County (Los Angeles). These counties will provide governance for the multitude of incorporated suburbs in the nation's city-states.

Regardless of where these urban pods are located, they share common attributes. They are suburban and prosperous. They have good schools and public services. Mega-malls provide wonderful shopping. Crime rates are low because "those people" don't live here, and their police aggressively enforce the law. They have sameness, because they are a collection of the same standardized corporate building blocks—Wal-Marts, Home Depots, McDonalds, Walgreens, and Mediquicks. They are home to the fortunate fifth and far removed from the unfortunate classes just a few miles away in the next city or county.

The evidence is that symbolic analysts are seceding from the rest of society. Witness the widening divergence in incomes, growing difference in their working conditions, regressive shift of the tax burden, growing disparity in the quality of primary and secondary schools, growing disparity in their access to higher education, and increasing difference in recreational facilities, roads, security, and local amenities available to them. Insulated from social problems in their gated, guarded pods, they have shown an unwillingness to share their new wealth with others in this and other societies. But they could be just hiding their heads in the sand.

The goal of progressive nations is to create a just and stable society. We know from twentieth-century history that the most important stabilizing force in a modern industrial society is a large and prosperous middle class. As we have shown, the health and size of the nation's middle class is eroding, as more and more

Americans are forced into the fringes of our economy by globalization. As more Americans are marginalized, they are being segregated in the city-state's worst housing and neighborhoods, usually in the central city. This group has become known as the *underclass.*

America's growing underclass is a heterogeneous grouping of families and individuals outside the mainstream of the American and global economy. They are poorly educated, they lack training and skills, and they suffer from long-term unemployment or underemployment. They share similar problems: low income, poor health, inadequate housing, poor education, and cultural and linguistic differences that separate and isolate them from the mainstream of society. Structural changes in the global economy, along with the decentralization of business and industry from the central city to industrial parks and commercial centers on the fringe, have led to the segregation and isolation of our most disadvantaged citizens. Potent barriers prevent their full participation in the nation's economy. Social scientists call it the inequality of place. When people are segregated in the central city, they tend to be cut off from information on outlying labor markets. The time and cost of commuting is an additional barrier to employment. Residential segregation inhibits contact between groups, lessening the chances of interaction and eventually assimilation, and it is a major factor in the perpetuation of inequality in our society. Therefore, one's life chances are circumscribed not only by social class, but also by one's residential location within the city. This is especially true of children. When education and skills are vital for full participation in a global economy, these children go to the society's worst schools. During a communication and information revolution, these children have no Internet access. During a period of prosperity, these children are denied adequate health and child care. During a revolution called globalization, a particularly pernicious form of poverty is being created that is structural and cyclical in character (Belsie, 2000).

The twentieth century is called *America's century.* During this century, we found our national character and became a superpower. The evidence is strong that the twenty-first century may be America's century, too. Here are the qualities that Thomas Friedman (1999) and Robert Reich (1991) think will make America succeed:

- We are blessed with geography. We are on the Pacific and Atlantic rims with economic and cultural ties to the vibrant economies of Asia and Europe.

- We are blessed with an ethnically, racially, and religiously diverse society that has links to most of the nations in the world. Although multicultural, multiethnic, and multilingual, we are bound together by a single language—English—the language of world commerce. We openly accept immigrants and their talents and money. We protect their constitutional rights, and we embrace them as citizens.

- We have the most diverse, innovative, and efficient capital markets in the world.

- We have an honest legal and regulatory environment, and our government, financial institutions, and corporations are the most transparent in the world. We have a legal right to government and financial information.

- Our system of bankruptcy laws encourages people to take risks and, if they fail, to try again.

- We have a relatively fluid stratification system. We are becoming a society based on merit.

- We have a decentralized decision-making process in our federal system capable of changing to meet the needs of our society in the twenty-first century.

- We have an open and mobile workforce.

- We accept the innovator, the oddball, and the maverick. Just look at John McCain.

- Our corporations have already gone through downsizing, privatizing, networking, deregulation, reengineering, streamlining, and restructuring in order to exploit the democratization of finance, technology, information, and decision making. These corporations excel in a fast-moving, networked global economy.

- Our system is deeply rooted in entrepreneurship, and our tax system allows the risk taker to keep what he or she earns.

- We have environmentally protected open spaces and small towns.

- We have the largest and best system of higher education in the world.

- Finally and most important, we have the world's largest pool of symbolic analysts. We have the richest and most diverse innovation clusters in the world where our symbolic analysts live, work, and learn from one another.

In short, our society is designed for the global economy in the twenty-first century. Whether or not we reach this promise will be determined by the centrifugal forces that will tear at our social fabric.

I reported staggering statistics earlier. By 2020, the top fifth of American earners will account for more than 60 percent of all income earned by Americans, the bottom fifth 2 percent. Symbolic analysts are withdrawing into ever more-isolated enclaves, within which they pool their resources rather than share their bounty with less-fortunate Americans. Now that the Bush administration's massive tax cuts have become law, an ever-smaller proportion of the fortunate fifth's incomes will be taxed and invested in the nation's common good. There are other troubling trends. Government spending on education, training, and infrastructure continue to decline, and this decline will continue in the post–Iraqi War period. And as the federal government shifts more of the service burdens to lower levels of government, poorer cities, counties, and states will be in an even more precarious position. In the midst of the worst fiscal crisis at the state and city level, this nation is becoming two nations—one rich and one poor.

The basic questions are, "Will we choose to act fairly and compassionately in the face of globalization?" "What will the meaning of American citizenship be in a global economy?" We agree with Robert Reich's call for a positive economic nationalism. Each nation takes responsibility for enhancing the capabilities of its citizens, each nation gives all its citizens full and productive lives, and our national purpose becomes investing in our most valuable asset, our people. In this way, we can smooth the transition from the old to the new world economy. By doing these things we create stronger, more diverse, and more vibrant cities—the basic building block of the global economy (Halal & Varey, 1999).

Summary

In this chapter, we explored the social revolution called globalization and its consequences for cities. Francis Fukuyama (1992) sees a more prosperous and safer world shaped by the principles of free-market capitalism and liberal democracy. Samuel P. Huntington (1996) presents a compelling counterargument. He agrees that technologies like the Internet and the end of the Cold War have led to the economic changes we call globalization. Rather than a world moving from integration to interdependency, Huntington and others see the emergence of a multicultural-, multipolar-, multiconflict-oriented world, not a globalized, homogenized culture or a new era of world peace and prosperity. Globalization may mean that nation-states have lost control over the movement of ideas, images, capital, technology, and people across their borders. Improvements in transportation and communication technology have produced more frequent and more intense interactions among people of different civilizations than at any time in history. But this movement of people, ideas, and capital has also created the potential for more frequent and more dangerous conflicts among nations because, according to Huntington and his followers, they are on the fault lines of civilizations.

Although Fukuyama and Huntington differ in their future vision for the world, they agree that we are in the midst of a revolution bringing about rapid and basic changes in the social, political, and economic institutions of societies around the world. I used two books—Thomas Friedman's *The Lexus and the Olive Tree* and Robert Reich's *The Work of Nations*—to analyze these changes. Thomas Friedman argues that all societies in the world have two wants. First, people want and need roots—family, home, neighborhood, and culture—and things lasting and satisfying. Friedman represents them with the olive tree, which is deep rooted and long lived. People also want things represented by the Japanese luxury automobile, the Lexus. They want a higher standard of living made possible by the promise of a global economy. The new conflict in the world, according to Friedman, is not between competing ideologies; rather, it is between the human needs represented by the olive tree and the Lexus. The dilemma is that societies must embrace the social and economic changes necessary to compete in a global economy, while at the same time preserving the uniqueness of their culture and the quality of their environment.

This revolution was made possible by the democratization of technology, finance, information, and decision making . These changes lowered the barrier of entry into markets, empowered consumers, shortened the product cycle, and unleashed the creative power of people through free-market capitalism. In the first decade of this revolution, globalization has created more wealth than at any other time in history. It also has created enormous inequality within and among nations and threatened the integrity of cultures and the environment.

The nation's economy grew by roughly $1.8 trillion between 1989 and 2001. Since September 11, 2001, the value of stocks has been halved, investors have lost trillions of dollars in equity, hundreds of firms have failed, and the nation's economy is in recession. Was Friedman's analysis of globalization wrong? He foresaw globalization and the technology upon which it is based integrating world markets, transportation, and communications systems to a degree never witnessed before. Friedman is right; we live in a faster, smaller world. And he accurately described the draconic role of the markets in correcting economic excess. But I don't think Friedman could have anticipated the level of fraud, manipulation, and abuse made possible by globalization. And he didn't foresee how the technology that makes it possible to manage markets worldwide also permits super-empowered individuals to do unimaginable harm.

According to Friedman and Reich, in the United States and in the world, corporations have been transformed from national to global entities; the economy has shifted from high-volume to high-value-added production; and human capital has become the nation's most important asset. As part of the global economy it helped to create, the well-being of our citizens is tied to the value they add to products through their talents, skills, and know-how. As the nation leaves its longest economic expansion in history, this transformation has created an unprecedented amount of national wealth, but not all Americans have shared in it. Those who contribute most to the global economy, our nation's symbolic analysts, have watched their standard of living soar, while most Americans (routine production workers and in-place service workers), trapped at the margins of the revolution, have watched theirs stagnate and decline. Therefore, globalization is a mixed blessing. The floor under the billions of the world's population living in absolute poverty has risen, but, at the same time, the income disparity between the rich and the poor within countries (relative poverty) has grown. The same is true among nations. Nations that have the infrastructure and human capital to take advantage of the system have experienced unprecedented growth, and the average income of their citizens has soared relative to those nations ill equipped for globalization.

The problem is that historical forces over which a single society has no control are pushing the rules of globalization forward. If you don't embrace the system, then your people will experience a declining standard of living. If you embrace change, then your society and its culture may begin to look like all the other societies in the world. There is no more intrusive and powerfully norming process in the world than globalization. As a result, political agendas that attempt to preserve a society's way of life are becoming secondary to economic agenda. The rules of the global economy are not being enforced by governments, but by the invisible hand of the market.

This economic and social revolution has been accompanied by a revolution in the world's geography. A borderless world has changed the geographical units upon which economic competition takes place. The most sweeping change is that continents are replacing nations as a basic geographic unit in the global economy. The North American Free Trade Agreement is an example. Goods and services now move freely from Mexico's southern border with Guatemala to the Arctic Circle. NAFTA has accelerated the integration of regional economies along our southern border with Mexico. The region's cities are now being integrated socially, economically, and culturally into vibrant regional economies.

Globalization has simultaneously pushed power up to the international level and down to the local level. As city-states have risen in stature, state governments have become less important in economic development. Although states are delegated enormous powers by our Constitution, the global economy may reduce their role to collecting taxes for schools, roads, and human services. The economic engines in the global economy are city-states and their regional economies, not state government.

Similarly, Robert Kaplan (1999) found that globalization and the emergence of a two-tier economy mean a change in the way we construct communities. He even suggests that we may be seeing the end of citizenship. In the future, cities, even nations, will compete for citizens, and the community with the highest quality of life will win. He found that symbolic analysts and other well-off citizens increasingly live in segregated, isolated urban pods, cut off from society's problems.

Thus, our society is faced with basic questions such as, "Will we choose to act fairly and compassionately in the face of globalization?" and "What will the meaning of American citizenship be in a global economy?" I agree with Robert Reich's call for a positive economic nationalism in which each nation takes the responsibility for enhancing the capabilities of its citizens, each nation gives all its citizens full and productive lives, and our national purpose becomes investing in our most valuable asset, our people. In this way, we can smooth the transition from the old to the new world economy. By doing these things we create stronger, more diverse, and more vibrant cities—the basic building block of the global economy.

Notes

[1] Francis Fukuyama in his 1992 book, *The End of History and the Last Man,* has gone so far as to argue that this victory represents the end of history. He argues that the historical conflict between competing ideologies represented in the Marxian dialectic by communism and capitalism has not ended in the emergence of industrial communism as the only ideology in the world; rather, it is liberal democracy and free-market capitalism. Fukuyama, however, sees the end of the Cold War as America's political and economic institutions writ large through benign means. The political geographer Saskia Sassen has a different perspective. She calls globalization a new and sophisticated form of American Empire. Unlike previous empires, America's empire accommodates the world's 196 sovereign states. According to Sassen, the United States is not interested in winning the hearts and minds of a nation's inhabitants or in controlling a nation's government. (This is where colonial powers ran into trouble.) All the United States demands is the adoption of world standards of trade and commerce, so its international corporations can operate inside a nation's borders. A nation doesn't want to make the changes? Then, it can't join the international club. After all, the United States controls all the international organizations that run the global economy. If a nation has something the United States needs—markets or raw material—and it still doesn't want to make the changes? Then the United States will make the changes for them. The United States can use force if necessary because, remember, there is only one superpower left, and it is in a position to change global norms and behavior. Robert Kagan (2003) in *Of Paradise and Power: America and Europe in the New World Order* is an apologist for this position. Kagan is the intellectual architect of a neoconservative interventionism that seeks to promote democracy and American values internationally, even, if necessary, by force. The Iraqi War is an outgrowth of this policy position.

[2] Former President Bush initiated the Free Trade Agreement of the Americas (FTAA) in 1994. FTAA will include thirty-four countries in the Western Hemisphere except Cuba, and it is scheduled to start in 2005. The FTAA seeks to eliminate trade and regulatory barriers and to increase trade and investment across the hemisphere. The FTAA is not a new idea. The dream of a unified hemisphere reaching from the Arctic Circle to

Tierra del Fuego has inspired statesmen and thinkers in both the North and the South since the 1960s.

[3] Throughout the 1990s Alan Greenspan and the Federal Reserve were credited with keeping inflation down and growth up in the U.S. economy. In a recent article "One Nation Under Wal-Mart," Jerry Useem argues that Wal-Mart, not the Fed, was responsible. Wal-Mart's corporate headquarters in Bentonville, Arkansas, are just fifteen miles north of my campus. The *Fortune* reporter argues "by systematically wresting 'pricing power' from the manufacturer and handing it to the consumer, Wal-Mart has begun to generate an economy-wide Wal-Mart Effect. Economists now credit the company's Everyday Low Prices with contributing to Everyday Low Inflation, meaning that all Americans—even members of Whirl-Mart, a 'ritual resistance' group that silently pushes empty carts through superstores—unknowingly benefit from the retailer's clout." A 2002 McKinsey study, moreover, found that more than one-eighth of U.S. productivity growth between 1995 and 1999 could be explained "by only two syllables: Wal-Mart." "You add it all up," says Warren Buffett, "and they have contributed to the financial well-being of the American public more than any institution I can think of." His own back-of-the-envelope calculation: $10 billion a year (Jerry Useem, *Fortune*, February 18, 2003).

[4] During the boom of the 1990s, nothing exemplified the globalization and the new economy more than just-in-time supply chains and lean manufacturing techniques designed to make a company's output more sensitive to customers' needs. Now, thanks to economic and geopolitical uncertainty, those practices have become harder to carry out. New regulations on border crossings by the Homeland Security Department, intended to protect the nation from terrorism, are making just-in-time just too difficult and many companies are abandoning the practice. Many of the productivity gains in the new economy were due to these manufacturing techniques. Efficiency lost means higher prices (Altman, 2003).

[5] New rules recently implemented by the Department of Homeland Security mean tighter borders and less free flow of goods and services across all our borders. Increased waiting times at Canadian and Mexican checkpoints slowed the nearly $1 trillion a year trading relationship between the three NAFTA members in 2002 (Krauss, 2003). The West Coast longshoreman strike in 2002 along with slowdowns in the nation's busiest ports by these new security regulations showed the vulnerability of the nation's "just-in-time" inventory and manufacturing system. The threat of terrorism is reducing the productivity gains made possible in a smaller and faster global economy (Krauss, 2003).

[6] The gaps between the rich and the poor and between whites and minorities have grown wider in recent years, the Federal Reserve reported in 2003. Wealth, measured by *net worth,* includes stocks, retirement funds, homes and other assets minus all outstanding debts. The differences in median wealth between the 10 percent of families with the highest incomes, and the 20 percent of families with the lowest incomes jumped 70 percent from 1998 to 2001. The gap between whites and minorities grew 21 percent. Median net worth for all families rose 10 percent to $86,100 in 2001 from 1998 and was up 41 percent from 1992. Net worth for the lowest income group, whose median pretax income was $10,300 in 2001, rose 25 percent to $7,900. Net worth for the top 10 percent of household income, with a median income of $169,600, however, rose 69 percent to $833,600. Growing wealth inequality mirrors growing income inequality in the United States (Hagenbaugh, 2003).

[7] Many of Robert Reich's fears have come to pass. At this writing, the 2004 federal budget is in the conference committee. The House budget includes $750 billion in tax cuts, targeted to the wealthy, while cutting billions of dollars in programs that provide food stamps, school lunches, health care for the poor and the disabled, temporary

assistance to needy families, veterans' benefits, and student loans. An analysis of the House budget by the Center on Budget and Policy Priorities found that proposed cuts in child nutrition programs would eliminate school lunches for 2.4 million low-income children; cuts in Medicaid would eliminate health coverage for 13.6 million children; and cuts in the food stamp program would lead to a reduction in the average benefit from 91 cents to 84 cents per meal (Center for Budget and Policy Priorities, 2003).

[8] These are income figures. What about wealth? In 1989, less than one-third of families owned stocks (either directly or through a mutual fund or retirement account). By 1998, half did, according to the Federal Reserve. And the median value of those holdings more than doubled from $10,800 to $25,000 over the same period. But the wealth hasn't been evenly distributed. Families earning at least $100,000 have seen their portfolios skyrocket 300 percent while those earning between $10,000 and $25,000 have seen a rise of 50 percent. Furthermore, that doesn't count the other half of families that don't own any stocks. If they're included, the median value of stock holdings falls considerably. Even among middle-income earners (families earning $25,000 to $50,000 a year), it amounts to $400 (Belsie, 2000).

3

GLOBALIZATION AND URBANIZATION IN THE LESS-DEVELOPED WORLD

Introduction

In 1950, 275 million people were living in cities in the less-developed world—38 percent of the world's total urban population. By 1975, this figure reached 1.6 billion, with more than half of this number living in the metropolitan areas of the developing world. Today, 2.2 billion of the world's 3.3 billion urban dwellers (66 percent) live in the cities of the less-developed world. In the twenty-five years from 1975 to 2000, the cities of the less-developed world had to accommodate nearly 1.3 billion new inhabitants. More often than not, these millions moved to the world's largest cities. Only one city in the less-developed world had more than 5 million inhabitants in 1950; today, there are forty cities of this size. By 2015 there will be 58 cities housing 604 million inhabitants (United Nations Population Division, 2003a).

In the span of just fifty years, the world has seen the greatest migration in history, not from one nation to another, but from the countryside to the city. Increasingly, this migration is focused on one city, a megacity. Although the poor dominate these megacities, modern skyscrapers, wealthy urban pods, luxurious shopping centers, and world-class restaurants also share the urban landscape. Shantytowns and slums are in the shadow of these monuments to the gifts of a global economy. Underdevelopment and overdevelopment exist side by side.

Mexico City, the capital and largest city in Mexico, is a striking example. Now home to 16.5 million people, it is expected to grow to nearly 20 million by 2015. It is a crowded and dirty city of many contrasts. From the vantage point atop one of the downtown office buildings, one sees high-rise buildings decked with the logos of multinational corporations—Hyatt, Hilton, Citibank, and Chase. From this vantage point, a modern city spreads out before you—a university campus, medical complex, government ministries, and the luxurious neighborhoods of the wealthy. A web of modern highways binds the city into an organic whole.

Walking on the street twenty floors below, one experiences the familiar. The crush of pedestrians wears mostly Western dress, but an occasional local reminds you that you're someplace else. Familiar chains—McDonalds, Subway, and KFC—dot the streetscape along with the ubiquitous Nike and Adidas shoe outlets. The power of multinationals is felt in Mexico City because this downtown, like the centers of all other major cities in the world, is created out of the same standardized, interchangeable, multinational corporate elements—luxury hotel chains, international banks, fast-food restaurants, and retail outlets.

But the vast majority of the residents live starkly different lives in the hidden, less-visible parts of the city. Over half of Mexico City's population lives in the sprawling squatter settlements and shantytowns on the outskirts of the metropolis. Most of these residents have never had a real job and make a living in the city's informal economy. Fewer residents have jobs in factories owned by multinationals making clothing and other commodities for world markets. A small elite of symbolic analysts have internationally competitive salaries by selling their knowledge and talent in the global economy (Thinkquest, 2000).

As we saw in chapter 2, urbanization cannot be studied in isolation. It is related to population change and linked to the processes of economic development and modernization shaped by globalization. This chapter explores the urbanization process in the developing world and focuses on the three major facets of this process—demographic, economic, and social/cultural change. First, global population and urban patterns will be presented, and the underlying demographic patterns will be discussed. Fertility, mortality, and migration patterns will be explored, the theory of demographic transition will be presented, and the impact of these changes on cities will be assessed.

Second, issues surrounding economic development will be presented. The relationship between the more- and less-developed countries of the world will be discussed, along with the relationship between cities and their rural hinterlands. Primacy, the phenomenon in which the population of a country's largest city outstrips that of all others, is explored. The phenomenon of megacities will be presented, as will the formal and informal economies found in these cities.

Urbanization and economic development change the way people organize and live their lives. A third section of this chapter will explore the revolutionary change in society's norms, values, and roles that accompany the development process. The contrasts between the old and the new values and the formal and informal economies of these societies will be explored in the context of the spontaneous settlements found in the cities of the developing world. Special attention is given to spontaneous settlements and the role they play in the development process.

The chapter ends with a discussion of the major theories used to explain the world patterns of urbanization, economic development, and modernization. We will once again visit globalization in this section and discuss how this revolution shapes the people and cities in the developing world.

World Population Growth

I was born in 1947. The year I was born, the earth's population was a mere 2.5 billion people. By the time I reached thirty, the earth's population had nearly doubled to 5 billion. On my fiftieth birthday, near the year 2000, the world's population exceeded 6 billion people (United Nations Population Division, 2003a). In the course of my lifetime, one of the greatest events in the planet's history has occurred: the domination of the earth by a single species, homo sapiens. This domination has had disastrous consequences for the earth's ecosystem. Population pressure has led to the extinction of thousands of species, the destruction of the ozone layer, global warming, the destruction of the world's rain forests, desertification, widespread famine, and a host of other ills. The media identifies chemicals like chlorofluorocarbons, atmospheric CO_2, and acid rain as the culprits, but, in reality, the increase in these chemicals in our atmosphere is linked to the unprecedented growth of human population.

Population growth does not take place in a vacuum, but rather within societies. Throughout the text, I will make a distinction between two types of societies—more-developed countries (MDCs) and less-developed countries (LDCs). Following the lead of the World Bank and the United Nations, I use these terms over others, like developed and developing, because it reflects the shifting economic relationships among nations of the world. Argentina is a country with enormous natural wealth, and a century ago it was considered a more-developed country. Mismanagement by a succession of military governments from the 1950s through the 1980s left its economy in ruins. Argentina returned to civilian rule following the Falklands War, but this legacy lives on. In the late 1990s, the World Trade Organization forced Argentina to· make painful structural changes in its economy. The changes did not work. Today, Argentina is on the brink of bankruptcy, and this nation is considered an LDC.

The same is true for the United States, but in the other direction. The twentieth century has been America's. For the past fifty years, the United States has dominated the world's economic order, and we are poised to continue this dominance well into the twenty-first century. The United States has the world's largest economy and its most productive industry, but globalization has changed the rules of the game. In 1980, Japan, a country the size of California, displaced the Soviet Union as the world's second-largest economy, and Americans worried that they might be next. Japan, however, has been unwilling to make the painful changes necessary to compete in a global economy, and it is now in its tenth year of economic recession. The Soviet Union no longer exists, and Russia is an economic basket case. The economic unification of Europe in 1992 was another challenge to our preeminence but is only now providing the bounty it promised.

The U.S. economic juggernaut continues; in the 1990s the United States increased the size of its GDP by $2 trillion, about the size of Germany's economy. Therefore, the United States is developing faster than other nations, and over time, our relative position to other nations has changed. This shuffling and reshuffling of nations on the economic ladder is an ongoing process, but a general pattern continues. Today, it is generally agreed that MDCs include the United States, Canada, the nations of Europe, Russia, Japan, New Zealand, and Australia. The economic tigers of Asia—the Republic of China (Taiwan), South Korea, and Singapore—have recently become MDCs. The nations in the rest of the world are considered LDCs (World Resources Institute, 1999).

Level of Development and Population Growth

How is population growth related to a nation's level of economic development? The contributions of the more- and less-developed regions to world population growth are shown in Figure 3.1. Until 1900, the population growth of MDCs equaled or exceeded LDCs. This pattern began to change in the 1930s, and by the end of World War II enormous differences existed in the growth rates of the two regions.

Today, the less-developed countries of the world contain approximately three-quarters of the world's 6 billion people. Since the end of World War II, these nations have grown from 2 to 3 percent per year. On average, their populations double in size every 27 years. Contrast this pattern with the experiences of more-developed countries. Most MDCs grew no more than 1 to 1.5 percent a year during their period of most rapid population increase in the nineteenth century. Today, the birth rate in most European nations is below replacement level, and as their populations age, they will experience slow population decline. The same is true in the United States. The U.S. population grows through immigration, not through the natural increase of its American-born citizens. In other parts of the world, the growth rate of MDCs is below 1 percent, and their populations double, on average, every 111 years (United Nations Population Division, 2003a).

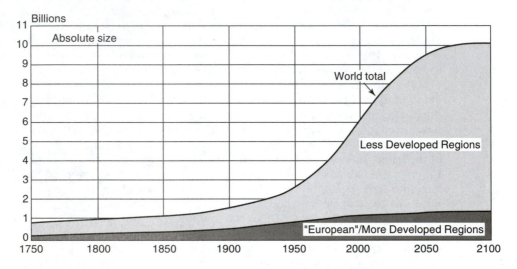

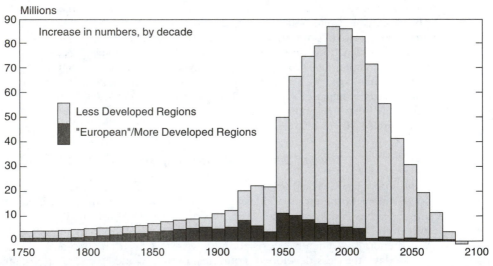

Figure 3.1 *World, Developing and Developed Regions, Population Growth: 1750–2100 (Source:* Thomas W. Merrick, with Population Reference Bureau staff "World Population in Transition." *Population Bulletin* 41, No. 2 [April 1986]: Figure 1, p. 4.)

Why the differences in the growth rates of MDCs and LDCs? The population growth of LDCs in the postwar period can be contributed to one factor—the importation of death-control technology from MDCs. DDT and other insecticides, first introduced fifty years ago in the tropical regions of the world, have controlled one of the great scourges of humankind, malaria. Modern sanitation, improved water supplies, childhood immunization programs, and other public health measures have dramatically lowered mortality rates in LDCs (World Resources Institute, 1999). This decline in death rates in LDCs, however, has not been offset by a decline in birth rates. The gap between these two vital events has led to rapid population growth. We live in a world of more than 6 billion people. Nearly 5 billion of these people live in the less-developed countries of the world, and this disparity will continue to grow. In the next twenty-five years, nations like India will grow from 985 million to 1.4 billion and Brazil from 168 million to 217 million (United Nations Population Division, 2003a).

The Theory of Demographic Transition

A number of competing theories describe these demographic processes, but by far the most important is the theory of demographic transition introduced by Kingsley Davis more than fifty years ago (Davis, 1945). The theory of demographic transition posits a close relationship between economic development, modernization, and demographic processes. As societies move from less developed to more developed—from traditional to modern—conditions are created encouraging low fertility. The theory suggests people in modern societies have fewer children because they no longer want large families. One reason is the great reductions in mortality, especially the deaths of infants and children. Couples no longer need to have large families to ensure several will reach adulthood. Other changes in modern societies, including mandatory education and child labor laws, have greatly diminished the economic value of children. Children no longer are economic assets but economic burdens. Therefore, fertility patterns follow mortality patterns. Mortality usually declines first, and then, after several generations, fertility declines to a level close but never as low as mortality (Davis, 1945; Davis & Golden, 1954).

Stage 1

The transition process is graphically depicted in Figure 3.2. In Stage 1, one finds traditional societies with high and stable rates of fertility and high and unstable rates of mortality (famine and epidemics periodically kill thousands). Because the rates are both high, they tend to balance each other out, and the size of the population remains stable. These societies have high growth potential because any improvement in the food supply or in death-control technology can lead to a rapid increase in population.

The vital events in Stage 1 societies profoundly influence all aspects of life—their institutions, values, norms, and roles. Life is short; life expectancies range between twenty-five and forty, and as a result these societies use ascribed status to fill key positions. Orphans and widows are common, so these societies have extended families. Only in this way can society be assured children will be cared for if their parents die. The values, norms, and roles of the extended family ensure high fertility. Women in these societies have few options outside the roles of mother and homemaker, and the social pressure to

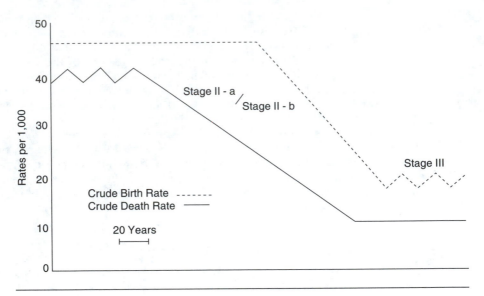

Figure 3.2   *Graphic Representation of the Classical Demographic Transition Model*

have children is intense. It is not a question of if, but how many children a wife will bear (Goldscheider, 1971).

Stage 2

Stage 2 is a phase of transitional growth. The industrialization that accompanies economic development improves the quality of life. Improved diets, cheaper and more abundant clothing, fuel, and shelter as well as public health measures lead to dramatic declines in death rates. The birth and death rates for Mexico from 1895 to 2025 are shown in Figure 3.3. Note the decline of mortality from 50 per thousand in 1920 to 5 per thousand in 1995, but also note the high and stable birth rate that remained at 30 per 1,000 population until 1976. Since then it has declined by almost half to 20 per 1,000 in 2003. The difference is natural increase on an unprecedented scale. The explanation for this lag is that institutions change slowly. The values and norms of an extended family continue to encourage high fertility, but as parents learn most of their children will survive to adulthood, as the nuclear family becomes the dominant family form, and as women find alternatives to the role of mother and homemaker, birth rates decline. Although Mexico is making progress, many LDCs are in this transition stage, and they are experiencing unprecedented rates of natural increase.

Stage 3

In Stage 3, societies have low and stable death rates and low but unstable birth rates (remember the post–World War II baby boom and the much-touted baby bust). The result: populations are stable in size or change slowly. Life expectancies are long, over seventy years, which permit new social patterns. Achievement

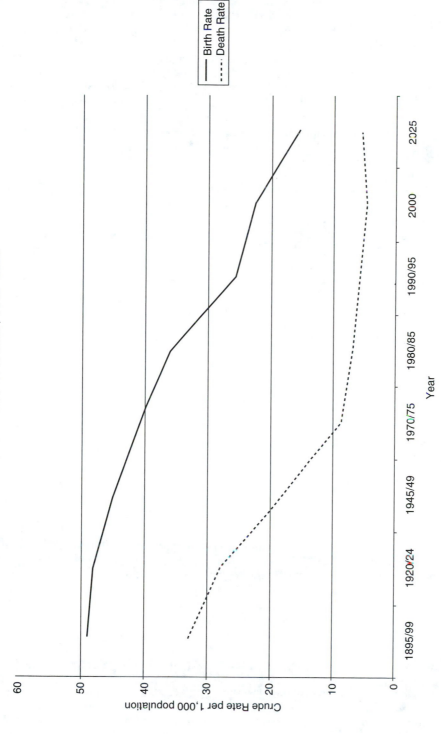

Figure 3.3 *Birth and Death Rates for Mexico, 1895–2025* (*Sources:* 2000 and 2025 data from U.S. Census Bureau. 2001. *International Data Base Summary for Mexico* [Internet] U.S. Census Bureau [cited September 9, 2001]. Available from *www.census.gov/cgi-bin/ipc/idbsum.?cty=mx*. Historical data from Thomas W. Merrick, *Population Pressures in Latin America*. Washington, D.C. Population Reference Bureau, Table 2, p. 8.)

rather than ascription is used by society to fill key positions. The nuclear form sup-plants the extended family. Women have alternatives to the roles of mother and homemaker, and the values and norms of the nuclear family encourage smaller families. Therefore, the values, norms, institutions, and other patterns in society are intertwined with its vital events (Goldscheider, 1971).

The theory of demographic transition has been tested and refined over the past fifty years. In general, the theory reasonably describes the course of vital events in most industrialized nations, but it has never been able to predict levels of fertility and mortality or the timing of these events. This is because the theory is based on the experiences of societies that have already experienced the transition—more devel-oped countries. The conditions under which MDCs developed in the nineteenth and early twentieth century are very different from those LDCs face today. Few MDCs had birth rates as high as those of LDCs, nor were their levels of mortality as high. And, as we have already noted, mortality decline in MDCs was the result of economic devel-opment created through innovation and invention from within, not through technol-ogy introduced from outside the society (Goldscheider, 1971).

Importing technology rather than creating the technology internally suggests that the demographic transition in LDCs will differ from MDCs. The United Nations reports public health measures in LDCs have reduced mortality to a minimum, and in the future, these efforts will have little impact on population growth. Therefore, any attempt to bring about significant reductions in the rate of population growth in these countries must focus on changing fertility.

The problem is that death control can be applied without the knowledge of the individual through public health; birth control requires the participation of individuals. In the past, fertility decline was correlated with the development process. As development proceeded there were fundamental changes in the underlying fertility and mortality patterns of a society. In the Western world this was true; in the developing world, the relationship is not as clear cut. The improvement in birth-control technology over the past fifty years has lowered its cost and simplified its distribution. The result: the fertility rate in LDCs has declined faster than economic development. Whereas, in England it took 100 years to reach low rates of fertility, in some LDCs the same transition is being com-pressed into a single generation. For example, the Population Institutue estimates that the average family size in Mexico will reach replacement level of just 2.1 chil-dren per couple by 2015. Although there is hope for future trends in world popu-lation growth, a major gap still exists between birth and death rates.

On closer examination of the demographic data for the world's LDCs, one finds enormous differences within and between countries. In Latin America, infant mortality for women with no education is five times higher than for women with eight years of education. Therefore, one must not only understand the general demographic patterns shared by LDCs, but, in addition, appreciate the variation in vital events within the nations we refer to as less developed (United Nations Population Division, 1996).

The Effects of Rapid Population Growth

The economic growth experienced by European nations during the nineteenth and early twentieth century was associated with the first sustained population growth in history. Population growth, then, was viewed as good because more people meant larger markets for newly burgeoning industries. The population that could not be absorbed in cities emigrated to the sparsely populated regions of the world—North and South America, Australia, and New Zealand. Growth rates were moderate by today's standards, seldom exceeding 1 percent, and the process was gradual, spanning a century (Goldscheider, 1971).

The situation is different today. Growth rates in LDCs run between 2 and 3 percent per year, and populations double in less than thirty years. Rapidly growing populations distort the age structure of a society, and one finds in LDCs a disproportionate share of a society's population in the young, unproductive age categories. Consequently, less-developed countries face enormous service burdens. Children require schools, hospitals, housing, food, clothing, and other services, but they are not old enough to work and contribute to the nation's economy. More serious, LDCs cannot export their surplus populations: there are no virgin, undeveloped territories left in the world. In addition, LDCs must compete in a world dominated by the advanced economies of the more-developed nations. Thus, at a time when LDCs must expand their technology; improve their infrastructure of roads, communications, and public facilities; and modernize their agriculture to compete in a global economy, they are saddled with enormous service costs to a young, unproductive population (Gugler, 1990).

Research shows high population growth slows economic growth and exacerbates the inequality between more- and less-developed nations in at least two ways. First, an increase in population means an increase in the number of workers. More workers mean that, on average, each worker produces less per worker in relationship to the land and other resources available in the society. Second, as the number of children per worker increases, there are fewer savings to go into industry and technology to increase productivity. Resources go to schools, health care, and food instead of for roads, electrical systems, factories, and other parts of the capital stock necessary for competition in world markets. Thus, many of the problems faced by LDCs are linked to population dynamics (Gilbert & Gugler, 1992; Gugler, 1990).

World Urban Growth

In the last half of the twentieth century, the world's population problems became the world's urban problems. Underemployment and unemployment, poor public services, inadequate housing, nonexistent medical care, and poor nutrition are now concentrated in their most visible and pernicious forms in cities. In LDCs, population growth on the national level is unprecedented; urban growth is astounding. As we noted earlier, 275 million people, or 38 percent of the world's urban population, lived in the cities of the less-developed world in 1950; by 2000, the world's urban population exceeded 3.2 billion, and 66 percent of this population was in the cities of the developing world. The United Nations Population Division estimates that by the year 2025, the world's urban population will be more than 5 billion, and 78 percent, or 4 billion people, will be living in the cities in the less-developed world. Therefore, in the next twenty-five years, the cities in LDCs must absorb 1.8 billion people—a task that would strain the managerial talent of any nation, much less an LDC (United Nations Population Division, 2003b).

Contrast this with the urbanization experience of MDCs. In the nineteenth and early twentieth centuries, during our period of rapid urbanization, population growth was relatively low, incomes high, rural to urban migration manageable, and the diffusion of innovations slow by today's standards. The process was painful, but the adaptation of our political, economic, and social institutions was carried out over the span of a century. Urbanization in LDCs will be different. First, the rate of natural increase and the magnitude of rural to urban migration are much higher today than in the past.

Second, in the nineteenth century, rural to urban migration reduced the population pressure on agricultural land in MDCs. In LDCs, high rates of natural increase in both urban and rural areas have kept the ratio of population to arable land high.

Third, unlike MDCs, innovation and technology in LDCs is imported and diffuses rapidly throughout the society. The process has been accelerated in the global economy. Imported communication technology informs farmers and villagers of the opportunities in cities, and imported transportation technology lowers the cost of migration to these centers.

Fourth, in MDCs when rural to urban migration threatened to overwhelm the cities there was a safety valve—emigration. North and South America and the far-flung colonies of the European empires provided virgin territory for settlement. Today, international migration is controlled, and in LDCs, cities, not colonies, have taken on the role of absorbing surplus rural population.

Therefore, the urbanization in LDCs will be both qualitatively and quantitatively different from MDCs. These societies will be forced to absorb more people in less time than any societies in history. Experiences will vary from country to country, but, in general, the vast majority of this urban population will be poor with few skills, and LDCs will be saddled with two problems—absorbing this growing population and carrying out economic development (Gilbert & Gugler, 1992). A question for the world's planners is, "Will the promise of globalization help or exacerbate these problems?"

Current and Projected Growth

The previous discussion cites general patterns. There is enormous variation between and within the world's regions. Estimated and projected urban population for selected countries in the world's regions is provided in Table 3.1. Note that as late as 1950, 60 percent of the world's urban population lived in MDCs. By 2000, however, two-thirds of the world's 3.2 billion urban population lived in the cities of LDCs. Thus, between 1950 and 2000, the urban population of LDCs grew 670 percent from 275 million to 2.1 billion, while MDCs grew by 144 percent from 448 million to 1.1 billion. Some regions grow faster than others. During this same fifty-year period, urban populations in Africa grew an astounding 981 percent, from 32 to 346 million; Latin America 585 percent, from 68 to 466 million; and Asia 641 percent, from 176 million to 1.3 billion (United Nations Population Division, 2003a, 2003b).

Another view of this urbanization process based on annual growth rates is provided in Table 3.2. Annual growth of the world's urban population has not fluctuated a great deal since 1960 and was not predicted to change much before the turn of the century, but this summary measure masks the enormous variations

Table 3.1 Size of Urban Population in Major World Regions and Selected Countries, 1950–2025 (in thousands)

	1950	1975	2000	2025
World Total	724,147	1,560,860	3,208,028	5,065,334
Developed Regions	448,929	767,302	1,092,470	1,089,003
Developing Regions	275,218	793,558	2,115,558	3,976,331
Africa	31,818	103,032	345,757	804,239
Algeria	1,948	9,024	28,021	33,675
Egypt	6,532	16,346	37,048	60,519
Ethiopia	761	3,273	15,140	37,929
Ghana	727	3,193	10,843	21,934
Kenya	336	1,592	8,125	32,616
Morocco	2,345	6,551	19,704	26,917
Nigeria	3,595	11,449	45,041	146,948
Senegal	563	1,070	3,002	10,506
South Africa	5,261	11,934	30,109	46,673
Sudan	572	3,722	16,551	27,075
Zambia	428	1,704	6,260	11,647
Latin America	67,511	193,366	466,234	600,679
Argentina	11,205	20,436	28,875	43,083
Brazil	19,064	66,621	163,027	204,791
Chile	3,588	8,044	13,460	17,684
Columbia	4,334	16,946	41,779	41,592
Ecuador	911	2,971	8,564	13,456
Guatemala	921	2,269	6,384	13,389
Mexico	11,348	37,318	102,293	117,222
Nicaragua	397	1,163	3,396	7,072
Paraguay	474	1,003	2,708	6,475
Peru	2,811	9,619	24,132	30,653
Venezuela	2,739	9,795	21,125	33,791
Asia	175,618	490,570	1,297,719	2,718,435
Bangladesh	1,786	6,838	32,095	78,430
India	59,247	127,177	360,688	629,757
Indonesia	9,362	25,079	76,612	167,398
Iran	4,087	14,959	43,138	92,491
Iraq	1,819	7,272	20,366	36,436
Nepal	183	550	2,275	16,959
Philippines	5,695	15,244	43,988	77,622
South Korea	4,347	16,682	37,807	50,987
Sri Lanka	1,106	3,359	8,660	10,660
Syria	1,677	3,393	10,105	23,311
Turkey	4,441	17,106	45,482	79,102

Source: Adapted from World Resources Institute. 1996. *World Resources: A Guide to the Global Environment.* New York: Oxford University Press, Table A1, pp.150–151.

Table 3.2 Urbanization Patterns in a Sample of Less-Developed Countries

Country	Per Capita GNP Level (1997 U.S. $)	Size of Population (in millions) 1975 Urban	1975 Rural	2000 Urban	2000 Rural	Percentage of Population (Urban) 1975	2000	Compound Growth Rate (Urban) 1970–1975	1990–2000	Compound Growth Rate (Rural) 1970–1975	1990–2000
Type 1											
Argentina	8,950	20.3	5.1	29.2	3.6	80.0	89.2	2.0	1.2	−1.1	−1.6
Mexico	3,900	37.4	21.8	103.6	28.7	63.2	78.3	4.6	3.8	1.3	0.9
Columbia	2,180	16.0	9.9	40.4	11.1	61.8	78.4	4.8	3.2	0.9	0.2
Brazil	4,790	65.2	44.5	162.2	50.3	59.5	76.3	4.5	3.3	0.9	0.3
Type 2											
Algeria	1,500	8.4	8.4	26.0	10.7	49.9	70.8	5.7	3.9	1.0	0.7
Egypt	1,200	17.9	19.6	41.5	23.1	47.7	64.3	3.9	3.1	1.2	0.4
South Korea	10,500	16.1	17.9	36.0	16.0	45.9	67.0	4.8	2.5	−0.1	−0.6
Philippines	1,200	16.0	28.5	45.6	47.1	36.0	50.9	4.8	3.9	2.7	1.2
Malaysia	4,530	3.6	8.4	9.9	12.1	30.2	45.1	4.7	3.5	2.2	0.8
Type 3											
Senegal	540	1.3	3.2	3.5	4.7	28.4	42.7	4.1	4.1	1.8	1.4
Ivory Coast	710	1.0	3.9	3.7	5.9	20.4	38.7	6.5	4.8	1.7	1.6
Nigeria	280	11.4	51.5	40.9	94.0	18.2	30.3	5.0	5.2	2.2	2.4
Sudan	290	2.4	15.9	8.9	30.0	13.2	22.9	5.5	5.1	3.0	2.9
Kenya	340	1.5	11.8	6.4	24.6	11.3	20.7	6.1	5.8	3.0	2.9
Upper Volta	110	0.5	5.6	1.7	9.2	8.3	15.7	5.2	4.9	2.1	2.0
Type 4											
Pakistan	500	19.0	51.6	62.3	84.6	26.9	42.4	5.3	4.4	2.4	1.5
India	370	131.7	481.4	342.1	717.2	21.5	32.3	3.7	3.7	2.1	1.2
Indonesia	1,100	26.2	109.8	74.7	162.8	19.3	31.4	4.7	3.9	2.2	1.2
China, People's Republic	860	196.9	641.9	414.1	733.8	23.5	36.1	3.3	2.9	1.2	−0.4

Source: United Nations Population Division, Department of Economic and Social Affairs. 1999. *Urban and Rural Projections from 1950 to 2000.* New York, Table 2; and Population Reference Bureau 1999. *1999 World Population Data Sheet.* Washington, D.C., Population Reference Bureau.

in growth rates in the world's regions. The growth of urban populations in MDCs dropped by half between 1950 and 2000 to 1.2 percent. The rate for LDCs also declined but not as rapidly. There is regional variation. Africa's urban growth peaked in the late 1970s at 5.1 percent per year (the highest ever recorded). This rate has declined but remains high—4.6 percent in 2000. Rates in Asia and Latin America, in contrast, peaked around 4.6 percent a year in the late 1950s and early 1960s, but declined to 2.9 percent in 2000 (United Nations Population Division, 2003a, 2003b).

Where do these people come from? A society's urban population comes from three sources: reclassification (a town's population grows large enough to be considered an urban place by the nation's census), migration, and natural increase (births exceeding deaths). UN data suggest most urban growth in LDCs comes from the high fertility of urban residents. In 2000, only one-third of urban growth in LDCs was attributable to rural to urban migration and reclassification; two-thirds came from natural increase. In MDCs the pattern is reversed. These figures are somewhat misleading because of the selective nature of migration. Migrants in more- or less-developed nations are similar—young and better educated and skilled than those left behind. The selective nature of migration is important because those who move are in their prime reproductive years. Therefore, the unprecedented growth of cities in LDCs is attributable to both the high rate of rural to urban migration and the high fertility of these new migrants to the city (Goldscheider, 1971; United Nations Population Division, 2003a).

Migration

Two questions remain: why do people migrate to the city when conditions there are often so deplorable, and which cities are they likely to choose? The answer to the first is simple: People relocate because it is rational for them to do so. Just as in this country, migrants move from low-wage to high-wage areas of a nation. The young are in a strategic point in the life cycle to recoup the cost of migration, and research shows that migrants seem to be better off, on average, than those who stay in the countryside.

The answer to the second question is that migrants usually choose the largest city in the region. Transportation networks are usually keyed on a nation's largest city with the result that transportation costs to the primate city are low. Second, migration does not occur randomly but along clearly defined migration streams. Kin and neighbors from the old village are usually found in neighborhoods within the large city and can aid migrants in their transition to urban life. This network helps the migrant find employment, housing, and financial support. In general, when a primate city is home to 20 percent of the nation's total population, everyone will have at least one relative in that city (Gilbert & Gugler, 1992).

A Typology of Urbanization Patterns in LDCs

We have been generalizing about urban patterns throughout this chapter. As we have already noted, there are enormous differences in the demographic patterns among the major regions of the world and within regions. One way to study the urbanization of LDCs is to ignore region and identify similar under-lying demographic patterns. Four patterns of urbanization in LDCs can be identified.

Type 1

This group includes countries like Argentina, Mexico, Columbia, and Brazil. These are countries in which the urbanization process is well underway. The population is already half urban, and incomes are high by international standards. In 2000, 75 percent of their populations were urban. The rural areas of these nations experienced absolute declines in population (United Nations Population Division, 2003b).

Most Type 1 societies are in Latin America. They underwent industrialization and economic development for most of the twentieth century, and these processes have encouraged rural to urban migration. These societies are characterized by enormous inequality in both their cities and the countryside. The benefits from development, especially in the area of public services, are directed to middle- and upper-income families. As a result, one finds massive numbers of poorly housed, poorly educated, and poorly serviced people in both rural and urban areas (Gilbert & Gugler, 1992).

Type 2

This group includes the nations of East Asia and North Africa, such as Algeria, Egypt, and the Philippines. In these societies urbanization is more recent, and today more than half of the population is urban. Incomes are low by interna-tional standards, but these countries have been successful in creating employ-ment and raising incomes. Urban services are improving but are still below those found in MDCs. In general, these nations have few natural resources, and their success in the future depends on careful population control and invest-ments in their human capital (Gilbert & Gugler, 1992; United Nations Popula-tion Division, 2003b).

Type 3

These countries include the sub-Saharan nations of Senegal, Ivory Coast, Nigeria, Sudan, and Kenya. They are predominantly rural but urbanizing at a tremendous rate—between 4 and 5 percent a year. Even at this rate, these societies were still rural in the year 2000 because of high birth rates in their rural populations. It is unlikely per capita income will rise in these societies as population growth out-strips agricultural, oil, and other natural resources (Gilbert & Gugler, 1992; United Nations Population Division, 2003b).

Type 4

India, the People's Republic of China, and Pakistan dominate this group of coun-tries. These nations are predominantly rural, subsistence-level societies. They are all experiencing severe pressures on their land and other natural resources. Although their cities are growing rapidly, general population growth is also high, so in 2000 half their populations were still rural, living in absolute poverty. Although these nations will continue to have massive rural populations, urbanization is occurring on an unprecedented scale. India, for example, absorbed 210 million people in its cities and 236 million people in its country-side between 1975 and 2000. China, in contrast, has been able to stabilize its overall population growth, control rural to urban migration, increase per capita income, and reduce inequality. China is still a poor country, but its few resources are more equitably distributed to its billion-plus population. One measure of its success is that average life expectancy in China now approaches those of most MDCs (United Nations Population Division, 2003b; World Resources Institute 1999).

This typology is a convenient tool for grouping the urbanization patterns of the world's LDCs (see Table 3.3). What these groupings do not show is the patterns of urbanization found in these societies. If one were to make a general-ization, the population of societies around the world—MDCs and LDCs—are

Table 3.3   *Population and Annual Growth Rates for Selected Countries, 1975–2000 (population in millions)*

Urban Area	Population 1985	Growth Rate 1975–1985	Population 1995	Growth Rate 1985–1995	Population 2015	Growth Rate 1995–2015
Type 1						
Mexico City	14.4	2.5%	15.6	0.8%	18.8	0.8%
Buenos Aires	9.9	1.2%	11.0	0.7%	12.4	0.5%
Sao Paulo	12.1	3.1%	16.4	2.0%	20.8	0.9%
Rio de Janeiro	9.1	1.5%	9.8	1.5%	11.6	0.8%
Bogota	3.5	3.2%	5.6	3.1%	7.7	1.1%
Type 2						
Cairo	7.7	2.4%	9.7	2.3%	14.5	2.2%
Seoul	9.6	3.4%	11.6	2.0%	13.2	0.3%
Manila	6.9	3.2%	9.3	3.6%	14.7	1.8%
Type 3						
Kinshasa	2.8	4.7%	4.2	4.2%	9.9	4.5%
Lagos	5.8	5.7%	10.3	5.1%	24.4	3.6%
Type 4						
Shanghai	12.4	0.8%	15.1	2.0%	23.4	1.9%
Peking	9.8	1.4%	12.4	2.3%	19.4	1.9%
Jakarta	7.4	4.4%	11.5	4.4%	21.2	2.3%
Calcutta	9.9	2.3%	11.7	1.7%	17.6	2.3%
Bombay	9.9	3.7%	15.1	4.2%	27.3	2.6%
Karachi	6.3	4.6%	9.9	4.3%	20.6	3.4%
Developed Nations						
London	7.4	0.0%	7.4	0.0%	7.4	0.0%
New York	15.8	0.3%	16.3	0.4%	17.6	0.4%
Paris	9.1	0.4%	9.5	−0.1%	9.6	0.3%
Tokyo	23.3	1.7%	26.8	1.4%	28.7	0.1%

Source: United Nations Centre for Human Settlements (HABITAT). 1996. *An Urbanizing World: Global Report on Human Settlements 1996.* Oxford, England: Oxford University Press, Table 4.

increasingly being accommodated by cities so large that they dwarf all others in the country. This urbanization pattern is known as *primacy*.

The Question of Primacy

The post–World War II period has experienced explosive growth of cities in the LDCs. These cities, already large at the end of the war, have experienced explosive growth in the fifty years that followed. Mexico City, with just 2.9 million inhabitants in 1950, grew to 16.56 million by the end of the century. Sao Paulo, with 2.1 million in 1950, was not far behind with 16.53 million in 2000. In 1950 only ninety cities in LDCs had populations over 1 million; in 2000, 300 did (United Nations Population Division, 2003b). See Photo 3.1.

This rapid growth of cities in the less-developed world demonstrates a second trend—the continued concentration of population in the largest cities in the more- and less-developed world. If we define urban as cities of more than 100,000 inhabitants, the pervasive trend has been the growth in population of those living in cities of more than 1 million. Between 1950 and 2000, the proportion of the urban population in LDCs living in these large urban centers grew from 38 to 65 percent. Most of this population, however, was absorbed in cities of more than 8 million. In 1975, million-plus cities already contained 13 percent of the world's population; by century's end this figure was 33 percent (United Nations Population Division,

Photo 3.1   *La Paz, Bolivia has an urban form shared by many metropolitan areas in the less-developed world. Downtown high-rise buildings serve the middle- and upper-income residents in nearby neighborhoods. The poor live on the city's periphery. (Source: © Alison Wright/CORBIS.)*

2003b). More important was the growth of megacities, cities with at least 8 million inhabitants. In 1950, there were only two megacities—New York and London. In 1995, there were twenty-three with seventeen of them in the developing world. By 2015, the number is projected to grow to thirty-three with most of these megacities in Asia (United Nations Population Division, 2003b). Table 3.4 shows the expected growth in megacities.

The growth of one large city at the expense of other cities is called *primacy*. Mark Jefferson introduced the terms *primacy* and *primate city* in the 1930s, and they refer to one large city that dominates all other cities in a country and through time "draws away from all of them in character as well as size" (Jefferson, 1939, p. 227). Primacy is measured simply by comparing the population of the largest city with that of the second-largest city.

Table 3.4   *Megacities: Expected Growth in Cities with Populations of 8 Million or More, 1995 and 2015*

City	Population (Millions)	
	1995	2015
Tokyo, Japan	26.96	28.89
Mexico City, Mexico	16.56	19.18
Sao Paulo, Brazil	16.53	20.32
New York, United States	16.33	17.60
Bombay, India*	15.14	26.22
Shanghai, China	13.58	17.97
Los Angeles, United States	12.41	14.22
Calcutta, India	11.92	17.31
Buenos Aires, Argentina	11.80	13.86
Seoul, Korea, Rep.	11.61	12.98
Beijing, China	11.30	15.57
Osaka, Japan	10.61	10.61
Lagos, Nigeria*	10.29	24.61
Rio de Janeiro, Brazil	10.18	11.86
Delhi, India	9.95	16.86
Karachi, Pakistan*	9.73	19.38
Cairo, Egypt	9.69	14.42
Paris, France	9.52	9.69
Tianjin, China	9.42	13.53
Metro Manila, Philippines*	9.29	14.66
Moscow, Russian Fed.	9.27	9.30
Jakarta, Indonesia*	8.62	13.92
Dhaka, Bangladesh	8.55	19.49

Source: United Nations Population Division. 1996. *Urban Agglomerations, 1950–2015.* New York: United Nations Population Division.

Cities expected to grow by more than 50% by 2015.

Primacy's Relationship to Development

Historians, geographers, ecologists, and demographers have studied the nature of primate cities and their relationship to economic development for the past seventy years. Many of these researchers believe that primate cities in developing nations are "parasitic" and hold back economic development. Why parasitic? Many of the world's primate cities are in countries that have agriculturally based economies with a fledgling industrial sector. Agriculture does not create the large profits that industry does, so there is less money to be reinvested in other areas of the economy for development. Cities are expensive to build and maintain; they tax the limited financial resources of these nations. In other words, money that might have gone into industry, tractors, mining, or irrigation projects is spent on the support of a large urban place (Gilbert & Gugler, 1992; Smith, 1996).

Another aspect of primate cities—their power to attract migrants—exacerbates this problem. Large numbers of the rural population, especially the young, are drawn to the city by the prospect of jobs and other opportunities. Although some find jobs, most remain unemployed or underemployed, continuing the drain on the nation's resources. The term *overurbanized* refers to those nations whose urban population is too large in relation to the level of economic development (Gilbert & Gugler, 1992; Smith, 1996). The cost of providing food and shelter for this nonproductive population also detracts from economic growth.

Lowering the rate of economic development, however, is not the only consequence of high primacy. Uneven economic development occurs as a government makes large investments in the primate city while ignoring the needs of the country's other regions. This large investment in the primate city encourages industrial and commercial activities to locate there. Through time, a vicious cycle develops. Industrial growth means more jobs, but new jobs also increase the attractiveness of the primate city to new migrants from other parts of the country. This population movement detracts from the growth that might occur in other cities, and economic development in other regions of the country stagnates (Smith, 1996).

Primacy also has political ramifications. Many primate cities are national capitals and become governmental, educational, and religious centers as well as industrial centers. The concentration of a nation's political, business, and religious elites in one city leads to major social and political division within a country. The primate city becomes the center of wealth and power, and the countryside becomes the habitat of the poor and powerless. Evidence seems to suggest that this process is accelerating (United Nations Population Division, 2003b).

Thailand is one example of a country that has a large percentage of its population in urban places, but a disproportionate number of urban dwellers in a single primate city. In 1996, 19 percent of Thailand's population was living in urban places, but a disproportionate number of these inhabitants were living in one city, the capital and its twin city, Bangkok-Thomburi. Bangkok-Thomburi had a population of almost 6 million in 1996, but the second-largest city, Chiengmai, had a population of little more than 117,000. Thailand's primacy index was 51: the nation's largest city was fifty-one times larger than the second-largest one. The rapid urbanization of Thailand and its capital is occurring faster than the rate of change in its economic and social institutions, leading to what some consider overurbanization (World Resources Institute, 2003).

Social scientists call the uneven rate of change in various elements of a society *cultural lag*. The problems of primacy and overurbanization are good illustrations of the concept. Medical technology has been introduced into LDCs, but comparable institutions for handling the ensuing population growth have not accompanied it. Vast numbers of peasants have been pushed off their land through the introduction of high-yield grains and other farm technology. This new technology requires a higher capitalization per acre, and fewer farmers are needed to produce more food. Traditional handcrafts and indigenous industries are unable to absorb the surplus population, and nearby villages, towns, and small cities offer few job opportunities. These products have no market in the global economy. With nowhere else to go, the surplus rural population migrates to the city where institutions of government often find it impossible to provide basic city services. Thus, the city is only one part in the larger encompassing society, and change in one part of this system inevitably has an impact on the city. The urbanization patterns of Thailand and its massive urban problem are not isolated phenomena but are shared by many developing nations.

An Alternative View: Primacy as a Solution

There is an alternative view. If LDCs are going to develop, they must shift population from rural/agriculture to urban/industrial employment. If LDCs are going to industrialize, they must compete in a world market, and if they are going to compete in a world market, they must take on the financing, marketing, and management patterns that the global market demands. In many cases, LDCs have no choice. Large multinational corporations dictate industrial development. The World Bank, the International Monetary Fund, and the General Agreement on Tariffs and Trade frame the economic relationships among nations, and the more-developed countries control them all. Thus, the MDCs set the rules and control the playing field. The LDCs have not yet developed the transportation, communication, financial, marketing, management, and the host of other corporate services international corporations demand. More important, their educational systems have not produced the managers, bankers, accountants, computer experts, and other specialists necessary to support a modern industrial society. With so few skilled people, the only way these societies can provide the manpower necessary for modern enterprises is to concentrate millions of people in one primate city. Additionally, only in the primate cities of LDCs does one find the transportation, communication, and other corporate services upon which these operations depend. The location of a large industry in a primate city attracts a constellation of other enterprises—suppliers, utilities, banks, and corporate service firms. The presence of these firms creates an environment favorable for additional growth. Growth feeds growth (Gilbert & Gugler, 1992; Gugler, 1990).

Many researchers feel the social, economic, and political costs of this process are unacceptably high, and therefore, LDCs must pursue alternative policies of rural and urban development. The idea is simple: If opportunities were available in other parts of a country, rural migration could be directed there instead of to the primate city (Baker, Epstein, & Pollin, 1998; Smith, 1996).

However, migration is an efficient way to reallocate the human capital of a society. The question facing all societies is where to find the best location for new industry, jobs, and housing. In some cases, it may be a second city in another region of a nation; in others, rural areas; in still others, the primate city. The question is, who can best make this decision?

Locational decisions are individual decisions. Individuals respond to the perceived economic and social situation in their present community versus others. If the information given citizens accurately reflects the true costs of a move, then people will make rational decisions, and the population redistribution will be cost effective for society. This is seldom the case, because an important public policy overlay distorts this process. We are all aware of the growth of the Sunbelt in the United States. Millions of Americans have migrated from Snowbelt states to the South and West. Few Americans are aware of the massive federal subsidy that made this migration possible. The subsidy is hidden in military budgets and in an implicit industrial policy buried in the tax code (Schwab, 1992).

In general, public policy in LDCs favors primate cities over smaller cities and rural areas. Public services are usually better in primate cities. Industrial protection policies, price controls on agriculture products, and national budgets usually favor cities. Taken as a whole, they motivate rural residents to migrate to the city.

Large cities, therefore, exist because they provide an environment conducive to industrial production. Certain economies of scales entice industry to locate in cities, including the clustering of suppliers and customers, and access to a wide range of corporate services. Financing, legal services, and advertising are facilitated in an urban environment. Substantial savings on transportation, communication, and training further reinforce the tendency for these cities to grow.

There are also disadvantages. As the city grows beyond a certain size, transportation, land, and service costs increase. Size increases the distance between place of residence and place of work, and the time and cost of transportation increases. Increased size and population increases congestion, pollution, and a host of other costs for consumers. Friedman (1999) describes a day trip he took with a friend during a 1996 visit to Bangkok. They left early in the morning for a tour of the countryside, but gave up after four hours. They had moved four miles. Travel in many of the world's megacities, usually primate cities, is nearly impossible. Why do they grow? They grow because people are rational, and cities usually have higher incomes and opportunities not found in the small towns or the rural hinterlands.

The Internal Structure of the City

The timing, scope, and magnitude of urbanization varies from region to region, and we have explored this process by grouping nations by their level of economic development—more and less developed—and by the magnitude of their vital events, classified as Types 1 through 4. However, we have said nothing thus far about the internal structure of cities in LDCs. How are these cities organized? Where are business and industry located? Where do the people live? Are these cities organized the same way as the ones in MDCs? The answers to these questions are complex. Just as in the case of the urbanization process, urban patterns found in the major regions of the world vary enormously. There are, however, underlying similarities in the physical form of these cities because cities reflect the characteristics of their societies and are, therefore, shaped by similar social, economic, and ecological forces.

The physical form of the city can be described along two dimensions. The physical dimension encompasses the streets, buildings, neighborhoods, and commercial, industrial, and political areas of the city, while the organizational dimension of the city includes the family, ethnic, class, and associational groups found there. A complex interrelationship exists between the social structure and the physical reality of the city. In general, social change that takes place on the societal level is manifested first and most clearly in the use of space within cities. One can tell a great deal about a society by exploring the characteristics of its cities.

The Premodern City

Large cities are not new to the less-developed world—they originated there. Only since the sixteenth century have European cities gained prominence. Before that time, the world's major cities were in LDCs, and some of these cities reached remarkable size and organization. Many were ancient religious and political centers, including cities like Bangkok, Mecca, Mandalay, and Kabul. Others developed after the sixteenth century and were established by European empires. Outposts like Capetown, Bombay, Calcutta, Hong Kong, Singapore, and many Latin American cities played a crucial role in the exploitation of these societies by the colonial powers. The empires of France, Great Britain, Germany, and other colonial powers were dismantled after World War II, and their colonies were replaced by self-conscious nation-states, but one still finds remnants of these much older cities at the core of many of the largest cities in the less-developed world.

Four distinct patterns are associated with the premodern city. First, these cities were compact and densely settled. Houses were packed together along an irrational street pattern. They were pedestrian cities. Since everything had to be within walking distance, the spatial patterns of these cities were constrained by the transportation technology. Transportation still constrains cities in LDCs because per capita income is so low that automobile and mass transportation is beyond the reach of the average city dweller (Schwab, 1992). Second, people were segregated into precincts based on tribe, caste, or ties to a rural village. Even today in India caste plays an important role in determining the residential structure of the city. In Africa, the tribe plays a similar role.

Third is the absence of specialized areas of the city based on function. Premodern cities had ceremonial centers and quarters that housed the elites, but the rest of the city was a hodgepodge of homes, shops, and industry.

Finally, the wealthy live near the city's center and the poor at its periphery. This is opposite to what one finds in MDCs.

In general, the premodern city can be characterized as dense, compact, and residentially segregated on the basis of tribe, caste, or village. There is little functional specialization of land use and an inverse status gradient with the wealthy living at the city's center and the poor at the periphery. This pattern characterizes all societies where the transportation technology is poorly developed. This was the case in the nineteenth and early twentieth century American city and this pattern was found in the cities of the less-developed world in the twentieth (Schwab, 1992).

The Modern City

Improved transportation and communication technology permits an entirely different type of spatial organization in the modern city. Population densities decline, and residential segregation is based on social class and family type as well as ethnicity. Specialized subareas emerge according to economic function; areas of the city are specialized in industry, education, banking and finance, and government. There is also a direct distance-status gradient—the poor live near the city's center, the wealthy at the periphery.

Although societies around the world differ in history and culture, research suggests that as development proceeds, the spatial patterns of cities move from the premodern to modern form. Primate cities are the first to take on the modern spatial form because they are the portals for change. Over time these innovations to modern urban forms diffuse to other cities. Change, however, does not occur smoothly. In most cities in the less-developed world, one usually finds elements of both forms—areas of the city that look and feel like any city in the West and vast areas that have a premodern form. This is especially true of the spontaneous settlements found in the largest cities of most of the less-developed world (Shunnaq & Schwab, 2000).

Spontaneous Settlements

Housing is the most visible problem facing less-developed countries in their struggle to develop and modernize. Sprawling shantytowns, slums, and squatter areas are permanent features of most large cities in the less-developed world. In primate cities, one finds square mile after square mile of dilapidated structures patched together from scraps of cardboard, corrugated iron, and discarded wood. In general, these areas lack even the most basic services—safe drinking water, sanitation, and drainage. Electricity, schools, clinics, and police protection are unimaginable. Any Westerner passing through a squatter settlement would agree that something needs to be done. But what is the appropriate way to attack the urban housing problem in the developing world? How can the housing and service needs of over a billion new urbanites be accommodated in a single generation? What are the alternatives to spontaneous settlements when the average incomes of most of the people in the world is less than $1,000?

Shantytowns are not the only type of housing found in the cities of LDCs. There are spacious suburbs, luxurious high-rises, and large and prosperous working-class neighborhoods, but spontaneous settlements are the primary source of housing for the poor. Most owners, squatters, and renters in the less-developed world live in homes and neighborhoods that started out as spontaneous or unplanned settlements. LDCs are not the only place one finds spontaneous settlements. We all too quickly forget our own less prosperous past and our shameful present. Hoovervilles graced the Mall in Washington, D.C., and other American cities during the Great Depression, and today this nation's homeless inhabit the streets, abandoned buildings, culverts, overpasses, and spontaneous settlements in virtually every major American city. These settlements vary enormously in size and form, and it is difficult to generalize from one society to another. Moreover, the terms *squatter settlements, squatments, shantytowns, slums,* and *spontaneous settlements* are value laden and represent the biases of those who use them. The term *squatter settlement* is misleading because many of these structures are built on purchased land. *Shantytown* is inappropriate because many middle-class homes started out as shanties but have been upgraded into nice homes. *Spontaneous settlement* is misleading because community leaders in cooperation with politicians have carefully planned many of these developments. Even with these qualifications, I still prefer the term *spontaneous settlement* because it represents the innovation that the poor bring to their housing problems.

Spontaneous Settlements Defined

There are four basic types of spontaneous settlements: *invasions*, when structures are built without permission on another's land; *pirate settlements*, where the land is purchased but lacks planning permission; *rental settlements*, where the structure is built on rented land; and *usufruct settlements*, where the tribe, local government, or owner has given permission to build (Gilbert & Gugler, 1982). See Photo 3.2. Regardless of type, spontaneous settlements share two or more of the following characteristics. First, most dwellings have been built and are occupied by the original settlers. Second, the settlement was built on another's land or lacked planning permission. Third, the settlement was built without basic services and in many cases still lacks services. Fourth, poor people occupy the settlement. Fifth, there is usually an element of self-help: The occupants carry much of the construction out, although some of the work is contracted out (Aldrich & Sandhu, 1995).

A general idea of the scope of spontaneous settlements in the major regions of the world is given in Table 3.5. Note that the incidence rate in cities in Africa range from as high as 85 percent in Addis Ababa, Ethiopia to a low of 50 percent in Lusaka, Zambia. In North Africa and the Middle East the rate ranges from as high as 54 percent in Cairo, Egypt to as low of 1.5 percent in Beirut. The cities in low-income Asian nations like India, Indonesia, and Pakistan have rates which range from a high of 50 percent in Karachi to 40 percent in Delhi. Cities in the Philippines, and other middle-income Asian nations are in the 40 percent range. Cities in Latin America and the Caribbean display a wide range from a low of 32 percent in Sao Paulo, Brazil, to as high as 59 percent in Bogotá, Columbia. Half the people in the world's largest city,

Photo 3.2   *Spontaneous settlements house tens of millions of the world's urban poor. The World Bank now funds projects that harness this process to provide safe and affordable housing in the less-developed world. (Source: © Photo Collection Alexander Alland/CORBIS.)*

Table 3.5   *Proportion of City Population in Illegal Housing in Selected Third-World Cities*

City	Population (Millions)	Percentage of Population in Illegal Housing
Jakarta	8.0	62
Manila	5.6	40
Delhi	7.5	40
Karachi	8.0	50
Ankara	2.0	51
Addis Ababa	1.6	85
Dar es Salaam	1.0	60
Cairo	5.7	54
Beirut	0.9	1.5
Lusaka	0.8	50
Mexico City	16.0	50
Sao Paulo	13.0	32
Bogotá	5.5	59
Lima	4.6	33
Caracas	3.0	34

Source: R. Baker and J. Van der Linden. 1998. *Land Delivery for Low-Income Groups in Third World Cities.* Aldershot: Avebury.

Mexico City, live in spontaneous settlements. Percentages mask the tremendous number of people who live in these areas. If one multiplies these percentages by the populations of these nations, we are looking at hundreds of millions of people who are housed in vast unplanned areas of cities (Fernandes & Varley, 1998).

Spontaneous settlements, therefore, are significant and permanent features of most cities in LDCs. They represent the only way that developing nations can absorb the millions of new inhabitants of their cities. On the surface, they may appear to be squalid and pathological, but researchers have found a complex social system below the surface. Support networks of family and kin, employment, education, and banking cooperatives based on the caste, tribe, or village of the residents, mutual aid societies, schools, churches, retail and wholesale establishments, factories, and industries are all found within the boundaries of spontaneous settlements. In some countries a significant proportion of the nation's food supply comes from these settlements. For example, in Brazil more than 50 percent of pork production comes from spontaneous settlements (Aldrich & Sandhu, 1995).

The Life Cycle of Spontaneous Settlements

Research in Latin America and the Caribbean shows that spontaneous settlements follow a life cycle that sometimes results in middle-income housing. In the first stage known as the *bridgehead*, recent migrants, renters, and the poor invade land they do not own or land they own but have been denied planning permission—there is an element of illegality. There is strength in numbers, and the invasion is often highly organized by community leaders with the tacit permission of local politicians. The invaders are taking a calculated risk. They are betting that once settlement takes place, local officials will be unwilling or unable to evict them. In the bridgehead stage, the areas lack basic services, and the structures are usually shanties.

As the area gains political strength and a quasi-official identity, the area moves into the second stage—consolidation. Political clout means local authorities can be pressured into supplying water, electricity, waste disposal, paved streets, schools, police, and clinics. With the threat of eviction removed, homeowners slowly replace the cardboard and scraps with more substantial materials. Slowly the spontaneous settlement moves into the final stage, an area with the characteristics and identity of an ordinary suburb (Fernandes & Varley, 1998).

Why People Settle There

Why do people choose spontaneous settlements? What would you rather be, a renter or an owner? Given the choice, would you rather slowly develop equity in a home or pay rent to a slumlord? People living in spontaneous settlements are as rational and as economically sophisticated as we are. The consolidation process has been found to be slow but consistent. When money is available, residents improve their dwellings. When times are hard, they need not worry about eviction and can use their money to buy food. When the price of food, fuel, and clothing rise, the cost of housing remains the same. Therefore, in the best of circumstances, spontaneous settlements provide a cheap and flexible way to house the poor of the less-developed world. In the worst of circumstances, crowding and a lack of basic services lead to high infant mortality, chronic illnesses, and lowered life expectancies. The absence of schools, bus service, and employment diminishes life chances and perpetuates inequality, just as the slums in this nation diminish the life chances of our poor. The dilemma for the less-developed world is that there is probably no other alternative to this pattern of urban development.

In the past twenty years there has been a dramatic change in policy on spontaneous settlements by governments in LDCs. In the past, spontaneous settlements were seen as blight to be removed from the city as soon as possible. Borrowing planning principles from the MDCs, urban renewal removed spontaneous settlements and replaced them with showcase projects. As in the United States, these short-sighted plans, designed to help the poor, actually exacerbated their conditions. In recent years, the United Nations, the World Bank, and other international agencies have funded projects to harness the spontaneous settlement process. The Indonesian government with the help of the World Bank has pursued a program to provide spontaneous settlements with basic city services. As a result, 62 percent of households in Jakarta have basic city services. Currently twenty-two nations are experimenting with preemptive planning with funds from the World Bank. Undeveloped urban land is subdivided into small lots and provided with basic services. Lots are provided at little or no cost to the poor, and building regulations are relaxed so the slow consolidation process can occur (Aldrich & Sandhu, 1995). Take a look at recent grassroots efforts spearheaded by NGOs around the world at the UN-Habitat web site, *www.unchs.org* (UNCHS, 1999).

When one studies the social, economic, and physical characteristics of the major cities in less-developed countries, one often finds two cities sharing the same site. In former colonial outposts, the old European quarter persists: broad tree-lined streets, Western-style homes, and spacious administrative centers and country clubs. These areas stand in sharp contrast to the native quarters developed with their own vernacular architecture and chaotic street plan. There are literally two worlds: one native and one European.

The nineteenth-century city continues to affect the present. The society's elites have replaced the colonialists; central business districts look like those in MDCs; middle- and upper-class citizens have taken over the high ground; and the poor are segregated in vast areas of the city—often in spontaneous settlements.

These spatial divisions are reflected in political, economic, and social divisions as well. There are usually two sectors to the local labor market, one formal and one informal. The formal sector is modeled after those found in MDCs and employ well-educated middle- and upper-income people in industry, business, and government. These are usually high-skilled, high-paying jobs; entry is restricted by educational level or family connections; and the activities are regulated and taxed by government. They often participate in the global economy. The informal sector, in contrast, employs the poor and very poor who have recently migrated to the city. They are employed in a variety of occupations ranging from native crafts, street vending, and shoeshining, to small-scale retailing and manufacturing and the sex industry. These are small-scale operations often carried out in the household. People working in this sector are self-employed or family employed, with low skill, and their enterprises are unrelated and untaxed by government (Smith, 1996).

The social structures also differ. The prosperous areas often reflect the lifestyles and family form of the middle class found anywhere in the world: nuclear families, middle-class value systems, a concern for the education and experiences of children, and middle-class consumption norms. One often finds in the spontaneous settlements traditional lifestyles followed by the most recent migrants to the city. In some cases, the social structure of the village has been effectively transferred to the center of the city. Therefore, two physical realities, two economies, two social structures—two worlds—inhabit the same city at the same time (Shunnaq & Schwab, 2000).

The physical and social realities of these two worlds have sobering implications for their respective inhabitants. The characteristics of nonsquatter and squatter settlements in Manila, Philippines, are presented in Table 3.6. Regardless of the social indicator, the health and quality of life of those living in squatter settlements is lower. School dropout rates are 75 percent higher; hospital bed ratios are 1:300 for nonsquatter, 1:4,000 for squatter; the infant mortality rate is nearly three times higher for squatter, the birth rate six times higher, and the TB rate nine times higher. Although data are sparse, these patterns reflect the gulf between the people who live in spontaneous settlements of the cities of the world and those who live in traditional areas.

This is the reality. This pattern is tied closely to the tremendous population pressures that exist in these societies because of high birth rates and low death rates.

Table 3.6   *Characteristics of Nonsquatter and Squatter Urban Settlements in Manila*

Parameter	Nonsquatter	Squatters
School dropouts before high school (percent)	20	35
Hospital-bed-to-population ratio	1:300	1:4,000
Infant mortality rate (per 1,000 live births)	76	210
Birth rate (per 1,000 population)	33	177
Neonatal mortality rate (per 1,000 live births)	40	105
Tuberculosis rate (per 100,000 population)	800	7,000
Gastroenteritis rate (per 100,000 population)	780	1,352
Third-degree malnutrition (percent of population surveyed)	3	9.6
Second-degree malnutrition (percent of population surveyed)	21	37.5
Anemia (percent of population surveyed)	10	20
Per capita food intake (calories)	1,700	1,550
Typhoid rate (per 100,000 population)	33	135
Diphtheria rate (per 100,000 population)	48	77
Measles rate (per 100,000 population)	130	160
Clinical signs of vitamin A deficiency (percent of populations affected)	50	72

Source: Adapted from Samir S. Basta. (1977). *Nutrition and Health in Low Income Areas of the Third World.* Ecology of Food and Nutrition. Vol. 6, pp. 113–24.

Spontaneous settlements reflect the momentous shift of population from rural to urban areas and the difficulty that LDCs have in absorbing massive numbers of people in their cities. Spontaneous settlements are ubiquitous in the cities of the world because these societies and the governments that lead them have no alternatives. The World Bank and other international agencies are recognizing spontaneous settlements as one of the few ways LDCs have to house their people. Demonstrations projects have shown the feasibility of harnessing this process, but the question remains, are things getting better or worse?

Are Conditions Getting Worse?

A review of the literature suggests that conditions in the cities of LDCs have gotten worse. A perusal of UN data shows housing construction in LDCs has fallen behind population growth. Spontaneous settlements continue to grow unchecked. Unfortunately, many students of housing equate the growth of spontaneous settlements with a decline in the quality of urban life, but as we have seen, spontaneous housing may be the first step on a long process of consolidation. As time passes and these areas receive water, electricity, and other services, conditions improve. This is not to diminish the population, housing, health, and service problems the vast majority of nations face, but the biases of researchers, either Westerners or those trained in the West, lead us to apply inappropriate standards to these societies. This problem, combined with the lack of valid and reliable data, makes it impossible to assess accurately conditions in the cities in LDCs. One must also remember, regardless of how appalling the conditions are in the cities, more people have access to potable water, sewerage, drainage, electricity, clinics, and hospitals than those who live in rural areas (Brandon, 2000; de la Barra, 1998).

The process of development brings change across a society. The United States is undergoing a painful adjustment to the emergence of a global economy. In the previous chapter, we described the plight of routine production and in-person service workers. This society, with a $10 trillion GDP, is grappling with the problems of education, housing, and inequality. Imagine the problems faced by societies in the first stages of the development process. Imagine the problems of transforming a traditional/rural economy to a modern/urban one in a single generation. These nation-states seek to improve agricultural productivity at just the right pace so people can be shifted to more productive industrial activity, but not so fast that cities are overwhelmed by migrants. They attempt to create an infrastructure of roads, rail, telecommunications, and electricity upon which modern enterprises depend and a system of universal education, health, and social services that can produce the trained people needed to compete in a global economy. Development entails providing housing and other services and a humane standard of living for those who live in the cities and the countryside. It is a Herculean task that would strain the human and economic resources of any society, much less a less-developed one.

Theories of Development

In more-developed countries economic development and urbanization were linked together in the process of industrialization, modernization, and urbanization. As we have shown, in the less-developed world, urbanization is occurring at an unprecedented rate, but economic development lags far behind. This state—population growth without economic growth—was not supposed to happen.

Predictions Gone Astray

After World War II, theorists from a number of disciplines developed a neat scenario on how LDCs would change. These theorists considered LDCs underdeveloped because they were agricultural and rural. They argued that development would occur with industrialization. Moreover, industrialization requires shifting labor away from farming, mining, and forestry to manufacturing, and because industries are located in cities, a massive redistribution of population from rural to urban centers was required. Thus, industrialization and urbanization were viewed as inseparably linked, with one supporting and facilitating the other.

Manufacturing, however, requires a population with higher skills and literacy than does agriculture. Therefore, one of the prerequisites for economic growth was the creation of a national system of mandatory education and the inculcation of a value system that supports an industrial economy. New values, new norms, new roles supporting things such as entrepreneurial personality types, a money economy, achieved status, and the nuclear family were viewed as both a prerequisite and a facilitator of rapid social change. It was assumed the rise of cities and an urban way of life would quickly replace the rural/traditional way of life found in these societies.

Development requires a revolutionary change in the economic, social, and cultural patterns of developing societies. Many of these changes were expected to be generated internally as the process of development proceeded; however, implicit in this argument was that much of the innovation would come from the West. Innovation would first diffuse from more- to less-developed societies. Cities would be the portals of change from which this innovation would be diffused to the rest of the society. Therefore, cities, especially primate cities, played a central role in this development model.

Economic development and modernization in LDCs has not occurred as predicted. Two theories—the modernization theory and the world systems theory—give different reasons for why less-developed societies have not developed as expected.

Modernization Theory

The modernization theory is part of the efforts of a group of mostly American social scientists writing after World War II. Drawing on the works of Karl Marx, Weber, and Durkheim, the modernization theory posits that industrial development follows a coherent pattern of growth and would, in time, produce certain common social and political structures across different countries and cultures. By studying advanced industrial countries like Britain and the United States that industrialized and democratized first, one could unlock the path that all countries would eventually follow. In the 1950s and 1960s these researchers worked with great enthusiasm to harness their new social science to the task of helping the newly independent countries of the third world develop economically and politically.

Modernization is an ethnocentric concept referring to the social and political changes that accompanied the industrialization and modernization process in Europe and North America (Bendix, 1964). Among these changes are urbanization, achieved status, a money economy, wage labor, universal education, representative government, and a concern for individual rights. Modernization involves the diffusion of these characteristics from more-developed to less-developed regions, and built into the concept is the notion of a time lag. It is argued urban areas tend to change first, and rural areas tend to lag far behind. The result: two cultures coexist in the same society—a modern one associated with large primate cities and urban areas and a traditional one associated with rural areas. Modernization theorists argue development has not occurred as predicted because the modern is in conflict with the traditional. They maintain the only reason a modern sector exists at all is because colonial powers imposed their alien system upon a traditional order through military coercion. The resulting dualism in these societies pits urban/modern against rural/traditional. Modernization theorists argue the inconsistency in the development process—the state of population growth without development—results from the resistance of traditional segments of less-developed societies to industrialization and urbanization (Fukuyama, 1992).

There are many sources of resistance. The first comes from the people themselves. Culture is a blueprint for living—values, norms, roles, and institutions—that permits people to deal with the problems of day-to-day living. Many members of society prefer the traditional to the new and refuse to adopt the modern way of life, impeding the development process (Chirot, 1986).

A second source of resistance comes from the traditional elites, including large landowners, clerics, and village elders, whose power, wealth, and prestige is linked to the traditional social order. Development changes the social structure, achievement replaces ascription, rationality replaces tradition, and change undercuts the power and prestige of the old order. Therefore, both forces, the masses who resist the imposition of an alien culture and the elites who have a vested interest in maintaining the old system, work in concert to encapsulate the change in the major urban areas and prevent its diffusion into the larger society. Growth without development is the result of this duality—two incompatible cultural systems sharing the same society (Chirot, 1986). Huntington's work, *The Clash of Civilizations*, elaborates on many of these same themes.

Numerous examples in history illustrate colonial powers intruding into the traditional societies in Latin America, Africa, and Asia, setting up modern sectors with cultural and economic ties to the motherland, but few with the indigenous population. The smoldering resentment of subjugated peoples toward colonial powers led to the dismantling of empires in the postwar period. In most cases independence has not resolved the conflict between modernists and traditionalists. The attack on the World Trade Center by Osama Bin Laden and his Al Qaeda terrorist organization is the most recent manifestation of this anger. (Berman, 2003)[1]

The modernization theory eventually fell victim to the accusation that it was ethnocentric; that is, it elevated the Western European and North American development experience to the level of universal truth without recognizing its own cultural bounds. Some critics wrote that it reified one model, the Western model, as the only valid end state to societal evolution. As we will see in a few pages, the critics were probably wrong.

Dependency/World Systems Theory

In the 1950s, it was fashionable to attribute the underdevelopment of the third world to the global capitalist system. It was argued that early developers in Europe and America had in effect structured the world economy in their favor and condemned those who came later to dependent positions as providers of raw materials.

The dependency theory or world systems theory is more recent than the modernization theory. Its advocates are usually neo-Marxian and often citizens of developing nations. Modernization theory blames the traditional social system for resisting modernization; dependency theory blames the world capitalist system for underdevelopment. The model of the class system used to describe the stratification system in a single society is used by dependency theorists to describe the relationship among nations in the world economic system (Fukuyama, 1992; Smith, 1996).

Dependency refers to an imbalanced economic relationship in which one side enjoys advantageous economic control over another. The dominant nations in the world, core nations found in North America and Europe, have diversified economies and are modern and highly industrialized. Although their populations are small, the size and power of their industrial economies and their control of the organizations that control world monetary relationships—the World Bank, the International Monetary Fund, and GATT—allow them to hold economic sway over peripheral nations (Wallerstein, 1974).

Peripheral nations often have little industry, swelling populations, and economies specialized in the export of a narrow range of raw materials, including coffee, cotton, ore, hemp, and petroleum. A few nations in the world display the characteristics of both core and peripheral nations, and they are known as *semi-peripheral nations*, such as South Korea and Taiwan. Therefore, we find a world community in which a relatively small number of nations in the core, because of their economic, political, and military might, exploit peripheral nations for their own ends. Moreover, resistance by peripheral nations to this exploitation will be met with resistance by the core through overt military force or covert political and economic action. Dependency theorists would argue that you need look only as far as the Iraq War for proof.

How does this exploitation take place? The fundamental mechanism is the domination of peripheral nations by foreign firms and investors who control their economies. This, in turn, has several consequences. First, profits from overseas investment flow back to the core nations, denying the peripheral nations development capital. Second, foreign investors are in a key position to control what types of industries are carried out in a peripheral country. Core nations have a vested interest in selling high-value-added manufactured goods to peripheral nations and, therefore, invest in agricultural and extractive processing rather than in plants that produce manufacturing goods. This forces peripheral nations to depend on an export economy that condemns them to poverty. Why? Raw materials are subject to the vacillations of a world commodity market. Commodity sales depend on the demand by consumers in the core nations. A drop in consumption in core nations can devastate a peripheral nation's economy. Recent health concerns in the United States reduced the demand for palm and coconut oil almost overnight, devastating the economies of a number of peripheral nations. In 2001, world coffee prices dropped fifty cents a pound, throwing the Brazilian and Colombian economies into turmoil. Falling soybean prices decimated the Bolivian agricultural economy. Economic recession and energy conservation in core nations wreaked havoc on OPEC nations in the late 1990s. Remember a few years ago when a gallon of gasoline cost less than bottled water (Wallerstein, 1974)?

According to the dependency theory, peripheral nations with specialized export economies have distorted economies. Their development tends to be concentrated in relatively few sectors of their economy, often centered in primate cities, and low capital returns mean there is little money or motivation to develop other regions of the nation.

Dependency is implicit in colonialism, and the mechanism by which colonial powers exploited their colonies is well understood. The political and economic exploitation of colonialism ended for the most part with World War II. Systems theory replaced dependency theory in the postwar period, but the mechanisms were the same. The principal agents are large multinational corporations head-quartered in core countries. AT&T, General Motors, Ford Motor Company, and mammoth oil companies are all examples of corporations headquartered in core nations and with more employees and larger budgets than most nations in the world. These corporations use their economic power to influence the political and social life of the societies in which they operate to their own benefit, not necessarily to the benefit of the host nation (Wallerstein, 1974).

The Theories Revisited in the Age of Globalization

Modernization Theory

Modernization theory looks far more persuasive today than it did a generation ago when it came under heavy attack in academic circles. In the first decade of glob-alization, those societies that have achieved a high level of economic development have come to look increasingly similar to one another. Modernizing countries from Spain and Portugal to Taiwan and South Korea are liberal democracies based in free-market capitalism. Their propensity is tied to their use of knowledge and information-based technology. They have become successful because they have invested heavily in their human capital and have created a highly educated and skilled workforce. As a result of these policies, which took decades to implement, they now have a prosperous and stable middle class. Their corporations and symbolic analysts compete globally. Their governments and corporations are becoming transparent. They are urban. They are industrial. They share common communications and transportation technology. The invisible hand of the market shapes their economies. Powerful international norming processes controlled by supranational organizations and huge multinational corporations shape their societies. English is their second language, the language of the global economy. But by far the most important of these changes is the emergence of liberal democ-racy and free-market capitalism as the dominant form of political and economic organization in these nations.

What has caused this unplanned revolution? According to Fukuyama (1992), modern natural science is largely responsible for the process we call economic development. Science is the most efficient way humankind has developed for gath-ering and verifying knowledge. Technology is the application of science to real-world problems, and this process was responsible for the Industrial Revolution that began more than two centuries ago and continues today. As we noted earlier, industrialization is not simply the application of technology to the manufacturing process. It is also the process of bringing human reason to bear on problems of social organization, specifically the creation of a rational division of labor. The par-allel uses of reason—the creation of new technology and the organization of pro-duction processes—have succeeded beyond anyone's wildest dreams. And we know now from the experiences of the United States, Europe, and newly industri-alized nations (NINs) around the world that economic development produces cer-tain uniform changes in all societies, regardless of their prior social structure. What are these common characteristics? They are urban because only in cities does one find an adequate supply of skilled labor required to run modern enterprises. They have mobile labor markets because labor is sold in a global economy. They have replaced traditional groupings like tribes, clans, extended families, and religious groups with bureaucratic systems. Finally, they are meritocracies because the global economy rewards knowledge, skill, and talent; achievement, not ascription, drives the social stratification system.

How did these changes occur? Who planned them? Fukuyama (1992) argues that, like globalization, this was an *unplanned* revolution. It was made possible by modern natural science. This revolution has replicated itself in all industrialized countries whether the country was capitalist or socialist and in spite of the differences in the religious and cultural backgrounds out of which these societies arose. The revolution continues to shape the character of postindustrial societies like the United States, just as it does societies in the first stages of industrialization.

Why capitalism? According to Fukuyama, capitalism was the victor over socialism because it proved itself to be far more efficient than any other type of economic organization in developing and using technology in a rapidly changing global economy. The dominance of free-market capitalism has led to another unplanned and gradual revolution—the unification of humankind into a single global market for Daimler-Chrysler cars, Malaysian flat-screen monitors, Dutch flowers, Japanese electronics, Chinese clothing, Bolivian soybeans, and American music and movies. Not only does capitalism allow products to move faster and more efficiently around the globe, but fads, crazes, tastes, fashion, music, art, and slang move faster too. Globalization shapes both social organization and popular culture. It appears that the traditionalists who resist change are being overwhelmed by the onslaught of global change. Today, reformers are reshaping the social landscape of Iran, and the Communist party is loosening its control over the economic and social life in China. Fukuyama would argue this is a natural outcome of the globalization process. But the themes in Friedman's and Huntington's works are equally compelling.

Dependency/World Systems Theory

The dependency theory has its origins in the analysis of colonial relationships. The world systems theory was a natural extension of this theory in the postcolonial period. In the opening decade of the twenty-first century, the dependency/world systems theory has developed into a powerful tool for analyzing problems involving global change. This approach conceptualizes uneven development and inequality as inevitable results of the expansion of the global economy. Like its predecessors, it argues that the unequal exchange between core and peripheral nations leads to stunted or distorted growth in peripheral nations. According to these theorists, nations like India may have gained independence from Britain in 1947, but their former masters have relegated them to a marginal position in the world's economy. The terms may have changed from *colonial power* and *colony* to *core* and *periphery,* but the relationship of economic dependency remains the same in the global economy.

David A. Smith (1996) in his book *Third World Cities in Global Perspective* uses this theory to examine urban patterns in the less-developed world. Like theorists before him, Smith believes that the position of a nation in the global economy matters. He extends this work by arguing that this position—core, peripheral, or semi-peripheral—constrains and directs the type of urban development likely to occur. In his research, Smith found that timing was important. When a nation becomes part of the world system predicts the trajectory of a nation's urbanization. For example, early European domination of non-Western areas generally led to primate city patterns. Why? Europeans keyed the transportation and communication networks on a primate city to facilitate the export of a single commodity. This skewed city growth created a legacy of underdevelopment and overurbanization that persists today. Smith found that later domination by Europeans of non-Western nations usually led to more even urban development.

Smith's research also shows that these factors affect urbanization in peripheral nations in other ways. Colonial powers developed relationships with local elites to exploit their colonies, and these indigenous elites dominate the social structures of these nations to this day. They direct investments in their society's infrastructure, and these investments, in turn, determine urban structure. A good example is technology. Smith found that technology is not value neutral. The way a new technology is used in a society is the product of struggles between competing political and economic interests. Roads, railroads, shipping facilities, airports, and telephone and telecommunications networks are all outcomes, not of a smooth, natural process of innovation and diffusion, but of political conflict. These are usually one-sided battles, however, and the interests of the wealthy and powerful usually win. These class and power relationships explain why urbanization in the less-developed world is so different from the more-developed world, why the life chances of people in urban and rural areas are so different, why resources are concentrated in capitals and primate cities, why there is a growing disparity between the masses and a small wealthy elite, and why these imbalances retard economic development.

The global economy plays a part in this process in many ways. First, local elites make decisions about infrastructure and human capital development, which in turn affects urban development. These decisions are not made in a vacuum but through a web of relationships with leaders in more-developed countries who control the global economy.

Second, as we discussed earlier, investors make many national, regional, and local decisions in the global economy. A business decision made thousands of miles away in London, New York, or Hong Kong can profoundly affect the well-being of other nations and cities.

Third, global decision making appears to reflect an urban bias. As we discussed earlier, primate cities provide the communication, technology, and business services vital to the operation of the global economy.

Fourth, urban elites and symbolic analysts wherever they live are linked to the global economy via the Internet. They have insulated themselves from nearby poverty and squalor in gated, guarded communities.

Therefore, global change plays itself out on the national level by affecting investments in infrastructure. Since a city is the accumulation of millions of individual decisions that have occurred within the economic, transportation, and communication constraints placed on it by the encompassing society, understanding the roles of elites in a society's social structure is crucial. They determine what investments are made. They negotiate state partnerships with multinational corporations. They all too often pursue strategies in their best interest, not the interest of their society.

The implications of this research are many. International dependency imposes constraints on the urban development of peripheral nations. History matters. When a nation first enters the world system profoundly influences future growth. And not all nations will follow the Western path of urbanization and development.

Who's Right in the Era of Globalization?

In the previous chapter on globalization, we argued that we are in the midst of a revolution that has created a global economy. This revolution was made possible by the democratization of technology, finance, information, and decision making. These changes lowered the barrier of entry into markets, empowered consumers, shortened the product cycle, and unleashed the creative power of people through free-market capitalism. In the first decade of this revolution, it has created more wealth than at any other time in history. It has also created enormous inequality within and among nations and threatened the integrity of cultures and the environment. For people like Friedman (1999) and Fukuyama (1992) the creation of a global economy is our best chance to solve the global problems of poverty, overurbanization, and underdevelopment. They would argue that the less-developed world is suffering from too little, not too much, capitalism.

A far different voice comes from the 1992 Nobel Peace Prize winner, Rigoberta Menchu Tum. She calls attention to the failure of the current economic model. In one speech to the world summit on Sustainable Development she implored the international financial institutions to alter their "backward economic schemes" that result in the impoverishment of poor people. She contends globalization is geared toward opening international markets to a global economy based on the assumption that the benefits of the expansion of economic activities will trickle down to all. She argues that, in reality, the benefits of a global economy, rather than trickling down, have been systematically and increasingly concentrating wealth in fewer and fewer hands. She feels that the ultimate beneficiaries of the global economy are multinational corporations, which have gained the ability to produce where raw material and labor costs are cheapest and where labor and environmental regulations are most lenient. These corporations sell where markets are most profitable and transfer profits to countries where taxes are lowest (de la Barra, 1998; Mander & Goldsmith, 1996). So who is right? Friedman and Fukuyama? Or David Smith and Rigoberta Menchu Tum? Let's look at some of the evidence.

In 1998, the richest country in the world possessed 115 times the per capita income of the poorest. The 20 percent richest of the world's population had a per capita income 13 times that of the 20 percent poorest. Almost a quarter of the world's inhabitants lived in poverty (Melchior, Telle, & Wiig, 2000). Have things gotten better or worse in the globalization era? Is inequality increasing or decreasing among the nations of the world? Researchers at the Norwegian Ministry of Foreign Affairs found that global inequality has actually decreased over the past four decades. There has been a modest reduction in absolute poverty in the world (people living on less that $1 per day) from 28.3 percent to 24.0 percent. In the East Asia and Pacific region, which is characterized by both rapid overall economic growth and increasing integration into the global economy, the number of poor dropped from 418 million to 278 million during the same period, or from 26.6 percent to 15.3 percent (Melchior, Telle, & Wiig, 2000).

Figure 3.4 gives a better picture of global income disparities. Note the tremendous disparities between the high-income countries and the rest of the world. Simply, most of the benefits of globalization have gone to high-income countries. East Asia and the Pacific, South Asia, the Arab States, and Latin America and the Caribbean showed major gains. Sub-Sahara Africa and Central and Eastern Europe experienced major setbacks. But taken as a whole, the world

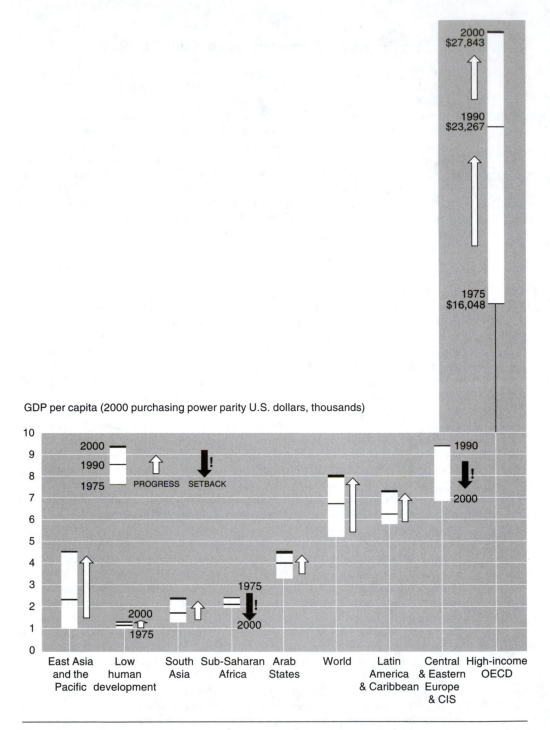

Figure 3.4 *Global Disparities in Income: Are Regions Closing the Gap? (Source: From Human Development Report 2002 by United Nations Development Programme, copyright–2002 by the United Nations Development Programme. Used by permission of Oxford University Press, Inc.)*

experienced increases in incomes between 1975 and 2000 and less inequality (Center for Global, International and Regional Studies, 2003).

But do these data reflect the experience of the average citizen? National averages mask internal differences. A nation's average income could increase by the rich getting richer and the poor, poorer. This is what has happened in the United States over the past decade. The Norwegian researchers, however, could find no clear link between the inequality within nations and globalization. Half the nations in their sample had increases in inequality, half declines (Melchior, Telle, & Wiig, 2000).

How are globalization and a nation's income related? Globalization has wrought many changes, but one of the most important is the change in labor—it is now bought and sold in a global market. We know from our own experiences that low-cost imports from East and South Asia have displaced most of the MDCs' production in textiles and electronics. But trade is a two-way process. When a country like China sells clothing to MDCs, MDCs sell more machinery to China. Thousands of textile workers lose jobs in MDCs, but new jobs are created in their machinery industries. In China thousands of new textile jobs are created, but the new machinery puts inefficient plants out of business. Therefore, trade benefits both nations, there are winners and losers in both labor markets, and the economies in both countries are forced to restructure. As this process is repeated across the globe, national economies are forced to become more rational and efficient. Since globalization is technologically based, the multinational corporations that drive it diffuse modern technology worldwide. As we showed in chapter 2, this is why the largest manufacturer of computer hard drives and flat screen monitors can be Malaysia. And remember the major point in Robert Reich's work: The benefits of globalization go to the nation's citizens who contribute most to a product through their skills, talents, and education. Therefore, globalization provides a way for LDCs to tap into the value added to products in international markets. Countries like South Korea and Taiwan have demonstrated that sustained investment in a nation's human capital pays dividends in the long run; they are now MDCs. Similarly, the world's two most populous countries, China and India, have proven that high technology is no longer reserved for the rich. The diffusion of high technology to LDCs is what is unique about the globalization process.

But these figures also show that growth in one region of the world has been accompanied with stagnation in another. The map in Figure 3.5 shows the growth competitiveness of the world's nations—their potential for growth in the next decade. In many respects it is a stacked deck. Finland is the most competitive, and the United States second. Zimbabwe is seventy-ninth and Haiti eightieth, the least competitive nations in the rankings. If you look at these rankings over time, they don't change much. The reason is that already-established industrial nations have economic inertia. Inertia allows them to compound their advantage over time. These nations are the seedbed for innovations, and their institutional structures permit them to influence subsequent growth. Once an economic activity is concentrated in a nation, it has a self-perpetuating momentum. In short, some nations, because of rapid industrialization, generate their own conditions for growth. Therefore, it is extremely difficult to break into the MDC club (World Economic Forum, 2003).

But maybe something else is going on. Compare Figure 3.5 with Huntington's map of the World's Civilizations (Figure 2.2). See a pattern? Maybe unequal development is rooted in the history, traditions, and culture of civilizations.

Plenty of evidence supports the position of Friedman and Fukuyama. There have been economic miracles. South Korea, Taiwan, and other Asian counties have

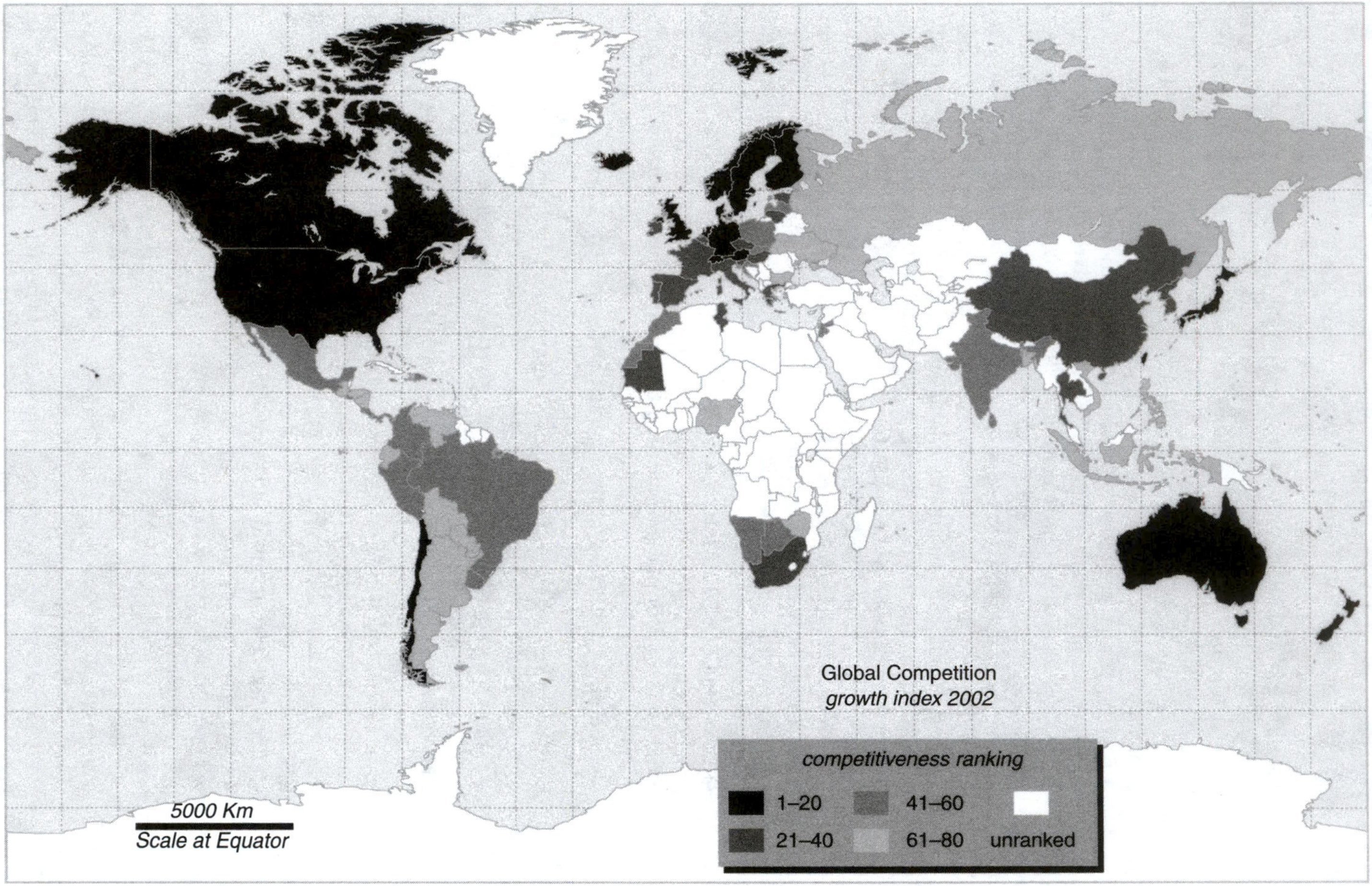

Figure 3.5 *Growth Competition Rankings Around the World (Source: World Economic Forum—Global Competitiveness Report 2002–2003, table 1, page 5.)*

Global Competition
growth index 2002

competitiveness ranking

1–20   41–60

21–40   61–80

unranked

5000 Km
Scale at Equator

invested in their infrastructures and human capital and reap the benefits of the global economy. As a group their GDPs have increased between 5 and 8 percent per year for the past generation. The disposable income of their people has increased dramatically. They have a large and stable middle class, and military rule has been replaced by democracy. Even after the economic meltdowns of several Asian economies in the late 1990s, these nations had the political will, expressed through free and open elections, to restructure their economies. Their economies have recovered.

But Smith and Tum would point out that South Korea has only 47 million people, and Taiwan only 22 million. They would ask, "What about an Indonesia with 212 million or an India with 986 million people? Can these societies ever hope to catch up? Can these societies ever generate the necessary capital to make the investments needed to participate in the global economy?" Take a look at the GNP figures in Table 3.2. Type 1 societies like Brazil and Mexico have per capita GNPs in the thousands and are capable of becoming full participants in the global economy. But what of Type 3 and Type 4 countries with per capita GNP measured in the hundreds of dollars?

Cisco Systems recently ran an ad that touted the power of the Internet the corporation helped to create with its servers and routers. A talking head says, "Seventeen million people in the world join the Internet daily." "There is ten times more e-mail than snail mail." "E-business will someday be the only business." They claim a world ripe for e-commerce. But Smith and Tum would point out that 93 percent of the world is not ready for the global economy. You can't have e-commerce if you don't have a population that can read and write and that live in societies without a stable banking systems, credit cards, a money economy, reliable mail and phone service, and disposable incomes high enough to buy stuff in the first place. None of the Type 3 and 4 countries have the transportation, communication, and energy infrastructure to support an industrial economy, much less to participate in a globalized electronic boom. If you've ever tried to use a credit card or cash a check in an LDC, you know what I mean.

If the past tells us anything, in the future the vast majority of people in the world will live in absolute poverty. All nations in the world have underdeveloped regions. The United States has its Mississippi Delta and Appalachia. In the future, underdeveloped nations and even underdeveloped subcontinents will not participate in the global economy. Similarly, the urban pattern in LDCs of opulent wealth side by side with poverty will reproduce itself around the world, even in the United States. We already see nascent examples here. Technology allows the wealthy in this nation to isolate themselves from the poor. This same technology will permit a similar pattern in LDCs. A small segment of this population will live first-world lives in less-developed countries. They will be full participants in the global economy, creating world-class products through their knowledge and creativity. They will bypass their nation's inferior telecommunication system and communicate by voice and Internet via satellite. They will live in isolated urban pods. Insulated in their fenced and guarded neighborhoods, and linked by roads to similarly protected environments in the city's core, they will have world-class shopping, restaurants, entertainment, health care, and business services in the midst of unimaginable human suffering. Cheap and reliable air service from their capital's world-class airport will whisk them and their products anywhere in the world within hours (Slambrouck, 1999). This isn't a farfetched prediction; we already have this settlement pattern in the silicon valleys of the developing world like Bangalor, India, Singapore, Kuala Lumpur, Malaysia, and Zhongguancun/Hebei, China (Allbritton, 1999; Deshmukh, 2003).

There are elements of the modernization and world systems theory in the process called globalization. In its early formulation, modernization stressed the continuing resistance of traditional cultures and elites to economic development. Large landowners, privileged families, clerics, and a rural population holding traditional values are the central culprits that cause underdevelopment in LDCs. In its present reformulation by researchers like Fukuyama, the universal adoption of modern natural science means that free-market capitalism will overwhelm any resistance by traditional elites. Nations will change along international lines, or they will be shut out of the global economy. The evidence suggests globalization will bypass much of the less-developed world.

The dependency theory, on the other hand, stresses the hegemony of Western nations over the world economic order and the ability of their proxies—multinational corporations—to perpetuate inequality. The inequality among nations and the control of organizations like the World Bank, IMF, GATT, and WTO by core nations give support to this theory. The purpose of the International Monetary Fund and its sister organization, the World Bank, was to provide financial stability for a chaotic global trading system in the post–World War II period. Founded by 36 nations in 1946, its roster now totals 182 nations, including Russia, China, and most of the world's trading nations. Under IMF rules, however, each member bears votes in accordance with a "quota" that is assessed roughly in proportion to its share of the world economy. Thus, the United States carries 17.4 percent of IMF voting power, while states with tiny economies carry a fraction of 1 percent. Between annual meetings, all IMF decisions are made by a 24-member executive board, in which only the United States, Japan, Germany, France, the United Kingdom, Saudi Arabia, Russia, and China have permanent seats. The other member states are formed into sixteen groups, with one representative from each casting the proportionalized votes of all the members in their group in board decisions. Thus, the present voting is a stacked deck, preserving the status quo in the global economy. Many in the less-developed world are asking, "Why should governments in the more-developed world still dominate the decision making of these organizations? Now that free-market capitalism dominates the global economy, shouldn't the World Bank and IMF shift their focus to eradicating the poverty that persists, and worsens, in so many of its member countries?"(Cobban, 2000).

I would argue that the two theories complement each other and explore different aspects of the same problem. Whereas modernization theory describes the social and cultural changes within societies, which contribute to and inhibit development, dependency theory explores those factors external to LDCs that profoundly affect the course of development. A clearer understanding of the development process requires a fusion of the two perspectives, and this fusion is the process called globalization.

Should we despair for those living in the less-developed world? Recently, Thomas Downey, a former Democratic congressman from New York, and Richard Williamson, assistant secretary of state under President Reagan, suggested a solution that may be palatable to both schools of thought. Downey and Williamson cochair the board of trustees of Enterprise Works Worldwide, an antipoverty organization in Washington, D.C. They note that the developing world's primary workforce is self-employed small producers—2 billion entrepreneurs involved mainly in agriculture and low-tech manufacturing. They point out that these entrepreneurs aren't competitive in the global marketplace and have a hard time turning a profit. Most earn less than $2 per day. Inefficiencies abound, resources are underused, business infrastructure is woefully lacking, and unsustainable production methods are damaging the environment at an alarming rate. They believe the best strategy to fight world poverty is to enhance workers' productivity, increase their income, and help them connect to the global economy (Downey & Williamson, 2000).

They call it fighting poverty with profit, and they suggest focusing on helping the world's small producers by upgrading their businesses in economically and environmentally sustainable ways. By sharing the industrialized world's technical knowledge of how to improve product quality, how to add value to products through innovation, and how to create links to new and larger markets, they believe they can succeed. By implementing this strategy on a massive scale, they believe many of the negative by-products of globalization can be overcome. No government involvement would be needed, because nongovernmental organizations would help. International financial institutions could provide low-income loans. But Downey and Williamson insist that the private sector should be the major player. The key strategy is for corporations to partner with local enterprises and provide them with a modest investment to upgrade facilities. The corporate partner would agree to buy the producers' upgraded products at a globally competitive price, once the producers meet international standards. The international corporation gets a new supplier; the local producers get a higher price for their commodities and links to the global economy.

A recent example is Starbucks Coffee. In 1997, Starbucks financed the upgrading of two Guatemalan coffee-processing plants at a cost of $37,500 each. When their product reached international standards, Starbucks bought the region's entire 1998 coffee-bean crop. The Guatemalan coffee growers' incomes rose 20 percent, and they now have a reliable outlet for their crop. Meanwhile, Starbucks has gained a new supplier and helped forge an important economic link between a group of small producers and the global economy. Implemented on a massive, global scale, this and other grassroots strategies could improve the welfare of billions and contribute to a just and stable global community.

Summary

Change is occurring at an unprecedented rate on this planet, and much of this change is related to the unprecedented population growth. From 1950 to 2000, the world's population grew from 2.5 billion to more than 6 billion people. Increasingly this population is being absorbed in the world's cities.

Population growth must be studied within the social, economic, political, and cultural context of society. Throughout this text, a distinction is made between more-developed countries and less-developed countries, reflecting the fact that all societies are developing, some more rapidly than others. These two categories of nations are used to explore the relationship between urbanization and economic development.

The theory of demographic transition describes the relationship between economic development and demographic processes. The theory argues that as societies move from less developed to more developed, conditions are created encouraging low fertility. Families in more-developed nations have fewer children because it is in their economic interest to limit fertility. The theory suggests a three-stage transition process from traditional societies in Stage 1 with high fertility and mortality and stable populations, through societies in transitional growth with high fertility and declining mortality and rapidly growing population (Stage 2), to societies in incipient decline with low fertility and mortality and stable populations (Stage 3). Most LDCs are in Stage 2 and imported death-control technology has dramatically reduced mortality but not fertility. Death-control technology can be applied without the consent of the individual through public health. Birth-control technology requires the cooperation of couples. Equally important is the persistence of the values in traditional families that encourages large families. The consequence of rapid population increase in LDCs is the retardation of the development process as money that would go into development is invested in a large unproductive young population.

In the last half of the twentieth century, the world's population problems have become the world's urban problems. Underemployment and unemployment, poor public services, inadequate housing, nonexistent medical care, and poor nutrition are now concentrated in the cities. Two approaches were used to examine these patterns. The first employed level of development—more developed versus less developed. The second grouped less-developed nations into four types based on the characteristics of their demographic patterns. Applying the first criterion, it was observed that urban growth in LDCs is unprecedented. In 1950, 275 million, or 38 percent of the world's urban population, lived in the cities of the less-developed world; by 2000, the world's urban population exceeded 2.1 billion, and 66 percent of this population was in the cities in the developing world. The experiences of LDCs differ sharply from those of MDCs in the timing, scope, and magnitude of urbanization.

Four types of societies were examined. Type 1 societies are in Latin America. They have been undergoing economic development for most of the twentieth century and ended the urbanization process by 2000 with 75 percent of their populations in cities. Type 2 nations are found in East Asia and North Africa, and more than half of their populations are in cities. Urban life in these societies is slowly improving as economic development proceeds. Type 3 nations are located in the sub-Sahara. They are rural but urbanizing rapidly. Even at this rate most were still rural in 2000. Population growth in these nations will outstrip the resources of these societies, leading to a declining standard of living. Type 4 nations include India, China, and Pakistan, and the rapid population growth in these subsistence-level societies exerts tremendous pressure on the natural as well as urban environment.

Increasingly, the world's population is being accommodated in large cities. This is true for both more- and less-developed countries. The situation in which the population of one city in a nation outstrips that of all other cities is called primacy. Primacy has been studied by social scientists for more than fifty years. Two schools of thought have developed around this concept. The first group views primate cities as parasitic. These scientists argue that primate cities often exist in societies based in agriculture. Cities are expensive to build and maintain, and these large urban populations drain away the limited financial resources of an entire nation. Primate cities also polarize a nation politically, socially, economically, and culturally because the major institutions of these nations tend to locate in the primate city.

The second group argues that primate cities operate to create a critical mass of talent necessary for development to take place. They argue there are so few people with the skills necessary to run modern enterprises, the only way to bring the necessary people together is to concentrate millions of people in one place. Additionally, only in primate cities does one find the infrastructure—banking, finance, transportation, and communication—necessary for modern enterprises to exist.

The internal structure of the city can be described along two dimensions—a physical dimension and an organizational dimension. The physical dimension includes streets, buildings, neighborhoods, and commercial and industrial areas. The organizational dimension includes the family types and ethnic, class, and associational groups found there. A complex interrelationship exists between the two. In general, the characteristics of the larger society are reflected in the city's physical structure.

A distinction is made between the structure of the premodern city and the modern city. Premodern cities are densely settled, compact, and residentially segregated on the basis of tribe, caste, or village. There is little functional specialization of land use and an inverse status gradient. This pattern is related to the low level of transportation technology. Modern cities, in contrast, have lower population densities; residential segregation based on social class, family type, and ethnicity; and specialized areas based on function. There is also a direct distance-status gradient with the poor living near the city's center and the wealthy at the periphery. Although societies around the world differ markedly in history and culture, research suggests that as development proceeds, the spatial patterns of a city move from the premodern to modern form with primate cities the first to experience change in the society.

Spontaneous settlements are a permanent and visible element of most cities in LDCs. Spontaneous settlements around the world share at least two of the following characteristics: most are occupied by the original settlers, most have been built illegally, most lack basic services, most are occupied by the poor, and most are built with an element of self-help. The number of people housed in spontaneous settlements varies from region to region, but the total is in the hundreds of millions. Research suggests many spontaneous settlements follow a life cycle from an initial settlement or bridgehead, through a period of consolidation in which the area gradually improves, to a final stage when the area takes on the characteristics of an ordinary suburb. These settlements, once viewed with alarm by government officials and often destroyed by urban renewal, are now viewed by many as the only way LDCs can provide housing for its citizens.

Two physical and social systems usually share the same city in LDCs. The modern sector shares the economic and social characteristics of cities in MDCs: nice housing, wage employment, and middle-class value systems. A traditional sector of spontaneous settlements houses the poor, poor housing, high unemployment, and lifestyles more closely resemble village life. Therefore, two physical realities, two economies, and two social structures—two worlds—inhabit the same city at the same time in much of the less-developed world.

In more-developed countries economic development and urbanization were linked together in the process of industrialization and modernization. In less-developed countries population growth is occurring without development. This pattern goes against many of the theories developed after World War II to predict the course of development in LDCs and to guide the spending of development funds.

Two theories have been developed to explain this deviation—modernization theory and dependency or world systems theory. Modernization refers to the social and political changes that accompanied the industrialization and modernization process in the West. Modernization involves the diffusion of these changes from more-developed to less-developed regions of the world. This process began in the sixteenth century and continued into the twentieth as European powers subjugated native populations into their empires. These powers imposed an alien culture on a traditional one and set up a dualism between the modernists and traditionalists, a source of conflict even today. This theory argues underdevelopment is the result of the resistance of traditional elements of less-developed societies to industrialization and urbanization.

The dependency theory is more recent than the modernization theory and is neo–Marxian. Modernization theory blames the traditional social system for resisting modernization; dependency theory blames the world capitalist system for underdevelopment. Dependency theory argues that core nations, MDCs, have used their economic and military might to control the world economic order and to structure economic relationships in a way to perpetuate dependency. During the colonial period, this domination was direct in the form of political and economic control. In the neocolonial period the control is indirect and is carried out by large multinational corporations, headquartered in core nations, which exert economic sway over peripheral nations. Multinational corporations exert this control by targeting investments, manipulating foreign governments, and perpetuating export economies in peripheral nations. All these techniques distort local economies and facilitate the exploitation of peripheral nations over time.

Thus, the two theories posit different explanations for growth without development. Modernization stresses the continued resistance of traditional cultures and elites to economic development. Dependency theory stresses the hegemony of Western nations over the world economic order and the actions of their proxies in perpetuating inequality among nations.

Note

[1] History repeats itself. Mohammed Ahmed Ibn el-Sayyid Abdullah was the Osama Bin Laden of the nineteenth century. He and his followers came to be known as the Mahdi, and they carried out a decade-long revolt in the Sudan in the 1880s against Britain and its client state Egypt. By 1890 they had created an Islamic state covering a million square miles, an area larger than England, France, and Germany. The Mahdi ruled the Sudan with the same fundamental Islamic principles as the Al Qaeda in Afghanistan. Both regimes came to the same end. See Moorehead, A. (1960). *The White Nile.* New York: Harper & Brothers Publishers.

The Iranian revolution in which Mullahs, Bazarine merchants, and peasants overthrew the Peacock Throne is another example of the resolution of this dialectic—a revolution that "cleansed the nation of the corrupting influences of the West" by executing or expelling the modernizers, returning Iran to theocratic traditionalism (Abrahamian, 1986). Iran is in the midst of its second revolution in a quarter century. This time it was conducted through the ballot box, as reformists trounced the Mullahs and traditionalists in the 2001 parliamentary elections. Iran's recent experiences suggest modification of modernization theory is needed.

4

THE CITY IN EVERYDAY LIFE

Introduction

I lived in Cincinnati as a child, and in Columbus, Ohio; Charleston, South Carolina; New York City; Fayetteville, Arkansas; and Irbid, Jordan, as an adult. I've always been fascinated by the city's people and spaces. Although I've lived in cities my entire life, the one experience that taught me more about the city was my first trip to New York.

I had just finished my freshman year in college, and I learned from a friend about the summer job of all summer jobs as a seaman in the U.S. Merchant Marine. The problem was I had to move to New York City to ship out. I remember it was early May when my parents drove me to the Cincinnati airport. Everyone in the car was tense. We all tried to make small talk, but it didn't work. I sat glumly asking myself, "Why am I doing this?" I'm sure my parents were asking themselves why they had ever said, "It sounds like a wonderful experience." But I had bought the plane ticket. I had cleaned out my bank account and converted my savings to traveler's checks. My bags were packed. The die was cast. I was shipping out.

My plane landed at La Guardia. As the plane was taxiing to the terminal, it hit me. I was in one of the largest cities in the world, I didn't know a soul, and I didn't have a clue what I was doing. I remember walking into the terminal and seeing a crush of people who shared only two things in common: They were late, and they didn't care who I was. Somehow I managed to navigate through the crowd to the baggage claim area, collect my bags, and follow the signs to the cabs and buses. Before I knew it, I was on my way into Manhattan.

On my bus ride into the city, I had a bird's-eye view of the cityscape. And what a cityscape it was—row houses, walk-up apartments, high-rise apartments, retail strips, clusters of retail shops, commercial warehousing, industrial centers, and the Manhattan skyline off in the distance. To my untrained eye, it was chaos, just a jumble of buildings. Then, a tunnel ride under the East River, and I was in one of the most densely populated places on earth, Manhattan.

I stayed at a YMCA at Seventh Avenue and Fifty-Fourth Street called the Sloan House. It was cheap, I was told it was a fairly safe neighborhood, and it was just a couple of blocks from Madison Square Garden and Penn Station. I checked in, dropped my bags off in my room, and headed for the National Maritime Union Hall on Seventh Avenue and Thirteenth Street.

I remember pausing in the lobby to check my map and then walking through the doors into a world of strangers. My first memory of Manhattan was a ConEd crew blocking two lanes of traffic in front of the Y. The crew was drinking coffee and looking down a manhole, indifferent to the drivers of hundreds of cars, cabs, trucks, and buses who were leaning on their horns in unison. When my eyes turned to the sidewalk, I noticed white people, black people, Chinese-looking people, Eastern European-looking people, well-groomed people, and shabby-looking people, each on their own mission, indifferent to my existence. I moved my wallet from my rear to my front pocket and made my first hesitant steps toward the subway station.

In the late 1960s, the graffiti artists had not yet plied their trade on the New York Subway System, but the stations and the trains had a tired look. I was unnerved making my way down into the station for the first time and became disoriented. I asked directions several times, and much to my surprise people were helpful. I remember one guy even asking me, "You from Cincinnati?" It was nearing the lunch hour when I made it onto my train, and I had to stand. I checked out the people sitting around me. No one was talking. A few passengers were reading folded newspapers or books, but most stared into empty space. Their bags and briefcases were locked between their feet or held close to their bodies. I caught the eye of one or two people, and they quickly looked away. I had caught a local rather than an express train, so we stopped at every station. As people milled in and out at every stop, I noticed that everyone was careful to avoid physical contact. As the train restarted and the new crowd settled in, the people standing were careful to keep their distance from those around them.

I remember getting off at my station and walking into the daylight. The first thing I remember is that there were fewer people. Some of the buildings looked newer. As I walked down Seventh Avenue and looked down the side streets, they had a residential look and feel to them. The streets were tree lined, and just a few people were in sight. I found the environment less threatening, and I even began to relax a little bit. I continued to walk a few more blocks. I looked up, and there it was, the International Headquarters of the National Maritime Union. Even a kid from Cincinnati could figure this one out. The building's windows were shaped like a ship's portholes.

In the next three months, I sailed to the Caribbean and the west coast of South America. They were experiences of a lifetime, but my home port was New York. When in port, I began to better understand the people and spaces of the city. These were experiences that led me to become an urban sociologist.

This chapter explores the social psychology of the city. In this chapter we will explore the city as a world of strangers. As we will see, even though we may not personally know another person, we still know a lot about her or him. We will explore the techniques we all use to make strangers known and less threatening. We will discuss our use of mental maps—the maps we all carry around in our heads that guide our behavior. We will explore how we divide space into private, parochial, and public realms and how these realms contribute to our sense of community, safety, and well-being. We will discuss changes in the nature and character of our cities in the last half of the twentieth century. We will see how these changes, in the eyes of many critics, have destroyed community and diminished the quality of urban life. We will use this same lens to examine crime and your chances of becoming a victim. First, we will explore how changes in the public realm have affected crime. Then, we will shift our focus to crimes on campus and how campus architecture, and the people who live and work there, affect your chances of becoming a victim. Finally, I will present some urban survival strategies that have served me well in cities all over the world. These strategies work well for the students I take to the Middle East each year. Most of us use these same strategies every day without ever thinking about them.

A World of Strangers

To live in a city is, among many other things, to live surrounded by large numbers of persons whom one does not know. To experience the city is, among many other things, to experience anonymity. To cope with the city is, among other things, to cope with strangers.

—*Lyn H. Lofland*

    This paragraph from the opening pages of Lyn H. Lofland's *A World of Strangers* (1985) captures the quintessential quality of the city: In the city we are surrounded by people we do not know. In the great expanse of human history, people were surrounded by people they knew. They were born and reared in small hunting and gathering societies or small villages. When they reached adulthood, they married a person from a nearby clan or village, raised a family, and died within the same social grouping. In these societies, strangers were viewed as a threat, and they were killed, run off, or made nonthreatening in some other way. In these societies, banishment was a death sentence. See Photo 4.1.

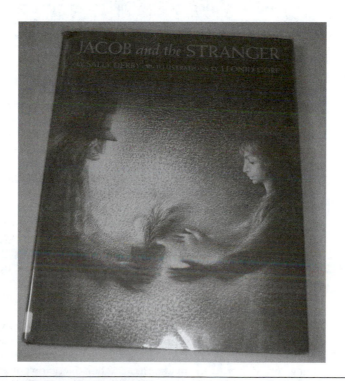

Photo 4.1   *The stranger is a common theme in the folk tales and literature of all societies. A recent example of this centuries old tradition is Sally Derby's children's book,* Jacob and the Stranger. *The spatial and appearential order of the city allows us to make strangers known and safer.* (*Source:* Beaura Kathy Ringrose/Houghton Mifflin Company College Division.)

This changed 10,000 years ago with the creation of the first cities. For the first time, humans found themselves surrounded by people they did not personally know. Given the biological and psychological characteristics of our species, Lyn Lofland believes we shouldn't be able to live in cities. She asks, "How is city life possible?" Her answer is that city life is possible because we actually know a great deal about the strangers who surround us. We know strangers by ordering the city's people through their personal appearance and location. These clues are generally reliable and allow us to navigate the city in relative safety.

The Role of Language in Ordering the Urban Environment

Our gift of language is the key to structuring the city and making it manageable. Language allows us to categorize and label all kinds of things—buildings, streets, neighborhoods, cities, and even people. We then use these categories to direct our behavior. Here's a good example. Yesterday in my general sociology class, I asked my students to describe some of the groups in their high schools. They came up with a long list that included preps, APs, jocks, ropers, druggies, boarders, and gothics. I then divided the class into small groups and asked the groups to describe each category. They came up with roughly the same descriptions. They based their descriptions on social class, dress, and behavior. For example, the preps, APs, and cheerleaders were at the top of their high schools' social ladder; the ropers, druggies, and boarders were at the bottom. The gothics just scared them.

Appearential Ordering

Like my students, we use our knowledge of our social structure to create social categories. If you know the person's position in the social structure—their status—then you know a lot about the person. The most obvious category is the person's socioeconomic status. Are they rich? Are they poor? Do they look employed or unemployed? We ask other questions. Are they male or female? What's their race? Are they ethnic looking?

We use other cues. How are they dressed? Are they wearing a uniform? Is their clothing upscale or threadbare? What about their haircut? Tattoos? Piercing? How do they walk? How do they use their props? How do they use language? Once we determine a stranger's status, we know the behavioral repertoire, or roles, associated with their status, and we use this information to predict behavior. The steps are straightforward: categorize, classify, draw on knowledge of status and roles, then act. In this way urbanites make strangers routine and safe.

Going back to the chapter's opening vignette, why did New Yorkers classify me as new to the city, scared, lost, and not a threat? The evidence was straightforward. I was young, blond, dressed differently than the natives with a funny midwestern accent. From my clothes, posture, demeanor, and use of language they could tell I was middle class. A few people knew I was from the Midwest, and one person even knew I was from Cincinnati. How? When I couldn't understand their New York accents, I said, "Please," to get them to repeat themselves. In the Cincinnati area, when you can't understand someone you don't say, "huh," or "pardon," you say, "please." The German immigrants to the region used the word *bitte* when they didn't understand someone. The English translation of the German word *bitte* is, you guessed it, *please.*

The dilemma is that this process is fraught with errors. We can misclassify people, or we can use the wrong scripts from our behavioral repertoires. There have been some glaring examples in the news lately. Racial profiling by police departments has led to a series of public relations disasters and multimillion-dollar lawsuits. It even became an issue in the 2000 presidential campaign, and the practice is now banned in many states. Similarly, Danny Glover couldn't get a cab in New York City. Why? Glover, a black actor, believes the city's cabbies were doing some racial profiling of their own. We have all been misclassified at some time in our lives. I'm often misclassified when I walk into a Home Depot on the weekend in my lawn-mowing clothes.

The city may be a world of strangers, but it doesn't mean that the city dweller is bereft of a spouse, children, relatives, friends, neighbors, coworkers, and church and club members. We live in social networks, and our network is intertwined with the social networks of others. These interlocking webs of relationships span continents and the world. Stanley Milgrim demonstrated nearly fifty years ago that most people in the United States are only four or five steps removed from every other American. You've probably played the name game yourself. You meet someone at a party or in line at the bank or the grocery, strike up a conversation, and ask, "You don't happen to know my friend (Insert name) in (Insert city or area of the city)?" Why do people ask such seemingly inane questions? Because they get a connection once in a while. The stranger next to you in line may not be a stranger at all, just a friend of a friend.

Spatial Ordering

More than 200 racial, ethnic, and religious groups coexist in the United States. In large cities like New York, Chicago, and Los Angeles most of these groups are represented. Beyond language and appearances, a third process at work in the city masks much of this diversity. It's called segregation. Even in our smallest metropolitan areas, we segregate residential, commercial, industrial, office, and retail activities in different parts of the city. Most of the time segregation occurs through zoning, but racial and ethnic exclusion is at work as well. Even the smallest metropolitan areas have a financial and commercial district, a dining and entertainment center, and an area that houses the community college or the university. Retail is concentrated in the mall. Medium and heavy industry is zoned in the city's industrial park, and high-tech businesses in the technology park. The hospital and the majority of doctors' offices are in or near the city's medical center. Smaller retail and commercial centers are scattered around the city. What would an American city be without its retail strips?

The segregation of economic activities is accompanied by the segregation of people. Neighborhoods are segregated by income, race, and ethnicity, along with factors like lifestyle and stage in life cycle. Think about the city in which you live or the city in which you were raised. Where do the elderly live? Young families with children? Young singles? The wealthy? The poor? Is there an ethnic neighborhood? Predominantly African American, Latino, or Asian neighborhoods? This isn't just a process found in the United States; it is a process that has been at work in all cities in all places at all times in history.

In categorizing these places, we have spatially ordered the city. Most of us have a mental map of the city to guide our behavior. You know what types of economic activities are found where. You have an idea of where categories of people live and work. You know where you can walk and drive safely, and you know the areas you should avoid. If you don't know, if you are new to a city, then, the police may add *victim* to your name.

Applying Appearential and Spatial Ordering to Strangers

We combine appearential ordering with spatial ordering and make routine our interaction with strangers. If people and places match up, then there is no problem. But if someone is someplace he or she shouldn't be, then an alarm goes off in our heads—be careful! Here's an example from my family. My son and I came to campus this summer. He's twelve. He has been on this campus his entire life, and he feels comfortable here. When I come to the office in the summer to pick up my mail, I usually give him a couple of dollars to play video games at the union and say, "Meet me at my office in thirty minutes." He goes to the union on one side of campus, and I go to my office on the other. Why does Judd feel safe here? First, he is familiar with the appearential ordering of the campus. What are his expectations? He expects to see students, faculty, administrators, and staff people like secretaries, janitors, and groundskeepers. The campus also has a spatial ordering: fraternity and sorority row, the athletic complex, the graduate center, the fine arts complex, the union, and so on. Different parts of campus serve different segments of the university community, and this pattern is pretty much the same everywhere. It is a predictable order.

This summer he came back to my office early. I could tell he was shaken, and I said, "That was quick. What's up?" Judd blurted out, "Dad, there was this really weird guy in the union." So I asked him to describe him, and he said he was dirty, shabbily dressed, and stood in the center of the union talking to himself. I knew right away who he was. The students call him Mr. Kotter because his hair looks like Abe Kaplan on the old TV sitcom. Our Mr. Kotter is a schizophrenic who has been hanging around campus for years. He's harmless. The campus police don't even hassle him anymore. But Judd didn't know him. He had expectations for the appearential and spatial ordering of campus. He also had behavioral expectations. When they didn't jive, he did what I have taught him to do—flee.

Life in the city frequently deviates from a predictable order. A homeless person wanders into an upscale office building or retail area. Someone calls the police. Or it can go the other way. A well-dressed person wanders into a tough, high-crime area and is mugged. This mismatch is a common plot in TV series like *Law and Order.* The running gag in Chevy Chase's vacation movies is his inept navigation of cities. Remember the scene when Clark Griswald takes a wrong turn and finds himself in the middle of East St. Louis, one of the most dangerous cities in the nation? He and his family leave the city a lot poorer.

These experiences are repeated billions of times each day in the world's metropolises. We all carry around with us a mental map of the city. We have expectations for the spatial, appearential, and behavioral order of the city. Our expectations help us make strangers known others because we can predict, with a high probability of being right, the behavior of others. Most of the time this process is subconscious. It only comes to the surface when a mental alarm goes off. The question remains, "How do we organize and store information about the city?" The answer is that we use mental maps.

Mental Maps of the City

The Physical Realm

Kevin Lynch in *The Image of the City* (1960) and *What Time Is This Place* (1972) was one of the first to explore the process by which we develop mental maps of the city. Lynch created a vocabulary to describe a city's spatial elements and discovered how people perceived them and how people put these elements together to create mental maps. These maps help us make sense of the physical world, guide our behavior (allow us to avoid areas), contribute to our sense of well-being (enjoyment, awe, fear, trepidation), and over time become part of a city's culture.

Do a little experiment. What mental images come to mind when you think of Boston's cityscape? The Commons? Harvard Square? Beacon Hill? What about St. Louis? What element of this cityscape is best known? Would you say it was the Arch? What comes to mind when you think of Chicago? Is it Lake Shore Drive? Lake Michigan? The Loop? If you know these symbols, you have a handhold on four of the five terms Lynch uses to describe the cityscape. The Commons, Harvard Square, and the Loop are districts, the Arch is a landmark, Lake Shore Boulevard is a path, and Lake Michigan is an edge. The only term missing is *node*, a place where paths and edges converge. Lynch and his colleagues found that people use this information on a city's paths, edges, nodes, districts, and landmarks to create a common mental image of their city. They also discovered how residents use these maps to navigate and how they use these maps to do mundane things like give directions. Here is an example. "Take Center Avenue five blocks until it dead ends at the park (a path meets an edge to form a node). Take a right and keep going until you see the courthouse (a path meets a landmark). Drive past the courthouse, and the restaurant is two blocks on the right (the path continues from the landmark to your final stop)." It's so simple. We do it everyday without thinking about it.

A city's residents, therefore, share a common language of the city using the vocabulary of paths, edges, nodes, districts, and landmarks. But cities are incredibly complex places, and no one can know all areas of a city. As a result, we fill in the gaps with a broad brush. Depending on your position in the social structure, you might describe an area as, "*those* people live on that side of town." Or, "I wouldn't drive through that area during the day much less at night." Or, "I could never afford to live in an area like that." Statements like these reflect people's attitudes about racial segregation, crime, and income. These statements have consequences when large numbers of people share them. A few isolated assaults reported on the evening news may cause thousands of residents to define a safe, livable neighborhood as dangerous. If this label sticks, it becomes a self-fulfilling prophecy and the neighborhood declines.

Closer to home, we apply a finer brush. People use concepts like face blocks, defended neighborhoods, and communities of limited liability to describe the areas of the city in which they live. You know intimately the street you live on (your face block) and the few blocks surrounding it (your defended neighborhood). Moving out of these areas you know the stores, groceries, schools, bars, and police and fire stations in your general part of the city (your community of limited liability). Your area may even have a name like the Near East Side, Huntington Place, or Washington Heights. You and your neighbors may know the name of your defended neighborhood, but the vast majority of a city's residents do not. They can't describe its boundaries, and they probably don't know who lives there. Outsiders find out about these areas when they wander into one. These spatial units are part of the mental maps shared by most residents of a city.

The Social Realm

Whereas Lynch focuses on the public images of the city, Lofland writes about the social realm (Lofland, 1973.)[1] Whereas Lynch explores the physical side of the city, Lofland explores the social spaces of the physical city. She divides the city differently based on the type, density, and intensity of the social interaction that takes place in these spaces. In her research, Lofland discovered three types of social realms: the private, the parochial, and the public.

The private realm is the place where our most intimate interaction takes place. It is our home—a house and backyard, condo, apartment, or dorm room—over which we exercise exclusive control. The boundaries of private space are clearly marked and recognized by neighbors and strangers—the front door, a backyard privacy fence, and a line of bushes separating the sidewalk from the front lawn. Students often decorate their dorm doors so other students know this is their private space. The sign on a child's bedroom door, "Keep Out or Die" sends a clear message to the family that this is her private space (Lofland, 1998).[2]

The social interaction of the face block and defended neighborhood makes up what Lofland calls the *parochial realm*. This is where much of the ebb and flow of daily life takes place. These are the streets, yards, and parks where children play. This is where children attend elementary school. This is where you are a neighbor. This is the social space in which you interact with the clerks at your neighborhood market, pharmacy, and gas station. You meet your friends here at hangouts—the neighborhood bar, restaurant, or video arcade. See Photo 4.2. Although residents usually don't have total control over the parochial realm, they do exercise some control over who comes and goes. For example, driving into many cities and suburbs you will find, right below the city limit sign, a small green sign. The sign reads, "Green River Ordinance Enforced." Thousands of communities have adopted the ordinance, which prohibits door-to-door sales. Last year when a door-to-door salesperson showed up at my door, I told her, "No thank you, and by the way, our city enforces the Green River Ordinance." I didn't call the police, but I noticed that within fifteen minutes the police showed up to escort her out of the area. It was our neighborhood watch program at work, and neighbors use this and other techniques to keep strangers out of their parochial spaces.

The third social space is the public realm. This is truly public space, and everyone has the right to be here. This is where we interact with strangers. These are streets in the central business district, the train and bus stations, and the public parks—the places where we use appearential and spatial ordering and behavioral expectations to make strangers safe. Although the city appears chaotic, Lofland found orderliness and predictability. A city could not exist without the cooperation and rule playing by the millions of people who live there. Lofland spent endless hours observing the public realm and found a rich set of rules that guide behavior. Make some observations of your own. Buy a soda or a cup of coffee, and find a seat near a busy

Photo 4.2   *The thrill, excitement, and pleasure of urban life often occurs at the boundary between parochial and public spaces. Note the iron fence that marks the transition between the two. (Source:* Tibour Bogn/CORBIS/Bettmann.)

pedestrian walk or flight of stairs. Hundreds of people will pass you in a few minutes without mishap. They will change their gait, they will slip to their right or their left or slow or quicken their pace to avoid contact. Similar sets of rules guide behavior in places like elevators or waiting in line. No one taught any of us these rules; we picked them up informally through socialization. What fascinates sociologists is not the disorder and chaos of the city, but its orderliness and predictability.

Rules for Navigating the Public Realm

Through her thousands of hours of observation, Lofland found some unwritten rules for navigating the public realm. We might call them the *Book of Urban Etiquette*. Here are the five most important rules.

> **Rule I: Cooperative motility.** These rules cover walking and navigating in public space. Walk on the right side of a busy sidewalk. Slower walkers keep to the outside. Watch the traffic in front of you; change your gait to avoid walking on the heels of the person in front of you. Be considerate of the elderly and disabled.

> **Rule II: Civil inattention.** Thou shalt not violate other people's privacy. Read a paper or a book. Ignore people who are different. Fiddle with your purse, briefcase, package, or some other prop and keep busy. No props? Glance around quickly, look out the window, look into empty space, or look down at the floor, but never, never stare down a stranger.

Rule III: Audience role prominence. The public realm is a stage. Be a member of the audience, not an actor. Cities have street performers and vendors who get your attention and your pocket change, but there are other dramas as well. A couple's argument spills out from a bar into the street. The police roust a panhandler. A street preacher draws a small crowd. The list of dramas is endless. Watch. Do not interfere. Do not get involved, unless, of course, you discuss the drama with the stranger standing next to you.

Rule IV: Restrained helpfulness. Give directions, make change, or ask, "Does anyone want my paper," when leaving a coffee shop. By doing these things, you add to civic life.

Rule V: Civility toward diversity. Cities are the great equalizers because the vast majority of people are strangers. The last and most important rule of the public realm is civility. Being friendly is not the same as being civil. Being civil is treating everyone with dignity and respect; in turn, they will treat you with respect. Polls show that the quality of life in New York City has increased tremendously in the 1990s. Former Mayor Guillione is given much of the credit. Why is New York a better place to live? Because the police have curbed incivility. Police have cracked down on aggressive panhandling, car window washing, three-card monte con artists, boom boxes, and the street vendors and the homeless who had taken over the city's sidewalks. It's come at a cost. Many civil libertarians feel the police are trampling people's civil rights. See Photo 4.3.

Photo 4.3 *The behavior in public places often appears random and disorderly, but Lofland's research shows that it is guided by a complex set of rules.* (*Source:* Alan Schein/CORBIS/Bettmann.)

Acquiring Information and Survival Skills

Up to this point we have argued that urbanites cope with strangers by using appearential and spatial ordering. We also explored mental maps, the social realms, and the rules of urban etiquette. Several questions remain: How do we acquire an understanding of the people and places in the urban environment? How do we learn to interact with strangers? How do we build our behavioral repertoires? The answer is simple. We learn through the normal socialization process. Throughout life we learn, retain, modify, and discard information about the environment in which we live. We all share similar experiences. I remember as a child, my parents would say things like, "Stay away from the Millers' house" (they never told me why). Or, "Don't you and your brother dare go across Millville Avenue," which was a busy street and the western boundary of our neighborhood. Or my parents would make offhand comments when we drove around town like, "Those houses must be thirty-thousand-dollars!" Or, "Goodness, look at what's happening to the old neighborhood." Like a sponge I stored it all away. Gradually, I learned about the city's people, where they lived, how they acted, and how I should interact with them. When I started to drive, I began to compare my impressions of people and places in my community to reality. Most of my impressions were right; others were very wrong. Thus, the learning process is most intensive during childhood and adolescence, but the process continues into adult life. Anytime we move, change jobs, or change our social status in some way, learning takes place. Why? Because the timing and patterns of our daily life change. We come into contact with new spaces and new people at different times of the day. And we must learn two types of new information. First, we must acquire new meanings for the people, places, and behaviors of the city. And second, we must modify our behavioral repertoires—where to go, how to dress, and how to act.

We learn the meaning of places through personal experiences and by word of mouth. We learn the coding for restaurants by using them. We learn the coding for bars and coffee shops from friends. We learn the coding for streets, parks, shopping areas, and neighbors from multiple sources. Some of this is based on actual experiences, but most is based on media reports and second- and third-hand reports from friends, family members, and acquaintances. All these sources of information have distortions, and we build these distortions into our mental maps.

Learning the meaning of people is more difficult today than in the past. Cheap international travel and liberal immigration policies mean that American cities are far more heterogeneous than in the past. The segregation of economic activities masks some of this heterogeneity, but in the public realm these people come together. The problem is that our mass culture, steeped in mass merchandising, has erased many of the class distinctiveness of clothing. Just look around one of your large introductory classes. You know there are major socioeconomic differences among the students, but most students are wearing jeans. This doesn't mean you can't use appearential ordering, but you have to combine it with other information.

Appearential and spatial ordering of the public realm is by no means a total solution to the problem of dealing with strangers. It provides a relatively stable and accurate way of identifying and dealing with the strangers around you. Having this information and knowing what to do with it, however, are two different things. The second part of this process is developing the skills necessary to respond appropriately—a behavioral repertoire. Building a behavioral repertoire is a complex process because it is based in social interaction which itself is a complex process. Social interaction is the mutual and reciprocating influence that two or more people have on each other's thoughts and actions. Interaction involves receiving clues from another, interpreting these clues, drawing upon our knowledge of statuses and roles, and then responding appropriately. After we respond, others must interpret our actions. It's a ping-pong game with visual, verbal, and nonverbal behavior being passed back and forth. The first person acts, the second person interprets and responds, and then the first person interprets and responds to the actions of the second person who has interpreted and responded to the first person's behavior. Confused? It gets even more complicated. In complex, heterogeneous societies like our own, behavior is culturally specific. You have to know something about the subculture to respond appropriately. How do we learn these skills? The majority of this learning takes place during childhood socialization. But anytime you move to a new community or change your daily routine, the learning continues. Social scientists still poorly understand this incredibly complex and haphazard learning process. What is remarkable is that the vast majority of us do it successfully. We learn the urban survival tools, we shape our behavior in anticipation of others, and we do it correctly most of the time.

Decline of the Public Realm? Decline of Community?

During the 1990s, the United States experienced unprecedented prosperity. We enjoyed the longest economic expansion in our history. Disposable family income and homeownership were at historic highs. Employment was at a historical high. Unemployment was at a historic low. The divorce rate was down, and the marriage rate was up. Crime rates were down. Almost every measure of economic and social well-being was rising, yet polls showed an uneasiness in American society. Many Americans felt something was wrong with their lives; some vital element was missing. Was it work? Was it family life? Was there another explanation? Could there be something wrong with our communities?

Robert D. Putnam touched a nerve in his book *Bowling Alone: The Collapse and Revival of the American Community* (2000). Putnam uses bowling as a metaphor for community. Bowling is an important sport in America. More people bowl in a year than attend most sporting events. In the past, people bowled together in leagues; it was a communal experience. Today, bowling is the recreation of couples and families; Americans bowl alone. To Putnam, bowling mirrors changes in the larger society. He sees a basic change in the way we connect with other people, even in informal and leisurely ways. Putnam's book overwhelms the reader with charts, statistics, and examples, but these data all show the same thing: Americans are no longer connected in the way they once were to neighborhoods, churches, and clubs. In Putnam's opinion, this sea change in community relations has meant a loss of social capital, the glue that holds our communities together. In comparison to the previous two generations, fewer Americans vote, join civic clubs, and run for local office. Simply, fewer Americans are engaged in their communities. Putnam contends this lack of civic engagement has led to a decline in the quality of the public realm. Lessening support for the local community means less investment in our civic culture. Less investment in civic culture results in a decline in the quality of community life. What is the culprit? According to Putnam, urban sprawl is a major cause. The link is straightforward. For every ten minutes of commuting time, people have 10 percent less time for every other form of social activity, whether it be going to church or attending clubs and public meetings.

James Kunstler explores sprawl in his book *The Geography of Nowhere* (1993). He sees the building of suburbia as a destructive and tragic act. He paints a dismal image of a suburban landscape of car-clogged highways, strip malls, tract houses, franchise restaurants, and parking lots. In the process of building nowhere, Kunstler believes we have junked cities and ravaged the countryside. In our haste to build suburbia, he believes we have lost sight of an urban form that has deep historical and social significance to this society—the village and the small town. Without links to these past urban forms, Kunstler believes the living arrangements Americans now think normal are bankrupting the nation economically, socially, ecologically, and spiritually. In Kunstler's mind, this is not merely a symptom of troubled cities, but a sign of a troubled society. Kunstler, like Putnam, feels that we, as a nation, have squandered the very thing that creates a civil, civic society, the public realm.

So what is the public realm? The public realm includes schools, community colleges, public universities, hospitals, libraries, courthouses, county office buildings, post offices, museums, galleries, parks, streets, squares, and sidewalks. The public realm is those places shared by the public for the public. Everyone has the right to be there. WE own it. This is where we interact with strangers. These are the buildings, institutions, and places that gave rise to civic culture. Civic culture means civilization—the lifestyle found in cities. The public realm is the heart of civic society, and in the minds of many critics of the city, we have squandered this heritage.

It is no accident that the words *communicate* and *community* share the same Latin root, "to put in common." Sociologists have known for decades the importance of communication in creating community and the role that public realm plays in this process. As Lyn Lofland shows, most of the interaction in the public realm is with strangers. Most of it occurs by chance. It is associated with going to work, taking the kids to school, running errands, and going out to dinner or a movie. When sociologists study the content of the verbal and nonverbal communication that takes place in the public realm, it is utterly trivial. But the sum of this communication is not trivial at all. It is the stuff that creates community.

Relationships in the Public Realm

Lyn Lofland identified the constellation of relationships that takes place in the public realm.[3] We have already explored the process by which we make strangers safe and known. Other types of interaction take place in the public realm and contribute to our sense of community. By far the two most common are fleeting relationships and relationships with categorically known others. These contacts last between a few seconds and a few minutes. Most involve no verbal communication at all. Examples of fleeting relationships abound. A young father catches the smile of an old man watching his five-year-old take her first hesitant ride on a two-wheeler. Sitting on a park bench, the old man scowls at a teenager interrupting his solitude with a boom box. Examples of interaction with categorically known others include ordering a sandwich from the counter help at McDonalds or asking directions from the security officer at the mall. The uniforms guide the interaction. We enter into these types of interactions so often, we don't even think about them.

There is really nothing unique about these relationships. They exist in even the smallest communities. There are, however, two additional types of relationships that are important in the community-building process. The first is what Lofland calls quasi-primary relationships. These are emotionally infused temporary relationships shared by dog owners, sidewalk superintendents, people you are forced to sit next to on buses and trains, or the student sitting next to you in a big intro class. These relationships last from minutes to hours rather than seconds to minutes. What's interesting is that personal information is often exchanged: "I'm from . . . " "I have two sons and a daughter." "I'll be a sophomore next fall." "We live just up the street, and we haven't had water all morning either." These relationships share a common element. Once the focus of the interaction is gone—the victim of the accident you both witnessed is driven off in an ambulance—the relationship ends. But funny things happen in these chance meetings; sometimes, a friendship or love affair can emerge.

Intimate-secondary relationships are the final and most important type in community building. They are of long duration and involve the exchange of personal and, at times, intimate information. Let me give you some personal examples. My family has intimate-secondary relationships with Carl Collier, the owner of a local drugstore. We are on a first-name basis. Carl, through the prescriptions he fills, knows a lot about the health of my family. He knows the names and ages of my kids and where they go to school, where we live, where we work, and where we attend church. We aren't friends, but we are friendly, and we often share personal information about our families and kids. This relationship has continued for the past twenty-five years.

I have developed other intimate-secondary relationships. At our local farmers' market, I've been buying my produce from the same truck farmer for twenty years. I know the names of his wife and kids. I know what colleges his kids attended. I know when and with whom they married. I know all about his grandkids. I even know what they look like because their photos are tacked up on the back of his pickup. My life in this community is filled with these relationships. I know a lot about these people, where they are from, how many children and grandchildren they have, how long they have lived in the area, and what their work routines are, but, in many cases, I don't know their last names. These relationships may appear to be superficial, but they are not. These intimate-secondary relationships are vital to the community-building process because they create our public identity. These relationships are the links between you, your family, and the local community.

The Importance of These Relationships

Sprawl doesn't mean that these relationships don't exist, but when they are combined with the McDonaldization of America, their numbers have diminished. Wal-Mart is the largest corporation in the United States. Wal-Mart was founded in Bentonville, Arkansas, in 1971. The founder of Wal-Mart, Sam Walton, knew he couldn't take the big retailers, like Sears and K-Mart, head on, so he opened his stores where the big retailers weren't—in small towns.[4] In doing so, he transformed community life in rural and small-town America.

A lot of good and bad is associated with the rise of Wal-Mart. On the one hand, when a Wal-Mart opens on the edge of a small town, the range of goods and services available to the residents improve. On the other hand, the opening of a Wal-Mart usually means the closing of the local pharmacy, grocery, hardware, and clothing store. There is disagreement over the impact of Wal-Mart on communities. One group of researchers argues that Wal-Mart destroys the local community by destroying the web of primary-secondary relationships between residents and locally owned businesses. Other researchers argue that Wal-Mart contributes to the community-building process by providing jobs and goods and services heretofore unavailable in small towns. Maybe the answer to this question is as simple as asking, Is the welcome by the greeter at the local Wal-Mart equivalent to the welcome by the owner of a local store? Does the greeter know you? Does this relationship contribute to your community identity? Does this interaction evolve into intimate-secondary relationships? Will Wal-Mart employees become a strand in the web of relationships that create the network of relationships we call community?

Community and Crime

A lot of angst focuses on the state of the community in America. This angst is nothing new. Probably the majority of the words written about the city in the past fifty years have been on its decline. I believe that most social scientists would agree that the way we live our lives in communities today is very different from fifty years ago. Tracking these changes provides a history of community life. How do we chronicle these changes? One way is to study one of this society's major social problems, crime. The number and types of crimes and how our communities control them tell us much about community change over the last half century.

Crime Statistics

The United States is one of the most crime-ridden societies in the world. Each year the FBI publishes the Uniform Crime Report (UCR). The UCR is a compilation of all the crimes reported to police. In 1999, the FBI reported 11.6 million offenses that fit into eight categories: murder, forcible rape, aggravated assault, robbery, burglary, motor vehicle theft, larceny-theft, and arson. Nine out of ten of these crimes were property crimes: burglaries, motor thefts, and larceny thefts. Murders and rapes get the most press, but they make up less than 1 percent of all crimes in the United States each year (Federal Bureau of Investigation, 2000).

The UCR lists crimes reported to the police. The National Institute of Justice (NIJ) collects a different type of crime data. Each year the NIJ conducts the National Crime Victimization Survey. Questionnaires are sent to a scientifically drawn sample of Americans. The questionnaire explores the respondents' experiences with crime in the preceding year. These self-reported data give a more disturbing picture. In 2001, 24 million Americans were victims. The experiences of these people, however, mirror the UCR data (Bureau of Justice Statistics, 2003). Most crimes involved minor assaults or minor larceny. Most of these crimes were so minor that they weren't worth reporting to the police. If we were to make some generalization, most crime is against property, not people. The crimes against persons are usually minor. But there is an irony in these data. Overall crime rates have fallen throughout the 1990s. The drop in reported crime was 16 percent between 1993 and 2002 (Federal Bureau of Investigation, 2003). We live in a much safer society than we did a decade ago. But this is not the perception of most Americans. The fear of becoming a victim is far greater among most Americans than odds of becoming one. I believe this fear may reflect changes in community.

Crimes may be reported to federal agencies like the FBI and the NIJ, but they occur locally in our private, parochial, and public realms. We have already discussed the complex relationship between the physical and social forms of the city. We know from our own experiences that the form of community shapes the ebb and flow of our daily lives. The layout of streets, the location of schools, hospitals, shopping centers, and office complexes affect the mundane things we do in life such as getting to work, shopping for groceries, or making a doctor or dental appointment. When we combine our schedules with thousands of others, these schedules intersect at certain times of the day, and we find ourselves walking a street with thousands of other people. Time and space interact in complex ways in cities. As we move through our daily lives, we move in and out of parochial and public spaces without even knowing it. By just being in these spaces, we contribute to and deter crimes without knowing it. For example, when thousands of people break for lunch and fill downtown streets, their presence prevents serious crimes like assault, murder, and rape. But their presence contributes to other types of crimes like petty larceny.

The Shape of the City: Now and Then

Transportation and communication technology determines who will meet, when they will meet, and how far they will travel to meet. This technology also determines how and where we will travel during the day to meet our daily needs of work, child care, shopping, and entertainment. Therefore, one of the general principles of understanding crime is to understand how people and goods move around the city. Prior to 1950 metropolitan areas were organized around a single central business district where most retail and commercial activities were located. Trolley, rail, and major thoroughfares radiated from the core, determining the location of other land uses. Industry located near rail lines and waterways. Warehousing needed access to the center's businesses so it located on the periphery of the central business district. Retail and small-scale commercial activities located at the major intersections. Residential neighborhoods filled in the rest of the space. There was a clear pattern to the location of these neighborhoods. Groups with lower socioeconomic status lived near the city's center; those with higher socioeconomic status located near the fringe. Neighborhoods were more densely settled. Few Americans owned cars, so people's ability to move around the city was limited. Most of a family's needs were met near or within the neighborhood.

The automobile transformed the metropolis. We no longer have a single central city; we have a multinucleated metropolis. In most metropolitan areas, the central business district is no longer the commercial, financial, and retail center of the city; these activities are spread across the metropolis. They are most often found in edge cities. Edge cities have at their center large, privately owned malls (Garreau, 1992). Adjoining the malls are office parks, apartment complexes, and retail, entertainment, and restaurant clusters. All these businesses have plenty of free parking near their buildings. A problem is that the activities within the edge city are accessible only by car. You usually can't walk from, say, your office to a nearby restaurant. There are no sidewalks.

A more important change in this form of urban development has gone largely unnoticed: These spaces are not in the public realm. Malls are privately owned. The owners control who can and who cannot be there. The fringe's largest land use is private, low-density residential areas. One of the least appreciated aspects of urban sprawl is the precipitous decline in public space, the realm that creates community. These changes have fundamentally altered not only the way we create our communities, but also the way we maintain social control. Therefore, changes in transportation and communication technology permitted the rapid development of the fringe. The character and form of this development resulted in the rise of the private realm and the decline of the public realm. These changes taken in concert contributed to the high crime rate in our society.

The Importance of Informal Social Control

There is probably no better book to contrast cities of the 1950s with the cities of the twenty-first century than Jane Jacob's *The Life and Death of Great American Cities*. Jacobs shows how the key to safety in our cities is the informal social control that comes from mixed land use. Ironically, she shows how cities work at their best by describing the experiences of an old, rundown Boston neighborhood known as the Near North End, a type of area sociologists call an *urban village*.

In the 1950s, the Near North End was a working-class neighborhood. Puritans settled in this neighborhood in 1630. Many years later, Irish immigrants moved in, then Russian and Polish Jews, Portuguese and Spanish fishermen, and finally Italians. Today, the North End is one of Boston's most trendy neighborhoods with more than 100 eating places. Through much of its history, however, the neighborhood provided low-cost housing to a succession of immigrants. When planners looked at the neighborhood in the 1950s, they saw a slum ready for renewal. The managers of banks and savings and loans agreed and stopped lending money in the area. Only the inspired leadership of a group of community activists saved the neighborhood from the wrecking ball.

Where planners saw a slum, Jacobs saw something different. She saw a viable neighborhood that met the special needs of its residents through a diversity of land uses. The neighborhood was densely settled with walk-up apartments, duplexes, and single-family homes. Intermixed with the residences were groceries and shops. Kids could walk to the neighborhood schools. Residents were only minutes from their jobs in and near the central business district. Applying the building standards of the day, Near North End was technically a slum. But the Near North Side had few of the social pathologies usually associated with a slum. In fact, the crime rate in this neighborhood was one of the lowest in Boston. Why? Because the neighborhood's physical layout and mixed land use contributed to informal social control. Neighbors, not the police, maintained order, and informal social control is far more effective than the formal control afforded by the police.

By studying the Near North End, Jacobs discovered the three elements needed for safe streets and neighborhoods. First, there must be a clear demarcation between public, parochial, and private spaces. People must know where they can go and where they cannot. Second, there must be eyes on the street all the time. And third, sidewalks and public places must be busy. The very things that make the city unique—its size, density, and heterogeneity—contribute to its safety. Stores, shops, businesses, bars, and restaurants mix with public spaces like schools, libraries, public squares, and parks, and together they contribute to a neighbor-hood's security by keeping people in the public realm day and night. As people leave stores, shops, and businesses at the end of the workday, other activities take over like grocery shopping, eating out, or just meeting friends on the front porch, at local hangouts, or in public squares and parks. These activities work together in different and complex ways, but together they contribute to the neighborhood's safety by keeping the public realm under continuous surveillance. Other forces are at work as well. Storekeepers and other small businesspeople are stakeholders in the neighborhood. They have a vested interest in keeping crime and disturbances low. They are effective guardians. Remember those intimate-secondary relation-ships? During times of trouble, local guardians can draw upon this network of rela-tionships. Therefore, Jacobs found that once a street and neighborhood create a clear demarcation between public and private spaces, offer a diverse range of activ-ities, and create an unplanned but effective system of informal surveillance, the more strangers the merrier. Strangers become an asset on the street because their presence deters crimes and adds to the quality of urban living. These cities were far from perfect. Crime existed in these cities, but the areas of high crime rates were the central business district, warehousing districts, and transportation corridors. The police were more effective in maintaining social control in these areas.

Dependence on Formal Social Control

Contrast the city of the past with today's city. Through zoning and other tech-niques, we have created a city of specialized land uses: malls and retail centers, commercial and business centers, medical and educational complexes, and resi-dential areas segregated by income, race, and ethnicity. These specialized areas are not used continuously. Commercial and business centers are empty after business hours and on weekends. Residential areas are abandoned during the day. There are few eyes on the sidewalks and streets most hours of the day. Com-pounding the situation, commercial buildings are oriented to the parking lot, and homes and apartments are set back from the streets. People may look out onto these spaces from their offices or homes, but whose space is it? If a crime is in progress—if a car is being broken into, for example—who is responsible? Who provides social control? The parking lot isn't exactly private and it's not parochial. It's quasi-public—not everyone has the right to be there. The police or private security guards are responsible, right? The result: ambiguity reigns in the fringe.

Other important changes in the urban fringe have contributed to much higher crime rates. First, low-density residential, retail, and commercial construction means more roads and bigger parking lots. As the private realm expands, the pub-lic and parochial realms shrink, and the safety that comes with safety with others and eyes on the streets declines. With a decline in the effectiveness of informal social control, communities depend on the police. But low-population densities mean the police must patrol larger and larger territories, thus lowering their effec-tiveness (Felson, 1998).

Second, accompanying sprawl has been an explosion in the number of American households and a change in household composition. Adult children don't live with their parents. Few elderly parents live with their children. In a society with one of the highest divorce rates in the developed world, divorce creates two new households. In addition, the number of people living alone has exploded. There is an even more important change in the household composition of this society. In 1950, 25 percent of women over twenty-five years of age were in the labor force; today it's 70 percent. Fewer people are home fewer hours a day, interacting with neighbors less and providing less of a deterrent to crime. Research shows that when people are spread over many households, there are proportionately more property crimes and violent crimes.

Third, driving alone on an eight-lane highway, hermetically sealed in an air-conditioned car, may lull you into a sense of safety, but there's one flaw in your thinking: Eventually you will reach your destination. That walk across the deserted parking lot to the mall, doctor's office, or office complex puts you at risk for crime. Isolated parking also leaves a vast number of unsupervised vehicles at risk. There are plenty of places for criminals to hide. The police are ineffective because they can't be everywhere at once. And don't be lulled into security with that expensive alarm system. Someone has to be around to hear it.

Contrast the urban fringe with an urban neighborhood that works. For example, Jane Jacobs described how the physical character of the Near North Side produces natural conversations over the backyard fence or on the front stoop. Jane Jacobs showed that by mixing residences with groceries and shops, a network of intimate-secondary relationships develops to provide informal social control. Sprawl disperses people and households and reduces the interaction with neighbors, but it increases the face-to-face interaction with people who live miles away. Changes in transportation technology liberate people from local attachments like nosey neighbors. The car allows friendships to be based on taste rather than space. But ask yourself, does a friend two miles away provide eyes on your street?

In general, sprawl means that people are dispersed over more households, and these households are taking up more of the urban fringe. This low-density development has forced residents into their cars because virtually all activities are away from the home and the neighborhood. To accommodate this travel, miles of streets and acres of parking lots have been built in the fringe. The following statistic reflects that new reality: The typical American travels more than twenty-five miles per day to complete daily routines. Fringe communities have made only small investments in the public realm. There are relatively few truly public spaces. The end result is that traditional means of social control no longer work. The capacity of neighbors to control their environment and to prevent crime has been diminished. The result is predictable—crime.

College Campuses

Colleges and universities are wonderful labs for studying crime. First, there is a lot to steal. Students bring stereos, VCRs, TVs, Walkmans, computers, clothes, books, cars, and money to campus. They live in communal settings or apartments. There is an abundance of young, unmarried males, the most crime-prone segment of our population. Alcohol and drugs also abound. Turnover in the living communities is guaranteed—it's called the academic year. After some well-publicized rapes and murders, Congress passed a law requiring colleges and universities to report annually the types and frequency of crimes on campuses. In general, crimes reported to campus police departments across the nation mirror the rest of society. Like the FBI's reports, most campus crimes go unreported. In a recent survey of students, however, 25 percent reported that they were victims of one or more crimes during the academic year. As in society, most of these crimes were minor and were against property, not people. Murder was rare, rapes were usually by acquaintances, and assaults were usually alcohol related (Fisher, Sloan, Cullen, & Lu, 1997).

There are lots of other stuff to steal and people to assault on every campus. Every office on campus has a computer with printer and other peripherals. Computer and science labs are full of wonderful things. University bookstores are often understaffed. The staffing in libraries is even worse. My campus even has a breeder reactor. Could terrorists be lurking about?

Campuses have areas that resemble urban villages and the sprawling metropolis. They have public, private, and parochial realms. Student unions, theaters, stadiums, basketball arenas, sports complexes, libraries, squares, sidewalks, and lawns are in the public realm. Offices and dorm rooms are in the private. Common areas in dorms and fraternity and sorority houses, staff and faculty break rooms, and the faculty dining room are in the parochial realm. Public streets, major thoroughfares, and acres of parking lots on the periphery of most campuses are quasi-private. More important, we use a mixture of informal and formal social control to control crime and maintain social order on our campuses.

Lawrence Cohen and Marcus Felson's *opportunity theory* is a good vehicle to understand campus crime (Felson, 1997). The theory in a nutshell is that three things must be present for crime to occur. First, there must be motivated criminals. Second, there must be suitable targets. And third, there must be an absence of effective guardians. Let's use a few examples. When is someone more likely to steal something from your dorm room, at the beginning or end of the semester? If you check with your campus police, you'll find that it is at the beginning of the semester. Why? There are lots of suitable targets and ineffective guardians. Most new freshmen are from small towns and suburbs and are oblivious to their risks. They forget to lock their doors when they go to dining hall or class. In addition, no one knows the neighbors. No one knows who belongs and who doesn't belong on the floor. There are no effective guardians. The result is that petty larceny is at the highest at the beginning of the semester. By the middle of the semester, you or a friend has had something stolen, so you keep your door locked. Your susceptibility as a victim has declined. More important, you've developed friends and acquaintances on your floor, and they'll keep a watch on your room. Dorms are like the urban village. A network of primary and intimate-secondary relationships keeps eyes on your parochial space and maintains order through informal social control.

Where are you most likely to be physically assaulted or robbed on campus? On most campuses it is in the quasi-public spaces on the periphery of campus. Why? Motivated criminals have easy access to these areas. There are usually plenty of good places for them to hide along walls, in, or between cars. You are highly susceptible because you are alone. Thus, the third factor of the opportunity theory is that there are no eyes on the lot, and the campus police, a formal control agent, are ineffective guardians because they have dozens of buildings, miles of streets, and acres of parking lots to patrol.

Campuses are cities in microcosms. Time and space interact in complex ways on our campuses, bringing students, faculty, and staff together at certain times of the day and dispersing them at others. Without knowing it, we both facilitate and deter crime. The goal is to use this knowledge of place and space to make the campus safe.

Summary

In this chapter we explored the social psychology of the city. We explored the city as a world of strangers. We explored how we divide space into private, parochial, and public realms and how these realms contribute to our sense of community, safety, and well-being. We described how the decline in the public realm has led to a decline in social capital and a decline in the quality of life in our communities. We saw how changes in the public realm have affected crime and how crimes on campus, campus architecture, and the people who live and work there affect your chances of becoming a victim.

In the great expanse of human history, people were surrounded by people they knew. But in cities today we live in a world of strangers. We make strangers known by ordering the city's people through their personal appearance and location. Language is the key to this process. Language allows us to categorize and label types of people. We combine this information with our knowledge of social structure to create social categories. When we combine this information with our knowledge of which groups live in which areas of the city, we are able to correctly classify the vast majority of strangers with whom we come in contact. If the strangers with whom we come in contact with fit our social categories, and they are in the right part of town, there is no problem. When there is a mismatch, our defenses go up.

Kevin Lynch (1960) explored the city's physical realm. He was one of the first to uncover the process by which people develop mental maps of the city. Lynch created a vocabulary to describe a city's spatial elements—paths, edges, nodes, districts, and landmarks. He also discovered how people perceived them and how people put these elements together to create mental maps.

Whereas Lynch focused on the public images of the city, Lyn Lofland (1985, 1998) explored the social spaces of the physical city. Lofland divided the city according to the type, density, and intensity of the social interaction that takes place in these spaces. In her research, Lofland discovered three types of social realms—the private, the parochial, and the public. The private realm is the place where our most intimate interaction takes place—our homes and our yards. The social interaction of the face block and defended neighborhood make up what Lofland calls the parochial realm. The third social space is the public realm, those areas where everyone has the right to enter. Although the city's public realm appears chaotic, Lofland found orderliness and predictability. She shows that a city could not exist without the cooperation and rule playing by the millions of people who live there. Lofland described the rich set of rules that guide behavior in the public realm.

Currently there is a heated debate on the future of the community. In his book, *Bowling Alone: The Collapse and the Revival of the American Community* (2000), Robert Putnam describes the dramatic decline in social capital and civic participation in American society. Similarly, William Kunstler in his work, *The Geography of Nowhere* (1993), argues that we have junked our cities and ravaged the countryside through sprawl. Both authors view these changes as destroying the public realm—places shared by the public for the public. Lofland sees the decline in the public realm as a decline in the relationships that take place there. Intimate-secondary and primary-secondary appear to be the most important relationships in building our sense of community. As Wal-Mart and other large chains replace locally owned stores, these community-building relationships have declined.

The United States is one of the most crime-ridden societies in the world. However, most crime in this society is against property, not people. In this section, we showed the complex relationship between the physical and social forms of the city. Time and space interact in complex ways in cities. For example, when thousands of people break for lunch and fill downtown streets, their presence prevents serious crimes like assault, murder, and rape, but facilitates minor crimes like purse snatching and petty larceny.

We also explored the changing form of the city. Jane Jacobs, in *The Death and Life of Great American Cities,* showed how the key to safety in our cities is the informal social control that comes from mixed land use. In the past, densely settled neighborhoods provided an environment in which there were always eyes on the street. Today, none of these basic elements exist in the fringe areas of cities. Today, we typically find on the fringe edge cities that have at their center large, privately owned malls. Adjoining these malls are office parks, apartment complexes, and retail, entertainment, and restaurant clusters. A problem is that the activities are accessible only by car. According to these critics, one of the least appreciated aspects of urban sprawl is the precipitous decline in public space, the realm that creates community. These changes have fundamentally changed not only the way we create our communities, but also the way we maintain social control. Rather than using informal means to maintain social control, we must rely on formal means—the police and private security—which are far less effective. The result is predictable: Crime is epidemic.

Colleges and universities are wonderful labs for studying crime. Students bring stereos, VCRs, TVs, Walkmans, computers, clothes, books, and cars to campus. In general, crimes reported to campus police departments across the nation mirror the rest of the society. Crimes are minor. Most crimes are against property and not people. Most crime is so minor that it is never reported. Campuses have areas that resemble urban villages and the sprawling metropolis. They have public, private, and parochial realms. Dorms, offices, and sorority and fraternity houses resemble the urban village. Places like student unions, theaters, stadiums, basketball arenas, sports complexes, libraries, squares, sidewalks, and lawns are in the public realm. But public streets, major thoroughfares, and acres of parking lots on the periphery of most campuses are quasi-private. Our universities use a mixture of informal and formal social control to control crime and maintain social order on our campuses.

Notes

[1] The following section is based in part on Chapter 5 of Lyn H. Lofland, 1973, *A World of Strangers: Order and Action in Urban Public Space* (Prospect Heights, IL: Waveland Press).

[2] Please see Chapter 2, "The Normative or 'Legal' System: Patterns and Principles," in Lyn H. Lofland, 1998 *The Public Realm: Exploring the City's Quintessential Social Territory* (New York: Aldine De. Gruyter).

[3] Please see Chapter 3, "The Relational Web: Persons, Places, Connections," in Lofland, *The Public Realm: Exploring the City's Quintessential Social Territory.*

[4] The expansion and growth strategy, pioneered by Sam Walton, is called *reverse, hierarchical diffusion.*

5

COMMUNITY IN THE MODERN WORLD

Introduction

Few ideas in Western thought are more widely shared than the belief that modern society has destroyed the community. Our literature, movies, criticism, philosophy, social theory, and folk sociology share the belief that we have lost a simpler and better way of life where relationships were based in kin, friendship, and neighborhood. In earlier times consensus reigned, and when conflict did occur, it was handled informally, neighborly, over the back fence or in the parlor. Today, critics argue, we find in its place a way of life that is somehow void—void of feeling, void of relevance, void of intimate friendships, supportive kin, and caring neighbors. More disturbing to many is the unsettling feeling that we have lost a sense of belonging, a sense of place, a sense of community. How did this happen? Who is responsible? Theorists and citizens alike blame modern life. Historical forces converged in the twentieth century to create this new way of living, but in its wake tradition was destroyed. Church leaders, politicians, and social critics point to the products of this destruction: soaring crime rates, disintegrating families, a loss of faith in our basic institutions, and the reduction of society to a group of atomistic, selfish, egocentric, and alienated individuals.

Social philosophers argue that the city plays a crucial role in this process of community destruction. Modern social and technological innovations were forged in the city. It was here the factory, the joint stock company, new forms of finance and administration, transportation and communication breakthroughs, modern political arrangement, and new forms of social control were created. Few critics question the role of the city in creating this web of economic, political, and social relationships responsible for the modern way of life. The question is whether this way of life is better or worse than the past.

This chapter explores the community and the social aspects of urban life. What is community? Are the images of the community of the past correct? Has modern society destroyed community? Do members of modern societies have shallow and superficial relationships? Are there no ties to kin and neighbor? Is the city the villain? We will answer these questions by examining the evolution and present usage of the concept of community. In the first section, the contributions of nineteenth-century community theorists Sir Henry Maine, Ferdinand Tönnies, and Emile Durkheim are explored in terms of the historical factors that shaped their works. Next, the works of Robert Park and other members of the Chicago School are discussed in relation to the influence of both the nineteenth-century community theorists and the conditions in American society. In chapter 6, the community as a social unit in contemporary society is examined. In the final section of the chapter, today's most exciting research on community—social networks—is explored.

Evolution of the Concept of Community: Premodern to the Modern Era

Though the concept of community has been of concern to sociologists for nearly 200 years, there continues to be disagreement on its exact definition. Early ideas about community were developed before cities had reached their present-day size and scope, at a time when societies were smaller and less complex and when large population centers were few. The early concepts of community focused on the relationship of individuals and groups to their society. How societies maintained order and the forces that produced and maintained rules of conduct were the central concerns in the perspective of nineteenth-century sociologists.

Societies have changed radically since the nineteenth century, and the concept of community has changed also, but not to the same degree. Though in many respects the nineteenth-century sociologists' concepts of community are not relevant to today's communities, these concepts continue to shape current expectations of the ideal community. This cultural heritage, combined with the fact that what constitutes a "good" or "ideal" community is a subjective evaluation, leads to definitional problems. The problem of defining the concept of community is highlighted in a 1955 article by the sociologist George Hillery, "Definitions of Community: Areas of Agreement." Hillery conducted a thorough review of the sociological literature on community and found ninety-four separate definitions in use. The only point of total agreement among them was that communities "deal with people!" The diversity of definitions is due to the fact that sociologists work from several different theoretical perspectives, study a wide variety of phenomena, and adopt the definition that is most compatible with their theoretical approach.

Although Hillery concluded that there was no overall agreement beyond the fact that community involves people, he did find substantial agreement among the majority of authors on three points. First, community involves groups of people who reside in a geographically distinct area. Second, community also refers to the quality of the relationships within this group. The idea that members of a community are bound together by common characteristics such as culture, values, attitudes, and the like was shared by a majority of the authors. Third, community refers to a group of people who are engaged in sustained social interaction—neighboring, for example. Therefore, for the purposes of this text, a *community* is defined as a group of people who share a geographic area and who are bound together by common culture, values, race, or social class.

Although an operational definition of community has been established, what level of community is meant? A city? A small town? A neighborhood? The concept of community has evolved from earlier concepts. To understand its present use and the types of geographic units to which it refers, one must understand its evolution.

The concept of community was a central element in the works of most of the founders of sociology—Auguste Comte, Alexis de Tocqueville, Sir Henry Maine, Ferdinand Tönnies, Frédéric LePlay, Karl Marx, and Emile Durkheim (Nisbet, 1966).

Photo 5.1   *The term modern was first used to describe Western Society in the early 1800s. This photo, taken at the turn of the twentieth century, is the form of the city experienced by Emile Durkheim and the other community theorists of that era. (Source: CORBIS/Bettmann.)*

See Photo 5.1. These men were living and writing during the nineteenth century, a period of profound change in Western society. Change was so rapid and pervasive that it can best be described as revolutionary. Industrialization, urbanization, and bureaucratization were the forces shaping society. Many negative by-products of transformation were manifested. It was in this atmosphere that the modern concept of community first emerged. Community during this era was often thought of in romantic terms as a way of life destroyed by the forces of the modern world. Community was equated with the good life, and industrial society was often contrasted with the community of the past. Thus, the concept of community first was used for the purpose of contrast—the past versus the present—and examples of this usage can be found in the works of Maine, Tönnies, and Durkheim (Bell & Newby, 1972).

Sir Henry Maine: Family versus Individual Status

Maine, an Englishman writing in the middle of the nineteenth century, was primarily interested in the origins of codified or written law.[1] His book, *Ancient Law*, was not concerned with community as such, but his work greatly influenced other thinkers of his age, especially Tönnies. The major contribution of Maine is his demonstration that one cannot understand a society's legal system without first understanding its social system. The contrast he makes between societies from different ages is based primarily on ascribed status and tradition versus achieved status and contract.

The Family and Tradition

Maine describes these differences clearly in the following statement:

> *Society in primitive times was not what it is assumed to be at present, a collection of individuals. In fact, and in view of the man who composed it, it was an aggregation of families. The contrast may be most forcibly expressed by saying that the unit of ancient society was the family, of a modern society an individual. (1870, p. 126)*

In many ancient societies, the individual was not recognized in law; the family was the legal entity. The individual's position in society was based on the family into which he or she was born. Stated another way, the status of the individual in society was ascribed by family membership. In addition, solutions to the problems of day-to-day living were drawn from the experience of past generations or tradition rather than based on reason.

In contrast, the individual, not the family, is the important unit under law in modern society. Some modern societies even protect the individual from her or his family (for example, in cases of child abuse)—a practice unknown to society in primitive times. The individual's position in modern society, although influenced by family membership, depends mainly on the person's skills, training, and education. Ideally, the individual rises to a social status based on achievements rather than on family membership.

The Contract

The contract is another important element of modern society. To Maine, the contract was a revolutionary social invention that made possible an entirely different form of society. A contract is simply a binding agreement between two or more individuals or parties. The agreement states certain terms and conditions that, when fulfilled, relieve both parties of any further obligation. It permits two strangers to come together, carry out a business transaction, and then go their separate ways once the terms of the agreement have been fulfilled. Contractualism makes possible an ordered society composed of individuals.

Maine's distinctions between the legal systems of *primitive* and *modern* societies were explicitly recognized and taken into account by sociologists who later attempted to understand and explain change in the social relationships among persons in industrial societies. The influence of Maine is clear in the writings of Tönnies and Durkheim.

Ferdinand Tönnies: Gemeinschaft and Gesellschaft

Tönnies's book *Gemeinschaft and Gesellschaft* (usually translated as *Community and Society*) was first published in 1887. It has provided a constant source of ideas for students of community ever since. Drawing on the earlier works of Sir Henry

Maine, Otto von Gierke, and Fustel de Coulanges, Tönnies described several dimensions along which European society had changed (Nisbet, 1966). The basic changes were threefold. First, the basis of one's social status had changed from ascription to achievement. In other words, a person's position in society was becoming less dependent on the family into which he or she had been born and more dependent on the individual's accomplishments. Second, the individual was increasingly viewed as the basic unit of society. As Maine noted, by the nineteenth century, the individual was recognized in the legal system of Western societies as a person rather than simply a member of a communal organization. Third, the character of societies themselves had changed from sacred-communal to secular-associational (Nisbet, 1966).

Tönnies, like many nineteenth- and twentieth-century theorists, employed a technique known as *ideal types* to structure his analysis. Ideal types do not exist in reality but represent the essential qualities of the phenomenon being studied. Researchers construct ideal types by examining a category of things and then identifying those qualities that set the members of that grouping apart from all others. For example, psychologists use this technique to develop profiles of potential terrorists, bank robbers, or child abusers. The ideal type "terrorist" does not really exist; rather, it represents those qualities shared by all persons who are terrorist.

Tönnies employed the ideal types *Gemeinschaft* and *Gesellschaft* to describe the characteristics of two different types of societies, the human relationships within those societies, and the process by which society is transformed from one type to another. These ideal types are at polar extremes of a continuum and represent the essential characteristics of traditional versus modern communities. *Gemeinschaft* translates easily into community. *Gesellschaft* is more difficult to interpret; its translation is society. The problem is that community is a part of society, but the concept becomes clear when one examines the types of societies to which Tönnies was referring.

Gemeinschaft

Gemeinschaft refers to communities that are small and relatively homogeneous. Members of the community normally spend their entire lives in the same locale and have very little geographic mobility. The social structure is relatively simple but rigid. Each person has a clear understanding of where he or she belongs in society; this position is determined by the social status of the family of the person's birth. *Gemeinschaft* leads to a communal life based on tradition, with strong sentimental attachments to the moral code and conventions of the place. There is nearly universal agreement among the members on the way things should be done. Deviations from this code are punished informally. Because people, places, and things are familiar to everyone, the individual cannot escape this collectivity. The basic unit of the social structure is the family. The individual's life has meaning only in the context of the family and the larger community. Therefore, the moral code is clear, strongly held, and enforced by the family and the church.

The social structure of *Gemeinschaft* is made possible by the nature of day-to-day interaction among its members. In *Gemeinschaft*, social relationships are warm and personal, with strong ties among individuals and between the individual and the community. The members of *Gemeinschaft* are like a family, and, as in a family, the rules of conduct are understood, not codified into law. Harmony, naturalness, depth, and fullness are words often used to describe the intimacy and pervasiveness of the relationships among members of *Gemeinschaft* (Nisbet, 1966). Under these conditions, individualism and privacy are at a minimum.

Gesellschaft

In polar extreme to the ideal type of *Gemeinschaft* is the ideal type of *Gesellschaft*. Tönnies saw *Gesellschaft* as a new phenomenon, the end product of social change occurring in the nineteenth century. *Gesellschaft* refers to large, complex, heterogeneous societies composed of individuals who differ in their racial, ethnic, and socioeconomic characteristics. The social structure is complex and fluid. The individual has been freed from the constraints of the family and ideally may rise in the social structure to her or his own level of achievement. *Gesellschaft* is a rational society that one can join or leave at will. The basic unit of the social structure is the individual, and as a result the traditional means of social control—family and church—are supplanted by what is called *rational-legal authority*, the police and the court system, for example. Deviations from the normative order are no longer sanctioned informally but are penalized by formal institutions such as the courts and the police.

In *Gesellschaft*, each individual is guided by self-interest. Human relationships become impersonal; egoism and competition begin to dominate interpersonal relationships. Sharing and concern for others are minimal. Because economic self-interest guides the relationships between individuals, a formal device—the contract—must be used to ensure that both parties abide by an agreement. Moreover, in *Gesellschaft*, the size and complexity of the social structure make it impossible to know the social status of each person. Tangible symbols of a person's social standing, such as cars, clothing, and home, become important.

Gesellschaft is a contractual, individualistic society in which the accumulation of property has a greater importance than close personal ties among individuals. The modern corporation and its complex economic and legal relationships symbolize *Gesellschaft* best. Relationships are based not on kinship and friendship, but on rationality, calculation, and contractualism.

Gesellschaft refers not just to a concept of society, but also to a process by which society is transformed from one type to another. As a society is transformed from *Gemeinschaft* to *Gesellschaft*, the nature of its social organization is changed. Social relationships become more contractual, based on self-interest. Consequently, communal ties are weakened, social solidarity decreases, and the individual is more isolated and potentially more alienated.

Gemeinschaft and *Gesellschaft* are concepts that reflect a great many factors—legal, economic, cultural, and intellectual—but at the core of each concept is an image of a type of social relationship and a state of mind. As Nisbet (1966) notes, the importance of Tönnies's work is not simply classification of community types but rather his historical and comparative use of these types, which gives insight into the fundamental social change caused by the processes of urbanization, industrialization, and bureaucratization.

To Tönnies, *Gemeinschaft* was humankind's natural habitat, and it was the basis of what he thought modern society should be. Tönnies considered the industrial society of his day to be dehumanizing and artificial, in contrast to the natural structure of *Gemeinschaft*. This viewpoint was a major source of disagreement between Tönnies and his contemporary, Emile Durkheim, who held that industrial societies could be as satisfactory as Western societies had been before the Industrial Revolution.

Emile Durkheim: Mechanical and Organic Solidarity

Durkheim shared with Tönnies many concerns about the direction of modern society. He differed from Tönnies, however, in that he believed modern society could be as natural and organic as the *Gemeinschaft* societies of the past. A major theme in Durkheim's work is social solidarity, or the social glue that holds societies together. If modern societies are large, complex, and heterogeneous, what is the social glue that holds individuals together to form a functioning society? Durkheim's work covers a broad spectrum of topics, but, for the student of community, his analysis of the types of social solidarity is the most important.[2]

Mechanical Solidarity

Durkheim made a distinction between two types of social solidarity—mechanical and organic. Mechanical solidarity is found in small homogeneous societies, similar to Tönnies's *Gemeinschaft*. In such societies, the division of labor is simple, and each family unit can carry out most of the functions necessary for society. The division of labor is based on the age and sex of individuals. Moreover, each member knows every other member, and people agree on what society should be. Durkheim called this agreement the *collective conscience*, the values, beliefs, and sentiments held in common by the members of society. The operation of the collective conscience is reflected most clearly in society's norms or rules of conduct and by the types of punishment used when these rules are violated. Durkheim agreed with Maine that law reflects the underlying character of society, its institutional structure, and the form of social solidarity.

   In societies based on mechanical solidarity, legal rules are repressive; violation of rules demands retaliation and punishment. In general, offenses against the collective conscience in these societies evoke an immediate and direct response, and this punishment guarantees conformity in other members. Such punishment serves to reinforce the collective conscience. In the context of a *Gemeinschaft* society, deviants serve a positive social function. Deviation from a norm elicits an immediate response from society. It reinvigorates the collective conscience and increases solidarity among its members.

Organic Solidarity

In small societies, an individual can know the roles of every other member. Modern societies, in contrast, are large and complex, composed of diverse groups of people of which an individual has little or no knowledge. In these societies, the division of labor is complex, based in many cases on specialized skills learned through years of formal training. Because society is composed of diverse groups, there is much less agreement on what society should be. For example, few crimes in these societies would be viewed as "a crime against society." Treason is one, but only two people have been tried and convicted of that crime in the United States in the past twenty years. The question posed by Durkheim was, if this type of society is composed of individuals and diverse groups of people and if there is no single uni-fying collective conscience, what keeps it together? Durkheim suggests that modern societies have a special type of social cohesion—organic solidarity.

In modern complex societies, an individual is dependent on a great many other people for day-to-day existence. An urbanite, for example, depends for basic sustenance—food, clothing, and shelter—on thousands of other people with whom he or she has no personal contact. Organic solidarity occurs in societies in which separate groups perform many different functions. A living organism is a good anal-ogy of how organic solidarity works. The functioning of each organ in the body depends on the functioning of every other part. Each organ is composed of spe-cialized cells that collectively carry out a specific function. All organs work together to accomplish a single purpose—life. A similar interdependency among diverse groups in society (cooperation necessary for survival) provides social cohesion.

The change in the nature of a society's solidarity is reflected in law. With organic solidarity, law is no longer repressive but restitutive. Civil lawsuits, for example, attempt to bring parties together to reconcile differences so that society can work more smoothly. Contractualism and the legal system that emerges to enforce it exemplify this new form of organic solidarity. However, the collective conscience does not cease to exist. Durkheim notes that although a contract is often made between strangers, a contract cannot exist unless it is built on an explicit social foundation. The parties know when they enter into a contract, soci-ety will enforce it. Therefore, a collective conscience is present—a set of beliefs and sentiments—but it operates indirectly on an individual through modern society's institutional structure. In societies characterized by mechanical solidarity, the indi-vidual is bound directly to society without this intermediary. In addition, mechani-cal solidarity continues to exist within modern societies, not in society as a whole but within specialized groups. In metropolitan areas, for example, the viability of tight-knit ethnic neighborhoods is based largely on mechanical solidarity.

This brief review of the works of three sociologists of diverse national ori-gins—French, English, and German—shows how each explored the changing nature of human association. Although written a century ago, the questions raised by these theorists are still central to the discipline of sociology, especially the liter-ature on community. Collectively they had an important influence on all of sociol-ogy, but particularly on the works of Robert Park and other members of the Chicago School. The influence of the European social philosophers on Robert Park and the contributions of the Chicago ecologists to the study of community are examined in the following section.

Robert Park and the Chicago School

In general, Tönnies, Maine, Durkheim, and other European theorists documented both the destruction of the small, tightly integrated community and the emergence of community in its modern form. The works of these sociologists give a negative impression of urban life—a life in which egoism, isolation, and anomie pervade the community. Interestingly, early American sociology continued in this tradition, as is particularly evident in the works of Robert Park and other members of the Chicago School. Louis Wirth, in his 1938 essay, "Urbanism as a Way of Life," summarized the major viewpoint of this school: City growth, with its concomitant increases in the size, density, and heterogeneity of population, leads to a substitution of secondary relations for primary ones and a greater dependency on formal means of social control. Moreover, the traditional sources of community solidarity and control—the family and the church—were believed to be largely ineffective in the urban setting, and social disorganization was thought to be a predictable outcome of these underlying changes. Through the works of these sociologists, social disorganization became a central theme in the theoretical and empirical works in American sociology for the next two decades. The obsession of the Chicago ecologists with disorganization is reflected in the titles of their works: Thrasher's *The Gang*, Anderson's *The Hobo*, Shaw's *Delinquency Areas*, *The Jack-Roller*, and *Brothers in Crime*, Zorbaugh's *The Gold Coast and the Slum*, Wirth's *The Ghetto*, and Faris and Dunham's *Mental Disorders in Urban Areas*.

Influence of Nineteenth Century Community Theorists

There is an important difference between the sociology of Tönnies, Maine, and Durkheim and that of the Chicago ecologists. The nineteenth-century theorists used the concept of community in a broad sense and considered whole societies. The Chicago School referred to cities, like Chicago. Thus, community is synonymous with city in much of their work. In addition, the concept of community was defined ecologically as the "patterns of symbiotic and communalistic relations that develop in a population; it is in the nature of a collective response to the habitat; it constitutes the adjustment of organisms to the environment" (Hawley, 1950, p. 2). Although these ecologists defined community narrowly, both groups wrestled with essentially the same problem—how to maintain order in society. Park's sociology in particular attempted to identify the "control mechanism through which a community composed of several quite different subcommunities can arrange its affairs so that each of them maintains its own distinctive way of life without endangering the life of the whole" (Stein, 1972, p. 17). This statement is reminiscent of Durkheim's work because Durkheim greatly influenced Park. Durkheim addressed the same problem in his interpretation of the transition from mechanical to organic solidarity as the basis for order in society. Like Park, Durkheim saw a role for each type of solidarity in modern society: The bonds of mechanical solidarity held subgroups within society together, whereas in the larger society the cohesive forces of organic solidarity prevailed. Park examined the relationships between subcommunities (natural areas) and the encompassing community. The major thrust of both of their works, therefore, was how organic solidarity can be achieved (Stein, 1972).[3]

Achieving Solidarity in the Modern Community

To Durkheim, the integration of complex societies was based on the role of occupational subgroups. Each subgroup—physicians, lawyers, tradesmen, and skilled workers—would develop its own code of ethics through which the behavior of their members would be restricted. Moreover, in order to survive, each subgroup had to integrate its functions with the larger society. In this way, the self-interest of the occupational subgroup and the necessities of organic solidarity could be reconciled.

Park approached the same problem but from a somewhat different perspective, subcommunities. Subcommunities were simply another type of subgroup in society that were defined spatially. The behavior of the members of these subcommunities could be controlled either through a complex set of social institutions (police, courts, welfare agencies) or through the operation of the informal control mechanisms of the residential subgroups. The operation of these informal control mechanisms within subcommunities was of greatest interest to the members of the Chicago School.

Natural Areas

The urban landscape is not homogeneous and undifferentiated, but is composed of a mosaic of social worlds. These subcommunities, or *natural areas* as Park called them, are often strikingly different in makeup, but most large cities share many of the same types of subareas. For example, every large city has a central business district, slums, ghettoes, and middle- and working-class areas. Most large cities have a "skid row," a "bright lights district," and a "Greenwich Village," where "life is freer, more adventurous and lonely than elsewhere" (Stein, 1972, p. 21). To Park, these areas were the product of unplanned biotic forces, the product of sorting individuals and groups into homogeneous subareas based on common culture and language, race, or occupational and socioeconomic status. The reason for their emergence was framed in purely ecological terms. Natural areas emerged simply because they helped a group of people with similar characteristics satisfy "fundamental needs and solve fundamental problems" (Park, 1952, p. 194). Park reasoned that as long as the problems remained, natural areas would continue to exist.

According to Park, there is another important characteristic of natural areas. Through time, each natural area develops its "own peculiar traditions, customs, conventions, standards of decency and propriety, and, if not a language of its own, at least a universe of discourse, in which words and acts have a meaning which is appreciably different for each local community" (Park, 1952, p. 201). New residents of the natural areas through time are socialized and take on the norms of their new community. Therefore, once a natural area comes into existence, it has a tendency to perpetuate itself. Thus, Park, like Durkheim, saw subgroups, defined spatially within the larger community, as developing a moral code to regulate the behavior of the members. In addition, natural areas must make a contribution to the functioning of the encompassing community. This functional interdependence among subareas of the city was the basis for the integration and solidarity of the larger community.

Why Social Disorganization Was Emphasized

The question remains of why Park and the Chicago School emphasized social disorganization. The answer relates to Park's notion of natural area. Natural areas were viewed not as static but as dynamic phenomena. Park reasoned that within a city, individuals, groups, and institutions are constantly being sorted and relocated. During periods of rapid population growth especially when there is an influx of large numbers of diverse ethnic or racial groups, the stability of certain natural areas is upset as the subareas undergo the invasion-succession process. As a result of this transition, the mechanisms for social control within natural areas are weakened and social disorganization occurs. Most natural areas maintain their solidarity, but in some areas the control mechanisms break down.

In the 1920s, Chicago gained more than a half million people. This rapid growth affected all areas of the city to a degree, but nowhere was the effect greater than in the slums. In the slum, ghetto, and "hobohemia," the Chicago ecologists saw an absence of any effective means of social control. In these areas, the traditional forms of social control—the family, church, and neighborhood—had been undermined and such secondary agencies as the police, courts, newspapers, schools, and settlement houses had taken their place.

Criticism of the Natural Area Concept

The image of a community, a city, as a planless outgrowth of ecological segregation, along with the view that homogeneity and stability characterize a city's subcommunities or natural areas, has persisted and influences the present image of community. Is this image correct? Did natural areas, as the concept was advanced by the Chicago School, exist in the 1920s, and, if so, do they exist today?

The social order of the slum and ghetto ignored. A review of the works published by the Chicago School in the 1920s and the research on subcommunities completed since that decade suggests that Park and the Chicago ecologists may have overstated their case. First, were the slums, ghettoes, and hobohemias as devoid of social order and institutional structures as this school suggests? In *The Gold Coast and the Slum* (1929), Zorbaugh begins with this general statement on the slum, which he characterizes as a collection of isolated individuals:

> *The slum is an area of freedom and individualism. Over large stretches of the slum men neither know nor trust their neighbors. Aside from a few marooned families, a large part of the native population is transient: prostitutes, criminals, outlaws, and hoboes. Foreigners who come to make a fortune, as we used to go west, and expect to return to the Old Country as soon as they make "their stake," who are not really a part of American life, and who wish to live in the city as cheaply as possible, live in the lodging-houses of the slum. Here, too, are the areas of immigrant first settlement, the foreign colonies. And here are congregated the "undesirable" alien groups, such as the Chinese and the Negro. (p. 128)*

Zorbaugh in this paragraph lumps a number of diverse groups under one heading—slum dwellers. Moreover, he implies that they are unorganized. But it is interesting to note that within a few pages he describes the manner in which the immigrant community is organized:

> *As the colony grows, the immigrant finds in it a social world. In the colony he meets with sympathy, understanding and encouragement. There he finds his fellow-countrymen who understand his habits and standards and share his life-experience and viewpoint. In the colony he has status, plays a role in a group. In the light of the colony's streets and cafes, in its churches and benevolent societies, he finds response and security. In the colony he finds that he can live, be somebody, satisfy his wishes—all of which is impossible in the strange world outside. (p. 141)*

Commenting on other areas, Zorbaugh notes:

> *The life of this area is far from unorganized. The Gold Coast has its clubs;*
> *intimate groups gather in "village" studios: the foreign areas have numerous*
> *lodges and mutual benefit societies; the slum has its "gangs . . . " And these groups*
> *may play an enormously important role in the lives of their members. (p. 192)*

During the same period other researchers, including H. A. Miller (1920), Robert Park, Fredrich Thrasher (1926), and Louis Wirth (1928), identified similar organizations within the slum, but their attention continued to be focused on social disorganization. Why were findings of organization in slums reported by the Chicago ecologists and then ignored? Suttles (1972) and Whyte (1943) suggest that the theoretical and political perspectives, as well as the class and social backgrounds of the researchers themselves, biased their research.[4] Whyte (1943) observes:

> *Apparently Zorbaugh began his study with the conviction that the slum*
> *represents the Gesellschaft ideal type. [This idea is expressed in the first quote.]*
> *His discussion of the evidences of social organization does not fit the ideal type.*
> *However, by calling them [organizations] interstitial phenomena, he manages to*
> *dismiss them from further consideration. (p. 36)*

Zorbaugh found that lower-class organizations were closely bound to the local area and had no "community-wide loyalties." Because these organizations were very different from the middle-class ones with which he was familiar, he dismissed them as unimportant. More recent ethnographic works, however, have outlined in detail the social organization and the normative order in these districts. Whyte's *Street Corner Society* (1955), Liebow's *Tally's Corner* (1967), Gans's *The Urban Villagers* (1962), and Suttles's *The Social Order of the Slum* (1968) are four of the dozens of community studies that have reported in detail the social processes operating within slums.

Park's Influence on Research

Apparently Park's influence at the University of Chicago over both the types of research and the researchers themselves led to biases in the school's works. Park looked back with nostalgia to the days when the family, the church, and the neighborhood provided a natural order for a community. In the present, he looked to secondary institutions such as schools, newspapers, and social agencies as potent forces in reconstituting a community—that is, a city. Within this scheme, natural areas were viewed as a social unit that could provide a social order similar to that of an earlier and simpler time. Therefore, Park saw the combining of two worlds, the *Gemeinschaft* in the subcommunity within the encompassing *Gesellschaft* society.

Difficulty in Identifying Natural Areas

The natural area concept has a second weakness. Natural areas were viewed by the Chicago School as emerging through the operation of basic ecological or biotic forces. To these ecologists, the most distinctive characteristic of these areas was that they were unplanned or artificially constructed, but developed out of millions of individual decisions based on different moral, ecological, political, and economic positions. The city from this perspective was a mosaic of social worlds loosely organized by larger political and administrative structures of the metropolis. In other words, each natural area had a unique quality that resulted from the combination of the area's ethnic and racial mix, physical characteristics, and other factors, including the income and occupation of its residents.

Readers of this literature are left with the impression that all one needs to do to delineate the boundaries of each natural area is examine the racial, ethnic, income, and occupational characteristics of a city's population or examine its housing and land-use characteristics. That is, a city is seen as a gigantic jigsaw puzzle, and natural areas are the pieces. In this scheme, boundaries do not overlap, and the world is neat and ordered.

In the 1930s, 1940s, and 1950s, published research called into question the validity of the natural area concept. For example, Davie (1938), Hatt (1946), and Form and colleagues (1954) were unable to find clearly bounded, culturally homogeneous areas in the cities they examined. By the mid-1940s, the concept of natural areas and the theoretical foundation of the Chicago ecologists had been seriously undermined.

As a result of these findings, most research since the 1940s has shifted from the physical characteristics of urban subareas to the social character of these areal units. Although the term *natural area* is seldom used, Keller (1968) suggests that many of the key components of this concept have been integrated into the popular term *neighborhood*. Since the 1940s, the major areas of sociological research on the neighborhood have been urban-rural differences in neighborhoods, formal and informal participation in neighborhood activities, family adaptation to new residential environments, social networks in urban areas, propinquity, and neighboring and symbolic communities.

Social Construction of Communities

Much recent research is directed to identifying the present nature of communities. Janowitz (1961), Greer (1962), Suttles (1968, 1972), and Hunter (1974) address two questions about the modern community. First, what is the relationship of communities to changes in the scale of the larger society? Second, do local communities have recognizable names and boundaries, and are these names and boundaries known to their residents and members of the larger metropolis as well?

Societal Scale and the Local Community

A consensus seems to have developed about the relationship between societal scale and the nature of a local community. Increasing societal scale, as indicated by increasing use of nonhuman energy and increased per capita output, results in a loss of autonomy and fragmentation of local groups and increased dependency on secondary and formal institutions, especially in the area of crisis intervention. Concomitantly, increasing societal scale leads to greater social and physical mobility and a decreasing dependency on the local community.

Separation of Physical and Social Neighborhoods

The validity of this point is found in the research of Morris and Mogey (1965). These authors found in their studies on neighboring a decreasing correspondence between social and physical groupings in urban areas. They concluded that the growth of secondary institutions, such as schools and welfare organizations, and increased physical mobility have led to a separation between physical and social neighborhoods. As Keller (1968) states, these changes have altered the social relationships among neighbors from "neighboring of place to a neighboring by taste" (p. 55). Transportation innovations, in particular, have drastically changed the nature of human relationships within urban areas. In the past, because of poor transportation, people either worked within the home or lived within walking distance of their place of employment. The individual was closely tied to the subcommunity because there were no alternatives. Today, the automobile gives Americans great physical mobility and many alternatives. The place of employment is normally far from one's place of residence. Urbanites have been released from the constraints of the local area, and they can be selective in choosing friends. Ties to the local community have been weakened, but new forms of social relationships have emerged (Meier, 1968; Tobin, 1976).

The Community of Limited Liability

In contrast, Janowitz (1961) explored in detail the effect of an increasing societal scale on the subareas of the city. To Janowitz, the most important change brought about by increasing societal scale was the metamorphosis of community from a primary grouping to a more voluntary and less involving institution. Janowitz (1961) introduced the concept of *community of limited liability* to describe this phenomenon and defined it as the "intentional, voluntary, and especially the partial and differential involvement of residents in their local community" (p. 47).

Janowitz discovered this pattern in specific areal units while studying the local community press. He found that neighborhood newspapers sold weekly within the metropolis's subcommunities provided not only an advertising medium for the local merchants, but also a communication mechanism for the social and cultural integration of the local area. During the same period, Hawley and Zimmer (1970), Axelrod (1955), and others found large numbers of voluntary associations operating within local areas, organized to argue their community's position on metropolitan issues. The Clintonville area of Columbus, Ohio, provides a good example. In 1975, the city of Columbus decided to widen and thus destroy a beautiful tree-lined street in the Clintonville area known as Northwest Boulevard. The local area's weekly, the Booster, in a series of front-page stories, publicized the city's plans. As a result, several local concerned citizens' groups were formed, monies were collected for attorneys' fees, and the city's plans were blocked in the courts. The point that Janowitz and others have made is that the neighborhood or "the community of limited liability" is no longer a primary group, but it is still an important source of social contacts for a large proportion of the metropolis's residents.

Symbolic Communities

Suttles (1968, 1972) provides additional support for the concept of the community of limited liability and also addresses the question of whether local communities have recognizable boundaries that are known both to their residents and to members of the larger metropolis.

Suttles's research suggests that the individual simplifies and makes comprehensible the complexity of the metropolis by developing a simplified mental or cognitive map of the city. In large cities, those mental maps were found to consist of three symbolic structures: the face-block, the defended neighborhood, and the community of limited liability.

The Face-block

The most elementary grouping in urban areas is a network of acquaintances known as the *face-block.* "These are acquaintances who are recognized from face-to-face relations or encounters and seen regularly because they live on the same block, use the same bus station, shop at the same stores, and for any number of reasons continually cross one another's pathways" (Suttles, 1972, p. 55). The basis for this association is not ethnicity, race, or socioeconomic status but rather familiarity because in the back of each person's mind "is the knowledge that this person lives close by or uses the same facilities" (Suttles, 1972, p. 55).

Face-blocks are only loosely organized and do not constitute a neighborhood because only the residents living within them normally know the boundaries of these units and these boundaries remain unknown to outsiders. The areal unit is real and important for the people living within its boundaries, however. Parents often use the face-block as the area in which their children are permitted to play. As a result, these units become the basis of the child's peer-group activities. In addition, adults use this unit to organize block clubs, "a common adult form of organization for acquiring better public services" (Suttles, 1972, p. 56).

Social process carried out in the face-block. Thus, the face-block that surrounds the household is an important and inescapable part of any household's environment. Here the problems of social order are clearest because the play of children and child-adult and adult-adult relations must be regulated within this areal unit. If misunderstanding and conflict arise, the orderly performance of the household may be interrupted. In addition, the social interaction that takes place on this level is in many respects determined by the nature of the physical environment. In apartment-house districts, the communication level is low because of the lack of common or overlapping space and because of a separation of the work and leisure routines of the residents. In these areas, greater dependence generally is placed on the rules of the building and the formal authorities that enforce them.

In familistic areas, social interaction is greater. As Suttles notes, it occurs among persons whose paths must cross—in adjoining backyards, bus stops, schools, on sidewalks, and in playgrounds. Interaction with one's neighbors is unavoidable (Michelson, 1970).

Although the face-block is a social unit for both adults and children, Suttles believes that it is not based on the ties suggested by Park in the natural area concept. Although age, race, ethnic, and socioeconomic status do bring about the general sorting of individuals into subareas of the city, physical closeness and small area are the basis of the face-block.

The Defended Neighborhood

The defended neighborhood is composed of numerous face-blocks. It is commonly the smallest area within the metropolis that has an identity known both to its residents and to outsiders. Suttles (1972) defines it as that area outside the face-block in which residents have a high degree of familiarity and a relative degree of security on the streets compared to adjacent areas (p. 57). These units vary considerably in size depending on the characteristics of the area's inhabitants, but normally include the schools, churches, and grocery and retail stores that an area's residents use on a day-to-day basis.

Zorbaugh's *The Gold Coast and the Slum* and many of the other works by the Chicago School explored the operation of defended neighborhoods. Park and his followers give the impression that these areas were homogeneous, occupied by a single ethnic, racial, or occupational grouping. Suttles, however, suggests that very few of these defended neighborhoods now have, or ever have had, homogeneous populations and that most inner-city neighborhoods have always undergone a continuous process of invasion-succession. Interestingly, although these areas' populations have completely turned over, the character and boundaries of many of the areas have remained the same. This persistence is due to the fact that these units have been incorporated into the cognitive maps of residents of the larger community. As Suttles remarks:

> *[Some neighborhoods] may be known as snobbish, trashy, tough, exclusive, dangerous, mixed or any number of other things. Some neighborhoods may simply be unknown, and reference to one's residence may arouse only puzzlement and necessitate one's explaining one's guilt or virtue by residential association. In any case, neighborhood identity remains a stable judgmental reference against which people are assessed, and although some may be able to evade the allegations thrown their way, they nonetheless find such evasions necessary. (1972, p. 35)*

These units are also used in the cognitive maps of city residents to guide other types of behavior, specifically travel. In large metropolitan areas, one must be concerned about one's personal safety. In many areas of a city it is not safe to travel day or night. The cognitive map held by individuals simplifies the choices they make on spatial movement within the city, such as areas of travel, time of day, type of transportation, and appropriate number of people in the group.

Finally, although some people may have strong sentimental attachments to a defended neighborhood, this feeling is not the basis for social cohesion in these areas. Though there may be underlying similarities in race, ethnicity, and income, solidarity appears to be simply a matter of common residence. Defended neighborhoods are a grouping and as in any other grouping "members are joined in a common plight whether or not they like it" (Suttles, 1972, p. 37). The fate of a defended neighborhood often depends on city planners, realtors, politicians, and industry. This common fate and common experience provide the cohesion of the neighborhood. A threat to the neighborhood will lead to a defensive response that generates cohesive solidarity.

Community of Limited Liability

A defended neighborhood may or may not be known to members of the larger community. A community of limited liability, in contrast, is a unit of analysis that research has shown to be symbolically important to residents of an area and to members of the larger metropolis as well. More important is the fact that in some cities governmental agencies on the federal, state, and local levels reinforce the boundaries of these units. Physical and symbolic boundaries of these areas do not always reinforce each other. However, physical characteristics of a city such as parks, railroads, waterways, highways, and major distorting features in the terrain normally lead to a clear demarcation of these areas.

Formation of communities of limited liability. One aspect of the boundary-forming and boundary-maintenance process that Suttles believes has largely been ignored by sociologists is the role of external organizations in defining residential group-ings. Both Suttles (1972) and Hunter (1974) report that the boundaries, as well as the names used by residents to identify their communities, have often been imposed by planners, developers, booster organizations, and realtors. "Once symbols and boundaries come into existence numerous external adversaries or advocates are anxious to claim a constituency or market and keep it intact" (Suttles, 1972, p. 49). Unlike the other cognitive structures identified by Suttles, a commu-nity of limited liability has an official identity that requires its name and boundaries to be institutionally secured by governmental acknowledgment. More important, although an external force imposes this official identity, the boundaries and symbols are often incorporated into the cognitive models of the residents of the neighborhood and the wider metropolis as well (Hunter, 1974, p. 25). The validity of the concept can be seen in Hunter's research on the community areas first delin-eated by Burgess and his students in the 1920s. At that time, Chicago was mapped into seventy-five exhaustive and mutually exclusive areas. Kitagawa and Tauber (1963) outlined the criteria used in this mapping process in the introduction to the 1960 edition of the *Local Community Fact Book for Chicago Metropolitan Area*:

> . . . *When community area boundaries were delineated . . . the objective was to define a set of subareas of the city each of which could be regarded as having a history of its own as a community, a name, an awareness on the part of its inhabitants of community interests, and a set of local businesses and organizations oriented to the local community. (xiii)*

Although the names and boundaries were imposed on these areas nearly fifty years ago, for a large proportion of Chicago's residents these community areas still operate as meaningful symbolic communities or natural areas (Hunter, 1974). A significant percentage of the residents sampled were able to name the commu-nity area and its boundaries in a way consistent with the *Fact Book.*

In terms of the mechanisms by which these symbols were transmitted from generation to generation, Hunter points to the role of local community organiza-tions, neighborhood newspapers, government agencies, and real estate interests as crucial in maintaining symbolic stability through time. The gradual socialization of a new member of a community into an area through initial contacts with schools, shops, realtors, and neighbors is another dimension of this process. Both Hunter and Suttles provide general support for the existence of these areal units in Chicago. Similar units are found in many other cities, including Cleveland. A com-munity of limited liability develops when the similar interests of residents are transformed into common interests based on the degree to which the vital resources of a household are involved, such as public schools and government services. The residents of a community of limited liability are therefore function-ally interdependent, often with a single adversary. Communication in a community of limited liability takes place through two channels: the community press and local voluntary organizations. Organizations such as homeowner associations are more important in ordering behavior, whereas the press is the more effective channel of communication.

Participation in Local Community Affairs

What relationships do local voluntary associations and the community press have to the residents of an area? Greer and Orleans (1962), Greer (1970), and others studied the interaction of the community press and the local voluntary associations in the participation of residents in local community affairs. These authors suggest that approximately 90 percent of a city's population fits into one of three categories: isolates, neighbors, and community actors.

Isolates

Isolates are people who are literally disengaged from the organizational structure of a local community. They operate as neighbors slightly if at all and belong to none of the voluntary organizations in the area. In general, they rarely vote. They seldom read the local community newspaper except to see the advertisements. As a result, they are generally ignorant of most local community affairs. For example, they are unable to name local leaders or important current issues in the community.

Neighbors

Neighbors are the second-largest group. They are involved in their immediate social environment. Generally, they live in the small world of the face-block, and their social life revolves around casual social interaction and family friendships. They tend to be young families, and, like isolates, they have low rates of participation in politics, but are likely to read the local community newspaper and to know the names of local community leaders. They participate in the local area, but this participation is limited to their face-block or defended neighborhood.

Community Actors

Community actors are the smallest group but are the most influential because of their involvement in local organizations. Generally they are "joiners" involved in voluntary associations at many levels—a church group, the chamber of commerce, or the Lions Club. They are a disproportionately large part of the local electorate (approximately 70 percent of them vote versus 30 percent of the isolates), and they are the most knowledgeable on local issues. Interestingly, this group, which carries out most of the public affairs in a local community, is self-selected. Interest in local community affairs is so low that literally anyone who has the time and the interest can be a community leader. Therefore, it is the community actors who speak for the interests of the local community, normally through a community-based voluntary association. This group could be likened to a ruling class who through their influence has a disproportionate role in determining the outcome of local community issues.

The other less-interested groups benefit from the actions of these self-chosen community actors, however, and frequently identify with them. The community actors serve an important watchdog function in the community and defend it from outside adversaries. If a threat to the local area is particularly severe, this group uses the local community press and their overlapping memberships in voluntary associations to publicize the problem. In certain circumstances, they can elicit the help of neighbors and, in extreme circumstances, even of the isolates.

Transition in Local Communities

Although face-blocks, defended neighborhoods, and communities of limited liability appear to be present in Chicago and other cities, these units are in a process of continuous change. In a face-block, for instance, a dispute among the block's central clique may cause members to switch their loyalties to other adjacent areas. Likewise, the defended neighborhoods in inner cities regularly undergo the invasion-succession process that may influence both their solidarity and identity. The boundaries and identity of a community of limited liability may also change as groups of advocates and adversaries compete for influence over the constituencies of these areas. The identification of the areas is complicated by the fragmentation of authority on the local level. Municipal governments are often familiar with the natural or symbolic communities but seldom use their boundaries explicitly to determine the jurisdictions of various public agencies. Suttles (1972) and Hunter (1974) found little overlap in the boundaries of Chicago's community areas, political wards, school districts, and police districts. Residents often are members of more than one community of limited liability. In one case, the boundaries may coincide with a school district, in another an improvement district. The split loyalties that result from the fragmentation of local authority partly explain the high failure rate of local community groups. It is difficult to raise interest in a particular issue when residents of an area are involved in other issues.

In general, when one examines how an urbanite defines and uses space, a somewhat confusing picture of the urban landscape emerges. Boundaries between the various areal units are not clear and sharply delineated but instead overlap and in some cases are superimposed over one another. The pattern contrasts to the neat patchwork that results from social area analysis. Social area analysis provides a tool for examining the broad structural form of a city, but it is less useful in analyzing the actual operation of a city on the social level.

This is not to say that the social area dimensions are unimportant in analyzing the social basis of community life. Family status, ethnic status, and social status however, have each been identified as important factors influencing social interaction and the size of the various symbolic community units. For example, in lower socioeconomic areas of the city—areas characterized as low in both ethnic and social status—distrust among residents is often high, and the defended neighborhood may be a single building (Suttles, 1968). Suburban areas, in contrast, are characterized by high family, ethnic, and social status, and normally their defended neighborhoods are large, covering many square blocks.

Relationship of a Community to the Larger Society

The discussion of community suggests that local communities, whether they be face-blocks, defended neighborhoods, or communities of limited liability, are best described as partial communities unable to perform within their boundaries all the functions traditionally carried out in *Gemeinschaft* communities. In the past, the services provided by local merchants, bankers, and schools were important in generating a sense of community. Today, most local communities depend on numerous institutions and organizations outside their borders for basic, day-to-day services. Most local communities, for example, have chain stores, branch banks, schools, and churches that serve the local community but are affiliated with metropolitan or national organizations. These ties that Warren (1978) calls "vertical patterns of integration" are important in that they integrate the local area into citywide and national social and economic systems. There are, however, costs. Because of these ties, subcommunities do not perform on their own a full range of community functions often necessary to generate a sense of community. However, mechanisms and institutions within the local community promote cohesiveness. Ideally, the community press, local voluntary organizations, and locally based networks of friends and kin, as well as awareness of a common bond, bring about the internal integration of a local community. This horizontal pattern of integration combined with vertical patterns leads to the orderly operation of a local community in the metropolitan system.

Summary

In this chapter the evolution of the concept of community is traced from its use by nineteenth-century social philosophers to its present use in American community studies. The nineteenth-century community theorists Maine, Tönnies, and Durkheim used the community concept to analyze the changing relationship between the individual and society. Community was also applied as an ideal by which life in industrial societies could be compared with life in communities of the past. Although the concept of community is a theme in many of their works, each theorist explored a different aspect of this phenomenon. Maine explored the legal systems of societies, contrasting the family-centered traditional societies with the individual-centered modern societies.

Tönnies employed the ideal types *Gemeinschaft* and *Gesellschaft* to analyze the qualities of past and present societies. *Gemeinschaft* refers to small, homogeneous communities based on tradition, communities in which an individual is guided by the norms and conventions of the community and is tied to the institutions of family and church. *Gesellschaft* stands in polar extreme to *Gemeinschaft* and refers to large, complex, heterogeneous societies composed of individuals. In these societies reason prevails, and contracts define the relationships between people.

Durkheim's concern was with the "social glue" that holds society together. He identified two types of social solidarity: mechanical and organic. Mechanical solidarity is found in small, homogeneous societies in which there is nearly universal agreement on the values, beliefs, and norms of the community—a collective conscience. Organic solidarity prevails in modern societies that have large, heterogeneous populations and a complex division of labor. The all-encompassing collective conscience cannot exist in such societies because of their size, but the functional interdependency that develops among specialists forms the basis for social solidarity.

In general, these sociologists concluded that three basic changes had occurred in community. First, the basis of one's social status had changed from the family's status to one's individual achievement. Second, an individual was increasingly viewed as the basic unit of society. Third, the character of societies had changed from sacred-communal to secular-associational.

Park and the Chicago School were influenced by the writings of the nineteenth-century sociologists. Their interest, however, was not in "community" in a broad sense, but in cities and their subcommunities. Although this school's unit of analysis differed from that used in the earlier works of Durkheim, Tönnies, and Maine, both groups were interested in essentially the same problem—order in society. Park, in particular, combined the ecological notion of natural areas with Durkheim's concepts of mechanical and organic solidarity to explain how a community composed of several different subcommunities could allow each of them to maintain its own distinctive way of life without endangering the life of the whole community.

Durkheim greatly influenced Park. Like Durkheim, Park felt that the city was held together by both mechanical and organic solidarity. Park viewed natural areas as homogeneous in their family, social, or racial and ethnic characteristics. Their mechanical solidarity was based on their commonly held norms, values, and beliefs. However, each of these specialized natural areas made a functional contribution to the operation of the entire city, which produced organic solidarity. Major weaknesses in Park's approach have been identified. The natural areas concept has been called into question, as has the emphasis of the Chicago School on social disorganization. These notions, nevertheless, continue to influence the present image of community.

Recent research by Suttles, Hunter, and others suggests that areal units continue to influence life in urban places. Face-blocks, the most elementary grouping in urban areas, are based on the familiarity among people who live on the same block or use the same parks, stores, or other local facilities. This unit is important because it is where children play and where adult-child and adult-adult relationships are regulated.

The defended neighborhood corresponds to the areas identified by Zorbaugh and other members of the Chicago School. It is the larger area outside the face-block that people use on a day-to-day basis.

The most distinguishing characteristic of the community of limited liability, the largest of the three symbolic communities, is that it is normally known by the people who reside within it and by the larger community as well. These units are normally composed of numerous defended neighborhoods and come into existence through the actions of builders, planners, or booster groups. Most residents of these areas are classified as isolates or neighbors and have little involvement in community affairs. The few community actors who hold membership in many community organizations provide the political direction for the community.

Social critics suggest that the crime, isolation, poverty, and alienation in the urban setting are the result of the destruction of community. Is this a fair criticism? The city is composed of a mosaic of social worlds, each subcommunity serving the needs of a special subgroup in society. Certainly, problems are severe in some subcommunities. They always have been. But for the majority of Americans living in urban areas, the partial communities in which they live provide a satisfactory and satisfying solution to the recurring problems of day-to-day life in large, complex societies.

Notes

[1] The discussion of Maine, Tönnies, and Durkheim is based in part on the following books: Robert A. Nisbet, *The Sociological Tradition* (New York: Basic Books, 1966); Lewis A. Coscr, *Masters of Sociological Thought* (New York: Harcourt Brace Jovanovich, 1971); David A. Karp, Gregory P. Stone, and William C. Yoels, *Being Urban: A Social Psychological View of City Life* (Lexington, MA: D. C. Heath and Co., 1977), Chap. 1; and Larry Lyon, *The Community in Urban Society* (Chicago: Dorsey Press, 1987).

[2] The following material is based in part on Chapters 3, 4, 5, 6, and 8 of *Emile Durkheim: Selected Writings*, ed. and trans. by Anthony Giddens (Cambridge, England: Cambridge University Press, 1972).

[3] This material is based in part on Maurice Stein, "Robert Park and Urbanization in Chicago," in *The Eclipse of Community: An Interpretation of American Studies* (Princeton, NJ: Princeton University Press, 1972) (expanded edition).

[4] This material is based in part on an article by William F. Whyte, "Social Organization in the Slums," *American Sociological Review* 8 (1943): 34–39.

6

THE COMMUNITY IN THE POSTMODERN ERA

Introduction

In Chapter 2, we reviewed the work of Francis Fukuyama, who argues that with the end of socialism, only one ideology exists in the world today—free-market capitalism guided by liberal democracy. He reasons that since there are no competing ideologies in the world, we have seen the "end of history." Over the past twenty years, other scholars have proclaimed "the end of politics," "the end of work," "the end of the family," "the end of liberalism," "the end of medicine," and "the end of ideology" (Pescosolido & Rubin, 2000, p. 52). These themes suggest a world in the midst of rapid and profound social change: change so rapid that our children will live in a world different from their parents, change so basic that traditional theories on how the world should work no longer apply, and change so profound that some scholars argue we have made a break with the past and have entered a new era—the postmodern era.

Sociology traces its roots to the late eighteenth and early nineteenth centuries. This too was a period of profound social, political, and economic upheaval. The world witnessed the first ideologically based revolutions, the American and French Revolutions; the first modern war, the American Civil War; the social and economic upheavals that came to be known as the Industrial Revolution; and the first wave of globalization, made possible by the telegraph and the steamship. Less appreciated were revolutions in agriculture, commerce, and urban living that made these changes possible. Thus, the founders of sociology, theorists like Comte, Marx, Weber, and Durkheim, described the transformation of society brought on by modernity and the rise of capitalism.

Today, a new generation of social scientists is trying to describe the transformation of society brought on by globalization. They ask questions like: Has there been a break with the past? Do we live our lives differently than our parents and grandparents? How has globalization, and the social and technological revolutions upon which it is based, affected our day-to-day lives? Do we fall in love, find a partner, make friends, and raise our children differently than past generations? Has global interdependence and technology, so central to postmodern thought, meant the end of community? If community still exists, how is it different from the past?

Postmodernism and Globalization

The modern era begins with the rise of capitalism.[1] According to David Harvey, capitalism has gone through three stages, and each stage is associated with a distinct technology, form of social organization, and social problems. *Early-market capitalism,* for example, evolved during the eighteenth and nineteenth centuries and is linked to steam-driven machinery. *Mid-monopoly capitalism* evolved in the early twentieth century and is linked to the internal combustion engine. *Late-multinational capitalism* evolved in the second half of the twentieth century and is associated with nuclear power and the computer. According to Harvey, the problems of massive rural to urban migration, the rise of great cities, the transformation and exploitation of industrial labor, and the emergence of new family and community forms are problems associated with early-market and mid-monopoly capitalism. These were the conditions that led to the classic works of Marx, Durkheim, and Weber. Our age, the age of late-multinational capitalism, is the focus of postmodern thought.

So when did the postmodern era begin? Many postmodern scholars point to a series of events that culminated in the early 1970s. These were the closing years of the great post–World War II economic expansion. European and Asian economies had finally recovered from the ruin of World War II. These nations grew their economies through the wholesale adoption of modern production and management techniques pioneered in the United States. These nations also pioneered a strategy of high-value added over high-volume production that was to become the norm in the global economy. The result was that by 1975 a quarter century of American economic hegemony had come to an end. U.S. corporations responded to this challenge with massive downsizing, deindustralization, and a shift to overseas production. Global corporations emerged through this process, and these changes set the stage for globalization. The rise of postmodern thought, therefore, parallels the changes associated with globalization.

The postmodernists point to the response of other institutions to this sea change in the economy. Our political institutions face a host of intractable problems brought on by globalization. For example, what is the role of central governments when multinational corporations are larger and more powerful than countries? What is the role of central governments when city-states develop their own foreign and economic policies? Or how does government control the countervailing forces of dissent when thousands of the world's nongovernment organizations (NGOs) organize their protests across national boundaries using the Internet. Demonstrations at the meetings of the World Bank, the World Trade Organization, and the International Monetary Fund are vivid examples.

From the postmodern perspective, the cultural change wrought by globalization is the most important. Today, not only capital, but images, ideas, fads, crazes, fashion, norms, values, and beliefs flow unimpeded across national boundaries. Popular culture is no longer nationally, but globally spun. These global forces shape even your appetite. Your nearby grocery store is a wonderful example. In 1947, the average American grocery store carried 150 items. Today, the typical supermarket carries 40,000–50,000 items. In 1947, 95 percent of the items in a grocery store were produced within twenty-five miles. See Photo 6.1. Today, only 5 percent of the items are produced locally. Increasingly our food stuffs come from abroad—grapes from Chile, bananas from Costa Rica, kiwis and lamb from New Zealand, tilapia and catfish from China, brie from France, and a dizzying array of specialty items from every region of the world. In the United States, salsa outsells catsup, and dishes from Thailand, China, and India grace the menus of restaurants in even our smallest cities. The global influence extends well beyond food. In the United States, Islam and Buddhism are the nation's fastest growing religions, and parents ask their kids, "What's a Pokemón?"

Photo 6.1 *The Modern Supermarket—a Metaphor for Postmodern Angst* (*Source*: © David Katzenstein/CORBIS.)

Culture is the blueprint for living. But according to postmodern thinkers, culture is no longer a meaningful guide because it changes so quickly and because so many divergent forces shape it. The traditional guideposts have even changed. For example, in the past quarter century, the social contract between citizens and their government, workers and their employers, patients and their physicians, and children and their parents have changed. Uncertainty and ambiguity reign when medicine fails to provide health care to millions for a lack of insurance, schools fail to teach all but the most fortunate, religion is sullied by scandal, and politics benefits only the wealthy and powerful. No wonder John McCain hit a resonant cord with so many Americans. Here at last was a savior! Here was someone who will stop the special interests! Postmodernists argue that these same patterns, in slightly different form, repeated themselves in societies around the world. Regardless of the society, words like *inequality*, *insecurity*, and *uncertainty* describe the economy, and *fragmented*, *incoherent*, *rootless*, and *unsatisfying* describe the culture.

Postmodernism According to David Harvey

The ideas surrounding macroeconomic change are abstract. David Harvey gives some examples of how changes in the postmodern age affect our day-to-day lives. One of his examples is our changing perception of such fundamental concepts as time and space. He argues that these new definitions, in turn, have modified the way we order our private and public lives. Key to his analysis is new transportation and communication technology like the Internet, Palm Pilots, satellite phones, Fed-Ex next-day delivery, and cheap and reliable international travel. Why? Because they allow people and things to move faster, farther, and at a lower cost than ever before. Relationships and patterns of production that could not exist only a generation ago are very much a part of our postmodern world. As we have already shown, designing a car in one country, financing it in another, building components in a half dozen countries on two or three continents, and then assembling, advertising, and marketing them in forty or fifty countries was unimaginable a generation ago, but it is the standard way of doing business today. Why? Because communication and transportation technology allows us to compress space.

According to Harvey, the compression of space leads to the compression of time. Since goods, services, plans, and ideas are moving around the world farther and faster, we all have more things to do and less time to do them. E-mail, just-on-time delivery, and 24/7 services blur night and day, the workweek, and the weekend. Many of us wonder where is work and where is home. With a note-book computer connected to the Internet the task is important, not where you do it. Consequently, our lives become a blur and less meaningful because we cannot compartmentalize our lives. We can't separate the private from the public. Employers can demand unreasonable working hours because their investments must be protected. This means little free time for family and friends and less time for *you*. When do you have time for the dentist or the doctor? How do you work in the parent-teacher conference? Can you make it to your child's soccer game or school play? The travails of the characters in the Dilbert comic strip hit uncomfortably close for many of us.

The compression of time and space means a faster, smaller world and the destruction of national and cultural barriers. Things ranging from cars and computers to art, fashion, and music are no longer designed for a single society but for the global market. Citizens of advanced industrial societies are used to change, but what happens when these new images and products diffuse to more traditional societies? When change occurs slowly, a culture has time to adapt. The term *cultural lag* refers to the process by which one part of a society lags behind other parts during periods of rapid social change. But today postmodernists write about cultural shock to describe social change. *Culture shock* traditionally described the experiences of missionaries, Peace Corps volunteers, and travelers entering a strange, alien culture for the first time. It refers to the disorientation and alienation that occurs when you lose all that is familiar around you. Postmodernists think culture shock no longer strikes the world traveler, but many who stay at home in a rapidly changing and increasingly alien culture. Culture responds to social change by creating new meaning. But what happens to a culture when the new meanings have no meaning because they are obsolete before they can be adopted? Or what happens when members of a society can no longer adapt because they are no longer able to adopt?

Here are a few examples of changing meaning in a globalized world. If jobs can be immediately exported overnight to another country because of lower-priced labor, then workers' beliefs about corporate loyalty must change. Graduates must change their conceptions about how to develop a career. Workers must change their attitudes about training and retraining. Executives must rethink their companies' commitments to local communities. And governments must recast import/export, labor market, and corporate policies. All these new meanings must be incorporated into a culture. Technology and markets can change rapidly; people and cultures cannot.

What about changes in community in a postmodern world? Who are you? Who and what give you your identity? In the past, your reference group, drawn from your immediate social surroundings, provided the meanings to create your *self.* We used categories like race, ethnicity, and social class. Your profession was often your reference group. Schools, neighbors, churches, and those secondary primary relationships that Lyn Lofland writes about created your public identity. But with the compression of time and space, people are constantly exposed to a new array of social categories. These categories may not even be local, but global. Skinheads, the Aryan Nation, and other extremists groups do their most effective recruiting over the Internet. They are not local groups; you, and the FBI, really don't know where these groups are in cyberspace. Also, millions of Americans follow Islam, Buddhism, and other Eastern religions in their search for spiritual meaning. In the United States today, there are more followers of Islam than Judaism. Are we now a Judeo-Christian-Islamic nation? Where are the stable cultural markers?

A community is, among other things, a web of relationships. In the past, locally owned banks, markets, pharmacies, funeral homes, churches, bars, and restaurants provided the social fabric upon which community was formed. Lofland called them *primary secondary relationships.* We know what happens to many of these businesses when a Wal-Mart comes to a small town. But the postmodernist asks, "What happens when it's an e-Wal-Mart?" What happens to community when we do most of our shopping in cyberspace, and our groceries, prescriptions, and books magically arrive at our front door without any interaction with a human? What happens to the web of relationships that creates and sustains communities? What happens to the very act of shopping? Shopping should be an inherently enjoyable activity. Is it? Should you have loyalty to a local company? Is the concept of a local business obsolete? Has there been a fundamental change in the nature of human relationships upon which community is based? Is the word *community* obsolete?

In the last quarter of the twentieth century, postmodern thought has taken root in many disciplines: art, music, architecture, popular culture, the humanities, especially English, history, and philosophy, as well as the social sciences. There are a bewildering number of schools of postmodern thought, but they share a common theme: Global interdependence and technological change have brought about unprecedented social change. They believe this change is so profound that the theories social scientists use to give meaning to society are no longer relevant. This change has shattered the comforting definitions of reality that described early times, leading to a failure of our social and political institutions and a renegotiation of the social contract. Without these institutions, people live in uncertain and insecure times. This change means people live ambiguous, chaotic, and fragmented lives in societies guided by a polyglot and meaningless culture. The postmodernists' views clash with the basic, underlying assumptions of the modern era—emphasis on individual freedom, rationality, progress, and the promise of science to improve the human condition. Postmodernists give us a bleak and unpleasing picture of society's experiencing dissolution and fragmentation. They describe a society of detached and isolated individuals and fragmented communities. Whereas Marx used *alienation*, Durkheim, *anomie*, and Weber, *rationalization*, postmodernists use *fragmentation*, *isolation*, *ephemeral*, and *chaotic* to describe the human condition.

Postmodernism leads us to ask a series of new questions about the nature of institutions and individual behavior in an increasingly complex, interdependent world. It requires us to rethink our understandings about social relations and social structures in a world made smaller and faster by innovations in technology, finance, information, and decision making. The postmodern vision of the world, however, is a dismal one. It envisions a fragmented world created by the globalization juggernaut. It is chaotic, uncertain, and insecure, a world that changes so rapidly computers are obsolete the day they are purchased and where the culture of your birth is different from the one of your death. It's cultural shock for the nontraveler. Since culture no longer provides a blueprint for living, where are life's guideposts? It's no longer the family, the neighborhood, or the community; they no longer provide recognition, security, and support. So where does one look for direction? The media? The Internet? Postmodernism paints a dark and brooding present, and an uncertain, insecure, and fragmented future.

But is it as bad as the postmodernists say? I thought about my life while writing this chapter. I also talked with a friend who is an urban sociologist about his day-to-day life. We came to the conclusion that we live rich, productive, and satisfying lives. We have long and successful marriages. Our children, in spite of us, have become fine adults. We have nice homes in stable neighborhoods. We have good neighbors, because they are just that, neighbors. They keep an eye on our houses when we are away and lend us the occasional cup of milk or sugar. We have ties to the community. We are active in our churches, and we do volunteer work for local nonprofits. We have a wonderful circle of supportive friends. We like our jobs, in large part, because we have good colleagues. We are not alienated by the technology; we embrace it. Our lives are made better and richer with e-mail, the Internet, and the computer. The technology permits us to maintain personal and professional relationships easier and over greater distances than before. We both have book projects, but our projects are much easier with the help of the word processor and the Internet. Rather than mailing manuscripts back and forth to our editors, we attach our manuscripts to e-mails. We can do in seconds what once took weeks. As a result of the technology, our social networks have grown larger and wider. We have friends and colleagues around the world, and we keep in touch via e-mail. I have a major project in Jordan, and I manage the project, pay vendors, and maintain my network from my office 6,000 miles away from my office at Yarmouk University in Irbid, Jordan. The technology has also enriched our private lives. We occasionally wrote our parents and siblings; now, we e-mail several times a week. Technology, rather than fragmenting our lives, integrates it. Globalization, rather than making our lives insecure and uncertain, has made them more secure, certain, and richer. Although we are exposed, like everyone else in the world, to a blizzard of conflicting images and meanings, we have no problem interpreting them through our cultural lens.

Maybe we are not representative. We are sociologists, after all, armed with intellectual tools to fight postmodern angst. We don't think so. Our students aren't any more fragmented, insecure, and uncertain than we were at that age. In fact, they may be more secure than our generation without the draft and a Vietnam war to worry about. Our friends, colleagues, neighbors, and acquaintances have never admitted to lonely lives of quiet desperation. They seem to be managing their lives quite well, thank you. As noted earlier, Americans were feeling pretty good about themselves in the 1990s during the first decade of the global era. After all, it was the longest economic expansion in our history. Although there has been a downturn in the economy and war in Iraq, the unprecedented prosperity of the 1990s has meant that most measures of social well-being are still high.

If you examine your life and the lives of your kin, friends, and neighbors, you will probably come to the same conclusion. Most people live satisfying lives in supportive communities. So why all the nihilism? Could it be that critics are looking in the wrong place for community? Could they be looking for community in local areas with clearly defined boundaries? Perhaps people no longer operate in spatially bound communities? Could modern transportation and communication technology allow people to construct tailor-made communities—personal communities? This is precisely what researchers find when they study social networks.

Social Networks

> Individuals' bonds to one another are the essence of society. Our day-to-day lives are preoccupied with people, with seeking approval, providing affection, exchanging gossip, falling in love, soliciting advice, giving opinions, soothing anger, teaching manners, providing aid, making impressions, keeping in touch—or worrying about why we are not doing these things. By doing all these things we create community. And people continue to do them, today, in modern society. The relations these interactions define in turn define society, and changes in those relations mark historical changes in community life. (Fischer, 1982, p. 2)

This quote from Claude Fischer's book, *To Dwell Among Friends*, demonstrates an exciting alternative approach to the study of community. Whereas Janowitz and Hunter explore community structures like face-blocks, defended neighborhoods, and communities of limited liability, Fischer and other researchers explore the world of intimate social relationships—social networks.

Students sometimes have trouble relating to concepts like communities of limited liability because they haven't experienced them in their day-to-day lives. All of us know social networks because we live in them. Take a moment and explore your own social network. From your perspective, personal relationships emanate outward from you—first to kin and close friends; then to other students, coworkers, and church members; then finally to people in the local community and friends back home. Community from this perspective isn't simply a jigsaw of local structures but a complex web of relationships, a latticework of interpersonal ties.[2]

Creating Social Networks[3]

As a child our networks are centered in family, and we have no control over this choice. But, as we grow older we are free to choose our friends, coworkers, and associates, and by the time we are young adults, our social networks have been forged. An interesting thing occurs in creating our networks: we tend to choose friends, coworkers, and associates from people like ourselves. Social networks are homogeneous. They tend to be inbred, composed of people of the same social class and ethnic and racial group. Why? Because we are not totally free to choose our network. Our alternatives are limited by society. This notion that we make choices from socially constrained alternatives is known as the ***choice-constraint model***. The model assumes decisions are rational. It recognizes that all relationships have costs and benefits. It accepts the fact that relationships are double edged. They contribute to our sense of well-being but can also destroy it. More important, it reminds us that even in a small town we can only know a minuscule number of people. We have to decide whom we're going to spend time with and whom we're going to ignore. Throughout this analysis is the recognition that we have freedom to make these decisions but freedom within constraints. See Photo 6.2.

Our position in the social stratification system is the most important force in determining our networks. Simply, the higher your social status, the larger your personal network. If you have money, you can buy more long distance, plane tickets, and ski weekends with friends and these investments pay off. Research shows the wealthier you are, the larger, more encompassing, and supportive your network. At the bottom, you find people with few alternatives: few housing alternatives, few employment alternatives, and few network alternatives. Many of the problems of the poor are linked to their small personal networks. When researchers include other factors in their analysis—stage in the life cycle, age, gender, race, religion, and level of education—they can predict with uncanny accuracy the size and scope of social networks.

Photo 6.2 *As college students, young adults forge friendships that last a lifetime. As with other links in our social networks, they tend to be homogeneous, composed of people of the same social class, ethnic and racial group. (Source: © Catherine Wessel/CORBIS.)*

Personal networks are constrained by the social structure, and they are constrained by the local community. They are constrained by the schools we attend, the jobs we hold, the places we shop, and the organizations we join. The location of housing, businesses, jobs, public transit, and public institutions affect networks. Seemingly unrelated factors, like the weather, traffic, and crime, also affect the choices and constraints we face in building our personal networks.

Things get more complicated. We don't sit idly by and simply react to our environment; we interact with it. Americans are the most mobile people in the world. If a neighborhood or community doesn't suit us, we move and find one that does. Self-selection, therefore, affects neighborhoods, communities, and in turn our personal networks. Regardless of where you live, you know where the rich, the poor, the working folk, the professionals, and the minorities live. Students are usually segregated in campus dorms or nearby apartment districts. Young singles seek out the excitement of central-city neighborhoods; retirees seek the quiet of retirement communities and small towns; and parents choose suburbs because of the children. These areas come into existence when people select neighborhoods that meet their needs. Once a neighborhood takes on a special character, the reinforcing nature of the self-selection process perpetuates it, in some cases for generations. Choices within the constraints of society and community, along with self-selection, explain much of the community-making process.

Alternative Approaches and Theories of the Community[4]

Claude Fischer in *To Dwell Among Friends* uses social network analysis to explore urban life in the last quarter of the twentieth century. Fischer and his colleagues interviewed 1,050 adults living in fifty northern California communities. Residences of San Francisco high rises, Oakland slums, suburban tract homes, and small farm communities were interviewed and the size and quality of their social networks measured. Fischer's research gives us a glimpse into personal networks; their links to kin, neighbors, coworkers, and friends; their structure and spatial form; and their role in creating subcultures. He also tests many of the assumptions of the decline of community theory.

The Decline of Community Theory

The decline of community is a theme woven throughout much of the last chapter. Traditional theorists believe that urban life weakens ties of family, kin, and community. In the past, we lived, worked, and worshiped with the same people, so relationships were rich and multistranded. Today, we live in one area of the city, work in another, and shop in a third, and each one of these roles involves a different set of people. Since few of these relationships overlap, traditional means of social control don't work, and the rich and overlapping network of the traditional community no longer gives people a sense of belonging and a shared commitment to the group. Crime, vice, mental illness, suicide, and social disorganization are predictable outcomes because traditional means of social control can't work. The public is comfortable with this explanation. It seems to make sense. It explains at a gut level the murder and mayhem in New York, Washington, D.C., and Miami.

The Subcultural Theory of Urbanism

There is an alternative explanation, the subculture theory of urbanism. The theory holds that the diversity of the city—its size, density, and heterogeneity—fosters an environment ripe for the creation of subcultures. As we stated earlier, our social networks are inbred, and we choose our networks from among those like us. In a large city, you can be choosey because there are more alternatives. If you're a trekie, an environmentalist, or gay, there will probably be enough people like you in a big city to form a club, an association, or even a subculture with its own values, beliefs, and norms.

There's more. Cities not only create the critical mass necessary for the birth of subcultures, they also provide the conditions necessary for subcultures to become a world unto themselves. They provide an environment where Italians, Latinos, or Vietnamese can create a community within a community, each with its own culture, language, and food, its own schools, churches, hospitals, stores, and savings and loans. When subcultures become associated with certain parts of the city—Little Italy, Pole Town, the Castro District—physical as well as social barriers are erected to the outside community. Rather than a community of isolates, Fischer argues we have a mosaic of social worlds. Cities, rather than being a random collection of isolated individuals, are filled with people with complex attachments to a rich variety of subcultures. From this perspective, the carnage in Washington, D.C., and in New York isn't the lawlessness of individuals, but the product of subcultures—gangs, organized crime, and leverage buyout artists. The behavior of these groups is normal because it is guided by the goals, values, and norms of subcultures.

Thus, we are faced with two contradictory explanations. Has the community declined or is the behavior we see the result of competing moral communities? Fischer attempts to resolve this question by testing three assumptions of the decline of community theory. It has long been assumed that urbanism leads to psychological strain, reduced social involvement, and a decline in traditional values.

A Test of the Decline of Community Theory

Psychological Strain[5]

Since the heyday of the Chicago School, Americans have believed that large cities are unhealthy places and lead to psychological strain. A casual reading of the statistics would lead many Americans to conclude that this is indeed the case. A cornucopia of social ills are associated with the city: drug use, suicide, murder, crime, vice, and corruption. In the opening decades of the twentieth century, Park and Wirth found a higher concentration of personal disorganization in the central city than elsewhere (Schwab, 1992, pp 3–11). This is still the case. Most measures of collective mental health—admissions to mental hospitals, outpatient mental health services, drug treatment services, and suicide rates—seem to support the contention that cities are psychologically stressful places to live.

There's another way of looking at these statistics, however. A great deal of evidence shows that people already suffering from mental illness drift to the larger cities of a region. Bizarre behavior deemed intolerable in small towns may go unnoticed in a big city. Cities are also the places where you find the region's services: homeless shelters, soup kitchens, the Salvation Army, and drug treatment centers, as well as illicit drugs and services. There also may be more admissions to mental hospitals and outpatient programs because cities have larger, better staffed, and better funded service organizations. What we may be seeing is a statistical artifact of selective migration and not a link between urbanism and psychological strain.

Fischer's survey (1982) of 1,050 respondents was extensive. Interviewers asked respondents 131 questions from a fifty-three page survey. A series of questions touched on the urbanism-strain hypothesis. Respondents were asked how nervous, worried, and pleased they felt about their lives. These answers were combined in an overall mood scale. Decline of community theory predicts that as urbanism increases, morale decreases. This is not what Fischer and his colleagues found.

Figure 6.1 summarizes the results from the mood scale. Along the x-axis is a measure of urbanism; the four community categories are arranged from semi-rural to the regional core. The y-axis presents the scores on the mood scale. First, note that the mood scale doesn't vary much across the four categories of places. The average for all four groups was at the forty-fifth percentile, and semi-rural residents were slightly above it; at the other end of the urban scale, residents of the regional core had the highest score. Respondents living in towns and metropolitan areas had the lowest scores in the study.

We know from our own experiences that certain life events like the death of a family member, a serious illness, or unemployment can affect our mood. Fischer was able to statistically correct the data for these life events and for background variables that may have biased the scale. The dashed line represents these

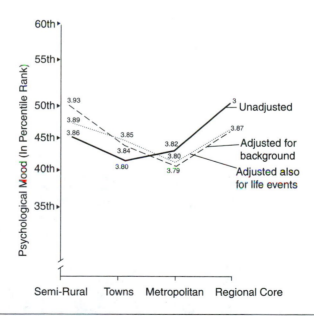

Figure 6.1 *Mean Respondents' Psychological Mood, by Urbanism* (*Source*: Claude S. Fischer. 1982. *To Dwell Among Friends: Personal Networks in Town and City.* Chicago: The University of Chicago Press, Figure 3, p. 47.)

corrected data. Even with these corrections, Fischer found no relationship between urbanism and psychological stress.

Urbanism and Social Involvement[6]

Community decline theorists state that the city creates isolated individuals. They argue that frenzied daily schedules pull urbanites in many directions. We live in one place, work in another, send our children across town to school, and meet with our club or professional association somewhere else. The end result: Relationships become superficial and meaningless. They just aren't the social stuff that creates community. Or are they?

Fischer found that urbanites are engaged in a wider variety of activities than their counterparts in other parts of the region. The self-selecting nature of the core accounts for most of these differences. The core attracts young, unmarried, and well-educated people, and they are more active wherever they live. But the idea that they lack meaningful relationships is quite a different matter.

Figure 6.2 is similar to the previous one. The x-axis measures urbanism; the y-axis summarizes the number of persons named by respondents as part of their networks. The two lines at the top are the total number of persons named. The

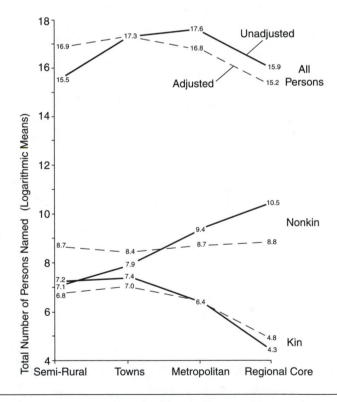

Figure 6.2   *Number of Persons Named, by Urbanism (Source*: Claude S. Fischer. 1982. *To Dwell Among Friends: Personal Networks in Town and City.* Chicago: The University of Chicago Press, Figure 4, p. 57.)

dark line is the unadjusted figures; the dashed lines are scores adjusted for background factors. Notice, there is no clear linear relationship between urbanism and social involvement. In general, core residents had about two fewer associates than did respondents living elsewhere, but this doesn't represent isolation. The differences aren't great, but they do exist, and self-selection appears to be responsible for much of the difference in the size of the networks. The bottom half of the table throws some light on these differences. Here, the curves at the top of the table are divided into their kin and nonkin components. Note that those living in the regional core report fewer kin in their networks, but they balanced this out by having more nonkin. The results do say something about the relationship between urbanism and familism, but there is no evidence that urbanism produces social isolation.

The decline of community theorists would argue that Fischer has missed the point; it's not the number but the quality of the relationships. Fischer looked at levels of intimacy and length of friendships and found no evidence that the quality of urban relations was inferior to those of small-town residents. Thus, there seems to be little support for the second hypothesis drawn from the decline of community theory.

Urbanism and Traditional Values[7]

The 1990s were rough on small towns. There were a third fewer farmers at the end of the decade than at the beginning, and the communities that depended on the farm economy withered. Scores of small towns closed stores, boarded up schools, and shut down hospitals and other services. The media dutifully recorded these personal and collective tragedies, but it also sparked a debate about our national character. Commentators insisted American values were tied to the land, farm, and small town. Some critics likened the dying of these small towns to the death of the last member of a species. Some had the unsettling feeling that a thread in the national fabric was lost and the bolt weakened. The media and the public agreed that our modern, urban way of life destroys traditional values.

Urbanism weakens traditional values. Fischer discovered that residents of the regional core were more likely to live out of wedlock, more likely to have no religious identity, and more likely to be gay. The decline of community theorists argue that this happens because attachments to kin, friends, and neighbors are the most powerful form of social control. The small town's rich network of overlapping and intertwined relationships is effective in reducing deviance and bringing about conformity. In the city, these all-encompassing networks fall apart and individuals can be just that, individuals free to act as they wish. Simply, deviance and nonconformity result from a breakdown of traditional values.

Fischer provides an alternative explanation. Rather than a breakdown of traditional values, he argues for a buildup of competing moral orders. The presence of a critical mass of similar people creates subcultures with their own values, beliefs, and norms. It isn't a paucity of values but a rich environment of competing value and normative systems that accounts for the nontraditional behavior. Behavior from the perspective of one subculture is deviant, from another normative. Thus, the decline of community thesis and the subcultural argument predict a decline in traditional values as urbanism increases. Deviant behavior from the perspective of the traditionalists is a breakdown of traditional means of social control. Subcultural

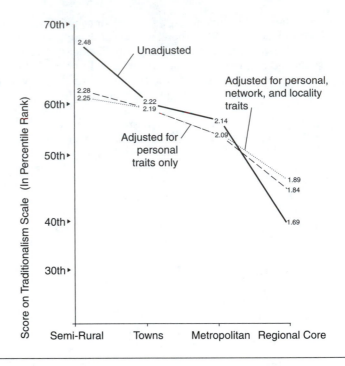

Figure 6.3   *Traditionalism, by Urbanism* (*Source*: Claude S. Fischer. 1982. *To Dwell Among Friends: Personal Networks in Town and City*. Chicago: The University of Chicago Press, Figure 5, p. 69.)

theorists say, first, it may not be deviant, depending on the subculture, and second, it results from the growth of competing moral orders.

Fischer developed a traditionalism scale by measuring respondents' opinions on social issues (sex before marriage, abortion, legalization of marijuana, and allowing homosexuals to teach in public schools). The results are summarized in Figure 6.3. Again, the x-axis measures urbanism, and the y-axis summarizes the scores on the traditionalism scale. The solid line is the unadjusted scores; the dash and dotted lines are the curves corrected for personal and network traits. The relationship is clear: The more urban a community, the lower respondents' traditionalism scores. It's a strong relationship. The respondents in semi-rural communities were near the seventieth percentile, the ones in the regional core near the fortieth. In a complex analysis of the networks of the respondents, controlling for involvement with kin and nonkin, the pattern is the same, traditionalism declines with urbanism.

Of the three charges against urban life, that it is psychologically stressful, socially isolating, and nontraditional, only the last hypothesis is supported by the study. Urban centers are no more likely to lead to psychological stress than other communities. Nor are people living in cities more likely to be socially isolated. Those living in the urban core have slightly fewer people in their networks, but there is no evidence that these relationships are less intimate. Urbanites, nevertheless, are more tolerant of nontraditional behavior, and it appears that urbanism itself contributes to these rural/urban differences. But, is a decline in traditional values such a bad thing? Remember, traditional values include elements of racism, sexism, and intolerance.

Fischer offers another explanation. He contends that the items in his scale on abortion, marijuana, and homosexuality don't just tap permissive behavior but also the progressive attitudes of our day. In Fischer's mind, it is not individual license that is the key to understanding these results, but the liberal ideology in our popular culture—feminism, gay rights, and personal privacy.

A Second Look at Social Networks

Fischer's research shows that community has not declined, is not lost, but has simply changed. Fischer's book was groundbreaking for its time, but it was written a generation ago. A classmate of his at Harvard, Barry Wellman, explores the community question in a somewhat different way by analyzing personal communities. In his 1999 book, *Networks in the Global Village: Life in Contemporary Communities*, Wellman ignores local areas, like neighborhoods, altogether and explores people's personal networks wherever these network ties take them. It is a complex process. Through surveys and interviews, Wellman and his colleagues mapped the social networks of 845 residents of Toronto and their nearly 4,000 network members. He measured the content, range, intimacy, and contact within these social networks. He asked, Is a person's network composed of kin or friends? What is the network's range? Is it compressed into a few blocks of a neighborhood or does it cover the entire city, nation, or world? Are networks homogeneous or heterogeneous? Do people have network members from different social classes? Different races? How many links involve intimacy? Which links provide emotional support? Financial help? How often do people see each other? By answering these questions, Wellman addresses the community question in the postmodern age: Is community lost, saved, or liberated?

Sociologists who believe in *community lost* argue that the profound economic, social, and technological changes wrought by globalization have destroyed community and created isolated and fragmented individuals. As we have seen, this has been a pervasive theme in sociology in the modern and postmodern era.

Sociologists who believe in *community saved* argue that community has not withered away but merely changed in response to the forces of globalization. They argue that communities today, as in the past, continue to buffer households against large-scale forces, provide mutual aid, and serve as a secure base to engage with the outside world. This is what Claude Fisher found.

Sociologists who believe in *community liberated* argue that our images of the community are highly romanticized. *Gemeinschaft*-like communities of close-knit kin, supportive friends, and helpful neighbors seldom existed in the past, and when they did, they were often unpleasant places to live. These communities may have provided people with secure, certain, and integrated lives, but at a cost— conformity and stifled individualism. This group of thinkers argues that revolutions in transportation and communication technology have liberated people from the tyranny of spatially constrained communities. People now are free to create a community based on taste rather than space.

Wellman's Community Typology

Which position is correct? What is the state of community in the postmodern age? Is it lost, saved, or liberated? Table 6.1 summarizes these positions in social network terms.

Table 6.1   *Wellman's Community Typology*

	Community Lost	Community Saved	Community Liberated
Kinship	Low	High	Low
Friendship	High	Low	High
Contact	Low	High	High
Range	Low	Low	High
Intimacy	Low	Low	High

Source: Wellman, B. (1992). Networks in the global village; Life in contemporary communities. Boulder, Co: Westview Press, Table 1.10, p. 71.

Wellman analyzed the personal communities of the participants in his study and ranked each high or low on the four personal community measures (kin/friends, contact, range, intimacy). He came up with 16 possible community types (4 measures squared = 16 types). Interestingly, most of the participants fell into one of four personal community types that correspond to the community lost, saved, and liberated positions. Summaries of the four types follow.

I. Community liberated: high intimacy, range, contact, and friendship. This was the most common personal community. People with this type of personal community are intensely involved in a large, diverse, sparsely knit network of friends. These people typically interact with each person in their personal network separately; therefore, most of the people in these networks don't know one another. As a result, people who live in a community liberated are linked to many social worlds, each social world meeting a special need or interest. In community liberated, when a mutual interest ends, the tie withers. These personal communities span great distances, and there are few ties to local areas. Without community attachments, there is little community solidarity, and when a neighborhood or school problem arises, people in community liberated vote with their feet—they move.

II. Community estranged: high intimacy with immediate kin; low range and contact. These people have few ties in their networks; they have few friends. The ties they do have are with a small, homogeneous, intimate set of kin with whom they have few contacts. For the most part, these are lonely, isolated people. Their contacts with kin usually occur during holidays or other family gatherings.

III. Community lost: high friendship; low intimacy, range, and contact. People with this type of personal community have small, homogeneous networks built around nonintimate friends who are not in frequent contact. Again, these are lonely, isolated people with few resources in their networks even during times of emotional or financial need.

IV. Community saved: high contact and immediate kinship; low intimacy and range. These people have a small, homogeneous network built around nonintimate, immediate kin who are in frequent contact. People with this type of network are intimate with one or two members of their kin network but interact often with other kin. In this type of personal community, many ties lack intimacy because contact with kin is required in a closely bound neighborhood. People often are forced to interact with people they really don't like because they are related to them and live down the street.

The Community in the Twenty-First Century

Interestingly, there isn't overwhelming support for any one of the four community types. The community type most frequently found was community liberated, but if you collapse "community estranged" and "community lost," into one category, then the community lost position has more support. Also remember that a significant number of the subjects had personal communities of the *community saved* type. Our question is, should we be surprised by these findings? I don't think so. Nearly a century ago, the founders of American urban sociology described cities as a mosaic of social worlds. Why would we expect things to be any different? If anything, our societies have become more complex, not less, and the complexity of Western society is reflected in the complexity of our communities. Rather than social networks bounded in a local area, technology permits us to create personal communities that transcend space.

How do people construct community in the twenty-first century? The following section summarizes what we know about the community at the beginning of twenty-first century. These findings also suggest how people will create their personal communities in the future.

Community ties are narrow, specialized relationships, not broadly supported ties. We receive five benefits from our personal communities: emotional support, companionship, large and small services, and financial aid. Most North Americans still think of communities as local areas filled with webs of broadly based, multi-stranded relationships. When we have a crisis, we imagine that help will come from an array of community members. There's one problem—research shows that personal community ties are highly specialized and are often not locally based. If you need emotional support, you go to the people in your social network who are intimate friends. If you need financial help, you probably will go to close kin—parents, siblings, or children. If you need someone to hold the ladder while you clean out the gutters, that's when you ask a next-door neighbor. And if you need emergency child care, that's when you turn to the parents of your child's best friend. The reality is that people can no longer assume that network members will supply the range of resources needed for daily life. The specialized nature of support in personal communities means that people must maintain a variety of ties to obtain the services and resources they need for the good life. If you are looking for community in a neighborhood, you are not going to find it. But if you broaden your perspective and look at the way people meet the needs of day-to-day life, community can be found. Community spans metropolises, nations, and continents.

People are not wrapped up in traditional densely knit, tightly bounded communities but are maneuvering in sparsely knit, loosely bounded, frequently changing networks. The classical view of community is that people interact frequently and freely with neighbors, friends, and kin in a local area. In reality, most people live in highly fragmented social networks, and members of an individual's personal community don't live in the same neighborhood and seldom know one another. Personal communities, therefore, are fragmented, specialized, and widely dispersed. People can no longer depend on solidarity of the local community to provide aid in times of crises. The time when a community took care of its own is in the past. Instead, people get out of the personal communities what they invest in them. Why would one invest time and energy in a local area when you receive most of your benefits from a geographically dispersed personal network? In personal community, investing in individual ties becomes crucial.

Research shows that the larger, more heterogeneous, and denser your network, the more support you will receive during times of need. As we showed in the opening paragraphs of this section, interpersonal skills, combined with structural characteristics like social class, affect the size and character of our personal communities.

What about the future? Will technology accelerate the decline of local areas? The answer is yes. If you derive benefits from your metropolitan-wide personal community, why would you invest your time and money in the local area? These changes suggest a continued decline in local solidarity and less commitment by neighbors to solving collectively community problems. And how will personal communities be bounded? In his Toronto study, Wellman found the best way to predict the bounding of a person's personal community is whether the participants lived in the same calling area and within a one-hour drive. What happens now that MCI, SBC, and other phone companies offer unlimited local and long distance for a low, monthly fee? As the cost of communicating with each other falls, the range of personal networks will expand. As e-mail and Internet chat rooms grow, the number of people with whom you can be in contact expands from a few dozen people to hundreds or even thousands.

Communities have moved out of neighborhoods to dispersed networks that continue to be supportive and sociable, but local areas still matter. Consider your own network and the networks of your family and friends. From your own experiences, you know that most people know few of their neighbors. And from your own experiences, you know that most members of personal communities live at some distance. Close-knit spatially bound personal communities, now as in the past, exist when people have no alternatives. In the past, it was because of poor transportation and communication technology; today, it's because people are trapped by age or poverty. It's nice to be young and rich. Community has not disappeared; it's just different than in the past. Dispersed networks are still supportive and sociable, but they will probably be even more dispersed in the future.

Today, the array of communication technology—wireless phones, the Internet, e-mail, flat-rate long distance—combined with fast and cheap transportation allows people to build and maintain personal networks over immense distances. For the past two decades, most network members lived within the same calling area or within an hour's drive. Revolutions in communication technology, however, are removing time and space restrictions. It's already happening. You need look no farther than the international students on college campuses.

I have always had a special place in my heart for our international students. Many of them learn English in a classroom setting and have a terrible time in a lecture class. I try to help, but most of these students are lost, isolated, and terrified. I can only imagine the challenges they face. Until a few years ago, airfare and long distance were prohibitively expensive, so international students banded together and formed student associations to help with the adjustment process. I have recently discovered from our students that technology has created some remarkable new solutions. My international students start their day reading the electronic edition of their hometown paper. They listen to their hometown radio station via the campus's high-speed computer network. They keep up to date with family news via e-mail. Some students even get weekly snapshots from home via the Internet. A few students have invested in Internet-based phone software. It's still primitive (a lot like a CB radio) but it's free long distance to friends back home in China, Malaysia, and the Middle East. Several of my students even tweak their satellite dishes and receive dozens of stations from India and the Middle East. They have created a remarkable array of virtual ties to home. The downside is that they interact less often with American students and don't participate as much in the student culture, but their experiences model the future of personal communities.

It is important to remember that place still has consequences. Where you live still locks you into the social and spatial structure of the local community, and spatial structures have social and symbolic meaning. There always will be Beacon Hills, North Shores, and the "wrong side of the tracks." Where you live tells us much about who you are. Where you live also determines where your children go to school; your access to parks, shopping, and employment; and your safety and quality of life. Community liberated may give you freedom to pick and choose your personal community, but it doesn't liberate you from barking dogs, meddling neighbors, or the people down the street who never mow their lawn. But the problem with personal communities is that people have few local ties that bind. When problems arise in the local schools or the neighborhood, people are more likely to move away than to try to solve them. In sum, dispersed personal networks mean less solidarity for local areas, less-effective schools, and less-democratic local government.

Private intimacy has replaced public sociability. In the past, neighborhood parks and local restaurants, bars, hardware stores, and hangouts provided vital links in the community-building process. But today, in two-parent families and single-parent families, parents work. When you combine work schedules with commutes and the demands of children, few couples have time to go out. Research shows that people are eating out more, but at fast-food rather than sit-down restaurants. Fewer people are going to movies; they are watching HBO or cable or renting movies. National franchises dominate the restaurant and entertainment of most communities. Since personal communities are no longer local, people reaffirm their personal ties by meeting as couples or in small groups for drinks or dinner. These informal meetings are used to reaffirm their ties by discussing the single interest that binds them together—jobs, the children's soccer, or school. Another important trend is home entertaining. An increasing number maintain their networks through informal entertaining at home. Architecture reflects this trend. Fewer homes have dining rooms and living rooms; more homes have great rooms.

Communities have become domesticated and feminized. Home is now the home base for relationships, and they are more voluntary and selective than in the past. Fewer network ties exist in the public realm in neighborhood associations, fraternal organizations, and work. Personal community networks are based on shared tastes rather than physical proximity. We come in contact with fewer people with whom we are forced to interact. People therefore have developed homogeneous networks of people with similar interests, attitudes, and lifestyles. As a result, the home has become the center of personal communities, and women, who have traditionally been the kin keepers anyway, have become the personal community keepers. They not only keep the kin informed with Christmas, anniversary, and birthday cards, they also make the party plans and schedule the children's school, social, and sport events. As Wellman points out, women bear more than a double load of domestic work and paid work; their triple load now includes community "networking."

As a result of these changes, people are less dependent on community for necessities. The goods and services that community members exchange are matters of convenience, rarely of necessity, and hardly ever of life and death. Community is no longer about men doing things together; it's about couples doing things together. The privatization and domestication of ties has transformed the nature of community. The domesticated community ties interact in small groups in private homes rather than in large groups in public spaces. Women create the ties that bind and in so doing create personal community.

A Picture Is Worth a Thousands Words

Throughout this section, we have argued that shifts in social networks represent an important way to understand social change. Changes in the nature of network ties have important consequences for the individual, the group, and society. An article by Bernice A. Pescosolido and Beth A. Rubin (2000) in the millennial issue of the *American Sociological Review* contrasts social networks in premodern, modern, and postmodern societies.

Premodern Social Networks

Figure 6.4 represents the social networks in premodern societies. Note that they form concentric circles. Participation in the smallest group implies participation in the larger groups. For example, your birth gives you automatic membership into an extended family, a clan, a neighborhood, a community, and a society. Institutions are interlocking and self-supporting. Statuses and roles are ascribed. Beliefs, values, and norms, universally accepted, prescribe behavior. Social networks are dense, multistranded, and spatially bounded. Individuals usually live their entire lives in a community of interlocking and overlapping social networks and share a common cultural orientation. The concentric nature of network means that there is a large safety net; few people fall through the cracks. It is a secure, certain, and integrated life. For conformists and people born to high status, it is a satisfying life where goals are clearly defined and the means clearly prescribed. The tensions in this social form come to the individualist, iconoclast, or deviant. Society's solution to these problem members is shunning, imprisonment, expulsion, or death.

This concentric pattern doesn't mean that everyone has the same network structure. There is plenty of room for variation. Men have very different social networks than women. Members born to families with high status operate in

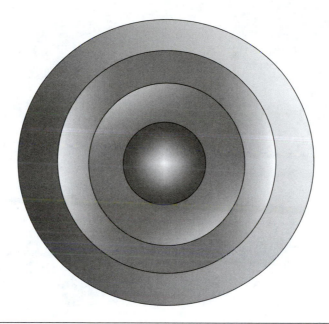

Figure 6.4 *Social Network Formation in the Premodern Era Depicted as Concentric Circles (Source:
B. A. Pescosolido & B. A. Rubin. 2000. The Web of Group Affiliations Revisited: Social
Life, Post modernism, and Sociology. American Sociological Review 65(1): 52–76.)*

different social worlds than low-status individuals. This ***Gemeinschaft*** community
is held together by mechanical solidarity.

Modern Social Networks

Figure 6.5 represents the social networks in modern society. The circles represent
groups, and the individual's social network is made up of overlapping, not concentric, circles. The most important change in this social form is that we inherit
some groups, like family, but have the freedom to choose other group memberships like neighbors, coworkers, and organizations. Furthermore, the place of
work is separated from the place of residence, so the social network of family no
longer circumscribes the network of work. Family networks still matter. Family
connections often affect occupational choice.

Thus, in this modern form, individuals have freedom and choice. As a result,
individuals are unique in the statuses they hold, the roles they play, and the
groups in which they participate. Large organizations are flexible enough to
accommodate individual differences. Laws and the contracts prescribe the rights of
the individual and the power of the state.

This modern network form has its strengths and weaknesses. The strength is
individualism, freedom, and choice. One weakness is psychological tension.
Individuals must reconcile their needs with the needs of the group to which they
belong. They often face the double bind—following the norms of one group
may very well alienate members of another group. There is also a decline in the

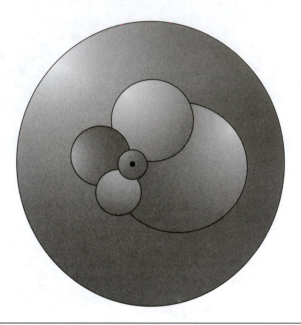

Figure 6.5   *Social Network Formation in the Modern Era Depicted as Intersecting Circles*
(*Source*: Pescosolido & Rubin, 2000.)

number of multistranded, locally bound personal communities—a decline in the local community. As a result, in modern societies an increasing number of members are alienated and anomic. Since the community no longer provides the safety net, the state steps in with programs like social security, unemployment insurance, and Medicare. This ***Gesellschaft***-like community is held together by organic solidarity.

Postmodern Social Networks

Social networks in postmodern society are depicted in Figure 6.6. Note that the spokes radiate from the individual to groups and the groups don't overlap. Links in the network tend to be single stranded, voluntary, ephemeral, and interest based. Many of the ties in the network are not even face to face, but computer or telephone mediated. Therefore, the individual has an almost infinite number of possible network configurations. Unlike premodern and modern social forms, individuals are not enmeshed in groups; in fact, few people in a social network know one other. Individual needs are paramount. Without overlapping membership, it would not be unusual or contradictory for a person to be a member of a Catholic Church and a Buddhist group. One group would meet the person's need for ritual, while the other the person's inner spiritual needs. Thus, individuals in the course of their lives have connections to many workplaces, many families, many voluntary organizations, and, perhaps, ties to many local areas. It is not unusual, given the instability of marriage in the postmodern world, that an individual may have biological parents, a stream of stepfathers, stepmothers, and live-in significant others, stepbrothers and -sisters, grandparents, stepgrandparents, brothers and sisters, half-brothers and -sisters, and

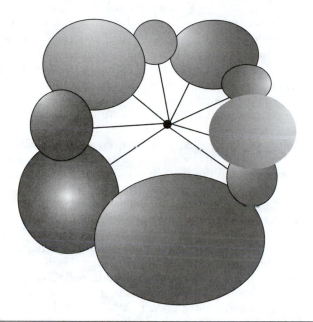

Figure 6.6   *Social Network Formation in the Contemporary Era Depicted as the Spoke Structure* (*Source*: Pescosolido & Rubin, 2000.)

an array of nephews and cousins. One has more kin, but less emotional attachment to them.

As a result, all the major spheres of life—family, work, and religion—are becoming transitional, ephemeral, and contractual. An individual is faced with an unprecedented scale of freedom and choice and is free to create new social arrangements in response to the changing personal and occupational circumstances. Therefore, social arrangements can no longer be taken for granted; they require constant attention. If they are ignored, they will wither.

In sum, the strength of social networks in the postmodern world is freedom and flexibility. The weakness in this freedom is insecurity, isolation, and fragmentation. The problem with these networks is that they require flexibility, skill, and the ability to reaffirm social relationships on a continuous level. People who thrive in this social form will be the well educated and the highly skilled. They are the symbolic analysts who drive the global economy. They are the people who hone their interpersonal skills through continuous interaction with others economically and socially. Most members of a society, however, will face a far less secure and certain world.

Summary

The work of Fischer and others in network analysis has opened up a new way of looking at the community. Rather than looking at historical forces or community structures, Fischer explores the web of personal relationships that combine to form social structures and, in turn, societies. The complexity of this research is mind-boggling, and the analysis, even with a sample of only 1,000 respondents, requires a mainframe computer. The work is valuable because it introduces a new tool for exploring the community and the city. It is also important because it provides another technique for analyzing theories, like the decline of community theory.

The present generation always laments what it has lost in the past. Somehow life was always better back then. Time is a powerful filter. It strains out the tension, conflict, and misery of the past. It ignores the tyranny of the majority and the suffering of minorities that have committed no sin other than being different. Fischer's work is indispensable reading for anyone interested in community because it shows us that we put our lives and communities together as we always have. The setting has changed, and transportation and communication technology has allowed us to organize community differently. But that's the point: The community is different, not better or worse.

We all carry around mental baggage—values, beliefs, and prejudices that sometimes crumble under close scrutiny. We hold to these things because they are comfortable, and public opinion holds dear the belief of community decline. It is interesting to watch our leaders dredge up the decline of community theories to justify a new drug policy or a police crackdown. Tragically, public opinion and public beliefs, rather than research findings, guide social policy. I find Fischer's work exciting because it opens up new vistas on community, and it suggests alternative remedies to the most serious problems facing present-day society.

Social network analysis is one of the newer approaches to the study of community. Social networks are often spatially dispersed rather than concentrated in a single locale. These networks of kin, friends, coworkers, and shared memberships in churches and voluntary associations can span an entire metropolitan area. Friends in one network may share friends in another, and a complex interconnected social network can emerge across the city.

Social networks are homogeneous. They tend to be composed of people of the same social class, ethnic, and racial group. Social structure is responsible for this homogeneity, and the choice-constraint model was introduced to describe the selection process. The model assumes that people are rational, that they enter into relationships because they are rewarding, and that the choices they make are from alternatives constrained by the social structure. One's social class is the most important constraint in determining one's network, but other factors like race, stage in the life cycle, characteristics of the local community, and self-selection are also important in limiting alternatives.

The decline of the community is a common theme among the theorists in this chapter. These theorists believe that urban life weakens traditional ties of family, kin, and neighborhood and that social disorganization results. They argue that informal means of social control have been replaced by the police and the courts and that people's intimate, close-knit ties to the family, neighborhood, and the community have been replaced by relationships in which individuals pursue their own self-interest.

Claude Fischer provides an alternative thesis—the subculture theory of urbanism. Fischer argues that the diversity of the city—its size, density, and heterogeneity—creates an environment ripe for the creation of subcultures. Subcultures are like all cultures: They develop their own goals, values, beliefs, and norms, and through the socialization process they perpetuate themselves. Consequently, rather than seeing the city as a haphazard collection of unattached individuals, subcultural theorists argue for a rich environment of competing moral communities.

Fischer uses network analysis to test three of the basic assumptions of decline of community theorists: Urbanism leads to psychological strain, reduced social involvement, and nontraditional values. Only one of the three assumptions was supported by Fischer's analysis. There was no evidence that urbanism was related to either psychological strain or reduced social involvement. There is a close relationship between urbanism and nontraditional values. Fischer reports profound differences in the values held by urban and rural residents. Urbanites tolerate nontraditional behaviors and accept many of the core values held by the liberal ideologies in our popular cultures—feminism, gay rights, and personal privacy.

The nature, scope, and functions of local communities have changed dramatically in the past century, and these changes mirror the underlying scale of society. The increasing scale of society has brought major improvements in transportation, communication, and energy technology that make the all-encompassing *Gemeinschaft* communities of the past unnecessary. A common human failing is to remember the past selectively. In many respects, this is what has happened to the concept of community. The *Gemeinschaft* type of community is romanticized and continues to be described by the words *harmony*, *naturalness*, *depth*, *fullness*, and *family-like*. Such communities, however, are not without their costs. They preclude free expression and individualism. The local community, as it is known today in urban America, is neither better nor worse than those of the past, just different.

Social critics suggest that the crime, isolation, poverty, and alienation in the urban setting are the result of the destruction of community. Is this a fair criticism? The city is composed of a mosaic of social worlds, each subcommunity serving the needs of a special subgroup in society. Certainly, problems are severe in some subcommunities. They always have been. Nevertheless, for the majority of Americans living in urban areas, the partial communities in which they live provide a satisfactory and satisfying solution to the recurring problems of day-to-day life in large, complex societies.

Notes

[1] Many social scientists argue that the modern era begins with the Age of Enlightenment. The *Age of Enlightenment* refers to the writings and thought in Europe and in the American colonies during the eighteenth century prior to the French Revolution. The word *enlightenment* was frequently used by writers of the time to describe their movement as one whereby Western society was emerging from centuries of darkness and ignorance into a new age enlightened by reason, science, and a respect for humanity. The basic assumption of the enlightenment was an abiding faith in the power of human reason. This was a period of great discovery in science and geography. Through the use of reason, humankind could discover the underlying laws of nature and society. People came to assume that through the use of knowledge, unending progress would be possible. Positivism, the belief that the scientific study of society could lead to the creation of a better society, is an outgrowth of the enlightenment and a common element in early sociology, especially the work of Comte. Positivism was very much a part of the

tradition of social science in the United States in the nineteenth and twentieth centuries. The principle that knowledge of society comes from only experience and observation guided by reason (the application of the scientific method) to society is at the foundation of most of American sociology. Through the thoughts, writings, and actions of enlightenment thinkers, most notably Benjamin Franklin and Thomas Jefferson, the United States was founded on the principles of the enlightenment.

[2] The origins of network analysis can be found in an essay published by Georg Simmel in 1922, titled "Social Circles." In this essay, Simmel discusses the different types of relationships possible in modern urban societies and contrasts them to those in rural and premodern societies. Simmel employs the concept of **social circles**, which we now call **personal networks**, to contrast the two. Simmel's article was not published in English until 1955, explaining, in part, the slow introduction of this concept into the urban literature. See Georg Simmel. (1955). ***Conflict and the Web of Group Affiliations.*** (Trans. and Ed. by Kurt Wolff and Reinhard Bendix). Glencoe, IL: Free Press.

Interestingly, the first empirical use of network analysis was done in anthropology, not sociology. For an excellent overview of the historical development of this approach, see Berkowitz. S. D. (1982). ***An Introduction to Structural Analysis: The Network Approach to Social Research***. Toronto: Butterworths.

[3] This section is based in part on section 1, "Networks," in Claude S. Fischer et al. (1977). ***Networks and Places: Social Relations in the Urban Setting***. New York: Free Press, and Chapter 1, "Personal Community," in Claude S. Fischer. (1982). ***To Dwell Among Friends: Personal Networks in Town and City***. Chicago: University of Chicago Press.

[4] This section is based in part on Chapter 3, "Personal Networks: An Overview," in Claude S. Fischer. (1982). ***To Dwell Among Friends: Personal Networks in Town and City***. Chicago: The University of Chicago Press.

[5] This section is based on Chapter 4, "Urbanism and Psychological Strain," in Claude S. Fischer, ***To Dwell Among Friends***.

[6] This section is based on Chapter 5, "Urbanism and Social Involvement," in Claude S. Fischer, ***To Dwell Among Friends***.

[7] This section is based on Chapter 6, "Urbanism and Traditional Values," in Claude S. Fischer, ***To Dwell Among Friends***.

7

READING THE CITY

Introduction

Whenever I visit a major city, a New York, Chicago, Atlanta, or Los Angeles, I have a mix of emotions—awe, fear, and fascination. At first, I am overwhelmed by the sheer size and complexity of the place, but as time passes, I do what all social scientists do: I look for patterns and relationships. There are many to be found. You can get a feel for the physical patterns of the city anytime you drive from the countryside to the city's center. It doesn't have to be New York or Los Angeles. Any large city will do because all cities share many of the same patterns. Think back to your last trip on the interstate into a major city. Thirty or forty miles outside the city you begin to sense a change. The exits aren't as far apart. Rather than an isolated gas station, a quick mart, and a fast-food outlet at the exit, you notice a small Wal-Mart, a grocery, and an isolated housing development off in the distance. The landscape is still dominated by farms and open space, but there's a noticeable change. Social scientists called this urban region *Exurbia* a generation ago. Today, I'm not sure what we call it. Sprawl? Sprawl is a good description because the infrastructure laid down now in these isolated pockets will set the stage for low-density suburban growth twenty years later.

As your drive continues, this pattern repeats itself, but exits come closer together, until finally, almost without noticing it, the isolated clusters of suburban housing, adjoining farms, and open spaces are replaced with housing that stretches from horizon to horizon. The exits are no longer isolated islands, but highly developed clusters of gas stations, mini-marts, fast-food outlets, sit-down restaurants, and national motel chains. Off in the distance, you may even see a strip development with big national retailers—a Wal-Mart Supercenter with a Target across the street, next door to a Home Depot, Lowe's, Best Buy, and Circuit City. From then on, you don't have to look for an incorporation sign because every few miles another suburb repeats this pattern in cookie-cutter fashion. This is suburban sprawl at its height—low-density housing supported by national grocery, retail, and food chains. Every American city has this type of development. In our largest metropolitan areas, there may be a hundred square miles of sprawl ringing the central city.

Driving at seventy miles an hour, this is all that you will see for the next fifteen or twenty minutes before you notice the next change in the cityscape. The interstate first widens to three, then, four lanes. Ahead, cars are starting to slow and merge to the exit ramps on the right. The road signs on the pylon overhead inform you that your interstate is about to cross the city's outer belt. This is one of the most accessible spots in the entire metropolis, and because of its accessibility, a very different type of development takes place here. Off to the right you see the city's largest mall. Located to your left are an upscale office park and a cinema complex. You even notice a hospital with what looks like an adjoining medical arts center. Interspersed throughout this development are high-rise office and apartment buildings and every imaginable restaurant and motel chain. This is one of the metropolis's edge cities.

The outer belt may not be the official boundary between the suburbs and the central city, but the character of the city changes rapidly after this. It still feels like suburbia, but it's different somehow. The homes are smaller, 1950s and 1960s vintage, with mature trees and established landscapes around them. But many of the neighborhoods have a worn appearance. By now you can just make out the downtown skyline, but there is still a lot to see on your car trip. In the next mile or two you notice that low-rise apartments and row houses are slowly replacing single-family dwelling. Many of the neighborhoods look seedy, some of the housing looks abandoned, but when you look to the right and to the left, you notice a neighborhood once and a while that looks like it's on the upswing. By now, the interstate has widened to six lanes to handle the wave of commuters who use the central city during the day and who return to the fringe at night. Soon housing disappears altogether, replaced by warehouses, railroad yards, truck depots, small-scale factories, and service shops. The next exit is marked downtown, and as if by magic, you find yourself in the canyons and the frenetic pace of the central business district.

We have all made this trip. For some of you this is part of your everyday routine. For others, it's a special event. Regardless of how often you experience it, there are patterns. Let me describe a few of them. The most obvious is that low-density, low-scale development is found on the city's periphery and high-density, high-scale development is found near the city's center. There is one exception—the zone adjacent to the central business district.

You probably noticed that the newest neighborhoods, offices, and retail developments were on the periphery and in the city's center. If you use housing style to gauge neighborhood age, you probably noticed that the age of development varies with distance from the city's center.

If you exited the interstate and drove on the city's streets, your windshield survey would uncover other patterns. The city offers a mosaic of social worlds. Each neighborhood provides housing and a host of services to a specific group of people. Using information like the type and condition of housing, the types of stores and restaurants, and the appearance of the people who live in an area, you can come up with a remarkably accurate description of the social class and racial, ethnic, and even occupational characteristics of the people who live in these neighborhoods.

The sheer size and complexity of the physical city is mind-boggling. Its social complexity is even greater. Social scientists have been trying to describe the social and physical characteristics of the city for nearly a century, and we know a lot about how cities grow and change over time. When a city was founded profoundly influences its future growth. For example, the nation's oldest cities in the Northeast and Midwest have different patterns from those found in the South and West. We also know that the economic base of a city profoundly affects its development. Industrial cities are patterned differently from those with commercial, service, and governmental bases. Similarly, the transportation technology at the time of a city's settlement affects its future urban development. Cities founded in the eighteenth and nineteenth centuries, shaped by the horse, railroad, and streetcar, are of higher population density and have evolved differently from those cities shaped by the automobile.

So why the intense interest in these variations in urban forms? Most of this research is driven by scientific curiosity. There, however, is a more utilitarian reason. If you can describe the underlying structure of the city and understand the forces that shape it, you can make a lot of money. Planners, bankers, Realtors, developers, investors, and speculators are among the cadre of people who shape the city. They all need to know these patterns in order to mediate their investment risks. You need to know these patterns if for no other reason than that you are a consumer of urban services. Someday the vast majority of you will be homeowners; nearly 70 percent of Americans are. You need to protect your investment. And a basic understanding of the forces and processes that shape our cities might help.

In this chapter we will learn how to read the patterns of the city. In the first section, we will examine the early attempts by sociologists, economists, and geographers to develop urban models. Drawing from a century of research, we will see how these models have changed and how we can use a general model, a template, to read the patterns found in most North American cities.

We then look at urban development through two very different lenses. The first lens is the work of the political economist and geographer David Harvey. Harvey uses a Marxist lens to describe a group of powerful and influential actors who shape the cityscape for their own ends, profit. He uses evidence from Baltimore to support his argument. We then see the city through a lens provided by a group of social scientists from southern California known as the Los Angeles School. They use a postmodern lens to describe a decentered, decentralized, randomly patterned cityscape made up of a series of new urban elements like edge cities and privatopias. They describe a city shaped by the positive and negative by-products of globalization.

Classical Theory of Urban Land Use

What amazes social scientists is that cities, left to their own devices, will order themselves in a rational manner. More interesting is that land-use patterns are the result of millions of decisions, made over the life of a city, by individuals, businesses, and industries in their search for a new location. Together these decisions determine the broad outline of land use within a city. A decision made by a city's leaders to locate a dump on the east side of town will stop the use of adjacent land for other purposes like expensive residences. Past decisions, therefore, determine present urban form and shape future locational decisions.

Not all decisions and decision makers are equal. The wealthy and powerful can profoundly influence the spatial form of a city. A developer may choose to build a shopping center on the city's periphery, or a bank executive may decide not to make loans in a central-city neighborhood. These decisions are direct, and the consequences of these actions are highly visible.

In most cases, people's decision making is subtler and less easily observed. The decision of a minority member to move into a white neighborhood and the decision of a white resident to move elsewhere are not significant in themselves.

But when these decisions are combined with hundreds of similar decisions, the process of invasion-succession results, and the social character of a neighborhood changes. Consequently, when our decisions on where to live, work, shop, and play are combined, the result is an urban form shared by most North American cities.

For most of the twentieth century, students of the city tried to develop a general theory that describes the distribution of people and activities across the urban landscape. Three of these theories—Burgess's concentric zone theory, Hoyt's sector theory, and Harris and Ullman's multiple nuclei theory—have been the starting point for so much research that they are known as classical theories. Three points must be made before we discuss the classical theories. First, each theory is based on ideal constructs or a set of generalizations about land-use patterns. Because the theories were designed to be general and to describe patterns in many cities, no one city will fit the models perfectly. Secondly, the theories are based on patterns found in American cities, and they may not describe land-use patterns of cities in other parts of the world. Finally, all three theories are dynamic and predict how the spatial patterns of cities change over time.

Burgess's Concentric Zone Theory

The Burgess theory, first published in 1925, was one of the first attempts to describe and explain general urban land-use patterns (Park, 1952; Park, Burgess, & McKenzie, 1925). Burgess posited that land uses in the modern city assume a pattern of concentric zones. These zones are ideal constructs, and no city will fit the pattern exactly because physical barriers such as rivers, ravines, and hills distort each zone. Major transportation lines further divide the zones into segments. The famous Burgess model is shown in Figure 7.1. A description of each zone follows.

Zone I

The central business district (CBD) is the zone that has the greatest accessibility from any point within the city. High accessibility means high demand for land, and only those activities that need a central location and can afford the high land costs are located here. Skyscrapers, department stores, hotels, restaurants, theaters, and specialty stores occupy Zone I. It is an area of retail trade, office and service facilities, light manufacturing, and commercialized recreation.

Zone II

The zone surrounding the CBD is the zone of transition. Unlike the CBD, the zone of transition is residential, populated by groups lower on the socioeconomic scale, immigrants, and rural migrants. Interestingly, the land use in this zone deviates from the type one would expect from most land-use models. Theoretically, the proximity of this zone to the CBD should cause the rents in the area to be among the highest in the city; however, its rents are among the lowest. The character of the zone of transition is the result of investors speculating on the future use of the land in the area. Zone II is in the path of business and industrial expansion. Investors buy land in this zone hoping that business and industry will invade the area and buy their property at a much

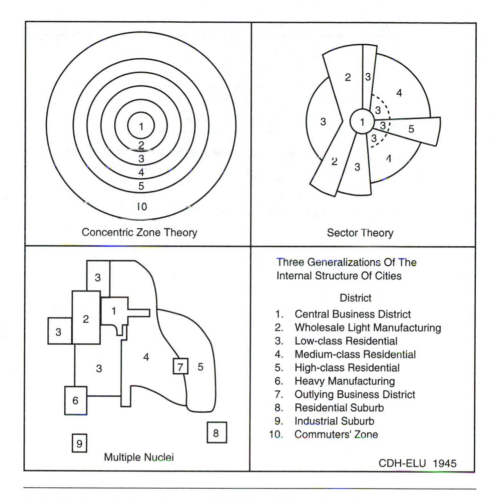

Figure 7.1   *Concentric Zone, Sector, and Multiple Nuclei Models* (*Source*: Reprinted from C. D. Harris and E. L. Ullman. 1945. The Nature of Cities. *The Annals of the Academy of Political and Social Science*, 242, figure 1, p. 107.)

higher price. Because the investors expect the structures they own to be torn down, they have little incentive to pay for their upkeep.

Zone III

The zone of working people's homes is superior in physical appearance to the zone of transition, but in size and quality its houses fall short of those in middle- and upper-class residential zones. Individuals who live in this zone have relatively low incomes. In comparison with wealthier families, they pay a larger part of their total budget for transportation costs. Low-income working families, therefore, tend to live near their place of employment in or near the CBD. This area also has a large number of neighborhoods made up of second-generation immigrants to the city, people who have escaped the slum conditions of the zone of transition but have not yet joined the ranks of the middle class.

Zone IV

The zone of middle-class homes is the residential area of clerical and managerial people, professionals, and owners of small businesses. The higher incomes of this group permit them to absorb higher transportation costs and therefore escape the noise and pollution of more centrally located housing.

Zone V

The commuter zone is the area of satellite towns and suburbs, sometimes thirty or forty miles from the CBD in large cities and normally acting as bedroom communities outside the political boundaries of the central city. In Burgess's time, these communities were served by commuter railroads that carried commuters to the CBD for employment. Because of the high transportation costs, this area is beyond the reach of most residents of the city, and it is therefore limited mainly to the wealthy.

The Dynamic Nature of the Theory

The concentration of the dominant groups in the CBD is the key to the entire model. Burgess noted that as a city grows, so too does the demand for land at the city's center. Through time the CBD expands, invading the adjoining zone of transition, taking over this land for nonresidential use. Because the property in this area is largely renter-occupied, landlords can turn over their property quickly by simply evicting their tenants. The people displaced by the invading land uses must have housing, so they move outward into Zone III, and the ecological process of invasion and succession continues outward toward the periphery of the city. Burgess, therefore, conceived his theory as a dynamic one that describes the process of city growth over time. As a city grows, it must reorganize spatially, and, although transportation lines, rivers, and hills introduce distortions, Burgess believed that a concentric pattern of land usage described most North American cities. See Photo 7.1.

The Burgess theory, although first introduced more than seventy-five years ago, still is of great interest to students of the city. Literally hundreds of articles have been written to interpret, test, and refute the model. Reasons for this interest are numerous, but among the most important is the fact that Burgess's theory, unlike the works of Hoyt (1939) and Harris and Ullman (1945), is part of a more general theory of the city. Equally important is the fact that it was the first to be published and thus provided a point of departure for other researchers. The theories of Hoyt and of Harris and Ullman were written in response to Burgess's theory.

Hoyt's Sector Theory

The sector theory was an outgrowth of a study conducted by Homer Hoyt (1939) for the Federal Housing Administration during the depression years of the 1930s. The study was an intensive analysis of the internal residential structure of 142 American cities, and it involved calculating the average residential rental values for each block of every city in the sample. By representing these data graphically on a map (see Figure 7.1), Hoyt found that sectors rather than concentric zones

Photo 7.1   *The Concentric Zone Model hypothesized by Burgess is vividly shown in this photo of Detroit from the 1920s. Note that the downtown high-rise buildings are surrounded by the multistory buildings in the Zone of Transition. In the foreground is the densely settled Zone of Workingmen's Homes. Not shown in this photo but farther out from the CBD are the Zone of Middle-class Homes and the Commuter Zone.* (*Source*: Eliott Erwitt/Magnum Photos, Inc.)

could better characterize the general spatial pattern of cities in the United States. Hoyt's study uncovered other important differences from the patterns suggested by the concentric zone theory. Industrial areas tended to develop along river valleys, waterways, and railroad lines rather than around the CBD. Moreover, a significant amount of this industry was at the city's periphery rather than near its center. In addition, the highest-rent areas were not in the last concentric zone but in one or more sectors usually on one side of the city. In general, these high-rent sectors were along the major axial transportation lines, which provided the residents easy access to the city's center. Low-rent areas, in contrast, tended to be more centrally located near the CBD, often in or directly opposite the highest-rent sectors. Middle-income rental areas were generally on either side of the highest rental areas or on the peripheries of low-rent residential sectors (Hoyt, 1939).

How Hoyt's Theory Operates

On the basis of these empirical findings Hoyt rejected the concentric zone theory and proposed his sector theory. As in the case of Burgess's work, Hoyt's theory was dynamic, designed to predict where the city will expand as it grows. The key to Hoyt's theory was the changing location of the city's dominant group—the wealthy.

In his analysis of housing rents, Hoyt discovered that high-rent neighborhoods do not skip around at random in the process of movement—they follow a definite path in one or more sectors (see Figure 7.2). These sectors, besides being along established transportation lines, also tended to develop on high ground, free from the risk of floods, or along lake or riverfronts not in use by industry. In addition, high-rent resi-

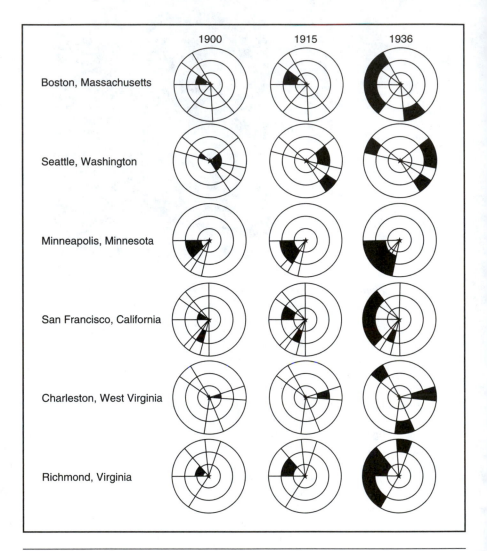

Figure 7.2   *Shifts in Location of Fashionable Residential Areas, 1900–1936 (fashionable residential areas indicated by solid black). This figure from Hoyt's original 1939 work shows the shift of high-rent areas at three time intervals. Note that in most cases high-rent districts have moved from the interior of a sector to its periphery. According to Hoyt, this movement was made necessary by the growth of commerce and industry in or adjacent to the central business district. It was made possible by an improved automobile technology. (Source: H. Hoyt. 1939. The Structure and Growth of Residential Neighborhoods in American Cities. Washington, D. C.: Federal Housing Administration, figure 40, p. 115.)*

dential areas tended to expand toward open country and away from dead-end sections of the city. In general, high-rent areas initially are near the CBD, but as the CBD expands and industry grows, the wealthy abandon these neighborhoods to escape the noise, traffic, and pollution. As this group moves outward in the same sector toward the newer areas at the periphery of the city, their former homes are taken over by members of groups lower on the socioeconomic scale. These homes are often large, multistoried, and prohibitively expensive to maintain as single-family dwellings by anyone but the wealthy. However, they are easily converted into flats and apartments for rental purposes. Because of the age and character of this housing as well as its proximity to the CBD, it is typically investor owned and is used as described in the discussion of the zone of transition (Hoyt, 1939).

According to the sector theory, the sorting of various income groups in the city occurs in the following way. The wealthy consume the best land—the high ground in the open areas of the city along major transportation lines. The low income groups have few or no housing alternatives and either consume the obsolete housing of the wealthy or live in other undesirable areas. The largest group, the working and middle-income people, consume the remaining residential areas of the city. In sum, the theory predicts that cities will grow axially or in only one or two directions at any one time and that the location and movement of high-rent residential areas are the most important organizing principles in this growth. Hoyt's theory also reflects changes in automobile technology that made the rapid expansion of wealthy suburbs possible in the 1920s. A major weakness of this theory is that it largely ignores land-uses other than residential, and it places undue emphasis on the economic characteristics of areas, ignoring other important factors such as the race and ethnicity of the residents.

Harris and Ullman's Multiple Nuclei Theory

Harris and Ullman (1945) recognized the shortcomings of both the concentric zone and sector theories and presented an alternative approach known as the *multiple nuclei theory*. This theory suggests that as a city grows it is differentiated into homogeneous areas or nuclei, but these nuclei do not necessarily form concentric zones or sectors. Harris and Ullman contended that in many cities land-use patterns do not focus on a single center, the CBD, but on multiple centers (see Figure 7.1). These centers include retail areas, warehousing districts, and concentrations of manufacturing and industry, as well as university, governmental, and financial centers. Moreover, these nuclei are often in different parts of the city.

Rules Useful in Predicting Land-Use Patterns

In the presentation of their theory, Harris and Ullman identified several rules useful in predicting the location and future growth of these specialized areas. First, certain activities require specialized facilities and concentrate where these facilities are available. Industry and manufacturing, for example, require transportation facilities, and these activities often locate near rail lines, waterways, and ports.

Second, similar activities benefit from being close to each other. Retailers locate near one another to increase the pedestrian traffic in front of their stores and hence their sales.

Third, certain dissimilar activities may be disadvantageous to each other. For example, because of its pollution, industry would be viewed as a nuisance to retailers and residents of high-income residential areas.

Finally, some activities could benefit from a centralized location in or near the CBD but cannot afford the rents. Warehousing or grocery wholesaling are examples of activities that require large structures and would benefit from a central location but must locate elsewhere because of the prohibitively high rents in the city's center (Harris & Ullman, 1945).

Harris and Ullman's theory has many of the same shortcomings as the preceding two. It is overly simplistic and does not state the limiting assumptions associated with the model. More important, Harris and Ullman are geographers and bring to this theory the unique focus of their discipline—the spatial distribution of specific land-uses. Little attention is given to the process that leads to the sorting of people and institutions across the urban landscape.

Tests of the Classical Theories

The three theories of urban residential structure are an important part of the sociological literature. Most introductory texts provide a synopsis of the theories, and urban texts devote at least a part of a chapter to them. There hasn't been a Graduate Record Exam in memory without at least one question on these theories. The coverage is all the more remarkable when you consider the youngest of the three, the multiple nuclei theory, was published a half century ago (Harris, 1998). The reason for the interest is that they have spawned thousands of research papers. All the theories have been tested, but the Burgess model has received the most scrutiny. This is due to the fact that it was the first published, it is the only one of the three tied to a more general theory of the city, and it is the easiest to analyze.[1]

The Burgess model has been tested in two major ways. First, armed with ruler, compass, and map, researchers have tried to find the hypothetical zones or a systematic difference in concentric zones as one moves from the CBD to the periphery. Second, researchers have analyzed status gradients, or the tendency for the housing and population characteristics to change as the distance from the CBD increases. Past studies show many variables—density, socioeconomic status, housing costs, and ethnicity—vary with distance. Few studies found sectoral variation. Less attention has been devoted to the multiple nuclei model.[2]

In the1960s, researchers found that all three theories had some validity depending on what characteristic one studies. For example, family types are distributed in a concentric zone pattern, social class by sectors, and ethnic and racial groups by a spatial pattern resembling multiple nuclei. Over the next decade, studies of U.S. and Canadian cities confirmed these findings (Anderson & Egeland, 1961).

The three major theories were published before World War II, and many of the tests of the theories are one or two generations old. Much has changed since the end of World War II: the emergence of a service economy, the dominance of the automobile, the decline in the size of the American family, the growth of the suburbs, the decentralization of business and industry, the increase in the role of the federal government, the growth of the Sunbelt, and the emergence of a global economy, to name a few. Anyone living through these tumultuous times knows cities today differ from those of the past. Can models conceptualized on cities of the 1920s, 1930s, and 1940s be relevant in the twenty-first century?

Michael White (1987) in his book, *American Neighborhoods and Residential Differentiation*, provides the definitive test of the models. White explores the spatial structure of twenty-one American cities on thirty-four variables with a variety of research tools. The analysis of the distribution of characteristics by distance from the CBD is one of the techniques he uses. Previous research has shown that distance from downtown is important in understanding a neighborhood's history and current status. To accomplish this, White calculated the average value of social characteristics for four concentric zones around the CBDs of twenty-one metropolises. Each zone contained 25 percent of the metropolitan area's census tracts. If distance is related to a variable, the average score of the variable should increase or decrease as one moves from Zone 1 to Zone 4. This is precisely what he found. Variables such as housing age, children in single-parent families, low income, population density, median household income, single-family dwellings, and owner-occupied dwellings changed in ways predicted by the Burgess model.

Let's look at one of these variables in detail, socioeconomic status (SES). SES is a master variable that correlates with many other variables. One measure of SES is occupational prestige and a commonly used variable is the percentage of white-collar workers in a neighborhood's workforce. If Burgess's theory is correct, then white-collar employment should increase with distance. In nineteen of the twenty-one metropolitan areas, White found that the percentage of white-collar workers increases between the first and second ring. Between the second and the third ring, the trend is still upward, but between the third and the fourth rings, the trend decreases. What's the explanation? We know there has been a massive movement of retailing, business, and manufacturing to the suburban ring in the past two generations, and this decentralization of business activity is reflected in the mix of status groups in the outermost ring. White-collar workers still commute to the CBD, but they also have jobs in nearby office parks; clerical workers drive to nearby suburban businesses; and high-wage blue-collar workers travel to nearby manufacturing or assembly plants. The Burgess model correctly predicts this pattern.

Let's take another variable, race. Race is a master status variable, and black Americans continue to be the most residentially segregated group in this society. Burgess, in his original formulation of his model, recognized the tendency of blacks and other ethnic groups to be clustered in enclaves. Assimilation models predict that as members of a group move into the mainstream of society they should disperse outward from the central city. White found the predicted variation. There is variation from city to city reflecting the racial composition of the local population, but, in general, black population declines as one moves from the center to the periphery.

In general, the physical characteristics of a city—housing age, density, and dwelling type—are the most differentiated by ring. These characteristics are followed by income and poverty measures. In the middle range is a complex mixture of life cycle, ethnic, racial, and SES indicators. Found at the bottom of the scale are measures of mobility and several occupational and life cycle measures; these characteristics are not distributed by zones. Therefore, the relationship between distance from downtown and population and housing characteristics remains an important factor in describing the urban landscape.

What do all these results tell us? Which model is correct? It is clear that the physical characteristics of the metropolis, its housing stock, and population density are quite symmetrical and oriented around downtown as predicted by the concentric zone theory. Generally, higher income and status groups live farther from the center than low-income groups, again, reflecting the importance of distance in the organizational structure of the city. Neighborhoods differ very little in their family characteristics regardless of where they are located except for household size, which is related to distance. Although racial and ethnic groups tend to live in enclaves, none of the models predict their location with any accuracy.

Social scientists are just that, scientists, and the goal of science is to develop theories. During this century, students of the city attempted to create a general theory of the residential structure of the city. But cities in this society differ in age, size, history, economic base, population, and housing characteristics. Herein lies the problem. A city's age and when it reaches metropolitan status profoundly influence the present character of the city. Streets are the dinosaurs of urban sociology. Even after cities like San Francisco, Chicago, Hiroshima, Nagasaki, Rotterdam, and Leningrad have been leveled by war or fire, they have been rebuilt along the old street pattern. Thus, the past constrains the present and shapes the future. This is why the Burgess theory, created seventy-five years ago, remains relevant to the physical structure of the city. Much of the old is still around, it may be underground, but it still shapes the present city. However, even this seventy-five-year pattern of a mono-nucleated city is being modified with the emergence of edge cities on the outer belts of our largest cities.

The economic and social structure changes more rapidly than the physical city, and the Burgess model is less relevant to the social side of the metropolis. The number of women in the labor force, fertility, household size, income distribution, occupational structure, and the economy have changed dramatically this century. The city isn't free to accommodate these changes. The housing stock, the clustering of structures into neighborhoods, and the location of schools, hospitals, shopping, parks, and other facilities continue to influence the locational decisions of families. Therefore, social changes must work themselves through the physical city. It takes generations to change these patterns. For this reason, the Burgess concentric zone model will continue to describe the physical characteristics of the city, along with characteristics like income, housing expenditures, and housing size. The model, however, must be modified to accommodate other characteristics of the city, and this is precisely what Michael White does in the closing chapters of his book.

White's Model of the Twenty-First-Century City

How do we use this massive amount of research to read the patterns of the city? White (1987) provides a guide that works well in understanding the North American city at the beginning of the twenty-first century. The model has only seven elements (see Figure 7.3).

The Core

The CBD remains the focus of the metropolis. Its functions may have changed over the years, but it still houses the major banks and financial institutions, government buildings, and corporate headquarters. The region's cultural and entertainment facilities—museums, libraries, galleries, zoos, botanical gardens, arenas, and stadiums—are also located here. Retailing has declined over the decades. A few large department stores keep their flagship stores downtown, but most retailing is out where the money is in the suburbs. Those that remain are specialty stores catering to the daytime commuters.

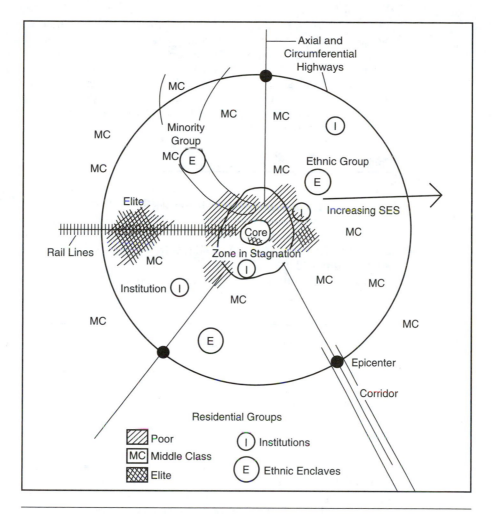

Figure 7.3   *The Shape of the Late Twentieth-Century Metropolis (Source: Michael J. White, "The Shape of the Late Twentieth Century Metropolis." In American Neighborhoods and Residential Differentiation. ©1987 Russell Sage Foundation, 112 East 64th Street, New York, NY 10021. Reprinted with permission.)*

The Zone of Stagnation

Burgess referred to the ring around the CBD as the zone of transition—an area composed of slums, flophouses, red-light districts, warehouses, and industry. Back then, the area's dilapidated state was the result of speculation. Investors expected the CBD to expand into the zone, and it was the future not the present use of the property that determined its value. Property declined as owners reinvested their money elsewhere.

Burgess was wrong. The CBD did not expand outward but rather upward in skyscrapers. Interstate highway construction, slum clearance, and the shifting of warehousing, trucking, and other activities to the suburbs dealt the zone additional blows. In older cities like Cleveland's "flats" district, warehouses and old factories have been converted into entertainment, shopping, and residential areas. Other cities attempted to convert old ethnic slums into upscale housing: Cincinnati's Over-the-Rhine District is an example of a failed attempt. In 2001, most of the city's riots were located in this district. Younger cities without nineteenth-century buildings in the zone have abandoned the zone altogether. The first time I drove into Dallas, Tulsa, and Kansas City, the vacant land that surrounds the CBD struck me.

Pockets of Poverty and Minorities

Slums are areas that house people with no housing alternatives. White (1987) found in all the cities in his study, highly segregated groups of disadvantaged people living at the fringes of society: addicts, the homeless, and the underclass. They are often members of minorities, and one also finds a concentration of dysfunctional families here. Their surroundings reflect their status—deteriorated housing in blighted neighborhoods. Most of these areas were in the inner city, some skirted the zone of stagnation, but a few were located in older suburbs.

Elite Enclaves

The poor have the fewest housing alternatives, the wealthy the most. White found that the wealthy were able to insulate themselves from many metropolitan problems, wherever they lived. Most of the elites lived in neighborhoods on the periphery where expensive houses could be built on spacious lots. Many gilded neighborhoods still existed in the central cities of older, larger metropolises.

The Diffused Middle Class

The middle class occupies the largest area of the metropolis. Spatially, this group is concentrated in neighborhoods on the outer edge of the central city extending to the metropolis's fringe. There has been a massive decentralization of business, retailing, and industry to the suburbs in the past fifty years. The social diversity long associated with the central city now describes the suburbs. In the interior sections of the middle-class region, one finds older settled neighborhoods. These neighborhoods are in transition now that the original settlers have raised their children and are either dying off or moving to other dwellings. These older neighborhoods, often adjacent to the central city, are attracting the black middle class. Although African Americans have moved to the suburbs in large numbers in the past decade, they remain highly segregated.

As one moves farther out, one finds the suburban communities inhabited by married couples with small children living in single-family, detached homes, built on spacious lots. The suburbanization of business and industry means that other groups are present too. Working-class families live in more modest neighborhoods, the elderly live in garden apartments and retirement communities, singles in apartment complexes, and ethnics in their own enclaves. A nucleated pattern describes the location of these groups best. In many ways, this settlement pattern dominates the fringe. The term *urban sprawl* describes the low-density development that engulfs more and more of the urban fringe.

Institutional Anchors and Public Sector Controls

Hospitals, universities, research and development centers, industrial parks, business and office centers, corporate headquarters, and other large institutional property holders exert an enormous influence over land-use patterns and residential development. The location of a large mall complex, for example, can shape the growth of an entire side of a metropolis.

Institutional actors and other members of the growth machine can pressure city government to change zoning, lower taxes, and build highways and sewer and water systems. These concessions often benefit special interests, not nearby neighborhoods. Thus, the location of these activities is important in shaping the residential structure of the city.

Epicenters (Edge Cities) and Corridors

After World War II, people moved to the suburbs in unprecedented numbers, but so, too, did business and industry. Today, there is more business and industry in the suburbs than in central cities and rural areas.

One of the most distinguishing features of the evolving metropolis of the twenty-first century is the emergence of epicenters on the periphery of most metropolises. Usually located at the convergence of an outer belt and an axial super highway, epicenters or edge cities provide a range of services that rival the CBD: retailing, professional, and office services, warehousing, and manufacturing.

Corridor development has also become a permanent feature of the emerging metropolis. Highways connecting the central city to the suburbs and beltways are a focus for intensive economic activity. This corridor development has become part of our vocabulary. How often have you heard the term, *beltway bandits*, in reference to the consulting firms along the Washington, D.C., I-495? Silicon Valley near San Jose, Route 128 near Boston, and the Johnson Freeway in Dallas are other examples of corridor development. The residential structure, in turn, is affected because executives and other highly paid workers live nearby in high-status neighborhoods.

This is the White model. It reflects the latticework of high-speed highways built over the past fifty years at government expense that permits the diffusion of population and economic activity to the urban fringe. This transportation system created a new locational calculus, and as a result we have become a suburban nation: More people now live in suburbs than in central cities or rural areas. These technological innovations and federal policies, unforeseen by theorists fifty years ago, have shaped the city. Still, the research by White (1987) and many others show that the city is still a giant sorting device that matches people with an appropriate residential environment. Most important, this sorting takes place in traditional ways. As we see in White's model, the patterns first identified by Burgess and others in the opening years of this century, with modification, still describe the city.

The City Through Different Lenses: Political Economy

In the earlier sections of this chapter we discussed the contributions of Robert Park and other members of the Chicago School to the understanding of the residential structure of the city. Park and his followers saw the city as the end product of ecological processes within a dominance-competition framework. From this perspective, the city is the accumulation of millions of individual decisions. In each decision people pursue their own self-interest, selecting a location that balances their financial resources with the qualities of a place. In Park's view, this impersonal process creates a natural economy of space; in the economists' view, market forces create an efficient distribution of land-uses across the urbanscape.

Violation of the Assumptions of the Classical Models

The problem with the classical schools is they assume a level playing field. They picture a city where there is no interference by government in market operations and a world where social facts like race and ethnicity don't distort the bidding process. More important, they ignore the fact that the free competition for privately owned property only occurs in capitalism, an institution created through a political process. They also ignore the fact that certain groups distort the land-bidding processes for their own ends through political and economic power.

In all fairness to these early theorists, the conditions in their time were closer to the market conditions they assumed in their models. Beginning in the first decades of the twentieth century, a number of political changes violated many of the assumptions of their work. These changes were (1) comprehensive zoning that regulated land uses in cities, (2) the growth of the role of government in providing the city's infrastructure, (3) an increase in the role of the federal government in the operation of the housing market, and (4) urban renewal and redevelopment. These changes moved the allocation of land away from market to political processes.

Zoning

The first comprehensive zoning ordinance was adopted by New York City in 1916, and in the decades that followed, zoning was adopted by almost every city in the United States. At present, Houston is the only major American city without a comprehensive zoning ordinance. In this same decade, Cincinnati adopted the first master plan that not only restricted land use but projected future use of undeveloped land as well. Master plans are also widely used in American cities.

Zoning ordinances change the rules on how land is priced. It freezes parts of the city to a specific land use and in a sense creates monopolistic markets. By creating an artificial scarcity of land of a particular use, land costs rise. Changing a parcel from one land use to another isn't determined by market forces but rather by a political process. Observe the cast of characters at a rezoning hearing sometime. Money speaks. Citizens with economic clout often manipulate the political process to their own ends.

In short, one of the underlying assumptions of the classical models no longer exists. Disinterested market forces no longer determine land prices, local governments do. Planning commissions, rezoning boards, boards of adjustment, city councils, and planning departments are key actors in shaping the form of the metropolis.

Infrastructure

Think of a city without the interstates, water and sewerage systems, schools, universities, police and fire stations, parks, stadiums, and the other facilities and services we take for granted. Consider also the role of government on all levels—local, state, and federal—in creating these facilities.

The connection between these investments and land values is clear. Undeveloped land with utilities is far more valuable than underdeveloped land without them. In this society, we do not tax away the marginal value created by public investments; this money goes to the landowner. Enormous profits can be made if you buy agricultural land with the knowledge that the city is planning to extend services your way. The plot of the movie *Chinatown* and its sequel, *Two Jakes*, explores corruption in Los Angeles and the attempt by members of the growth machine to control public expenditures for private gain. The fiction in movies reflects reality in many cities.

The Federal Role in the Housing Market

To the degree government controls the housing market, it controls the sorting and movement of people within the city. The federal government was involved in the housing market for most of the twentieth century. Its first foray was in the 1930s. During the Great Depression cities faced a housing crisis, and Washington D.C., provided money for public housing. During these same years, the federal government demonstrated the feasibility of thirty-year fixed mortgages.

After the war, housing subsidies were expanded to special groups through financing programs sponsored by the Veterans Administration and Federal Housing Administration. These low-cost home-financing programs along with federal grants for highway and sewer and water systems financed the massive suburbanization process in the 1950s and 1960s. There were other hidden subsidies. The most widely used is the provision in tax laws allowing homeowners to deduct mortgage interest from their federal income taxes.

An invisible hand of the federal government also guides the housing market. The Federal National Mortgage Association (Fannie Mae) and the Government National Mortgage Association (Ginnie Mae) are quasi-government agencies that control the amount of money going into the housing sector. In addition, the Federal Reserve, by controlling interest rates, indirectly controls the cost of housing for millions of Americans.

These benefits are not evenly distributed across our society. They are welfare programs for the middle class. Those who rent—the poor, minorities, recent immigrants, female-headed families, and increasingly the lower middle class—are shut out of these subsidy programs. Subsidies for other groups dwindled in the 1980s. The homeless problem is attributable to the 80 percent reduction in federal programs for low-income housing during the Reagan years. The Clinton administration reinstated some of these programs, but federal housing subsidies for the poor are still far below those of the pre-Reagan years. Therefore, the federal government through its control of housing financing along with its housing programs exerts a powerful influence on the residential structure of the city.

Urban Renewal and Urban Redevelopment

After World War II, this nation faced the most serious housing crisis in its history. During the Great Depression, there was little money for housing construction, and during the war money that would have normally gone into the housing market was diverted to the war effort. In an attempt to solve the mounting urban crisis, Congress passed the Urban Redevelopment Law of 1949. The law allowed cities to create redevelopment authorities with the power of eminent domain to purchase, condemn, demolish, and resell property in blighted neighborhoods. Once large parcels of land were cleared, they were sold to private developers at bargain prices. Developers, in turn, agreed to redevelop the land at higher intensity uses. The rationale was that intensive uses would increase property taxes and eventually repay the subsidy. A provision in the law required that those displaced by redevelopment be provided safe and affordable housing. Since the federal government didn't provide funds for subsidized housing, those displaced were often given a moving allowance and then quickly forgotten.

The abuses by developers and the unintended consequences of urban redevelopment forced the federal government to abandon the program in the 1960s, but by then the self-reinforcing cycle of inner-city neighborhood decline was established. Critics often point to our lack of a coherent urban policy (or for that matter, transportation, energy, housing, education, and population policy) as a major contributor to the problems of our cities.

The federal government's role in city redevelopment has diminished, but decisions by local and state governments still shape the redevelopment of the city. Downtown commercial anchors like stadiums and sports arenas are usually built at government expense. Highway construction, mass transit, and subsidized housing are projects that use government power and money to shape the urban environment.

The City and the Political Economist

Today, few urban sociologists accept the tenets of classical urban ecology. Rather, they believe the allocation of space is the result of political and economic power. Political economists argue that the value of land is not determined by market forces alone, but in markets shaped by political forces like zoning, tax policies, banking regulations, and redevelopment plans. Some of these theorists focus attention on what they call *collective consumption*—government-financed roads, sewers and water systems, schools, office towers, and hospitals. These investments benefit some groups and not others and shape urban residential structure.

Other political economists study the class interests of speculator-developers and the role of large institutions, like banking and lending institutions and government, in shaping the building environment.

David Harvey (1985) presents an alternative approach on residential structure in his book, *The Urbanization of Capital*. In this work, Harvey shows how Baltimore's housing market creates housing submarkets for specific social classes. Class segregation, Harvey argues, leads to the exploitation of these groups by landlords and speculator-developers through monopolistic rents.

Harvey argues that speculator-developers can only profit when they control the market system. He shows how this market has come to represent their interests and not those of consumers. Speculator-developers, therefore, play a crucial role in land-use decisions in a capitalist society. Moreover, the role of this group doesn't occur in a vacuum but in a complex institutional framework involving government and finance. First, there are bureaucratic regulations by federal, state, and local government. From the top, regulations by the Federal Housing Authority and other federal agencies work their way down to the local level. Federal regulations also affect large private institutions like banks and lending institutions, but these organizations also have their own agenda for pursuing profits. Thus, urban submarkets are created by

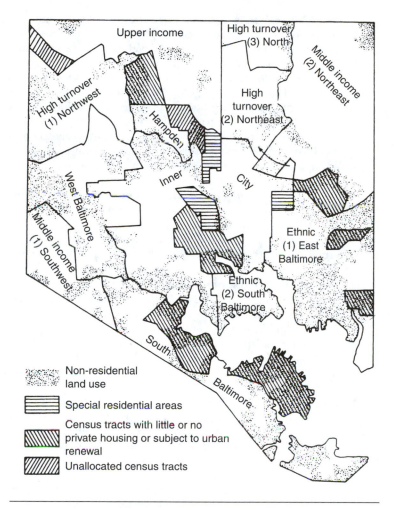

Non-residential land use

Special residential areas

Census tracts with little or no private housing or subject to urban renewal

Unallocated census tracts

Figure 7.4   *The Housing Submarkets of Baltimore City, 1970 (Source: Harvey, David. The Urbanization of Capital: Studies in the History and Theory of Capitalist Urbanization, pp. 73, Fig. 10. © 1985 [Copyright Holder]. Reprinted with permission of The Johns Hopkins University Press.)*

these large public and private institutions, and within this matrix landlords and speculator-developers operate.

Baltimore's submarkets created by the forces identified by Harvey are shown in Figure 7.4. Each submarket houses a specific social class, and according to Harvey this status segregation allows landlords and speculator-developers to exploit these neighborhoods. A description of a few of these submarkets follows.

The ***inner city*** houses low-income and predominantly black renters. In the 1970s, banks would not lend in these markets—a practice called redlining—and most sales were by private loans and cash transactions. There was also little government intervention, and conflict between landlords and tenants was endemic.

White ethnic neighborhoods were stable, housing was affordable, and most people owned their own homes. Most home sales were financed through locally controlled thrifts, and speculator-developers were kept out of the neighborhood. There was little conflict in these neighborhoods.

West Baltimore housed low- and moderate-income blacks. In the 1970s, banks and savings and loan institutions didn't make loans in west Baltimore, and few federally assisted programs operated there. Speculator-developers rose to fill the gap by selling the property they had redeveloped through land contracts. Land contracts are expensive to consumers but profitable to speculator-developers and this financing became a source of conflict. Local residents resented this *black tax* on housing, and under government pressure land contracts were eventually replaced by other financing schemes.

In the 1970s, ***areas of high turnover*** were financed through FHA-insured mortgages. The FHA program along with the enforcement of antidiscrimination laws created a predominantly black, low-income housing market. Speculator-developers manipulated this market to create high turnover and high profits. Government corruption and poorly administered federal programs contributed to the problems in this submarket.

The ***middle-income submarkets*** of northeast and southwest Baltimore were owner-occupied areas of the city with housing financed though conventional bank and S & L loans. During the time of the study, the inner edges of these neighborhoods were undergoing racial change. Banks withdrew their financing, and speculators moved in to exploit the situation. More-affluent submarkets used conventional financing, and their neighborhoods remained stable over the years.

Compare Harvey's map to White's in Figure 7.3 and notice the overlap. The geographical structure of the submarkets in Baltimore around 1970 formed the framework within which individual households made their housing choices. Most people made safe investments and chose already established neighborhoods. What few consumers realized was that the present residential structure represented the accumulated decision making of individuals, groups, and institutions over the preceding centuries.

To Harvey, the creation of urban structure is a continuous process, resulting from the conflicts and struggles of identifiable groups (speculator-developers, landlords, consumers), public and private institutions, and market forces. Urban structure changes slowly, and in the short run it provides a more or less rigid framework in which different groups pursue their class interests. But according to Harvey, there must always be the realization that urban structure is the end product of capital's search for profit. It is a continuous process in which groups compete for scarce space in a city shaped by our capitalist system.

The Postmodern Lens

We are in the midst of a revolution called globalization. We explored this revolution in chapter 2. We showed that this revolution was made possible by the democratization of technology, finance, information, and decision making. These changes lowered the barrier of entry into markets, empowered consumers, shortened the product cycle, and unleashed the creative power of people through free-market capitalism. In the first decade this revolution has created more wealth than at any time in history. It has also created enormous inequality within and among nations, and many critics believe it threatens the integrity of cultures and the environment.

In the United States, corporations have been transformed from national to global entities, the economy has shifted from high-volume to high-value-added production, and human capital has become the nation's most important asset. As part of the global economy it helped to create, the well-being of our citizens is tied to the value they add to products through their talents, skills, and know-how. As the nation leaves its longest economic expansion in history, this transformation has created an unprecedented amount of national wealth, but not all Americans have shared in it. Those who contribute most to the global economy, our nation's symbolic analysts, have watched their standard of living soar, while most Americans, trapped at the margins of the revolution, have watched theirs stagnate and decline.

Global economic change is mirrored in the world's geography. In a global economy, national borders are less important as money, goods, and services move seamlessly around the world. Gone, too, are the traditional functions of the federal, state, and local governments. Some researchers even believe that the character, form, and functions of cities have changed. We presented the new concept of city-state as an example of the metropolitan-wide reorganization that meets the demands of a global economy.

There are several recurring themes in our discussion of globalization. First, there has been a revolution in transportation and communications technology. Second, there has been a shift from high-volume to high-value-added production. (It is also called *post-Fordism flexible production*.) Third, symbolic analysts have gained, but most workers have lost in the new economy. Fourth, this has led to greater class, race, and ethnic polarization (fewer haves and more have-nots). And fifth, globalization is rapidly changing cultures. Many social scientists ask, "With the enormity and speed of this change, have the rules of the land-use game changed? Shouldn't we detect these changes in the cityscape?" The answer is yes, but it is a long and complicated answer. It starts with the changing assumption of the classical theories.

The concentric zone theory described the city as a series of concentric zones. Subsequently, Hoyt and Harrison and Ullman found sectors and multiple nuclei. Regardless of the theory, each is based on a manufacturing technique called *Fordism*, named after the founder of the Ford Motor Company. Fordism is a type of production characterized by large, vertically integrated companies employing mass-production techniques. Companies used new technologies and workplace organization to increase productivity, profits, and the wages of their workers. High wages, in turn, permitted high consumption. Mass marketing and mass consumption of standardized products are a part of Fordism. The height of Fordism in the United States occurred between the 1920s and the 1960s when the United States had the fastest-growing and most highly productive economy in the world. Chicago is a Fordism city. Chicago and the other great cities of the era grew up around one of the nation's great industries. Detroit was the center of the automobile industry, Pittsburgh steel, Akron rubber, and Chicago, the railroad. These cities were also shaped by the same technology. Their transportation systems were dominated by rail, and after World War II increasingly by the automobile. Their communication systems were mail, telephone, and telegraph. Given these limitations, a vibrant center was necessary to coordinate the activities of the metropolis.

And the classic theories reflected this reality: Change at the center sent ripples of land-use changes through the residential, commercial, and industrial areas of the Fordism city (Harvey, 1990).

As Fordism disappeared in the 1970s, a new set of economic arrangements called *post-Fordism* or *flexible production* took its place. (Robert Reich calls it *high-value production*.) This new system of production is characterized by the growth of small firms that produce small numbers of many different kinds of products rather than large numbers of standardized products. Flexible production is based in new, computer-driven technologies that can be quickly adapted to changing demand. This new production system replaced the Fordist assembly line that requires the large production runs of standardized products to be profitable. The term *flexible production* not only refers to this type of manufacturing, but increasingly to the way the entire economy is becoming reorganized. These changes in the nature of production, when combined with the revolutions in cyber, communication, and transportation technologies are restructuring the metropolis. Rather than the center driving the spatial reorganization of the city, the driver is now the periphery. Rather than transportation and communication technology dictating land-use, the superhighway and high-speed, fiber-optic networks have liberated locational decisions (Harvey, 1990).

The LA School's City of the Twenty-First Century

In the 1920s, a group of sociologists came together to study the prototypical city of the Fordism era, and it became known as the Chicago School. During the 1980s, a group of researchers, planners, and advocates came together in southern California to study the prototypical city of the post–Fordism era, and it became known as the Los Angeles School. Just as Chicago became the model for the urban development at the beginning of the twentieth century, members of the Los Angeles School believe that southern California is the urban model for the twenty-first century. The school is decidedly postmodern. Its proponents believe the rate of economic, cultural, social, and urban change represents a clear break with the past. They focus on the restructuring of the metropolis driven by deindustrialization and reindustrialization, the birth of the information economy, the decline of nation-states, the emergence of new nationalism, and the rise of the Pacific Rim. They believe LA is a prototypical city in a globalized, postmodern society. Its spatial order is decentered and decentralized because the underlying assumptions of urban development are different. In the post–Fordism era of flexible production, the use of space is increasingly flexible, disorganized, and eclectic. Whereas zones, sectors, and clusters described the Fordism city, the LA school found a random pattern. They coined the term *Keno Capitalism* to describe the lotto-style character of land-use decisions. This is not to say there is no order to the postmodern city—far from it. New urban forms have appeared in the past thirty years, elements which all U.S. cities share, but ones researchers can see in their clearest form in LA. Descriptions of a few of these new spaces follow (Arvidson, 1999; Dear, 2000; Dear & Flusty, 1998).

Edge Cities

In 1991, a *Washington Post* reporter, Joel Garreau, published an influential book called *Edge Cities*. He based his book on years of travel across the country, and he described what he considered a new urban form found on the fringe of most

American cities. In this chapter's opening vignette we described an edge city, a cluster of commercial, residential, and retail activity anchored by a regional mall located at the intersection of the city's outer belt and a major interstate. Edge cities emerged because of the locational freedom made possible by the city's highway and communication networks. According to Garreau, Los Angeles is the "great-granddaddy of edge cities." In 1991, Garreau found twenty-six edge cities within a five-county area in southern California. Southern California started it all, but in the appendix of his book, Garreau lists the edge cities found on the periphery of every major American metropolis. Edge cities, in turn, have shaped all fringe development leading to the sprawl that many critics feel is the most serious urban problem facing this society. Other parts of the cityscape are affected as well, especially the central business district, which has had to reorganize itself in order to compete with development at the periphery.

Privatopia and the Urban Pod

Robert Kaplan calls them *urban pods*; Michael Dear and Steven Flusty call them *privatopia*. Regardless of the term, they are becoming the dominant residential form in the postmodern city. We all know them. Some of you may have grown up in one. These are the walled and gated communities found on the fringe of most of our cities. These developments tend to be graded by housing type and price, and each development caters to a particular income, occupational group, or family type. They also represent a new political form called *common-interest associations* or *homeowners associations*. These associations have the right to tax, fine, and exclude people from their development. They have grown rapidly in the past forty years. In 1962 there were only 500 of these associations in the United States, by 1992 the number had grown to 150,000. These associations now govern 11 percent of the nation's housing stock, and the lives of 32 million Americans. They are a private, not public, entity—the nation's shadow government. Critics call them undemocratic and anti-community because they are based in exclusion, control, and nonparticipation in the larger community (Dear & Flusty, 1997).

Kaplan (1998) found urban pods in much of the United States. According to Kaplan, they are emerging as a vast conglomeration of mini-fortresses linked by the Internet to other pods across the region and the world. The county is emerging as the political unit of the urban pods—Johnson County (Kansas City), Dade County (Miami), Montgomery County (Washington, D.C.), and Orange County (Los Angeles). Counties, not cities and incorporated places, provide governance for the multitude of unincorporated suburbs in the nation's cities.

Regardless of where these urban pods are located, they share things in common. They are suburban and prosperous. They have good schools and public services. Edge cities provide wonderful shopping. Crime rates are low because *those* people don't live here, and their police aggressively enforce the law. They have sameness. It is the home of our society's most prosperous citizens, who live far removed from the unfortunate classes just a few miles away, in the next city or county.

Cultures of Heteropolis

Germans, Greeks, Swedes, Norwegians, Japanese, Koreans, Chinese, Laotians, Vietnamese, Ethiopians, Nigerians, Kenyans, French, British, Irish, Russians, Italians, Croatians, Poles, Czechs, Hungarians, Cubans, Mexicans, Salvadorans,

Nicaraguans, and the list goes on. This is a glimpse of the ethnic richness of the nation called the United States. No nation in history has accepted as its citizens, albeit sometimes reluctantly, more people from more backgrounds than the United States. As a result, something interesting happened in the 2000 census: Anglo-Americans were no longer the majority population in California. In fact, the census showed an important shift in the ethnic and racial composition of the nation. Hispanic Americans displaced African Americans as our nation's largest minority. More telling was the dramatic increase in the number of Asian Americans. If these trends continue, approximately 25 percent of the U.S. population will be of Hispanic origin by the year 2050. It is clear that the ethnic character of the United States is shifting from Europe to Latin America and the Pacific Rim.

In every city with a sizable ethnic population, one finds evidence of this rich ethnic heritage in the names of the areas in which these groups are segregated: German Town, Pole Town, Little Taipei, China Town, the Barrio, the Ghetto. Even when the ethnic group isn't identified in the name of a neighborhood, certain areas of a city come to be associated with certain groups. But southern California is different in the size and vigor of its ethnic communities, and the underlying cultural dynamics have led to a kaleidoscope of ethnic adaptation fusions. It is reflected in Wolfgang Puck's fusion cuisine, fusion music, and new art forms, as well as in the architecture of the city's neighborhoods. Without dominant Anglo-centric culture dictating urban form, one finds in LA's heteropolises competing architectural styles and neighborhood forms—each urban element reflecting a different voice of the postmodern city (Scott & Soja, 2000).

Dreamscapes

LA's mild Mediterranean climate allowed it to pioneer the architectural dreamscapes. The most famous is Disneyland in Anaheim, California, but Michael Sorkin (1992) in his work, *Variations on a Theme Park*, argues these fictive landscapes dot LA's cityscape. Synthetic stucco and other new building products mean every neighborhood, office building, and retail and commercial development can take on the character of any historical period or architectural style. Low-skill labor can fashion beamed Tudor homes as easily as Craftsman-style bungalows. Dreamscapes have been widely copied across the nation in developments with names like Savanna, Ridgemont Estates, and the Alhambra. The architecture promises a lifestyle seldom realized. Sorkin argues that modern telecommunications technology has rendered the old locational calculus obsolete, and functionally effective, yet architecturally fake dreamscapes have been created randomly across the cityscape. See Photo 7.2.

The Fortified City

One of its negative by-products of the class and ethnic polarization wrought by globalization is a high crime rate. The fortified areas of the central city are a spatial outcome defined by motion detectors; surveillance cameras; private security firms; walled, gated, and guarded communities; bunker-style architecture; and the destruction of public spaces. There is growing evidence that these technological and architectural solutions do little to solve these problems (Scott & Soja, 1996).

Photo 7.2 *The once-standard Chicago School logic has given way to a seemingly haphazard juxtaposition of land-uses scattered across the landscape. New urban forms—edge cities, privatopias, the heteropolis, dreamscapes, fortified cities, and interdictory spaces— have evolved in this new environment. As a result, patterns of zones, sectors, and multiple nuclei are replaced by a random pattern of land-use that is decentered, decentralized, and fringe-, not core-driven. Shown here is the Santa Monica Third Street Promenade, typical of contrived spaces in the postmodern city.* (*Source:* Thomas Mannfred Carlsson.)

Interdictory Space

Michael Dear and Steven Flusty (1997) used the term *interdictory space* to describe the application of modern security technology to the entire city. It doesn't stop with electronic monitoring and surveillance cameras. Electronic and private policing are elegantly combined with physical and psychological barriers to keep unwanted groups out. Fortress-style high rises, heavily guarded apartment complexes and pods, and police profiling and harassment tactics are designed to make certain groups feel unwelcome or out of place. The result is a further fragmentation of the city landscape.

Postmodern Urbanism

There is general agreement that urban growth is increasingly spatially decentralized. These new land-use patterns result from the complex interplay of two-tier labor markets; globalization of capital and production; deindustrialization; technological changes in transportation, communication, and computing; a shift in immigration to Latin America and the Pacific Rim; and the continued pursuit of a consumer-oriented lifestyle. Underlying changes in transportation and communication technology combined with the shift to high-value, flexible production techniques have changed the locational calculus. No longer is a centralized location necessary or desirable. In fact, location across the cityscape is more or less irrelevant. Communications and transportation limitations no longer dictate the close proximity of producers, suppliers, and support activities. The once-standard Chicago School logic has given way to a seemingly haphazard juxtaposition of land uses scattered across the landscape. Large-scale developers now know that the sheer scale of their mega-developments create their own ambience regardless of where they are located. An area's character is less relevant. Small-scale, flexible producers now know that they need low rents near low-cost labor to stay in business. Transportation and communications costs are no longer a factor. Symbolic analysts can just as easily live in an urban pod on the periphery as in the city's center as long as the security and bandwidth are good. Ethnic groups will assimilate as they always have, although the speed and the character of this process will change. The poor will locate as they always have, in what's left over, and the police as in the past will watch and keep them in control. Thus, the LA School's characterization of land-use decisions by Keno Capitalism has a ring of truth (Dear, 2000; Dear & Flusty, 1998). See Figure 7.5.

But are concentric zones, sectors, and multiple nuclei irrelevant in analyzing the city? The answer is no. The land-use decisions of past generations will shape the present and constrain the future cityscape. The pattern of streets and highways, the location of schools, parks, playgrounds, public spaces, buildings, colleges, hospitals, and all the infrastructure underground—water mains, sewers, and electrical and communications conduits—are potent limits on future development. And don't forget the political wildcards like zoning, master plans, and angry citizens' groups. Yes, new urban forms will be built in Chicago, Detroit, or New York, but they will be accommodated within the existing city form, just like the first skyscrapers were a century ago. This nation's suburbanized, modern, industrial metropolises will be transformed into exurbanized, postmodern, service and information cities supported by global capitalism. But it is going to be a long, ongoing process because the new will be accommodated within the old. And just as you walk around the downtowns of all our major cities today and find a nineteenth century brownstone or row house tucked in between two high-rise buildings, you'll find the same thing in the twenty-second century city. And these post-postmodern structures will be built along the same streets laid out one, two, three, or even four centuries earlier.

Summary

This chapter explores the social, economic, and ecological processes that lead to the sorting of groups and individuals into homogeneous subareas of cities. In the first half of the chapter, general theories of location were introduced to illustrate the operation of locational forces.

Of Burgess's concentric zone theory, Hoyt's sector theory, and Harris and Ullman's multiple nuclei theory, the Burgess theory was the first published and

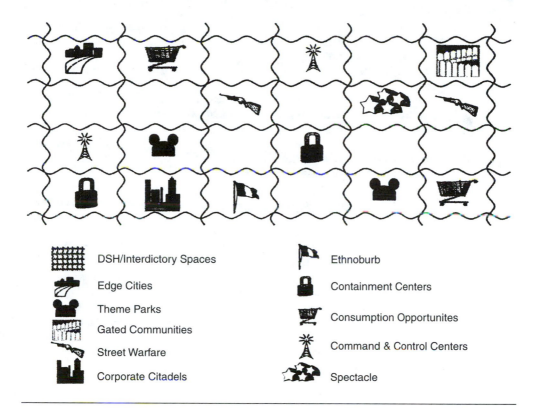

Figure 7.5   *Keno Capitalism: A Model of Postmodern Urban Structure* (*Source*: Dear, Michael, and Steven Flusty. *Postmodern Urbanism.* Annals of the Association of American Geographers, 1998, 88[1], figure 4, p. 66.)

the most controversial. Burgess posits that land uses are distributed into homogeneous concentric zones through impersonal economic forces. Burgess's theory, however, focuses on the types of people who live in each zone; it has a sociological emphasis. Hoyt's theory, in contrast, is based on an analysis of housing rents; it is more empirical than theoretical and asserts that economic groups are distributed across a city in a sectoral pattern. Harris and Ullman's theory places less emphasis on groups and more emphasis on the distribution of business, industry, commerce, and other economic activities.

The Burgess and Hoyt theories are dynamic, stressing the principle that a city must reorganize spatially as it grows. Burgess points to an expanding CBD as the cause of urban change; to Hoyt, both an expanding CBD and a mobile upper class are causes of change. Harris and Ullman's theory, in contrast, is more static, emphasizing present rather than future land-use patterns.

The Burgess theory has come under the greatest scrutiny by students of the city, and the model has been tested in two ways. Some researchers have tried to find the hypothetical zones, and others have analyzed status gradients or the tendency for urban characteristics to change as one moves from downtown to the suburban ring. A test of the models by Michael White from his benchmark work, *American Neighborhoods and Residential Differentiation*, was presented. In general, the study showed physical characteristics of a city, its housing stock, and population density to be symmetrical and oriented around downtown, as predicted by the Burgess model. High-income and status groups live farther from the center than low-income groups, reflecting the importance of distance in the organizational structure of the city. Neighborhoods differed little in the life-cycle characteristics with the exception of household size, which was distributed radially. None of the models predicted the location of racial and ethnic groups well. White found high-status groups, minorities, and the poor segregated from one another in a nucleated pattern. Few patterns were found to be distributed by sectors. In general, distance from the central business district, as described by the Burgess model, is still important in the spatial structure of the American metropolis. The other models fared less well in the analysis.

The city of the past continues to affect the present and shape the future. This is why the physical characteristics of the city still conform to the Burgess model. Social characteristics fit the model less well but are still influenced by the physical city. An alternative to the classical model is presented—Michael White's model of the late twentieth-century metropolis.

A summary of the works of political economists was presented as an alternative lens to seeing the city. Zoning, the role of government in providing the city's infrastructure, the role of the federal government in the operation of the housing market, and urban renewal and redevelopment violate the assumption of the classical theorists. The political economists assume that the allocation of space in the city is the result of political and economic power, not disinterested market forces. A case study on Baltimore by David Harvey was used to demonstrate how housing markets can be manipulated by speculator-developers for their own interests.

The final section presented the postmodern perspective of the Los Angeles School. Through this lens urban growth is seen as increasingly spatially decentered and decentralized. These new land-use patterns result from the complex interplay of two-tier labor markets; globalization of capital and production; deindustrialization; technological changes in transportation, communication, and computing; a shift in immigration to Latin America and the Pacific Rim; and the continued pursuit of a consumer-oriented lifestyle. Underlying changes in transportation and communication technology combined with the shift to high-value, flexible production techniques have changed the locational calculus. No longer is a centralized location necessary or desirable. In fact, location across the cityscape is more or less irrelevant. Communications and transportation limitations no longer dictate the close proximity of producers, suppliers, and support activities. The once-standard Chicago School logic has given way to a seemingly haphazard juxtaposition of land uses scattered across the landscape. New urban forms—edge cities, privatopias, the heteropolis, dreamscapes, fortified cities, and interdictory spaces—have evolved in this new environment. As a result, patterns of zones, sectors, and multiple nuclei are replaced by a random pattern of land use that is decentered, decentralized, and fringe, not core driven. I argue that the past will continue to affect the city of the future, and in the century to come, elements of the classical models will be found in postmodern and post-postmodern cities.

Notes

[1] Chauncey Harris (1998) analyzes the diffusion of the concentric zone, sector, and multiple nuclei models in the academic literature. He discovered 128 citations of his 1945 article and 309 reproductions of the models in books since its original publication in 1945. As late as 1995, there were 20 republications of his work in new textbooks. This analysis doesn't begin to measure the derivative publications based on the classical theories. See the biography for a complete citation of Harris's 1998 work.

[2] For a more detailed discussion of the test of the classical models, see my 1992 book, *The Sociology of Cities.*

8

CHOOSING A PLACE TO LIVE

Introduction

I still remember the closing on our first home. As we pulled into the lot of a non-descript office building, I looked over to my wife and said, "Are you sure you want to go through with this?" We looked at each other, shrugged, got out of the car, and walked into the real estate office. Within a few minutes the office filled up with people, mostly strangers. Sitting directly across from us was the builder. Only the week before, the builder had torn our low-ball offer to shreds and thrown our Realtor out of his home. To the builder's left was his attorney. To our left was our Realtor. At one end of the table was the representative from the bank, and at the other end of the table was the closing agent from the title company.

The closing agent welcomed us and then laid a one-inch thick stack of papers in front of us. The builder and his wife were given a much smaller stack. She said, "I'll give you a few minutes to look these over." My wife and I took a half an hour to read the HUD Settlement Statement, the promissory note, mortgage, survey, flood certification, Federal Truth in Lending Statement, loan payment letter, initial escrow account disclosure, termite clearance form, final inspection addendum, final affidavit on liens, and the agreement for escrowing funds after closing. It was all in legalese, and our Realtor carefully explained each document. The builder and his wife, who had obviously done this before, finished in five minutes and spent the rest of the time sighing and fidgeting. I remember only two numbers, the selling price, which took my breath away, and the due date of our last mortgage payment, fifteen years away.

After reading all the documents, my wife and I looked at each other and said in unison, "Where do we sign?" We must have signed twenty documents. Then reality set in. The banker handed us a check for our loan, asked us to endorse the back, and said he would deposit it in our checking account. He excused himself and left the room. The word *debt* took on new meaning as the door closed. Then the closing agent showed me a figure at the bottom of the sales contract, and said, "Would you please write a check to J & M Builders for this amount?" I had to write the check four times before I finally wrote it correctly. I had never written a check this large before. The builder and his wife signed their papers, took our check, and left the room. Then, I wrote a check to the Realtor to cover his commission. I wrote a check to the title company to cover their costs for the closing. I wrote a check to the bank to cover escrow costs for insurance and property taxes. I wrote another check to the bank to cover the prorated interest on our loan for the month of June. I wrote a check to our lawyer. I wrote a check to cover the tax stamps at the recorder's office. But we left the office proud new homeowners.

Purchasing a new home is the largest investment most Americans make in their lifetimes. And most buyers know that if they make a bad home purchase, it will haunt them for decades. This is why buying a new home is so stressful. You have hopes. You have dreams. You may even think you know what you are getting yourself into. But do you? You are dealing with a cast of professionals: real estate agents and brokers, Realtors, seller's agents, buyer's agents, lawyers, bankers, appraisers, inspectors, abstract searchers, closing agents, and, of course, the sellers. They all know what they are doing, with the possible exception of the sellers, but you don't. You are at a disadvantage in this process.

Deep down you also know the less obvious. You know you are not just buying a house, you are buying neighbors and a neighborhood. You are buying a lifestyle. You are buying into a social network. You are buying schools. You are buying safety. You are buying access to shopping, parks, and entertainment. You are buying access to jobs. You are buying the status associated with your house and your neighborhood. In short, you are just not buying a house, you are buying a bundle of housing services. This is why this decision is so important and why the consequences of this decision are so profound (See Photo 8.1). You have every right to be nervous. And this angst is shared by millions, as mirrored in the self-help books available on buying and selling houses. At my local Barnes and Noble, I found three shelves of books on buying and selling real estate. Here is a sampling of the titles:

Buying a Home on the Internet

Guide to Buying Your First Home

The Complete Idiot's Guide to Buying and Selling a Home

Photo 8.1   *If only choosing a home was this easy. Our decision to move and our search for a new home are two of the most expensive and complex purchases we make in our lifetimes. A mistake can haunt you for years. (Source: © Images.com/CORBIS.)*

The 106 Common Mistakes Homebuyers Make (And How to Avoid Them)

How to Buy the House You Want for the Best Price in Any Market

If You Are Clueless about Buying a Home

Home Buying for Dummies

Mortgages for Dummies

10 Steps to Homeownership: A Workbook for First-Time Buyers

I think the words *idiot, clueless, dummies,* and *mistakes* in the titles sum it all up.

This chapter will explore the how, why, when, and where of housing. We will explore people's decision to move and what factors enter into this decision. We will examine how, why, and where people search for a new home and where they eventually locate. We will discuss the consequences of these decisions on neighborhoods, communities, and society. The next chapter is a house-buying primer. The primer describes the steps in purchasing a house, tips on being a good consumer, and how to uncover information on houses, neighborhoods, and communities using the Internet and other sources.

Why Housing Is Important

North Americans are the most mobile people in the world. In the United States approximately 20 percent of our population, or 50 million people, move every year. The majority of these people move a short distance, only a few blocks or miles, and many of these moves are repeat moves. College students, for example, may move several times in a single year. The poor are often forced to move repeatedly. But these moves add up, and over a five-year period approximately half of our 270 million people will change their residence.

Demographers make a distinction between migration and residential mobility. The criteria used to distinguish between these two terms are complex, but for the purposes of this book, migration refers to a permanent change of residence that is too far to continue commuting to the same job. Residential mobility or intraurban migration is a move that allows commuting to the same job (Clark, 1986). The emotional and financial costs for migration are usually much higher than for residential mobility. The major reason is that you cannot maintain your old social network of friends, kin, and coworkers when you move far away. You must create a new network, which is a long, costly, and stressful process. Most of this chapter will focus on residential mobility.

Housing is a basic human need. How well a society houses its citizens is a litmus test of how well a government provides for its citizens. Since the 1930s, the U.S. government has been involved in the housing market. Over the decades it has expanded its role, and it now provides public housing, subsidized housing for low-income people, and subsidized housing for middle- and upper-income Americans through the mortgage interest income-tax deduction. The federal government also affects the housing market in unseen ways through quasi-public agencies like Fannie Mae and Freddie Mac. These agencies operate in the secondary mortgage market and buy loans from local banks and lenders. The purchase of these loans frees up more capital for loans in these communities. The federal government also supports housing by subsidizing highways and water and sewerage systems though grants and loans. These policies have been remarkably successful. No industrial nation in the world has a higher rate of homeownership than the United States.

Homeownership reached a historical high in 2000 when 67.8 percent of all American households owned their own homes.

Although our nation's rate of homeownership is remarkable, these housing policies have failed millions of Americans. It is estimated that between 400,000 and 2 million Americans are homeless. An additional 15 million households are inadequately housed or saddled with housing costs that exceed half their incomes. A new phenomenon, the middle-class poor, has recently been reported in the national media. These are well-paid professionals who have been priced out of the housing market in expensive, high-growth areas like Silicon Valley. In Silicon Valley some of these people have high-paying jobs during the day, but live in shelters at night.

There are many reasons for these housing problems, but housing professionals have identified two major causes. First, beginning in the early 1980s, federal low-income housing programs were slashed. Although many of these cuts were restored in 1995, the stock of low-income housing has declined by one-third in the past twenty years. Second, during this same period the U.S. government shifted national low-income housing policy from construction to filtering. Filtering is based on the assumption that the best way to provide low-income housing is to subsidize the construction of housing for upper-income groups. The rationale is that as upper-income groups buy new homes, their old homes trickle down to lower-income groups. These policies have not worked for two reasons. First, the poor often inherit housing that is inappropriate for their needs. The house may be too large or located away from jobs. Second, older housing requires more upkeep, and low-income families can ill afford these expenses.

Even with those problems, the federal government's role in promoting homeownership appears to be good public policy for many reasons. First, homeownership means a family is a stakeholder in a community. Homeownership is a potent vaccine toward promoting healthy neighborhoods and communities. If you have a large investment in a house, you are going to protect your investment and your neighborhood. Second, high rates of homeownership are associated with stable communities. Stable communities are associated with effective schools and lower crime rates. Third, homeownership is the major way middle-class Americans create wealth. The mortgage payment most Americans make each month can be thought of as forced savings. Fourth, the building, selling, financing, and furnishing of houses is a major part of our national economy.[1] In 2003, housing construction alone accounted for 4.5 percent of our Gross Development Product (GDP), or $1.9 trillion (U.S. Department of Commerce, Bureau of Economic Analysis, 2004). A healthy housing market means a healthy economy. Finally, an open and dynamic housing market means that people can move to other more prosperous parts of a city. People can find new and better housing. They can find better and more-fulfilling jobs. They can shorten their commute. They can send their kids to better schools. In short, they can find a neighborhood that is a better fit for their lifestyle.

A lot of sociology surrounds residential mobility. How and why people decide to move, how they search for a new home, and where they locate has been of interest to many sociologists. The reasons are straightforward. The process of residential mobility reveals a great deal about a city. The general movement of people from one area to another tells us how well the city is spatially and socially integrated. Social differences between groups are reflected in the spatial distances between the neighborhoods in which they live. High rates of racial segregation, for example, block the free movement of people from one part of the city to another. Thus, changes in the level of segregation in a city may reflect broader changes in society. Put another way, a change in a city's spatial barriers mirrors change in the social barriers between groups. Finally, the free movement of people from one part of a city to another reflects a community's ability to use the skills and talents of its people efficiently.

Residential mobility and the individual decisions surrounding it are the fundamental processes that build cities. The decision by a family to move from one neighborhood to another, whether voluntarily or involuntarily, is unimportant in and of itself. But when this decision is combined with hundreds of similar decisions, the ecological process known as *invasion-succession* occurs. All social science models of city structure, like the Burgess Concentric Zone Model and the Filtering Model, are based on the dynamics of residential mobility (Munro, 1987). Understanding residential mobility gives us a fundamental understanding of the city building process.

Residential mobility also reflects the relationship between individuals and households to their immediate environment—how they perceive it and how they use it. As simple as it may sound, house hunting is shopping behavior—the stakes are just higher. House hunting, as we will see, involves overcoming many practical difficulties. How households manage to overcome these difficulties from time to time gives us an insight into the decision-making process in a complicated market (Munro, 1987).

Why People Move

One way to think of the city is as a giant sorting machine in which individuals and families of different incomes and sizes are matched with the appropriate areas of the city. In many cases, individuals and families have some freedom in choosing the location of their residence and neighborhood.[2] The wealthy have the greatest locational freedom because their wealth allows them to absorb the transportation and housing costs anywhere. As family income declines, so too does locational freedom. The poor have few housing alternatives and the term *slum* refers to those areas of the city inhabited by people with no housing alternatives. Income, however, is not the only factor influencing residential location; race, ethnicity, family size, employment, and lifestyle are other important factors.

Regardless of the family's financial or ethnic status, choosing where to live is one of the most important decisions a family will make. Housing is a major part in every household budget, whether a person rents or owns. The average American spends nearly 40 percent of household income on housing. For the very poor in some parts of the United States, housing costs may represent as much as 75 percent of the household budget. And the house and neighborhood one chooses determine the quality of schools and the environment, one's personal safety, the types and number of friends and neighbors, access to jobs, and availability of parks and recreational areas.

The Decision to Move

Peter Rossi's *Why Families Move* (1955) was the first systematic study of residential mobility. Rossi conducted an exhaustive survey of Philadelphia residents and found that before families moved, they had experienced significant dissatisfaction with their housing conditions that *pushed* them out of the homes. The sources of their dissatisfaction included overcrowding, landlord problems, and neighborhood conditions, as well as the physical condition of the dwelling itself. In studies that followed in different cities other factors were found to be significant, such as a gap between a household's social class and that of their neighbors. The geographer Julian Wolpert (1965) was the first to develop a general theory of how personal, neighborhood, and housing factors interact to influence a family's decision to move. Although Wolpert's work was published nearly forty years ago, it still is relevant today. He showed how personal, neighborhood, and housing factors interact to influence a family's decision to move.

Wolpert's basic argument was that a family's decision to move is a response to a wide range of social, psychological, and economic conditions. First, families over time undergo change, which corresponds with their life cycle. The size of the family first increases and then decreases as children are born and grow to maturity. Divorce or widowhood may also change a family's housing needs. Second, the household's major income earner may experience career and social mobility. In addition, families vary considerably in their emotional attachment to a particular house and neighborhood, and these attachments change over time. These factors can be divided into four basic dimensions for use in the analysis of residential mobility: (1) the family life cycle, (2) social mobility, (3) characteristics of the residence and the neighborhood, and (4) the family's emotional attachment to and participation in the neighborhood. Researchers have found that these factors vary in a systematic way.

Family Life Cycle

In the United States, on average a family will move eight times in its lifetime, and most of these moves will be related to its life cycle. The stages of the family life cycle normally include (1) family-formation, (2) pre-child (constant size), (3) childbearing (increasing size), (4) child-rearing (constant size), (5) child-launching (decreasing size), (6) post-child (constant size), and (7) widowhood (family dissolution) stages. This doesn't describe all households. There are gay households, dual-income no-kids households (DINKS), young urban professionals (yuppies), and people who choose to live alone or live with another person unmarried. Although there are exceptions, the vast majority of Americans marry, and for the majority of these households the family life cycle describes their experiences.

The propensity to move is not constant throughout the life cycle. Researchers have found that younger families in the family-formation and child-rearing stages move more often than families at other stages. The major reason for moving is dissatisfaction with the amount of room in the old dwelling. The birth of a new child or newlyweds living in a spouse's old apartment may overtax the dwelling. Therefore, the decision of a family to move appears to be closely tied to changing space needs. The propensity to move is greatest during those stages of the life cycle when the size of the family is either increasing or decreasing—the family-formation, childbearing, and child-launching stages—and lowest during the child-rearing and post-child stages when family size remains constant. Other factors outside the life cycle—divorce, desertion, death, and remarriage—also influence mobility among family members.

Social Mobility

Researchers have found a close relationship between a family's expectations of upward social mobility and their decision to move. Sometimes a family's decision to move is a strategy for minimizing the social distance between the family and the group to which it belongs or wishes to belong. Sending the kids to the right schools, joining the right clubs, and, of course, moving into the right house in the right neighborhood are well-known strategies for moving up the social hierarchy. Since most Americans die in the social class in which they are born, social mobility probably affects the decision to move far less often than life cycle factors.

Characteristics of the Residence and the Neighborhood

As a city grows, it reorganizes spatially. In some cases subareas of the city undergo a process known as *invasion-succession* where a different land use or population displaces the original residents. Hoover and Vernon (1959) suggested that neighborhoods, like people and families, have a life cycle of five stages—development, transition, downgrading, thinning out, and renewal—corresponding with this transition process. As the neighborhood undergoes the life cycle process, the socioeconomic status of the neighborhood or its ethnic and racial composition may change. The reactions of the current residents of these transitional neighborhoods depend on their view of their new neighbors and their own self-perceptions. If there is a major discrepancy between the two, these changes in the neighborhood will increase the chances that a family will move. "White flight to the suburbs" and "panic selling" are phrases used in the popular press to describe this process.

Attachment to the Neighborhood Environment

The degree of attachment a family has with the immediate residential environment is an important element in the decision to move. Families who interact extensively and intimately with friends and relatives in their neighborhood are less likely to move than families with few attachments. In general, as the family's length of residence in a home increases, their propensity to move decreases. This tendency reflects both increased attachment to neighbors and general satisfaction with the living environment. The converse is also true. Families who have close ties with friends and relatives may decide to move if those people move. Moreover, interaction with neighbors is not always pleasant, and unresolvable conflicts with neighbors may increase the chances that a family will move.

Other factors such as homeownership, ethnic status, and the housing and neighborhood aspirations of families have also been identified as important factors in the decision to move. For example, it is much easier for a renter to move than a homeowner because of the small financial commitment of renters in their housing. Homeowners, in contrast, have a greater stake in what happens to a neighborhood, and homeownership is usually a powerful deterrent to neighborhood deterioration. In addition, ethnic groups commonly have strong "symbolic attachments" to the churches, schools, meeting halls, and other institutions in their subarea. These attachments can be so strong that these people will remain in an area although the structures are declining physically (Gans, 1962a).

Finally, family members may have definite ideas about the ideal home and neighborhood, and the match between the ideal and their actual residence will affect housing satisfaction and the family's propensity to move.

The Decision-Making Process

These four sets of background variables represent the environmental and personal characteristics that influence the decision-making process. The decision-making process begins when an individual (head of household) or family compares his or her personal characteristics (space needs, emotional attachments, etc.) with the characteristics of the residential environment. If they match, there should be a high degree of satisfaction; if not, some degree of dissatisfaction. An individual who is dissatisfied with the residential environment initiates a search for alternatives. The search does not necessarily involve a move, however. Adding a room or finishing an attic may solve a family's space needs. The family may look for housing elsewhere but find that better housing is out of its price range. This search ultimately leads to a decision either to move or stay. If the decision is made to move and nothing else intervenes, the family moves.

An important point made by Wolpert (1965) and others is that dissatisfaction with the residential environment does not cause the move directly; rather, "dissatisfaction initiates a search for more satisfying alternatives and the decision to move is one such alternative" (Bach & Smith, 1977, p. 147). If families can reduce their dissatisfaction by some other means, they are less likely to move.

The Search for a New Home

What happens when a family is dissatisfied with its current residence, has evaluated all its alternatives, and has decided to move? The household at this point must decide the type of dwelling needed and the best location within the metropolitan area. These decisions are not independent of each other. High-rise apartments, for example, are not normally found on the periphery of cities, but are more centrally located. The opposite would be true of single-family dwellings. Other factors such as the family's income, their desire for schools, recreation areas, and shopping, and the dwelling's location in relation to the household's places of employment, are all part of this decision-making process. The final location decision, therefore, is a complex one in which a large number of personal, economic, and urban characteristics must be evaluated. The search process involves matching the characteristics of the family with the characteristics of the available housing. The key variables in this process are summarized in Table 8.1. A short discussion of each of these variable sets follows.

Family Income–Housing Price

Of the four family characteristics listed in Table 8.1, the family's income level is by far the most important. In the final analysis a family's locational decision is tied to its ability to pay both the costs of housing and the costs of transportation. The importance of housing and transportation costs in the decision-making process declines with rising family income. The rich can afford to live any place, and in most instances the poor have few choices. In the past fifty years in the United

Table 8.1   *Factors in the Residential Location Decision*

Individual Characteristics	Housing Characteristics
Income	Price
Stage in life cycle	Type of home
Lifestyle preferences	Neighbors; type of community institutions
Attitudes toward journey to work	Location with respect to place of employment

Source: Adapted from Phillip H. Rees. 1970. Concepts of Social Space. In *Geographic Perspectives on Urban Systems*, edited by B. J. L. Berry and J. Horton. Englewood, Cliffs, N.J.: Prentice Hall, p. 313.

States and Canada, however, locational freedom has increased significantly for most income groupings as the automobile became the dominant form of transportation. In the past, the location of the working class, for example, was restricted to those areas of the city accessible to industry either by foot or mass transit. Since World War II, many industries have located on the periphery of cities. This trend, combined with the widespread use of the automobile, has extended the areas of possible location for the working person to almost the entire metropolis. The families with the fewest location choices are those who cannot afford to purchase and operate an automobile (the poor and the old). The location of these people is constrained by the availability of mass transit, a system that is of poor quality in most American cities.

The Role of Lending Institutions

Another important link between family income and housing is banking and lending institutions. These institutions analyze a family's income and credit history and determine the total amount they will lend. These institutions also play a crucial role in determining where a family may locate. In the past, the practice of redlining, where lending institutions refused to lend money to prospective buyers in certain parts of a city, eliminated those areas as locational alternatives. Although this practice is now illegal and bank-lending patterns are now scrutinized by the Federal Reserve, the practice of steering has replaced it. Lenders, by manipulating interest rates and terms of a loan, make purchasing a home in one part of a community more appealing than in others. Therefore, the availability and amount of mortgage money, as well as where these monies are likely to be lent, limit the housing alternatives for many families.

Stage of the Life Cycle Related to Housing Type

The stage of the family in its life cycle determines not only the type of family dwelling but also its size. Young couples in the family-formation stage may desire an apartment or duplex. Families in the child-producing and child-rearing stages will probably prefer single-family dwellings with yards for children. Couples in the child-launching and post-child stages may desire a smaller home or an apartment.

At each stage, families need different types of housing, and these housing types are often found in different parts of the city. Housing type and size, combined with the price range that a family can afford to pay, limit the areas where the search will take place.

Lifestyle–Neighborhood Preference

The predominance of single-family dwellings on spacious lots in the suburban ring provides a physical environment conducive to raising children—the lifestyle called *familism*. In the central city, however, the diversity of housing and neighborhood types provides physical environments that can support a more varied number of lifestyles. Gans (1962b), in his article "Urbanism and Suburbanism as Ways of Life," describes some of the types of residents found in the central city. They include cosmopolites, the unmarried or childless, the deprived, the trapped, and the ethnic villagers. A new lifestyle called the *digital nomad* has recently emerged. Each category is associated with a distinctive lifestyle; people with different lifestyles inhabit specific types of housing in different parts of the central city.

Cosmopolites

The cosmopolites include students, artists, writers, musicians, actors, and members of the professions. They live in the centralcity because they want to be near the specialized cultural facilities found there. The majority are unmarried or childless, but those couples who do have children are often absentee parents, delegating much of the responsibility for raising their children to sitters or preschools. In general this lifestyle is incompatible with familism, and an attempt to live in the suburban ring by a cosmopolite will often be of short duration.

The Unmarried or Childless

The unmarried and childless in the past were in a transitional stage of their life, enjoying the urban core until they married or had children. Today, for millions of Americans this is no longer a transitional stage but a chosen lifestyle, which is in many respects similar to that of cosmopolites. The major difference between cosmopolites and this group is that the unmarried and childless are young white-collar workers, many of whom initially moved into an apartment to escape parental supervision. They normally locate within easy access to their place of employment and the city's entertainment facilities at the city's center. People in this group who enter the family-formation and child-producing stages of the life cycle normally return to the suburbs.

Ethnic Villagers

Ethnic villagers also live in the central city by choice. The forces of tradition and kinship tie the members of these groups to their old neighborhoods. Their concentration in these areas permits them to support neighborhood schools, churches, fraternal organizations, and stores, and these institutions in turn permit this group to maintain its language, culture, and group structure.

The Deprived and Trapped

Unlike the cosmopolites, unmarried and childless, and ethnic villagers, the deprived and the trapped live in the central city of necessity. The deprived are the very poor, the mentally ill, and the physically handicapped. In the United States, the majority are nonwhite. Through the years, discrimination has limited their locational alternatives to specified parts of the city. A high proportion of this group are ghettoized in low-income areas. The transient live in flophouses in skid row areas or, if their income permits, in the city's rooming-house district. A trip to the downtown of any major city reminds one of the thousands of homeless that live in the alleys, doorways, and abandoned buildings of our central cities. In general, the deprived have few housing alternatives and live in the least-desirable areas of the city.

The trapped, in contrast, are victims of change. In most cases they are elderly people who have raised their children and have lived most of their lives in the same neighborhood. When the area undergoes the invasion-succession process, they stay in the neighborhood either because of a deep sentimental attachment or because they are too poor to move.

The Urban Homesteader

Urban homesteaders are people who have traditionally lived in the suburbs but who have opted for a home in the central city because of unusual housing opportunity. They are predominantly middle class. In many cases, they are willing to assume the risk of restoring an older house in a rundown neighborhood because it is the only kind they can afford to buy. Their efforts have led to the remarkable revitalization of older neighborhoods in Washington, D.C.; Columbus, Ohio; Minneapolis, Minnesota; and other American cities. As more and more central cities become revitalized, urban homesteaders will continue to be an important element in the ecology of central cities (London & Palen, 1984).

Digital Nomads

For less than $2,000, a person can create a home office that includes a state-of-the-art computer, a color monitor, and a combination color printer/copier/fax/scanner. For an additional $500, the desktop machine can be replaced with a notebook computer. Powerful portable computing combined with the revolution in wireless communication has fundamentally changed the nature of work. A notebook computer with wireless capabilities means your office can be anywhere you are. In 1996 for the first time in history, more information was available in electronic rather than printed form. With the Internet, an executive now has access to all the records of his or her company anywhere in the world (Makimoto & Manners, 1997).

This revolution in communication, computing, and information technologies has created the lifestyle called the *digital nomad*. Since English is the language of this realm, digital nomads are citizens of the world—people without nations. People with skills that are in such high demand around the world can live in the United States one year, Saudi Arabia the next, and Brazil the next.

Globe-trotting techies and consultants are one manifestation of this revolution, but the home-bound entrepreneur is a more common lifestyle. People with technical prowess have high incomes, and high incomes give these people the ability to live anywhere. One-half of the growth in the nation's GDP is the result of high technology. Susan E. Clarke and Gary L. Gaile in *The Work of Cities* (1998) describe the strategies the nation's communities are using to attract high-technology firms and the digital nomads. Of the 103 cities included in their study, the researchers found that 82 of these communities were active in recruiting and keeping these high-tech firms. In most cases, these activities included multimillion-dollar investments in high-speed fiber-optic systems and similar technologies. They have also made investments in their infrastructures that affected quality of life, such as investments in schools, downtown entertainment centers, parks, and recreation.

Lifestyle preferences, therefore, have considerable influence on the locational decision. The lifestyle of ethnic villagers would be impossible without the infrastructure provided by neighborhood facilities. The lifestyles of the cosmopolites and the unmarried and childless require easy access to the cultural and entertainment facilities of the central city as well as a high degree of personal freedom. Only the high-rise or the apartment complex in the central city provides the anonymity and freedom necessary for these lifestyles. The familism lifestyle is not suited to these conditions. Parents raising children in high-rise apartments find it difficult to supervise their youngsters and to exert the degree of social control needed for their socialization. Cosmopolites would be stifled by the neighboring obligations of the suburban ring. Digital nomads could not work without high-speed Internet access. Lifestyle preferences, therefore, reduce the areas in which the housing search takes place.

Attitudes Toward the Journey to Work

This final category of factors influencing the search for a home is probably the most idiosyncratic. In the past this aspect of the locational decision has been based largely on the time needed for the major earner in the household to journey to work. The rise in car ownership and the growth of the urban fringe have combined to make commuting a nightmare in many cities. The increased number of road rage incidents supports the time and psychological strain of long commutes. Commuting times continue to rise in the United States, and people are beginning to more carefully assess the true costs of transportation in terms of both time and money.

The computing and telecommunications revolution, however, has profoundly changed the relationship between location and transportation costs. Although society is in the early stages of this revolution, telecommuting is one of the less-visible changes. In Washington, D.C., for example, an estimated 20 percent of the federal workforce now telecommutes. Many workers travel to their agency's headquarters only one or two times per week for face-to-face meetings with their colleagues. The federal government has pursued other telecommuting strategies as well through the creation of interagency suburban work centers. These centers are usually one floor of an existing office building that has been divided into dozens of Dilbert-style cubicles. The cubicles are spartanly furnished with a computer and basic office supplies. Telecommuters reserve a cubicle every week or two to complete work that needs access to classified computer files. These workers may never visit their agency's headquarters in the District of Columbia.

Similar changes are occurring in the private sector. Ernst and Young, one of the nation's *big four* accounting firms, is a good example. Their consultants are issued high-end notebook computers when they join the firm. Since their consultants work in their clients' offices most of the time, they only provide one desk for every two employees at their home office in Chicago. The firm slashes overhead, clients are happy having an on-site accountant, and the employee has greater locational freedom in choosing a home. This revolution and the changes in the realm of work will profoundly affect lifestyles and the shape and character of the metropolis in decades to come.

Where Does the Search Take Place?

The search process involves the matching of the individual or family with housing of the appropriate type and size in an area of the city conducive to the household's lifestyle. The search process does not include the entire city, only certain well-defined areas delineated by income constraints, housing preferences, neighborhood characteristics, and geographic location. Information on these alternative areas is extremely important to the search process. People in large cities ordinarily have a general knowledge of the social status and ethnic and racial characteristics of different subareas of the city. However, in the process of constructing a mental map of a city, people do an enormous amount of stereotyping. Large areas of the city with which the individual is unfamiliar may be classified inaccurately as slum, ethnic, or rich. These mental maps, if shared by a great many people, can have unintended consequences for a neighborhood. For example, a racial incident in a neighborhood school reported in the city's newspapers may lead prospective home buyers to avoid an area although the incident may have been minor. Self-fulfilling prophecies can occur if large numbers of the city's residents share similar distortions in their mental maps. Therefore, the final choice of a house may not be the best location for the household but the one perceived as the best alternative in the areas searched. The areas searched in turn depend on the information available.

Sources of Information

Once a household decides to move, the household begins the search process. This search is primarily an information-gathering activity. Interestingly, Rossi (1955) found that the sources of information on which the search process was based were quite varied. More than one-half of his Philadelphia sample of households found their new home through personal contacts, one-fourth found housing by "windfall" or accident, and about one-fifth found it by riding around in a car.

The use of acquaintances suggests the parochial nature of the housing search. The social network of the average household is limited in a patterned way in the city. People of similar social class, race, and ethnicity tend to be delimited spatially in the city. The result is a distinct sectoral bias in the interaction and travel patterns of the average city dweller. In even a moderately large city, an urbanite living on the east side of town knows little about the residential areas, shopping, and schools on the west side. People tend disproportionately to associate with others living in the same sector of the city as themselves (Simmons, 1974). The slang word *GUD*, for a "geographically undesirable date," used by young single males in large metropolitan areas reflects the spatial bias in dating. As a result spatial choice is limited by the sectoral activity space of the potential migrant (Johnson, 1981). Simply, the household bent on moving is likely to remain within the same general area of the city. There are two basic reasons for this: (1) Most of the personal information about other neighborhoods comes from people living in the same general area, and (2) people perceive the sectoral pattern of segregation in the urban area, and they judge their own sector to be suitable to their social requirements (LaGory & Pipkin, 1981).

Regardless of the source of information, distortions and biases are inevitable. The most important distortions are those of income and race. In the final analysis, residential relocation is a search for a house of a certain type in an affordable price range, but this search also includes a strategy for finding a neighborhood that minimizes the physical distance between the members of the household and the income, racial, and ethnic group to which it belongs. This is especially true of race. Although federal and state laws outlaw discrimination in the sale and rental of housing, the United States remains one of the most highly segregated nations in the world. In general, whites avoid neighborhoods inhabited by blacks or areas undergoing racial transition. Whether by the restrictions placed on housing by its price or by prejudicial attitudes and discrimination, African American and other minorities have fewer housing alternatives than other groups. The search process carried out by members of these minority groups normally takes place in those areas deemed acceptable by the dominant group in the larger society.

The Search Process

The residential location decision process is graphically shown in Figure 8.1. The individual or family occupies a position in social space determined by the household's economic and family status, point S. The stage of the household in the family life cycle and the occupation, education, and income of the head of the household are the determining factors. In Figure 8.1, a household located in social space at point S might be headed by a salesperson with some high school education and average income; it might also be the household of a single person or couple in the family-formation (childless) stage of the life cycle. This household would be matched with a dwelling located in a parallel position in housing space, H. In this case, the corresponding housing would be a medium-density, low-rise apartment of average rent. The position of this dwelling in a neighborhood can be described by the social- and family-status characteristics of all the neighborhoods in the city. In this case, the household is located in community space at the position C. Finally, from the analysis of the general models of urban geometry, the location of these subareas would resemble the fourth figure in Figure 8.1 (Rees, 1970). Family-status characteristics are distributed by concentric zones, economic-status characteristics by sectors. The physical location of this household would represent a compromise between price and lifestyle. Because familism is low, the dwelling could be centrally located. The price range would place it in a middle-income sector of the city. An examination of the available alternatives would lead to the final decision to locate in dwelling 3 at point L.

To some of you the literature on the search for a new home may seem far removed from your own experiences. In the following chapter we apply these findings to the experiences of two couples, Mike and Elizabeth and Anne and Bill, all former students of the author.

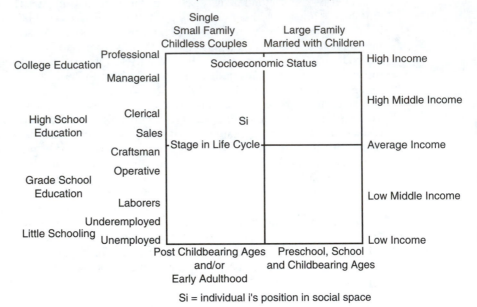

SOCIAL SPACE
(Units: Individual or Families)

Single
Small Family   Large Family
Childless Couples   Married with Children

College Education Professional   Socioeconomic Status   High Income

Managerial

High Middle Income

High School   Clerical   Si
Education
Sales   Average Income
Craftsman   Stage in Life Cycle

Operative
Grade School
Education   Low Middle Income

Laborers

Underemployed
Little Schooling Unemployed   Low Income

Post Childbearing Ages   Preschool, School
and/or   and Childbearing Ages
Early Adulthood

Si = individual i's position in social space

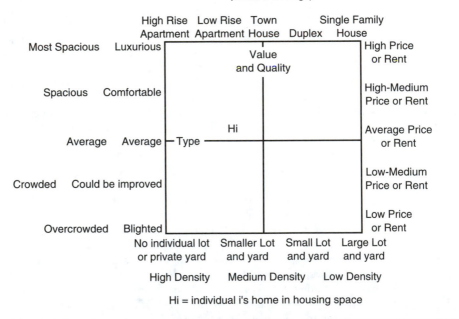

HOUSING SPACE
(Units: Dwellings)

High Rise   Low Rise   Town   Single Family
Apartment Apartment House   Duplex   House

Most Spacious   Luxurious   Value   High Price
and Quality   or Rent

High-Medium
Spacious   Comfortable   Price or Rent

Hi   Average Price
Average   Average Type   or Rent

Low-Medium
Crowded   Could be improved   Price or Rent

Low Price
Overcrowded   Blighted   or Rent

No individual lot   Smaller Lot   Small Lot   Large Lot
or private yard   and yard   and yard   and yard

High Density   Medium Density   Low Density

Hi = individual i's home in housing space

Figure 8.1 *The Residential Location Decision Process* (*Source*: P. H. Rees. 1970. Concepts of
Social Space. In *Geographic Perspectives on Urban Systems*, edited by B. Berry and
J. Horton. Englewood Cliffs, NY: Prentice Hall, p. 313.)

COMMUNITY SPACE
(Units: Tracts or Larger Sub-areas)

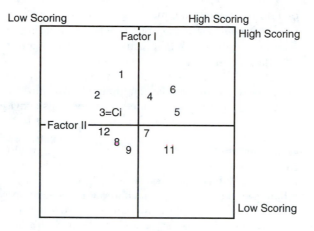

Ci = the community in which i's home is located

LOCATIONAL OR PHYSICAL SPACE
(Units: Tracts or Larger Sub-areas)

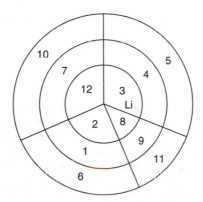

Li = the zone in which the community in which i's home is located

Figure 8.1 *Continued*

Summary

This chapter explores the how, why, when, and where of housing. The purchase of a home is one of the most important decisions a household makes because it is not just buying a structure, but a bundle of housing services. Where you live determines how you live. Where you live also determines the schools your children will attend and your access to a whole range of services.

Housing is also important to society, and it is one measure of how well a society provides for its people. The federal government was involved in the housing market for most of the twentieth century. This activity appears to be good public policy because homeownership means a family is a stakeholder in a community, and high rates of homeownership are associated with stable communities with low crime rates and good schools. Homeownership is also the major way middle-class Americans accumulate wealth, and housing is an important part of the nation's economy. A great deal of sociology focuses on residential mobility. Knowing where people live tells us much about the society in which cities exist. Residential mobility is also one of the fundamental processes in city building.

The decision to move and the search for a new home are complicated processes involving a wide range of factors that can be analyzed in terms of family life cycle, social mobility, characteristics of the residence and neighborhood, and neighborhood attachment. In general, incongruency between the personal characteristics of an individual and the characteristics of his or her residential environment cause dissatisfaction. Dissatisfaction with the residential environment does not cause the move directly, but initiates a search for more satisfying alternatives. The decision to move is one such alternative.

If the individual or family decides to move, factors influencing the decision include income, stage in the life cycle, lifestyle, and attitudes toward the journey to work. The search process involves the matching of these individual or family characteristics with an appropriate subarea of the city. The individual, however, has only limited information on the neighborhoods in the city, and this information is biased. As a result, the location finally chosen is normally not the best alternative, but the best of the sites visited.

Each individual decision, when combined with millions of others, leads to the emergence of homogeneous areas of the city—areas that when ranked on economic, family, and ethnic status are distributed in a pattern described by the models of urban structure discussed in chapter 7.

Notes

[1] In 2003 the Gross Development Product (GDP) for the United States was $11.1 trillion, and personal consumption accounted for $7.4 trillion of this figure. Out of personal consumption, Americans spent $400 billion on household equipment and furniture, $1.1 trillion on household services, and $396 billion on household operations—electricity, gas, water, and other household operations. Residential construction in 2003, when seasonally adjusted, totaled $1.9 trillion. New single-family home construction in 2003 was an estimated 1,514,000 units. Housing costs grew in the decade ending in 2003. The sales price of a new home in 2003 was $197,600. As you can see, the housing sector

is an extremely important part of the national economy. A healthy housing sector means a healthy U.S. economy (U.S. Department of Commerce, Bureau of Economic Analysis, 2004).

[2] This section is based on the following work of the author William A. Schwab. *Urban Sociology: A Human Ecological Perspective*. Boston: Addison-Wesley Publishing Co., 1982, Chapter 7, "The Use of Space Within Urban Areas."

9

A HOME-BUYING PRIMER: WHEN THEORY MEETS THE ROAD

A First Case Study: Mike and Elizabeth

Mike and Elizabeth have been married for three years. Mike graduated in May before their marriage, and Elizabeth completed her degree the following December. Mike is an elementary schoolteacher, and Elizabeth has a good job with a large computer company. With raises over the past three years, Mike makes $25,625 per year. Elizabeth's computer science degree has paid off, and with raises and bonuses over the past three years, her income is now $48,441. They are a responsible young couple and have tried to live off of Elizabeth's salary and save Mike's, but it hasn't been easy. With rent, student loan payments, two car payments, and the purchase of furniture, they have had to dip into savings from time to time. But they have nearly $25,000 in their savings account.

They live in a townhouse complex. Most tenants are young couples like them, but mixed in here and there are college students. Unfortunately, two of them, Aaron and Rod, live next door. They aren't around much during the week, because they go to school and work, but weekends are hell. Mike and Elizabeth have tried to be good neighbors. They went next door after a particularly noisy night last fall to clear the air. It didn't work. Since then there have been regular phone calls to the apartment manager and the police have shut down parties by 1:00 A.M. The mere presence of these two on the other side of a wall has been a constant irritant. Elizabeth wants everyone to like her and finds Aaron's and Rod's stares when they meet in the parking lot stressful. They have decided to stay because the rent is cheap, the complex is safe, the townhouse is close to both of their jobs, and they like most of their neighbors. In fact, George and Rosemary, the tenants on the other side, are their best friends.

Things changed this past August with a blue tip on the end of a home pregnancy test. They weren't planning on having a child this early in their careers, but it raises all kinds of questions. Can Elizabeth quit her job and become a full-time mom? Would it be better if Mike stayed at home with the baby and Elizabeth worked since she makes twice the money? If they can't afford to live off of one income, what about child care? Can they raise a child in a two-bedroom townhouse? Would it be worth staying where they are just so their baby could keep the two yahoos next door awake all night? They decide it's time to move and buy their first home. The only way to buy a house is for both of them to work. The other decisions will have to fall in place.

Mike and Elizabeth's problems are similar to many young couples. See Photo 9.1. Although their decisions are deeply personal, they share similar ones with millions of other Americans. Buying a new home is similar to other buying behaviors, but it is a far more complex process. Following are the steps in buying a home. Let's follow Mike and Elizabeth through their search.

1. Make the decision to move
2. Make a decision to buy or rent
3. Figure out how much you can afford
4. Decide what kind of home you want
5. Decide what kind of neighborhood you want
6. Prequalify or preapprove a loan
7. Decide if you should use a real estate agent
8. Find an appropriate neighborhood
9. Begin house hunting
10. Inspect houses
11. Make offer
12. Apply for a mortgage
13. Have a professional inspection
14. Close the transaction
15. Move in

Photo 9.1 *Mike and Elizabeth. Their son Will was born two months after the move.* (*Source*: Photo by the author.)

1. Make the Decision to Move

We know from Rossi's (1955) famous work, *Why Families Move*, that families move because of push-and-pull factors. They are either pushed out of their home by the condition of the house or the neighborhood or they are pulled from the house because of a new job or a new house and neighborhood that better meets their needs. As we showed earlier in chapter 8, these factors can be summarized into four categories: changes in the family life cycle, social mobility, changes in the neighborhood or residence, and attachment to the neighborhood. What factors are at work in Mike and Elizabeth's case? The most obvious is Mike and Elizabeth have entered the childbearing stage of the life cycle. The prospect of raising a child in a two-bedroom townhouse is daunting, especially with the college students next door. The couple's social status hasn't changed and neither has the neighborhood—it's still a townhouse complex with no playgrounds or green space. They still have attachments to the area. Their best friends live next door. It's convenient to their jobs and shopping. It's safe. It's a known quantity. But the lure of a home of their own with a spacious lot is a strong pull factor. It's something that they have been saving for for the past three years. After talking it over for several weeks, Mike and Elizabeth decide it's time to move.

2. Make a Decision to Buy or Rent

There are lots of reasons not to buy a home. First, there are a myriad of lifestyles, and some lifestyles are found only in parts of a city that cater to renters. Second, if you are likely to move out of the area in the next two or three years, the moving and front-end costs of buying a home make it a bad financial decision. Third, if you are in a declining real estate market, renting is the best option. Fourth, if you don't have job security, homeownership could be risky. Fifth, if you don't want to fool with home maintenance, you shouldn't own. Most experts agree that you should plan on spending 1 percent of the value of your home on maintenance each year. On a $125,000 home, that comes to $1,250 per year. This does not include regular maintenance like mowing the lawn, raking leaves, cleaning gutters, washing windows, changing light bulbs, and fixing the little things that go wrong with any house. It does include the big-ticket items, and household equipment does fail in predictable ways. For example, roofs last fifteen to twenty years. Houses have to be repainted every ten years. Refrigerators, dishwashers, dryers, and water heaters last between twelve and fifteen years. Furnaces and central air conditioning have a life span of twenty years. So if you don't want to deal with all these things, rent, and let a landlord take care of them.

There are an equally large number of reasons to own. First, it is an investment. Homeownership is forced savings. It is the major way middle-class Americans accumulate wealth. The monthly payment has two parts, principal and interest. You can think of the payment on the principal of your loan as savings you can tap into with a home equity loan if the need arises. You can think of the payment of interest as rent. You have to live someplace, and the federal government helps you out with this rent by allowing you to deduct this interest on your federal taxes.

Second, there are strong cultural reasons to own. The American Dream is closely tied to homeownership, and this cultural value has been translated by lawmakers into public policy. When the economy is robust and interest rates are low, homeownership becomes affordable for more Americans. This has been especially true in the past decade as homeownership has become affordable for more Americans than at any other time in our history; African Americans and Hispanic Americans have particularly benefited from this trend (Fannie Mae Foundation, 2003).

Third, homeownership integrates you into the social fabric of a community. You become a stakeholder in a community. You and your neighbors have a vested interest in protecting your investment. There is rootedness associated with home-ownership. This benefits both residents and the community.

Fourth, homeownership guarantees access to a whole array of social services, especially schools. Although federal courts have changed attendance boundaries, the neighborhood you live in usually determines the school your children attend. Crime rates are usually lower in owner-occupied areas of the city as well. Factors such as access to jobs, shopping, and recreation are tied to your neighborhood.

Fifth, homeownership is intricately tied to lifestyle. Whether it be families with small children, yuppies, or retirees, neighborhoods are age and lifestyle graded. How you live is tied to where you live. The area of residence, if well chosen, should provide significant support for the lifestyle you have chosen.

So what about Mike and Elizabeth? They are entering into their childbearing years. They want a secure environment in which to raise their new baby. They want neighbors that share their lifestyle and eventually playmates for their child. They want good schools. They want safe streets, and they want roots. They don't plan on leaving their hometown anytime soon. They have secure jobs with a good income. The decision is clear; they will buy.

Just because this decision was easy for Mike and Elizabeth, the decision for others may not be as easy. Mike and Elizabeth have an annual family income above the national average. A couple with an average income might not have the option to buy. Similarly, a couple who has chosen a different lifestyle may not face factors conducive to buying. They may decide to move but rent in another area of town.

3. Figure Out How Much You Can Afford

Many factors go into the decision on how much you can afford. In the past, the rule of thumb was that you shouldn't pay more than 20 percent of your gross monthly income or 25 percent of your net monthly income for housing. Those were the good old days when housing costs made up a smaller portion of a family's budget. The median cost of a new single-family dwelling in 2003 was $197,600 (U.S. Commerce Dept., 2004). The average American household spent 38 percent of their gross income on housing in this same year.

To give you an idea of how much you can afford for housing, I have repro-duced in Table 9.1 a homebuyer worksheet used by banks, savings & loans, and real estate firms. The worksheet gives you a ballpark idea of how much you can afford. Let's look at Mike and Elizabeth's finances.

They have an annual gross income of $75,036, or a gross monthly income of $6,253. The rule of thumb used by banks is that long-term financial obligations should not exceed 38 percent of a family's monthly income, or in Mike and Elizabeth's case, $2,376. Line 4 is important because it reflects past and future finan-cial obligations. Mike and Elizabeth have student loans totaling $280 per month and

Table 9.1   *Home Buying Worksheet for Elizabeth and Mike*

1. Gross Annual Income (before taxes)	$75,036
2. Gross Monthly Income Line 1 divided by 12 months	$6,253
3. Monthly Allowable Housing Expense and Long-Term Obligations Line 2 multiplied by .38	$2,376
4. Monthly Allowable Housing Expense Line 3 minus monthly obligations—credit cards, child support, car loan, etc.	($654) $1,722
5. Monthly Principal and Interest Payment Line 4 multiplied by .80	$1,378
6. Estimated Mortgage Amount Line 5 divided by 7.34 multiplied by $1,000*	$187,740
7. Estimated Affordable Price Line 6 divided by .90 (90% is the mortgage loan amount, assuming a 10% down payment. Use .80 for a 20% down payment.)	$208,600

Source: The table is based on general guidelines found in the buyers' guides provided by most banks and real estate firms.

*This is the interest rate factor for an 8% loan. For the rate factor for other interest rates see www.bankrate.com.

two car loans (one car will be paid off in a few months) leaving a $374 payment for a total of $654 of long-term obligations. They pay cash and have no credit card debt. This leaves $1,722 ($2,376 − $654) for monthly housing expenses.

Monthly housing expenses cover a lot of ground. You have the principal and interest on the loan, plus insurance, taxes, homeowners association dues, and other fixed costs. Usually banks take 80 percent of the allowable housing expense figure (.80 × $1,722) or $1,378 to cover principal and interest. Assuming that Mike and Elizabeth get an 8 percent fixed thirty-year mortgage, and the bank permits them to put up a 10 percent down payment, they can look for housing at around $208,600.[1] They can borrow $187,740. But this would wipe out most of their savings, and they still need money to move and to furnish their new home. They also have a child on the way, and child-care expenses will average $500 per month. They don't want to be house poor so they decide not to have a mortgage that exceeds $1,100 per month. This limit means they can borrow no more than $150,000, and with a 10 percent down payment, they can look for a home in the $166,000 range.

Worksheets like the one presented in Table 9.1 are helpful, but potential home buyers should not stop here. The numbers in the column mask a lot of family financial history, and a realistic appraisal of their financial health should guide their financial decisions. First, the gross income figure. How secure are their jobs? Mike and Elizabeth are in the early stages of their careers and have to ask themselves, "Will our incomes rise?" Mike's probably won't; Elizabeth has a much rosier income future. Note their modest level of debt. Few Americans carry no credit card or installment debt. Note the interest rate and years in the loan. The monthly payment on a fifteen-year mortgage at the same interest rate is only around $150 more per month. Why not a ten-year mortgage? Why only 10 percent down? Can they get some help from their parents to raise their down payment to 20 percent? Would another financial strategy work? Why not put down as little as possible, and invest their money in the booming stock market? Do they have a blemish on their credit history? If they do, the bank may want a higher down payment and may approve only a smaller loan. These and other facts must be factored into this decision. In its final analysis the lender will decide how much Mike and Elizabeth can afford, but if Mike and Elizabeth come up with a more conservative estimate, they should stick with that.

4. Decide What Kind of Home You Want

Do your tastes run toward neoclassical, federal style, cape cod, ranch, or contemporary? How many bedrooms will you need? Do you want a master bedroom suite away from the kids? How many baths? Do you like to cook? Do you entertain often? Do you want a formal living room? A formal dining room? Do you like to garden and landscape? Do you have lots of stuff to store? Will you need a basement? A two-car garage? What things do you really want in a home? It's time to make a wish list. But you'll have to make some hard choices later when your wishes clash with reality.

Questions about location are also crucial. Housing, location, and lifestyle are closely linked. Do you want to live in an urban, suburban, or rural area? A house in the central city may give you greater access to jobs, shopping, museums, concerts, restaurants, clubs, and universities. Central cities usually have mass transit, so you'll have less dependence on a car. But if you want a new house, you may need to look elsewhere. Houses in the central city are usually older and smaller and seldom have large yards. Crime rates are often higher in central cities. Pollution may be a problem. Do you have children? Do you want to raise them in an urban environment? Do you feel comfortable having them play in the street or walk unaccompanied to a nearby park to play? What about schools? Central city schools often have problems. Can you afford private schools if you live in the central city? You have a lot to consider.

What about suburbs? Suburbs conjure up images of large homes on spacious lots, puttering in the garage, mowing the lawn, chatting with neighbors, attending PTA meetings, and watching the kids' baseball and soccer games. Having some space between you and your next-door neighbor may be important to you. How important are good schools? If you are single and never intend to marry or if you and your partner never intend to have children, schools are not a factor. Good schools, however, are a major reason families move to the suburbs. Do you live in one suburb and work somewhere else? If you do, you'll have to consider transportation costs. How far are you willing to commute? Can you and your spouse or significant other commute together? What about getting the kids to school? Getting them home at the end of the school day? If one person works and the other stays at home, can you afford two cars? What if you can't? What about the mental health of the person left alone at home all day without a car?

Whether you settle on a central city, suburban, small-town, or rural location, you must consider the dominant lifestyle of the neighborhood in which you plan to live. If you are yuppies, will you enjoy living in a neighborhood dominated by young couples with small children? Or what if you are a gay couple living in a straight neighborhood? A mismatch in lifestyles usually means problems.

There are lots of factors to consider when evaluating what kind of neighborhood is best for you, and you should think carefully about your preferences. But for most people the primary factor guiding their location is cost. The house you can afford may not be the house you want. And it may not be in the city or neighborhood in which you want to live. Compromise is the guiding word in finding a new home.

Mike and Elizabeth have come up with their wish list. Let's review their work. In terms of the property, a view would be nice, but it is not that important to them. They would like a colonial-style house, but they are open. A swimming pool? You have to be kidding. A deck/patio is essential. They use the one in their townhouse all the time. Elizabeth really wants a two-car garage because she's sick of clearing snow and ice from the windshield. Mike wants a garage for his stuff.

They have clear ideas about the interior of their new home. They want a one-floor house because of the baby. Three bedrooms with a large master suite are a must. The second bedroom would be the nursery. The third bedroom would be a guest room/office. A large bathroom/dressing room off the master suite plus a second bathroom in the hall are also important.

They entertain a lot but informally. Elizabeth's parents had a formal living room and dining room when she was growing up, but they never used it. They decide that a large family/great room plus a large eat-in kitchen would best meet their needs. Houses are not built with basements in their region, so a basement is out.

They live in a rapidly growing city of 60,000 and in a metropolitan area of 350,000. Everything is within a fifteen or twenty minute drive, but they do like their present location. They are both within ten minutes of their jobs. Regardless of where they live in their hometown, elementary and junior high schools are minutes away. Mike's school is only one block away from day care, so that is not an issue. The crime rate in their community is extremely low, and the city, regardless of where one lives, has excellent police and fire protection.

New or used house? They want a new home. For them it has the same allure as the smell of a new car. They also realize that as their family grows, they'll probably need a larger home in five or ten years. They decide that a new home will have lower upkeep in its first decade, and they know they are going to be house poor for a few years. They are also concerned about resale. They know as a new neighborhood becomes established and the new landscaping matures, prices will probably rise. They also know that newer homes have higher resale value in their area. Mike's dad has persuaded them to follow his home-buying strategy: Buy the lowest-cost home in a neighborhood. His dad's thinking is correct—the higher value of their neighbors' homes will pull up the value of theirs over time. The question remains, can they find their dream house in their price range?

5. Decide What Kind of Neighborhood You Want

We have already discussed the relationship between housing, location, and lifestyle. Location is the most critical factor affecting a house's value. Houses in the most desirable neighborhoods tend to hold their value over time, so it makes sense to buy a home in the best neighborhood you can afford. The reason is that when you buy a home, you are actually buying a bundle of housing services. Good neighborhoods have a good bundle of services—proximity to good jobs, good pubic schools and facilities, nearby shopping, medical services, recreation, well-maintained homes, and a low crime rate. Homeowners in prestigious neighborhoods usually invest heavily in upkeep and landscaping. These neighborhoods have great windshield appeal and hold their value.

The best neighborhoods are usually the most expensive neighborhoods, putting them out of reach of most first-time home buyers. The general rule is to trade off amenities like an extra bedroom for a better neighborhood. Another strategy is to look for a home in a neighborhood that is likely to be in high demand in the future. Buying and renovating a home in an area in the first stages of gentrification is one option. Cities also tend to grow in one direction for several decades until they outstrip their infrastructure in that sector. So another strategy is buying a home in a solid neighborhood on the edge of a city's growth area. Review the theories of urban structure in chapter 7 and apply your sociological imagination.

Also use your sociological imagination to uncover neighborhoods on the move. Track *for sale* signs and newspaper ads for changes in sales activity in a neighborhood. Do a windshield survey of potential neighborhoods and note changes in the general upkeep of houses and lawns. Have a large number of homes recently been remodeled? Does the neighborhood look like it is on the upswing? Are there a large number of elderly living in the neighborhood? The neighborhood might go through another life cycle. Research shows that people age in place, and as the original families in a neighborhood die or move away, young families move in. What about the schools? What about the crime rate? What about access to jobs and other amenities?

The quality of schools and the crime rate have the greatest impact on the desirability of neighborhoods. The most important factor for people in the child-rearing stage of the life cycle is the quality of schools. Real estate in areas with good schools appreciate in value rapidly while those neighborhoods in bad school districts have stagnant or declining home values. How do you find out about the quality of schools? If you are new to a community, one way is to ask around. Talk to the central office of the school district. Ask for an attendance map. Ask to see test scores. Contact PTAs. Drive by the school and look at its upkeep. Talk to the principal. Realtors know the quality of schools like the back of their hands. If you are using a Realtor, ask her or him.

If you're moving from out of town, you can do some of your homework through the Internet. Most school districts now have web pages. They often give national test scores by district, by school, and by grade level. These scores show how well the local school does in comparison to national standardized tests. A number of web sites give loads of data on school districts across the United States. Take a look at Homefair (*www.homefair.com*). Homefair provides data on subjects like the location of schools within a district, district-by-district comparisons, student-teacher ratios, average class size, and the availability of after-school programs.

You can also tap into the data on the web site of the specific school district in which you are interested. I found, however, that the quality of these web sites varies enormously. Could the quality of a school district's web site give you an insight into the quality of the school system? Take a look at the web page of the school district in Mike and Elizabeth's community at *http://fayar.net*.

Although the crime rate has been declining in the United States for the past twenty years and we live in a far safer society than in the past, the majority of Americans still fear crime. How can you find out the crime rate of a neighborhood? All police departments must report crime statistics to the federal government for a publication called the *Uniform Crime Report*. These statistics are available by city, neighborhood, and even ZIP codes. Some police departments maintain web sites, but most don't. To find information on the Internet, search on the keywords *crime statistics* and *law enforcement*. Also include the name of the community in your search field. *Homefair.com* also provides crime data for most cities in the U.S. and Canada.

For those departments that don't have a web site, you can call the city's public or community relations officer. These data are public, so ask them for the crime rates for the city and specific neighborhood in which you're interested. Tell the officer you are thinking about moving to the city and ask him or her some pointed questions about the safety of different areas in the city. What areas would she or he avoid? In what neighborhoods would he or she live?

What about finding out general things about the community? Is there a college or university? Good hospitals? If you are a movie buff, how many movie theaters and how many screens are in town? If you live to eat out, what about the restaurants? Is there live entertainment? The list is almost endless. One strategy is to subscribe to the local paper for a few months before you move. Large metropolitan daily papers are available in most libraries, or you can buy a copy at your local bookstore. Better yet, check out the local paper on the web. The majority of papers now have web pages. Here are the URLs for the local papers in my area, northwest Arkansas. Take a look at them and see what's going on in this community. Are there any stories that suggest troubled neighborhoods, schools, or government?

www.nwarktimes.com

www.nwark.org

www.ardemgaz.com

As odd as it may sound, I read the Yellow Pages whenever visiting a new city. All businesses have phones, and you can get an uncanny snapshot of a community with a fifteen minute visit to the Yellow Pages. Did you know Columbus, Ohio, has three firms that specialize in flocking? (Flocking is that fuzzy stuff on wallpaper.)

Finally, any community with a chamber of commerce has a web site. I spent a couple of hours surfing the web and found an enormous number of city sites. They vary considerably in quality and usefulness, but it's a start. Search on the city's name and state. The URLs for the city of Fayetteville are *www.uark.edu/aladdin/cityinfo/cityweb/* and *www.Accessfayetteville.org* and the Fayetteville Chamber of Commerce is at *www.fayettevillear.com*.

What about Mike and Elizabeth? They were both born and raised in their community. As a teacher, Mike knows the school district intimately. He not only knows the school district's test scores; he also personally knows most of the teachers in the district. More important, he knows the ones to avoid. Mike and Elizabeth also know where the crime rates are highest, the neighborhoods to avoid, the neighborhoods that are on the rise, and the ones that are in decline. They decide the elementary school their child will attend is the most important factor in their housing decision. They decide they want to be in the Vandergriff Elementary School attendance area. See why. Take a look at why they made this choice at Vandergriff's home page at *http://fayar.net/vandergriff*.

Like most cities, the distribution of housing by age, type, and quality and by the people who live in these homes follow a distinct pattern. Mike and Elizabeth have lived with these patterns their entire lives. There is a large university in their city, and most of the students live in apartments in a wedge starting at the edge of campus and moving due west. Aaron and Rod their noisy neighbors, have persuaded them to avoid this area like the plague. Low-income families live directly south of the downtown and in a neighborhood adjacent and east of downtown. There is a historic district close in and northeast of downtown, but these houses are out of their price range. They would love to live there, but they couldn't afford the house or the upkeep. The Wilson Park area is near the university, but families are paying a $30,000 premium to live there. Their city has been growing rapidly (25 percent this decade), and most of this growth has been concentrated in one sector on the northeast edge of town. This area is near their townhouse. The area is convenient to their jobs, shopping, and their good friends. If they live there, their child would go to the best elementary and middle school in the district. They also would be on the other side of town from Mike's parents—another plus. They decide to look for a new home on the northeast edge of town. But they will pay a premium to live there. Take a look at neighborhoods across the nation at *www.neighborhoodfind.com*.

Interestingly, Mike and Elizabeth's search behavior is the same as that followed by the vast majority of people moving within the same city. People tend to relocate in the same sector of the city in which they already live. Why? The obvious reason is familiarity. They know where everything is. Another is that staying close decreases disruption in their lives. Their children can go to the same schools. They can keep the same jobs. They can maintain the same social network. Networks will change, though. A move of only a few blocks will bring about changes in their social networks because the patterns of their day-to-day life will change in subtle ways. They may change grocery stores or shop at a different time. If they do, they will run into a different set of people. They will have new neighbors. Their children will play with new kids. In short, there will be change in neighbors, friends, and acquaintances—their social network. I wonder if Rosemary and George will still be Mike and Elizabeth's best friends next year at this time.

6. Prequalify or Preapprove a Loan

The mistake that many first-time buyers make is that they do not get prequalified or preapproved for a loan. First, you really don't know how much you can spend on a house until you find out what the lender is willing to loan you. Second, and more important, you can demonstrate to a seller that you have the financing to close the deal—you are a genuine buyer—not someone shopping around.

There is a big difference between prequalification and preapproval. When you are prequalified, the lender asks you a dozen or so questions and based on what you say, issues you a letter stating that you are qualified to get a mortgage up to a certain amount. The prequalification is really nothing more than the opinion of the bank officer, but it is in the form of a letter and it carries some weight with sellers. One of the roles of a real estate agent is to prequalify buyers.

Better yet is getting preapproval for a loan. When you get preapproval, you go through the entire process of getting financing, except for identifying the actual piece of property. The lender does a credit check and a verification of employment and assets. If you pass muster, the lender issues you a formal letter. You have been approved for a loan up to a specific amount at a specific interest rate and term. This is something a seller can count on, and it puts you in a far stronger bargaining position with a seller.

You can get prequalification and preapproval at a local lender; however, an increasing number of buyers are buying their mortgage online. We will discuss e-commerce in the section on applying for a loan.

7. Decide If You Should Use a Real Estate Agent

When I bought my first home nearly thirty years ago, the agent who drove me around was full of helpful advice. She told us, "You don't want to buy there because of the schools." "You don't want to buy there because the city has plans to widen the street." "You don't want to buy there because *those people* are moving into the neighborhood." (I never found out who "those people" were.) What the agent didn't tell us was that she really didn't represent us. She was a licensed broker, and her role was to bring a buyer and a seller together for the sale. But, and this is a big but, she was legally bound to meet the seller's full asking price. When we told her in confidence that we couldn't afford the asking price but we could go up another $3,000 or $4,000 on our original offer, she was legally bound to tell the seller to hold out for a higher price. The eleventh commandment is to never confide in a real estate agent.[2]

A lot has improved over the past three decades, in large part, because of a rash of lawsuits against real estate agents. Virtually all real estate firms now provide standard disclosure forms that clearly state the nature of the company's role. In fact, the National Association of Realtors has urged states for years to pass laws that require full disclosure. Ask your agent if he or she represents you or the seller. In real estate the agent can owe a fiduciary responsibility to the buyer, the seller, or both. Another possibility is to hire a buyer's agent. Buyer's agents work for you, not the seller. There is no potential for a conflict of interest. They can be paid on a flat or hourly fee basis.

With these caveats, should I hire a real estate agent or a broker? There are a lot of good reasons to hire a broker. First, an agent can help you estimate the price range of homes you should consider. Second, if the agent knows the local market, he can hone you in on the neighborhood and home you really want. A real estate agent can save you time and mistakes. Third, if the agent knows the market and the city, she can steer you away from potential problem neighborhoods and toward neighborhoods with a real future. Fourth, a broker should have access to the Multiple Listing Service (MLS) offered by your area's local real estate board. The MLS is a listing of homes for sale in your area. Member brokers cooperate in order to provide sellers with the widest possible exposure of their property to potential buyers. The MLS book usually offers photos of property and a detailed description, including age, square footage, number of bedrooms, and days on the market. According to the National Association of Realtors, 75 percent of the homes for sale in the nation are listed through the MLS. Increasingly, the MLS is available on the web. Take a look at *www.cyberhomes.com* to see what the MLS looks like on the web. The bottom line is that a broker can be worth every penny, saving you time and problems in the long run.

On the down side, real estate services don't come cheaply. Typically the real estate commission will be between 6 and 8 percent of the selling price. In rural areas, the real estate commission can be as high as 10 percent. On a $150,000 house a 7 percent real estate commission is $10,500. The seller pays this fee, but you can be sure this commission is factored into the cost of the house. In addition, like any other profession, there is the wide range of talent in the real estate industry. You face the possibility of hiring a bad one.

Between 15 and 20 percent of the homes for sale in the United States are for sale by owner (FSBO). You might be able to get a lower price, but don't count on it. FSBOs usually don't know the local market well and, like many of us, they tend to overvalue their property. Second, since there are fewer FSBOs on the market than listed properties, the type of homes in the neighborhoods in which you are interested may not be available. But saving $10,000 or $12,000 makes it worth looking into these properties. The local paper is the first place to look. FSBOs are increasingly found on the web. Search the web on the key words *For Sale by Owner*, *FSBO*, and the name of the city, or explore *www.mls-fsbo.com* for one example.

If you decide to use an agent, use your sociological imagination. Use your social network. Ask people in your network if they have recently purchased a new home or if a friend has. Personal references are usually the best way to find a good agent. If you are new to an area, drive around and look at the names of listing agents on homes for sale in the community. Go to several open houses and meet a number of agents. Ask for references. Check with your state board of real estate to see if the agents you are interested in working with have past or pending actions against them. A nice thing about being a buyer is that you can use more than one real estate agent at a time.

What about Mike and Elizabeth? Since they are buying a new home, they know that real estate firms usually negotiate a lower fee with builders. They decide they have everything to gain and little to lose in using an agent. They use an old family friend as their agent.

8. Find an Appropriate Neighborhood, and 9. Begin House Hunting

I have combined these two steps because they are inextricably tied together. The factors in the residential location decision are summarized in Table 8.1. Individual characteristics are linked to housing characteristics. Family income determines the range of affordable housing. The stage of the life cycle determines the size and type of house the family needs. Lifestyle preferences determine the type of neighborhood and the neighborhood's location relative to the center of the city. And attitudes toward the journey to work will determine the distance between the new home and the owner's place of employment.

Housing types and neighborhoods are not distributed randomly across the city; they follow a distinct pattern. Chapter 7 presented theories on the structure of the metropolis. In general, most neighborhood and housing characteristics change in systematic ways as one moves from the city's center to its periphery. The distribution of some of these characteristics is common sense. The oldest houses and neighborhoods are near the city's center; the newest are on the periphery. Population density is another variable. The older and more centrally located neighborhoods were built at higher density than newer neighborhoods located on the city's edge. Income, owner occupancy, median house value, and household size are characteristics that change in a systematic way with distance from the city's center.

Knowing these patterns gives you framework to begin your search. There are a variety of ways to fill in your framework with information. If you have the time, get a city map and do a windshield survey of the city's neighborhoods over a few

Sundays. See which neighborhoods have windshield appeal. Also note neighborhoods where there are lots of for sale signs. Something is going on. It may be good or bad. Check it out.

You can use this system to quickly come up with a broad brush picture of a city. The next step is the U.S. Census. The census collects detailed demographic and housing information by census tracts. Census tracts are approximately the same size as most neighborhoods, but they are not the same thing. A neighborhood may straddle two census tracts. The Census Bureau collects this information at the beginning of each decade, but many communities have special censuses that update this information more often. Develop your own neighborhood profile with this information: housing type, housing age, mean housing value, number of families, number of children, and percent owner-occupied. You can get census tract information directly off the web. Take a look at the search engine on the U.S. web site at *www.census.gov*. More general information on cities and neighborhoods is available on the Internet. Fillout the questionnaire on MSN's house and phone link, and they will find it for you. (*http://houseandhome.MSN.com*). We have already discussed collecting information on schools and crime rates.

Check the Sunday real estate section of the local paper. In addition, most newspapers' archives are cross-referenced. Many libraries keep clipping files. Take a look at these files on the neighborhoods in which you are interested. City planning departments and neighborhood associations are other good sources of information. Just talking to people at a neighborhood coffee shop or a grocery can give you insight into what's going on in a neighborhood. Of course, people in your social network can be a wonderful source of information. You will be surprised how many of your friends have friends who know someone who lives in a neighborhood across town. Of course, a knowledgeable real estate agent who knows the local housing market can give you invaluable advice. Remember that every source of information is biased. The best way to protect yourself is to get as much information from as many sources as possible.

With this framework, you can fill in more-detailed information. The price of housing will limit the neighborhoods that you can afford. Your stage in the life cycle and your lifestyle will further reduce the number of neighborhoods you will consider. Finally, your attitudes toward commuting will affect neighborhood choice. My advice is think time, not commuting distance. You obviously can travel much farther on an interstate than on city streets. Drive in different directions from your place of employment at different times of the day. If your limit is twenty minutes, see how far you can travel in twenty minutes in each direction. Mark the map. Use the mark and your place of employment to set the width of a compass. Place the sharp point of the compass on your job site, spin 360 degrees. Voila, you have your search area. What if you are a two-income family? If the two circles intersect, there may be only one neighborhood in a metropolis that meets your commuting criterion. If they don't intersect, the fun begins. You have the final parameter of your search.

This is the rational approach, but there is a lot of irrationality and serendipity in finding a new home. The research that I have done shows that about one-third of people in my region find their home by serendipity. My graduate student and her husband are a good example. They had just moved to town, and they stopped and asked an elderly woman, watering the shrubs in her front lawn, directions to the street where they were meeting their Realtor. She asked, "Are you looking for a house?" They ended up buying her house without the Realtor.

What about Mike and Elizabeth? They have a lot of bias built into their search. For example, they could be far better off moving to the community just north of their city. It is a blue-collar community, but it has a sound school system, and the housing is significantly cheaper. It would add only five minutes to their commuting each day. They won't even consider it.

There are also some wonderful new houses on the western edge of town near another new elementary school. These homes are cheaper and closer to Elizabeth's job. They just don't like the west side. They have their heart set on the side of town where they now live.

After driving around after dinner for two weeks, they have located four possibilities. Two of the houses aren't even completed and they would be able to pick paint colors, wallpaper, and floor coverings. All the homes are in the Vandergriff attendance area, and all four homes are in their price range.

10. Inspect Houses

Mike and Elizabeth have decided on location, price range, and style of house. They have a detailed wish list. Since they are looking at new construction, they really don't have to worry about roofs, foundations, and mechanicals. Their major concern is curb appeal, the types and quality of homes surrounding them, and the types of neighbors. They completed a walk-through on four possibilities. They carefully evaluated the floor plan of each house and checked the traffic flow between the kitchen, great room, bedrooms, and utility room, and access to the yard, green space, and neighborhood park. But the most important question they asked themselves, "Did the house have the right feel." One did, and it was just a mile from their townhouse.

11. Make Offer

Once you find a home you want to buy, you will want to pay the lowest price possible. The problem is that the sellers want to get the highest price for their property. You have to negotiate.

Most people are uncomfortable negotiating the price of a car, much less a home. But remember we negotiate all the time in day-to-day life. The thrust of the symbolic interactionist's perspective in sociology is the negotiated order. Think of negotiating for the price of a home with a seller as just an extension of the process that defines the symbolic world.

Today negotiating has been routinized to the point where face-to-face negotiations are unnecessary. In some cases, you may not meet the sellers until the closing. Formal offers outlining what you are willing to pay and the conditions of the purchase are shuttled back and forth between buyer and seller by a real estate agent. The buyer makes an offer; the seller responds with a counteroffer. The buyer makes a counteroffer to the counteroffer, and the process continues until a deal is reached or one party walks away.

How do you decide what to offer? You need to do your homework. You need to know the market. Ask your agent for a market update. Know how long housing, in general, and this house, in particular, have been on the market. If you don't do your homework, you can pay too much for a house or you can lowball the seller, who then becomes a tough negotiator. Or you can even lose the home to another buyer who is better informed and who makes a more reasonable offer.

I think the best outcome of this process is a win-win situation. Through the operation of the negotiation process, the market determines the fair price for the property and both parties are satisfied.

Mike and Elizabeth are shopping in the most desirable part of town. New homes, in particular, are in high demand. Most new homes typically sell while under construction. Their Realtor suggested making an offer at the asking price. There was no negotiation. They chose the second home they looked at in a new subdivision. The average home in the neighborhood sells for $172,000; they bought one of the smaller homes at $158,000. It has everything they were looking for on their wish list: 2,100 square feet, great room, large eat-in kitchen, three bedrooms with master suite, two baths, two-car garage, and a deck. They will be living in a neighborhood that will appreciate over the years, and their child will attend Vandergriff School.

12. Apply for a Mortgage

For the millions of Americans buying a home each year, finding a home is only half the challenge. The other half is finding the right mortgage. There are a bewildering array of mortgage instruments and a bewildering number of actors in the mortgage market today. The nice thing is that with so many mortgages and so many actors, you can get a mortgage that meets your needs. The bottom line is that buying money is like buying any other commodity. Shop around for the best price. E-commerce is making this much easier.

First, check with your local savings and loans, commercial banks, and credit unions. Interest rates and points are often published in the local paper.

Second, try the web. In 2002, approximately $111 billion of mortgage financing was obtained online. E-mortgages are in their infancy, however. In this same year, total mortgage financing totaled $4.6 trillion (National Bankers Association, 2004). Where do you find mortgage web sites? I found more than a dozen in a five-minute search of the web. The best designed site I found on the web is *www.eloan.com*. It has virtually any type of loan you could want. It clearly identifies the costs associated with each type. It also has a wizard that analyzes your specific needs and suggests a type of mortgage. Most of the large national real estate companies and banks offer mortgages online. Take a look at Coldwell Banker, Century 21, Chase Manhattan, and the Bank of America for a start. The major search engines—Google and Yahoo—have real estate links.

The Department of Housing and Urban Development does not offer mortgages, but it has a web site that offers a wealth of information on mortgage hunting (*www.hud.gov*). Freddie Mac and Fannie Mae are quasi-government agents that operate in the secondary mortgage market. Their web sites are fairly technical but are a good source of information for the more-advanced mortgage hunter (*www.fanniemae.com* and *www.freddiemac.com*).

Regardless of where you search for a mortgage, the seven-step process is the same: (1) get preapproved, (2) determine the type of mortgage you need, (3) check out interest rates and costs for the mortgage, (4) apply for the mortgage, (5) get the necessary documentation, (6) get formal approval, and (7) track the mortgage until you close the deal.

Most of the steps are self-explanatory. The only two I want to comment on are step 2, determining the type of mortgage you need, and step 3, check out interest rates and costs for the mortgage. There are an enormous number of mortgage instruments on the market today, but the two most basic types are the fixed-rate and the adjustable-rate mortgages.

With a fixed-rate mortgage you pay a set monthly payment based on a fixed interest rate for a specific term—usually fifteen or thirty years. The monthly payment doesn't change over the term of the loan. There is security for the borrower with a fixed-rate mortgage.[3]

The real estate lending industry had a disastrous decade in the 1980s. Savings and loans, in particular, were saddled with billions of dollars of low-interest, fixed-rate mortgages during a period in our history of double-digit inflation. Thousands of lenders failed, and since the deposits on the savings upon which loans were secured were guaranteed by the federal government, the federal government picked up the tab. To date, the federal government has spent around $333 billion in the S & L bailout.

The adjustable-rate mortgage (ARM) emerged during this period. Essentially, the ARM shifts risk from the lender to the borrower by adjusting the interest rate on the loan one or more times a year. ARMs are normally tied to a national rate like the Federal Reserve's discount rate or the interest rate on the thirty-year treasury bill. The advantage of this type of loan is that interest rates are usually lower at the start. If inflation remains low, the cost of the loan may be lower over the life of the mortgage. The disadvantage is risk. The interest on an adjustable-rate mortgage can vary enormously, and the payment can change from year to year. Most ARMs have an annual interest cap and a cap on interest for the life of the loan. For example, a lender may cap any annual interest rate increase at no more than 2 percent and place an overall cap on the loan at 12 percent. I have yet to find a lender that will lower the interest on an ARM below the initial interest rate.

The other important step is checking out the interest rate and the cost of the mortgage. The federal government requires all lenders to supply consumers with information on the interest and the annual percentage rate (APR) of a mortgage. The APR is typically higher because it includes the interest rate plus other charges. Your monthly payment for the term of the loan will also be shown.

The lender may also charge points. A point is a charge for servicing the loan, and a point is 1 percent of the loan amount. Points are paid up front. One point on Mike and Elizabeth's loan would be $1,500 (.01 × $150,000). So when you check out interest rates, check out the points. You will find that loans with zero points have higher interest rates than loans with points. If you have savings, you can pay points and get a lower interest rate and lower monthly payments. If you have no savings and pay no points, you will face a higher interest rate and a higher monthly payment.

Terms are the last element when comparing home loans. It is simply the number of years of the loan. For convenience, terms are usually fifteen or thirty years, although most lenders will negotiate any term. The important thing to remember is to always compare loans of the same type (fixed or ARM) with the same number of points and the same term (fifteen or thirty years).

One other element to consider is *garbage costs*. In addition to points and interest, many lenders now add charges to cover a variety of other costs, including appraisal fees, title searches, recording fees, lawyer fees, preparation fees, and photocopying. In the past, lenders simply covered these charges with their interest charges. Lenders in today's intensely competitive mortgage market use these fees to increase their yields without increasing the loan's APR.

A good way to see how all this works is to use the mortgage wizards found on the web pages of many lenders. I think the one on the Intuit web site (*www.quicken.com/mortgage/*) is the best. Like everything in the world of commerce, caveat emptor. I found some wizards on the web lie or are biased toward a particular type of loan, especially ARMs. Another warning: If you use the web, be sure you know with whom you are working. Anyone can put up a web site. If you use e-commerce, I think you are better off working with larger, more established lenders. They use encryption software that ensures the confidentiality of any information you send over the web.

13. Have a Professional Inspection?

The answer is yes. A home purchase is the largest single investment most people make in their lifetime. A house is a complex system, and many things can go wrong. A foundation that fails could jeopardize the entire structure and make the resale of your home almost impossible. Your Realtor can recommend a professional inspector. You can also find them listed in the Yellow Pages. Be sure to interview the inspectors on the telephone and find out how many years they have been in the business in the area. Ask them about their education and training. Some states license home inspectors. A good choice is an inspector who is a member of the American Society of Home Inspectors (ASHI). ASHI is a national trade association of home inspectors, and members must meet education and training standards. Also ASHI has a code of ethics.

A home inspection will cost anywhere between $200 and $500. This fee is usually paid by the buyer. Most buyers put a home inspection clause in their offer and acceptance. If the inspector finds serious problems in the structure, the deal could be ruined and the buyer could be out hundreds of dollars. In my opinion, it is money well spent.

14. Close the Transaction

Closing occurs when all the terms and conditions of the purchase agreement have been met. The closing ritual varies from region to region, but as I showed in the opening vignette in Chapter 8, there is a huge cast of characters involved in the closing. Important issues must be resolved before the closing. The most important is the title. That is, who holds legal ownership to the land and the structures that sit on it? In some regions, abstract companies search the title. In other regions, lawyers do this type of work. Regardless, investing in the services of a lawyer is a good practice.

If you use a real estate agent, have her or him explain the closing process ahead of time. Get to the closing early and review the documents and know what you are signing. Ask questions about documents that you do not understand. Leave the room if necessary and phone your attorney if he or she is not present. Remember, you are probably entering into the largest investment of your life. Be sure you know what you are getting into.

Mike and Elizabeth were first-time owners of their home, and they had a clean title. The abstract companies had prepared the documents several days in advance, and Mike and Elizabeth met at the office an hour before the closing. They had read and understood all the documents before the closing. The closing took fifteen minutes. They arrived at noon and were the proud owners of a home at 1:20 P.M.

15. Move In

Mike, with the help of Aaron and Rod at $8 an hour, a U-Haul, and a case of beer, had the furniture in the townhouse moved to their new home in one afternoon. Aaron and Rod turned out to be pretty nice guys after all. Mike had a few bumps and scratches, but the furniture and breakables were fine. The new house is 1.2 miles from the townhouse. They still see Rosemary and George, but they don't get together as often. They have become close to their new next-door neighbors, Tina and Sean.

A Second Case Study: Anne and Bill

Mike and Elizabeth are a best-case scenario. They have college degrees. They have steady, well-paying jobs. They have savings and little debt. We chose them because we could walk you through the entire home-purchasing process. But what about the millions of Americans who don't have Mike and Elizabeth's education and income? A biography of Anne and Bill follows. Let's follow them in their search for a new home.

Anne and Bill have been married for three years. They were high school sweethearts, and they attended their state's land grant college together. Anne graduated with a social work degree and started working for a local social service agency after graduation. Anne loves her job. She thinks she is making an important difference in the lives of the families she works with, but her salary is low, only $21,245 per year.

Bill didn't finish his degree. His parents just couldn't afford to help with his college expenses. Even with a minority achievement scholarship and student loans, he still had to work two jobs. Exhausted and beaten by the grind, he decided not to return to college after he was suspended for low grades his sophomore year.

Bill doesn't like his job, but he knows he has a great future with his firm. He was selected for a management development program last year. He knows his company promotes only from within, and his quarterly evaluations have been excellent. They will even help him earn his college degree after he finishes the program. He makes $19,550. They have a combined income of $41,195, about $6,000 higher than the nation's average family income.

Anne and Bill are the first members of their families to attend college, and they received little financial help from their parents. Their parents just didn't have the money. They have always had it rough financially. They both had scholarships and worked during college, but they had to use student loans. Together their student loans total slightly more than $32,000. They have debt problems. Their first financial decision as a married couple was to buy a new car. Bill had a twenty-mile commute to his job and his old clunker just wouldn't make it, so they purchased a new Honda Accord in the first month of their marriage. Anne drives their old standby, an older model

Nissan. The only other debt is their credit card. Like many newlyweds, they misused their credit setting up their household in the first year of their marriage. Since then, they have consolidated their debt on a single card and have worked it down to under $1,000. It will be paid off in six months. Even with the credit card paid off, they have $650 in monthly payments toward long-term obligations. With rent, utilities, loan payments, and living expenses, they have saved only $1,800 in the past three years.

Like Mike and Elizabeth, they have lived in an apartment for the past three years. The apartment is OK. It was Bill's during college and only two blocks from campus. The turnover in the apartments is nearly 100 percent each year. Given their work schedules they really haven't met many of their neighbors. Being the only African Americans in the complex has also been a barrier. Most of their friends live in other parts of town.

Anne and Bill want to own their own home. They plan to have a family in a few years, but only after Bill has moved into middle management. They are worried that if they don't buy soon, they will be priced out of the housing market. Their city is experiencing California-style growth, and housing has been appreciating at an alarming rate. They decide it's time to think about buying a home and building a little equity.

Anne and Bill face the dilemma of many young couples. Anne will get her master's in social work in a few years, and Bill will probably finish his degree. He also has a great future with his company. But they brought a high level of debt to their marriage, and loan payments and the living expenses have made it nearly impossible to save. Let's see how differences in income, debt, savings, and race affect the search process. We will not go into the detail of the first case study and will touch only the high points of the process.

1. Make the Decision to Move. Anne and Bill haven't been students for more than three years, and frankly they are sick of living in an apartment complex that rents to college students. It's not just the noise; it's having no neighbors their own age. They know it's time to move. Whether it's a home or another apartment in a different part of town, they decide to move.

2. Make a Decision to Buy or Rent. Anne and Bill are worried that they will never be able to afford a home if they don't buy soon. Housing prices in their area have been rising 8 to 9 percent a year. Last week, they drove by a house on the market a few blocks from their apartment. It looked like a home they could afford. They called the real estate company as soon as they returned home and were shocked at the $89,000 asking price. They decide they need a starter home in a safe area of town. A home that will likely appreciate in value. A home where they can build some equity. A home where they can start their family in a few years. They decide it's now or never. They decide to start looking for a home to buy.

3. Figure Out How Much You Can Afford. As we described in the first case study, many factors go into the decision on how much you can afford. We'll once again use the Home Buying Worksheet to get a ballpark idea of how much Anne and Bill can afford. Let's look at their financial situation in Table 9.2.

Table 9.2   *Home Buying Worksheet for Anne and Bill*

1. Gross Annual Income (before taxes)	$41,195
2. Gross Monthly Income, Line 1 divided by 12 months	$3,432
3. Monthly Allowable Housing Expense and Long-Term Obligations, Line 2 multiplied by .38	$1,304
4. Monthly Allowable Housing Expense, Line 3 minus monthly obligations—credit cards, child support, car loan, etc.	($650) $654
5. Monthly Principal and Interest Payment, Line 4 multiplied by .80	$523
6. Estimated Mortgage Amount, Line 5 divided by 7.34 multiplied by $1,000*	$71,000
7. Estimated Affordable Price, Line 6 divided by .90 (90% is the mortgage loan amount, assuming a 10% down payment. Use .80 for a 20% down payment.)	$78,889

Source: The table is based on general guidelines found in the buyers guides provided by most banks and real estate firms.

*This is the interest rate factor for an 8% loan. For the rate factor for other interest rates see www.bankrate.com.

Anne and Bill have an annual gross income of $41,195, or a gross monthly income of $3,432. The rule of thumb used by banks is that long-term financial obligations should not exceed 38 percent of a family's monthly income, or in Anne and Bill's case $1,304. Line 4 is important because it reflects past and future financial obligations. Anne and Bill have student loans and a car loan payment for a total of $650 of long-term obligations. This leaves $654 ($1,304 − $650) for monthly housing expenses.

Monthly housing expenses cover principal and interest on the loan, plus insurance, taxes, homeowner association dues, and other fixed costs. Banks take 80 percent of the allowable housing expense figure (.80 × 654) or $523 to cover principal and interest. Assuming that Anne and Bill get an 8 percent, fixed thirty-year mortgage, and the bank permits them to put up a 10 percent down payment, they can look for housing at around $78,889. They can borrow $71,000. But they don't have the $7,100 down payment, and their parents can't loan them the money. Anne, however, read about a new Federal Housing Authority (FHA) program that allows first-time home-owners to reduce their down payment to only 3 percent (Federal Housing Administration, 1997). They have $1,800 in savings. They can just qualify for a $60,000 home.

4. Decide What Kind of Home You Want.   Above all else, Anne is a realist. She knows that you can't buy much for $60,000. After driving around, reading the newspaper, talking to friends and visiting several open houses, they think they have only three options. Option 1 is to buy a builder-financed townhouse on the edge of town. The townhouses are small, 1,100 square feet, with only two bedrooms, one and a half baths, and a galley kitchen. The neighborhood is also on the wrong side of town. Option 2 is to buy a new house in a new FHA-financed development in a small town six miles from the city. The town is in the growth area of the city. Traffic is becoming a problem on the winding two-lane highway, but it's still only a fifteen or twenty minute drive to work for both of them. Option 3 is to buy a handyman special in one of the older areas of the city. If they find a neighborhood on the upswing, they could do very well when they resell the house.

5. Decide What Kind of Neighborhood You Want. They have always liked the city in which they live. As an African American couple, the only problem is the small African American community. In the eight-county region of the state in which they live, only 4 percent of the population is African American. The population is so small that none of the local businesses carry makeup and hair products for African Americans. They have to stock up when they visit their parents back home. They are active in the Methodist church in the small African American neighborhood that is adjacent and south of the downtown, but this is a low-income area. Most members of their ethnic group are employed by the university or the three major corporations that dominate the region's economy. These people have high salaries and live in neighborhoods based on their income, not their race. As a result, the level of segregation in the region is among the lowest in the nation. Although they live in the South, the schools and housing in the region have been integrated for fifty years. They plan to stay in the area and build their personal community based on choice not place.

They carefully review their options and decide that a townhouse really wouldn't be much better than what they have now. They are also concerned about resale because condominiums and townhouses just don't sell in this area. In addition, they have eliminated the FHA house in the rural town. They really had bad vibes when they visited the model last week. An African American couple in a white working-class neighborhood just doesn't appeal to them. They decide to look for a small, older home in good shape in a stable area of the city. They are not planning to start their family until Bill gets his promotion, but they know the importance of schools on resale value.

6. Find an Appropriate Neighborhood and Begin House Hunting. Anne and Bill carry out a systematic search for a neighborhood and a new home. First, they talk to friends and school officials and find that there were two elementary schools to avoid. They already know where the high crime areas are in the city. Once they have eliminated these areas, they discover that they are priced out of virtually all the neighborhoods in the city. They know their search must be focused in the city's older, inner neighborhoods on the west and south side. Thoroughly discouraged after weeks of searching, they are about to rent a new apartment when Bill mentions their plight at work. One of his coworkers describes his neighborhood. It is tucked in behind an elementary school on the west side. He is right. You really couldn't find it if you didn't know it was there. It is a neighborhood of forty small bungalows built in the early 1960s. The architecture isn't much, but the houses have been well maintained, and the mature trees and shrubs give the neighborhood a nice feel. Anne and Bill discover that most of the homes are occupied by the original owners, who had raised their children and stayed in these homes for their retirement. The only way they come on the market is when one of the owners dies or moves to a rest home. Most sales are word of mouth. Anne and Bill think to themselves, "What has this world come to? In a city of 60,000, there are only forty homes we can afford."

7. The Process Completed. Anne and Bill's patiences is rewarded after six months when Mrs. Bowen decides it is time she moved in with her daughter's family. Bill's

Photo 9.2   *Anne and Bill's new home—older, well-built, in an established neighborhood, purchased from the original owner. (Source: Photo by the author's son, Judd Schwab.)*

friend Jim had put feelers out in the neighborhood, and Mrs. Bowen called him as soon as she made her decision. She really likes Anne and Bill when they look at the house. The young couple decides that the kitchen and bathroom will need to be remodeled in a few years, but the home inspector says the house has been well maintained and is in good shape. A little paint and decorating will make it a wonderful first home. After a few anxious weeks, the loan is approved. They move into their home almost one year after they began their search for a new home. See Photo 9.2.

The fascinating thing about the city is that the deeply personal decisions made by these two couples are shaped by the structure of the city. In turn, their decisions, when combined with others, shape the city. Anne and Bill, for example, are the first blacks to move into an all-white neighborhood. If other African American couples follow their lead, the process of neighborhood change will occur.

There are other patterns as well. The incomes of the couples reflect their position in the social stratification system, and their position in the stratification system determines their life chances. Incomes, one of our best measures of social rank, is mediated by lending institutions and determines housing options. Housing options, in turn, are shaped by city structure because housing is not distributed randomly across a city. Neighborhoods are graded by lifestyle, income, and race. In the final analysis, Mike and Elizabeth's social status and income gave them many housing options. They could purchase a home in most of the neighborhoods in the city. Anne and Bill, because of the unique events in their lives, had far fewer options, really only one. But the city is a giant matching machine, and both couples found housing they could afford in neighborhoods that met their income, lifestyle, and life-cycle needs.

This chapter is a home-buying primer. The experiences of a young married couple, Mike and Elizabeth, are followed through the fifteen-step home-buying process. The sociological research on the decision to move is brought to bear on this process. Practical advice on deciding to move, buying or renting, determining how much you can afford, deciding on what kind of home and neighborhood you really want, using a Realtor, hunting for and inspecting houses and neighborhoods, applying for a mortgage, closing, and moving in are discussed. We also follow the experiences of a second couple, Anne and Bill, through their home-buying process. Anne and Bill are African American and just starting out in their careers. They face a different set of challenges, but follow the same steps in finding the right home for them.

Notes

[1] There have been important changes in home financing in the past decade. Banks and other lending institutions, depending on your credit history, may allow you to put down as little as 5 percent on a home purchase; FHA downpayments can be as low as 3 percent. This covers the full range of homes from the modest starter home to the mansion. This is a factor you may want to consider.

[2] People use the terms *agent*, *Realtor*, and *broker* interchangeably to refer to people who sell real estate. Not all agents are Realtors and not all real estate agents are Realtors. Only a small percentage of agents are licensed real estate brokers.

The title, Realtor, begins with a capital letter because it is a proper name and a trademark. A real estate agent with the title, Realtor, is a member of the National Association of Realtors, the major and politically powerful professional association of the real estate industry. Members of the National Association of Realtors must subscribe to the Realtor Code of Ethics. Realtors often have advanced education and credentials. Real estate brokers are licensed by each state to act as agents for the buyers and sellers of property. Brokers can be individuals or large businesses like Coldwell Banker or ReMax. One real estate broker can have many real estate agents working for her/him. Depending on the firm, these agents may or may not be Realtors.

[3] The fifteen- or thirty-year monthly amortized home loan that Americans take for granted is relatively new. Until the 1930s, when the federal government introduced this new loan instrument, a family would take out a short-term loan, usually three to five years, put back money over the term of the loan, and pay off the loan or refinance on the due date. The uncertainty of the process meant that few Americans owned their own home. Once the federal government demonstrated that the risks for the thirty-year home loan were low and provided government loan guarantees, homeownership became a reality for most American households.

10

THE SUBURBANIZATION PROCESS

Introduction

Suburb. Few other concepts in the field of urban sociology evoke as many contradictory images. To some Americans, the word *suburb* means dreams realized—homeownership, spacious lots, and a good environment to raise the kids. To other Americans, the word conjures up a far less flattering image—tacky bungalows lining treeless streets named oak, maple, and chestnut. To baby boomers like myself, there is no value judgment associated with the suburb; it was the way everybody lived. Since we were raised in the suburbs, we accepted as normal the child-oriented culture, the convenient schools and shopping, and the dependency on the automobile. Rarely did we visit the central city.

In reviewing the literature on the suburbs, one finds, along with these divergent images of the suburb, a complex overlay of myth and distortion. One myth is that suburbs are something new and unique to the twentieth century. The truth is, as long as there have been cities there have been suburbs. When the elite of the ancient city of Ur wearied of the noise and filth of the city, they retired to their suburban villas. Archaeologists also have found evidence of a suburban region around Rome, Athens, and other ancient cities—again for the benefit of the wealthy. As early as 1820, the U.S. Census evoked the category *suburb* to describe the urban development that had taken place on the outskirts of our largest cities. By the census of 1890, most of the nation's large cities had well-developed suburban rings. The most telling of all census dates are 1890, 1920, and 1970. In 1890, the Census Bureau could no longer trace a frontier land, and we had become a nation that spanned an entire continent. In 1920, the Census Bureau reported that more people lived in cities than in rural areas—we had become an urban society. In 1970, the Census Bureau reported more Americans lived in suburbs than in central cities or rural areas—we had become a nation of suburbs.

Defined broadly as that area outside the central city but within the boundaries of the metropolitan statistical area, suburbs now hold 157.4 million of our nation's 281 million population (U.S. Census Bureau, 2001). Suburbs are not new, and the image of the romantic and bucolic suburb has a European rather than an American origin, but American suburbs share four characteristics that make them unique in the world. Americans live in suburban areas far from their place of work, in homes they own, which are built in the center of yards that are enormous by world standards and that are surrounded by other households of the same social class. Therefore, low population density, homeownership, homogeneous residential social status, and journey to work are the elements that make America's suburbs unique.

The process of suburbanization has been studied for most of this century, yet it is still poorly understood. A review of the literature on the suburb shows that at times suburbanization has been viewed as the solution to and at other times the cause of urban ills. For example, as early as 1905, the sociologist Charles Zueblin declared, "The future belongs not to the city but to the suburb." In a little more than fifty years, the process framed as a solution to urban problems was redefined as a problem itself. In the 1950s, authors like Reisman (1958) voiced the concern that the movement of the middle class and their skills and money to the suburbs was draining the vitality from central cities and aggravating the problems of poverty and racism.

In the past three decades, a new generation of sociologists has begun to study suburbs, and they are questioning the images of the suburb developed in the past. They ask: Are suburbs a new phenomenon, or do they represent the normal fringe development of a city? Are the images of the suburb as the bastion of the well-educated, white, affluent middle class and the central city as the home of the poor, uneducated, and minorities correct? Are suburbs all alike or are there different suburban types? Does suburban growth intensify the political, social, and economic problems of central cities, or is this a myth? Are the needs of women, the elderly, and minorities met in the suburbs? These questions are addressed in this chapter. The goal of this discussion is to separate the myth of the suburban process from the reality by studying the suburbanization process in the broad perspective of the metropolitan area as a whole.

Our Changing Image of the Suburb

Our image of the suburb has changed dramatically over the past century. Once considered a process that would solve urban ills, suburbanization was later thought to contribute to them. This shift in attitude can be explained by changes in the perceived nature of cities and changes in the social and intellectual biases of the researchers conducting suburban studies.

The Suburban Image of the 1920s

Harlan Douglas published one of the first comprehensive books on the suburb in 1925, *The Suburban Trend.* In this work suburbs were viewed positively. To Douglas, the suburbs represented the early states of development of an exciting new urban form. They combined the amenities of the city with the low density of the countryside, a place that brought together the best of both worlds. Douglas was writing during a period of history when many of the negative by-products of industrialization and urbanization were manifesting themselves in cities. The filth and squalor, as well as the crime, political corruption, and social disorganization found in cities, suggested to him that a new urban form was needed. The suburb was thought to be the place where the traditional forms of social control could be brought to bear on these evils. Such an attitude is not surprising. Douglas and many of the other urban researchers of his era had been raised in small towns and rural areas. These were the social forms with which they were most familiar and in which they placed the greatest hope (Douglas, 1925).

The Suburban Image in the 1950s

Ironically, a little more than twenty-five years after the publication of *The Sub-urban Trend*, the process framed as a solution to urban problems was rede-fined as a problem itself. After World War II, liberalized lending policies of the Federal Housing Authority and the Veterans Administration made suburban housing affordable to working- and middle-class people. The explosive growth of fringe areas of cities in the decade ending in 1960 led many students of the city to worry about the future of American civic culture. Reisman voices these sentiments in an article written in 1958:

> *The city [before World War II] represented the division and specialization not only of labor but of attitude and opinion; by discovering like-minded people in the city, one developed a new style, a new little magazine, a new architecture. The city, that is, provided a "critical mass" which made possible new combinations—criminal and fantastic ones as well as stimulating and productive ones. Today, however, with the continual loss to the suburbs of the elite and the enterprising, the cities remain huge enough for juveniles to form delinquent subcultures; but will our cities be able to continue to support cultural and educational activities at a level appropriate to our abundant economy? (p. 5)*

Reisman was part of a new generation of sociologists whose background was not in the countryside but in the great cities. These people were accustomed to the noise, filth, and social disorganization of the city, but appreciated its diversity and complexity. Rather than focusing on the negative aspects of urban life, they saw the city as a vital element of American culture. Their work is the basis of the present image of the suburb—single-family homes, crabgrass-free lawns, picture windows, familism, station wagons, backyard barbecues, and neighborliness. Suburbanization meant not only more spacious living but also a more gracious lifestyle.

This group was aware that suburbs had existed around the nation's largest cities since the nineteenth century. This group, however, believed suburban growth in the post–World War II period was a unique phenomenon because of the rate and magnitude of the growth. Moreover, this group viewed suburban growth as negatively affecting city life in many ways. First, these critics argued that as the middle and upper classes moved to the suburbs, the city would be deprived of its traditional leadership. Second, as these groups moved outward, leaving behind the poor, the old, and the minorities, the problems of poverty and racism in the city would become worse. Third, these critics suggested that the movement of the middle class to the suburbs would cause an erosion of the tax base and that cities would have fewer financial resources with which to solve their problems. Finally, these sociologists suggested that the financial plight of cities was worsened by suburbanites' practice of living on the city's fringe in politically autonomous com-munities but working at the city's center, consuming city services but not paying for them. In this sense, the poor in the central city were viewed as subsidizing the affluent in the suburban ring.

These authors also directed their criticism to the structure and lifestyle of the suburbs. Planners argued that suburbs squandered the nation's resources. Because of their low density, suburbs consumed large amounts of land in housing con-struction. Normally built on a modified grid pattern, they used water, sewer, gas, road, and electrical systems inefficiently. Socially, they were viewed as negatively affecting both men and women—the housewife isolated in the cape cod with the children by day was ignored at night by the breadwinner exhausted from commuting to the city. Thus, the critics thought the modern suburban lifestyle was unique and inevitably transformed the character of suburbanites.

The Suburban Image in More Recent Decades

In the decades that followed, other generations of sociologists began to study the suburbs and to question the prevailing image of suburban life. Scott Greer (1962) was among the first to interject a cautionary note into the central city-suburban debate. He pointed out that suburbia, in the strictest sense, is only an artifact of the static boundary lines of the central cities. Most new construction takes place outside a city's boundaries because undeveloped land is unavailable in central locations. In addition, Greer noted that the population attributes used by Reisman and others in the 1950s to characterize suburbs (white, middle class, and familistic) are shared by people living in many of the central city's neighborhoods (Greer, 1962).

In the forty years since Greer's cautionary remarks, two generations of urban sociologists have explored the suburbanization process. Many of these researchers were raised in the suburbs, and their background shaped their outlook just as the experiences of earlier generations shaped theirs. These newer cohorts, however, benefited from hindsight, and by testing the work of others, they achieved greater objectivity in their research.[1]

The Suburbanization Process in Historical Perspective

As we have seen, in the field of urban sociology a new generation of researchers has built on the work of the past to create a better understanding of suburbanization. This same process is underway in urban history. By far the most important recent history on suburbia is Kenneth T. Jackson's award-winning book, *Crabgrass Frontier: The Suburbanization of the United States*, published in 1985. Housing is one of the most telling artifacts of culture, and the theme woven throughout the work is that the way we have chosen to house our people is a reflection of our national character. Jackson argues that the suburbs that ring all our cities reflect the values and preferences that we as a people have always shared. Since colonial time, Americans have preferred detached dwellings to row houses, owning to renting, and rural to urban life. The suburbs represent a confluence of these values along with other technological and political factors. First, new building technology, especially the balloon or stick-built house, lowered the skill level of the labor needed to build homes and thus lowered housing costs. Second, changing transportation technology affected suburbanization. Walking distances determined the size, density, and character of our earliest cities. In the nineteenth and twentieth centuries, a series of transportation innovations—first, the horse-drawn omnibus and the horse-drawn trolley, then the electrified trolley, and finally the automobile—revolutionalized accessibility and land costs. Third, this nation's abundant resources, especially plentiful land and cheap energy, made suburbs as we know them possible. Finally, there is the often overlooked role of the federal government, whose innovative financing and massive subsidies made suburbanization possible.

According to Jackson, these factors led to the creation of a suburban form unique in the world. The majority of middle- and upper-income Americans live in single-family, detached suburban homes built in the center of lots that are enormous by international standards and that are located far from one's place of work. The following section traces suburban development from 1800 to the present.[2]

Early Suburbanization—The Colonial Period to 1890

With the exception of a few years in the 1970s, cities have grown faster than rural areas since 1820, and suburbanization has always been a part of this process. As early as the 1760s, suburbs could be found around major cities like Boston and Philadelphia. These were not the suburbs we know today but a mixture of rural, village, and urban life. Many of these communities provided country homes for the wealthy, but other activities too noxious for the nearby cities—soap making and tanning—along with farming and village life were found side by side in the urban fringe.

Traditionally, historians and urban sociologists assumed that the fringe simply responded to changes in the central city. Transportation innovation, for instance, might make the fringe more accessible and ripe for development. Henry Binford in his book on the early suburbs of Boston found this not to be the case. In the early 1800s, Binford found suburban entrepreneurs building toll roads, canals, bridges, docks, factories, and warehouses to foster economic development and to draw Boston's citizens to their newly platted subdivisions. These early suburbs, therefore, did not simply react but played an active role in the city's development. In the case of Boston, the city responded to the capital improvements made in suburban communities.

The Effects of Primitive Transportation Technology

During the years 1800–1890, the United States was undergoing the early stages of the Industrial Revolution. In fact, by 1890 several American cities had become very large. Chicago had grown to 1.1 million, New York to 1.5 million. Although large, these cities were quite compact. Transportation technology was primitive, and the cost of moving goods and people was high. In short, transportation technology defined the geographic possibilities of American cities. Because of their dependency on humans and horses as sources of power, cities like Chicago and New York had a radius of densely built-up area of only four to six miles, respectively (Jackson, 1985; McKelvey, 1963).

The limitations imposed on cities by primitive transportation technology affected many other aspects of life. Weber (1963), writing in this period, remarked with alarm on the appalling congestion of cities. High density combined with the lack of elementary sanitation led to dreadful levels of mortality during the more or less regular epidemics of cholera, typhus, influenza, and other diseases. The visitations of these diseases to New York City can be seen clearly in the graph in Figure 10.1. Note the extreme fluctuations in the graph during most of the nineteenth century and the decline and flatness of the curve in the twentieth century. Public health measures, especially the chlorination of drinking water, greatly influenced this mortality decline, but the lowering of density levels (decongestion) was also an important factor (Rosenberg, 1962).

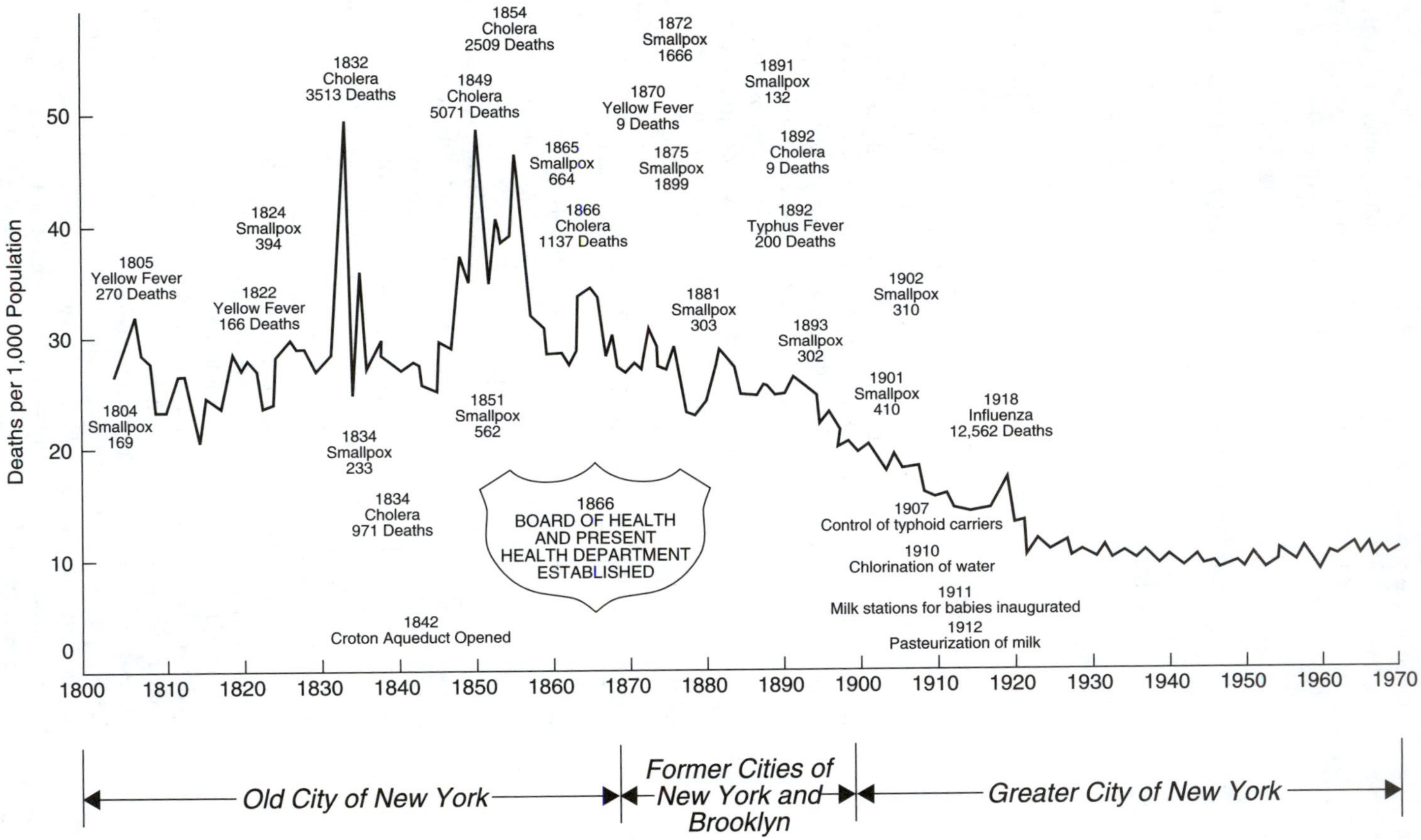

Figure 10.1 *Mortality Transition in New York City* (*Source:* New York City Department of Health, *Summary of Vital Statistics, 1965: The City of New York.* New York: City Department of Health, 1965.)

The Internal Structure of Cities

The internal structure of cities was shaped by transportation technology. In the early stages of the Industrial Revolution, only the wealthy and the small middle class could afford a ride on the omnibus or the horsecar. Most people lived either in the building where they worked or within a short walking distance of their place of employment. Transportation, therefore, did not permit much spatial separation between social classes. Then, as today, the wealthy could absorb the costs of transportation, and many of them lived in the suburbs or satellite towns serviced by steam railroads. Only a small minority of a city's population could afford to commute, and therefore the railroad had little impact on the spatial structure of the city. The horse-drawn trolley or horsecar was a common means of urban transport but only the middle and upper classes who could afford the fares escaped to other parts of the city. In general, the wealthy, the poor, the artisan, and the factory worker lived near one another and near the factories, wharves, and offices of the city (Warner, 1962).

1890–World War I

Before 1890, residential cities were built primarily within the limits of horsepower. This limitation combined with the spectacular growth rates of cities like Chicago and New York led to severe congestion. In 1888 the diffusion of cities' population was made possible by a technological innovation—the electric streetcar.

The introduction of the electric streetcar on the Richmond Union Passenger Railway in 1888 was so successful that within three years more than 175 systems were in operation in the United States. In 1890, 60 percent of all street railways (by mileage) were operated by horses; by 1902 this figure had dropped to 1 percent even though the street railway mileage in this country had more than doubled (Tobin, 1976). This new and efficient form of transportation lengthened the radius of the densely built-up areas of cities like Boston and Chicago to ten miles.

The United States during the decade ending in 1900 was growing at a rate of 1.3 million persons per year, and most of this growth was centered in cities. New York grew from 1.5 million to 3.5 million and Chicago from 1.1 to 1.7 million. Similar growth rates characterized many other cities in the heartland region of the United States. As these cities grew, so did their suburbs. Warner (1962), in his analysis of the streetcar's impact on Boston's suburban development, gives an estimate of the effect of this new transportation form on population diffusion. In 1850, one of every four Bostonians lived in suburbs; by 1900 more than one-third were suburbanites. Boston's population had grown by fourfold between 1850 and 1900, but the population in its suburbs was six times as large in 1900 as in 1850. This pattern was shared by many American cities. The electric streetcar enabled urban populations to spread out and thereby dramatically reduced residential densities.

The Influence of Streetcar Technology

Transportation technology greatly influenced the physical form of cities. Pedestrian cities were usually circular because any place on the periphery could be reached from the center by foot or horse in about the same time. Streetcars, in contrast, ran on rails that are expensive to build and maintain, and they were economically feasible only if they were built between points of high ridership. Initially, streetcar lines were built to connect the central business district with outlying satellite towns eight to ten miles from a city's center. During the early years of a line's operation, the trolleys would travel outside a densely settled city and pass through several miles of undeveloped farmland before reaching their destination. These satellite communities, then, provided the necessary ridership to justify the lines' initial construction. Through time the undeveloped land between the city and the satellite was settled in a pattern prescribed by the transportation technology.

The satellite towns had come into existence originally because of the steam locomotive. Because their economics of operation demanded that a string of cars be pulled, steam engines were not suited to schedules requiring frequent stops. As a result, large expanses of undeveloped land extended between a city and its satellites. Homes in the satellite towns were clustered around a small retail center dominated by the railway station, within easy walking distance. The streetcar, in contrast, was not only based on a more efficient power source—electricity—but was quiet and fast. Cars could be run separately or in tandem depending on ridership demand. Because power could be applied uniformly to the wheels, frequent stops were possible. Therefore, because of the streetcar's speed and its ability to make frequent stops, residential construction could occur on land adjacent to the line between a city and its satellite towns.

In general, the new streetcar technology led to the emergence of the following spatial pattern. Initially, streetcar lines radiated from a city's center in a pattern resembling the spokes of a wheel. Housing construction in the city's undeveloped fringe was limited to areas within easy walking distance of a trolley stop; the stops were frequent and more or less uniformly spaced along the entire line. Through time, the city changed from a circular pedestrian form to a star-shaped form made up of a densely populated core and appendages of streetcar suburbs. The areas between the built-up streetcar corridors were largely undeveloped; they were inaccessible because of the limitation of this form of transportation technology (Ward, 1964; Warner, 1962).

The Growth of Suburbs

This new transportation technology permitted a much-needed decongestion of American cities. For example, Baltimore grew by 10 percent between 1900 and 1910, but its suburbs grew by 45 percent; Chicago grew by 29 percent, and the area surrounding the city grew by 88 percent; Los Angeles tripled in size during the decade, but its suburbs grew by 533 percent. Many of the nation's cities, especially in the Northeast, underwent similar suburban growth (Tobin, 1976).

The Internal Structure of Cities

Another and equally important change in the nature of cities resulted from the electrified streetcar—the spatial differentiation of cities according to class, family type, and ethnicity. Groups that differ in socioeconomic, racial, and ethnic character have always been separated from one another in cities, but primitive technology kept these groups in relatively close proximity to one another. The internal structure of the American city was transformed between 1890 and World War I by several interrelated trends. First, the metamorphosis of society from rural-agrarian to urban-industrial was completed by 1920. This increase in the scale of society was accompanied by changes in the social structure, especially in the percentage of society considered middle class. Second, industrialization brought about more efficient exploitation of natural resources and greater per capita wealth. Greater wealth meant that society could provide housing and other amenities previously impossible. Third, transportation technology permitted the interaction of these two trends and thus led to the greater spatial and functional differentiation of the cities. Therefore, in the quarter of the century ending with the opening years of World War I, American cities were transformed from a preindustrial to a modern metropolitan form.

Suburbanization during this period primarily benefited the middle class, and the city and its fringe began to differ in its social, family, and ethnic characteristics. Although the suburbanized fringe was predominantly middle class, the housing in the area was graded into price and style groupings. The populations in these suburbs were differentiated spatially by income and occupational characteristics, and cities changed in turn. By the start of World War I, American cities were spatially more complex, social distance between groups was reflected in greater physical distance between them, and subareas of the city became associated with different racial, ethnic, and socioeconomic groups (Warner, 1962).

World War I to World War II

It is difficult to define specific periods for any process, but in this analysis dates that correspond to cataclysmic national events are used for good reason. During war, resources that normally would go into housing construction and other areas of the economy are diverted to the war effort. In postwar periods, a nation must undergo major economic and social readjustments as industry shifts from war production and millions of men and women leave the military service and join the civilian workforce. In the post–World War I years this readjustment included the most rapid expansion of suburbs that had ever occurred in America. In the 1920s, for example, central cities grew at a rate of 19.4 percent from 29 million to more than 34 million people, while suburban areas grew by 39.2 percent from 11 million to more than 15 million inhabitants. This development was nationwide in scope; suburbs grew faster than central cities in 70 percent of all United States metropolitan districts. Tobin (1976), commenting on this suburban growth, writes:

> *Many cities experienced rates of suburban growth that would never again be equaled in these urban areas. The central city of Boston grew by 4%, the suburbs by 20%. Cleveland showed a 12% population increase, while its suburbs grew by 125%. New York gained over 1.5 million inhabitants between 1920 and 1930, some 23%, even as the suburbs gained 400,000 persons, a growth of 67%. Saint Louis grew by 5% while the population of the suburbs increased by 107%.* (p. 103)

Suburbanization slowed dramatically during the depression but the metropolitan growth that did occur followed the patterns established during the previous decade, "with new residential construction primarily taking place in the suburbs" (Tobin, 1976).

The Effects of Automobile Technology

This large-scale suburbanization occurred simultaneously with the widespread adoption of the automobile. The undeveloped areas between the streetcar corridors in the city's fringe finally were accessible by means of this transportation innovation. The automobile during this period first competed with and then began to displace the streetcar as the dominant form of urban transportation. The reasons were varied, but cost was a major factor. After World War I, mass production lowered the unit cost of the automobile into the price range of the middle class. Cars also became more reliable and convenient. By the 1920s, the electric starter had replaced hand cranks, and technical improvements reduced the number of breakdowns that had so often plagued the automobile a few years earlier. Also, more gas stations and garages had been built, and more mechanics had been trained to keep the machines running.

An urban population that disliked public carriers readily adopted the automobile. "Mass transit was characterized by crowding, discomfort and inconvenience . . . Streetcars remained crowded and dirty, routes were fixed, service was irregular and unpleasant social intermingling persisted" (Tobin, 1976, p. 101). The private automobile enabled the owner to avoid all these problems and provided other benefits as well. This multipurpose vehicle could be used for commuting, recreation, and shopping. Moreover, it gave the owner a high degree of mobility and access to a more varied choice of goods and services, while at the same time providing privacy and segregation from undesirable groups. Most important was the fact that the automobile was fast and comfortable and permitted the owner to schedule his or her activities at will (Tobin, 1976).

In the decades between the great wars, the automobile became the dominant form of intraurban transportation in the United States. Although rates of adoption differed among cities, figures for St. Louis indicate how rapidly this shift from public to private transportation occurred. "In 1916, 83% of the persons entering the St. Louis' central business district came by streetcar, with 17% coming in automobiles. By 1937, 45% used cars, 12% buses and 27% streetcar" (Tobin, 1976, p. 105). Kansas City and Washington, D.C., made this transition even earlier.

Post–World War II

In terms of sheer numbers, the post–World War II period was the decade of the greatest suburban expansion in United States history. Most of this suburbanization was based on no other transportation than cars, trucks, and buses. An indication of this dependency is reflected in the number of registered motor vehicles. In 1945 about 25 million motor vehicles were registered in the United States; by 1973 this number had grown to more than 100 million vehicles (Tobin, 1976). It would be wrong to suggest that the automobile and other motor vehicles were solely responsible for this suburban development, however. Cars, trucks, and buses permitted the low-density development of retail, manufacturing, and residential areas in the urban fringe, and thus transportation technology set the broad limits within which this expansion could take place. Changes in other spheres of society, however, determined how metropolitan areas would develop within these limits. See Photo 10.1.

Specifically, in the post–World War II period several interrelated changes took place in American society. The baby boom between 1945 and 1960 generated demands for housing that simply could not be met in the existing housing market. Because little housing construction had taken place during the depression years and World War II, the nation was faced with a critical housing shortage.

The federal government through the FHA and VA housing programs made long-term, low-down-payment mortgage money available for the first time. These model programs were copied by saving and lending institutions that provided

Photo 10.1 *The private automobile and hundreds of billions of dollars of public investment in the nation's super highway system made the post–World War II suburbs possible. Shown here is a 1950s highway, a solution that many policy makers thought would solve the problems of urban congestion.(Source: CORBIS/Bettmann.)*

twenty-year loans to the general public for the first time. Previously, the purchase of a home had required a large down payment and a loan period of only four or five years. These changes made homeownership a reality to many socioeconomic groups previously priced out of the housing market. The new mortgage availability also permitted the building of the nation's first "mass-produced suburbs," suburbs of hundreds and in some cases thousands of homes with a standard floor plan and architecture.

In addition, the central areas of many older, industrial cities were undesirable in several respects. First, the housing was old and lacked the modern conveniences that the middle class had come to expect in a suburban home. In the city of Cleveland, for example, the average age of a home was forty-five years in 1960. Second, the pollution from industry and the high density made a central-city location undesirable in some cities. Third, in many cities the only available land was in the fringe (Schwab, 1988).

Finally, technology affected many aspects of urban life, especially the workplace. A revolution in the technological level of American industry in the post–World War II period enabled fewer workers to produce larger outputs of goods and services, which in turn created higher per capita income. This income provided the additional capital necessary for the rapid expansion of the urban fringe (Jackson, 1985).

Suburban Development in the 1970s and 1980s

Suburbs in the 1970s and 1980s underwent a process of consolidation and social and economic integration. The massive decentralization of people and businesses in the postwar period created a set of unique problems, and new urban forms emerged to solve these problems. One of the most important is the edge city. According to Joe Garreau (1991), an edge city is a major concentration of retailing, employment, entertainment, and other activities formerly found only in the central business district. Usually, an edge city has at its center a large regional shopping center, and on its periphery smaller shopping centers and retail strips develop. Over time, office buildings, apartment buildings, hotels, restaurants, and other facilities are built. Edge cities often have retirement communities, medical complexes, entertainment facilities, and wholesale and professional activities nearby. Many of these edge cities have become so large that they have come to rival the CBD.

The King of Prussia, Pennsylvania, was one of the first, located just twenty miles northwest of Philadelphia. At the nucleus of the complex is King of Prussia Plaza, the metropolitan area's second-largest super regional shopping mall, with 1.8 million square feet of selling space, six major department stores, and two hundred smaller shops. Distributed about the vicinity within a five-minute drive of the mall are dozens of highway-oriented retail facilities, including two community shopping centers, one of the region's largest industrial park complexes, one of General Electric's leading research and manufacturing facilities, a variety of office parks and buildings, the Valley Forge Music Fair, five first-run cinemas, at least a dozen fine restaurants, one of the area's best-known cabarets, numerous superior-quality high- and low-rise apartment complexes, and six large motels (Muller, 1981).

King of Prussia is not an isolated example; Garreau was able to find them around every major metropolitan area. Tri-county near Cincinnati, the Galleria in Dallas and Houston, and the edge cities that have developed around the nation's major airports, including Hartsfield Jackson in Atlanta and O'Hare International in Chicago, bear testimony to the emergence of edge cities as a new urban form in the history of our suburban development. Unfortunately, Garreau points out, edge cities are seldom planned, so the different activity centers are built without concern for the rest of the center. Because there is no coordination of activities, consumers must drive from one place to another.

Census 2000's Portrait of America's Suburbs

In early 2001, the Census Bureau began the release of Census 2000. The results paint a portrait of an increasingly complex American society and of the metropolitan areas that reflect this complexity. Most metropolitan areas continued their century-long process of accommodating growth by expanding at their fringe. But there were other surprising changes. Some of our oldest and most troubled central cities experienced a renaissance. Businesses expanded in their downtowns and their populations stabilized and in some cases grew, reversing decades of decline. Other changes occurred on the fringe and new terms like *boomburbs* and *edgeless cities* entered our language to describe them.

The Census Bureau uses the official term *metropolitan statistical area* (MSA) to describe metropolitan areas. An MSA is composed of a central city with at least 50,000 or more people and with one or more counties that are politically, socially, and economically dependent on the central city. Another geographical unit, the urbanized area, is used by the Census Bureau to describe a different part of the MSA. The urbanized area is the central city and the densely populated area that surrounds it. The suburban ring, therefore, is either the population outside the central city but within the urbanized area (a conservative measure) or the population outside the central city but within the counties that make up the MSA (a more liberal measure). I will use both measures in this chapter.

Metropolitan Statistical Areas

In 2000, 80.3 percent of Americans (226 million people) lived in metropolitan areas. The population within MSAs increased by 14 percent during the 1990s. Almost one-third (30 percent) lived in metropolitan areas of at least 5 million people. The New York MSA was the most populous metropolitan area, surpassing 21 million and making up 7.5 percent of the total U.S. population. Los Angeles was the second-largest metropolitan area with 16.4 million or 5.8 percent of the total. The top ten largest metropolitan areas experienced healthy growth in the 1990s, with Dallas experiencing the highest growth rate, 29 percent, and Philadelphia the slowest, 5 percent. Metropolitan areas with population of between 2 million and 5 million in 2000, grew the fastest during the decade, up 20 percent. Las Vegas was the fastest-growing MSA in the 1990s, growing 83 percent. Although central cities and suburbs grew during the decade, most of the metropolitan growth was still in the suburban fringe. Suburbs grew 18 percent during the decade, central cities 11 percent. By the end of the decade, less than 44 percent of the nation's metropolitan population lived in central cities (U.S. Census Bureau, 2001).

Central Cities

Census 2000 revealed that many of the nation's central cities experienced population decline, but many others had remarkable growth during the 1990s. Eighty-seven of the nation's central cities grew by 10 percent or more; 55 cities grew between 2 and 10 percent; 20 cities remained unchanged; and 33 cities declined. Las Vegas and Plano, Texas, led the high-growth group with increases of 85.2 percent and 72.5 percent, respectively. Other high-growth cities included Irvine, California, and Winston-Salem, North Carolina. With only a few exceptions, these high-growth central cities were in the Sunbelt, particularly in the West. At the other end of the spectrum were central cities that lost more than 2 percent of their population. St Louis, Missouri, and Hartford, Connecticut, had the ignominious distinction of experiencing population declines of more than 12 percent during the decade. Other big losers were Buffalo, New York, with a 10.8 percent decline, and Cincinnati, Ohio, with a 9 percent decline. With only a few exceptions, all of these cities were in the Midwest and Northeast. Thus, there were distinct regional differences in growth rates. The average growth rate for cities in the West was 19.5 percent; the South, 12 percent; and the Midwest, 3.4 percent. Cities in the Northeast had the slowest growth, with many of the region's central cities losing population during the decade (Glaeser, 2001).

Why did the South and West grow so well? The simplest explanation is the weather. Cities in regions with harsh winters grew by less than 5 percent while cities in regions with mild winters grew by 15 percent or more. Why is weather so important? One explanation is that generations of Americans have been correcting the mistake made by the original European settlers. For the past 50 years, Americans have been leaving the cold and wet of the Northeast for the warm or dry of the South and West. Another explanation is technological—air conditioning made the region habitable, and cheap transportation allowed businesses to take advantage of the Sunbelt's cheap labor and benign climate (Glaeser, 2001).

There were other patterns as well. Cities with highly skilled and educated populations grew by 16 percent; those without grew by only 7.5 percent. Cities tied to the new economy grew by 13.3 percent; cities dependent on manufacturing grew by less than 5 percent. Cities built for cars grew by 16 percent; cities designed for mass transit and pedestrians by 3 percent. So if you put it all together, the reasons for the regional differences are tied to the city's time of settlement and to its economic base. Cities in the Northeast and Midwest are older. They have an industrial and manufacturing base, a higher concentration of ethnic and racial groups, and densities high enough to support mass transit and pedestrian travel. Cities in the South and the West are the opposite. They are newer. Their economies are tied to service, distribution, and the new economy. They have ethnically and racially diverse populations, but they are members of the newest wave of immigration, Hispanics and Asians. Finally, they are automobile dependent because of their low population densities (Glaeser, 2001).

The new census figures also confirm some disturbing trends—whites continue to abandon many of America's cities. In the past decade, eight of the nation's ten largest cities, and most of its top 100, saw their white non-Hispanic population fall. And as they leave, they take businesses and jobs with them. The result is a declining tax base, and city budgets are squeezed ever more tightly. St. Louis is a good example. It lost almost a quarter of its white population in the 1990s. Baltimore, lost nearly one-third. So many whites have left Detroit, nearly half, that the city's population slipped under the million mark for the first time in decades. Evidence suggests that it's not just a racial issue; it has more to do with class and income. In Detroit, for example, the city lost not only a large share of its upper- and middle-income whites but also upper- and middle-income blacks. The city's poor schools, lack of service, and high taxes pushed them out of the city and into the suburbs.

Downtowns

In the 1970s and 1980s, downtowns in most metropolitan areas became ghost towns at night. High-rise office buildings and a few of the flagship stores of large department store chains dominated downtowns. To be sure, restaurants and specialty shops catered to office workers, but, for the most part, few people lived downtown. The people who worked in the downtown lived in the suburbs or other parts of the central city.

Oh, what a difference a decade makes. In a recent study by the Fannie Mae Foundation, researchers found that among the twenty-four cities in their sample, eighteen cities saw increases in their downtown populations. The population increase in downtowns is small compared to the growth in other parts of the metropolis, but the trend is reflecting a significant reshuffling of people in all parts of the nation's metropolitan areas. Interestingly, an increase in the white population is leading the resurgence in downtown living. This is in sharp contrast to the general decline in the white population in other parts of the central city. Cities in the study where both the central-city and its downtown populations are up include Houston, Seattle, Chicago, Denver, Portland, Atlanta, Memphis, San Diego, Colorado Springs, Los Angeles, Boston, and Des Moines. Cities where the central-city population is down but the downtown population is up include Cleveland, Norfolk, Baltimore, Philadelphia, Detroit, and Milwaukee. In a few cities downtown populations were down—Charlotte, San Antonio, Lexington, Phoenix, Cincinnati, and St. Louis—but they were in the minority (Sohmer & Lang, 2001).

Why the growth? Baby boomers are becoming empty nesters. Without children, empty nesters often change their lifestyle in a way that favors downtown living. Many are ready to trade the hassle of suburban homes for apartments or condominiums. Many have the leisure time to dine out and to take advantage of the cultural and other events that the downtown has to offer. Not to be underestimated is the importance of a dramatically declining crime rate. Downtowns were significantly safer in the 1990s than in previous decades. A central location, proximity to mass transit, work, museums, art galleries, sporting events, and shopping mean that the nation's downtowns should continue to grow into the next decade (Sohmer & Lang, 2001).

Growth in the Suburbs

Although Census 2000 pointed to some promising signs that central cities and their downtowns are doing better, the fact remains that suburbs grew faster than cities during the 1990s. The central cities in the nation's 365 metropolitan areas grew by 11 percent; their suburban population grew by 18 percent. Major regional differences mirror the changes in central-city populations that we have already discussed. The central-city population of Austin, Texas, grew by 33 percent, its suburban population by 48 percent. Atlanta's city population grew 6 percent, its suburban population by 44 percent. Chicago grew a modest 4 percent, but its suburbs grew by 12 percent. For decades Washington, D.C. has been plagued with financial mismanagement, poor schools, and high-crime rates, and its population abandoned the district for the suburban ring. The city's population declined 6 percent during the decade, but its suburbs grew by 17 percent. St. Louis, long used as an example of the urban crisis, lost more than 12 percent of its population, but its suburbs continued to grow, totaling 5 percent during the decade (Katz, 2001).

Metropolitan areas don't grow evenly at their fringe; they tend to expand in one direction until they outstrip their transportation network and other infrastructure needs like water and sewer systems. The Chicago MSA is a good example. The MSA is composed of eight counties in three states, Illinois, Indiana, and Wisconsin. The city grew by 4 percent, and Cook County in which the central city is located grew by 5 percent during the decade. But most of the Chicago MSA's population growth went to outlying areas. Will and Kendall Counties, for example, grew by 41 percent and 38 percent, respectively (Katz, 2001).

Sprawl

Most metropolitan areas are like Chicago. They are growing through a process known as *sprawl*. They are adding urbanized land at a much faster rate than they are adding population. Between 1982 and 1997, the amount of urbanized land in the United States increased by 47 percent, from approximately 51 million acres in 1982 to 76 million acres in 1997. During this same period, the nation's population grew by only 17 percent. Of the 281 metropolitan areas included in a study by the Fannie Mae Foundation, only 6 percent became denser during this period (Fulton et al., 2001).

The conventional thought is that metropolitan areas in the South and West are the sprawlers. In reality, metropolitan areas in the Northeast and Midwest are the sprawlers, and their new fringe development is at extremely low densities. See Photo 10.2. Of the 179 metropolitan areas that experienced slow or no population growth in the 1980s and the 1990s, 65 percent of them were located in these two regions. Fifty-six of the two regions' metropolitan areas lost population during this period, but they increased their land area by an average of 8 percent. Boston is a good example. Boston's central city population grew by only 6.7 percent in the 1980s and 1990s, but the MSA's land area grew by almost half (46.9 percent). Fragmented metropolitan government, an old housing stock, a manufacturing and industrial economic base, poor schools and public services, and large minority and ethnic populations contribute to the move of middle- and upper-class residents to the suburban fringe (Fulton et al., 2001).

The West, in contrast, had the highest metropolitan densities of any region. Ten of the fifteen densest metropolitan areas in the nation were located in Pacific Coast states like California, Oregon, Washington, and Hawaii. In fact, their population densities were significantly higher than even the older MSAs of the Atlantic Coast Region in New York, New Jersey, and Pennsylvania. The

Photo 10.2   *To many Americans, the "American Dream" is track housing in a new suburban development. Today, many policy makers ask, "Can we afford to build low-density housing on the urban fringe?"* (*Source*: Alan Schein/CORBIS/Bettmann.)

reason? Many metropolitan areas in the western United States are hemmed in by mountains and public lands. The region's cities also have a heavy reliance on public water and regional sewer systems. The region's central cities have a younger housing stock, their local economics are tied to the clean businesses of the new economy, and master-planned communities are more common in the West than in other regions. All these factors contribute to higher population densities. Cities in the South fall somewhere in between. Southern cities are accommodating most of their growth on the fringe, but at a rate lower than the Midwest and Northeast (Fulton et al., 2001).

Boomburbs

In the 1980s, a newspaper reporter named Joe Garreau introduced the term *edge city* to describe the concentration of retail, office, and commercial activities that had grown around large regional, suburban malls. In his 1991 book he identified edge cities around all the nation's major metropolitan areas. Social scientists felt edge cities were responsible for the sprawling suburbanization of the 1980s and 1990s.

Robert Lang and Patrick Simmons, researchers with the Fannie Mae Foundation, introduced the term *boomburb* in 2001 to describe a new type of large, rapidly growing suburban city that emerged in the latter part of the twentieth century. They suggest that boomburbs may replace edge cities as the ultimate symbol of the sprawling postwar metropolitan form.

Boomburbs are places with more than 100,000 residents that are not the largest city in their metropolitan areas. In addition, they have maintained double-digit rates of population growth over several decades (Lang & Simmons, 2001). Boomburbs develop around a major intersection on the beltways that ring most large metropolitan areas. Over time, development around these intersections include big-box stores, like Wal-Mart, K-Mart, Target, Home Depot, and Lowe's, a regional hospital, office parks, restaurants, multiplex theaters, and retail and commercial strip developments. Subdivisions dominated by single-family homes ring these commercial cores. Together they form a boomburb. Boomburbs, therefore, possess all the elements usually found in cities, but they lack a dense business core, and they have a much lower population density. They are totally auto dependent. Although the Census Bureau often defines these places as urban, they have a suburban feel about them.

In analyzing Census 2000, Lang and Simmons identified fifty-three boomburbs. Only one boomburb exists outside the Sunbelt, and just nine boomburbs lie outside the Southwest. Los Angeles, Dallas, and Phoenix alone contain thirty-two of the fifty-three boomburbs. Los Angeles, with eighteen, has the highest number of boomburbs and biggest cumulative boomburb population. The Phoenix MSA, however, has the highest percentage of its metropolitan population living in boomburbs, 42 percent. The boomburb population of this city exceeds the population of the central city. Most of the rapidly growing metropolitan areas east of the Mississippi, such as Atlanta, lack boomburbs. Chicago is the only MSA in the Midwest and Northeast with a boomburb (Lang & Simmons, 2001).

Why does the West dominate boomburb development? Hemmed in by mountains and federal lands, dependent on large, subsidized water projects, boomburbs in the West are often products of master-planned community development built in a single municipality. The South's suburbs, in contrast, are comprised of mostly small, fragmented municipalities that capture only a tiny fraction of metropolitan population growth. MSAs in the Northeast and Midwest share many of these same fragmented qualities.

Because of their fast growth, boomburbs face many growth-related problems, such as traffic congestion, poor public services, and sprawl. However, because of their large size and their potential to cooperate with other large municipalities, boomburbs may prove well positioned to participate in comprehensive regional solutions to these problems in the future. If, as many policy makers argue, regional cooperation is becoming more essential to take on problems like sprawl, then the West boomburbs may put the region at a distinct advantage (Lang & Simmons, 2001).

The final chapter of this book is devoted to urban planning, and we will explore the attempts of urban planners to address the problems of sprawl.

The Suburbanization of Jobs

As we have seen, the population of U.S. cities decentralized during most of the twentieth century. In the opening decades of the century, streetcar lines started the process. In the decades following World War II, the automobile accelerated it. As people left the central city for the suburbs in the 1950s, retail was the first to follow. As the workforce moved to the suburbs in the 1960s and 1970s, business and industry moved next. In the 1980s and 1990s, the process continued, but this time it was commercial office space. Although central cities are no longer losing population, the fact remains that central cities continue to lose their market share of the jobs created in metropolitan areas. Here are the figures for a few cities. Between 1992 and 1997, employment in Atlanta's central city grew by 14.5 percent, but employment in its suburbs grew by 30.6 percent. In metropolitan Chicago, job growth in the central city grew by less than 1 percent (0.6), but its suburban employment grew by 14.4 percent. In metropolitan Washington, D.C., the city lost 2.7 percent of its employment base, while its suburbs grew a healthy 18.8 percent (Katz, 2001).

A recent Brookings Institution report gives a broader picture. Researchers found that fifty-three of the ninety-two metropolitan areas in their study held less than half the jobs in their metropolitan areas (Brennan & Hill, 1999). They also found that more than half (fifty-two) of the cities had an increase in jobs, but their growth rates trailed the growth rates of their suburbs. One-quarter (twenty-three) of the central cities experienced employment losses while their suburbs enjoyed employment gains. Only 20 percent (seventeen) of the cities had positive employment growth rates that exceeded the growth rates in their suburbs. Even when central cities gained new jobs, the vast majority of them—seventy-five central cities—lost market share to their suburbs. This loss of market share is not confined to older industrial cities of the Northeast and Midwest. Cities in the South and West, which experienced strong employment growth between 1993 and 1996, were still outpaced by their surrounding suburbs (Brennan & Hill, 1999). Stated even more strongly, during the most rapid expansion of our economy in history, four out of five major cities were not able to stage a comeback. These were the boom times; how will cities fare during sour economies? There is a growing realization among policy makers that decentralization of employment is no longer just a Snowbelt issue. It is a national problem because central cities in all regions are losing employment. The loss is so great that the central cities of many metropolitan areas are no longer the economic engines of the region.

At the beginning of the twentieth century, poor transportation meant that most urban Americans lived close to where they worked. As late as 1950, the typical city still had a high-density core where most people worked, but a majority of these workers lived in the suburbs and commuted by car. As a result of these changes, census data shows that the distance between where Americans work and live has increased each decade during the last century. Are jobs sprawling along with the fringe? Researchers at the Brookings Institution tried to answer this question by counting the jobs within a three-, ten-, and outside a ten-mile ring around the central business district of the nation's 100 largest metropolitan areas. On average only 22 percent of people work within three miles of the city center. At the other extreme, 35 percent of people work more than ten miles from the city center. Jobs are indeed decentralizing. In fact, the central city may no longer be a relevant point to measure employment patterns. Most cities are now polycentric, and as we have seen in our discussion, boomburbs, like the ones around Phoenix, provide more jobs and homes than their central city. The researchers also found important regional differences. The Northeast has the least job sprawl, but several metropolitan areas in the West, including San Francisco, Portland, and Las Vegas, also have concentrated employment. This reflects the population trends we discussed earlier. Not surprising, the South is the region with the most job sprawl. As a result the average commuting times for residents of Atlanta, Houston, and Dallas are now the highest in the nation. The average commute in Atlanta is over an hour (Glaeser, Kahn, & Chu, 2001).

One of the truisms of urban sociology is that the changes taking place at the societal level appear first and most clearly in the use of space within cities. There has been no more important change in this society in the past quarter century than the emergence of a new, information-driven, global economy. These changes are mirrored in the remarkable shift of office employment over the past two decades. Since nearly half of all newly hired employees go to work in office buildings, trends in office space give researchers insight into the restructuring of the metropolis in response to global economic change.

In a recent study of the nation's thirteen largest commercial real estate markets, researchers found that between 1979 and 1999, suburbs in many cities, reached parity with central cities in their percentage of metropolitan office space. In 1979, 74 percent of office space was found in central cities, and only 26 percent was found in suburbs. By 1999, the central-city share of office space dropped to 58 percent while the suburban share grew to 42 percent. Some central cities held their office employment—Houston, Dallas, Chicago, New York, and Denver—but in the majority of metros, suburbs have captured more than half of the metropolitan area's office space. The most important finding is that office space is no longer found within a few high-density clusters. In 1999, while 38 percent of all office space was located in the traditional downtown, 37 percent was found in highly dispersed edgeless locations. These new office parks were spread over hundreds of square miles of the urban fringe (Lang, 2000).

People increasingly commute from dispersed locations to dispersed locations. Even the concept of well-defined suburban edge cities seems out of date, as metropolitan areas become edgeless. The home, not the city core or the edge city, is the main concern for most people. People locate their home where there is easy access to jobs, services, friends, and entertainment. The automobile, the Internet, the cell phone, and other technological changes give people flexibility that was unthinkable only a decade ago. If work is near home, fine; if not, commute, and do business on the cell phone. A planning strategy currently in vogue is matching housing construction with jobs. The problem with this strategy is that there is no guarantee that people will live near where they work. Planners once hoped that edge cities would develop like central cities and provide a population density high enough to support mass transit. But there is evidence that edge cities, which have grown up around the nation's large regional malls, are losing out to widely dispersed, unconnected office parks. You have seen them in large cities. They are the nameless office parks found near the exits of the beltways that ring the nation's metropolitan areas (Lang, 2000).

What's behind the decentralization of people, jobs, and almost everything else? From the 1920s until the 1960s, the nation's cities were based on the Fordism manufacturing technique, a type of production characterized by large, vertically integrated companies employing mass-production techniques. Automobile manufacturing is a classic example. Companies used new technologies and workplace organization to increase productivity, profits, and the wages of their workers. High wages, in turn, permitted high consumption. Mass marketing and mass consumption of standardized products is a part of Fordism. Chicago is a classic example of a Fordism city. Its transportation system was dominated by rail, and its communication systems by mail, telephone, and telegraph. Given these limitations, a vibrant center was necessary to coordinate the activities of the metropolis.

Fordism disappeared in the 1970s, and a new set of economic arrangements called post-Fordism or flexible production took its place. (Robert Reich calls it high-value production.) This new system of production is characterized by the growth of small firms that produce small numbers of many different kinds of products rather than large numbers of standardized products. Flexible production is based in new, computer-driven technologies that can be quickly adapted to changing demand. This new production system replaced the Fordist assembly line that requires the large production runs of standardized products to be profitable. The term *flexible production* refers not only to this type of manufacturing, but increasingly to the way the entire economy is becoming reorganized. These changes in the nature of production, when combined with the revolutions in cyber, communication, and transportation technologies are restructuring the metropolis. Rather than the center driving the spatial reorganization of the city, it is now the periphery. Rather than transportation and communication technology dictating land use, the superhighway and high-speed, fiber-optic networks have liberated locational decisions. The bottom line is that the costs of transportation and communication are so low, and every point in a metropolitan area so accessible, that people and the things people do can locate anywhere. The emergence of a polycentric, edgeless metropolis is the product of these changes.

Suburbia and Women, the Elderly, and Minorities

Women and the Suburbs

In the minds of many feminists, the gender inequality that pervades this society is manifested most visibly and clearly in the use of space within the city. In the 1970s, many writers on the concerns of women argued suburbs reflect a living environment designed by men for men; little concern has been given to the needs and roles of women in their planning and construction. Janet Abu-Lughod tells of her experience in the 1970s as the only woman attending a conference on design and the city. The male attendees were excited about a new social model that shortened the work-week to three days and allowed husbands to spend long weekends with the wife and kids in the suburbs. Dr. Abu-Lughod objected to the model as one designed by wealthy white males for wealthy white males. Her concern was that this model would further segregate the roles of men and women. The male participants responded to her concerns first with silence, and then, embarrassment (Rothblatt, Garr, & Sprague, 1979). In the 1950s and the 1960s, residential suburbs with their single-family houses centered on large lots and zoned from nonresidential activities were thought to be a perfect family environment. Men could commute to the world of work in the nearby city by day and escape from the pressures of the workplace in the bucolic environment of the suburbs at night. Women as mothers and home-makers had a relatively safe and protected environment to raise children. So what if the schools, pediatricians, groceries, and dry cleaners weren't nearby? That's what the family station wagon was for.

In the 1970s, this idyllic picture of the suburbs was questioned by a number of studies that showed that this spatial environment was not all that satisfying for women. Helena Lopata (1980) in a survey of Chicago women found that young, single women traveled to many parts of the city while pursuing their roles at home, school, and work—that is, until they married and the first child arrived. After children, the women felt tied down. If the couple moved to the suburbs for the sake of the children, things worsened. The combination of mortgage, trans-portation, and child costs—further exacerbated if the mother quit work—pushed many Chicago area families into a smaller and smaller social world often limited to neighbors. Herbert Gans found the same thing a decade earlier in his study of Levittown, New Jersey. He reported middle-class women, in particular, were frus-trated by the isolation of the suburbs, and they often turned to neighbors for friendship (Lopata, 1980).

These findings were buttressed by studies that compared the lives of subur-ban husbands and wives. Husbands, because they lived and worked in different places, had a far more extensive network of friends and associates outside the suburban neighborhood. The networks of wives, in contrast, were often restricted to the neighborhood. As with marriage, husbands were far more satisfied than wives with their suburban lifestyle (Booth & Choldin, 1985).

Wekerle (1980) and others concluded that suburbanization weighs heavily on women. Why? The separation of residential from nonresidential land uses in the suburbs often means that even the most basic services are not nearby. The segre-gation of families by their age and stage in the life cycle often means isolation from meaningful interaction. Therefore, the low-density suburbs of single-family homes segregated from nonresidential activities were thought to provide an envi-ronment for only one role—homemaker and mother. The contention was that higher density in the central city would provide women greater access to work, shopping, child care, and other services, reducing time pressures and enabling them to better integrate their various roles (Wekerle, 1980).

Things have changed, and the image of the suburbs that shaped our attitudes a decade or two ago may no longer be relevant. In 1950, when the first post–World War II suburbs were being built, only 25 percent of our population lived in the sub-urbs, and the bulk of this nation's business and industry was concentrated in our central cities. In 1970, the suburban population share jumped to 38 percent, exceeding for the first time the population of the central cities (31 percent). By 1980, 45 percent of this nation's population resided in suburbs and only 30 percent in central cities. As we noted earlier in this chapter, this population shift was accompanied by a massive decentralization of manufacturing and retailing. The suburbs now exhibit the diversity long associated with our cities. Peter Muller (1981) described the metropolis of the post-1970s as a polycentric city with a declining central city, an inner suburban ring, and an outer ring of suburbs with edge cities—multipurpose concentrations of shopping, jobs, and entertainment that were formerly found only in the downtown central city. In addition, most of the migrants to the suburbs in the 1950s and 1960s came from the central city. In the 1970s and 1980s, most people living in the suburbs were born and raised in the suburbs. The low-density lifestyle of the suburbs is what they consider normal, not the lifestyle of the central city.

Donald Rothblatt and his associates studied the suburban environment and its effects on women in San Jose, California. They concluded that environmental factors had little impact on women's overall sense of happiness or psychological well-being. Social influences like the age of women, marital status, the age of children, ethnic identity, and education seemed to be more important than environmental factors. The women in the study, however, reported that older interior suburbs and more distant comprehensively planned suburbs were more satisfying than mass-produced suburbs. In all likelihood, the sense of place of older and comprehensively planned communities along with greater accessibility to centralized shopping led to this greater sense of well-being (Rothblatt, Garr, & Sprague, 1979).

Christine Cook (1988) studied the needs of women heading single-parent households and found them to be more satisfied with housing in the suburbs than in the central city. Lower crime rates and less fear of crime were mentioned most often, but the quality of schools and the peace and quiet of the suburbs were other major factors contributing to the women's sense of well-being.

Other researchers report similar results from an analysis of housing data. They find that both men and women prefer suburban over central-city living. Although shopping, schools, and other services are closer in the central city, so were crime, poor schools, and other urban problems. They conclude that neither environment is particularly suitable for the majority of women who struggle to balance the demands of traditional and newer roles. Therefore, there are major gender differences between men and women in their residential preferences. The dramatic shift of employment, retail, and services to the suburbs now seems to better match the concerns of women with their need for transportation, accessibility, and safety.

In general, research shows a continued serious mismatch between the lifestyles of many households and the cluster of housing services found in the suburbs. Recent changes in the suburban ring, however, are beginning to give households greater access to a full range of goods and services once found only in the central city (Spain, 1988).

The Elderly and the Suburbs

Today, eight out of ten Americans can expect to live to retirement age, and as a result people over 65 are the fastest-growing segment of our population. This population will explode early this century when baby boomers retire, and society will be faced with a crisis in social security, housing, medical, and other services.

The changing age composition of our population has implications for society that far exceed those of social services; it also affects the very fabric of our cities. In the past thirty years not only has the elderly population grown, but their numbers in the suburbs have grown dramatically, too. In 1960, only 25.6 percent of the nation's elderly lived in the suburban ring. By 1980, this percentage had grown to 39.4 percent, and by 2000 this figure exceeded 50 percent. As with the general population, more elderly Americans now live in the suburbs than in the central city or rural areas. Providing housing, medical, transportation, and other services to the elderly poses special challenges for this society; therefore, the study of the suburbanization of the elderly has important policy implications. Unfortunately, there has been little research on the residential patterns of the elderly in the suburb; most has been focused on their experiences in the central city.

We do know from studies of the elderly in the central city that elderly Americans represent a unique segment of the housing market. First, since they have entered the last stages of the life cycle, they need less space but greater access to mass transportation and other social services. In other stages of the life cycle, families adjust to changing situations by moving, but the elderly are one of the least mobile segments of our population. Often they have strong emotional attachments to the homes and neighborhoods in which they raised their families, and most have built up large home equities that make the sale of a home more difficult. A number of critics have argued for innovative programs that would subsidize the movement of the elderly to smaller units closer to mass transportation, clinics, hospitals, and other services. They point out a second benefit: Housing needed by younger families with children would be freed up (Welfeld, 1985).

A second problem is the segregation of the elderly because most elderly age in place. Many of the elderly purchased their homes in the 1950s, raised and educated their children, and then stayed in their homes even when the home was too big for them. The surrounding communities no longer really served their needs because they were designed for families with children. This mismatch between the space and service needs of the elderly and the homes and neighborhoods in which they live causes problems, but a far more subtle and insidious problem is often ignored: The segregation of the elderly reduces contacts with other age groups and can result in social isolation.

Much of what we know of the elderly and the city has been gleaned from studies done in the central city. In a landmark study of the suburbanization of the elderly, Fitzpatrick and Logan (1985) found that many of the experiences of the elderly in the suburbs are different from the central city. First, although the suburbanization of the elderly has been dramatic, their segregation in the suburbs is modest and has actually declined over the past thirty years. The only exception is the South, where millions of retirees have settled, often selecting suburban communities that cater exclusively to the needs of older Americans. Second, the researchers found two distinct types of elderly suburbs. In the majority of cases, the elderly tend to be concentrated in denser, poorer employing suburbs. The second group of suburbs had the highest home values and rents in the suburban ring. In this case, high-income retirees had large equities in their homes and relatively low housing costs even though they were on fixed incomes (Fitzpatrick & Logan, 1985).

The policy implications of this research are clear. For many of the suburban elderly, social security, company pensions, savings, and large home equities mean a comfortable retirement in the suburban fringe. For the low-income elderly, the modest levels of segregation suggest the cost of providing services to them is spread across many communities. The downside of this residential pattern is that the efficiency of providing elderly services is low and the costs are higher than in the central city.

Minorities and the Suburbs

Suburbs are often thought of as affluent, predominantly white communities with good schools and little crime. While all suburbs have not conformed to this ideal, our popular conception of suburbs has been radically transformed in the past few decades. In an analysis of Census 2000 data for all 330 metro areas in the continental United States, John Logan (2001) found that while the total suburban population was only 18 percent minority in 1990, that figure had risen to 25 percent in 2000. The total suburban white population scarcely changed in the decade (up only 5 percent) while the number of black suburbanites grew by 38 percent, and the number of Hispanic and Asian suburbanites were up by 72 percent and 84 percent respectively. Whites continue to be the most suburban of all the major racial and ethnic groups; nationally nearly 71 percent of whites now live in suburbs. But minorities are starting to catch up: 56 percent of Asians lived in suburbs in 2000, up from 53 percent in 1990, and 49 percent of Hispanics, up from 46 percent. Lagging behind are African Americans (39 percent), although their current situation represents a significant increase from 1990 when 34 percent lived in suburbs (Logan, 2001). (Check out your metropolitan area at the University of Albany's Mumford Center *www.albany.edu/mumford/census.*)

In some metropolitan areas the shift has been more substantial: Blacks are more than 20 percent of the suburban populations in cities like Atlanta, Washington D.C., New Orleans, Fort Lauderdale, and Miami. Hispanics are a major presence in the suburbs in Miami (56 percent), Los Angeles (45 percent), and San Diego (27 percent). The Asian population, although smaller, is above 10 percent of suburban residents in San Francisco and Los Angeles. Thus, suburbs are beginning to display the income and population diversity that has long been associated with the central city (Logan, 2001).

General trends in the 330 metropolitan areas mask important metropolitan and regional differences. In a more focused study of 102 of the nation's largest metropolitan areas, William Frey (2001) found that minorities comprised more than 27 percent of the suburban population in 2000, up from 19.3 percent in 1990. If you limit the analysis to metropolitan areas of over a million residents, almost half of the minorities lived in the suburbs in 2000, compared to just over 40 percent a decade ago. This surge in minority representation in suburbs has been concentrated in just 35 metropolitan areas that Frey describes as *melting-pot metros*. The South and the West have experienced the most rapid suburbanization of minorities. Melting-pot metros such as Los Angeles, Chicago, Houston, Washington, D.C., and New York have the highest minority suburban populations because of a large influx of Asian and Hispanic immigrants. The regions with the lowest percentage of minority suburbanites are in the Northeast and Midwest—14.3 percent in cities with a large African American population (Frey, 2001).

African Americans returned to the South in record numbers during the 1990s. As a result of their influx to nineteen southern metropolitan areas, the South has regained its status as the home of the largest number of African Americans. The region also has the nation's largest black suburban population. Black in-migrants to the region are different from resident blacks. They are better educated, they are more likely to have managerial or professional jobs, and they have higher incomes. Therefore, they can live anywhere they like, and they have increasingly chosen to live in suburbs (Frey, 2001).

This trend is not just in the South. Across America's cities, African Americans are pulling out. Some observers call it "black flight" reminiscent of the "white flight" that shaped our cities in past decades. Increasingly middle class, they are drawn to the suburbs or pushed out of the cities by newer immigrants—in many cases, Hispanics. A booming economy in the 1990s, the effective enforcement of fair housing laws, and new home-financing programs has made homeownership a reality for more African Americans. Increasingly, these homes have been in the suburbs.

Black flight is most noticeable in California. Santa Ana, for example, saw its non-Hispanic black population drop by one-third, the biggest percentage decline of any of the nation's 100 largest cities. San Francisco was down 23 percent, Oakland and Los Angeles down 12 percent. One of the top black-flight cities outside of California was Miami, down 2 percent of its whites and 18 percent of its blacks. Washington, D.C., saw a 4 percent decline in its white population and a 14 percent drop in its black population. Seattle was one of the few metros that actually gained whites during the 1990s but still saw a 9 percent drop in its black population (Belsie, 2001).

Why black flight? Hispanics are moving into cities in large numbers, often taking over long-time black neighborhoods. In San Diego, for example, a 35 percent increase in Hispanics appears to have pushed out much of the black population from the city's traditional black neighborhoods. The city's black population declined by 8 percent. There were other factors as well. In the 1990s, a tight labor market and an expanding economy helped African Americans afford better housing. In addition, soaring housing costs and gentrification forced lower-income blacks out of the central city to the more affordable housing in older, interior suburbs of many cities (Belsie, 2001).

But does a suburban address guarantee better housing, quality schools, and a lower crime rate? The answer seems to be no. If you sort suburbs into low-, medium-, and high-status categories according to the education and income of their residents, low status suburbs are the home to a disproportionate number of black and Hispanic residents. These are usually older, interior suburbs, and they face many of the problems of the central cities: large numbers of high-cost citizens, a declining tax base, and faltering schools. For example, in 1990 low-status suburbs had a poverty rate that was nearly six times higher than the poverty rate in high-status suburbs, and 40 percent higher than the U.S. poverty rate. More than 40 percent of the suburban blacks and Hispanics live in low-status suburbs; fewer than 10 percent of black and Hispanic suburban dwellers live in high-status suburbs (Harris, 1999).

On the whole, high-status whites and Asians are better off spatially than high-status blacks and Hispanics. For them, suburban living means distance and isolation from lower-status groups, be it in the grocery store, the doctor's office, or school. But this is not the case for blacks and Hispanics (Sims, 1998). This suggests that while advantaged blacks and Hispanics can place some distance between themselves and lower-status groups, they are not able to totally escape being exposed to the conditions of lower-status neighborhoods. In general, well-off blacks and Hispanics live in neighborhoods less consistent with their social status.

Why the differences? Even when minorities have the financial wherewithal to live in high-status suburbs, they don't. If it's not income, then other factors must be at work. Voluntary factors explain some of this segregation, but discrimination plays an important role in the continued segregation of minorities in central cities and suburbs. Minorities face discrimination in all aspects of the housing search process. Field audits by the Department of Housing and Urban Development found that real estate agents provide less information to blacks and Hispanic clients than to whites. Whites are shown twice as many houses as Hispanics and three times as many properties as African Americans. Compared to whites, blacks and Hispanics are less likely to receive follow-up calls; and even when blacks and Hispanics express a desire for high-status suburbs, agents steer them to less-desirable areas (Yinger, 1995). All these factors affect the persistence of housing discrimination in the central cities and the suburbs. As a result, in this society there are two types of suburban experiences, one for Asian and whites and another for African Americans and Hispanics (Harris, 1999).

The Stratification of Suburbs

A social class is composed of people who, over time, develop similar access to the scarce resources of a society. A social class shares similar life chances and lifestyles, and its members may even have similar biographies. Objective measures like income, education, and occupation can be used to group people into social classes. When these classes can be arranged in a hierarchy on one or more of these dimensions, then one has a social stratification system. Measures of social status have been found to be a powerful tool in predicting a wide range of behavior ranging from voting to shopping patterns. Just as we can group people according to their social class, researchers have grouped the suburbs where they live. The reason is that the stratification of suburbs has implications for the well-being of people living in suburbs at the top and the bottom of the hierarchy. As we have already seen, African Americans and other minorities tend to live in lower-status suburbs. What is interesting is that once the social status of a suburb has been fixed, it tends to maintain the social status of its residents over time. Why?

The oldest and in many respects dominant theory on the stratification of suburbs is the persistence model. The persistence model argues that in the early stages of settlement a suburb's socioeconomic character and function are fixed and persist through time although the community may undergo rapid population and economic growth at a later date. This model posits the character of a suburb is shaped initially by its niche in the ecological structure of the metropolis—proximity to transportation lines, the central business district, industry, and amenities such as schools, recreation areas, and cultural facilities. Once secured, the character of the suburb persists over time. Why? Researchers have traced the socioeconomic status characteristics of a national sample of suburbs for time periods ranging from thirty to fifty years and have found remarkable stability in status over time (Stahura, 1987). The major reason given is the vested interests of homeowners and other users of land as well as banking and lending institutions. A change in the socioeconomic character of an area would adversely affect the investments of these groups; economic self-interest leads them to preserve the area's character. Thus, not only are there great differences in the character and function of these communities in the urban fringe, once their character is developed, this group argues that they will persist through time.

The stratification or political model of suburbanization draws upon the conflict perspective to explore the politics of place. As we have seen throughout the text, inherent in the character of place is a conflict between use value and profit value of property. Suburbs, like all other places, are in economic and political competition for the scarce resources of the metropolis. Just as opportunities are not equally distributed across groups in our society, some suburbs, because of the income, education, and occupations of their residents, have special access to the resources of the metropolis. High-income suburbs, therefore, are in a position to mobilize resources to benefit their communities. In the area of public housing, high-status suburbs can use tactics ranging from zoning and building codes to endless legal delays to keep out minorities, the poor, and public housing. Low-income suburbs, especially those adjacent to the central city, have no such access and can be expected to decline in status. In this model, not only would status differences persist, but inequality should increase over time.

Which theory is correct? Logan and Schneider (1981) found fluidity in the status hierarchy of suburbs under conditions of rapid population growth. This was particularly true of poorer suburbs in southern metropolises in the path of rapid fringe development. The low densities of southern cities meant that vacant and underdeveloped property could be purchased and quickly converted to other land uses. In northern metropolises where fringe growth had slowed by the late 1960s, the location of suburbs in the status hierarchy had crystallized, and persistence, not fluidity, characterized subsequent decades. As we have seen in earlier chapters of this text, the urban development in the South differed in significant ways from the North. Central cities in the South like Dallas and Houston have used preemptive annexation to bring large tracts of land under their political control, and city/suburban antagonism has been minimized. Northern fringe development has a quite different history.

Suburbs in the North were tools used by middle- and upper-income households to insulate themselves from the politics of the central city. This is also the region where laws passed by state legislatures made it difficult for cities to annex but easy for suburbs to incorporate. Political fragmentation has increased competition between political units and allowed high-status suburbs to use the political system to enhance their position in the hierarchy. In the North exclusionary zoning and a host of related techniques have been used by high-income suburbs to maintain their privileged high-status position (Logan & Schneider, 1981).

The Social Side of Suburbia

To this point, our analysis has shown that in spite of the major redistribution of population and economic activity since World War II, suburbs remain predominantly white, more affluent and more likely than the city to contain upwardly mobile families engaged in the process of child rearing. One wonders why this change has not had a greater impact on the suburban way of life. The answer is a complicated one, but it appears that the highly fragmented political structure of the American metropolis has been able to suppress the social consequences of much of this growth and change. In most American metropolises, many suburbs, smaller in size and politically autonomous, surround the central city. In 2000, the thirty-three largest metropolitan areas encompassed an average of 200 suburban non-school-system decision-making bodies. These political units have broad discretionary powers in the areas of taxation, zoning, and land-use planning. In other words, suburbs are in a position to control the size and quality of their population and to produce a socially homogeneous community. Although suburbs now exhibit the social complexity once found only in the central city, the political structure of the metropolis has minimized these differences by compartmentalizing groups similar in socioeconomic and racial characteristics.

The consequences of these residential patterns are straightforward. The more homogeneous a community, the more likely that a person will find others nearby whose interests and tastes are similar to his or her own. This, in turn, contributes to the development of social networks ("coffee klatching," for example) that often lead to the emergence of beliefs, values, and lifestyle preferences that are associated with suburban living. Therefore, it is not surprising that the behavior of people living in relatively homogeneous suburbs differs from similar groups living in central cities where they are more exposed to groups that differ in their socioeconomic and racial characteristics (Schwartz, 1979).

Lifestyles in Suburbia

The compartmentalized character of suburbs permits groups to pursue unique lifestyles. The lifestyle most closely associated with suburbia is familism. *Familism* refers to a lifestyle that emphasizes activities centered around home and children. The values associated with this lifestyle stand in sharp contrast to alternative American value systems centered on career success and conspicuous consumption. Since American culture stresses all three value systems, there must be a trade-off among them; if a person vigorously pursues a career, he or she will find less time for enjoyable consumption and family life.

Familism conjures up positive images. M. P. Baumgartner, in his thought-provoking book *The Moral Order of a Suburb* (1988), explores a less-flattering consequence of the suburban environment. Claude Fischer (1975) contributes to the discussion on the relationship between social disorganization and the city. Fischer argues that the city's ecological factors of size, density, and heterogeneity are crucial in creating a critical mass of similar people who over time form subcultures. These subcultures have their own value systems, some that reinforce the values of the larger society and some that do not. The conflict and social disorganization of the city, according to Fischer, is the result of an overly rich environment of competing moral communities rather than anomie as described by Wirth and others.

Baumgartner is a cultural anthropologist, and he studied a middle-class suburb the same way anthropologists would study a preliterate tribe. In the course of the study, the one pattern that struck him was the relative tranquility of middle-class suburbs. He discovered the reason; rather than an overly rich environment of moral communities, he found what he called *moral minimalism*. Baumgartner found most of his subjects had shallow, single-stranded relationships with coworkers, church members, and neighbors, when they moved, those relationships usually ended. The tenuous nature of these relationships along with the high mobility of Americans, Baumgartner found, led middle-class suburbanites to use avoidance as their major strategy for dealing with the petty day-to-day problems of life. Baumgartner found this to be true of a whole range of relationships. Middle-class families have large homes, and mom, dad, and the children live different lives during the day and often go their separate ways at night and on weekends. Moreover, the nature of the lifecycle in middle class families means that the kids will eventually go away to college and move away from the suburb. Rather than dealing with marital or child-rearing problems, these families often avoided them by staying in their rooms or staying away from home.

Moral minimalism also described the neighboring he observed. He found neighbors ignoring even the most extreme behavior. Baumgartner relates one case in which a man was seen frequently running around the neighborhood naked in the middle of the night. The neighbor's response: the kids had to stay away from Mr. X's house. Why wouldn't they do something? One reason is the time and emotional costs for intervening. The second, there was a pretty good chance that the problem would simply move away.

Baumgartner cautions that moral minimalism describes middle-class suburbanites living in detached single-family homes. Other class and ethnic groups display very different neighboring activities.

If you examine the literature of the suburbs, one is struck by the diversity of lifestyles represented in the fringe. The decentralization of millions of Americans to the suburbs in the postwar period has created suburban ghettoes, suburban ethnic enclaves, and suburban singles' communities, along with the familistic neighborhoods traditionally associated with the fringe. This mosaic of social worlds was heretofore found only in the central city.

The question remains whether the suburbs are to be understood simply as the product of ecological processes resulting from metropolitan growth or whether they represent a subculture with distinctive values, beliefs, and lifestyle preferences. In truth, there is probably an interaction between the two. American suburbs are usually age and class graded. That is, residents of a suburb often manifest similar demographic characteristics of age, ethnicity, homeownership, and family life cycle. Young homeowners with children in school obviously pursue familistic lifestyles and have a more direct concern in local rather than national problems. The characteristics of these homogeneous, class-compartmentalized suburbs give rise to suburban values and provide an environment supportive of these attitudes.

Why do people choose suburban housing over locations in the central city? Our discussion suggests that the availability of modern housing and schools unaffected by court-ordered school busing, as well as residential environments insulated from the urban ills associated with more centrally located communities, are major determining factors. Equally important is the presence of a residential environment conducive to a "local" and/or familistic lifestyle (Baumgartner, 1988).

The Consequences of Fragmentation

There are other consequences of fragmentation for the entire metropolis. In our federal system, land-use controls, such as zoning, and the provision and financing of public services are a local responsibility. In the minds of some researchers our fragmented governmental structure encourages the suburbanization of high-income households and contributes to the increasing income disparity between the city and the suburban ring. Why? A number of critics argue, political fragmentation creates an incentive for suburbs to pursue exclusionary growth policies. Upper-income families are low-service-cost citizens. The water, sewerage, and waste collection services they need are paid through user fees, and police, fire, and government costs are usually low and are handled through property taxes.

High-income households don't need the subsidized housing, day-care, medical, and other services required of low-income households. Therefore, it is in the best interest of many suburbs to keep low-income/high-cost citizens out, and they use restrictive zoning, minimum lot-size requirements, building codes, impact fees, and other techniques to keep subsidized and low-cost housing from being built within their borders (Logan and Schneider, 1981).

Once a pattern of exclusion is established, it perpetuates itself by influencing the way people choose a residential location. Likes attract and higher-income households usually settle in suburbs of the same social class. No high-cost citizens means higher-income suburbanites often receive excellent services at a cost lower than the mediocre ones found in the central city (Logan & Schneider, 1981).

There is a final and far more subtle effect of fragmentation. For most of this century, central cities could dictate policies for the metropolis because they had the largest populations and because most of the region's jobs were within their borders. The massive decentralization of people, manufacturing, industry, and trade in the past forty years means that central-city governments are no longer the dominant player, but rather just another player in the competition for the scarce resources in the metropolis. The loss of this leadership role has wide-ranging implications for the central city's ability to cope with the massive human, infrastructure, and fiscal problems they face.

The Impact of the Suburbs on the Central City

A broader issue related to the central city's loss of political power, pits the suburbs against the central city: Who pays for the services the suburbs cannot provide for themselves? Put another way, do suburbs pay their fair share of the central-city services they consume?

It now appears that the growth of the suburban ring has had measurable costs to the central city, especially in the area of public services. For decades, city officials and urban planners charged that the suburbs were exploiting the city. They argued that commuters use central-city services but escape paying for them by living in the suburbs. In the opinion of many critics their free ride exacerbates the fiscal problems of the central city in its struggle to provide basic services to the growing number of poor and disadvantaged.

Critics on the suburbs' side analyzed metropolitan data and found retail and office operations require fewer services than manufacturing and industry. They also found the cost of providing public services to manufacturing and industry exceeded the tax revenue generated, but with retail and office functions, the tax revenue exceeded the cost to government of providing services. In their opinion, the massive decentralization of manufacturing and industry to the suburban ring has reduced the service load of the central city. There is no free ride: Suburban commuters more than pay for the services they use in the city. This issue receded from the public agenda during the 1990s, but we believe it will reemerge as one of the more important policy issues in the first decade of the twenty-first century. Why? Simply because the problems of our cities will become more serious. Who will pay, how much, and for what must be addressed. This discussion, however, will occur with a different backdrop because of the massive reshuffling of people that occurred between America's cities and suburbs in the last decade of the twentieth century.

Summary

This chapter provides an overview of the changing relationship between the central city and its suburban fringe. Suburbanization is not a new process; it has been a part of this nation's history since its inception more than 200 years ago. However, low population density, homeownership, homogeneous residential social status, and journey-to-work are the elements that make America's suburbs unique.

The suburbanization process is described during four periods spanning more than 200 years, from 1800 to the present. In the earliest period, Early Industrialization, 1800–1890, most people walked; as a result, one's place of residence and employment were close together. Because of the primitive state of transportation technology, cities were settled at high density and took a circular shape. Moreover, groups that differed in socioeconomic status lived near one another. Only the wealthy could escape to the urban fringe. In the periods that followed, the introduction of new transportation technology, first the electric streetcar and later the automobile, changed American cities into their present-day form. The streetcar era, spanning the years from 1890 through World War I, permitted the first decentralization of the middle class to the suburbs. Later, improvements in automobile technology accelerated the process. In the post–World War II period, in particular, rapid population growth combined with environmental constraints, organizational changes, and technological breakthroughs in transportation and communication led to unprecedented growth of urban fringe areas. In the 1980s, suburbanization slowed, but in the 1990s, suburban growth accelerated, spurred on by the tremendous growth of the economy.

Census 2000 paints a complex picture of American society, and this complexity is reflected in metropolitan structure. More than 80 percent of Americans live in metropolitan areas, and almost one-third live in metropolitan areas of more than 5 million people. Surprisingly, the majority of central cities also grew in the 1990s, with metros in the West and the South experiencing the most rapid growth, followed by the Midwest and Northeast. Also surprising was the growth of residential populations in the nation's downtowns. The baby boomers' move into the later stages of the family lifecycle, along with a drop in the crime rates, explain this growth.

Although central cities and their downtowns have done better in the 1990s, the fact remains that suburbs grew faster than central cities throughout the decade. In older metropolitan areas in the Northeast and Midwest, these differences are pronounced. In general, cities are growing as they have for the past half century by expanding on their fringe through a process known as *sprawl*. Many policy makers view sprawl as the single most serious problem facing urban America. Counter to conventional thought, the metros in the Northeast, not the West, are the sprawlers. Western cities, often ringed by mountains and federal lands, and dependent on massive federal water projects, tend to be denser. The metros in the Northeast are the sprawlers because people are moving to the fringe to escape the problems of the central cities.

Whereas sprawl defines the suburbanization of the Midwest and Northeast, boomburbs define the suburbanization taking place in the Southwest. Boomburbs are places with more than 100,000 residents that are not the largest city in their metropolitan areas. In addition, they have maintained double-digit rates of population growth over several decades. Boomburbs develop around a major intersection on the beltways that ring most large metropolitan areas, and most city services are found there. Boomburbs, therefore, possess all the elements usually found in cities, but they lack a dense business core, and they have a much lower population density. Researchers at the Fannie Mae Foundation identified fifty-three boomburbs with Census 2000. Most lie in the region from Texas to the Pacific Coast. Los Angeles, Dallas, and Phoenix alone contain thirty-two of the fifty-three boomburbs. Los Angeles, with eighteen, has the highest number of boomburbs and the biggest cumulative boomburb population. The Phoenix MSA, however, has the highest percentage of its metropolitan population living in boomburbs, 42 percent. Because of their fast growth, boomburbs face many growth-related problems, such as traffic congestion, poor public services, and sprawl. However, because of their large size and their potential to cooperate with other large municipalities, boomburbs may prove well positioned to participate in comprehensive regional solutions to these problems in the future.

Jobs have followed people to the suburbs. A recent Brookings Institution report found that the central cities in fifty-three of the ninety-two metropolitan areas in their study held less than half the jobs in their metropolitan areas. Moreover, even when central cities gained new jobs, the vast majority of them—seventy-five central cities—lost market share to their suburbs. These changes are mirrored in the remarkable shift of office employment to the suburbs during the past two decades. The most important finding is that that office space is no longer found within a few high-density clusters. In 1999, nearly 40 percent of office space was sited in highly dispersed edgeless locations. The reason is that the costs of transportation and communication are so low, and every point in a metropolitan area so accessible, that people and the things people do can locate anywhere. The emergence of a polycentric, edgeless metropolis is the product of these changes.

In recent years researchers have studied the experiences of women, minorities, and the elderly in the suburbs. A common theme in the literature on women and the elderly is that the low density of the suburbs combined with the lack of crucial social services create an environment that makes the lives of these citizens more difficult. Recent research suggests that some of these services are now becoming available in the suburbs. African Americans moved to the suburbs in record numbers during the 1990s. An improvement in their socioeconomic status in a booming economy along with the enforcement of fair housing laws appear to explain much of this growth. Blacks, however, are still segregated in the suburbs, and as a consequence black Americans receive far fewer returns from their housing dollar than their white counterparts. The numbers of suburban Hispanics have grown rapidly in the 1990s along with the nation's Asian population. In general, the experiences of African Americans and Hispanics in comparison with Asians and whites are very different in America's metros, with the latter group receiving the most benefits from living on the fringe.

Finally, suburbs, like people, can be ranked by socioeconomic status, and the location of suburbs in the stratification system has profound implications for the quality of life in these communities. Two theories were presented to describe changes in the stratification of suburbs. The persistence model argues that the socioeconomic character of a suburb is fixed early in its settlement and that a variety of community actors—real estate, banking, and other businesses—work in concert to maintain the socioeconomic character of the community through time. The political model argues that high-income suburbs have the ability to manipulate the system to their advantage because they can afford to hire the skilled professionals necessary to compete for the scarce resources of the metropolis. This model predicts change, not persistence, but with high-income suburbs maintaining or improving their relative position while low-income suburbs decline in socioeconomic status. Neither theory is completely supported, but northern metropolises fit the stratification model better than metropolises in other regions.

The stratification of suburbs reflects the political reality of the nation's metropolises—political fragmentation. In most American metropolises, many suburbs, smaller in size and politically autonomous, surround the central city. These political units have broad discretionary powers in the areas of taxation, zoning, and land-use planning and have used these powers to compartmentalize themselves into relatively homogeneous enclaves. These enclaves allow people to find suburbs with a physical and social environment conducive to their particular lifestyle or stage in the life cycle. Moral minimalism is one of many lifestyles supported in suburban communities.

Notes

[1] For a critical review of the problems facing contemporary American suburbia, see M. Baldassare, *Trouble in Paradise: The Suburban Transformation in America* (Columbia University Press, 1986).

[2] I would recommend two books on individual suburbs. M. H. Ebner, *Creating Chicago's North Shore: A Suburban History* (Chicago: University of Chicago Press, 1988) is a beautifully illustrated book. Using hundreds of photographs, period maps, and newspaper illustrations, the author provides a panorama of the development of the North Shore from its founding in the nineteenth century to its rapid growth and development in the twentieth.

Zane Miller in *Suburb: Neighborhood and Community in Forest Park, Ohio, 1935–1976* (Knoxville: University of Tennessee Press, 1981) chronicles the development of a postwar, mass-produced suburb, Forest Park, a suburb of Cincinnati. I grew up a few miles from Forest Park and found this work to be a fascinating account of the attempt by the developer to combine elements of new town planning with the need to make a profit. Forest Park is a predominantly black middle-class suburb, and the experiences of this community in dealing with the issue of racial integration are chronicled in this work.

11

THE SEGREGATION AND LOCATION OF GROUPS IN CITIES

Introduction

I'm from Cincinnati. One of my favorite places in the city is Findley Market. Findley Market was founded in the early 1800s, and it is wedged in the center of one of the city's oldest and densest neighborhoods, the Over-the-Rhine.[1] The Over-the-Rhine district was settled by German immigrants and the austere red-brick homes, apartments, and tenements are set one next to the other on narrow lots with no setback from the sidewalks. The market itself is a shed-like structure that runs the length of two city blocks. The inside is broken into open stalls with butchers, sausage makers, fishmongers, poultry sellers, and grocers specializing in butter and eggs, bread and cookies, pickles, sauerkraut—the list is almost endless. On market days, green grocers hawk their produce outside from open stands with only a canvas awning to protect them from the weather. Across the street on all four sides of the market are full-time businesses—butchers, groceries, and specialty stores—that meet the needs of Cincinnati's ethnic communities. It's said that if you can't find it at Findley Market, it's probably not available in town.

Wednesday, Friday, and Saturday are market days, and thousands are crammed into the few blocks of Findley Market. The crush of people and market activities assault every sense. The smell of butchered meat mixes with the sawdust on the floors and blends with the smells of cheeses, breads, produce, diesel exhaust, body odor, and the stink of storm drains—a smell that's both revolting and pleasing. And as you push your way through the crowds, you catch sight of people of every description: black, white, rich, poor, Yuppie, Preppie, Germans, Greeks, Italians, Mexicans, Vietnamese, and those in native dress from Africa, India, and other lands.

Three days a week one finds concentrated in the few blocks of Findley Market the diversity of the city that gives the tang, thrill, and excitement to urban living. The market is a metaphor for the diversity that characterizes the entire city. When people leave the market with their purchases, they return to the city's neighborhoods that have grown up to meet their needs. Cincinnati, like all cities, is a collection of neighborhoods, a mosaic of social worlds. For example, in Cincinnati blacks are concentrated in Avondale, Bond Hill, Oakley, and in older suburbs like Kennedy Heights; Jews in Roselawn and Amberly Village; third- and fourth-generation Germans in Mount Lookout; the wealthy in Hyde Park, Indian Hills, and Mariemount; yuppies in Mt. Adams; and the list goes on. Each group is separated from the others by a process known as segregation.

Urban sociologists have studied segregation for more than a century, and they have been as acutely aware as we have been of the deep social class, racial, and ethnic cleavages in American society. Social scientists recognize that these differences that divide the nation also shape the residential structure of our cities. For a century, we have known that the social distance between groups is reflected in the spatial distance between their residential neighborhoods. Blacks/whites, rich/poor, old ethnics/new ethnics live in and use different parts of the city. Knowing where these groups live, why they live there, and how their location changes tells us much about the processes that shape our cities and our society.

Segregation has social consequences. As previously shown, one's personal safety and accessibility to services like schools, jobs, and medical care are tied to where one lives. Therefore, measures of segregation are the litmus test for evaluating a wide range of social problems from housing to AIDS.

In this chapter, we explore the three forms of segregation—socioeconomic, ethnic, and racial. We will discuss the measurement of segregation; the theories that attempt to describe it; the ecological, voluntary, and involuntary factors responsible for segregation; and the spatial outcomes of this process. Segregation has its costs and benefits, and we will end the chapter by looking at the consequence of this process for the most highly segregated group in our society—African Americans.

Segregation: The Study of Groups

We live our lives in groups. We love, we hate, we gossip, we argue, we solicit advice and give it, we raise our young, we bury our old, we work, and we play within groups. Our earliest experiences as children are with groups—families, cliques, schools, neighbors, and athletic teams. And as our world expands as adults, we begin to encounter other types of groups, including bureaucracies, work groups, professional societies, and voluntary associations. To make sense out of this enormous array of groups, sociologists have identified four types of groups: statistical, societal, social, and associational (Bierstedt, 1974). The classification of groups into one of these categories is based on three criteria: (1) Do the members of the group have a consciousness of kind or a feeling of *we-ness*? (2) Do the members interact? (3) Do the members have an organized structure?

Statistical groups are formed not by the members themselves, but by social scientists. In general, members of these groups are unaware of membership and do not interact. These groups have no organizational structure. A label is simply applied to a group by a researcher for the purpose of study. Cohorts are a commonly used statistical group. A cohort is any group that has experienced an event at the same time—for example, the birth cohort of 1970, or men having coronary bypass surgery at age forty. Social scientists have found that by aggregating individuals into groups based on a shared experience, they have a powerful tool in predicting a wide range of behavior.

Societal groups differ from statistical groups in one important respect—consciousness of kind. Members of these groups are aware of their similarities—age, sex, skin color, language, race, and class—but they do not interact nor do they have a formal organizational structure.

Social and associational groups are similar to societal groups in that there is a consciousness of kind, but they are different in that social interaction takes place among members. **Social groups** are usually unstructured and include friendships, cliques, members of a classroom, and neighborhood groups. **Associational groups** differ from social groups in that they are organized and normally have a constitution and a formal structure with officers. Student government, fraternities and sororities, the League of Women Voters, Young Republicans, and service clubs like the Rotary, Lions, and Kiwanis are examples of associational groups.

All four types of groups are important to social scientists in understanding society, but most research on segregation has focused on the degree to which certain statistical and societal groups are segregated. Specifically, to what degree are social status (statistical), and ethnic and racial groups (societal) segregated in cities?[2]

Why Study Segregation?

The notion that the social distance among groups is reflected in the spatial distance between them is a basic sociological principle. The sorting of groups and individuals into homogeneous areas of a city leads to spatial isolation. Segregation reduces the personal contacts among groups and causes social isolation. Without close day-to-day interaction, contact between these groups tends to be formal and is confined to the market and workplace. The segregation of a population, therefore, influences the patterns of relationships among people and can have positive and negative consequences for a community.

On the positive side, as long as there have been cities, people with similar social position, language, race, and religion have lived together. When this segregation is voluntary, residents may find that living with others of similar backgrounds is satisfying and contributes to a sense of belonging and security. A group consciousness may emerge based on similar group attributes and common residence. Consequently, voluntary segregation of a group may affect the behavior of the residents positively. Similar characteristics provide common ground for friendships and neighboring or may lead to the creation of ethnically based groups such as fraternal organizations or political action groups. This nation has a rich history of ethnic enclaves. Virtually every group that has immigrated to the United States has created an enclave at some time in their history.

On the negative side, the involuntary segregation of groups can cut two ways. Segregation can lead to the emergence of community, but once community is created, it can act as a barrier restricting the life chances of its members. For example, African Americans are the most segregated group in this society, and many live in the least-desirable areas of cities where housing is poor and public services are inadequate. The children of these families are often forced to attend the worst schools in the city, a practice that has been found to perpetuate inequality (Wilson, 1987). An unintended consequence of this group consciousness is the riots and other forms of collective behavior that have marked the nation's history. Riots broke out in Cincinnati's Over-the-Rhine district in the spring of 2001. Once a German neighborhood, the district is now a predominantly African American community. Years of resentment by residents of the Over-the-Rhine over their treatment by the police ignited into violence when a nineteen-year-old man was shot and killed during a routine traffic stop.

The segregation of groups tells social scientists much about our cities and our society. First, the degree of segregation between groups is an indicator of the inequality in society. Second, measuring residential segregation gives policy makers an indication of the effectiveness of programs designed to address problems like housing and civil rights. Third, the study of segregation gives social scientists insight into the basic ecological processes that shape the internal structure of the city. Finally, the segregation or integration of neighborhoods in different parts of a city leads to the emergence of communities with different characteristics and institutional structures and with different behavioral patterns among its residents. Understanding the complex linkages of process, social structure, and behavior is a common goal of all social science.

Why Does Segregation Occur?

Social scientists have studied segregation for a century, and they have identified three sets of factors that influence it: ecological, voluntary, and involuntary.

Ecological Segregation

Populations that differ in lifestyle, race, social status, and culture normally separate themselves from others on this characteristic. In chapter 7, we presented the Burgess and other models of urban land use. We showed that neighborhoods are not distributed randomly across the urbanscape, but in distinct patterns according to income, stage in the life cycle, and lifestyle of their residents. Neighborhoods differ in the type and price of their housing, and groups differ in their occupations, stage in the life cycle, and incomes. Recent immigrants, for example, traditionally have been overrepresented in low-paying blue-collar and service jobs. When a group is overrepresented in a lower income category, their housing options are limited and they become segregated because of their income and occupational characteristics. Thus, ecological segregation occurs as the result of the normal operation of the housing market.

Voluntary Segregation

Some segregation occurs because of self-selection. A group with a common language or culture will have common problems and needs that can be addressed best if the members live close together. In ethnic enclaves, schools, churches, businesses, and stores spring up to meet the group's needs. The enclave also serves to socialize the young into the language and culture of the group perpetuating the subculture.

Additionally, a person's identity is closely interwoven with the people with whom he or she interacts, and a person's peers provide an important reference point for the evaluation of her or his behavior. Moreover, a person's public identity, the social class to which he or she belongs, is defined by the people with whom he or she associates. Because physical distance between people is a major factor in determining who associates with whom, choosing a proper residential location is a strategy for increasing the probability of desired contact. People who want to interact will live close to each other in order to lower the time and costs of interaction. People who want to avoid each other will live far apart to minimize the chances of accidental contact (Timms, 1971).

This explanation has two implications. First, it describes the psychological factors that influence residential choice. Second, it explains why neighborhoods keep their social character even though people are constantly moving in and out. Once an area becomes associated with a social group, people who wish to identify with it move into the area, perpetuating segregation.

Involuntary Segregation

Involuntary segregation can occur in several ways. A group may be required by law or custom to live in designated areas of a city. The apartheid policy in South Africa is an example of governmental action that created a segregated society. Involuntary segregation may also be the result of the collective action of individuals or institutions within a community. So-called "white flight," or whites moving out of a neighborhood as African Americans move in, is an example of how individual acts, when combined, tend to perpetuate racial segregation.

The role of real estate agents. Institutions have an important impact on land uses and the levels of a city's segregation. Real estate agents have traditionally been singled out as a major force in perpetuating segregation (Seitles, 1996). As late as the 1950s, the National Association of Real Estate Brokers included in their code of ethics the following statement:

> *A Realtor should never be instrumental in introducing into a neighborhood, by character of property or occupancy, members of any race or nationality, or any individual whose presence would be clearly detrimental to property values in a neighborhood. (U.S. Commission on Civil Rights, 1975, p. 11)*

This statement no longer appears in the association's code of ethics, but real estate agents are among the several gatekeepers in modern industrial cities who channel and control the activities of people looking for a new home. Normally, a real estate agent is one of the first persons with whom new residents come in contact. The real estate agent can influence the selection of clients, the houses shown, and the sale prices. The real estate agent often intervenes into the source and type of mortgage the buyer secures. The literature is filled with examples of tactics used by real estate agents to match the social class and racial characteristics of buyers to the existing social characteristics of neighborhoods. Although civil rights and fair housing legislation have put an end to many abuses, a recent study conducted for the Department of Housing and Urban Development suggests that the practices are still widespread (Seitles, 1996).

The role of government and lending institutions. Other institutions also greatly influence residential segregation. For many years, the Federal Housing Authority would not loan money to African Americans if their purchase of a home would upset the racial balance of an area. The practice of redlining by banks and lending institutions, as well as the decisions of planning commissions, zoning boards, and other agencies, influence residential land uses and the patterns of segregation. Although most of these practices have ended, their effects still linger in the residential structure of our cities (Seitles, 1996).

Interaction of factors. These factors do not operate alone but together in complex and interrelated ways. For example, ecological and voluntary factors may interact and limit the areas of the city in which people of high social status will reside. A wealthy family will not live in a slum; a poor family cannot afford to buy in a country-club estate. Thus, the distribution of housing types combined with the desire of high-status individuals to live near members of their own group contributes to the segregation. One goal in the following discussion is to identify those factors that seem to be most responsible for patterns of segregation. These factors interact in different ways depending on the particular social, ethnic, or racial group.

Measuring Segregation

Over the past decade there has been controversy surrounding the measurement of segregation. Currently, two measures, the dissimilarity index (D) and the isolation index are used. The dissimilarity index compares the residential location of pairs of groups—whites and Hispanics, for example—and gives a measure of the net percentage of one population who would have to relocate in order to produce an integrated community. The index (D) has values that range from 0 to 100. (The index is also presented on a scale of 0 to 1.0.) For example, if Hispanics and whites were evenly distributed in all the census tracts of a city, the index would be 0. No one would have to change her or his residence to maintain an ethnic balance. If the city was completely segregated and exclusively Hispanics or whites inhabited census tracts, the index would be 100. For example, Hispanics made up 25.1 percent of New York City's population in 2000. They, however, are highly segregated. The dissimilarity index for Hispanics and whites was 68.9, which means that 68.9 percent of the Hispanics or 68.9 percent of the white residents would have to move in order to have an integrated community (Callaghan, 2001).

The dissimilarity index was introduced more than eighty years ago, and it has come under attack in recent years. One major drawback of the index is that it has the tendency to register high values even when the minority group under study makes up only a small proportion of a city's population. For this reason, students of segregation have developed a variety of measures, but the alternative measure used most often today is the isolation index. (See Callaghan (2001) for a complete discussion of the indexes used to measure segregation.)

The isolation index shows the percentage of a racial or ethnic group in a neighborhood where the average member of that group lives. The isolation index for Hispanics in New York City in 2000 was 48.2, which means that the average Hispanic lives in a neighborhood that was 48.2 percent Hispanic. In contrast, Hispanics make up only 1.9 percent of the population in Sioux Falls, South Dakota, but they are segregated. The dissimilarity index is 43.7. The isolation index, however, is only 4.5. Why? Because they make up such a small percentage of the city's population. Hispanics are segregated on several city blocks, but they live in predominantly white neighborhoods. In contrast to New York City, Sioux Falls' Hispanics have a higher probability of chance encounters with their white neighbors. The same pattern occurs nationally. The average Hispanic lives in a neighborhood that is 44 percent Hispanic. The average non-Hispanic white, in contrast, lives in a neighborhood that is 6.3 percent Hispanic. (To find the figures for your city, go to *www.albany.edu/mumford/census.*) The dissimilarity and isolation indexes are widely used and give measures of segregation that allow comparisons from decade to decade and from city to city. Therefore, we will use both indexes to describe segregation patterns in this chapter.

Social Status Segregation

There are deep cleavages in this society. Race and ethnicity are one; social class is another. Social class or socioeconomic status is an important variable because it correlates so highly with so many other things. If researchers know your social class—your position in the social stratification system—they can predict, among other things, how you will vote, what you will buy, and how long you will live. Social scientists measure SES in many ways, but income, occupational prestige, and education are the variables used most often. Regardless of the measure, the distribution of wealth and income in American society is unequal and is becoming more so. Thirty-eight million Americans live below the poverty line, and nearly 2 million are homeless, while at the same time, 1 percent of the population controls more than a 40 percent of the nation's wealth and owns two-thirds of all stocks held by individuals. In our discussion of globalization in the opening chapters of the text, we showed how changes in the economy in the 1990s exacerbated inequality. A two-tier society is emerging: one well educated and paid in highly skilled jobs; the other poorly educated and paid in low-skilled jobs. The $1.3 trillion tax cut passed by Congress in 2001 will magnify the problem because the majority of the benefits go to the wealthiest 1 percent of Americans (Francis, 2004). Repeal of the estate tax and reduced taxation of corporate dividends further exacerbates inequality in this society.

The data presented in Table 11.1 show the percentage of this nation's income received by each fifth of the nation's families for the years 1947–1998. In 1998, the poorest fifth of the families in the United States received only 3.6 percent of the nation's annual income, whereas the richest fifth received more than 49 percent. In 1998, the average income of households in the bottom fifth of the income distribution was $9,223, compared with $127,529 among households in the top fifth of the income scale. Between 1970 and 1998 the average household income increased within each of the five groups, but the wealthiest households had the biggest gains. This pattern of income distribution has become more unequal since the end of World War II even with massive federal poverty programs carried out over the past four decades (Population Reference Bureau, 2001b). Given this inequality in American society, one would expect, and in fact find, high levels of segregation among groups that differ in their occupation, income, and education.

Table 11.1   *Percent of Income Received by Each Fifth of Families in the United States*

INCOME	RANK	1947	1950	1960	1966	1972	1986	1998
Lowest	Fifth	5.1	4.5	4.8	5.6	5.4	4.6	3.6
Second	Fifth	11.8	11.9	12.2	12.4	11.9	10.8	4.0
Third	Fifth	16.7	17.4	17.8	17.8	17.5	16.8	15.0
Fourth	Fifth	23.2	23.6	24.0	23.8	23.9	24.0	28.2
Highest	Fifth	43.5	42.7	41.3	40.5	41.4	43.8	49.2
Total		100.0	100.0	100.0	100.0	100.0	100.0	100.0

Source: Bureau of the Census. 1998. *Statistical Abstract of the United States, 1998.* Washington, D.C.: Government Printing Office.

Research on Status Segregation

Ecological Theories

The segregation of status groups was among the first studied by urban sociologists. Ernest Burgess (1925), one of the early Chicago ecologists, described in his concentric zone model that lower-status groups are centralized near the central business district, whereas upper-status groups are decentralized near a city's periphery. To Burgess, the residential segregation of these groups was the result of impersonal ecological and economic factors operating within the city. The mechanism is straightforward. A family will attempt to maximize its housing satisfaction while minimizing its costs by balancing the costs of transportation with costs of rent within the constraints of the family budget. Theoretically, a citywide pattern of land rents would be high rents and low transportation costs near the city's center and the reverse situation at the city's periphery. Only high-status families have true locational freedom, because only they have the income to absorb the costs of transportation and rent. Because high-status families prefer large houses on spacious lots in areas where there is little congestion or business and industry, they select locations at the city's periphery. The poor have little choice and live near the city's center where transportation and housing costs are lowest (Burgess, 1925).

In chapter 7, we explored the models of Burgess, White, Harvey, and the Los Angeles School. They all describe social status segregation. The researchers call them different things—zone of transition, zone of stagnation, or areas of high turnover—but all the models demonstrate that the greater the social distance between groups, the greater the spatial difference between them. This pattern is not limited just to this nation; it is found in all societies at all times in history. Where high- and low-status groups are located is a function of the level of development of society. In countries undergoing the modernization process, high-status groups tend to live near the city's center, low-status groups at the periphery. The reason? Poor transportation keeps the wealthy and powerful near the society's key institutions in the city's center. In more-developed societies the opposite pattern is true; low-status groups tend to live near the city's center, high-status groups at the periphery. Good transportation and communication technology allows people in these societies to escape the city. These patterns are changing across the globe as communication and transportation technology improves.

Factors Influencing Social Status Segregation

Social status segregation is the result of many factors, and its understanding is confounded by the effects of both race and ethnicity. African Americans and other minorities are overrepresented in the lower socioeconomic strata. As a result, cities with large African American and Hispanic populations will have more extreme social-status segregation than cities with small minority populations (Logan, 2001a). Moreover, ecological and voluntary factors appear to be the most important in explaining social-status segregation. Persons of high social status have the income to select houses and neighborhoods in accordance with their tastes; the poor do not. Even if the effects of occupation, income, and education are removed, residual segregation remains. Such segregation is probably the result of voluntary factors of self-selection that are difficult to measure statistically (Clark, 1986).

In sum, residential dissimilarity among status groups appears to be a universal phenomenon. If plotted, the pattern of residential dissimilarity is U-shaped with income groups at the high and low ends of the status hierarchy being the most segregated. The centralization of high- and low-status groups, however, is difficult to predict. Factors such as city age, a group's position in the urban hierarchy, and the level of development of the society appear to influence the centralization or decentralization of status groups across the urban landscape.

Ethnic Segregation

Germans, Greeks, Swedes, Norwegians, Japanese, Koreans, Chinese, Laotians, Vietnamese, Ethiopians, Nigerians, Kenyans, French, British, Irish, Russians, Italians, Croatians, Poles, Czechs, Hungarians, Cubans, Mexicans, Salvadorans, Nicaraguans, and the list goes on. This is a glimpse at the ethnic richness of the nation called the United States. No nation in history has accepted as its citizens, albeit sometimes reluctantly, more people from more backgrounds than the United States. On the one hand, it is one of the nation's strengths; we have brought together the talents and the perspectives of many cultures in defining our national character. On the other hand, immigration has been a source of great division, at times creating cleavages that weakened our political and social fabric. The American miracle is that such a diverse collection of peoples can live together in peace. See Photo 11.1.

In every city with a sizable ethnic population, one finds evidence of this rich ethnic heritage in the names of the areas in which these groups are or were once segregated: German Town, Pole Town, Little Taipei, China Town, the Barrio, and the Ghetto. Even when the ethnic group isn't identified in the name of a neighborhood, certain areas of a city come to be associated with certain groups. In Cleveland, eastern European Jews are associated with the suburbs of Euclid and Shaker Heights, Poles with Parma, Germans with Lakewood. The same is true for the city's other ethnic groups.

The twentieth century witnessed the transformation of the United States from a predominately white population rooted in Western culture to a society with a rich array of racial, ethnic, and religious minorities. At the beginning of the twentieth century, the U.S. population was 87 percent white. The nonwhite minority was composed primarily of African Americans living in the rural South. At the beginning of the twenty-first century, whites accounted for less than 75 percent of the U.S. population. Whites now make up less than half of the population in California, and they are a minority in the 100 largest cities in the nation (Schmitt, 2001). The minority population is comprised of nearly an equal number of Hispanics and African Americans, a surging number of Asians, and a small but growing American Indian population. By 2050, whites will make up a slim majority of Americans. Hispanics will be nearly one quarter of the U.S. population. African Americans, Asians, and American Indians together will make up the rest. In the next fifty years, the United States will become significantly more racially and ethnically diverse than it is today (Riche, 2000).

Globalization has been a theme throughout this book. Population trends reflect these fundamental changes in the economy and the world. But these changes are not new in our history. At the beginning of the twentieth century, many Americans were concerned about slowing population growth, and the

Photo 11.1   *More than 200 languages are spoken in the nation. No society has welcomed (at times reluctantly) more people from such diverse backgrounds than the United States. These differences have created what some sociologists call a "mosaic of social worlds" in our cities. Where these groups locate and where they move over time tells social scientists much about the experiences of ethnic and racial groups in our society. (Source: Herb Watson/CORBIS/Bettmann.)*

growing number of immigrants from eastern and southern Europe. Industrialization and urbanization were the forces transforming our nation and its economy. At the beginning of the twenty-first century, immigration is again a concern of Americans, but this time the immigrants are from Latin America, Africa, and Asia, and the forces of globalization are transforming the nation and its economy.

Our society was created out of successive waves of migration, but Americans are divided in their beliefs about the long-term effects of this growing diversity. Some see the rapid growth of minorities as a key to the revitalization of America and a logical continuation of our melting-pot tradition. Others see the rapid increase in racial and ethnic minorities as an unwelcome departure from America's European heritage. But at a time when racial and ethnic hatred is promoting violence in societies around the globe, how Americans create a multiracial, multiethnic society will be a model for the world—a model that well positions this nation in the global economy. But in the midst of our growing diversity, racial and ethnic segregation continues to divide our people.

Factors Influencing Ethnic Segregation

Region of Origin and Time of Arrival

Three waves of immigrants have shaped this society.[3] The first wave spanned the years from the first settlements in the New World through the first half of the nineteenth century, ending with the depression of 1857. This wave was composed of western and northern Europeans. Their Anglo-Saxon physical features and predominantly Protestant religion reinforced the character of the host society, and little assimilation was required. Most of this wave settled on farms, but those who settled in cities chose cities in the Midwest, including the lake and river cities (Weeks, 1996).

Thirty million people immigrated to the United States between 1860 and 1924, forming the second and largest wave of immigration. Although Germans, Scandinavians, and millions of Irish continued to immigrate, the origins of most of this immigration shifted from western and northern Europe to eastern and southern Europe. The majority of these groups settled in Atlantic Coast and lake cities. The new ethnics differed from the native population in physical features, culture, and, most important, religion; they were predominantly Catholic and Jewish. To native-born Americans, they seemed foreign or alien to the American culture, and prejudice and discrimination led to their segregation into ethnic enclaves and ghettoes (Weeks, 1996).

Three developments shaped the third wave of immigration. First, the passage of the 1965 amendments to the Immigration and Nationality Act of 1952 replaced a quota system based on national origin to a policy that stressed family reunification and the admission of aliens with needed skills. The law dramatically increased the number of legal immigrants. Second, massive immigration followed the fall of U.S. client states in Indochina and the fall of the Berlin Wall. Third, a pattern of international labor migration from less-developed nations to more-developed nations emerged worldwide during this period. In the past forty years, legal and illegal immigration has grown and shifted from Europe to Mexico, Central and South America, the Caribbean Basin, Asia, and Western Africa. In addition, the immigration stream is no longer directed to the large cities of the Northeast but to cities across the nation. In the 1990s, the population of the United States grew about 2 million people per year. The majority of this growth is the result of immigration or the fertility of recent immigrants. Not included in this figure are the 1 million to 3 million aliens who enter this country illegally each year. The problem of illegal migration for the nation became so serious in the 1980s that Congress responded by passing the Immigration Reform and Control Act in 1986 (PL 99–603).[4] The act provided amnesty for millions of illegal immigrants and imposed penalties on employers who employed undocumented aliens. These laws did little to stem the flow of illegal immigrants (Weeks, 1996). The Patriot Act passed in the months following September 11, 2001, is an attempt by the Bush administration to stem the flow of illegal immigration across our borders. The Immigration and Naturalization Service (INS) is now part of the Office of Home Land Security, and draconic measures are being used to reduce illegal immigration. Federal agents have stepped up security at airports and crossings on our northern and southern borders; the INS has implemented new visa restrictions; and illegal immigrants and visa violators are being rounded up, detained, and deported. Many civil libertarians are troubled by many of these changes. INS deportation hearings are now held in secret, requests for political asylum are almost impossible, and foreign nationals may now be kept in prison indefinitely without access to legal representation. Many critics wonder if these measures are worth the social, economic, and political costs.

In 2004 President Bush proposed to Congress a new temporary worker program to match foreign workers with U.S. employers when no Americans can be found to fill the jobs. The program would be open to new foreign workers, and to the undocumented men and women currently employed in the U.S. According to the president, this legislation would help meet the Nation's economic needs. Organized labor thinks otherwise. They feel that the incomes of America's low-wage earners would be hurt by this legislation.

The Influence of Technology

Region and time of arrival shaped the experiences of the different waves of immigrants in American cities, but other social, economic, and technological factors were at work as well. For example, in the first half of the nineteenth century transportation technology was poorly developed and people had to be able to walk from where they lived to where they worked. Business and industry were on a much smaller scale, and unlike our cities today, these activities were spread across the city. As a result, the Germans and Irish who immigrated before the Civil War were not highly segregated in our cities (Hanlin, 1969).

After the Civil War, industrialization and the transportation revolution brought about by the elevated railroad and the electrified trolley permitted the middle and upper classes to escape the city. For the first time, it was possible for large numbers of people to separate their place of residence from their place of work and to avoid groups they defined as undesirable. Since the second wave of immigrants was more distinctive than the first wave of old ethnics—Germans and Irish—greater assimilation was required. The consequence was segregation.

Other factors contributed to segregation. Industrialization brought about a growth in the size and scale of factories, and since the factories were dependent on the railroads, specialized industrial centers sprung up in cities. Thus, the new immigrants arrived in an entirely different type of city. Most of the immigrants arrived without money or skills, so they located near their jobs in the zone of transition adjacent to the central business district (Massey, 1985).

In short, the industrialization of the last half of the nineteenth century created structural conditions conducive to high levels of segregation. In turn, high levels of segregation created a critical mass of people that permitted the creation of ethnic enclaves. Within these enclaves, one still finds ethnic stores, churches, schools, hospitals, social clubs, newspapers, and benevolent societies designed to meet the needs of the ethnic group. Over time there emerged a community within a community, and this had major consequences for ethnic segregation. Once enclaves were established, they encouraged additional immigration, contributed to the group's sense of peoplehood, socialized the young into the subculture, and perpetuated ethnic identity. These factors also contributed to segregation (Bledea, 1979).

Congress ended the second wave of immigration in 1924 with the passage of restrictive immigration laws. And the Great Depression and World War II reduced immigration to a trickle. The third wave of immigration began at the end of World War II, and it continues to this day. Cities felt the full impact of the automobile in the postwar years. The automobile gave individuals greater locational freedom, accelerated the expansion of the suburbs, permitted the decentralization of business and industry, and reduced the structural pressures for ethnic segregation. The Hispanics and Asians who entered the nation after World War II are less segregated than previous groups. However, in the older industrial cities of the Northeast and in many Sunbelt cities, one still finds high levels of segregation of these groups. As in the past, our newest migrants are often poor and lack the education and skills necessary for high-paying jobs, so they must keep housing costs down. They tend to locate in older inner-city neighborhoods near low-paying service jobs (Massey, 1981).

Theories of Ethnic Segregation

An ethnic group is any group that is defined or set off by race, religion, national origin, or some combination of these categories. In addition, these categories have a common social-psychological referent that can serve to create a sense of weness, a sense of peoplehood. This label can be used by the group itself or by larger society. But implicit in our discussion of ethnicity is the notion that ethnicity is the immigration of a group into an already existing social structure. The charter group, those who control the host society, will determine the experiences of the ethnic group (Boal, 1981).

A charter group is usually the first ethnic group to enter a territory, and because they control the key institutions of a society, they make the decisions about who gets in and what their experiences are going to be. In addition, they form the social framework into which the immigrant group must adapt and fit. If the immigrant group is similar to the charter group, the process will be relatively smooth and rapid. If major differences exist, the process will be slow and erratic. The process of fitting an ethnic group into an already existing social structure is called *assimilation.* There are two types of assimilation—behavioral and structural. Behavioral assimilation is a process whereby members of a group acquire the behavior, attitudes, sentiments, values, language, and history of the host society. Think of behavioral assimilation as fitting into or disappearing into a new culture. Structural assimilation refers to the distribution of ethnic people through the social system of a society, the process by which members of ethnic groups move into key decision-making positions in government, business, and other spheres of society. Both types of assimilation are temporal processes, but they can occur at very different rates. A good example is African Americans in American society. African Americans have been behaviorally assimilated into American society for centuries; only recently have blacks begun to move into key positions in this society—to be structurally assimilated (Boal, 1981).

The relationship between the forces at work in society and those at work in cities is summarized in Figure 11.1. In this model, immigrants with few differences from the host society should be rapidly dispersed into the residential structure of the city. For example, I live in a small city in which there are a number of Australians. Other than speaking English with a strange accent, their dress, behavior, values, and customs are so similar to American society they have been dispersed across the city.

At the other extreme, immigrants with a high degree of distinctiveness in language, custom, or color require a high degree of assimilation. If these differences are not easily removed (in the case of color, they may never be removed), long-term or

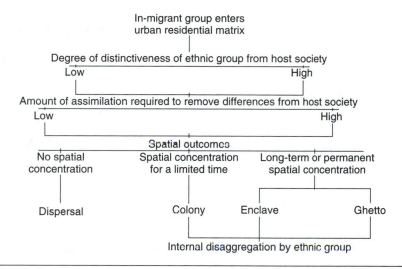

Figure 11.1   *Ethnic Groups, Assimilation, and Residential Spatial Outcomes* (*Source:* Adapted from
F. W. Boal. 1981. Ethnic Residential Segregation. In *The Geograpy of Housing*,
edited by H. Johnston. London: Aldein, figure 1, p. 43.)

permanent segregation will occur. There are two spatial outcomes—ghettoes and
ethnic enclaves. A *ghetto* refers to the residential area of a city where an ethnic group
has been involuntarily segregated. As we will see later in the chapter, housing discrimination is responsible for much of the residential segregation of African Americans. On the other hand, the term *enclave* denotes an area where an ethnic group
has voluntarily chosen to live in order to maintain the group's religion or culture. For
example, Russian Jews are one of the nation's most successful ethnic groups, yet they
remain highly segregated. Undoubtedly, some housing discrimination occurs, but the
high income of this group should mean more dispersal. In this case, voluntary factors
are probably important in explaining the segregation of this group.

The final case is those ethnic groups who are distinctive but who require only
a moderate amount of assimilation. They are concentrated for only a single generation into areas called *colonies*. A current example is the large British colony in
southern California. The colony, estimated to include more than 30,000 people,
preserves the food, customs, and English of Britain. Mick is a friend who lives in
LA's British enclave. He loves LA. He loves the climate, high wages, low taxes, and
lifestyle. But he hates Americans. He thinks we are loud, boorish, and ill man-
nered. For the most part, though, he doesn't have to deal with Americans. He lives
in the center of the British colony, works for a British company, shops at a British
grocery, drinks his favorite beer at a British-only pub, and plays darts on Tuesdays
and Saturdays just like he did in London. Except for the intrusion of an occasional
American, Mick and the other expatriates have successfully transported their way
of life from Britain to the United States. There are some cracks in Mick's idyllic life.
His wife, Penny, is a teacher, and her friends and colleagues are Americans. His
children went to American schools and have American friends and accents. Mick
had a couple of blows to his psyche last year. His son, Mark, was born in the
United States, and when he turned eighteen, chose U.S. over British citizenship.

His daughter provided the final indignity—she married a Yank. Mick may be able to wrap himself in the Union Jack, but his children have not, and the model predicts the colony will last only a generation.

While this model predicts the spatial outcomes of immigrants entering a host society, it does not describe the assimilation process. Ethnic assimilation is normally studied on the neighborhood level using the concept of invasion-succession. Invasion-succession refers to the process of neighborhood change that occurs when a new ethnic group enters a residential area and displaces the original inhabitants. Two different models are found in the literature, and they predict very different spatial outcomes.

The Melting-Pot Model

Members of the Chicago School believed that ethnic segregation was an aspect of social-status segregation. Ethnic segregation was seen as an artifact of their low social status in American society. Most sociologists thought that this social status was a temporary phenomenon and that as an ethnic group's standing improved, their segregation would gradually disappear. They hypothesized a four-stage process. (1) New arrivals seek cheap accommodations because of their poverty and desire to accumulate savings. The tenements in the zone of transition were cheap and close to jobs and became centrally located ethnic ghettoes. (2) Over time, the immigrants improve their socioeconomic status. Higher incomes permit them to pursue better housing, and they begin to move outward into other areas of the city through the process of invasion-succession. (3) The redistribution of this group into other areas of the city leads to less physical concentration and a breakdown of the old cultural solidarity. (4) Subsequent movements result in further dispersion of group members and their assimilation into the surrounding society. According to the model, ethnic segregation is the result of socioeconomic differences among ethnic groups and the fact that people who differ in socioeconomic status live in different parts of the city. From this perspective, ecological factors independent of ethnicity are responsible for the segregation of these groups (Burgess, 1928).

This ideal pattern is known as the *melting-pot thesis*. It has been taught in American high school history and civics classes for decades. However, several books written in the 1960s and 1970s called into question the melting-pot notion (Glazer & Moynihan, 1963). These authors pointed to the durable ethnic divisions that persist in our cities after many generations and suggest that these groups represent major cleavages within the city and our society. The accompanying box considers the example of Greek immigrants in Cincinnati.

Residential Patterns of Greeks in Cincinnati, Ohio

The melting-pot model argues that recent immigrants locate near the CBD, and as their socioeconomic status improves, they move to better housing in other parts of the city, often the suburbs. According to the theory, the move to the suburbs is accompanied by the diffusion of ethnic families, the destruction of their subculture, and the assimilation of the group in the mainstream of society.

These three figures from research by Bongkotrat Techatraisak (1978) illustrate the changing residential patterns of Greeks in Cincinnati, Ohio, from 1910 through 1976. Techatraisak uses a mapping technique called *centrography* to analyze the clustering and diffusion of this ethnic group. Note the points, ellipse, and crosshairs in figure 1. One point represents one household; the ellipse, the boundary that describes the cluster of Greek families; and the center of the crosshairs, the center of the ethnic community.

In 1910, Greeks were concentrated in a tight cluster adjacent to the CBD (see figure 1). However, over the next sixty-six years the group has dispersed. In figure 2, notice that the size of the ellipse has grown progressively larger and the center of the community has moved directly north of the central business district. According to the theory, the spatial diffusion of the Greeks should be accompanied by their assimilation. The evidence shows otherwise. As the Greek community has moved to better housing on the periphery, it has taken its institutions with it. The movement of the Greek Orthodox Church from 1908 to the present is shown in figure 3. Located in downtown Cincinnati in 1908, it is now located in the suburbs along with its members. Research in other cities has shown that ethnic groups maintain their ethnic identity after many generations, even when the ethnic neighborhood no longer exists. Ethnic churches, fraternal organizations, and family ties provide cohesiveness without propinquity (Agocs, 1981; Chrisman, 1981).

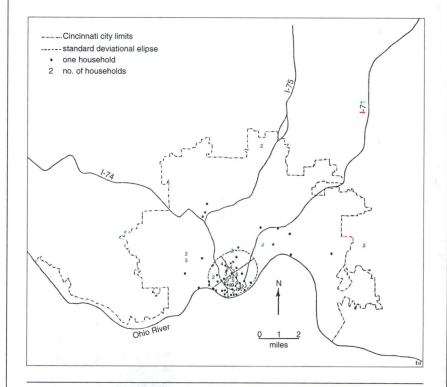

Distribution of Greek Households, 1910

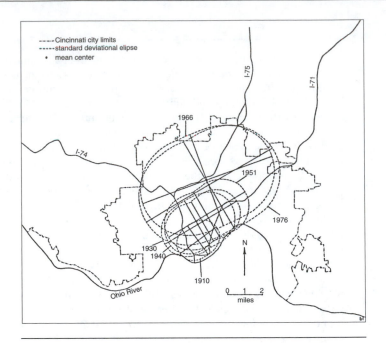

Comparison of all Standard Ellipses

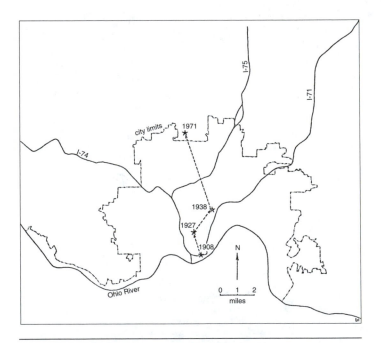

Movement of the Greek Orthodox Church in Cincinnati

The Ethnic-Status Model

The recognition of these unmeltable ethnics has led to the development of a second approach, the ethnic-status model. The model argues that ethnic status alone can account for residential dissimilarity among ethnic groups. In short, one's desire to maintain a particular ethnic identity may be translated into a preference to live near others with similar ethnic backgrounds. Once an enclave is formed, a critical mass of ethnic residents supports an institutional structure of schools, churches, stores, and associations. In turn, these institutions provide the enclave with a means to recruit and hold members and to socialize the young into the ethnic subculture—a means of perpetuating the community. Other forces may be at work. The group's distinctive character may trigger discrimination by other groups in society and prevent the group from participating in a citywide housing market. Thus, the status of an ethnic group may be derived both from processes at work within the community and from external societal forces. Regardless of the forces at work, this model predicts a different spatial outcome. Rather than spatial dispersal and assimilation of the ethnic group as the group improves its socioeconomic status, this model predicts that the group will remain residentially segregated regardless of social class. The question is, which model is correct?

Residential Patterns of Ethnics

In 1980, the Census Bureau asked Americans for the first time about their ethnicity or ancestry. Reynolds Farley and Robert Wilger (1987) used these data to study ethnic residential segregation in sixteen cities. They found that the descendants of the first wave of immigration were the least segregated from the charter group as illustrated by an average dissimilarity index score of 22 for Germans, 23 for Irish, 29 for French, and 30 for persons of Scottish ancestry. Descendants of groups in the second wave of immigration—Italians, Poles, and Hungarians—were more distinctive, required more assimilation, and even today are more segregated from the charter group. Their scores range from 37 for Italians to 59 for Russians (Farley & Wilger, 1987). Dissimilarity indexes for our newest group of ethnics—Hispanics and Asians—were 43 and 34, respectively. The researchers found remarkably low indexes for Asians. The major reason appears to be that only three cities, San Francisco, Los Angeles, and New York, have large enough populations to support Asian enclaves, so most Asians entering this country moved into predominantly Anglo neighborhoods. From this analysis one finds support for both models. The dissimilarity indexes for ethnic groups declines over time, but these groups have not been completely assimilated.

Hispanic Americans

With more than 35 million people and 8.4 million households, Hispanic Americans represent the fifth-largest Spanish-speaking population in the world behind Mexico, Spain, Columbia, and Argentina.[5] Demographers predict this group will become the second largest by 2010. Many people wrongly assume all Hispanic Americans share the same heritage; they don't. Mexican Americans, the oldest and largest group, account for almost two-thirds of the Hispanic population. Puerto Ricans, the second largest group, are not immigrants but rather citizens of the

United States. Cubans are third. Salvadorans compose the largest group from Central America, followed by Dominicans, Guatemalans, Nicaraguans, Colombians, Ecuadorians, and Peruvians (Ellison, 2001).

Hispanics are a product of one of the most important migration streams of the second half of the twentieth century—people moving from Latin America to the United States. Hispanic Americans are now the nation's largest ethnic minority. High immigration rates and birth rates have boosted the growth rate of the Hispanic population above that of any other major U.S. racial or ethnic group. The Hispanic population is projected to swell from 35 million in 2000 to about 100 million in 2050, or one-quarter of our population. Mexicans are the fastest-growing Hispanic population in the country for a simple reason: They live next door. The number of Mexican Americans grew by 7.1 million over the decade, accounting for most of the increase of 12.9 million in the nation's Hispanic population, according to the 2000 census. Nearly 21 million people reported they were of Mexican origin, and they make up more than 58 percent of U.S. Hispanics (Population Reference Bureau, 2001a).

Hispanics are more likely to work in lower-paying, semi-skilled jobs or service work than non-Hispanic whites or Asians. They are less likely to hold white-collar jobs, which range from managerial and professional to clerical positions. Those in white-collar jobs are more likely than whites or Asians to work as typists, clerks, or salespeople rather than as higher-earning managers or professionals. A large number of Hispanics work in the low-wage agriculture sector. Occupational segregation means low incomes, and low incomes limit housing choice, which translates into residential segregation (AmeriStat, 2001).

Although Hispanics historically have been less segregated from whites than have African Americans, the 2000 census revealed they are becoming more concentrated in their own ethnic neighborhoods. In Figure 11.2, notice that most of the points in the scatter plot fall above the diagonal, showing that most MSAs experienced increases in residential segregation between 1990 and 2000. Interestingly, Hispanics are increasingly settling in the suburbs. Nearly half of Hispanics (49 percent) live in suburbs. Hispanics are more than 25 percent of the suburban population in Miami (55.8 percent), Los Angeles (44.7 percent), Riverside (38.3 percent), and San Diego (27.0 percent) (Logan, 2001b).

For Hispanics, increasing segregation is largely related to the huge influx of immigrants in segregated neighborhoods. This change is especially marked in the larger metropolitan areas in the South. These enclaves follow a historical pattern for immigrants, who for generations have moved into neighborhoods with networks of relatives and friends, where others speak their language and can help them find work. The pattern tends to dissipate over time: the longer a group has been in this country, the less likely it is to be segregated. However, some sociologists and advocates are concerned that because newly arrived Hispanics are less educated than those of previous generations, they may be less able to pull themselves up economically and move out.

The assimilation problem is exacerbated by the school resegregation. Hispanic students increasingly find themselves isolated in poor schools. More than one in three Hispanic students attends a school with a heavy concentration of students from low-income families with high minority enrollment. As a result, school advocates believe that Hispanic children aren't receiving the quality education they need, and white students won't learn to live in a multiracial society (Nordell, 2001). Segregation and isolation, advocates worry, will slow the acquisition of English as a first language, placing Hispanic students at a disadvantage in school

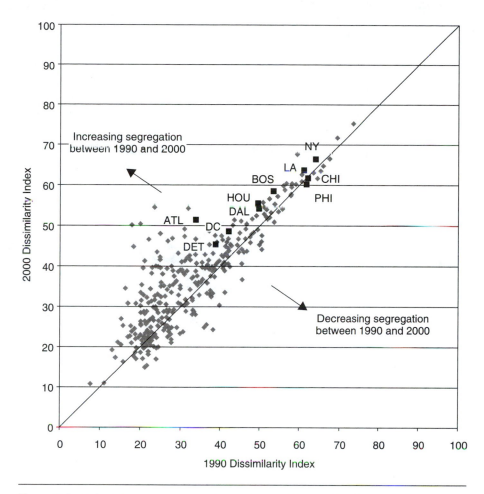

Figure 11.2   *Latino/Non-Hispanic White Dissimilarity in U.S. Metropolitan Areas, 1990 and 2000*
(*Source:* Examining Residential Segregation Patterns, by Shannon McConville and
Paul Ong with Douglas Houston and Jordan Rickles, July 19, 2001.)

(Pinal & Singe, 2001). Given their distinctive language, job skills, and social networks, Hispanic Americans tend to create durable residential enclaves, and their experiences in American cities will likely follow the ethnic-status rather than the melting-pot model of ethnic assimilation.

Asian Americans

The 2000 census revealed that the Asian American population nearly doubled between 1990 and 2000, and it is likely to double again by 2010.[6] The 10.2 million Asian Americans counted in the 2000 census make up 4.9 percent of the total U.S.

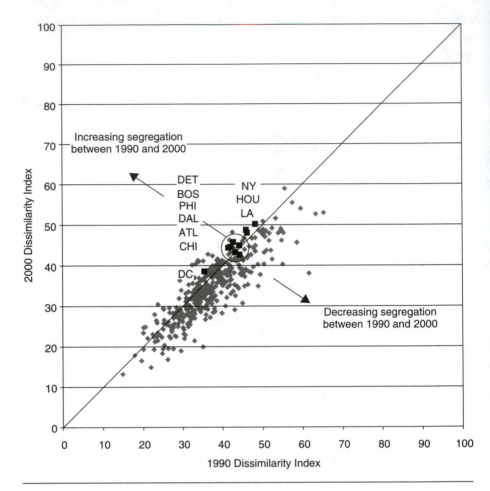

Figure 11.3 *Asian/Pacific Islander/Non-Hispanic White Dissimilarity in U.S. Metropolitan Areas, 1990 and 2000 (Source: Examining Residential Segregation Patterns, by Shannon McConville and Paul Ong with Douglas Houston and Jordan Rickles, July 19, 2001.)*

population, but their influence on U.S. society is accentuated by their geographic concentration in a handful of states and cities and their above-average income and educational levels. Immigration has fueled the dramatic growth of the Asian American population. Almost 70 percent of the U.S. Asians counted in the 2000 census were either immigrants who came to the United States after 1970 or the children of these immigrants. About 20 percent of the 2000 population arrived after 1990 (U.S. Census Bureau, 2001). Immigrants from Asia represent more than one-third of all legal immigrants admitted to the United States in recent years. The rapid expansion of the Asian American population has been accompanied by an ethnic diversity. In 1970, 96 percent of Asian Americans were Japanese, Chinese, or Filipino. In the 2000 census these three groups make up just over 50 percent of

Asian Americans. Asian Indians, Koreans, and Vietnamese now outnumber Japanese Americans (Asian American Federation, 2001). One indication of the size and diversity in this ethnic group is the number of Asian ethnic groups recognized by the U.S. Census. In 1970 the number was four; in the 2000 census thirteen were recognized, including Cambodians, Pakistanis, and Thais, among others (Population Reference Bureau, 2001a).

Their high average educational attainment, occupational status, and household incomes give Asian Americans many housing alternatives, and 60 percent now live in the suburbs, a percentage that equals whites (Logan, 2001b). This locational freedom has led to general declines in their residential segregation. The scatter plot in Figure 11.3 of dissimilarity index scores for the nation's MSAs shows that residential segregation for Asian Americans declined in the vast majority of MSAs. This group's high socioeconomic status, declining segregation, and dispersal to the suburbs suggests the melting-pot model will describe their assimilation into American society.

Ethnic Segregation in Other Societies

Canada

Canada, like the United States, is a nation of immigrants, and like the United States, Canada experienced three waves of immigrants. The first wave arrived before 1940 and included people from Britain, Poland, Scandinavia, and Russia. The second wave occurred in the 1950s and included French, Germans, and Dutch. The latest wave includes Italians, Asians, and Caribbeans, groups who entered Canadian society in the 1960s. Patterns of ethnic segregation parallel those found in the United States, except that the overall level of segregation is lower. The dissimilarity index between immigrants and native Canadians range between the 20s and 50s with an average of 30. As in the United States, northern and western Europeans have lower index scores than eastern and southern Europeans. In general, patterns of assimilation are similar to the United States. Ethnics locate in central-city enclaves and as time passes and their income improves, they move to other parts of the city where other factors become important (Massey, 1985).

Australia

Australia is also a nation of immigrants, but until World War II, the majority of immigrants were of British or Irish extraction. After the war, the government pursued a program to encourage immigration. Initially, most of the immigrants were from Britain, Ireland, and northern and southern Europe. In the past twenty years immigration has shifted to Asia, the Middle East, and Oceania. Today, 20 percent of Australians are foreign born and Australia's major cities are ethnically diverse.

The cleavage between northern and southern European immigrants, which characterizes Canada and the United States is also found in Australia but on levels comparable to Canada. The major ethnic division is between groups who speak English and those who don't. English-speaking immigrants have moved into white-collar occupations and tend to live in the suburbs; non-English speakers tend to be blue-collar workers who live and work in the central city.

The ethnic enclaves are dispersing in a manner similar to those in Canada and the United States (Massey, 1985).

Britain

Until the end of World War II, Britain was a homogeneous society with few ethnic immigrants. Unlike the United States, Canada, and Australia, it was a nation of emigration not immigration. After the war, Britain experienced two waves of immigration from within the commonwealth—West Indians (1947–1970) and Indians and Pakistanis (1960–1980). Today, ethnic people make up approximately 5 percent of Britain's total population, but the majority of the ethnic population is concentrated in Britain's largest cities. The factors affecting segregation in Britain were also different from the other nations we have discussed. The number of immigrants was smaller, there is less suburbanization, economic growth is slower, and government plays a larger role in housing than the other three nations. The dissimilarity index ranges from the 30s to the 50s with an average for both groups of around 50. Ethnicity has not been well studied in Britain, but ethnic enclaves are found in the central cities of most cities and their persistence is closely associated with the social status of their residents (Prandy, 1980).

Western Europe

After World War II, western European nations launched a massive rebuilding program, and this effort, combined with rapid economic growth, led to chronic labor shortages. By the 1960s, many western European governments were recruiting guest workers from Spain, Portugal, and Italy. And when this source of labor dried up, they turned to Yugoslavia, Turkey, and North Africa. Guest workers were seen as a temporary solution to a short-term labor problem, but as labor shortages persisted temporary immigration became permanent. By the 1970s western Europe contained 11 million foreign residents, comprising about 5 percent of the total population. As with immigrants in other societies, these groups gravitated toward the continent's largest cities, and by the late 1970s, the percentage of foreign-born residents in Brussels was 16 percent, in Paris 12 percent, in Berlin 18 percent, in Munich 15 percent, and in Amsterdam 5 percent.

Ethnic segregation has not been widely studied in Europe, but research in Germany shows that dissimilarity indexes range from 10 to 40. As in other societies the index scores are tied to the similarity between the immigrant group and the host society. Generally, these groups live in the oldest housing in the central city near the industries where they work and in isolated neighborhoods near suburban industrial centers (Massey, 1985).

In sum, other researchers have had mixed findings. Some researchers find that ethnic identification remains an important factor in the persistence of ethnic segregation (Bledea, 1979). Others find a close relationship between time of arrival and a decline in residential segregation (Farley & Wilger, 1987; Neidert & Farley, 1985). Regardless of the model, ethnicity remains an important division in this and other societies. I would argue that some ethnic groups may never be completely assimilated into this society, and there is plenty of evidence from societies around the world (see accompanying discussion). The ethnic Chinese in Vietnam, Jews in the pale of eastern Europe and Russia, and Koreans in Japan have retained their language, customs, and culture for centuries. Likewise, we find ethnic groups in the United States that have retained their strong ethnic identity for more than a century.

Deeply embedded in our national consciousness is the belief that all groups will eventually and inevitably be assimilated into the mainstream of our society. This is how we make Americans, after all. Although our mass media and popular culture are potent forces in bringing assimilation about, there are the countervailing forces of ethnic identification. I believe that elements of both models describe the experience of ethnic groups in American society. I also believe that ethnicity will continue to be important to understanding our cities and our society well into the twenty-first century. Rather than an assimilated society, America is becoming a more diverse and pluralistic one. Our national goal should be working toward a time when ethnic divisions are recognized, protected, and appreciated.

Racial Segregation

In the 1990 census, half a million people disregarded instructions to mark only one race and checked two or more races instead. The 2000 census allowed multiple racial responses, and 6.7 million Americans took advantage of the change in racial reporting. The new standards for collecting data on race provide a more accurate portrait of our nation, albeit a more confusing one. In all, the census offered a mosaic of sixty-three racial options, up from just five in 1990. This included the six single races, fifteen possible combinations of two, twenty combinations of three, fifteen of four, six combinations of five, and one grand mix of all six main categories—White-Black-Asian-American Indian or Alaska Native-Native Hawaiian or other Pacific Islander-Some Other Race. By matching these racial options against two ethnic possibilities—Hispanic or non-Hispanic—the census produced a matrix of 126 total combinations of race and ethnicity (Porter, 2001). Only 2.4 percent of Americans filling out the census questionnaire took advantage of this flexibility. But these data show a growing number of interracial marriages and more children being born to parents of different races. The nation will be a far more ethnically and racially diverse society in the future.

Race and ethnicity are social constructions. Humans cannot be scientifically classified into races on the basis of biological factors. Instead, race means that certain physical characteristics, such as skin color, are used to separate people into racial categories. Membership in racial categories, in turn, shapes the social status and experiences of individuals, from childhood to old age. Thus, racial identity is an important force in shaping the opportunities, rewards, and social experiences of groups in this society. For example, many racial minorities continue to have a higher poverty rate than whites. Health data show that they are more susceptible to diseases like diabetes, hypertension, and stroke. And poor health is linked to the poor health care many racial minorities receive (Lee, 2001).

As a society, we have recognized the reality of racial discrimination and have passed laws to curb it. The Civil Rights Act of 1965, the Voter Rights Act of 1967, and federal fair housing legislation are examples. In addition, the federal courts have used school busing and racial quotas to remedy past discrimination. And although many Americans believe that racial discrimination is part of our not-so-distant past, it is very much part of our present. See Photo 11.2. The U.S. Commission on Civil Rights issued a final report in June 2001 that some black Floridians who attempted to vote in the 2000 presidential election faced discrimination, including possible violations of the Voting Rights Act of 1965 (U.S. Civil Rights Commission, 2001). So as

Photo 11.2 *The modern civil rights movement began nearly 50 years ago, yet African Americans remain the most highly segregated group in our society. (Source: Courtesy of Do It Best Corp.)*

long as racial discrimination exists, the U.S. Census Bureau will collect data on the racial characteristics of our people (see Table 11.2 and Figure 11.4).

Racial and ethnic diversity has always been a hallmark of American society. Immigration from different parts of the world, and the different fertility and mortality rates among recent migrants, has kept our racial and ethnic composition in flux. African Americans are currently the second largest racial-ethnic minority in the United States, accounting for 12.3 percent of the population. About 12.5 percent of persons classify themselves as Hispanic; 3.6 percent are Asian or Pacific Islander; and less than 1 percent are American Indian or Alaska Native. The majority of the U.S. population, about 72 percent, is white.

Because of their relatively high migration and fertility rates, Hispanics now outnumber blacks. By 2025, Hispanics will account for 18 percent of the U.S. population, while only 13 percent of the population will be African American. Over the same period, the percentage of whites will decline by 10 percent to 62 percent. If current trends continue, almost half of the U.S. population will be nonwhite by 2050. Half the populations in California and Hawaii are already nonwhite, as are the populations of the nation's 100 largest metropolitan areas. In the next twenty-five years, minority concentrations are projected to increase in all parts of the country, but especially in the South, Southwest, and West. By 2025, New Mexico, Texas, and the District of Columbia should join California and Hawaii as states where minority groups account for more than 50 percent of the population (Population Reference Bureau, 2001a).

Amid this growing diversity, racial and ethnic segregation continues to divide our people. At a time of massive demographic change, we are still likely as ever to

Table 11.2 Residential Segregation of Race/Ethnic Groups with Non-Hispanic Whites in MSAs, 1990–2000

Metropolitan Area	Total Population	Non-Hispanic White	Black/African American		Latino		Asian/Pacific Islander	
		% of Total Population	% Total Population	Index Score	% Total Population	Index Score	% Total Population	Index Score
All MSAs								
2000	225,981,477	66.0%	13.5%	64.3	13.6%	51.0	4.9%	41.4
1990	198,400,277	73.2%	12.9%	67.8	9.7%	49.7	3.5%	41.2
Change	27,581,200	−7.2%	0.6%	−3.5	3.9%	1.3	1.4%	0.2
Large MSAs (over 1 million)								
2000	146,733,822	61.7%	15.1%	67.9	15.4%	53.9	5.9%	42.7
1900	127,830,800	69.7%	16.6%	71.5	11.1%	52.5	4.1%	42.0
Change	18,903,022	−8.0%	−0.5%	−3.5	4.3%	1.4	1.8%	0.7
Small MSAs (under 1 million)								
2000	79,247,655	73.9%	10.7%	54.9	10.3%	42.9	3.1%	36.7
1900	70,569,477	79.5%	9.9%	58.0	7.3%	42.1	2.4%	38.7
Change	8,678,178	−5.6%	0.8%	−3.1	3.0%	0.8	0.7%	−1.9

Source: D. Houston, S. McConville, J. Rickles, and P. Ong. 2000. Census 2000 Fact Sheet: Residential Segregation in United States Metropolitan Areas. Los Angeles, CA: University of California, School of Public Policy, Ralph and Goldy Lewis Center for Regional Policy Studies, Table 1.

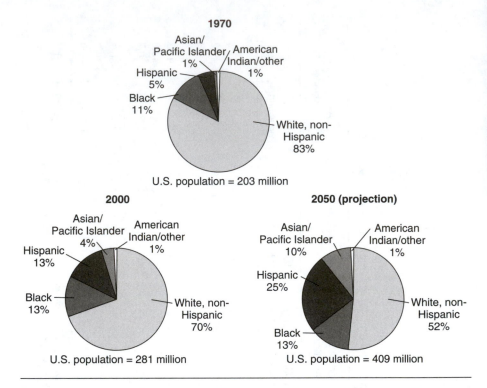

Figure 11.4   *U.S. Population by Race and Ethnic Group, 1979, 2000, 2050 (Source:* U.S. Bureau of the Census. 2003. *Current Population Report P25-1130.* Washington, D.C.: Government Printing Office.)

live in integrated neighborhoods. Distinct living patterns continue to hold sway in large urban centers where most of America's blacks, Hispanics, and Asian Americans live. In 2000, the typical white lived in a neighborhood that was 80 percent white, 8 percent Hispanic, 7 percent black, and 4 percent Asian American. The typical black lived in a neighborhood that was 51 percent black, 33 percent white, 12 percent Hispanic, and 3 percent Asian American. Although there were slight overall decreases in white-black residential dissimilarity, white-Hispanic residential dissimilarity increased in the decade ending in 2000 (Armas, 2001). The final section of this chapter explores the causes and patterns of racial segregation. We will focus our discussion on the experiences of the largest racial minority in this society—African Americans.

African Americans

The 35 million black Americans are this nation's most-segregated minority group. Americans of African heritage have roots reaching back to the founding of the nation, yet today the residential segregation of this group is higher than our most recent immigrants, Hispanics and Asians. Understanding why black Americans remain segregated after centuries reveals something about the forces that shape our cities as well as our society.

The Rural to Urban Migration of Black Americans

Through much of our history, America's black population has been mostly rural and southern. However, during much of the twentieth century a major redistribution of population occurred as blacks moved to urban areas in the North and the South. In fact, the migration of more than 5 million blacks from the rural south to northern industrial cities represents one of the largest migrations in history. In 1900, 76 percent of this nation's black population lived in rural areas, and nearly 90 percent lived in the South. By 1980, only 18 percent of this nation's black population lived in rural areas, and 47 percent lived in regions outside the South. The first significant out-migration of blacks from the South began with World War I and continued through the 1920s. The primary attraction of northern cities to southern blacks was jobs. The war cut off the immigration of cheap European labor to northern industries, creating a labor shortage. At the same time the mechanization of farming was creating a surplus of unskilled farm labor in the South. Therefore, black Americans in the 1920s and the decades that followed became a new source of cheap industrial labor.

The depression of the 1930s dramatically lowered the population growth of blacks in metropolitan areas. Later, with the rapid expansion of American industry during World War II, the flow of migrants accelerated, and this trend continued into the 1950s and 1960s. During the 1970s, migration slowed and the regional distribution of population by race stabilized.

The 2000 census shows that blacks ended the twentieth century by returning to the region that they spent most of the century leaving. Southern black population growth surged by more than 3.5 million people in the 1990s—more than the other three regions combined. This represents 58 percent of the nation's total black population gain. It also represents about twice the number of blacks that the South gained in the 1980s and lies well above the gain for the 1970s, the first decade when blacks began returning to the South. Still, the 1990s are distinct because of the sheer magnitude of black southern gains, and because it is the first decade this century where each of the other major regions registered a net out-migration of blacks, completing the century's reversal (Frey, 2001).

Migration streams. Enclaves and ghettoes serve many functions. They give a group a sense of peoplehood and allow a group to avoid a hostile host society. They provide a safety net of kin and friends and support stores, shops, schools, and other enterprises. They provide a haven to new immigrants. And once they reach a critical mass, they encourage additional migration. How? They do it through a network of old friends and relatives in the sending society. Money, letters, calls, and people pass back and forth between the sending and receiving societies, and over time migration occurs in streams. One of the largest migrations in our history is the Famine Irish who entered this country in the second half of the nineteenth century. Oscar Handlin (1969) in his book, *Boston's Immigrants: 1790–1880*, describes the factors that confined much of this immigration to a stream between Ireland and Boston. Douglas Massey (1987) examined Mexican immigration and described the network of kin and friends, the lines of communication, and the economic ties between Mexico and the United States that shaped the size and direction of this migration to the United States.

These same factors shaped black America's migration. Social networks and communication between friends and relatives channeled black migration into distinct migration streams. Between 1900 and 1970, blacks from the South Atlantic states of Virginia, North and South Carolina, Georgia, and Florida migrated to the metropolises of the Northeast and Middle Atlantic states, including Washington, D.C., Philadelphia, New York, and Boston. Blacks from Alabama, Mississippi, Tennessee, Arkansas, and Louisiana tended to follow migration streams along the valleys of the Mississippi and Ohio Rivers to the lake and river cities. Blacks from Texas and western Louisiana usually chose cities in the West.

In the return migration of the 1980s and 1990s, blacks located to many of the same metropolitan areas that attracted whites to the "New Sunbelt." Among the thirty-two metro areas that house more than 200,000 blacks, southern metros, led by Orlando and Atlanta, dominate the list of black high-growth areas. Other Southeast metros were also attractive to blacks, including Miami, Tampa, and Jacksonville in Florida; Charlotte, Raleigh, Durham, and Greensboro in North Carolina; Norfolk and Richmond in Virginia; and Washington, D.C. Like whites, blacks are attracted to the good economy, low-density living, and warmer climate. In addition, the past shapes the current migration streams: Many blacks are returning to city and states that their parents and grandparents left decades earlier (Frey 2001).

Residential Patterns in the 1970s and 1980s

In 1980, 82 percent of all blacks were urban, a percentage that exceeds that of their white counterparts (71 percent). The black migration from the South was predominantly a migration to the central cities of metropolitan areas. By 1980, the population of metropolitan areas had become 15 percent black, and blacks made up 7 percent of the suburban rings (Stahura, 1988). In the 1970s and 1980s, black Americans began to move to the suburbs, but the suburbs to which they moved were usually older and adjacent to the traditional black area of the central city. Black suburbs might be politically autonomous, but they shared many of the housing, employment, and service problems of central-city neighborhoods (Logan & Schneider, 1984; Stahura, 1988; Sterns & Logan, 1986).

The 2000 census revealed that the reverse stream of black migrants is different—it's overwhelmingly suburban. Approximately 88 percent of black southern in-migrants chose to live in metropolitan areas; and of these, 81 percent selected a suburban residence. Among all southern blacks, 76 percent live in metropolitan areas, and 43 percent reside in the suburbs. The fact that there is a suburban spreading out of blacks is evident from 2000 census results, which show that seven of the ten fastest growing counties for blacks are located in the suburban portion of metropolitan Atlanta (see Table 11.3). The migration is different in other ways: Black in-migrants tend to be of high socioeconomic status. Approximately 19 percent of all black in-migrants to the South are college graduates, compared with 13 percent of all black southern residents. Among labor force participants, nearly three out of ten black in-migrants to the South are professionals and managers. The special attraction that the South holds for professional workers is the existence of a large black middle class in many of the region's largest cities, providing opportunities for networking and upward mobility (Frey, 2001). Higher levels of education and income, an improved racial climate, and rigorous enforcement of fair housing laws have translated into more housing options for black in-migrants. The 2000 census revealed a general decline in black-white residential dissimilarity and the potential for greater racial integration in the future (Frey, 2001).

Table 11.3 Counties with Fastest Growing Black Populations, 1990–2000

Rank	County and State	Inside Metro Area	1990–2000 % Change	2000 Black Population	2000 % Black Populations
1	Gwinnett County, GA	Atlanta, GA MSA	343.9	79,781	13.6
2	Fayette County, GA	Atlanta, GA MSA	221.7	10,727	11.8
3	Douglas County, GA	Atlanta, GA MSA	215.1	17,499	19.0
4	Rockdale County, GA	Atlanta, GA MSA	198.8	12,940	18.5
5	Dakota County, MN	Minneapolis-St. Paul, MN-WI MSA	198.8	10,049	2.8
6	Henry County, GA	Atlanta, GA MSA	195.3	17,841	14.9
7	Clayton County, GA	Atlanta, GA MSA	185.6	122,957	52.0
8	Snohomish County, WA	Seattle-Tacoma-Bremerton, WA CMSA	183.6	13,160	2.2
9	Stafford County, VA	Washington-Baltimore, DC-MD-VA-WV CMSA	178.1	11,796	12.8
10	Cobb County, GA	Atlanta, GA MSA	166.5	116,346	19.1
11	Macomb County, MI	Detroit-Ann Arbor-Flint, MI CMSA	131.2	23,843	3.0
12	Collin County, TX	Dallas-Fort Worth, TX CMSA	130.4	24,713	5.0
13	Collier County, FL	Naples, FL MSA	127.5	13,124	5.2
14	Prince William County, VA	Washington-Baltimore, DC-MD-VA-WV CMSA	122.8	54,986	19.6
15	Osceola County, FL	Orlando, FL MSA	122.6	12,135	7.0
16	Salt Lake County, UT	Salt Lake City-Ogden UT MSA	116.3	11,256	1.3
17	Loudoun County, VA	Washington-Baltimore, DC-MD-VA-WV CMSA	105.7	12,603	7.4
18	Stanislaus County, CA	Modesto, CA MSA	104.9	12,515	2.8
19	Williamson County, TX	Austin-San Marcos, TX MSA	103.3	13,291	5.3
20	Denton County, TX	Dallas-Fort Worth, TX CMSA	99.1	26,513	6.1

Source: William H. Frey. 2001. Census 2000 Shows Large Black Return to the South, Reinforcing the Region's "White-Black" Demographic Profile. Ann Arbor, MI: University of Michigan, Population Studies Center, Table 4.

Trends in Racial Segregation

In the nineteenth century, the few blacks who lived in urban areas were not sep-arated from whites. Residential land use in the preindustrial city was not like the modern metropolis. Industry and commerce were dispersed across the city, and most people lived near where they worked (Hershberg et al., 1979). The cities were heterogeneous, but different populations lived side by side despite the eth-nic, racial, and social-status differences that separated them in other aspects of urban life. Dissimilarity indexes for free blacks in fifteen cities in 1850 are shown in Table 11.4. Note that the scores range from a high of 59.2 in Boston to a low of 15.8 in Louisville. But these indexes are based on ward data, and they can be deceiving, because they mask some segregation. We know from studies in Cincinnati, Detroit, and Philadelphia that if segregation patterns are analyzed on the street and block level, one finds that blacks were not evenly distributed within wards but tended to be concentrated on a few streets within each ward (Hershberg et al., 1979; Hershberg et al., 1981). For example, Taylor (1986) in his study of Cincinnati found that 52 percent of the black population of Cincinnati in 1850 resided on just 3 percent of the city's streets. In examining these clusters, he found that blacks were found to live together regardless of nativity, sex, house-hold structure, stage in the life cycle, or occupation.

In the past century, the size of the black urban population has grown, the forces shaping the city have changed, and the scale of urbanization has increased. But have segregation patterns changed? The answer is yes. The 2000 census showed that between 1990 and 2000 the segregation levels in 272 metropolitan statistical areas declined; in only 19 metros did they rise. It was the third straight decade in which segregation between blacks and nonblacks in the nation's cities

Table 11.4   *Free Black Indexes of Dissimilarity for Fifteen Cities, 1850*

City	Black Population	Percent Total Population	Index of Dissimilarity
Boston	1,999	1.46	59.2
Philadelphia	10,736	8.85	49.3
Pittsburgh	1,959	4.20	46.3
New Orleans	9,905	8.51	45.1
Cincinnati	3,137	2.67	37.5
New York	13,815	2.68	37.2
St. Louis	1,398	1.80	35.8
Brooklyn	2,424	2.50	31.8
Buffalo	675	1.60	25.1
Albany	860	1.69	25.1
Providence	1,499	3.61	24.2
Baltimore	24,442	15.05	21.4
Charleston	3,441	8.01	20.5
Washington, D.C.	8,158	20.39	20.4
Louisville	612	1.34	15.8

Source: L. P. Curry. 1981. *The free black in urban America: The shadow of a dream.* Chicago: University of Chicago Press, p. 56.

had declined. In a 2001 Brookings Institution report, *Racial Segregation in the 2000 Census: Promising News*, Edward Glaeser and Jacob Vigdor detail these and other trends in black segregation.

Glaeser and Vigdor (2001) found that between 1890 and 1970 segregation rose dramatically in U.S. cities. Starting in the 1970s, however, segregation began to fall. The sharpest decline in segregation occurred during the 1970s, when the average segregation level in metropolitan areas fell by almost 10 percent. Segregation continued to fall in the 1980s and 1990s, but at a slower rate. Changes in the average dissimilarity and isolation indexes for the period 1890–2000 are summarized in Figure 11.5. Note that the indexes peak in the 1950s and 1960s and then begin a dramatic decline after 1970. Note also that the level of black/nonblack segregation in the United States is at the lowest level since the 1920s. Data from the beginning and end of the 1990s give a good indication of the scope of this change. In 1990, the average African American lived in a neighborhood that was 56 percent black; by 2000, this figure had dropped to 51 percent, a decline of 5 percent (Glaeser & Vigdor, 2001).

The 1990 and 2000 indexes of dissimilarity for the nation's metropolitan statistical areas are plotted in Figure 11.6. Notice that the vast majority of the points fall below the diagonal, indicating declining segregation in these cities. Only nineteen MSAs reported increases, and most of these metros were in the South, communities like Pine Bluff and Texarkana in Arkansas and Alexandria, Baton Rouge, in Louisiana and Biloxi in Mississippi. But MSAs in the Northeast and Midwest were also represented, including Brockton, Maine, and Terre Haute, Indiana. Interestingly, several were home to large land-grant universities—Ann Arbor, Michigan; Champaign-Urbana, Illinois; Iowa City, Iowa; and Tuscaloosa, Alabama. At the other extreme were the forty-four MSAs that experienced declines in their indexes of 10 percent or more. Twenty-six of these cities were in the South and West, twelve in the Midwest, and six in the Northeast (Houston et al., 2001).

What is behind this decline? In general, the decline is the result of the integration of formerly all-white census tracts. For example, in 1960, 61.8 percent of census tracts in metropolitan areas were less than 1 percent black. In 2000, this figure had dropped to 23.1 percent. This is true across the range of integrated tracts. For example, in 2000, 45 percent of census tracts had between 1 and 10 percent African Americans, but only 13.6 percent of the metropolitan blacks lived in these tracts. More telling is the fact that almost half of the metropolitan black population now lives in a majority-nonblack census tract. Census tracts of very high percentage African American populations remained unchanged between 1990 and 2000, however, indicating that the integration of all-white tracts by blacks, not the integration of all-black tracts by whites, is driving this change (Glaeser & Vigdor, 2001).

There are distinct regional differences in these patterns. Metropolitan areas in the West have the lowest levels of racial segregation, closely followed by the South. The Northeast and Midwest regions continue to be highly segregated. This is especially true of the older industrial cities of the upper Midwest like Chicago, Cleveland, and Detroit that have extremely high indexes of dissimilarity—77, 78, and 84, respectively. In general, these regional differences reflect the age of cities and their economic bases. Cities in the West and South are younger and have local economies tied to distribution and commerce. Unlike the older industrial cities of the Northeast and Midwest, they are multinucleated; they were built at lower density; they have a younger housing stock and newer neighborhoods; and they do not have durable ethnic enclaves that resist integration (Glaeser & Vigdor, 2001).

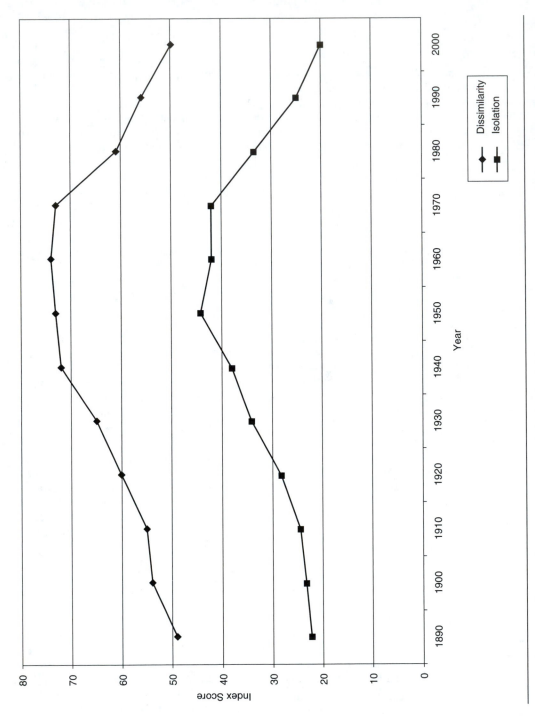

Figure 11.5 *Average Dissimilarity and Isolation Indexes, 1890–2000 (Source: E. L. Glaeser & J. Vigdor. 2001. Racial Segregation in the 2000 Census: Promising News. Washington, D.C.: The Brookings Institution, p. 4.)*

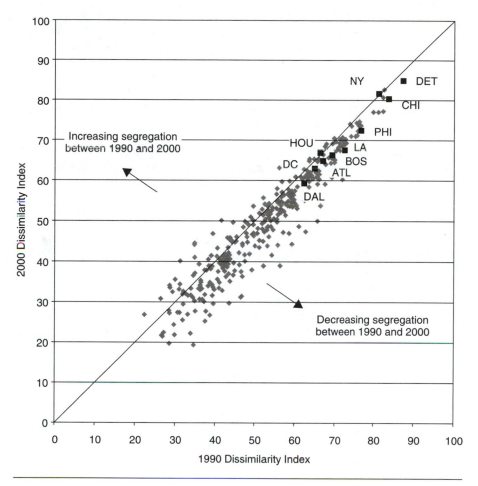

Figure 11.6   *African American/Non-Hispanic White Dissimilarity in U.S. Metropolitan Areas, 1990 and 2000* (*Source:* Examining Residential Segregation Patterns, by Shannon McConville and Paul Ong with Douglas Houston and Jordan Rickles, July 19, 2001.)

Other economic and demographic factors are also important. First, faster-growing cities had sharper declines in segregation. The reason: slowly growing MSAs accommodated change in their black populations within existing neighborhoods, a process that typically follows past residential patterns. Faster-growing cities have a clean slate. They accommodate residential change within new neighborhoods, free of past racial patterns. Similarly, MSAs with growing black populations reduced segregation because most black in-migrants move to newer neighborhoods in the suburban fringe (Glaeser & Vigdor, 2001).

Although the 2000 census gives promising news, it is important to remember that segregation remains extremely high in the United States. The index of dissimilarity of the nation's MSAs averages 65. Moreover, older industrial MSAs in the

Midwest—Detroit, Chicago, Cincinnati, Toledo, and Cleveland—continue to display hyper segregation with average scores over 70, but even these cities showed declines in segregation. The biggest change occurred in the rapidly growing cities in the South and West. As shown throughout the text, where you live determines how well you live. Integration means greater access to good schools, shopping, jobs, and a range of metropolitan services. The 2000 census suggests that the experiences of African Americans in the Sunbelt will be quite different from those in other regions.

A Community Within a Community

Patterns of segregation have changed in the past three decades in ways policy makers would have expected from the landmark civil rights legislation in the 1960s and the affirmative action programs in the late 1960s and 1970s. As the socioeconomic status of black Americans has improved, their residential mobility has increased, enabling them to leave the inner-city ghettos for other parts of the city, especially the suburbs. Although improvements have been made in the past three decades, segregation forces blacks of widely different social status to live closer to one another than do their white counterparts. Because of the persistence of segregation in American society, the "black community" in many large American metropolises has taken on some of the characteristics of the total metropolis of which it is a part. The most interesting of these is residential segregation according to class within the black community.

Mario Sims (1998) investigated this relationship among different status groups in the white, black, Hispanic, and Asian populations in five cities, Chicago, Los Angeles, Miami, New York, and San Francisco. He discovered that the residential closeness or propinquity between high- and low-status persons differed dramatically among racial and ethnic groups. Although whites with high income and education lived in census tracts with others of comparable status, high-status blacks did not separate themselves from low-status blacks. Well-off blacks and Hispanics are more concentrated in tracts with higher percentages of persons of dissimilar status than are well-off whites and Asians. This suggests that while advantaged blacks and Hispanics are able to place some distance between themselves and lower-status groups, they are not able to escape totally being exposed to the conditions of lower-status neighborhoods that are characterized with fewer services and harsher social and economic conditions. For the black upper class, social-status segregation means avoiding the inner ghetto and public housing, but it does not mean isolation from the black lower class. Unlike whites, higher-status black families shared schools, parks, and other facilities with lower socioeconomic groups, and since the neighborhood environment affects things like children's school performance, these findings suggest that propinquity may have consequences for social mobility (Sims, 1998).

Much has changed in the past decade. Average family income for black Americans has grown, and blacks in increasing numbers have moved to the suburbs. The black middle class has been able to do what whites have done all along—avoid groups that they define as undesirable—and isolate themselves in politically autonomous suburbs. The move to the suburbs may serve the interest of the black middle and upper classes, but it has consequences for those left behind.

William Wilson (1987) in his controversial book, *The Truly Disadvantaged*, explores the consequences of these changes in the black community. He makes an argument in opposition of Sims (1998): The lower class may have hindered the social mobility of the middle class, but the middle class has traditionally provided the leadership, role models, and values and norms for the entire black community. This occurred because blacks of all social classes shared the same area of the city. During the 1970s and 1980s, blacks experienced upward social mobility, and the black middle class abandoned the traditional community for other parts of the city. According to Wilson, the people left behind are the most disadvantaged element of the black community, the underclass.

The black underclass is a heterogeneous grouping of families and individuals outside the mainstream of the American occupational system. They lack training and skills; they suffer from long-term unemployment or have never worked; they engage in street crime and other aberrant behavior; and they have a long history of welfare dependence. They share similar problems: low income, poor health, broken homes, inadequate housing, poor education, and cultural and linguistic differences that separate and isolate them from the mainstream of society (Wilson, 1987).

Is the outward migration of the black middle class the only reason for the emergence of the underclass? The answer is no. Structural changes in America's economy have contributed to the problem. Chicago and other northern industrial cities have changed from manufacturing and distribution centers to administrative, information, and service centers. Gone are the high-paid factory jobs. Gone are low-paying, entry-level jobs. Growing are jobs that require high levels of education and training. Wilson argues that racism and discrimination have led to the overrepresentation of black Americans in lower occupational groupings, and these jobs are vulnerable to changes in the economy. Not only has there been a decline in the number of jobs in the low-wage sector, but those remaining are no longer found in the central city; they're in the suburbs. There is a mismatch between where people live and where the jobs are.

Therefore, structural changes in America's economy combined with the suburbanization of industry and the black middle class have led to the segregation and isolation of the most disadvantaged citizens in this society. According to Wilson, this isolation has contributed to the destruction of the black family, the growth of female-headed families, and the emergence of a set of values and norms that perpetuate inequality. For example, at a time when education is vital for success, the children of the underclass are going to the worst schools in the city. At a time when intact black families are experiencing upward social mobility, the pool of employed males available for marriage is shrinking. At a time when the fastest-growing segment of the poor is female-headed households, the stigma on unwanted pregnancy and illegitimacy in the ghetto is on the decline. And at a time when an intact family—one in which both the father and mother are present—has been found to be a major deterrent to illegitimacy, these families have become rare in the neighborhoods of the underclass.

Solutions? Wilson explores the failed programs of the past—the War on Poverty, Model Cities, and Job Corps—and claims that they failed because they were not broadly based. He contends that a program that will work is one that addresses structural problems faced by all Americans, not just those of color.

The work of Wilson has been corroborated by the research of others on occupational inequality. For more than thirty years, researchers have investigated patterns of racial socioeconomic inequality in cities. Occupation is one of the most important dimensions of social status because it is related to so many other factors. One's occupational status is correlated with one's education, income, lifestyle, social roles, and life chances. As with residential segregation, occupational status is an important indicator of racial inequality in American society.

Researchers have found a steady decline in socioeconomic differences between blacks and whites in the last forty years. And they have documented the growing equality in schooling, earnings, and access to employment (Massey, 1993, 1996). But major differences still exist. Why? Because of the ecology of place. People living in different places face different opportunity structures. Since the end of World War II, changes in transportation and communication technology have permitted the decentralization of industry from the central city to industrial parks and commercial centers on the fringe. When blacks are segregated in the central city, they tend to be cut off from information on outlying labor markets. The time and cost of commuting is an additional barrier to employment. Segregation means isolation and cutting blacks off from labor markets in the suburbs.

This is what Lewin-Epstein (1986) found in youth unemployment among blacks and whites. In the past decade there has been a growing disparity in labor market standing of black and white youth. While the employment of white youth has increased, unemployment rates among blacks have risen to twice that of young whites. Adolescents live with their parents, and they have no choice in residence. Few black youth own cars, and poor mass transit makes commuting costs to the suburbs prohibitive. The isolation of black youth "from life outside their communities and neighborhood restricts their ability to receive, organize, and put to use diverse labor market information" (Lewin-Epstein, 1986, p. 561). It appears that residential segregation not only inhibits contact between groups, lessening the chances of interaction and eventually assimilation, but it is also a major factor in the perpetuation of inequality in our society. Your life chances are not only circumscribed by your position in the social structure but also your residential location within the city.

Why Racial Segregation?

Ecological Factors

In the discussion of ethnic segregation three factors—voluntary, involuntary, and ecological—have been identified as being responsible for the segregation of these groups. The assimilation model presented in this section argues that the segregation of ethnic groups is an artifact of the group's social status. In the case of blacks, if ecological factors are responsible for segregation then poor blacks should live near poor whites, and rich blacks should live near rich whites. They don't. Even when the effects of income and education are removed, the dissimilarity index across metropolitan areas remains high. In the cities of Chicago, Detroit, Buffalo, Toledo, and Cleveland the indexes are consistently higher than the national average. Therefore, blacks are segregated from whites regardless of their income or education. Even among the highly educated, where you would expect to find racial tolerance, residential segregation is high. Therefore, it appears that the improving social status of blacks is unlikely, in and by itself, to alter the prevailing patterns of racial segregation (Farley, 1990).

Voluntary And Involuntary Factors

Even if involuntary and ecological factors in residential patterning could be eliminated completely, the segregation of races would persist for voluntary reasons:
Blacks would choose to live near blacks. However, the evidence is strong that
involuntary factors are responsible for much of black segregation. The nation's history is replete with examples of how violence, rumor, prejudicial insinuation, and
racial threats of declining property values and block busting have been used to
segregate black Americans. Racial minorities, because of their high visibility, are
the most easily manipulated real estate client groups. Because their housing
options have been limited by prejudicial feelings, a segregated market, and the
undemocratic rules to which they are subject, racial minorities have traditionally
had little choice in the matter of residential location. Nearly a century ago William
Graham Sumner, a founder of American sociology, stated, "stateways cannot
change folkways." It is true that federal legislation cannot change attitudes and
prejudices, but it can stop overt behavior in the form of discrimination. The 1964
Civil Rights Act and subsequent legislation have had a measurable impact on the
economic well-being of black Americans. These laws have reduced discrimination
in the economic sphere. The research we have reviewed in this section suggests
that residential patterns are beginning to change, too. Yet, changes in attitude
have not always translated into behavior. Whites still choose to live in neighborhoods that have few black residents, and, although there is evidence that it is
changing, blacks continue to live in a community within a community in the
nation's urban places.

Summary

This chapter addresses the segregation and location of socioeconomic, ethnic, and
racial groups in cities. Urban sociologists have discovered that the social distance
between groups is reflected in the spatial distance between them in their residential locations. These patterns can have positive and negative consequences for
society. Voluntary segregation can positively affect society by contributing to the
solidarity of groups and directly enhancing the individual's sense of belonging and
security. However, segregation can also lead to the physical and social isolation of
a group and form a barrier to its full participation in society.

Segregation is studied for several reasons. First, the degree of segregation
between groups is an indicator of the degree of social inequality in society.
Second, understanding residential segregation gives policy makers an indication
of the effectiveness of social programs and government policies in reducing
segregation. Third, the study of segregation gives the sociologist insights
into basic ecological processes that affect the overall structure and functioning
of society.

Three sets of factors have been identified as influencing the segregation
process. Ecological factors include impersonal economic and ecological forces
such as the location of housing types and the socioeconomic characteristics of
groups. Voluntary factors are ones of self-selection. Individuals of common culture
face common problems and needs and willingly choose to live near one another.
Involuntary segregation occurs as the result of laws or customs that prescribe

where certain groups can live. These three types of factors can operate alone but are usually interrelated.

The degree to which members of different status groups are residentially segregated from one another has been of long-standing interest to students of cities. Social-status segregation is a universal phenomenon; the gross inequality in the distribution of income in the United States is reflected in the residential patterns of its status groups. When the indexes of dissimilarity are plotted, the resulting U-shaped curve shows that the members of the highest and lowest status groups are the most segregated. The location of these groups depends on the level of development of the society and on the age and region of the city under study. Voluntary and ecological rather than involuntary factors are indicated in the segregation of status groups.

Ethnic segregation continues in many U.S. cities in spite of theories that predict the assimilation of ethnic groups. Three waves of immigrants came to this country, and their region of origin, time of arrival, and the dominant transportation and industrial technology in cities at the time of their arrival influenced their segregation. In general, those groups who were similar to the society's charter group—core English ancestry—were the most rapidly assimilated and least segregated. Two models were presented to describe the assimilation process, the melting-pot model and the ethnic-status model. The melting-pot model argues that ethnic assimilation is a function of the low socioeconomic status of recently arrived ethnic people. As the socioeconomic status of the groups improves, their segregation will decline. The ethnic-status model argues that a group's ethnicity operates independently of socioeconomic status and ethnicity acts as a marker affecting segregation. Although ecological factors such as income, occupation, and education explain some of this residential segregation, voluntary factors appear to contribute to the durability and resiliency of ethnic enclaves in American cities.

Black Americans are the largest and most segregated minority group in the United States. Blacks lived in mostly southern and rural areas until the early part of the twentieth century, when more than 5 million black Americans left the rural South for the cities. A majority of these migrants moved to the central cities of the North, where they formed durable racial communities. These communities have isolated black Americans, and this isolation has social consequences. The concentration and isolation of the poorest of this group have led to the emergence of an underclass. The social values, levels of education, and demographic and family structure make the participation of this group in the mainstream of American society difficult. The problems of the underclass have been exacerbated by the decentralization of jobs to the suburbs. Although nationally there were declines in the segregation of blacks in the decade ending in 1980, black Americans remain the most segregated group in our society.

The 2000 census showed that between 1990 and 2000 the segregation levels in 72 metropolitan statistical areas declined; in only 19 metros did they rise. It was the third straight decade in which segregation between blacks and nonblacks in the nation's cities had declined. Segregation in the United States is at the lowest level since the 1920s. This decline is the result of the integration of formerly all-white census tracts. Moreover, there are distinct regional differences in these patterns. Metropolitan areas in the West have the lowest levels of racial segregation, closely followed by the South. The Northeast and Midwest regions continue to be highly segregated. Although the 2000 census gives promising news, it is important to remember that segregation remains extremely high in the United States.

Finally, although voluntary factors cannot be eliminated, research has shown that ecological factors have little effect. In all probability racial segregation in the United States is due to involuntary factors. Although the 1964 Civil Rights Act has increased economic opportunities for black Americans, it has not increased the number of housing alternatives. Therefore, racial segregation will persist in the United States for the foreseeable future.

Notes

[1] See the Over-the-Rhine District in the movie, *Traffic*, starring Michael Douglas.

[2] Sociologists have studied the segregation of many groups including the very young and the elderly. Most of the attention of researchers is on social status, ethnic, and racial groups because they represent the major cleavages in American society and are important ecologically, politically, and socially.

[3] Smith and Zopf identify five distinct periods in the history of immigration to the United States. "The first embraces the years from establishment of the first settlements to the emergence of the national state in 1783; the second period of free immigration, ending about 1830; the third extending until 1882 was the period of state regulation; the fourth, beginning with the passage of the first national immigration act in 1882 and lasting until 1917, was a period of federal regulation with individual selection; and the fifth, the present stage of restricted immigration began in 1917" (Smith & Zopf, 1976, p. 473). For the purposes of this text, waves of migration have been classified according to the region of origin and this classification reflects the work of Douglas Massey (1996) and other students of ethnicity and assimilation.

[4] The nation's current immigration law still follows the framework of the Immigration and Nationality Act of 1952, which established a national quota system. However, with major revisions in 1965, the national-origins emphasis in this law was replaced by the governing themes of family reunification and the admission of aliens with needed skills. The Immigration Reform and Control Act of 1986 (PL 99-603) is built on the earlier legislation but addresses the control of illegal immigration by employer sanctions for the employment of unauthorized aliens, legalization of some undocumented aliens, and the legal admission of alien agricultural workers.

[5] Until the 1990s, *Hispanic* was the dominant term for referring to Spanish-speaking people in the United States or descendents of Spanish-speaking countries. Today, *Latino* and *Hispanic* are used interchangeably (Ellison, 2001).

[6] The Census Bureau classifies Asian Americans as a racial group. Asian Americans are also one of the America's most rapidly growing ethnic groups. I have chosen to discuss them under ethnicity.

12

URBAN PROBLEMS IN THE GLOBAL ERA

Introduction

Americans felt good about themselves in the 1990s. Following the 1990–1992 recession, the Clinton administration balanced the federal budget, created the largest budget surplus in history, swelled the ranks of the employed, reduced unemployment to a fifty-year low, and raised the incomes of even the poorest in our society. What was responsible? Politicians and social scientists alike pointed to a single event—the fall of the Berlin Wall on November 9, 1989. It marked the end of the Cold War and ushered in a new world order of globalization. Globalization unleashed the power of capitalism, and the United States, poised to take advantage of falling trade barriers, grew its economy by $2 trillion, roughly equal to Germany's GDP, the third-largest economy in the world.

Globalization depends on the free, unfettered movement of people, goods, money, and ideas across international borders. The attack on the World Trade Center on September 11, 2001, showed the fragility of this system and marks the end of the first phase of the globalization process. The plan for the rebuilding of the WTC is a good metaphor for what is in our future—a trade center and world that are less accessible and less vulnerable.

As I write this chapter in the spring of 2003, we occupy Iraq, the economy is in recession, unemployment hovers at 6 percent, the federal budget is poised to set a record $400 billion deficit, the Bush administration has passed a $330 billion tax cut that largely benefits the rich, and state and city governments are facing their worst financial crises since the Great Depression. With little debate and less media coverage more subtle and important changes are occurring in our society—the weakening of our social safety net. In the past decade, benefits have been reduced for Medicare, Medicaid, and Social Security recipients; traditional welfare programs have ended; and state programs for children and the disabled have been slashed. Corporations are reducing or eliminating pension benefits. Congress has reduced pension protection and the rights of citizens to use the courts to address government and corporate misconduct. And as we explored in the chapter on the postmodern community, American society is changing from a social world characterized by long-term stable relationships to one characterized by short-term temporary ones. These fundamental changes have altered the social contract between citizens and their government, workers and their employers, and residents and their communities.

Combined, these changes have shaken the underpinnings of our society. Less appreciated is that these societal changes profoundly affect the communities in which we live and the way we construct our lives. But social scientists can detect these community changes by studying where people live, where businesses and industries locate, and where neighborhoods prosper and decline. One of the principles of urban sociology is that social change is reflected first and most clearly in the spatial forms of our cities because this is where society touches the ground. I could devote an entire book to urban problems in the global era, but I have chosen three—the problems of inequality, housing, and public safety.

Earlier we reviewed Robert Reich's book, *The Work of Nations*. Reich argues that nations no longer shape their economies, global forces do, and that the well-being of our citizens is no longer determined by economic changes within our national borders but by what economic groups in our society contribute to the global economy. As Reich shows, the rules have changed and there are winners and losers. What happens to the losers? What are the consequences of downward social mobility for millions of Americans trapped in the margins of this revolution? How are these economic changes mirrored in our cities? This section explores one of the most important problems facing this society: What do we do for those left behind?

For some reason the plight of the homeless has slipped out of our national consciousness. What we do hear is that rates of home ownership are at record highs, and thirty-year mortgage rates are at historic lows. But millions of Americans live in substandard dwellings, and somewhere between 350,000 and 2 million Americans are homeless. In this section, we ask: Where are the homeless? Who are they? Why are they homeless? Are the numbers changing?

Public safety is one of the most intractable problems facing city governments, and the fear of crime is one of the factors that motivated millions of Americans to leave central cities for the fringe. An interesting point is that crime rates declined throughout the 1990s. We live in a far safer society than a generation ago. But most Americans are unaware of this trend, and the fear of crime has become a national obsession. Are police departments doing a better job or are other forces at work? Who is responsible for our, at times, irrational fear of crime? Urban crime and our attempts to control it are the third urban problem explored in this chapter.

All of these problems are national in scope, but are played out in urban places. As we will see in the final chapter of the book on urban planning, changing the way we build our cities may change the way we live in them.

INEQUALITY–A NATIONAL PROBLEM, URBAN CONSEQUENCES

Woven throughout this text is the theme that we are in the midst of the globalization revolution. This revolution made possible by the confluence of transportation, technological, political, and economic factors in the late 1980s permitted the democratization of technology, finance, information, and decision making and the creation of a global economy. These changes lowered the barrier of entry into markets, empowered consumers, shortened the product cycle, and unleashed the creative power of people through free-market capitalism. It also freed one of the most remarkable features of capitalism—the process of creative destruction. In markets shaped by unbridled competition, inefficient firms are forced out of business, and new, more efficient ones rise to take over their abandoned plants, offices, equipment, and labor. Enron is a good example. What is remarkable about Enron is not the greed of its chief officers, but our market's speed and efficiency in dismantling and absorbing Enron's parts into other companies. When this process is repeated thousands of times a year, the nature of our economy changes. Our cities are affected, in turn, because changes in the nation's economy must be worked out in cities. Globalization, therefore, has not only transformed our national economy but the economic base of every city. It has changed the relationship between cities in our system of cities, and it has affected where businesses and industries locate, what wages they pay, and where residents live, work, and play.

Globalization has also affected the fortunes of labor. As we have shown, well-educated and highly skilled workers who identify and solve problems are flourishing in the global economy. Poorly educated and unskilled workers who provide routine production and in-person services are foundering. As a result, the United States and nations around the world find themselves in the unusual situation where average incomes are growing at the same time inequality is rising.

This section explores the reasons for and consequences of a growing economic inequality in this nation. We ask: How has the labor force changed, and how is it expected to change in the future in response to the forces of globalization? Who have been the winners and losers? What are the consequences of this growing inequality? How have the changes affected the poor? Where do we see these changes in our cities?

Globalization Revisited

Two important themes come from Reich's *The Work of Nations* (1991). First, the world's economy has shifted from high-volume to high-value-added production. Second, global, not national, corporations dominate our economy. Combined they have changed our nation's economy and the fortunes of labor.

In the old world order, the welfare of all of us, rich and poor alike, rose and fell with the health of the national economy. But as Reich shows, today, different groups of Americans rise and fall in the global economy independent of each other. The standard of living of each group is determined not by the health of the American economy, but by what they add to the global economy. The reason is simple: Each economic group in the United States and everywhere else in the world competes against each other in a global economy. The value of a group's labor is determined by a global, not a national, economy.

Who are these groups? They are workers in routine production, in-person, and symbolic-analytic services. We used to call routine production workers blue-collar or factory workers. In the past, many of these workers belonged to unions. Their work is low-skilled, repetitive assembly-line work, and they are usually paid hourly or by the amount of work they do—piecework. In the new economy, this category includes office workers. These workers make up a quarter of our workforce, and these jobs are still very much in demand in the global economy. But in the global economy, many of these jobs can be done more cheaply abroad.

In-person services are also repetitive and low skill, and these workers normally need only a high school education. They differ from routine production workers in that their services cannot be sold worldwide. They provide consumer services. In-person servers include telephone operators, airline reservationists, retail clerks, waiters, janitors, telemarketers, hospital and nursing-home workers, and workers in the hospitality industry. This category of workers is one of the fastest growing in the nation, accounting for approximately 30 percent of our workforce. These jobs are usually low wage and seldom offer health insurance and other benefits.

Symbolic analysts usually have college educations, and their work includes problem-solving, problem-identifying, and strategic-brokering activities. They provide services to producers, not consumers. Since they add the most value to the things they help produce in the global economy, their incomes have grown dramatically in the global era. Symbolic analysts make up approximately 20 percent of the American workforce, and their number has grown dramatically in the past half century. They are not immune to recession. Hundreds of thousands of symbolic analysts in the information technology industry are unemployed and unable to find work in our current recession.

As we noted earlier, the future of each of these groups is determined by three factors: (1) their replaceability, (2) the value they add to a product or service, and (3) the value of their services to the global economy. In 1991 Reich predicted a bleak future for routine service workers because these workers are easily replaced, they add little to the value of a product, and their work can be done by workers in China or India at a fraction of what it costs in the United States. Reich also predicted slow downward social mobility for in-service workers. Computers are replacing telephone operators, and millions of immigrants threaten the jobs of others; in-service workers add little to the value of products; and workers in the world's other English-speaking nations can do many of their services more cheaply. Symbolic analysts have a brighter future. They are not easily replaced; until recently, there was a shortage of these workers worldwide, and their skills are still in high demand in the global economy. Reich called symbolic analysts the fortunate fifth. He predicted that most of the wealth created in the world in the 1990s would go to this group.

Was Reich right? Has there been realignment in the nation's workforce; have most of the benefits gone to the fortunate fifth; and has economic inequality grown? These are complex questions that require complicated answers, but, first, let's review a few points about social stratification and mobility.

A Short Review on Social Mobility

What we do for a living not only determines our income but also every other aspect of our lives. This is why social scientists have developed a special variable called socioeconomic status (SES) to measure it. The index usually includes income, occupation, and education variables because your level of education determines the occupations you can enter and your occupation determines your income. SES is social science's most powerful variable because if we know where you are in our stratification system, we can predict a lot of your behavior. Research conducted over the past century shows that your SES influences where you will live, how long you will live, how happy you will be, when and who you will marry, how many children you are likely to have, how you will raise them, who your friends will be, and what your tastes, attitudes, voting behavior, consumption patterns, and even your sex life will be. A multibillion-dollar industry has grown up around predicting consumer and voting behavior, and the work of all these research firms focuses on one concept, socioeconomic status.

Social mobility refers to the upward and downward movement of individuals and groups within our social stratification system. There are several types of social mobility, but structural mobility has affected the greatest numbers of people through history. Structural mobility is the movement of entire groups of people up or down the stratification system as the result of broad changes in the economy. The Industrial Revolution provides a good example. As our economy shifted to manufacturing and the industries found in cities, the number and prosperity of occupations associated with agriculture declined, and occupations associated with industry grew. The lives of millions of Americans were affected, rural communities shrank, cities grew, and the size and prosperity of entire occupations rose and fell. A more recent example is deindustrialization. When corporations close plants in the United States and shift their manufacturing to low-wage regions of the world, millions of workers in the manufacturing industry lose their jobs. In a perfect world these workers would quickly find high-paying jobs in other sectors of the economy. But as the nation discovered in the 1990s, replacement jobs are often in the low-wage service industry, and as a result millions of U.S. workers have experienced downward structural social mobility.

The Future Occupational Structure

Figure 12.1 shows occupational changes by sectors for most of the twentieth century. The patterns are clear. The mechanization of American agriculture caused

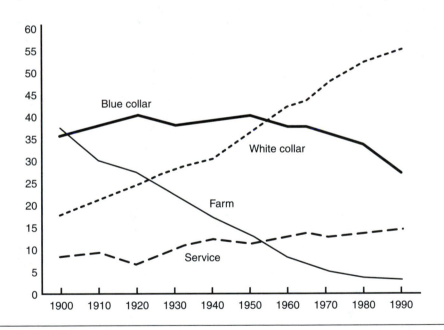

Figure 12.1 *Occupational Changes by Sectors (Source:* U.S. Census, *Bicentennial Statistics* [1976]; U.S. Department of Labor, *Employment and Earning* [1990]; Gilbert, *The American Class Structure in an Age of Growing Inequality* [1998]. U.S. Census, Statistical Research Division (1976). Bicentennial Statistics. R.R. 26–102. Washington, D.C.: Government Printing Office. U.S. Department of Labor, Bureau of Labor Statistics. [1990]. Employment and Earning. Washington, D.C. Government Printing Office. Gilbert, D. [1998]. The American class structure in an age of growing inequality. Belmont, CA: Wadsworth.)

the long steady decline in jobs associated with the farm sector. Today, farmers make up less than 3 percent of our workforce. Note the steady growth in white-collar employment. The rise of our urban-based industrial and postindustrial economy explains this trend. The number of blue-collar jobs peaked at the end of World War II and then began a slow downward drift in the late 1960s as the nation's economy shifted to high-value-added manufacturing. Deindustrialization accelerated this trend in the 1980s and 1990s. Service occupations have experienced a slow steady rise throughout the century, but this growth has not offset the decline in blue-collar jobs. Who are the winners and losers? In the first half of the century, the fortunes of farm occupations declined, and those associated with business and industry rose (Gilbert, 1998). At the beginning of the twenty-first century, the fortunes of symbolic analysts are on the rise, and those of routine production and in-person service workers are on the decline, just as Reich predicted.

The U.S. economy is expected to add millions of jobs in the next decade, and as always, new jobs will be created to replace those that are disappearing. Figure 12.2A and 12.2B show expected job growth and reductions by type of occupation through 2010. Note in Figure 12.2A that the winners in the next decade will be college-educated and highly skilled workers, symbolic analysts. Computer engineers and computer support and systems specialists top the list. But even those near the bottom of the list, physician assistants and surgical technologists, require postsecondary education. Information- and knowledge-based businesses are expected to grow in the next decade, which translates into a rosy future for the well educated and skilled. Now turn to Figure 12.2B, and note the occupations expected to decline—farmers, office workers, clerks, tellers, and equipment operators (Labor Department, 2003). Where do these less well-educated and skilled workers go?

Changing Incomes, Growing Inequality

This metamorphosis of the nation's labor force is reflected in our income distribution. Figure 12.3 shows the median household income from 1967 to 2001. Although average incomes have risen from $32,000 to more than $42,000 over the last thirty-four years, when inflation is taken into account, the buying power of the average American household actually declined 31.6 percent. Some groups in our society have fared better than others. White and Asian Americans had significantly higher mean incomes, and blacks and Hispanics had significantly lower ones. But the clear trend for most American families is less purchasing power (Jones & Weinberg, 2002). How have they made ends meet? The answer is dual-worker families. Note the dramatic change in the labor force patterns of families in Figure 12.4. The *traditional family* where Mom stays home and takes care of the kids and Dad works is a thing of the past; this group makes up only 7.5 percent of all households (AmeriStat, 2003). Although we have far greater diversity in our family types than a generation ago, today's reality is that both parents work to support their families (Employment Policy Foundation, 2000).

One of the consequences of these changes is growing inequality. Social scientists use something called a *Gini Index* to track changing inequality in a society. The Gini Index is interpreted exactly the same way as the segregation index we used earlier. The index has a range of 0 to 100; an index value of 0 means all groups in society have the same income—total equality. At the other extreme, an index value of 100 means that one group has all the income. Figure 12.5 shows the changes in the nation's Gini Index from 1967 to 1999. The general trend from

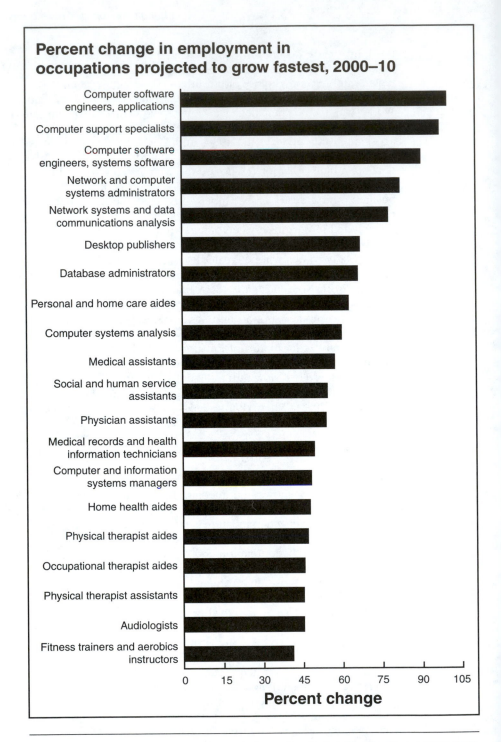

Figure 12.2A *Percent Change in Employment in Occupations Projected to Grow Fastest, 2000–2010 (Source: U.S. Department of Labor, Bureau of Labor Statistics. Retrieved from BLS site on June 15, 2003: http://stats.bls.gov/oco/images/ocotjc07.gif)*

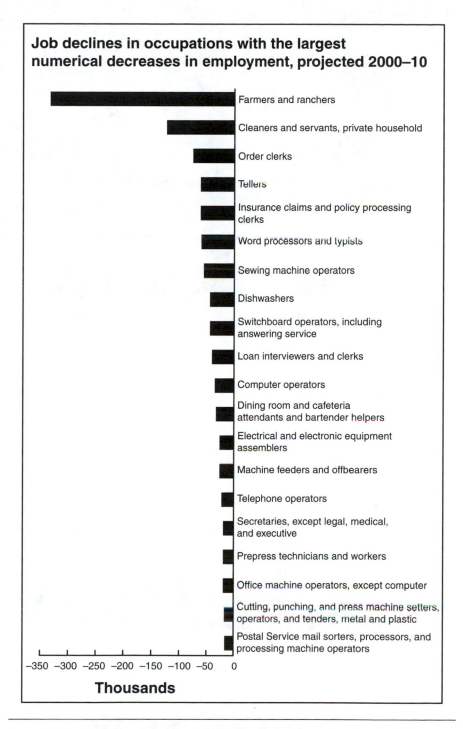

Job declines in occupations with the largest numerical decreases in employment, projected 2000–10

- Farmers and ranchers
- Cleaners and servants, private household
- Order clerks
- Tellers
- Insurance claims and policy processing clerks
- Word processors and typists
- Sewing machine operators
- Dishwashers
- Switchboard operators, including answering service
- Loan interviewers and clerks
- Computer operators
- Dining room and cafeteria attendants and bartender helpers
- Electrical and electronic equipment assemblers
- Machine feeders and offbearers
- Telephone operators
- Secretaries, except legal, medical, and executive
- Prepress technicians and workers
- Office machine operators, except computer
- Cutting, punching, and press machine setters, operators, and tenders, metal and plastic
- Postal Service mail sorters, processors, and processing machine operators

−350 −300 −250 −200 −150 −100 −50 0

Thousands

Figure 12.2B *Job Declines in Occupations with the Largest Numerical Decreases in Employment Projected 2000–2010 (Source: U.S. Department of Labor, Bureau of Labor Statistics. Retrieved from BLS site on June 15, 2003: http://stats.bls.gov/oco/ images/ocotjc09.gif)*

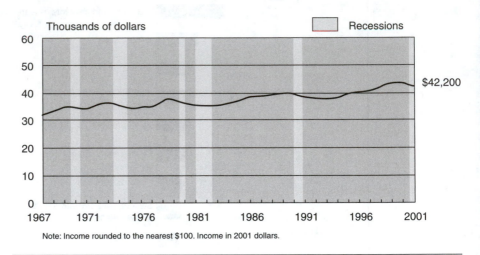

Figure 12.3   *Median Household Income, 1967–2001 (Source:* U.S. Census Bureau, Current Population Survey, 1968 to 2002. Annual Demographic Supplements.)

1968 on has been growing inequality. Starting in 1980, at the onset of high-value-added manufacturing, deindustrialization, and globalization, inequality in this society soared (Morris & Western, 1999). The reason: changes in the labor force are reflected in incomes. Figure 12.6 shows the change in after-tax family income from 1979 to 1997 for income fifths. Note that the bottom 20 percent actually lost income; the next 60 percent stood still; the top 20 percent experienced an 85 percent increase; and the top 1 percent of all families enjoyed a whopping 157 percent jump in income over this period. There is no better example of the reasons for growing inequality than in CEO pay. Figure 12.7 compares CEO pay, worker pay, and inflation for the 1990s. Whereas CEO pay grew on average 463 percent, worker pay grew by only 42 percent, slightly above the 36 percent inflation during the decade.

All general sociology texts have a chapter on social stratification. Typically the author will provide a figure showing the income distributions in preindustrial and industrial societies. The preindustrial stratification system is portrayed as a triangle with a broad base of impoverished peasants, a small middle class, and a small capstone of elites. Industrial societies, in contrast, are portrayed as a diamond, with a small lower class at the bottom, a larger working class, a middle class that takes up 40 percent of the figure, then a smaller professional class, and at the top, the elites, a capstone the same size as the lower class. The nation's income distribution approximated this pattern in the 1950s, when we had the most equitable distribution of income in our history. The income distribution of postindustrial societies is often depicted as an hourglass, with a large

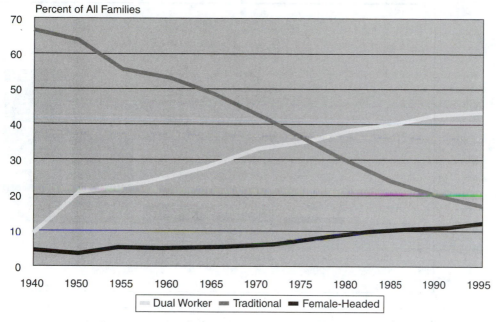

Note: Some categories have been omitted.
Source: Howard Hayghe, "Family Members in the Work Force," Monthly Labor Review, vol. 113, no. 3.

Figure 12.4 *Change in Family Labor Force Patterns* (*Source:* Employment Policy Foundation. The American Workplace 1998. Retrieved on May 14, 2003 from *http://www.epf.org/ labor98/98introf7.htm*)

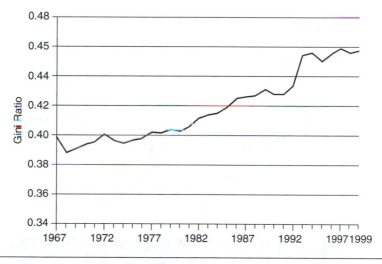

Figure 12.5 *Change in Gini Index, 1967–1999* (*Source:* U.S. Census Bureau [2002]. Gini ratios for families, by race and Hispanic origin of householder: 1947–2001. Downloaded on March 17, 2004, from *http://www.census.gov/hhes/income/ histinc/f04.html*)

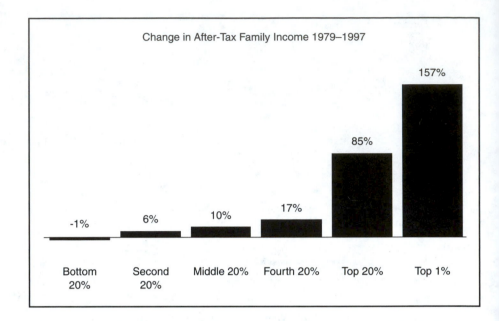

Figure 12.6 *Change in After-Tax Family Income, 1979–1997 (Source:* Inequality. Org. *Facts and Figures.* Retrieved on August 1, 2003, from *www.inequality.org/factsfr.html.* Used by permission of inequality.org. Data: Center on Budget and Policy Priorities, *Pathbreaking CBO Study Shows Dramatic Increases in Both 1980s and 1990s in income Gaps Between The Very Wealthy And Other Americans,* May 31, 2001: *http://www.cbpp.org/5-31-01tax.htm,* and Congressional Budget Office, Effective Federal Tax Rates 1979–97, October 2001: *http://www.cbo.gov/showdoc.cfm? index=3089&sequence=0)*

impoverished lower class, a small middle class, and a large upper class. Figure 12.8 shows the actual income distribution in the United States in 2000. It's not a triangle or a diamond or an hourglass, it's more like a pot-bellied stove. At the bottom of our society is a large group of very poor Americans with incomes well below the poverty line, above them is a larger group of near poor with incomes near the poverty line, and then a bulge of lower-income house-holds come in just above the poverty line. The bulge narrows, as one moves up through the middle and upper-middle incomes, to a long neck of high-income households (Rose, 2000).

Robert Reich's predictions were right. For the past two decades the United States has experienced rapid growth accompanied by widening inequality. Four-fifths of our families have declining or stagnant incomes, and because of structural and other factors, the incomes of the fortunate fifth are rising.

The Importance of Government Policy

Although the hidden hand of the market guides global change, government policies matter. Government programs can soften the transition to a new economy by providing unemployment insurance, retraining programs, and relocation

CEO Pay, Worker Pay, and Inflation, 1990–2001

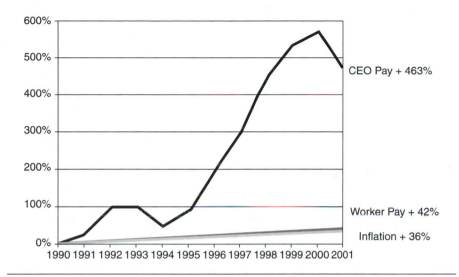

Figure 12.7 *Increase in CEO Pay, Worker Pay, and Inflation, 1990–2001 (Source:* Inequality.Org. *Facts and Figures.* Retrieved on August 1, 2003, from *www.inequality.org/factsfr.html.* Used by permission of Inequality.Org. Data: Institute for Policy Studies and United for a Fair Economy, *Executive Excess 2002,* August 26, 2002, citing the following sources: CEO Pay: *Business Week* annual executive pay surveys. Average Worker Pay: Bureau of Labor Statistics, Average Weekly Hours of Production Workers [Series EEU00500005] and Average Hourly Earnings of Production Workers [Series ID: EEU00500006]. Inflation: Bureau of Labor Statistics, Consumer Price Index, All Urban Consumers [CPI-U].)

expenses. The federal government provides many of these programs, but our social net is shrinking, not expanding. In fact, tax and policy changes over the past thirty years have disproportionately benefited the well-off. For example, changes in the tax structure during the Reagan administration allowed the wealthiest Americans to keep more income. Inequality grew rapidly in the 1980s as the Reagan administration cut federal programs for the poor and shifted the tax burden from upper- to middle- and lower-income Americans. Trickle-down economics (what George Bush called *voodoo economics,* and a policy that now shapes his son's economic policies) was supposed to fuel economic growth. It didn't. What it did was increase inequality. In fact, the nation registered the greatest transfer of wealth in our history during the Reagan years.

Inequality widened in the 1990s, although this was a decade of unprecedented economic growth in the U.S. economy. The greatest gains in wealth went to upper-middle-class Americans with significant holdings in the stock market. The greatest increase in incomes went to the fortunate fifth, as Reich predicted. At the other end of the income distribution, it was not so much that the poor got poorer in the 1990s; it was just that their incomes didn't keep up. In fact, it took most of the Clinton years for the poorest groups in our society to recover the income they lost in the 1990–1992 recession. The Clinton administration tried to address issues

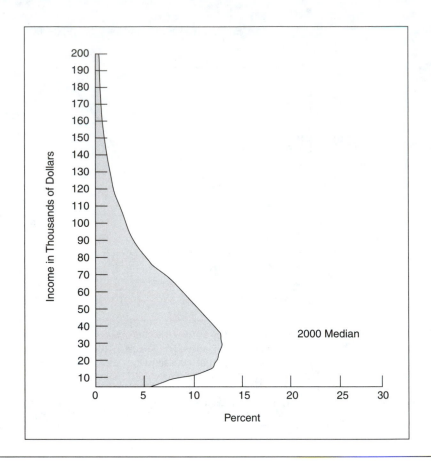

Figure 12.8   *U.S. Income Distribution, 2000 (Source:* DeNavas-Walt, C. and Cleveland, R.W. [2002]. Money Income in the United States: 2001. Current Populations Reports: Current Income P60–218. Washington, D.C. US Census Bureau, Table A.1.)

of minimum wage, uninsured health coverage for workers, continuing education, additional benefits for the poor, and a small increase in taxes for the wealthy. But inequality throughout the decade increased. Robert Reich was the secretary of labor in the first Clinton administration, and he pushed policies that increased investment in the skills and training of our workers. Yet President Clinton also announced the end of big government and federal welfare programs. Welfare, one of the key elements of our nation's safety net, ended in 1996 with the passage of the reform legislation known as Temporary Assistance for Needy Families (TANF). Unlike welfare, TANF provides only a four-year lifetime benefit of cash assistance, and adults with a child over the age of one are required to work (Sernau, 2001). In 2003, the maximum cash assistance for a family of three was only $223 per month. Single women with children have fared the worst under these new policies (Chapman & Bernstein, 2003).

The direction of inequality in the current Bush administration is clear. The recession early in the twenty-first century disproportionately affected low-income workers.

This, coupled with the tax cuts in 2001 and the $330 billion tax cut in 2003, largely benefited the wealthy. Congress has passed legislation that will end federal estate taxes in 2010—again, a change that benefits only the rich. At other levels of government, states dealt with budget crises in 2003 by slashing health, housing, and other programs for the poor. Cities were making similar cuts in dealing with their budget crises. Thus, globalization, the recession, current and past federal economic policies, and smaller state budgets mean greater economic inequality in the future. These forces working themselves through the U.S. economy over the past two generations, when combined with the social, labor, and economic policies of the past four administrations, have created the greatest inequality in our nation since the 1920s.[1] It is not surprising that lower- and middle-income groups are less well off today than a decade ago.

Economic Upheaval in Our Nation, Spatial Upheaval in Our Cities

Changes in what our economy produces, how it produces it, and where it is produced have a spatial as well as a social impact. As we have seen, as employment in this society shifted from manufacturing to services, the occupational structure of the nation changed. In turn, the shift in the occupational structure affected cities by changing the mix of businesses and industries in their economic bases. As with all change, there are winners and losers. Because of their economic base or strategic position in our nation's metropolitan system, some cities have prospered; others, those dependent on a single industry or saddled with obsolete infrastructures, have foundered.

In the 1980s, cities in the South and West prospered because of their lower labor costs, available land, huge federal subsidies, benign climate, and access to cheap oil, gas, and other resources. Known as the *Sunbelt,* this region was in a strategic position to attract manufacturing activities, usually from the North and upper-Midwest. Northern and Midwestern cities, in contrast, with local economies dependent on heavy industry and traditional manufacturing, foundered as our nation shifted to high-value manufacturing and a deindustrialized economy. Conditions were so bad in the region's major cities, like Chicago, Detroit, Toledo, Cleveland, and Buffalo, it became know as the *Rustbelt* (Sassen, 1990).

The U.S. economy's blistering 4.6 percent annual growth rate from 1992 to 2000 meant economic growth for most U.S. cities, but growth varied dramatically around the country. The nation's two global cities, New York and Los Angeles, rather than leading the nation, lagged far behind. The massive metropolitan regions that surround them lagged as well. The big improvements were in the Midwest and the South. After a period of painful readjustments, cities in the Midwest bounced back and built upon their universities and research centers and their historical domination of financing, marketing, and management. They prospered in the new knowledge- and information-driven economy. The word *Rustbelt* is no longer in our urban vocabulary. Cities in the South experienced solid economic gains. This, however, contrasts sharply with the West, especially California. Two Californias have emerged: a northern section that has experienced strong economic growth and a southern and central section in decline (Logan, 2002a).

Looking at the nation's metropolitan future, resurgent cities in the Midwest and the South are bright spots, and the future of cities in the Northeast and south and central California are causes for alarm. The future of the nation's two global cities, New York and Los Angeles and their regions, are of greatest concern. Given that they experienced little growth during the prosperous 1990s, many wonder how they might fare in a sustained recession. More troubling, what if they are indicators of America's metropolitan future in the global economy?

Social Inequality and the Internal Structure of Cities

These shifts in the economy also affect the internal structure of our cities. Although most U.S. cities benefited from the boom, the experience of groups within cities varied enormously. As Reich and others have shown, a dual economy has emerged in our cities—one that provides jobs to high-wage earners and another to low-wage earners—which explains the pattern of rising incomes with growing inequality. Our cities reflect this inequality because the social distance between groups is always reflected in the physical distance between them. As we know from our own experiences, different income groups live in different neighborhoods.

Although most Americans benefited from the 1990s boom, Census 2000 reveals that this prosperous decade did not yield greater income or neighborhood equality in our cities. In 2000, 225 million of the nation's 272 million people (83 percent) lived in the nation's 331 metropolitan areas. As in the past, suburbs continued to have the economic advantage. In the 1990s, increases in median income were twice as large in the suburbs as in the cities; the poverty rate was twice as high (18.2 percent vs. 8.6 percent) in the cities, remaining unchanged since 1990; and unemployment was nearly 40 percent higher in cities (8 percent vs. 5 percent) (Logan, 2002b).

Growing Spatial Inequality

Growing inequality was also reflected in the neighborhoods in which people live. Recent research by the Lewis Mumford Center explores how the 1990s affected two important aspects of people's lives—household income and the quality of neighborhoods—and they are surprisingly distinct. When you buy or rent a home or an apartment, with the dwelling comes the neighborhood's status, schools, safety, and access to jobs, shopping, and recreation. The Mumford Center researchers found that as whites and Asians earn more, they tend to move to neighborhoods that match their new economic standing. Simply, they translate growing income into a higher quality of life. Due to residential segregation, however, blacks and Hispanics are less able to move to better neighborhoods. Despite overall prosperity, the "neighborhood gap" grew in the 1990s, reflecting the growing income inequality in our cities. Blacks continue to remain the lowest-income minority group, and they also have the greatest neighborhood gap. On average blacks lived in neighborhoods with median incomes only 70 percent as high as whites. The surprising finding was that the gap is greatest for the highest-income blacks and Hispanics in the study. These groups were the least likely to translate rising incomes into better neighborhoods and schools, lower crime rates, and a higher quality of life (Logan, 2002c).

Race and ethnicity matter, but research shows that economic segregation is also growing. As inequality grew in the 1990s so too did the physical distance between economic groups in our society. Given the tremendous variation among metropolitan areas in their economic bases, housing markets, race and ethnicity, and poverty levels, the near universal increases in economic segregation suggest that a fundamental change is underway in the way people are sorted into neighborhoods (Jargowsky, 1996). This mirrors the theme woven throughout this book: The upheaval in our nation's globally linked economy is creating social and spatial upheaval in our cities. Therefore, understanding the future form of our cities will require greater understanding of the economic future of our citizens, especially the poor.

The Nation's Urban Poor

Journalists, novelists, social reformers, and social scientists have been interested in the plight of our nation's poor for more than a century. The federal government began to measure poverty systematically in 1965, and our current poverty line is based on this system. The poverty line is an estimate of the minimum income necessary to buy the basic necessities, such as food, shelter, and clothing. For a family of four with two dependent children the poverty threshold was $14,269 in 2001. For an individual, it was $9,214 or around $25 per day. Although the Census Bureau makes periodic adjustments for inflation, the calculation of the poverty line has never been revised to take into account changes in family spending patterns. Nor does the poverty measure take into consideration regional variations in the cost of living. For example, Boston, Massachusetts, and Greenville, South Carolina, had the same 19.5 percent poverty rate in 2001, but rent for a two-bedroom apartment in Greenville was $539, in Boston $979 (Proctor & Dalaker, 2002).

The unemployment rate at the time of Census 2000 was 3.9 percent, the lowest in decades. The strong economy during this time moved millions of individuals from welfare to work and improved the economic lives of many of the most disadvantaged groups in our society. Nationally, the percentage of people living below the poverty line declined from 13.5 percent to 11.7 percent between 1990 and 2000, but since the nation's population continued to grow the total number of poor decreased only slightly from 33.6 to 32.9 million people (Proctor & Dalaker, 2002). While the decline was significant, it was surprisingly small in light of the nearly decade-long economic expansion.

These national statistics do not reflect important changes in the nation's cities and suburbs. A recent study of Census 2000 data found that the economic outcomes for the poor were mixed. Traditionally, central cities have the metropolitan area's highest poverty rates, but in the 1990s the rates between central cities and suburbs converged as almost half of all central cities saw their poverty rates decline. These shifts caused the city-suburb poverty gap to narrow overall, but the rift remained wide, to the point that city residents remain more than twice as likely to be poor as their suburban counterparts. Although the share of the poverty population residing in the suburbs increased during the 1990s, most of this growth was in older suburbs adjacent to central city poor neighborhoods.

Even with the urban poor moving to the suburbs worst neighborhoods, half of all the poor in our nation's largest metro areas live in central cities, and the metropolitan poverty rate was unchanged from 1990. In fact, 2.5 million more people were living in poverty in the nation's largest metros in 2000 than in 1990 (Berube & Frey, 2002).

Concentrated Poverty

As we have seen, the definition of poverty is arbitrary—a family's income is compared to the costs of basic necessities. This poverty line does not capture the multiple ways that poverty degrades the quality of life of the poor and the way it limits the opportunities of those trapped in poverty. It doesn't capture the psychological costs for families struggling with their own poverty, much less the effects of the poverty of others in their neighborhood. And it does not measure the costs of the social ills that cause or are caused by the concentration of the poor in the nation's ghettoes, barrios, and slums. Simply, concentrated poverty magnifies the problems faced by the poor.

For nearly a century the conditions of the poor in our cities' poorest neighborhoods have attracted the attention of researchers. Starting in the opening decades of the last century, members of the Chicago School focused their research on the plight of those trapped in impoverished neighborhoods, and on the effects of this concentrated poverty for the larger society. More recent research by Kathleen Short and Martina Shea (1995) carry on in this tradition. Short and Shea measured the well-being of the poor and nonpoor in cities and showed the consequences of concentrated poverty on everyday lives of poor Americans. Interestingly, they found few differences in the household items owned by the two groups like televisions, stereos, refrigerators, and stoves. The real differences showed up in the housing conditions, neighborhood crime rates, diet, and access to health care. For example, the urban poor in the study were three times more likely than the nonpoor to live in a dwelling infested with rats, mice, or roaches, and where the toilet, hot water heater, or other plumbing did not work. Their dwellings were four times more likely to have exposed wiring and holes in the floor. The poor were more than twice as likely to live in a neighborhood where trash and litter were a problem. They lived in neighborhoods with large numbers of run-down and abandoned buildings and high crime rates. In fact, the poor were three times more likely to say they were afraid to go out at night. Compared to the nonpoor, the poor were twice as likely to be evicted, five times more likely to have their phones disconnected, and eight times more likely to have their gas or electricity turned off. The problems did not stop with their dwellings and neighborhood; the poor were sick more often because of their poor diet and housing, and when they became ill, they were half as likely as the nonpoor to receive medical care.

Children living in concentrated poverty suffer the most. Figure 12.9 shows the full range of consequences for poor children living in concentrated poverty. They lack the basic necessities in their homes; they live in dangerous neighborhoods; and their poverty often means lack of food, poor diet, greater family stress, fewer resources for learning, and housing problems. These conditions, in turn, lead to a host of individual problems including lower IQs, behavioral problems, lower school attainment, and short-term and long-term health problems (Sherman, 1997).

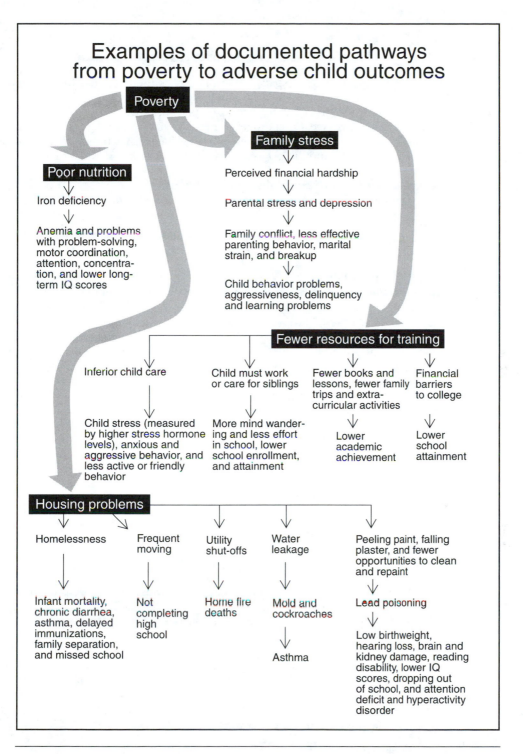

Figure 12.9 *Consequences of Poverty for Children (Source:* A. Sherman. 1997. *Poverty Matters: The Cost of Child Poverty in America.* Washington, D.C.: Children's Defense Fund)

The Growth of High-Poverty Neighborhoods

In the 1970s and 1980s, the spatial concentration of the poor rose dramatically in the nation's metropolitan areas. The number of Americans living in high-poverty areas doubled, and the chance of a poor black child living in a high-poverty neighborhood increased from roughly one in four to one in three. Most urban textbooks of the day focused on the nation's urban crisis as these blighted neighborhoods expanded and the poor became more isolated from the social and economic mainstream of society. The growth of high-poverty areas pushed other economic groups into the suburbs, which led to the general process of population deconcentration that created donut cities with depopulating and impoverished urban cores surrounded by prosperous and growing suburbs.

The Urban Underclass

One of the most influential books of the period was William Julius Wilson's *The Truly Disadvantaged,* published in 1987. Wilson argued that during the 1970s and 1980s, many blacks experienced upward social mobility, and the black middle class abandoned the high-poverty neighborhoods of the central city for the suburbs. According to Wilson, the structural changes in America's economy, combined with the suburbanization of industry and the black middle class, led to the segregation and isolation of the most disadvantaged citizens in this society. This isolation contributed to the destruction of the black family, the growth of female-headed families, and the emergence of a set of values and norms that perpetuate inequality, Wilson contended. For example, at a time when education was vital for success, the children of the underclass were going to the worst schools in the city. At a time when intact black families were experiencing upward social mobility, the pool of employed males available for marriage was shrinking. At a time when the fastest-growing segment of the poor was female-headed households, the stigma on unwanted pregnancy and illegitimacy in the ghetto was on the decline. And at a time when an intact family—one in which both the father and the mother were present—has been found to be a major deterrent to poverty, these families were becoming rare in the neighborhoods of the underclass.

Paul Jargowsky Tests Wilson's Model

Since the publication of Wilson's book, studies of neighborhood poverty have mushroomed. One of the more important works is Paul A. Jargowsky's *Poverty and Place: Ghettos, Barrios, and the American City,* published in 1997. Jargowsky uses tract data from the 1980 and 1990 censuses to study the nation's high-poverty neighborhoods, those with more than 40 percent of households below the poverty line. He then classified them according to their race and ethnic character—ghetto (black), barrio (Hispanic), and slum (white). Using these data, he tested Wilson's major hypotheses on the reason for the plight of the underclass: (1) deindustrialization, (2) deconcentration of employment, (3) middle-class black flight, (4) segregation, and (5) a culture of poverty. Jargowsky found the following.

- Little support for the first hypothesis on deindustrialization, except in Northern metropolitan areas. This region was affected most by the loss of high-wage union jobs.

- Support for the second hypothesis, industrial deconcentration. The shift of manufacturing and industry from central cities to the fringe appears to have created a mismatch between jobs in the suburbs and minority workers in the central cities. This led to declining incomes and the growth of high-poverty neighborhoods.

- Support for Wilson's third hypothesis that the flight of higher-income groups from minority poverty neighborhoods increased concentrated poverty.

- Little support for Wilson's fourth hypothesis that racial segregation is a key determinant of black poverty, and, therefore, indirectly creating and sustaining ghetto poverty. Although racial segregation is fundamental in understanding the presence of black high-poverty neighborhoods, it did not appear that racial segregation played a direct role in the recent growth of ghettos and barrios.

- Little support for Wilson's fifth hypothesis that there is a culture of poverty. If there were a culture of poverty, increases in economic opportunity would do little to break up ghettoes and barrios because the culture of poverty is self-sustaining, like any other culture.

A better test of the final hypothesis comes from Census 2000, which captures the social change during the booming 1990s. In his recent analysis, Jargowsky (2003) found that the strong economy in the 1990s dramatically altered long-term spatial concentration of poverty. The number of people living in high-poverty neighborhoods declined by a dramatic 24 percent, or 2.5 million people in the 1990s. The share of poor blacks living in high-poverty neighborhoods declined from 30 percent in 1990 to 19 percent in 2000. This improvement marked a significant turnaround from the 1970–1990 period, during which the population in high-poverty neighborhoods doubled. This does not mean that poverty declined in the United States in the 1990s. In reality there was very little change in the number of poor.

The implication is the residents of high-poverty neighborhoods in the 1990s benefited disproportionately from the boom, and so did others. In previous decades, central cities bore the brunt of economic downturn; in the 1990s, they were one of the major beneficiaries of the boom. One reason was the dual economy. High-income groups moved to the fringe and also reclaimed and gentrified older central-city neighborhoods. The housing they abandoned trickled down; as they abandoned dwellings, other income groups moved up to better housing. The poor, for the first time in decades, were able to abandon the nation's worst housing. However, they often moved only a few miles, across a political boundary, to an older, inner-circle suburb. High-poverty neighborhoods in central cities declined in the 1990s, but a careful inspection of suburban poverty over the 1990s reveals some disturbing trends: Poverty rates increased along the outer edges of central cities and in the inner-ring suburbs of many metropolitan areas.

What We Should Do: Policies for the Twenty-First Century

The concentration of poverty is an important public policy concern because it has dynamic effects on income distribution, undermines the political and social fabric of our cities, and restricts opportunity for the most disadvantaged in our society. The booming economy of the 1990s reversed several decades of increasing concentration of poverty in our central cities. The recent economic downturn and the erosion of conditions in older, inner suburbs suggest that greater poverty concentration is in our future (Jargowsky, 2003).

Currently, federal urban programs target at-risk neighborhoods through local economic development and enterprise zones. Jargowsky shows that these policies will be ineffective without larger economic changes in the metropolitan community. Without broader changes in the metropolitan economy and in rates of segregation, programs in barrios and ghettoes alone, including those aimed at changing behavior, are unlikely to have much success. He advocates federal intervention at the metropolitan level designed to increase productivity, lower inequality, and reduce spatial and economic segregation. These policy proposals mirror those of Robert Reich and others aimed at reducing ghetto poverty. But these proposals come with warning: As the national economy deteriorates, and if employed and higher-income people keep fleeing from the path of poor neighborhoods in the older suburban ring, no self-help program will stem the spread of the urban blight and the re-creation of concentrated poverty.

HOMELESSNESS

Introduction

Home is a powerful word, full of meaning. I've been sitting here thinking about the word. Home is, of course, the place I eat, sleep, and carry out my private life. It's where I keep my furniture. My things. My home is not just a structure, it's memories. There is the patch in the wall where my two-year-old rammed his toy. There is a dark spot on the carpet where Vicky Sloan spilled her red wine. There is my bookcase filled with my father's books. My wife and I picked the paintings together. The word *home* had special meaning when my mother recently sold my boyhood home, the only home that I had known for over forty years. The reason why the house was so difficult to give up was every nook and cranny of that home had meaning. I told my mother on the day of the sale, "This was a happy house. I hope the new owners have as much joy."

Home is other things. It is where I carry out my most important roles—husband, father, and friend. Home is my refuge. It's where I go to get away from the office. It's where I go during the day to think and write. It's that one place on earth where I can let my hair down and be me. Home is where I welcome and entertain my kin and close friends. My home also locks me into the community's social structure. The location of our home determines where my children go to school. The safety and the quality of our lives are tied to the location of our home.

Home. *Home* for most people is a word pregnant with meaning and social consequences. This is why being homeless is so devastating. It means not only not having a place to put your stuff. It means separation from friends and kin. It means disengagement and isolation from all those things that give our lives meaning and direction.

Beginning in the late 1970s, police, social workers, and citizens alike began to see an increase in the number of homeless. Some people were sleeping in doorways, others wandered the streets, and still others hung out behind buildings, in alleys, parks, and bus depots. Some came to our attention by panhandling, others by their disheveled and dirty appearance, and a few by their bizarre behavior. The most vivid images were those homeless heaping all that they owned in a shopping cart. Our individual experiences soon filtered into newspaper stories. Finally, newspaper stories began to show up in official statistics. Homelessness became a major social problem in the 1980s. A fascinating thing happened in the booming 1990s: The homeless were no longer a social problem; they were a nuisance. Cities used an age-old strategy to deal with the nuisance—out of sight and out of mind. From New York to San Francisco, cities passed ordinances to ban behavior ranging from panhandling to loitering. The goal: get the *problem* off the streets. The theme of Rudolph Guiliani's first mayoral race was "reclaim the streets for New Yorkers." And he was remarkably successful. Aggressive panhandling and threatening car window washing were stopped, boomboxes were banned, bag ladies and the homeless were rousted on the city's streets and public places, and city residents agreed that the public realm was much improved. Critics pointed it was done at a cost—the loss of the civil liberties of homeless people. Although the Congress, the press, and the academic community have examined homelessness for three decades, we still have difficulty in defining the concept, measuring the numbers of people affected, describing the types of homeless, or developing solutions. In this section, we will look at the history of homelessness in the United States and at how we define and measure homelessness. We will ask, Who are the homeless? How did they get this way? What can be done?

A Brief History of the Homeless

The Homeless in the Nineteenth Century

Homelessness is not new. One can find homelessness in one form or another throughout our history.[2] Prior to the Civil War, America was a rural nation, and poverty and homelessness were defined as a moral failure. The relatively small numbers of homeless were housed in almshouses or communal workhouses. Philadelphia's Bettering House was typical. Its operation was based on the premise that the poor chose their idleness and required the discipline of organized labor to stem their indolence.

After the Civil War, the rapid expansion of the national economy required a mobile workforce of unsettled laborers. Hundreds of thousands of transient workers, known as tramps, roamed the states looking for work in lumbering, herding, harvesting, and common labor. Tramps played an important role in the economic development of the nation. This was a period of massive rural to urban migration, massive immigration, and explosive urban and industrial growth. It was also a period of shameful economic exploitation of the working classes. Meager wages, injuries, and illness combined with periodic economic downturns led to this society's first experience with massive homelessness. Police were used to control the rising number of homeless. Idle men were arrested and housed in police stations and poorhouses. The numbers were staggering. Between 1867 and 1883, it has been estimated that one out of every twenty-three males experienced a station house arrest. On average, one out of every five American families had at least one member arrested for idleness during these years. New York City alone provided over 150,000 lodgings per year.

During these years, the press created an image of the homeless as "dangerous tramps." These public perceptions carried over into reform. Reformers holding an ideology of Social Darwinism argued that charity and church relief only made things worse, and they influenced state legislatures. By 1900, all but four states had enacted tramp acts: tramping became a criminal offense. The tramp acts required the homeless and idle to be imprisoned at hard labor in the nearest penitentiary. The police unable to cope with the massive number of homeless turned their backs on the problem, and by the first decade of the twentieth century, municipal lodging houses and rescue missions became the predominant way the destitute and homeless were sheltered.

The Homeless in the Twentieth Century

In the opening decades of the twentieth century, the election of populist and social-ist candidates to state and local offices, the rise of organized labor, the influence of muckraker journalism, and the creation of social work as a profession brought a new perspective to the problem of homelessness. The muckrakers contended that great wealth was often the result of exploitation, greed, and political manipulation. They also showed that poverty and homelessness were often the results of eco-nomic cycles and social injustice. Social workers also showed the public that the problem of homelessness was tied to social conditions rather than flawed characters.

Other forces were at work. The tractor and the combine dramatically reduced the need for farm workers. Mechanization revolutionized the lumber and mining industries. Automation meant more permanent jobs and less need for itinerant labor. These changes improved the conditions of the working class and dramati-cally reduced the number of tramps. As labor changed, so too did the nature of homelessness. By the 1920s, social workers began to characterize the sheltered homeless as individuals who were crippled, mentally ill, drug addicts, alcoholics, runaways, and epileptics unable to master the problem of self-support.

The Great Depression once again changed the character of the homeless. The number of poor and homeless exploded in the 1930s. Politicians and professionals were forced to acknowledge for the first time that homelessness was linked to economic cycles. Local governments were unable to cope with the swelling pop-ulation of homeless. For example, San Francisco sheltered 6,902 families in 1929, by 1932 the number had jumped to 55,789. The Roosevelt administration's New Deal programs brought the federal government to bear on the problem of poverty and homelessness for the first time. In a series of programs like the Civilian Con-servation Corps (CCC) and the Works Progress Administration (WPA), jobs, shelter, social insurance, and work projects were created. These projects along with other programs like social security, unemployment insurance, and public housing cre-ated the modern welfare state in the United States. These emergency programs evolved into permanent programs. By the 1940s a two-tiered welfare system had emerged in the nation. Citizens who paid into programs like social security received benefits they were entitled to—thus the name *entitlement programs*. Other welfare programs were designed specifically for the poor and were based on need, thus, the current title, *needs-based programs*.

The draft and the demand for industrial labor during World War II and the expanding economy in the postwar period dramatically reduced the incidence of homelessness. Rapidly rising mean family income between 1950 and 1970 reduced the ranks of the homeless. The homeless became associated with older single men surviving on pensions and marginal employment housed in flophouses and mis-sions on skid row. The homeless once again came to the nation's attention in the early 1980s with the worst economic recession since the 1930s. However, as our nation's attention shifted from recession to economic boom in the 1990s, public interest in the homeless disappeared.

Defining and Measuring Homelessness in the 1980s and 1990s

During the 1980s, the press played a central role in shaping our image of the homeless. Two images emerged in the national consciousness. There were the vivid images of the age-old problem of the skid row drifter—drunks, drug addicts, broken men with failed dreams. There was also the image of the new homeless, one that is apropos for the 1990s—victims of a changing economy and an indifferent government.

In the professional literature an even more diverse set of definitions of homelessness emerged. A variety of criteria were used, including *transience*—itinerant persons using shelters; *frequency*—the chronically homeless; *ecology*— those who lived in shelters or on the streets and alleys in run-down parts of town; *spatial marginality*—people who live in alleys, dumps, under bridges, and behind buildings; and *social marginality*—people who are isolated and detached from the social structure, family, and friends (LaGory et al., 1989). Which definition do you use to measure the homeless? Should you include the homeless who are doubling up with friends and relatives? Should you include women and children in battered women shelters who will most likely return to their homes? Do you include those who live in intolerable living conditions? Should you include prisoners? Those in mental hospitals? We have problems measuring homelessness because we have trouble defining the concept.

There is also a political dimension. Public agencies and government researchers tend to define homelessness in line with their agency's objectives or the administration's political ideology. Private groups often have a vested interest in making the problem as big as possible. Some censuses include only those who are living in public and private shelters. Others have included sheltered people and street people plus a guesstimate on the hidden population. Some counts have been used to minimize the problem, while others have been used to make it a problem of crisis proportions (Best, 2001).

At the low end, the Census Bureau calculated the emergency and transitional shelter population at 171,000 in 2000, a figure unchanged since 1990 (Smith & Smith, 2001). At the high end, advocacy groups like the National Alliance to End Homelessness estimates between 2.5 million and 3.5 million people experienced homelessness at some time during 2002 (National Alliance to End Homelessness, 2003). Thus, the number moves up and down depending on the definition used, the group doing the counting, and the motives of the counters. Therefore, the problem can be either a national crisis of historical significance or a temporary problem that will improve as the economy improves.

How many people are homeless? Calculations from different sources show that in the late 1990s at least 2.3 million, and perhaps as many as 3.5 million, people experienced homelessness at some time during the year. Because more families with children than single men and women enter and leave homelessness, families represent a relatively large share of the annual population. As a result, during a typical year, between 900,000 and 1.4 million children are homeless with their families. The scope of the problem is summarized in figures from a recent Urban Institute report. They estimate that 1 percent of the total U.S. population and as many as 10 percent of the nation's poor are homeless each year (Burt, 2001). See Photo 12.1.

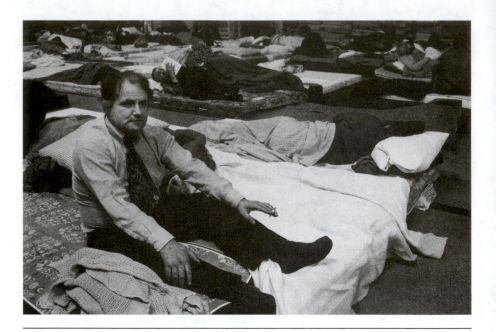

Photo 12.1   *The homeless—out of sight, out of mind, and out of the nation's political agenda.*
(*Source:* Giden Medel/CORBIS/Bettmann.)

More detailed data come from an annual survey on homelessness conducted since 1987 by the U.S. Council of Mayors. In presenting the latest survey results in December 2002, Boston mayor and conference president Thomas Menino said, "To address hunger and homelessness we must all work together to confront our national affordable housing crisis and turn around our sluggish economy." The survey showed requests for emergency shelter assistance grew an average of 19 percent over the past year in eighteen of the study's twenty-five cities, the steepest rise in a decade. People remained homeless for an average of six months in the survey cities, a figure that increased from one year ago in all but four cities. Single men comprised 41 percent of the homeless population, families with children 41 percent, single women 13 percent, and unaccompanied youth 5 percent. Single parents head 73 percent of homeless families in the survey cities. It is estimated that substance abusers account for 32 percent of the homeless, and persons considered mentally ill account for 23 percent. Twenty-two percent of the homeless in survey cities are employed; 10 percent are veterans (U.S. Conference of Mayors, 2003).

The survey also documented significant unmet need for shelter in cities across the nation. All the cities in the survey expect that requests for both emergency food assistance and shelter assistance will increase again over the next year. As need increased, the level of resources available to help the needy at emergency food assistance facilities decreased in 52 percent of the cities. And nearly two-thirds of the cities reported they had to decrease the quantity of food provided and/or the number of times people can come to get food assistance. An average of 16 percent of the demand for emergency food assistance is estimated to have gone unmet in the survey cities. The survey finds that 48 percent of those requesting emergency food assistance were members of families with children and that 38 percent of adults requesting such assistance were employed. "These are not simply statistics," said Nashville mayor Bill Purcell, who chairs the Conference's Task Force on Hunger and Homelessness. "These are real people who are hungry and homeless in our cities" (U.S. Conference of Mayors, 2003, p. 1).

Table 12.1 tracks hunger and homelessness in America's cities from 1987 to 2002. Notice that the change follows the economy—highest in the late 1980s and the 1990–1992 recession, lower during the late 1990s at the height of the boom, then rising again in 2001–2002 during another recession. Note also that the composition of the homeless has not changed much over the past sixteen years. The notable exception is the category "family with children": It has grown from 33 percent to 41 percent.

The statistics vary, but the message is the same. With the downturn in the economy, there is a large and growing number of homeless in the nation. The problem is not isolated in one city or region but is national in scope. Moreover, the problem has become so large that cities do not have the resources to cope.

Who Are Homeless?

A variety of people have been identified as homeless: winos, alcoholics, drug users, retired seamen, bag ladies, bottle gangs, vets, displaced families, runaway children, ex-convicts, AIDS victims shunned by their families, immigrants, and mothers with children. In the past, the homeless were mostly vagrants and tramps, usually white, middle-aged, alcoholic men. The new homeless are more diverse: They are younger, often female, sometimes entire families, and more likely members of minority groups. David Snow, one of the major researchers in the field, developed a general profile of the homeless through his ethnographic studies of the homeless. He found that a homeless person was typically a white male, in his mid-thirties, unmarried, poorly educated, likely to be a veteran, and most often drawn to the community in search of work (Snow & Anderson, 1993). Although many descriptions abound, four types of homeless are usually identified in the literature: homeless mentally ill, homeless women, and homeless alcoholics.

The Homeless Mentally Ill

In 1955 there were 560,000 residents of public psychiatric hospitals.[3] In 1981, this number had dropped to around 120,000. Since the 1960s, the catchwords among mental health professionals have been *deinstitutionalization* and *community-based mental health care*. The move toward community-based mental health care was motivated by many factors. First came the exposés on the horrors of mental hospitals. Second, there was a revolution in drug therapy, and it was thought that many patients could be safely returned to society. Finally, there was the belief that treatment in a community setting could be less costly, more humane, and less confining. There is evidence community-based programs have not worked. Many people on the street may be there because of deinstitutionalization.

How many of the homeless are mentally ill? Estimates vary. Some studies suggest the figure may be as high as 80 to 90 percent; other studies of sheltered homeless, like the U.S. Conference of Mayors survey, put the figure between

Table 12.1 Homeless in America's Cities, 1987–2002

Indicator	1987	1988	1989	1990	1991	1992	1993	1994	1995	1996	1997	1998	1999	2000	2001	2002
HUNGER																
Increase in demand for emergency food	18%	19%	19%	22%	26%	18%	13%	12%	9%	11%	16%	14%	18%	17%	23%	19%
Cities in which demand for food increased	92%	88%	96%	90%	93%	96%	83%	83%	72%	83%	86%	78%	85%	79%	93%	100%
Increase in demand by families for food assistance	18%	17%	14%	20%	26%	14%	13%	14%	10%	10%	13%	14%	15%	16%	19%	17%
Portion of those requesting food assistance who are families with children	67%	62%	61%	75%	68%	68%	67%	64%	63%	62%	58%	61%	58%	60%	54%	48%
Demand for emergency food unmet	18%	15%	17%	14%	17%	21%	16%	15%	18%	18%	19%	21%	21%	13%	14%	16%
Cities in which food assistance facilities must turn people away	67%	62%	73%	86%	79%	68%	68%	73%	59%	50%	71%	47%	54%	28%	33%	32%
Cities that expect demand for emergency food to increase next year	84%	85%	89%	100%	100%	89%	100%	81%	96%	96%	92%	96%	84%	71%	100%	100%
HOMELESSNESS																
Increase in demand for emergency shelter	21%	13%	25%	24%	13%	14%	10%	13%	11%	5%	3%	11%	12%	15%	13%	19%
Cities in which demand increased	96%	93%	89%	80%	89%	88%	81%	80%	63%	71%	59%	72%	69%	80%	81%	88%
Demand for emergency shelter unmet	23%	19%	22%	19%	15%	23%	25%	21%	19%	20%	27%	26%	25%	23%	37%	30%
Cities in which shelters must turn people away	65%	67%	59%	70%	74%	75%	77%	72%	82%	81%	88%	67%	73%	68%	44%	56%
Cities which expect demand for shelter to increase next year	92%	89%	93%	97%	100%	93%	88%	71%	100%	100%	100%	93%	92%	72%	100%	100%

Table 12.1   Homeless in America's Cities, 1987–2002 (*Continued*)

Indicator	1987	1988	1989	1990	1991	1992	1993	1994	1995	1996	1997	1998	1999	2000	2001	2002
Composition of Homeless Population																
Single men	49%	49%	46%	51%	50%	55%	43%	48%	46%	45%	47%	45%	43%	44%	40%	41%
Families with children	33%	34%	36%	34%	35%	32%	34%	39%	36%	38%	36%	38%	36%	34%	40%	41%
Single women	14%	13%	14%	12%	12%	11%	11%	11%	14%	14%	14%	14%	13%	13%	14%	13%
Unaccompanied youth	4%	5%	4%	3%	3%	2%	4%	3%	4%	3%	4%	3%	4%	4%	4%	5%
Children	NA	35%	25%	23%	24%	32%	30%	26%	25%	27%	25%	25%	NA	NA	NA	NA
Severely mentally ill	23%	25%	25%	28%	29%	28%	27%	26%	23%	24%	27%	24%	19%	22%	22%	23%
Substance abusers	35%	34%	44%	38%	40%	41%	48%	43%	46%	43%	43%	38%	31%	37%	34%	32%
Employed	22%	23%	24%	24%	18%	17%	18%	19%	20%	18%	17%	22%	21%	26%	20%	22%
Veterans	NA	26%	26%	26%	23%	18%	21%	23%	23%	19%	22%	22%	14%	15%	11%	10%

Source: U.S. Conference of Mayors. (2003). A Status Report on Hunger and Homelessness in America's Cities. Retrieved on June 20, 2003, from
http://www.usmayors.org/uscm/hungersurvey/2002/onlinereport/Hunger And Homeless Report 2002.pdf

20 and 30 percent. Snow and Anderson (1993) puts the figure much lower. Snow argues that many of the behaviors labeled as mental impairment may in fact be the result of living on the streets. Severe hypoglycemia (extremely low blood sugar) leads to confusion, tremors, and unfocused staring. A large percentage of those labeled mentally ill may simply be suffering from the effects of homelessness. In their opinion, changing the environment will in many cases change the behavior.

Homeless Women

There is probably no more depressing sight than a bag lady, a homeless woman carrying her worldly possessions in a grocery cart. There is evidence that the number of homeless women is increasing, and they may now constitute between 15 percent and 25 percent of the homeless population. Some are married and have left their children with kin, others are victims of marital abuse, and still others are victims of economic conditions (National Coalition for the Homeless, 2002).

Homeless Women and Children

The most recent HUD report (2003), *Homelessness: Programs and the People They Serve,* shows that 34 percent of homeless service users in the United States are members of homeless families. Among these homeless families, 84 percent are female-headed families, and more than half are minority. Nearly 75 percent of these women have never married or are separated or divorced, and nearly three-quarters have a high-school or less education. In a Boston study, researchers found a considerable overlap between these families and multi-problem welfare families. In the Boston study, 80 homeless mothers and 151 children were interviewed. Forty-five percent of the mothers were single and 45 percent were separated, divorced, or widowed. Their mean age was 27 years. They had an average of 2.4 children living with them in the shelter. Ninety percent were receiving Aid for Dependent Children (AFDC) benefits. The majority of women were raised in dysfunctional families. Nearly 25 percent of the mothers were under professional care for abuse or neglect of their own children. The majority of these women reported their move to the shelter was the result of eviction, nonpayment of rent, overcrowding, and housing conversions. Problems with other household members were also a major reason for moving to the shelter. This group of homeless people has not received much attention in the press. Unfortunately, little is known about them, and this lack of knowledge has hampered attempts to develop effective programs for them.

The Homeless Alcoholic

This is the group of men that have been most studied. They are often hardcore, skid-row alcoholics in the last stages of acute alcoholism. This group of homeless men is generally middle-aged and older and often isolates with little social contact. Studies show that the rate of alcoholism among sheltered men ranges from between 29 percent to 40 percent. Although widely studied, little is known about their actual drinking habits. Since shelters forbid drinking, much of their drinking is done clandestinely. There is evidence that alcoholism may mask mental health disorders of many of these men. Alcoholism is also a contributing factor to these men's health problems (National Coalition for the Homeless, 2002).

The New Poor

The earlier section on poverty and inequality explored the effects of globalization on the nation's economy. Millions of Americans have been economically marginalized. Many of the homeless are victims of the new economy and of changes in federal welfare and housing programs. As we have seen, growing numbers of these people are homeless youth and homeless families (Burt, 2001).

Why the Homeless Problem?

Structural, personal, and political factors influence the level of homelessness and determine where it will occur most often. Structural factors in the United States identified in a recent Urban Institute report identifies some of the structural factors responsible for the growth of the homeless (Burt, 2001).

- Changing housing markets for extremely low-income families and single adults are pricing more and more people with below-poverty incomes out of the market.

- Dwindling employment opportunities for people with a high school education or less are contributing to the widening gap between rich and poor.

- The removal of institutional supports for people with severe mental illness, epitomized by drastic reductions in the use of long-term hospitalization for the mentally ill, are leaving many individuals with few housing options.

- Racial, ethnic, and class discrimination in housing, along with local zoning restrictions that exclude affordable housing alternatives, persists in many areas.

These themes are familiar; we explored them in the first section of this chapter. Inequality has increased; housing costs relative to household income have risen; those on or below the poverty line now make up the majority of the homeless. Caught in a new economy without education and skills, the new poor find it difficult to earn enough money to raise their incomes above the poverty level, even when they are employed full-time and work overtime. Once structural factors have created the conditions for homelessness, personal factors like mental illness, disability, no family safety net, and alcohol and drug abuse increase a person's risk of homelessness.

Structural and personal factors don't tell the whole story. Affordable housing is considered housing that does not exceed one-third of your gross income. In the 1960s and 1970s, the federal programs provided millions of subsidized dwellings to low-income families. Note in Figure 12.10 the draconic declines in housing assistance that began in the late 1970s. As a result, the number of low-income housing units declined dramatically during the 1980s and 1990s. Market forces were at work as well. Skyrocketing housing values in most U.S. cities removed many of the marginal housing units from the market; low-cost rooms in residential hotels all but disappeared in large cities as they were converted into luxury apartments and offices; and gentrification removed additional units from the low-income housing stock during the 1990s (HUD, 2000).

As you can see, many factors contributed to the homeless problem. The first and most important factor is poverty. Poverty affects not only the homeless person, but

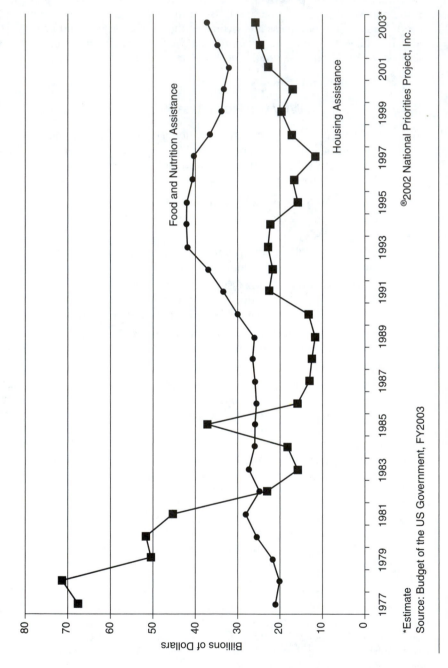

Figure 12.10 *Food and Housing Assistance, 1977–2003 (In constant $1996) (Source: National Priorities Project [2003]. Charts and Statistics. Retrieved on June 16, 2003 from the NPP site: http://www.nationalpriorities.org/charts/FoodHousing.html)*

also the person's social network of family and friends. Ultimately, family is the safety net of last resort. If this net has no resources, there is no place else to turn. As we have explored throughout the book, the 1990s were a period of economic restructuring. Job opportunities for low-skilled workers vanished as the economy shifted from industry to service and high tech. Contributing to those challenges are changes external to the individual, the most important being public policy. Expenditures on entitlement and needs-based programs declined, and the federal government largely abandoned its role in providing affordable housing for low-income Americans.

These structural patterns transcend the individual, but important individual patterns play a role as well. Once a person becomes homeless, a vicious cycle begins. Sheer survival—finding shelter, food, and clothing and protecting the few possessions you have—becomes an all-consuming task and there is little time for other activities like job hunting. How do you fill out a job application when you don't have a permanent address or a telephone to list on the form? Is a prospective employer going to hire someone who lives in a shelter? How do you shower and dress appropriately for a job interview? Thus, the labeling and stigmatization of the homeless create barriers to their reentry into society.

What Can Be Done?

In a perfect world, federal, state, and local governments along with private trusts and agencies would coordinate a comprehensive program for the homeless. The program would have elements of job training, education, substance abuse treatment, affordable shelter, health services, and psychological and family counseling. The question is, will it or can it be done? I think not. This nation is facing a bewildering set of problems: a declining infrastructure, schools, poverty, crime, drug addiction, lack of competitiveness, a changing political and economic world order, and a $7 trillion deficit. In a society with all these problems, how are priorities set? Which problems get the resources?

Homelessness in the final analysis results from powerlessness and marginality. By definition, these people are detached from the social fabric. They don't vote. They have no money. They are not a constituency. They will not be heard. The pressing problem of the homeless cries for federal intervention. It is a national problem played out in our largest cities. The political environment was right in the late 1980s, when Congress passed the Stewart B. McKinney Homeless Assistance Act of 1987. Because of this act and its annual modifications the homeless service system in the United States grew in the 1990s. Available beds more than doubled from about 275,000 in 1988 to about 607,000 in 1996. Emergency shelter capacity increased about 20 percent during this period. The availability of housing for disabled formerly homeless people also grew. But as the U.S. Conference of Mayors' study shows, as the homeless service network has grown, more people in desperate need have come forward. Look again at Table 12.1. If the nation were addressing this problem, the demand for food and housing would have declined. Instead, the demand for services has grown.

What should be done? Emergency food and shelter are only symptoms. Homelessness is only a small part of much larger issues involving the distribution of wealth and social justice. In the current political climate, these issues will not be addressed, and as a result the homeless will haunt our streets, alleys, and shelters well into the twenty-first century.

CRIME

Introduction

Two Teens Arrested in Fort Smith Murder and Robbery

No Mercy for Killer, Prosecutor Argues

Man Pleads Innocent in Case of Killing, Dismembering and Eating Dog

Man, 18, Sentenced for Groping Women

Bishop Quits After Hit and Run Arrest

Mother of Three Arrested for Abuse and Neglect

These headlines from today's *Arkansas Democrat Gazette* are all too familiar to Americans. TV and radio coverage, campaign speeches, advocacy ads, and sermons reinforce this message: We live in a crime-ridden society. But we need to remember, each group has a vested interest in exploiting crime data. After all, newspapers need to sell papers, news organizations need listeners and viewers, politicians need to win elections, advocacy groups need members, and preachers need parishioners. What most Americans seldom hear is that during the 1990s crime rates in the United States declined dramatically. In fact, if the rates that prevailed in 1990 had remained the same throughout the decade, there would have been 34,000 more murders, 6,715,000 more robberies, 5,547,000 more burglaries, and 2,569,000 more motor vehicle thefts than there were. Whatever the cause, the decline in crime rates prevented tens of thousands of deaths and millions of thefts (Conklin, 2003, p. 1).

The problem is that the decline in the crime rate has not been accompanied by a decline in fear. Americans fear crime. Urbanites are terrified of being victimized, and many people have changed their behaviors to reduce their risks. People stay in at night, barricade themselves in their homes, buy expensive security systems, and avoid risky people and places. Fear of crime also weakens neighborhood solidarity, limits mobility, and depresses real-estate prices. Are these fears justified? Some of you may be thinking, "You can give me all the national crime data you want, but I live in a city. I hear urban crime is at epidemic levels!" This section explores urban crime. What are the crime rates? How are these data collected? Why is the crime rate higher in urban areas? What are the causes of crime? Why have they declined? What can be done to further lower our crime rate?

Perceived and Actual Crime Rates

Sociology tells us that if something is defined as real, the social consequences will be real. The fear of crime rose dramatically in the 1960s and has remained high ever since. This public perception is a potent political issue. State and federal crime reports, along with stories in the media about them, can have a significant impact on local and national elections. They are particularly important in local elections and serve as grist for the political mill. Local elections have been won or lost over crime stories that created fear. Remember the random shootings in the Washington, D.C., metro area in 2002? Montgomery County, Virginia police chief Charles Moose became a national hero overnight. But what if the two assassins had not been caught? Where would Chief Moose and the metro area's other police chiefs be today?

In modern politics, the law and order issue first appeared in the 1968 and 1972 presidential campaigns of Richard Nixon and has been an element in every campaign since. Fear of crime continued to be a hot-button issue in the 1970s and 1980s and, in his 1992 campaign, Bill Clinton promised to put another 100,000 police on the streets. In the 2000 election, George W. Bush portrayed himself as Texas's "law and order" governor. He pointed to his state's record number of executions, high incarceration rate, and falling crime statistics.

The Gallup organization has been asking Americans a variety of questions on American's fear of crime since 1965. In a 1967 poll, Gallup found that 31 percent of Americans were afraid to walk alone at night. Our fear of a night stroll rose to 45 percent in 1975 and stayed in the mid-40s range until 1993. Not until the late 1990s did it begin to drop, but in 2002, after a decade of falling crime rates, 35 percent of Americans were still afraid to go out at night. Gallup found similar responses to other questions. In 2002, 45 percent of Americans worried about their home being burglarized, 43 percent having their cars stolen, 28 percent getting mugged, and 26 percent being sexually assaulted (Pastore & Maguire, 2003).

Is this public perception correct? First, a caveat. Official crime statistics are notoriously inaccurate. I'm always chagrined to hear statements on the evening news like, "The crime rate continues to spiral upward—another 2.0 percent increase this year." This is the official crime rate, the crimes reported to the police. The fact is that the vast majority of the crime that occurs in this society is never reported to the police. Most property crime is minor theft. Most assaults are a push or a shove. Violent crime? Murder seldom goes undetected, but most rapes and assaults never come to the attention of the police. As a result, the Department of Justice collects two types of statistics on crime in this society. The most familiar is the Uniform Crime Report (UCR) collected by the Federal Bureau of Investigation each year. This is a compilation of crimes reported to thousands of local jurisdictions throughout the United States and its territories. These are the figures usually reported in the press.

The National Crime Victimization Survey (NCVS) is a report published by the Bureau of Justice Statistics. The NCVS gathers information from a large representative sample of U.S. households. First conducted in 1973 and redesigned most recently in 1992, the survey can now trace a three-decade trend in criminal victimization. The 2001 NCVS report was based on a survey of 83,000 persons in 43,000 households about their experiences as victims of crime during the past year (U.S. Department of Justice, Bureau of Justice Statistics, 2003). These data include crimes both reported and not reported to the police, and many researchers feel these data more accurately report the level of crime in this society. According to the UCR, there were 11.9 million offenses in 2001; 24.2 million victimizations occurred according to the NCVS data (U.S. Department of Justice, FBI, 2003; Bureau of Justice Statistics, 2003).

Figure 12.11 summarizes victimization data from 1973 to 2001. The rates per 1,000 persons or households in 2001 for overall violent crime (simple assault) and property crime (burglary and theft) were the lowest ever recorded by the NCVS. Other crime rates registered their lowest rate in 2000 and remained unchanged in 2001. These included rape and sexual assault, robberies, aggravated assaults, and motor vehicle thefts. Data from the FBI's Uniform Crime Report mirror these changes. These losses would have incurred even if people were not fearful, but most Americans overestimate their risk of being a crime victim. The reality is that we live in a far safer society today than thirty years ago.

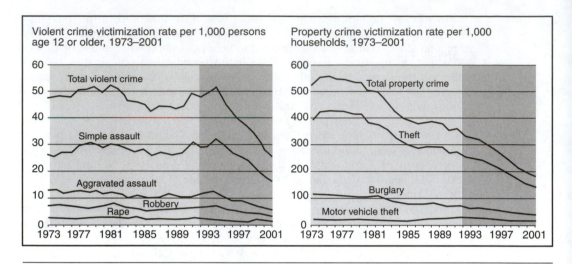

Figure 12.11   *Crime Victimization, 1973–2001 (Source:* U.S. Department of Justice, Bureau of Justice Statistics. [2003]. *National crime victimization study,* 2001. Retrieved June 3, 2003, from *http://www.ojp.usdoj.gov/bjs/pub/cv01.pdf)*

Crime and Cities

Since the beginning of the field of urban sociology, sociologists have known that the larger the city the higher the crime rate. Sociologists also have known for decades that crime is not evenly distributed across the urban landscape. Many behaviors considered deviant by the larger society—prostitution, juvenile delinquency, and violent and property crime—tend to be concentrated in the older and poorer sections of the city. Some of the earliest studies by human ecologists were on the distribution of deviant behavior in the city. One of the first by Shaw and colleagues (1929) showed that the level of juvenile delinquency declined in a regular fashion as one moved from the central business district to the fringe of the city. Shaw found that the same pattern existed for adult crimes (see Figure 12.12). Another classic study by Schmid (1960a, 1960b) conducted a more detailed analysis of crime in Seattle and found the crime rate highest in the areas near the downtown. Shoplifting, check fraud, burglary, and car theft were the most frequent crimes in the CBD. In the adjacent skid row and slum areas, crimes like assault, robbery, burglary, and disorderly conduct were the most frequent offenses.

Since these pioneering works, a large body of research has been completed on the variation in crime rates in metropolitan areas. The patterns first discovered by Shaw in the 1920s still exist today. Note in Table 12.2, that both violent and property crime rates are considerably lower in the suburbs than in the central city. This is why millions of Americans have moved there. Distance from the CBD is still an important variable in describing the geographical distribution of crime in metropolitan areas, but it is only a statistical artifact. As we saw in the first section of this chapter, high-poverty neighborhoods are concentrated in the central city and older, inner-ring suburbs. Since the urban poor are overrepresented in national crime statistics as perpetrators and victims, it should be no surprise that central-city crime rates are higher.

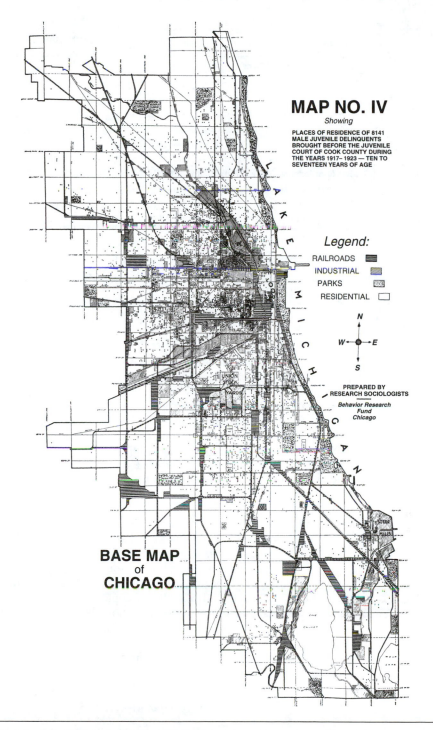

Figure 12.12 *Clifford Shaw's Map of Delinquency Areas, Chicago, 1927 (Source:* Shaw, C. R. [1931]. *The natural history of a delinquent career.* Chicago: University of Chicago Press, map 1, p. 13.)

Table 12.2   *Number of UCR Index Crimes per 100,000 Population*

	Violent Crimes	Property Crimes
United States (total)	506	3,656
Metropolitan statistical areas (MSAs)	560	4,475
Urbanized areas that include at least one city with 50,000 or more inhabitants, or a Census Bureau defined urbanized area of at least 50,000 inhabitants and a total MSA population of at least 100,000		
Non-MSA cities	393	4,450
Cities that do not qualify as MSA central cities and are not otherwise included in an MSA		
Suburban areas	291	3,312
Suburban cities and counties within metropolitan areas		
Rural areas	211	1,892

Source: Federal Bureau of Investigation. 2002. Uniform Crime Report, 2001. Retrieved on June 18, 2003 from FBI user site: *http://www.fbi.gov/ucr/cius_01/01crime2.pdf,* Table 2, p. 57

    The UCR and NCVS provide cold crime statistics, but they are only part of the information we use in assessing our risk of becoming victims. Street crimes—murder, armed robbery, assault, and rape—are the crimes the public fears most, and they are splashed across our TV screens each evening. We are one of the world's largest societies, and a lot of terrible things can happen among 280 million people. Even if an event is extremely rare, say, happening to only 2 out of every 100,000 Americans, 5,600 Americans are affected. A neighbor kidnaps a seven-year-old California girl and murders her. It is a terrible tragedy for her family and community. It is an extremely rare event, happening only a few times a year, but within hours it is transformed into a national story. What has changed is not murder, rape, assault, and robbery—we have always had these crimes—but the media technology that transforms local to national news stories. The consequence is fear of crime. See Photo 12.2
    Another example: Once the nation's murder capital, Washington, D.C., still has one of our highest metro murder rates. There were 396 homicides in Washington in 2001, about half the 1990 figure. Youth gangs, the drug trade, and the availability of handguns contribute to the number of deadly assaults in the nation's capital. Census 2000 counted 5 million people in the Washington, D.C., MSA. Moreover, closer examination of these data show that 232 of the 396 murders took place in the central city, and most of these in just a few neighborhoods. With less than one homicide per day in a population of 5 million, the odds of becoming a victim are pretty remote. You have a higher probability of being killed in a car or household accident, but knowing this does not help to reduce our fear of crime.

Why Urban Crime?

Over the years, numerous theories have been developed to explain deviance in general and crime in particular. Two general explanations focus on the higher incidence of crime in cities—cultural and structural.

Photo 12.2   *Most crimes are minor. Most crimes are against property, and crime rates have dropped. Yet Americans still fear becoming a victim. Social scientists are still trying to understand why the fear of crime hasn't declinied. (Source: CORBIS/Bettmann.)*

Cultural Explanations

In the opening chapter of this text, Claude Fischer's (1975) subcultural theory of urbanism was presented. Fischer's argument is straightforward: The size, density, and heterogeneity of the city provides an environment ripe for the creation of sub-cultures. Most of these subcultures develop a value and normative system that reinforces the values of the larger society. However, a few subcultures like street gangs lack strong external controls or strong motivations to conform and have the potential for lawlessness and delinquency. Urban gangs are nothing new. Thrasher in the 1920s identified more than 1,300 gangs in the city of Chicago (Thrasher, 1927). Today, as in the past, high schools in our largest cities bring thousands of students together five days a week. This critical mass of teenagers creates an environment conducive for the creation of groups like the National Honor Society, sports teams, cliques, and gangs. Gangs exist in all our major cities, and their involvement in the drug trade and their proclivity toward violence is played out in our electronic and print media almost daily.

Another version of the cultural theory was first introduced in the works of Edward Banfield (1970), James Q. Wilson (1983), and William J. Wilson (1987). Banfield argues that crime flourishes in areas of the city where lower-class culture is rooted. Elements of a lower-class culture include a strong present-time rather than future orientation, inability to defer gratification, low aspirations, and moral irresponsibility. These culture traits, according to Banfield, lead to situations where the poor victimize each other and anyone else who seems an easy mark. The poor are concentrated in the central cities of this society, and these conditions, according to Banfield, create an environment conducive for the creation and perpetuation of the lower-class culture.

James Q. Wilson echoed these same sentiments in his 1983 book, *Thinking About Crime*. According to Wilson, crime does not occur because people are poor, but because many of the poor hold lower-class cultural values. Marginality and a lack of commitment to the goals and values of the larger society are characteristics of this cultural group. These values, according to Wilson, reduce the effectiveness of informal social controls and ultimately destroy the local community. The destruction of the community is crucial to Wilson's argument because our public behavior is regulated by our concern for what our kin, friends, and neighbors think. Informal controls are powerful forces in maintaining conformity and respect for others and their property. Since these controls have broken down in slums, serious crime abounds, especially predatory street crime.

Wilson's interpretation of the link between poverty and crime has been widely criticized. His ideas echo the culture of poverty argument widely held in the 1950s and 1960s. The culture of poverty posited that values the poor held made their participation in the larger society impossible. Social programs from the 1960s like Head Start were designed to interrupt the transmission of these cultural values from parents to children. Wilson's solution to crime is more draconic. He argues that since criminal behavior results from a lack of commitment to common principles of decency, then the only remedy is to convince potential criminals there will be consequences for their behavior through swift and certain punishment. According to Wilson, social programs designed to improve the conditions of the poor won't solve the problem because these people are steeped in lower-class culture.

A more benign version of the cultural position is found in the work of the black sociologist William J. Wilson, especially his work *The Truly Disadvantaged*, which we reviewed earlier. In this work, Wilson tries to place the experiences of the ghetto in a larger social context. In the 1970s and 1980s, many black Americans experienced upward social mobility. Black Americans like all our other ethnic groups responded to this increase in social status by moving to the suburbs. The problem: people were left behind. In the past, segregation in the central city meant that middle- and lower-class blacks lived in the same communities. Importantly, small businesspeople, professionals, and church leaders provided the leadership for these communities. When these leaders left these neighborhoods for the suburbs, the ghetto was deprived of its leadership and role models. Those left, the truly disadvantaged, live in an environment bereft of stable families, appropriate role models, and traditional values. Over time the cultural values of the truly disadvantaged form barriers to participation in education and job training programs. Moreover, the barriers also limit their contacts to the network of gainfully employed people, a source of role models that could lead to employment opportunities.

Crime, according to Wilson, is a predictable outcome of isolating a group from the mainstream of society. Crucial to understanding the problem is the realization that the culture of the truly disadvantaged is like any culture. It reproduces itself from generation to generation through the socialization process. The problem is more serious than in the past because there is no way to break the cycle. Wilson's solution to crime is straightforward: Invest in our human capital regardless of race and ethnicity. Provide all members of our society with the education and skills necessary for full participation in society.

Structural Explanations

Wilson's research on the truly disadvantaged is a bridge between the two schools of thought. The structuralists believe important structural problems in our society contribute to the problem of crime. The United States is a society with a core value, *materialism*. Most members of our society hold this value, but not everyone is provided with the means to reach this goal legitimately. Poor schools, a lack of job training programs, and other social factors cut off millions from traditional means of social mobility. Unable to use legitimate means, many resort to illegitimate means. Some structuralists go as far as to argue that crime is a survival strategy for the poor. Many of the poor cannot live on the welfare benefits provided in most cities, so they turn to crime to supplement their incomes.

Marxist theorists like Manuel Castells (1977) make a similar argument. The city in capitalist societies reproduces the labor force. Here people are born, housed, fed, and schooled to provide the workforce necessary to keep the capitalist system working. According to Castells, capitalism benefits relatively few people. Any behavior that interferes with the reproduction of labor threatens the interests of the few. Moreover, those who control the means of production also control the political and police powers of the state, and they erect a legal system to protect their interests. The poor who deviate from laws created by these vested interests are labeled and stigmatized as criminals. White-collar criminals like the CEOs of Enron, Tyco, and WorldCom who bilked investors out of billions of dollars usually receive less severe penalties than street criminals. Why? Because a criminal justice system of their social class judges white-collar criminals.

Which Theory Is Right?

Little research has focused on why crime rates increase and decrease, so many of the explanations offered by sociologists and criminologists are based on theory rather than empirical evidence. John E. Conklin (2003) in *Why Crime Rates Fell* reviewed the major studies on changing crime rates. He asked, "Were the police, increased incarceration, drugs, firearms, age structure, or changing institutions responsible for the falling crime rates?" Conklin finds meager evidence that the police or the strategies they use have any effect on crime rates. Similarly, neither changes in drug use and drug markets nor shifts in the crime-prone 15–29 age group had much impact. The long-term decline in divorces, an increase in religion, and a shift in firearm possession had only modest effects on crime rates. The booming economy in the 1990s seems to be a more important factor. The availability of good-paying jobs and full employment for the first time in generations probably convinced some members of crime-prone groups to choose legitimate work over criminal sources of income. But the most important reason that crime rates fell, according to Conklin, was the rising rate of incarceration. There were 564,094 more prisoners in 1999 than there were in 1990. And Conklin estimates that the growth in prison population alone resulted in 10,800 fewer murders, 2,176,00 fewer robberies, 738,000 fewer burglaries, and 748,000 fewer motor vehicle thefts over the course of the decade. Others who have performed cost-benefit calculations estimate that incarcerating 1,000 more prisoners would cost $25 million but save $430 million in losses. Others come up with much lower estimates (Conklin, 2003). But these benefits came at a steep cost. State and federal governments have been forced to spend additional billions building new prisons, hiring new correctional officers, and caring for a half million new inmates. Also, the growing incarceration rate, especially for drug offenses, fell most harshly on young African American males from poverty-stricken urban areas. Thousands of Americans spent their most productive years behind bars, and their parents, spouses, and children also suffered. Legislatures may have passed laws with harsher penalties, and courts meted out longer sentences, but these policies were flawed. Eventually most of these prisoners will be released into society; many of the ex-convicts, embittered by arrests for minor drug offenses, will commit crimes again; and without a booming economy, government can no longer afford to lock up so many of its citizens.

What Can Be Done?

As we have seen, the relationship between crime and various social and economic factors is a complex one. Conklin's research seems to support the policy measures recommended in the cultural theories of Edward Banfield (1970) and James Q. Wilson (1983) and the economic measures supported by the structural position. Conklin's analysis, however, explored institutional factors; other researchers who look at the characteristics of offenders come up with other policy answers. First, there seems to be a close relationship between crime and family background. Nearly half of those in jail or prison grew up in homes with only one parent or in which they were raised by relatives. It is sobering to realize that in the 1990s one out of five children under age eighteen was living with one parent. Many of the offenders incarcerated for violent crimes were victims of childhood abuse. Moreover, most offenders have never been married. Thus, no or destructive attachments to the most fundamental of all our social institutions, the family, appear to be a contributing factor to criminal behavior that leads to incarceration (U.S. Department of Justice, Bureau of Justice Statistics, 2003).

Second, economic marginality appears to be a contributing factor to crime. Those in jail or prison have levels of education far below the national average. Most offenders were unemployed at the time of their arrest or lacked steady employment. Those employed were usually in blue-collar occupations, and few were working in their customary occupation. The average inmate was at the poverty level before entering jail and those with incomes received it from sources other than wages—welfare, disability benefits, and crime (U.S. Department of Justice, Bureau of Justice Statistics, 2003).

Crime can be addressed on two levels—dealing with the symptoms or dealing with the causes. Short-term solutions are defensive in nature. For decades, we have known the principles of defensible space. Designing doorways, windows, halls, and walks in certain ways can dramatically lower the crime rate in high-rise buildings and public housing. Neighborhood watch programs have been found to be an effective deterrent to crime (Felson, 2002). Today, one in three Americans lives in neighborhoods with active watch programs. But as Conklin (2003) notes, larger police forces, more effective patrolling, better community police relations, gang control, and gun control have little effect on crime rates.

In my opinion, inequality in this society is responsible for our high crime rate. Since the work of Durkheim we have known that attachments to social groups is the most potent force in bringing about conformity. Full participation in, commitment to, and vested interests in society would probably be the most potent vaccine to the problem of crime in our cities. Lessening inequality in this society through full employment legislation, providing greater access to good jobs through job training programs, and providing greater access to quality education, health care, and housing services to our citizens would attack the root causes of crime. In short, these solutions get at the heart of the issue of social justice—the social contract between our institutions and our people.

The politics of the next decade will pay little attention to issues of social justice or domestic issues like housing, education, and health care. The social contract of the nation has shifted from the well-being of our citizens to the protection and accumulation of property. We will continue to incarcerate more citizens than any society in the world, but this policy is defensive in nature and does not address the root causes of crime. The question is, can we afford to spend additional billions on prisons? Can we continue to squander our investment in the human capital that we put behind bars? If the structuralists are correct, investments in our society's most important asset, our human capital, may be the best way to keep the low crime rates in our cities.

Summary

All cities must maintain their infrastructure, provide services, and maintain social control. This chapter explores three serious problems facing cities in meeting these obligations: inequality, homelessness, and crime.

As employment in this society shifted from manufacturing to services, the occupational structure of this shift affected cities by changing the mix of businesses and industries in their economic bases. Some cities in the Midwest and South, because of their economic base or strategic position in our nation's system of cities, prospered in the 1990s; others, especially those in the North and the West, foundered in the late twentieth century.

These shifts in the economy also affected the internal structure of our cities. Although most U.S. cities benefited from the booming 1990s, the experience of groups within cities varied enormously. A dual economy emerged in our cities—one that provides jobs to high-wage earners and another to low-wage earners—which explains the pattern of rising incomes with growing inequality. Our cities reflect this inequality because the social distance between groups is always reflected in the physical distance between them.

Concentrated poverty concerns policy makers and the federal government has systematically measured it for forty years. The 1990s economy moved millions of individuals from welfare to work and improved the economic lives of many of the most disadvantaged groups in our society. While the decline was significant, it was surprisingly small in light of the nearly decade-long economic expansion. Traditionally, central cities have the metropolitan area's highest poverty rates. In the 1990s rates converged somewhat between central cities and suburbs, but the rift remains wide.

The poverty line does not capture the multiple ways that poverty degrades the quality of life of the poor and the way it limits the opportunities of those trapped in poverty. In the 1970s and 1980s, the spatial concentration of the poor rose dramatically in the nation's metropolitan areas. One of the most influential books of the period was William Julius Wilson's *The Truly Disadvantaged,* in which he argued that during the 1970s and 1980s, structural changes in America's economy combined with the suburbanization of industry and the black middle class led to the segregation and isolation of the most disadvantaged citizens in this society—a black underclass.

Paul A. Jargowsky tested Wilson's major hypotheses on the reason for the plight of the underclass and found support for the hypotheses on industrial deconcentration and middle-class black flight, but little support for deindustrialization, segregation, and culture of poverty. His study of Census 2000 found a dramatic decline in concentrated poverty in the 1990s. High-poverty neighborhoods in central cities declined in the 1990s, but a careful inspection of suburban poverty reveals poverty rates increased along the outer edges of central cities and in the inner-ring suburbs of many metropolitan areas.

The concentration of poverty is an important public policy concern because it has dynamic effects on income distribution, it undermines the political and social fabric of our cities, and it restricts opportunity for the most disadvantaged in our society. Jargowsky recommends policies that focus on broad economic improvement across metropolitan areas.

This society has always had homeless people, but conditions in the past decade have exacerbated an already bad situation. Through our history, the definition of the problem and the solutions that followed have changed. Prior to the Civil War, the homeless were deemed moral failures, and communities solved the problem by placing these people in workhouses. After the Civil War, the rapid industrialization of our society and the rapid settlement of the West required a large and transient workforce. These itinerant workers were known as tramps, and they were defined by society as a dangerous class. By 1900, tramping was illegal in most states. Cities couldn't jail all the homeless so they depended on municipal shelters and rescue missions. In the early twentieth century, the growth of populist government and social work professionals redefined the homeless as victims of circumstance, not flawed character. During the Great Depression, the link between homelessness and economic cycles was recognized, and all of the major programs in the nation's welfare state were established. In the post–World War II period, an expanding economy meant that the homeless were reduced to a relatively small number of older, single men surviving on pensions and marginal employment in skid-row areas of our cities. In the 1970s and 1980s, conditions changed once again and homelessness became a national problem.

One of the problems this society faces in dealing with the problem of the homeless is defining who are the homeless. Using conservative definitions, HUD estimates between 350,000 and 500,000 homeless in the nation. Other groups put the number much higher. One thing has become apparent: The homeless are not a homogeneous group, but one made up of the mentally ill, AIDS victims, alcoholics and drug abusers, women and children, and the new poor. Each group has specific problems and needs, requiring different solutions.

A changed economy, a decline in federal funding for low-income housing, and reforms in social programs are all contributing factors to the problems of the homeless. What can be done? The author feels that little will be done. The homeless by definition are marginal and isolated citizens and so do not form a constituency. With no one to represent their interests, this society will do little to solve the long-term problem of the homeless.

Crime in our cities is perceived as a serious threat to most urbanites. Forty-five percent of Americans are afraid to walk the streets at night. This fear has become a potent political issue. Is this fear justified? Crime is difficult to measure, and two sources of data are used to assess the amount of crime in this society. In its annual Uniform Crime Report, the FBI publishes the number of crimes reported each year to the police. These data show that crime declined during the 1990s. The National Crime Victimization Survey is a survey of American households conducted by the Bureau of Justice Statistics. The survey includes reported and unreported crimes, and many researchers feel it more accurately reflects the level of crime in this society. These data show that crime has declined to its lowest levels in thirty years.

The larger the city, the higher the crime rate. Sociologists have known for most of this century that crime is not evenly distributed across the city, but concentrated in poorer neighborhoods near the central business district. Two types of explanations have been posited. Cultural explanations argue that the size, density, and heterogeneity of the city create conditions ripe for the emergence of subcultures. Some of these subcultures have a value and normative system that diverges from those of the larger society. Edward Banfield and James Q. Wilson argued that lower-class subcultures are pathological and the behaviors that result need to be extinguished through the sure, swift retribution of the law. William J. Wilson, in contrast, explores the changes in the larger society that have created the subculture of the truly disadvantaged. He suggests that a massive investment in our people, regardless of race, would be the best solution to the problem of crime in our cities.

Structuralists argue that crime is a result of social structure. Poverty and inequality reduce the commitment of the poor to society. From this perspective, a lack of legitimate means of social mobility, a lack of attachments to social groups, and a lack of commitment to the values of the larger society are the major reasons for crime. Marxists and structural sociologists agree economic inequality and a lack of social justice are at the root of the problem of crime in our society. Recent research suggests that incarceration and an improved economy and labor market explain the falling crime rate. The first supports the cultural theory of Banfield and Wilson, the second, structural theory.

Notes

[1] Wealth is the accumulated property owned by a person or family. Although the Michael Jordans, Oprah Winfreys, and Sam Waltons have accumulated billions in the last generation, most wealth is inherited. The Rockefellers, Fords, Duponts, and Kennedys are best known examples.

As such, wealth is far more concentrated in the United States than is income. The wealthiest 1 percent of Americans controls more of the total wealth of the nation than the bottom 90 percent. The distribution of wealth hasn't changed much over the past fifty years; in fact, there is evidence that it hasn't changed much since the 1920s. The division of wealth now and in the past looks like this—the wealthiest 1 percent of Americans control one-third of the wealth; the next 9 percent one-third, and the remaining one-third goes to the remaining 90 percent of the population. The bottom

90 percent can be divided into halves—the top half controls most of the remaining one-third, the bottom 45 percent of our population has no or negative net worth.

[2] The following section on the history of the homeless in the United States is based on two works. The first is Carol L. M. Caton *Homelessness in Historical Perspective*. The second is Charles Hoch, *A Brief History of the Homeless Problem in the United States*. A complete citation for each work is found in the bibliography.

[3] Much of the following section is based on the book *Landscapes of Despair: From Deinstitutionalization to Homelessness* by Michael J. Dear and Jennifer R. Wolch. A complete citation for the work is in the bibliography.

13

URBAN PLANNING IN THE TWENTY-FIRST CENTURY

Introduction

In the closing months of World War II, Winston Churchill, looking toward his nation's massive rebuilding task, told his people, "We shape our buildings, and they, in turn, shape us." We, like the British, undertook a massive building program in the postwar years. We have built 70 percent of all the structures that have ever existed in our nation in the past half century (Kunstler, 1993). But what have we built, how have we built it, and how has it shaped us? For many critics, the answers are not good. James Kunstler (1993, 1996), for example, in *The Geography of Nowhere* and *Home from Nowhere*, points to suburban sprawl as a source of much of our nation's discontent. He describes the physical setting of the suburban fringe—a landscape of car-clogged highways, strip malls, tract houses, franchise restaurants, parking lots, junked cities, and a ravaged countryside—as not merely the symptom of a troubled culture, but also the major source of our social problems. He shows that another urban form, the village and the small town, is deeply rooted in our history and has resonance in our national psyche. He argues that the building of suburbia as a replacement for towns and cities was a destructive and tragic act. More important, he argues that this living arrangement, which most Americans have come to view as normal, is bankrupting the nation economically, socially, ecologically, and spiritually, and it cannot continue.

Robert Putnam (2000), in his book *Bowling Alone*, describes the decline in the nation's social capital, the glue that holds our communities together. In the past generation, there has been a precipitous decline in every form of social capital whether it is measured by voter turnout, membership in civic clubs, charitable donations, church attendance, or volunteerism. We are a far less civic and civil society than we were a quarter century ago. What is the cause? According to Putnam it is urban sprawl. His data show for every additional ten minutes of commuting there is a 10 percent decline in every form of social participation, whether it is the number of Americans going to church, giving dinner parties, joining clubs, attending public meetings, or bowling in leagues.

These public concerns have become part of our political agenda. In the 2000 presidential campaign, the candidates addressed the issue of *smart growth*, policies designed to curb urban sprawl. On the campaign trail, Al Gore's message was that "sprawl exacerbates a host of societal problems; transforming suburbs into lonely cul-de-sacs; creating road-rage-inducing, child-bedtime-story-missing commutes; and emptying main streets in older communities, leaving a nighttime vacuum filled with crime and disorder" (Smith, 2000, p. 49). Among his initiatives was a $2 billion federal aid program for urban smart-growth projects designed to protect threatened farmland, preserve open spaces, and redevelop downtowns. Similarly, George W. Bush told a gathering of big-city mayors that the federal government "should not be your rival but your partner in promoting smart growth and regional cooperation" (Smith, 2000, p. 49). But a more important indication of the scope of this movement was the initiatives on the November 7 ballots in more than 250 communities in thirty-one states. Most of them were growth-related ballot initiatives, and more than 70 percent passed. The most common were "open space" measures that set aside land for aesthetic and recreational purposes. In addition, measures passed in Florida and California expanded light rail and high-speed monorail. In a similar move, the federal government, bowing to intense political pressure, permitted states for the first time to shift highway money to mass transit (Li & Wachs, 2001). Has there been a shift in our nation's fifty-year automobile-oriented transportation policy?

The evidence is overwhelming that change is afoot. Words like *new urbanism, smart growth, sustainable urbanism,* and *neotraditonal neighborhoods* have entered our vocabulary. More important, a group of planners, researchers, and developers known as the *new urbanists* have translated these words and political initiatives into physical reality. The new urbanism applies the principles of the small town, village, and traditional neighborhood to new developments, whether they are in the central city or the suburban fringe. Guided by these principles, planners and developers have built hundreds of projects. The first and the most famous is Sea Side, a resort community on Florida's Gulf Coast. (It was the set for the movie, *The Truman Show.*) Other examples are Kentlands, a town twenty-three miles northwest of Washington, D.C., conceived by the planners of Sea Side as "an authentic town made up of distinct neighborhoods in the classic American tradition" (Duany, Plater-Zyberk, & Speck, 2000, p. 3). Or Laguna West, a community of 3,400 units, located eleven miles south of Sacramento. Designed as a pedestrian city, it is the first new community based on transit-oriented development (TOD) principles. Every metropolitan area has one or more of these new urbanism developments, and the new urbanism is even shaping my region, northwest Arkansas. We have three neotraditional towns and neighborhoods—Harber Meadows, Charleston Place, and the Commons. Centerton, a small, rural town just six miles west of Wal-Mart's corporate headquarters, has recently adopted a master plan based on the principles of new urbanism with the help of the University of Arkansas's Community Design Center.

This chapter explores urban planning in the United States. Today, the most serious problem facing the planning community is suburban sprawl. The irony is that during most of our history, high population density, not suburban sprawl, was the most serious problem facing our cities. The opening section describes urban sprawl, the social and environmental costs associated with it, and the economic and technological forces that shaped it. We will then turn to types of community planning in the United States and the pragmatic character of American planning in its attempt to address the health, housing, social, and transportation problems of American cities. Next is a discussion of this society's most recent attempts to deal with urban problems, smart growth and new urbanism. I will outline the history of this movement, the forces that created it, the principles that guide it, and solutions it proposes for our urban problems. We will examine the Kentlands and other new urbanist developments and ask, Have these communities met their promise? Are consumers willing to pay more for them? Do they increase social interaction and create community? The chapter ends with a peek at the city of the future and considers, what we can expect to see in the city of 2050.

Urban Sprawl

Once upon a time in America, there were small towns where people gathered in the square, shopped at the local markets, and generally lived a sort of Rodgers and Hammerstein existence. Those days are officially over, according to the U.S. Agriculture Department, which on Monday released a study heralding a new rise in suburban sprawl, particularly in areas just outside mid-size to small U.S. cities. From 1992 to 1997, the numbers proclaim, our forests and farmlands fell prey to development at a rate of 3 million acres a year, compared with 1.4 million acres that were snapped up annually from 1982 to 1992. It seems that the paving of America, previously associated with New York City and Los Angeles, has crept inward from the coast, and has taken root in a former cornfield just outside Des Moines.

—Jessica Reaves, 2001

Jessica Reaves's *Time Magazine* editorial (May 29, 2001) is sobering, but it doesn't give the entire picture. More land was developed between 1992 and 1997 than at any other time in our history, about 16 million acres. A more detailed analysis of these data from 1982 and 1997 shows that cropland declined by 13 million acres, pasture land by 14 million acres, and range land by 12 million acres. And while most of this development is associated with suburban sprawl, Department of Agriculture officials say it is now a prominent feature in small- and medium-sized cities as well. Although the loss of farmland is of major concern to agriculture officials, the biggest impact of development is on forests, with more than 6 million acres of forest cleared for development between 1992 and 1997. Established metropolitan areas are losing their trees even as the urban fringe grows. In 1973, trees covered 37 percent of the Washington, D.C., metropolitan area. By 1997, only 13 percent were left. If you combine suburban sprawl with deforestation of these urban and suburban areas, the quality of urban life in our cities is rapidly changing (Stevens, 1999).

Thus, the United States is facing some vexing land-use questions. At the federal and state level, should markets reign? We are a capitalist society after all, and markets are the most efficient way to allocate resources. But can or should aesthetic and ecological factors be included in market decisions? Should agriculture be given priority over urban land-uses? Should governments continue subsidies that encourage sprawl? At the local level, officials use growth to expand their tax base. But what impact does growth have on the character of a community and its quality of life? At the individual level, should a young family take advantage of the schools, safety, and lifestyle of a new suburb, or should they move closer in to an older, less-livable neighborhood? If you are a farmer, should you continue to work the land or sell it to a developer for $10,000, $20,000, or more per acre?

Every region of the United States is grappling with these issues. Like global warming, there's urgency in the decision making because policy makers fear that unless something is done now, the process will be irreversible. Here is an example. The American Farmland Trust (AFT) recently reported that 25 million acres of

Photo 13.1 *The principles of smart growth address the problems of sprawl. Shown here is fringe development in Southern California.* (*Source:* James Marshall/CORBIS/Bettmann.)

prime agricultural land is threatened by rapid urban development in the next two decades. Most of this loss is occurring in key farming states like Illinois, Texas, California, and Florida. See Photo 13.1. The twenty most-threatened prime farming areas supply half of the fruit, two-fifths of the vegetables, and nearly a third of the dairy goods produced in the United States. The AFT warns that if the destruction of highly productive farmland continues along with current rates of population growth, the United States could become a net food importer by the mid-twenty-first century (Tyson, 1997).

Other examples can be found at the regional level. In northern Illinois and southern Wisconsin, Chicago's sprawling suburbs are colliding with some of America's best farmland. From 1970 to 2000 the population of the Chicago metro area grew by 7 percent, while its land area expanded by more than 50 percent. The fastest-growing rural county in Chicago's growth area is Illinois's McHenry County about fifty miles southwest of the city. Its population increased 55 percent from 1980 to 2000. McHenry County is typical of many farming communities where farmland is under assault by developers, city dwellers, and suburbanites. These groups migrate deeper into rural areas in search of lower land prices and a higher quality of life. The county's farmland typically sells for $1,000 to $3,000 per acre when it's used for farming. But developers are willing to pay up to 10 times as much for it if it's in a prime location. Farmers close to retirement with children uninterested in farming grab the deals (Wood, 1997).

California's Central Valley is another good example. The state's $24 billion agricultural industry produces half the nation's fruits and vegetables. The state's

Mediterranean climate allows farmers three to four harvests a year, and crops like artichokes, almonds, walnuts, and olives grow no where else in the United States. With projections that the state's population will increase 18 million by 2025, the pressures on the land are enormous. California's cities must accommodate 800,000 new people per year, and increasingly these people are moving away from the congested coast to the Central Valley. As a result, the state's agriculture industry is losing 100,000 acres of prime land each year. Without new land-protection strategies, what happened to the Los Angeles basin and the Silicon Valley will be repeated again and again across the state (Wood, 1997).

This is the supply side of urban sprawl. What about the demand side, urban growth? You can get an idea of the dimensions of urban sprawl by looking at housing data for the thirty-nine largest metropolitan areas. Researchers group a city's housing into three geographical areas: the central city; the metro area, composed of the central city and its suburbs; and the fringe, outside the metro area but inside the county. In 1998 the thirty-nine largest U.S. metro areas covered an area of 191,575 square miles, or roughly the land area of California and Alabama. Only 7,697 square miles, or 4 percent of the metro, was in the central city, an area about the size of New Jersey. These figures do not include the land outside the official boundaries of the metro area in incorporated and unincorporated communities in counties. This area covers nearly 100,000 square miles, an area the size of Colorado (Hoffman, 1999).

The number of new housing units constructed in American's largest metropolitan areas grew by nearly 78 percent between 1991 and 1998, mirroring the rapid growth of the economy. There was healthy growth in some of our largest central cities, but it was dwarfed by suburban growth. More than 80 percent of the new homes built in the 1990s were in the suburbs. Furthermore, outlying suburbs, small cities, and towns in the fringe areas outside the official metropolitan area boundaries consistently attracted more new home building than central cities (Hoffman, 1999).

This growth was uneven, and there were some interesting patterns. First, it appears city size matters. Cities like Phoenix, Houston, and Dallas, with vast territories of more than 500 square miles, were able to produce urban sprawl within their city limits. These cities developed the undeveloped land and open spaces that they had preemptively annexed decades earlier. In contrast, older, smaller cities (less than 150 square miles) like Cleveland, Buffalo, and St. Louis found themselves surrounded by politically independent suburbs. The only way these cities could accommodate growth was on their fringes. Portland, Oregon, was an interesting case because it was one of the few cities to adopt metropolitan growth controls designed to concentrate urban development in the city. It seems to have worked. Portland's housing grew faster than its fringe (Hoffman, 1999).

Second, sprawl is associated with a healthy regional economy. Hot housing markets in the 1990s were Seattle, Orlando, Boston, Miami, Columbus, Portland, Tampa, New York, San Francisco, San Antonio, Phoenix, Houston, and Dallas. Cold housing markets were Baltimore, Providence, St. Louis, Sacramento, Detroit, Philadelphia, New Orleans, Chicago, Kansas City, and Los Angeles. There were distinct regional differences. With the exception of Boston, Columbus, and New York, the hot housing markets were in the Sunbelt or the Pacific Northwest. Cold housing markets, with the exception of New Orleans, Los Angeles, and Sacramento, were in the Frostbelt (Hoffman, 1999).

As you can see, it is dangerous to paint suburban sprawl with a broad brush. Yes, sprawl is a problem. It is occurring in almost every county and at a significant level in one-fifth of the nation's 3,200 counties. But not all regions are affected equally. Factors like the age and size of a metro's central city, the health of a region's economy, the region's climate, and the state and metro's history of land-use controls also affect this process.

Sprawl is a complex phenomenon with a great deal of ambiguity surrounding it. How complex and how ambiguous is reflected in a 1998 report by Robert Burchell and others titled *The Costs of Sprawl—Revisited*. The report, funded by the Federal Transit Authority, systematically reviewed and synthesized the literature in five major areas of research: operating costs, transportation costs, land/natural habitat preservation, quality of life, and social issues. The authors found that researchers agreed that sprawl was real and occurring in most metropolitan areas. They agreed on little else. For example, researchers disagreed on how to define sprawl and on how to measure it. They disagreed on the social, political, economic, and environmental costs of sprawl. Opponents like the new urbanists want laws enacted and policies changed to control sprawl because they believe it destroys community and harms the environment. Proponents, like developers and civil libertarians, don't want government interfering in the urban development process because they believe government will only make things worse. They also point to the fact that the United States has the highest rate of homeownership in the industrial world. Sprawl and the trickling down of older housing to the poor seem to be an efficient way of providing housing to most Americans. Who is right? Let's explore some of the issues surrounding sprawl.

How Do You Define Sprawl?

The urbanist Anthony Downs uses the following five criteria in his definition of sprawl (Burchell, 1998).

1. Low-density, primarily single-family residential settlement
2. Heavy dependence on the automobile for most travel
3. Saturation of job locations widely across the landscape in mainly low-density establishments
4. Fragmentation of governance authority over land uses among many relatively small localities
5. Widespread reliance on the filtering or "trickle-down" process to provide housing for low-income households

Another social scientist, Henry Richmond, includes the following eight criteria in his definition of sprawl (Burchell, 1998).

1. Low residential density
2. Unlimited outward extension of new development
3. Leapfrog development
4. Spatial segregation of different land uses
5. Decentralized landownership
6. Primacy of automobile transportation

7. Fragmentation of governmental land-use authority
8. Disparity in the fiscal capacity of local government

There is some overlap, but we like the working definition used in the Burchell report. Sprawl is

> *the spread-out, skipped-over development that characterizes the non-central-city metropolitan areas and non-metropolitan areas of the United States. Sprawl is one- or two-story single-family residential development on lots ranging in size from one-third to one acre accompanied by strip commercial centers and industrial parks, also two stories or less in height and with similar amount of land takings. (Burchell, 1998, p. 1)*

How Do You Measure It?

We have already reviewed the scope of the nation's urban development over the past generation. Sprawl is widespread but difficult to measure. Population density doesn't work very well because these data are collected at the township or county level. Since sprawl occurs in a leapfrog fashion, surrounding farms and open space mask population growth. Building permit data and subdivision plats show the process in great detail, but it is expensive research, and metro-to-metro and regional comparisons are difficult to make. Researchers make gross comparisons by tracking changes in population, housing, and building-code activity at the central-city, metro, and county level. Using these data, there is universal agreement that sprawl is occurring and that most of our cities accommodate growth in this way (Burchell, 1998).

What Form Does It Take?

In the United States, when we speak of sprawl, we are referring to the residential form—low-density residential development in rural and undeveloped areas. Five types of development are usually present: (1) leapfrog or scattered development, (2) commercial strip development, (3) large expanses of low-density or single-use developments, (4) low accessibility to open space, and (5) developments that are unconnected to each other. Other parts of the world can claim a nonresidential form of sprawl. Latin American, Asian, and Middle Eastern cities are surrounded by a vast fringe where low-density businesses and factories dominate.

Why Has It Occurred?

Sprawl has been a long time coming. In the opening decades of the twentieth century, high population density, tenement housing, slums, and incompatible land uses were viewed as our most serious urban problems. In the teens and twenties of the last century, reformers developed zoning and other tools to address these problems, and these reforms have shaped our cities ever since. For example, New York City adopted the nation's first comprehensive zoning regulations in 1916. Two years later, Cincinnati created the nation's first master plan. In 1922 Congress passed the Standard Zoning Enabling Act. In 1926, the U.S. Supreme Court ruled zoning laws constitutional. Congress followed this ruling by passing the Standard City Planning Enabling Act in 1928. With a legal framework in place, communities passed a barrage of "model" zoning and planning legislation in the next decade. Smaller communities saved money and adopted these "model" zoning ordinances. The result was that by the 1940s zoning and master planning, designed for our largest metropolitan areas, guided the urban development of most American cities.

Regardless of a community's size, zoning laws encourage segregated land use. Retail, commercial, industrial, and residential areas are segregated into different parts of the city. Small retail and single-family housing cannot exist in the same zone. Similarly, single- and multi-unit housing are usually zoned apart. Zoning covers subdivisions, and they are normally platted for a single housing type for a single socioeconomic group. This nation has always had racial and ethnic segregation, but the residential segregation of Americans by stage in the life cycle and lifestyle begins with these early zoning and subdivision regulations. Thus, zoning encourages low-density, specialized land use and contributes to sprawl. Although the fringe is demographically and economically diverse, it is different from the central city because groups and economic activities are separated from each other.

Local control of land-use decision making contributes to sprawl. There is no national land-use planning. Only a few states, like California, Washington, and Florida, have statewide land-use plans. We have regional planning of highways, water, and sewer systems, but local governments control most of the nation's infrastructure development.

Our culture and our national character contribute to sprawl. First, many Americans view the supply of land as virtually unlimited. The thirty-nine largest metropolitan areas in the United States cover an area the size of California and Alabama. The pro-growth lobby would say, "So what? This is less than 10 percent of the land area of the United States." Second, property rights are deeply ingrained in our national character. The U.S. Constitution protects them. The Supreme Court has limited the state's power to infringe upon them. Third, we distrust elected and appointed officials, so zoning regulations are written in exquisite detail. Bad people can't do bad things, but good people can't do good and innovative things, either. These social and cultural factors shape the planning profession. Planners and planning departments develop and approve plans within legal guidelines. They seldom question whether or not something should be developed in the first place.

Finally, there is the "American dream" of owning a single-family house on a spacious suburban lot. Our political process has translated this dream into reality. In the postwar period, the federal government subsidized suburban growth through the Interstate Highway Act of 1956, federal grants and loans for water and sewerage system development, subsidized FHA and VA home mortgages, as well as hidden subsidies like the mortgage interest income-tax deduction. The federal government encouraged fringe development in other, unintentional ways by making central cities less livable. Federally subsidized freeways made suburbs accessible, but destroyed viable neighborhoods. Ill-conceived federal urban renewal programs destroyed downtowns and inner-city neighborhoods rather than revitalizing them. Central cities became less livable, suburbs became more affordable, and millions of Americans moved to the fringe.

Other forces were at work as well. The baby boom had to be housed and schooled, and a postwar housing crisis had to be solved. In the 1930s, the housing sector came to a standstill during the Great Depression. In the 1940s, the war efforts swallowed the money and materials that would have normally gone into housing. By the 1950s, the nation was saddled with an old and worn housing stock and improved it by investing in the suburbs. Thus, a confluence of factors—legislative, judicial, cultural, and technological—played out over most of the twentieth century, creating the problem of sprawl that we face in the twenty-first century.

What Factors Affect Sprawl?

Los Angeles, whose traffic congestion and spread-out development have epitomized suburban sprawl for decades, doesn't have the worst sprawl after all. Nashville does. Several factors explain the extent of sprawl in a metro area. The availability of water is a major factor in limiting sprawl. For example, Las Vegas is one of the nation's most rapidly growing metro areas, but the scarcity of water forces developers to build close to the city's water lines. Similarly, oceans, mountains, and other natural barriers can force a metro to grow compactly. As much as critics malign Los Angeles, the Pacific Ocean to the west and mountains to the east constrain LA's growth. Regional planning tends to retard sprawl; a lack of it contributes to it. Powerful cultural forces also shape sprawl. Racial tensions and urban decay fuel white flight to the suburbs in metro areas in the Midwest and Northeast. Finally, local politics contributes to sprawl. Metros like Chicago and St. Louis, made up of dozens of municipalities each with their own zoning and planning power, make regional growth plans difficult (El Nasser, 2001). See *USA Today's* Sprawl Index at http://sprawl.usatoday.com for a ranking of 271 metro areas by sprawl, based on 1999 population data.

Sprawl Costs How Much?

Sprawl costs more than compact settlements. The Burchell report (1998) shows a growing consensus that we can no longer afford to build new infrastructure farther out while abandoning it in the central city and inner suburbs. The infrastructure costs for South Carolina are a good example. If sprawl continues, statewide infrastructure costs for the period 1995 to 2015 are projected to be more than $56 billion, or $750 per citizen per year for the next twenty years. Even with plans to curb infrastructure costs, the estimated cost of these improvements would require the state to increase the gasoline tax by 2 cents a gallon, increase the state sales tax by 0.5 percent, increase the property taxes by 12.5 percent, toll the state's interstates at thirty-mile intervals, impose impact fees on residential and nonresidential development of $2,000, and require a mandatory 10 percent set aside for infrastructure in all of the state's school districts (Burchell, 1998). Here is the dilemma: While state and local governments are building new roads, sewers, water systems, and other infrastructure improvements on the fringe, they are abandoning or underfunding existing infrastructure in the central cities and older inner suburbs. The complexity of the issue is reflected in the savings South Carolina would make if it immediately shifted to a managed growth policy; it would save only about 10 percent in the short run. The reason is that only part of infrastructure costs is growth related. Operating and maintaining the existing infrastructure of road, water and sewer systems, schools, hospitals, and public buildings make up the rest.

Policy changes should be driven by sound research. Dozens of studies have been published. They use different models, they are based on different assumptions, and they include different variables. Researchers usually compare current trends in land use (sprawl) with planned or compact development. Further complicating the research are the advocacy groups like 1000 Friends of Florida, 1000 Friends of Oregon, or the National Association of Homebuilders that fund much of it. But regardless of the study, infrastructure costs for compact development appear to be substantially lower than for sprawl. Roads and schools in compact developments cost 25 percent less, and water, sewer, and electricity 5 percent less. Governments have hidden many of these extra costs by subsidizing fringe growth through the deferred maintenance of the older infrastructure in the inner city and older suburbs. No longer. The 1990s saw higher home prices, larger mortgages, and higher utility bills for fringe developments, as these costs were passed on to consumers.

What Are the Other Social, Environmental, and Cost Issues?

Table 13.1 summarizes the pros and cons on each of these issues. As you can see, there is little agreement on any of them. The alleged negative impacts on transportation costs are more miles driven, longer travel times, more trips, and higher household travel costs. Alleged positive impacts are just the opposite—shorter commuting times, less congestion, lower governmental costs, and an efficient transportation system (Burchell, 1998, p. 42).

One would think that experts could agree on land/natural habitat preservation. They can't. The alleged negative impacts are a loss of agricultural land, reduced farmland, loss of fragile ecosystems, and reduced regional open space. The alleged positive impacts are enhanced personal and public open space (Burchell, 1998). As you can see in the table, debate over quality of life and social issues is even more contentious.

Consequently, with no consensus on the nature of the problem, there is little political will to change the status quo. Public opinion polls consistently show Americans favor sprawl development because it provides safe and economical neighborhoods removed from the problems of the central city. It also provides unlimited use of the automobile, segregates housing by race and income, fosters good schools, and requires lower property taxes. When residents wish to move, they typically leave in better financial condition, the result of almost certain appreciation of housing in fringe locations. Bankers, investors, and developers like sprawl development because the risks are known and manageable.

Until recently, the costs of sprawl have been cheap, but costs are beginning to increase. The recent jump in gasoline prices hurt the SUV market and gave many Americans pause about living on the suburban fringe. There is growing sentiment that current sprawl cannot continue and evidence that change is underway. The 1998 Transportation Equity Act funded transit bike paths and urban trails and allows states to shift money to mass transit (Li & Wachs, 2001). There are other signs as well. The majority of states have developed sustainable development regulations; government at the federal and state level has funded smart growth and open space land acquisition initiatives; and citizens approved $1.37 billion of bond issues for park and recreation projects in 1997 alone. There is growing support for public transportation, affordable housing, and environmental protection. Finally, and most important, the issue of sprawl has become part of the national political agenda.

Table 13.1   Alleged Negative and Positive Impacts of Sprawl

Substantive Concern	Alleged Negative Impacts	Alleged Positive Impacts
Public-Private Capital and Operating Costs	• Higher infrastructure costs • Higher public operating costs • More expensive private residential and nonresidential development costs • More adverse public fiscal impacts • Higher aggregate land costs	• Lower public operating costs • Less expensive private residential and nonresidential development costs • Fosters efficient development of "leapfrogged" areas
Transportation and Travel Costs	• More vehicle miles traveled • Longer travel times • More automobile trips • Higher household transportation spending • Less cost-efficient and effective transit • Higher social costs of travel	• Shorter commuting times • Less congestion • Lower governmental costs for transportation • Automobiles most efficient mode of transportation
Land/Natural Habitat Preservation	• Loss of agricultural land • Reduced farmland productivity • Reduced farmland viability • Loss of fragile environmental lands • Reduced regional open space	• Enhanced personal and public open space
Quality of Life	• Aesthetically displeasing • Weakened sense of community • Greater stress • Higher energy consumption • More air pollution • Lessened historic preservation	• Preference for low-density living • Lower crime rates • Enhanced value or reduced costs of public and private goods • Fosters greater economic well-being
Social Issues	• Fosters suburban exclusion • Fosters spatial mismatch • Fosters residential segregation • Worsens city fiscal stress • Worsens inner-city deterioration	• Fosters localized land use decisions • Enhances municipal diversity and choice

Source: Robert W. Burchell, Ed. 1998. *The Costs of Sprawl: Revisited.* Edited by R. W. Burchell, U.S. National Research Center. *Transit Cooperative Research Program.* Washington, D.C.: National Academy Press, p. 54.

Urban Planning

Around 2500 B.C.E., one of the world's earliest civilizations appeared in the Indus River system in what is now western Pakistan. Known as the Harappa Civilization, it imposed a uniform culture over an area of one-half million square miles. Its twin capitals—Harappa and Mohenjo-Daro—were remarkable in their size and uniformity. Straight, wide streets, running north-south and east-west, were laid out in a gridiron pattern forming rectangular blocks 1,200 feet by 800 feet. Each block housed a specific group: potters, weavers, brick makers, metal workers, and laborers. Most of the city's 20,000 inhabitants lived in rows of identical two-room dwellings. A small elite, though, lived in a segregated precinct near the city's center in houses built around courtyards. Many of these homes were multistoried and had wells and complex drainage systems. These cities also had refuse collection bins and a complex underground drainage system suggesting a concern for sanitation not shared by other urban societies at the time (Schwab, 1992).

Cities mirror the societies in which they are located. The archaeology of the Harappa's capitals suggests a powerful central government, a rigid social structure, and a preoccupation with public health. The Harappa Civilization also demonstrates that as long as there have been cities, there has been urban planning. The challenge to planners, then as now, is shaping the city's growth in socially valued ways. We stress *socially valued* because planners profoundly influence the quality of life of all urban residents.

When you buy a home you are actually buying a bundle of housing services. The location of your residence determines how far you live from work, school, parks and recreation, shopping, kin, and friends. It locks you into the community's social structure; it reflects your social status; it sustains your stage in the life cycle; and it shapes your lifestyle. Your personal safety, happiness, and well-being are all tied to where you live. Finding the right place to live is one of the most important decisions we make in life, and the fascinating thing about a city is that it is a product of millions of these individual decisions. People don't make these decisions in a vacuum, however. They make them within the city's physical and social structure, a structure shaped by planners at all levels of government.

The Planning Process

Metropolitan government in the United States is highly fragmented. In large metropolitan areas, thousands of people in hundreds of government units at the federal, state, regional, and local levels guide land-use decisions. Each group approaches land-use decisions with different goals, objectives, and interests. Regardless of the planning function, planning takes on at least four forms: (1) exploitive opportunity seeking, (2) ameliorative problem solving, (3) allocative trend modifying, and (4) normative goal oriented (Berry, 1973). I have added a fifth type, smart growth, a planning approach that fuses elements of the last two planning approaches with the smart growth social movement.

Exploitive opportunity seeking has deep roots in American communities. Used by community boosters, usually unelected business elites, it is growth for growth's sake. Because elected officials in these cities are often weak or incompetent, the business community fills in the vacuum. The business of business is business, and they have little concern for the infrastructure and social problems that unplanned growth creates. Small cities have traditionally used this approach to rapidly grow their economies, but a few big cities like Houston, Texas, still use this model. Houston has no zoning ordinances, nor does it have a master plan. It had one of the nation's most vibrant economies in the 1990s. It was also one of the nation's fastest-growing cities. But there were some trade-offs. The city has the worst air pollution, lowest water quality, and some of the worst traffic congestion, housing, and poverty rates in the nation.

When exploitive opportunity-seeking planning creates unmanageable urban problems, communities move to a planning model called **ameliorative problem solving**. This is a short-term reactive planning style dominated by elected officials and professional planning staffs. Power shifts to elected officials because the problems are so severe that business elites no longer have the time nor the will to tackle them. There is no long-term planning because planning departments spend most of their time taking care of emergencies. Often found in communities with a deep distrust of elected officials and professional bureaucrats, these cities usually have understaffed or underfunded planning departments that also limit their effectiveness. These first two planning styles are quickly dying out, however. In the twenty-first century, city governments must coordinate plans and programs with governments at the regional, state, and federal levels. Only full-time planning professionals have the education, experience, and time to cope with the complexity of the work. As a result, the vast majority of American cities have moved to other planning approaches.

Today, the **allocative trend-modifying** style of planning is the most common in large American cities. This style is proactive and dominated by planning professionals guided by policies approved by elected officials. In this planning approach, the business community is like any other special interest group, influencing the planning process through political means. With this planning strategy, planners and urban policy makers analyze past trends in population, land use, housing, and transportation and use these data to project future trends. They then use these projections to allocate resources to minimize costs and maximize benefits. Planners using this style emphasize citizen participation in the planning process, although it is often a hollow process. Experience has shown that the democratic element can reduce conflicts. It is a professionally oriented, top-down planning process.

So, too, is **normative goal-oriented planning**. This style is long associated with central planning in socialist and communist nations, but it is now part of most large regional and metropolitan planning departments. Often housed in a special division called "long-range planning," it is highly technical in nature and dominated by professional planning staffs. It is a proactive, long-range planning process. Planners create a vision of an ideal city, and they develop long range goals years or decades in advance. They receive feedback from other divisions in the planning department, and, when necessary, they advise city governments to modify existing trends to achieve their planning goals through regulatory means.

Slow-growth advocates, pro-growth advocates, inner-city advocates, and better-growth advocates are some of the grassroots groups promoting a new planning philosophy known as **smart growth**. Smart growth is reactive in the sense that the movement has grown to address the undesirable impacts of urban sprawl. It is proactive in the sense that it is based in four planning principles: (1) preserving large amounts of open space and protecting the quality of the environment, (2) redeveloping inner-core areas and developing in-fill sites, (3) removing barriers to urban design innovation in cities and new suburban areas, and (4) creating a greater sense of community and a greater recognition of regional interdependence and solidarity (Downs, 2001). This planning philosophy complements the previous two planning approaches. It is different because it is a bottoms-up, broad-based planning approach.

Smart Growth

Smart growth is a broad coalition of planners, developers, community activists, environmentalists, private nonprofit groups, and politicians. Although they disagree on many issues, they are united in their concern that current development patterns are no longer in the long-term interest of our society. Although supportive of growth, they question the economic costs of abandoning infrastructure in the city, only to rebuild it further out. They also question the social costs of the mismatch between new employment locations in the suburbs and the available workforce in the city. They question abandoning former industrial and manufacturing sites (*brownfields*) in older communities and developing the open space and prime agricultural lands at the suburban fringe. Demographic shifts, a strong environmental movement, increased fiscal concerns, and more balanced views of growth drive the smart growth movement.

Smart growth recognizes the connection between development and quality of life. It acknowledges that the features that distinguish smart growth vary from metro to metro and region to region. Smart growth focuses on restoring community and vitality to central cities and older suburbs. New smart growth developments are more town centered and pedestrian oriented and have a greater mix of housing, commercial, and retail uses. They also preserve open space, wetlands, and farms. Successful smart growth communities usually follow these principles:

- Mix land uses.
- Take advantage of compact building design.
- Create housing opportunities and choices.
- Create walkable communities.
- Foster distinctive, attractive communities with a strong sense of place.
- Preserve open space, farmland, natural beauty, and critical environmental areas.
- Strengthen and direct development toward existing communities.
- Provide a variety of transportation choices.
- Make development decisions predictable, fair, and cost effective.
- Encourage community and stakeholder collaboration in development decisions.

There is strong evidence that smart growth is fundamentally affecting the way we grow our cities. For example, the governors of twenty-six states championed smart growth initiatives in their 2000 legislative session. In Arizona the Republican governor Jane Dee Hull has championed statewide land-use planning since taking office. In 1997, the legislature passed her compromise legislation to better coordinate local and regional planning and created the Arizona Growing Smarter Commission. The commission limits sprawl in at least three ways: it provides citizens a real voice in community planning by giving them a vote on general plans; it requires development to pay for itself; and it allows cities and counties to restrict services to areas within their self-determined limits. The Arizona legislature passed the Growing Smarter Plus plan in 2000. The plan does away with piecemeal planning, subsidized growth, and irresponsible annexation. The package includes more than a dozen changes to the state's municipal zoning policies that encourage sprawl (Wells, 2001).

In 1999, Colorado's Republican governor Bill Owens introduced a package of incentives called "Smart Growth: Colorado's Future." The initiative created a Commission on Saving Ranches, Farms, and Open Spaces; established Colorado Heritage Communities; created the program Moving Forward to promote innovation and funding for transportation; and launched Opportunity Colorado to foster economic opportunity and entrepreneurship in Colorado's struggling communities. In the 2000 legislative session, Governor Owens helped win passage of six growth-related laws that provide tax incentives for developing low-income housing; funds for the redevelopment of brownfield sites (abandoned industrial and manufacturing sites); farm and open space conservation easements; and funds for the governor's Office of Smart Growth that coordinates regional planning in the Colorado Heritage Communities (Wells, 2001).

In Florida, Governor Jeb Bush launched two major growth-related initiatives shortly after taking office in 1999. The first, called Front Porch Florida, selected twenty inner-city communities for neighborhood revitalization. Governor Bush also signed the new Florida Forever law that extends the nation's most ambitious land and water conservation program. The program commits $3 billion over ten years to acquire, protect, and restore open space, greenways, and urban recreational land. It also funds certain water resource and supply projects. In 2001, the state partnered with the federal government's multibillion-dollar effort to restore the Everglades, the source of much of south Florida's water supply (Wells, 2001).

In an August 2000 address, Governor Bush outlined the way the state's land-use policies will change in the future. The newly created Florida Growth Management Study Commission will write the state's land-use master plan. This plan will guide Florida's development for the next quarter century. In the governor's charge to the commission, he urged members to require developers to assume a greater share of the costs of building in outlying suburbs, to give local governments more control of development decisions, to involve citizens in decision making, to protect the statewide environment, to preserve farmland, and to spend money on parks and other amenities to attract residents to live downtown (Wells, 2001).

Maryland has the nation's most comprehensive smart growth program. (See the state's web site, *Smart Growth* at *http://www.mdp.state.md.us/smartintro.htm*.) During his administration, former Democratic governor Parris Glendening pioneered a smart growth strategy based on targeting state investments. Under the law, counties work with the state to designate priority funding areas where they will encourage economic development and new growth. Local governments may plan for development outside the priority funding areas, but the state will not subsidize it (Wells, 2001).

In 2000, Maryland's General Assembly passed and funded the administration's entire package of smart growth bills. The package included the following:

> *Green Print:* a major initiative to protect Maryland's most endangered forests, greenways, wetlands, and other environmentally sensitive lands and to create an integrated network that links existing preserved areas to maximize environmental value. (Funded at $35 million in FY 2002.)
>
> *Neighborhood Parks and Playgrounds:* A competitive program that allows existing communities to establish or renovate parks and playgrounds, a

critical component of the overall quality of life that makes these neighborhoods attractive to residents. (Funded at $11 million in FY 2002.)

Community Legacy: A competitive program supporting neighborhood revitalization efforts, providing funds that fill in the gaps between existing programs and helping to focus communities on developing comprehensive strategies and approaches to revitalization. (Funded at $10 million in FY 2002.)

Special Secretary for Smart Growth: A small cabinet-level office that will provide a one-stop resource for communities, developers, and individuals seeking to use Maryland's toolbox of smart growth programs.

Mass-Transit Initiative: The General Assembly passed the majority of the governor's transit proposals, which will now invest more than $500 million in the next six years in upgrading mass-transit service and infrastructure and make significant progress toward the state goal of doubling ridership.

During the summer of 2000, Governor Glendening was elected chair of the National Governors Association (NGA) and created a new initiative "Where Do We Grow from Here?" Governor Glendening asked the NGA to focus on ways to help the nation's governors better steer future growth, increase preservation of our natural resources, encourage community revitalization, and assure that Americans maintain a high quality of life (Glendening, 2001).

Smart Growth Initiatives at the Local Level

State governments provide the legal framework for zoning and other land-use controls. State governments like Arizona, Colorado, Florida, and Maryland and twenty-two other states provide funding for programs that encourage smart growth, and legal frameworks that permit new land-use controls. But most land-use decisions are made at the local level by city and county governments. Evidence is also mounting that a fundamental change in development and land-use decision making is underway. We mentioned earlier the passage of hundreds of land-use initiatives in the 2000 election. You can get a feel for change by visiting the web sites of traditionally pro-growth organizations like the Planning Commissioners Journal (www.plannersweb.com). But the best way is to look at the plans of several communities.

The Greenline, San Jose, California

In 1950, San Jose was a modest city of 95,280 people living in a compact 17 square miles surrounded by farmland. In 1970, San Jose had expanded to 136 square miles with 445,000 people. Today, it occupies 174 square miles with a population of 835,000. After decades of uncontrolled growth of tract homes, shopping malls, and industrial parks, San Jose has adopted a long-term urban growth boundary, beyond which development will not be allowed. Planners call it the *greenline.* San Jose is one of a growing number of cities that has adopted smart growth strategies. Portland, Oregon, was the first, and Boulder, Colorado, and Minneapolis-St. Paul, Minnesota, soon followed. San Jose is the largest city to create an urban growth boundary. More important, more than a dozen smaller cities in northern California are considering adopting similar plans.

Studies funded by the city showed that extending urban services (roads, sewer, water, and schools) to new suburbs would cost the city more than it gained from any expected revenue increases stemming from the expansion. Setting growth limits is the strategy behind the city's 2020 General Plan, the city's road map for long-term urban development. The plan is based on an approach known as *in-fill development*. The idea is to shift growth to the inner part of a city, using vacant or underdeveloped areas for new housing and businesses. It accommodates growth within the city, with at least 126,000 new jobs and about 51,000 new housing units. The plan includes an "urban service area" boundary, which defines the area where urban services will be provided. The greenline is backed by the powerful Santa Clara Valley Manufacturing Group, which includes all the major Silicon Valley firms. But some developers argue that a green line is inflexible and represents an attempt to impose urban living on people who want to live in suburban conditions (Sneider, 1996).

Seattle, Washington

Washington State passed its Growth Management Act in 1990, and Seattle is an example of how a city can adapt to a state-mandated smart growth plan. Seattle, at the heart of the 2.5 million Puget Sound metropolis, actually lost population over the past thirty years. In 1970, it had a population of 530,000. By 2000, its population had dropped to just over half-million residents. Like most metro areas, growth was accommodated in suburbs and on the fringe. In 1970, Seattle housed 46 percent of King County's population; today it hovers around 34 percent.

Like San Jose, Seattle's master plan encourages in-fill. Seattle's plan defines three categories of urban villages. Five areas would be dense, commercially oriented "urban centers" where 45 percent of the city's 60,000 anticipated new housing units would be built over the next twenty years. Seven less-dense "hub urban villages" and seventeen "residential urban villages" would account for another one-third of expected growth. By concentrating growth in these areas, the areas surrounding Seattle that would normally be covered by suburban sprawl will remain undeveloped (Trumbull, 1994).

Even if the urban-village scheme succeeds in drawing the expected 72,000 new residents to Seattle, the surrounding region will still be growing faster than its biggest city. Although the city's vision may be headed in the right direction, observers worry that the costs may be exorbitant. Among the costs will be those for new parks, utilities, low-income housing subsidies, new bike and pedestrian paths, expanded bus service, and an experimental van transit program. Meanwhile, the school board is seeking more than $1 billion in construction bonds, and the three-county regional transit authority is considering spending twice that on new rail systems. There isn't a shortage of criticism of the plan. The local press contends, "The government class in this town has not faced up to the shortage of money and the shortage of voter confidence." An urban economist, James Hebert of Hebert Research Associates, notes, "Falling costs of electronic communication and transportation mean that fewer and fewer jobs are tied to big cities. There is no reason that people have to live in an urban environment at urban prices. The market doesn't have to grow into those boundaries at all" (Trumbull, 1994).

Centerton, Arkansas

Northwest Arkansas is the sixth-fastest-growing metropolitan area in the United States. The corporate home of Wal-Mart, the largest retailer in the world, it is also home to Tyson Foods, the world's largest integrated meat producer, and J. B. Hunt, the world's largest trucking firm. Some of the world's largest firms and hundreds of smaller ones have moved to Northwest Arkansas to service their Wal-Mart account. Proctor and Gamble, for example, has its second-largest office in northwest Arkansas, and for good reason; more than 20 percent of its world-wide sales come from this one account. The region's two counties, Benton and Washington, have grown by more than 57 percent, in large part because of the growth of Wal-Mart. What is fascinating to the press, and of keen interest to social scientists, is that the sprawl here is without a major central city (Glasser, 2001). Northwest Arkansas is not growing on the edge of a central city; it is blending four relatively small communities, Fayetteville, Springdale, Rogers, and Bentonville, into one, low-density, sprawling urbanized area. The largest city in the region in the 2000 census was Fayetteville with a population of only 55,000. Arkansas, a rural, populist state, has few state land-use controls. Northwest Arkansas has a regional planning office, but it is an information clearinghouse for local governments. Virtually all land-use decisions are left to local governments. The result is that Northwest Arkansas is making all of the same mistakes that every other region in the nation has made. Sprawl, and all of the problems associated with it, is very real in this region.

Centerton is a small, traditional farming community just six miles west of Wal-Mart's corporate headquarters. Overwhelmed by the region's sprawling development, community leaders decided to do something about it. They contacted David Glasser, the director of the University of Arkansas's Community Design Center and asked for his help. For the past decade, Glasser and his team of students from architecture, sociology, economics, business, and law have helped the state's small communities to revitalize through thoughtful design and development. With the Design Center's help, Centerton's City Council adopted in early 2001 a comprehensive plan to control sprawl. One of the interesting strategies the city used was the preemptive platting of the entire city. Developers have wide latitude in planning a subdivision. They purchase a farm or a block of land; hire an engineering firm to lay out the streets, lots, and setbacks; and submit the plan to the city's planning department. As long as the plan meets the city's general guidelines, the plan is accepted and the plat is recorded with the county. Developers typically build a subdivision with curving streets with plenty of dead-end cul-de-sacs. This is what the National Homebuilders Association tells them will sell. The result is isolated, unconnected developments. By platting the entire city, the council members, not the developers, are guiding the community's development. The city's street layout follows smart growth principles. It is laid out in an interconnected gridiron pattern, lots are narrow and deep, and the homes are built close to the street. Mixed housing types and mixed land use are permitted, and the neighborhoods are interconnected. The downtown zoning regulations reflects these same planning principles—human scale, pedestrian-oriented, and community-enhancing development. If a place like Centerton is using smart growth, I would argue, the nation is in the midst of a planning revolution.

Planning Solutions

So how does a community go about reshaping the development juggernaut? Here are a few of the tools used by communities pursuing smart growth planning.

Land-Use Regulations

Current smart growth regulations have evolved over the past twenty years from straightforward zoning controls and master plans into full-blown experiments with growth restrictions, fair share housing guidelines, and other techniques to guide and manage growth. These initiatives have altered the traditional roles of the public and private sectors in development and have generated thousands of lawsuits. Commonly used techniques include construction codes, setback requirements, height limitations, density requirements, and sewer hook-up restrictions. Development policies also include targeted areas for redevelopment, direct new housing development, and industrial parks development. These are the most conservative tools used by communities pursuing smart growth.

Job/Housing Balance

Much of the fringe development occurs in the boondocks. You have housing but none of the amenities associated with urban life. The job can be an hour away in one direction. The grocery twenty minutes in another. Even the most mundane things like taking the children to the doctor or making a hair appointment requires a major investment of time, money, and energy. The stress on commuters is high. The strain on family relationships is even higher. Long commutes have fueled the clamor for growth management in which the jobs/housing balance issue and traffic congestion play an important role. A relatively new solution to the problem of increased suburban traffic congestion is the concept of jobs/housing balance. Local and regional planners increasingly support the notion of expanding the supply of housing in job-rich areas and the quantity of jobs in housing-rich areas. Ideally, a ratio of one job for every dwelling unit would represent a balance. But in many households, more than one person is employed so that more jobs than housing would be a better balance.

Growth Management

This technique usually includes three elements: (1) orderly infrastructure development, (2) environmental preservation, and (3) quality of life and design considerations. This is becoming the dominant form of planning in the United States. Washington State, Florida, and Oregon currently use this approach.

In the past, cities have passed on the costs of transportation, water, and sewer systems for new development to all the rate payers. The philosophy of growth management is making developments pay for themselves. Impact fees on new projects are the most popular means of shifting the cost to developers. These fees provide a way to pay for facilities and avoid service shortages. A similar technique is called *orderly infrastructure development.* Typically, these policies support development, but channel it into areas already serviced by utilities. It prevents the leapfrog development associated with sprawl. At the end of the continuum are urban service boundaries, areas that cannot be developed. Portland, San Jose, and Seattle are examples of cities that have enacted this type of restriction on fringe development.

Environmental preservation/protection initiatives related to growth management gained prominence in the United States in the 1990s, especially in sensitive areas such as wetlands, coastal areas, and mountain environments. California and

Florida have coastal commissions. The Federal Emergency Management Agency (FEMA) is purchasing vulnerable properties in flood plains and returning it to wetlands. The federal government's flood insurance program no longer insures new coastal and flood-prone development.

The third focus on growth management involves quality of life issues and design guidelines for development, such as architectural control, setbacks, and land-use mixing, which are akin to the more traditional policy power of zoning.

Other Smart Growth Management Tools

There are numerous tools at the disposal under each of these groups. We have already discussed zoning. Other techniques include construction codes, setback requirements, height limitations, density requirements, and sewer hook-up restrictions. Finally, development policies include areas targeted for redevelopment, direct new housing development, or the creation of industrial parks. Naturally, all of these planning stages assume that planners can operate in a detached, objective manner. It is also assumed that planners can predict the effects of alternative plans. These assumptions have been strongly criticized by some. Molotch and Logan (1987) talk about the "growth machine"—bankers, developers, and construction firm owners who work alone and in concert to bias the outcomes of planning commissions and development departments. David Harvey (1985) suggests that planning is really a technique for redistributing wealth.

Backlash Against Smart Growth Initiatives

Maryland is a national leader in fighting urban sprawl, through a program called Smart Growth and Neighborhood Conservation that tries to manage new development while rejuvenating city centers. Advocates of smart growth say uncontrolled suburban development is economically irresponsible, socially destructive, and environmentally harmful. Thirteen other states have similar comprehensive programs, and the list is growing. As the movement gains momentum, so does the resistance. In Carroll County, Maryland, officials have responded to the state's Smart Growth program by taking matters into their own hands. In 1999, the county's three-person elected commission approved a zoning change that would allow a golfing community to build on a 425-acre farm. More recently, the commission voted to move forward with development in the county's vast watershed area, which contains the state's primary source of drinking water, Liberty Reservoir. Those decisions, pushed by Republicans, infuriated then-governor Parris Glendening, a Democrat and influential anti-sprawl crusader who chaired the National Governors Association. The dilemma is clear. While a family on one side of the development line is stuck on a money-losing farm, the Rash farm across the street can be sold for about $75,000 per acre (Brown, 2001).

There are similar backlashes occurring elsewhere. In Oregon, an approved referendum requires states to pay landowners when they lose money because of property-use restrictions. In Arizona and Colorado, voters last year rejected broad measures that would allow the states to manage local development. Dairy farmers in New England are facing the same difficulties as the crop farmers in other parts of the country.

The New Urbanism

Smart growth refers to the broad coalition of planning professionals, community activists, politicians, and ordinary citizens who are addressing the problems of sprawl. Spearheaded by private nonprofit organizations, like the Smart Growth Network, the coalition contends that cities can grow in socially responsible ways. It is a new voice in a planning process traditionally dominated by planners and the growth machine, and it is changing the nation's urban landscape.

The new urbanism movement is part of the smart growth coalition, and it refers to a group of architects, planners, and developers who are actually building neighborhoods and communities based on these new planning principles. People at the forefront of the new urbanism movement formed the Congress for the New Urbanism (CNU) in 1996. The *Charter of the New Urbanism*, signed in the spring of that year, states that new urbanists stand for "restoration of existing urban centers and towns within coherent metropolitan regions, the reconfiguration of sprawling suburbs into communities of real neighborhoods and diverse districts, the conservation of natural environments, and the preservation of our built legacy" (Congress for the New Urbanism, 2001). (See the complete charter at *http://www.cnu.org.*) The Congress developed guidelines for new public policies and development practices, stating that "neighborhoods should be diverse in use and population; communities should be designed for the pedestrian and transit as well as the car; cities and towns should be shaped by physically defined and universally accessible public spaces and community institutions; and urban places should be framed by architecture and landscape design that celebrate local history, climate, ecology, and building practice" (Congress for the New Urbanism, 2001).

The new urbanists have introduced a succession of new terms into the American lexicon like *sustainable development, traditional neighborhood development (TND), neotraditional neighborhood (NTN), suburban in-fill, central-city in-fill,* and *brownfield redevelopment* (Steuteville, 1998). These terms all refer to a set of design principles known as *neotraditional planning.* It is called neotraditional because these planners are using elements from traditional towns and villages, types of communities that have been important in our history. New urbanists use these principles to change the nature of development from sprawling conventional subdivisions to compact, interconnected communities. The key principles of new urbanism are as follows:

- Development occurs in compact, walkable neighborhoods with clearly defined edges and centers.
- Without excluding automobiles, their presence should be minimized.
- Diverse activities (residences, shops, schools, workplaces, and parks) should be accommodated.
- A wide spectrum of housing options should enable people of a broad range of incomes, ages, and family types to live within a single neighborhood.
- Existing urban centers should be restored within coherent metropolitan areas that protect the built legacy (Atkin, 1998).

The Nation's Rich Legacy of New Town Development

The new urbanism represents a continuation of a long tradition of new town development in this society. We carved our nation out of a frontier, and, in a sense, every community is a new town. But when we speak of new towns, we are referring to community building shaped by a religious or a social philosophy. Founders of new towns have a vision of a better society, and they believe they can create their vision by changing the built environment. For example, in the three decades prior to the Civil War, every conceivable form of communal living was tried in the United States. There were communities built on religious principles like the Shaker communities, Hopedale, and Brook Farm. The Oneida Community in upstate New York practiced an early form of eugenics called *stirpiculture*, the selective breeding of humans. And Old World reformers like Robert Owen and Charles Fourier created communities based in primitive communism and socialism. Remarkably some of the buildings and streets from these early experiments still survive in Cleveland, Ohio; New Milford, Massachusetts; and New Harmony, Indiana (Tyler, 1944). New town development resumed after the Civil War, but this time they were built not by religious and social visionaries, but by large corporations. Paternalism created Pullman, Illinois, and Hershey, Pennsylvania. Worker riots at Pullman ended that social experiment.

Responding to the horrific conditions found in the late nineteenth- and early twentieth-century city, a group of American reformers founded the American Garden City Movement in the opening decades of last century. Borrowing concepts from the British reformer and planner Ebenezer Howard, they built their first and most famous new community, Radburn, in 1928. Built in northern New Jersey, a few miles from Manhattan's George Washington Bridge, it was based on the neighborhood unit and had many of the design elements touted by today's new urbanists. The Great Depression ended the Radburn experiment, but others followed. During the depression, the federal government built three greenbelt towns—Greenhills near Cincinnati, Greenbelt near Washington, D.C., and Greendale near Milwaukee—following neighborhood-oriented, pedestrian-friendly principles. Although these communities have drifted from their original design principles, they are still viable communities today. Baldwin Hills in Los Angeles and Chatham Green near downtown Pittsburgh stayed true to their planners' vision, and today they demonstrate the promise of careful, thoughtful development (Stein, 1966).

In the postwar period, rapid suburbanization defined the nation's urban growth. As early as the 1950s, sociologists like Herbert Gans and William H. Whyte raised warnings about suburban sprawl. By the 1970s, the environmental, transportation, and social costs of suburban growth set the stage for a next round of new town development. This time it was on a much larger scale. James Rouse, the famous banker and commercial developer, began construction on Columbia, Maryland, in the early 1970s. North of the capital, in the rapidly growing Baltimore-Washington corridor, Columbia's design was based on the neighborhood and community unit. Neighborhoods had amenities like grocery stores; neighborhoods were clustered around a community center with recreation, schools, and shopping; and the communities were organized around a city center dominated by a regional mall. Today, Columbia has a community college, it is the summer home of the Washington Symphony, and 100,000 people call it home.

Reston, Virginia, south of Washington, D.C., was more upscale, but it was plagued with financial problems from the beginning. It, too, was designed around neighborhoods and community centers. It, too, had a city center, and it won a series of design awards. It was even able to attract a significant amount of local employment. But neither Columbia nor Reston or the other large-scale new towns of this era were very profitable. Faced with enormous front-end costs, land acquisition and legal problems, and opposition from local politicians and planning departments, this era in new town development ended by the 1980s.

The New Urbanism: The Nation's Newest Attempt at New Towns

New urbanism, therefore, is the continuation of a long heritage of new town development. The new urbanists have learned from the past. For example, they promote the integration of commercial and residential land uses. A convenience store is considered an appropriate use on a residential street corner. Small offices at the rear of residences and apartments above stores are part of their plans.

New urbanists believe that the optimal size of a neighborhood is the distance a person can cover in a five-minute walk, about a quarter mile. Conveniences like a dry cleaner, a grocery, and a cafe are a short walk away in the village center. Children can meet up with their friends and walk to the nearby public elementary school. To keep things within walking distance, neotraditional neighborhoods are more compact with smaller lots, and they have more multifamily units. Houses are close together and set close to the street. There is an unabashed element of nostalgia in the new urbanism movement. Homes in these neighborhoods are usually of traditional designs following styles found in Charleston, Savannah, Georgetown, or a New England village. Most homes have porches, reaching nearly to the sidewalks. Pedestrians rule in NTNs. Neighborhoods are linked to town centers, village squares, parks, and greenbelts by sidewalks. Streets are built in a gridiron pattern so the community is interconnected, not isolated into cul-de-sacs. Streets are usually narrow to slow traffic. Garages face alleys. NTNs are built to diminish, but not eliminate, the need for the automobile. New urbanists believe these design elements increase the number of chance encounters among residents. Chance encounters lead to neighboring and friendships, and these interactions are the stuff that creates community (Duany, Plater-Zyberk, & Speck, 2000).

As in other eras of new town development, there is an element of social engineering. The major goal of the new urbanists is to reduce the problems of sprawl. New urbanists also believe that many of our social problems can be linked to the segregation of groups in cities. They believe that the physical distance between groups breeds social distance between them. Mixed land use and mixed housing by type, style, and cost lowers the age, income, and racial segregation that characterizes today's suburbs. For example, a mansion and subsidized housing are built on the same street, so families of different incomes live side by side. There simply isn't the segregation of income and racial groups in neotraditional developments that one finds in current suburbs (Tu & Eppli, 1999). Again, the assumption is that chance, informal encounters on the sidewalk, corner store, library, or village center will bring about greater understanding between different groups.

Another important change is the integration of people in different stages in the life cycle. In neotraditional neighborhoods, a family can move through the life cycle and still live in the same neighborhood. Traditional suburbs cater to people in different stages of the life cycle. We segregate singles from young couples and couples with children from retirees. Americans usually accommodate change in family size by moving. In most cities, finding a new house means moving to a new neighborhood. And when you move, you disrupt your social network. In NTNs as a family grows, they can move to a larger house on the same street because there is mixed land use. When the children leave home, the parents can move to a smaller home on the next street. When the couple retires, there are apartments on the same block. And when a partner dies or divorces, there's a carriage house or a detached bungalow available nearby. There is continuity because moves don't disrupt social networks (Paul, 2001).

The first development inspired by the neotraditional approach was Seaside in Walton County, Florida. The biggest and best-known example, however, is Disney's 4,900-acre town of Celebration, Florida (see Photo 13.2), which eventually will have 8,000 homes and already has a $200 million town center. Other examples of new building inspired by the traditional neighborhood concept are Kentlands in Gaithersburg, Maryland; Harbor Town in Memphis, Tennessee; and Laguna West in Sacramento County, California. Five years ago, few neotraditional neighborhoods existed in the United States. Today more than 100 have been built, with an additional 200 on the drawing board. The movement's journal, the *New Urban News*, reports investment in NTNs has nearly doubled, from $1.2 billion in 1997 to $2.1 billion in 2000. Moreover, local planning boards in sprawl-plagued areas like Miami's Dade County are creating zones dedicated solely to such development. The trend is growing. In the 2000 legislative session, twenty-one states passed smart growth legislation (Padgett, 2001).

Photo 13.2   *Celebration, Florida, a few miles from Disney World, is based on the principles of the New Urbanism. Note the short setbacks, sidewalks, and nineteenth century style of the homes.* (*Source:* Photo by the author's son, Judd Schwab.)

Thus, the principles of the new urbanism are shaping hundreds of communities across the nation's urbanscape. The most familiar are new communities built from scratch on undeveloped land. But older cities and towns are reinventing themselves with central-city in-fills, and even rural communities are rethinking their growth and reshaping future development. Let's consider a few examples.

Kentlands, Maryland: A New, New Urbanism Community

Kentlands is a 352-acre project in Gaithersburg, Maryland, thirteen miles northwest of Washington, D.C. The original master plan included 1,600 dwelling units, 1 million square feet of office space, and 1.2 million square feet of retail space. Due to the excess supply of office space in the region, the office component of the development has been postponed (Tu & Eppli, 1999).

The neighborhood of Kentlands is designed by the planners of Seaside, Florida—Duany, Plater-Zyberk and Company—and applies the principles of the new urbanism. Designed for the pedestrian, it integrates homes, offices, stores, and civic buildings for a diverse population. Following new urbanism principles, it is sensitive to the ecology and culture of the local area. It is a compact, pedestrian-friendly community that offers residents greater opportunities for neighboring and participation in community life than most suburbs.

Sited on the historic Kent Farm tract, Kentlands includes a variety of public open spaces, which cover approximately 28 percent of the development. Wetlands preserves, greenbelts, and small town squares help to define individual neighborhoods. Each neighborhood has its distinctive character. For example, the Old Farm neighborhood surrounds the original Kent homestead, which currently serves at the town's cultural arts center. The Hill District overlooks the Old Farm and the wetlands and is centered on a community clubhouse. Housing types in Kentlands include single-family detached homes, town homes, condominiums, apartments, and carriage houses. Kentlands is not the ideal of economic diversity. While the homes do vary block by block—from $175,000 townhouses to $600,000 mansions—there is virtually no low-income housing. This is due, in large part, to the high real estate costs in the Washington-Baltimore corridor.

At first glance, the settlement seems old. Adorned with white picket fences and large front porches, the Colonial and Victorian homes vary in size, shape, and color. The sidewalks, meanwhile, funnel pedestrians into nearby village centers and parks, made possible in part by clustering homes closely together. As in most neo-traditional developments, the homes have short setbacks, and alleys replace the driveways and garages in front of houses. Kentlands has more than three miles of walking/jogging trails, and the community's youth center provides a cinema, CD store, pizza parlor, and skating rink for teenagers (Padgett, 2001). To encourage the use of public transportation, a shuttle service is provided to a nearby Washington Metro station. Neotraditional neighborhoods, classically styled architectural design, a greenbelt, parks, and recreation, with urban amenities only a short stroll from home set Kentlands apart from conventional subdivisions (Tu & Eppli, 1999).

Kentlands is a work in progress. The commercial Main Street area is completed, and the live/work units were scheduled for occupancy in 2001. The nearby community of Lakelands, which follows new urban design principles and borders and connects with Kentlands, was also set to open in 2001, and the two communities should provide a greater mix of commercial and residential uses and additional options for transit. With acres of connected greenways protecting the natural systems, the preservation of mature trees, and networks of pedestrian trails throughout the two communities, a new type of community is being created in Gaithersburg, Maryland (Kentlands Community Foundation, 2000). Read more about the community on the Kentlands Community Foundation web site at *www.kentlands.org* or *www.kentlandsusa.com.*

Broomfield, Colorado: The New Urbanism Reshapes an Old Community

Already-developed towns like Broomfield are examples of how a community can weave the principles of new urbanism into a complex world of zoning laws, property rights, road-engineering codes, the realities of the local economy, and citizen concerns. Framed by the Rocky Mountains in the rapidly growing Denver-Boulder corridor, Broomfield is a small farming community shaped by the area's agricultural and farming heritage. Broomfield, like many small communities, is being overwhelmed by sprawl. In an effort to curb sprawl, preserve open space, and save its small-town character, Broomfield is creating a new master plan and has hired Peter Calthorpe, one of the nation's best-known new urbanist architects, to create it. According to Calthorpe;

> *The problem for Broomfield and many cities isn't growth per se; it's how growth usually occurs that is so harmful to our environment and our sense of community. . . . The problem is that in appealing to people's desire for solitude, safety, and predictability, most modern suburbs are showcases for repetitious architecture that gobbles up open space and caters more to cars than people. (Salisbury, 1996)*

Broomfield's new master plan requires all future developments to be built in accordance with new urbanism principles. Broomfield's new downtown will mix retail outlets with office space and some residential apartments. At the same time, the master plan calls for the creation of a half dozen smaller village centers built near residential communities, where residents can walk to video stores, pick up their dry cleaning, or take out a book from a satellite library outlet. The new urbanism is still catching on. Broomfield is just one of a half dozen nearby communities using the new urban framework for planning growth. There is opposition. The idea of mixed use was controversial because people objected to the noise and traffic of commercial properties next to residential areas. Many in Broomfield didn't like the idea of high-population densities and mixing housing sizes and style into each city block. Community leaders modified Calthorpe's original plan, and new housing will be built at lower densities and segregated by income (Salisbury, 1996). See the master plan and learn more about Broomfield at *www.ci.broomfield.co.us.*

Paradise at Parkside: An Example of Central-City In-Fill

Paradise and Paradise at Parkside in Washington, D.C., are examples of what the new urbanism calls *central-city in-fill.* In the redevelopment of one of the district's most crime-ridden neighborhoods, planners have transformed a stark, high-rise development into a middle-class community called Paradise and its sister community, Paradise at Parkside. Paradise had all the ills associated with high-rise, low-income public housing. The architects, following new urbanism principles, reestablished a traditional Washington, D.C., grid, complete with a park square.

Once the high rises were demolished, the developers replaced them with town houses and larger condominium buildings on corner lots. All the units have small yards. Landscaping takes off the sharp edges. With comfortable houses, pleasantly scaled streets, and landscaped yards, the quality of life in Paradise has soared while crime rates have declined (Sands, 1998).

Paradise and Paradise at Parkside are just part of a larger program transforming public housing through HUD's HOPE VI program. The Congress for New Urbanism partnered with HUD in this successful revitalization effort, which offers communities a unique chance to incorporate the principles of the new urbanism in older inner suburbs and central cities. CNU developed a set of 14 Principles for Inner-City Neighborhood Design that will guide HUD's future public housing construction and redevelopment (U.S. Department of Housing and Urban Development, 1999 HOPE VI 52E).

Will They Work?

Will neotraditional neighborhoods work? Can they deliver on their promises, especially since amenities like community pools, hiking trails, and greenbelts can add more than 10 percent to the cost of homes? Can they sell a $250,000 home with a lot only about the size of its foundation? Will retailers move in before the community is finished? The jury is still out, but the evidence is mounting that the answer is a qualified yes.

Mark Eppli and Charles Tu, professors at George Washington University in Washington, D.C., wanted to find out if consumers were willing to pay more for single-family homes built in new urbanist communities than for those in conventional suburbs. To find out, they compared home prices of four neotraditional developments that opened in the early 1990s with conventional suburbs with similar housing types and styles. Their findings suggest that consumers are willing to pay significantly more for a home with the same amenities (about 11 percent) in a new urbanist community over comparable homes in conventional subdivisions. The researchers found that architectural design, walkability, public open space, and an enhanced sense of community were the elements that appealed most to consumers (Tu & Eppli, 1999).

In the past decade, developers have made mistakes in housing mix and design, poor consumer research, and overpricing, but they are learning their markets. Developers have learned that a convenience store or general store plus other retail shops are high-priority amenities that people want right away. Greenbelts, hiking and jogging trails, and small neighborhood parks are also high on consumers' wish lists. Market research shows lot sizes, which are generally smaller than in typical subdivisions, must be roughly compatible with buyer preferences in a particular market. As we have seen, consumers in the Baltimore-Washington, D.C., corridor will accept smaller lots; consumers in the Denver-Boulder corridor will not. As developers learn the rules of the new urbanism and learn how to fit their projects into local markets, they are enjoying better sales. Surveys of homeowners in neotraditional developments show that they expect their homes to appreciate faster than conventional developments (Muto, 1999).

Market research also shows that the smaller yards of NTNs don't appeal to established families with elementary- and junior-high-school-age children. But NTNs do attract young married couples, parents with young children, single parents who like the lower-priced units, and preretirement empty-nesters. Clearly, these communities are not for everyone (Atkin, 1998).

Will They Create a Sense of Community?

The premise of new urbanism is that a design that celebrates the public realm and planning features that enhance pedestrian over auto travel will facilitate social interaction and create a sense of community. Data from interviews with residents of Kentlands and several other NTN communities of the East Coast reveal that there is increased social interaction. Moreover, this interaction appears to strengthen communal relations and created a sense of community. Children are not isolated in a closed social system. They appear to be introduced to society beyond community boundaries like children in conventional subdivisions (Kim, 2000; Langdon, 1997).

Critics of the Smart Growth and the New Urbanism

Smart growth, elements of which have been adopted by twenty-one states, promises answers to the problems facing community leaders and planners. The new urbanism is a vision of recapturing community life. Critics note that smart growth only slows growth—it doesn't stop it—and that the new urbanism simply makes higher densities more tolerable. Critics of these approaches argue that neither approach can change the fact that growth in metropolitan areas will result in overcrowding, traffic congestion, and poor air quality, regardless of what we do. Gridlock is simply a function of too many people living in a metro area, and neither new planning doctrines nor money will solve it.

There are other solutions. A great deal of literature addresses optimum city size, but it is seldom discussed. In a democratic society can we tell people they can no longer move to a metro area? Can we tell people they must live someplace else, a less-desirable place, because there is no room? The former Soviet Union and the People's Republic of China tried it. It didn't work. There is no discussion on limiting growth, because there is no marketable alternative to current development (Carson, 2000).

Why do our cities continue to grow? Because our population continues to grow. By 2050, the United States will have 400 million people. Where is the discussion about population controls? Where is the discussion about immigration reform? Similarly, the 2000 census showed that we are becoming a nation of singles and small households. Where are the innovative programs that address the housing needs of this group? The bottom line: If we want to stop sprawl, we must address the underlying population issues. Neither smart growth nor the new urbanism addresses these issues.

Other critics note that the new urbanism movement attempts to influence and improve urban environments through changes in the physical design of neighborhoods. But neighborhoods have an organic nature and evolve in form over time. The imposition of new urbanism architectural standards, critics argue, impedes this process. Further, critics point out that the new urbanism promotes cultural and economic integration, but they build segregated communities, culturally biased in favor of the middle class. It is based on an exclusionary notion of community, (Lehrer & Milgrom, 1998).

Critics make other arguments as well:

1. Smart growth infringes on the property rights of citizens.
2. Markets, not government officials, should determine land-use. Dynamic markets have created a society with the highest rates of homeownership in the industrial world. Why change a good thing?

3. The process of urban growth and development is poorly understood. Smart growth principles may do more harm than good.

4. New urbanism developments are Disney-like and kitschy. There is a fakeness, naïve materialism, and sentimental attachment to Euro-American designs.

5. They are nostalgic designs from a bygone era. New urbanists have an unrealistic and incorrect interpretation of the good old days. Mixed neighborhoods in the past seldom worked like the new urbanists envision them. In the past, ethnically, racially, and income-mixed neighborhoods were a source of conflict, not understanding.

6. Smart growth and the new urbanism are elitist. It is a movement driven by people with a narrow, middle-class value system.

7. Critics note that it is a return to changing human behavior through design. They argue that an enormous body of evidence shows it has never worked in the past, so why should it work now?

8. The nature and character of communities is the result of unplanned natural forces that are still poorly understood. There are many unintended consequences, yet to be observed.

9. Smart growth planning may actually lead to more traffic congestion.

10. Developers are often left out of the process. The movement has never really addressed the issue of whether or not this type of development is profitable. (Calthorpe, 2000)

The Smart Growth Network is aware of this criticism and provides a biography of the works of the major critics of the smart growth and new urbanism movement on the web site at *www.smartgrowth.org/library/*

The City in the Future

American planners have looked to visionaries to shape the future of our cities. The famous architect Frank Lloyd Wright envisioned a decentralized garden city called *Broadacre City*. In Wright's vision there were no large buildings or high rises, and each family lived on at least one acre. It was an automobile-dependent community. In many ways his dream came to be; we call it *suburban sprawl*.

The French planner Le Corbusier's vision was the *Radiant City*. At the city's center, he saw skyscrapers surrounded by parks and open spaces. Nearby residential skyscrapers were organized into super blocks, again, surrounded by green space. In many respects his vision became reality, but instead of parks and green space, buildings, parking lots, and streets surround skyscrapers. We have already discussed Ebenezer Howard's vision of the *garden city*. Garden cities were built, and many are successful, but they have had only a minor impact on our nation's urban development.

What vision should we have for our cities in the future? What can we expect in 2050? We believe you need look only as far as the city around you, because the city of your children and grandchildren will look pretty much as it does today. Cities will change; planners will modify the built environment; but the cities we live in today will be the canvas upon which the cities of the future will be built. We can predict how our cities will change by revisiting some of the urban processes we have already explored in the text.

First, we live in the midst of the revolution of globalization. Globalization is fundamentally changing our economy and our society. It now appears that metropolitan areas and the regional economies in which they are embedded will be the economic units that compete for business in the global economy. We introduce the concept of city-state to describe this emerging urban form. City-states, not nation-states, will compete in the global economy. To compete successfully, a city-state must provide a safe, service-rich environment that appeals to international investors. They must also provide a high quality of life for the symbolic analysts who run the global economy. City-states must have vibrant central business districts with restaurants, shopping, and entertainment. They must have world-class medical complexes and universities, professional sport teams, museums, and other urban amenities. They must have good public education. They must have a transportation and communication infrastructure that works. Most important, they must have domestic tranquility, which means dealing with the problems of social inequality and justice. Regional and metropolitan government is a part of this vision of the city of 2050.

Second, suburban sprawl will no longer be the dominant form of urban growth in this society. In the 2000 legislative season alone, twenty-one states passed smart growth initiatives. States like California, Oregon, Washington, Colorado, Florida, and especially Maryland have comprehensive, statewide initiatives to control sprawl. So how will cities in 2050 grow? We believe they will use techniques like inner-city and suburban in-fill. Cities will shift costs to developers rather than spreading the costs across all the residents of a city. This change in the development calculus, along with reforms of zoning, master planning, and other traditional planning tools, will change the urbanscape. Housing and population density will grow as a result. Density levels may even become high enough for alternative forms of transit—like light rail.

Third, the automobile will continue to be the dominant transportation form shaping our cities. Although population densities will increase, U.S. cities will still have the lowest housing and population densities in the industrial world.

Fourth, the new urbanism will shape urban development in North American cities, but it will be one of many competing visions of the city. Money talks, and members of the growth machine will continue to have the greatest influence on urban development.

Fifth, propinquity and location will be less important in the city in 2050. Broadband Internet and related technologies will permit new forms of social organization. The city elements, like privatopias and dreamscapes, described by the LA School will be found in all North American cities.

Finally, every city has a signature space. San Francisco has Fisherman's Wharf and Union Square, Boston its Back Bay and the Commons, Seattle its Pike Street Market and Space Needle, and New Orleans its French Quarter and Garden District. Every city, regardless of how big or small, has a space that is just as distinctive. The city of 2050 or 2100 will have these signature spaces, too, because these cities will still hold these urban forms from the past. The city is always in a process of becoming, and the past will continue to determine the present and shape the city of the future.

Summary

This chapter explores the planning process and the role planning plays in the growth and development of our cities. Our discussion was framed by the problem of sprawl. We showed that this issue has become part of the nation's political agenda: 70 percent of the 250 growth-related ballot initiatives passed in 1997, and the legislatures in twenty-one states passed smart growth legislation in 2000.

Sprawl has become an issue because it is occurring so rapidly. Between 1982 and 1997, cropland declined by 13 million acres, pasture land by 14 million acres, and range land by 12 million acres. While most of this development is associated with suburban sprawl, sprawl has become a prominent feature in small- and medium-sized cities as well. Sprawl is occurring in almost every county, and at a significant level in one-fifth of the nation's 3,200 counties. But not all regions are affected equally. Factors like the age and size of a metro's central city, the health of a region's economy, the region's climate, and the state and metro's history of land-use controls also affect sprawl. Like global warming, there's urgency in the decision making because policy makers fear that unless something is done now, the process will be irreversible.

We defined sprawl as the the spread-out, skipped-over development that characterizes the non-central-city metropolitan areas and nonmetropolitan areas of the United States. Sprawl is one- or two-story single-family residential development on lots ranging in size from one-third to one acre accompanied by strip commercial centers and industrial parks, also two stories or less in height and with similar amount of land takings. We also reviewed how you measure it, what form it takes, why it occurs, and how much it costs.

We explored the role of planners in shaping the city and controlling sprawl. The challenge to planners is shaping the city's growth in socially valued ways because planners profoundly influence the quality of life of all urban residents. Regardless of the planning function, planning takes on at least four forms: (1) exploitive opportunity seeking, (2) ameliorative problem solving, (3) allocative trend modifying, and (4) normative goal oriented. We added a fifth type, smart growth as a planning approach that fuses elements of the last two planning approaches with the smart growth social movement.

Smart growth is a broad coalition of planners, developers, community activists, environmentalists, private nonprofit groups, and politicians. Although they disagree on many issues, they are united in their concern that current development patterns are no longer in the long-term interest of our cities, existing suburbs, small towns, rural communities, or wilderness areas. Smart growth encourages things like mixed land use, compact building design, housing choice, and walkable communities. They also promote making development decisions predictable, fair, and cost effective, and they encourage community and stakeholder collaboration in development decisions. Smart growth advocates are having an impact. For example, the governors of twenty-six states championed smart growth initiatives in their 2000 legislative session.

We reviewed smart growth initiatives in San Jose, California; Seattle, Washington; and Centerton, Arkansas. We reviewed smart growth tools like the modification of traditional land-use regulations, job/housing linkage, and growth management. We noted that a backlash has developed to these smart growth tools, and many of them are being tested in the courts.

The new urbanism movement is part of the smart growth coalition, and it refers to a group of architects, planners, and developers who are actually building neighborhoods and communities based in these new planning principles. New urbanists use these principles to change the nature of development from sprawling conventional subdivisions to compact, interconnected communities. The key principles of new urbanism are (a) development occurs in compact, walkable neighborhoods with clearly defined edges and centers; (b) without excluding automobiles, their presence should be minimized; (c) diverse activities (residences, shops, schools, workplaces, and parks) should be accommodated; (d) a wide spectrum of housing options should enable people of a broad range of incomes, ages, and family types to live within a single neighborhood; and (e) existing urban centers should be restored within coherent metropolitan areas that protect the built legacy.

We showed that the new urbanism is a continuation of a long tradition of new town development in this society. As in other eras of new town development, there is an element of social engineering. The major goal of the new urbanists is to reduce the problems of sprawl. But new urbanists also believe that many of our social problems can be linked to the segregation of groups in cities. We described Kentlands, Maryland; Broomfield, Colorado; and the central-city in-fill development Paradise at Parkside in Washington, D.C. We asked, "Will they work?" Research suggests they will. Consumers are willing to pay a 10 percent premium to live in them. Survey results also suggest that they create a sense of community. We also reviewed the criticism of the new urbanism that ranges from threatening private property rights to ineffective ways of stemming metro growth to kitschy, Disney-like development.

We ended the chapter by looking toward the North American city of 2050. We believe it will look pretty much the way it does today. City-states with regional government will emerge in response to the globalization of the world's economy. Suburban sprawl will abate as smart growth and other land-use controls are implemented. The automobile will continue to shape the metropolis, and members of the growth machine will continue to dominate land-use decisions. But propinquity and location will be less important as broadband Internet and other technologies free land uses from many past constraints.

Bibliography

Chapter 1

American Demographics. (1998). *What I love and hate about cities.* Ithaca, NY: Cowles Business Media.

Bissell, R. (1950). *Stretch on the river.* Boston: Little Brown.

Castells, M. (1977). *The urban question: A Marxist approach.* Cambridge, MA: MIT Press.

Davis, M. (1992). *City of quartz: Excavating the future in Los Angeles.* New York: Vintage.

Davis, M. (1998). *Ecology of fear: Los Angeles and the imagination of disaster.* New York: Metropolitan Books.

Dogan, M., & Kasarda, J. (Eds.). (1988). *The metropolis era: A world of giant cities.* Newbury Park, CA: Sage.

Fitzpatrick, K., & LaGory, M. (2000). *Unhealthy places: Ecology of risk in the urban landscape.* New York: Routledge.

Gould, P., & White, R. (1974). *Mental maps.* Baltimore: Penguin.

Hauser, P. (1963). *The population dilemma.* Englewood Cliffs, NJ: Prentice Hall.

Hawley, A. (1971). *Urban society.* New York: Ronald Press.

Keyfitz, N. (1967). Political-economic aspects of urbanization in south and south-east Asia. In P. Hauser & L. Schnore (Eds.), *The study of urbanization* (pp. 265–310). New York: Wiley.

Krupat, E. (1985). *People in cities: The urban environment and its effects.* New York: Cambridge University Press.

LaGory, M., & Pipkin, J. (1981). *Urban social space.* Belmont, CA: Wadsworth.

Lapham, L. (1976). City lights: A defense of New York. *Harper's Magazine, 252,* 8–14.

Logan, J., & Molotch, H. (1987). *Urban fortunes: The political economy of place.* Berkeley: University of California Press.

Mumford, L. (1961). *The city in history: Its origins, its transformations, and its prospects.* New York: Harcourt, Brace & World.

Planning Commissioners Journal. (1999). Sprawl resource guide. Retrieved December 1, 2001, from http://www.plannersweb.com/sprawl

Sassen, S. (1994). *Cities in a world economy.* Thousand Oaks, CA: Pine Forge.

Schwab, W. (1992). *The sociology of cities.* Englewood Cliffs, NJ: Prentice Hall.

U.S. Census Bureau. (2000). *The geography of the 2000 census.* Washington, D.C.: Government Printing Office.

Weber, M. (1958). *The city* (D. Martindale & G. Neuwirth, Trans.). New York: Free Press.

Whyte, W. (1958, January). Urban sprawl. *Fortune, 57,* 302.

Wirth, L. (1938). Urbanism as a way of life. *American Journal of Sociology, 44,* 1–24.

Chapter 2

Allbritton, C. (1999, November 7). It's a wired, wired world: Here's an atlas of digital hotspots. *Northwest Arkansas Times,* D9, D11.

Altman, D. (2003, March 15). Uncertain economy hinders highly precise supply system [Electronic version]. *New York Times.* Retrieved March 21, 2003, from http://nytimes.com

Arrow, K. J. (1972, Summer). Gifts and exchanges. *Philosophy and Public Affairs, 1,* 351–374.

Belsie, L. (2000, February 3). Where America's economic good times haven't reached [Electronic version]. *Christian Science Monitor.* Retrieved February 3, 2000, from http://www.csmonitor.com

Berman, P. (2003, March 23). The philosopher of Islamic terror [Electronic version]. *New York Times.* Retrieved March 23, 2003, from http://nytimes.com

Brandon, J. (2000, January 6). Raising the world's standard of living [Electronic version]. *Christian Science Monitor.* Retrieved January 6, 2000, from http://www.csmonitor.com

Brummett, J. (2000, January 30). On becoming a modern 'citistate.' *Arkansas Democrat Gazette,* J1, J8.

Center for Budget and Policy Priorities. (2003, April 3). The administration's tax cuts and the long-term budget outlook. Retrieved on April 3, 2003, from http://www.cbpp.org/3-5-03bud.htm

Clarke, S. E., & Gaile, G. L. (1998). *The work of cities.* Minneapolis: University of Minnesota Press.

Crutsinger, M. (1999, January 20). Stock market helps push up household wealth for average American family. *Northwest Arkansas Times,* 26.

Crutsinger, M. (2000, January 9). Typical U.S. family amassed 17% greater wealth in mid-'90s. *Arkansas Democrat Gazette,* A1, A10.

Dahrendorf, R. (1997). *After 1989: Morals, revolution, and civil society.* New York: St. Martin's Press.

Debre, G. (2000, March 11). In foreign affairs, a return of the city-state? [Electronic version]. *Christian Science Monitor.* Retrieved March 11, 2000, from http://www.csmonitor.com

DRI-WEFA Inc. (2001). U.S. metro economies: The engines of America's growth. Retrieved December 16, 2001, from United States Conference of Mayors site: http://www.usmayors.org/citiesdrivetheeconomy

Egan, T. (2003, March 3). New economy recedes in Pacific northwest [Electronic version]. *New York Times.* Retrieved March 3, 2003, from http://nytimes.com

Falvey Jr., J. J., & Wolfman, M. A. (2002, December 11). The criminal provisions of Sarbanes-Oxley: A tale of sound and fury [Special report]. *Insurance Coverage Litigation Report,* 1–9.

Francis, D. R. (2000, January 20). A widening rich-poor gap gets wider political play. *Christian Science Monitor,* 1, 10.

Francis, D. R. (2002a, March 4). New economy endures, and whole economy benefits. *Christian Science Monitor,* 1, 4.

Francis, D. R. (2000b, March 4). Enron may push regulatory wave across free enterprise. *Christian Science Monitor,* 6.

Friedman, T. L. (1999). *The lexus and the olive tree: Understanding globalization.* New York: Farrar, Straus, and Giroux.

Fukuyama, F. (1992). *The end of history and the last man.* New York: Free Press.

Grant, J. (2003, March 24). Battling the fog of finance [Electronic version]. *New York Times.* Retrieved on March 25, 2003, from http://nytimes.com

Greenfield, K. T. (2000, January 17). Do you know Cisco? *Time,* 72–74.

Hagenbaugh, B. (2003, February 17). Nation's wealth disparity widens but report shows 52% of families own stocks. *USA Today,* 1.

Halal, W. E., & Varey, R. J. (1999, February 3). Recognizing the emerging third way. *Christian Science Monitor,* 9.

Halberstan, D. (1993). *The fifties.* New York: Villard Books.

Harris, S. (2000, January 24). Keeping track: Income gap. *Christian Science Monitor,* 1, 3.

Huntington, S. P. (1996). *The clash of civilizations and the remaking of world order.* New York: Simon and Schuster.

Kalathil, S. & Boas, T. C. (2003). *Open networks, closed regimes: The impact of the internet on authoritarian rule.* New York: Carnegie Endowment for International Peace.

Kaplan, R. D. (1998). *The empire wilderness: Travels into America's future.* New York: Random House.

Kilborn, R., & Nichols, J. (2000, January 6). Costs of the WTO conference [Electronic version]. *Christian Science Monitor.* Retrieved on January 6, 2000, from http://www.csmonitor.com

Kilborn, P. T. (2002, February 16). Changes in world economy on raw materials may doom many towns. *Christian Science Monitor.* Retrieved on February 16, 2002, from http://www.csmonitor.com

Knickerbocker, B. (2000, February 3). New kid in the global arena. *Christian Science Monitor,* 12.

Krauss, C. (2003, March 23). Concerns about commerce as borders tighten. *New York Times.* Retrieved on March 23, 2003, from http://nytimes.com

Leach, S. L. (2003, February 20). The net effect. *Christian Science Monitor,* 3.

Luhby, T. (2002, December 4). Firms fined $8.25M for lost e-mail. *Newsday* (Business & Technology Section), A1.

McCaffrey, S. (2000, January 18). Income gap widens for nation, states. *Arkansas Democrat Gazette,* A3.

Nason, J. M., & Rogers, J. H. (1999). Investment and the current account in the short run and the long run. Washington, D.C.: The Federal Reserve Board.

Oster, S. (1999, December 31). China's lukewarm capitalism spirit. *Christian Science Monitor,* 6.

Peirce, N. R., Johnson C. W., & Hall, J. S. (1993). *Citistates: How urban America can prosper in a competitive world.* Washington, D.C.: Seven Locks Press.

Porterfield, E. (1999, July 26). Emerging 'Cascadia': Geography, economy bring northwest cities ever-closer. *Christian Science Monitor,* 3–4.

Reich, R. B. (1991). *The work of nations: Preparing ourselves for the 21st century capitalism.* New York: Knopf.

Scherer, R. (1999, December 6). WTO failure portends limits to 'open trade.' *Christian Science Monitor,* 2.

Scherer, R. (2000a, January 16). Can't keep a good boom down. *Christian Science Monitor,* 1, 4.

Scherer, R. (2000b, January 28). Rise and . . . rise of America inc.: Entrepreneurial spirit and technology fuel the longest economic expansion in U.S. history. *Christian Science Monitor,* 1, 9.

Scherer, R., & Eviatar, D. (2000, February 1). High-churn American workforce: Bigger salaries and plentiful jobs are offset by higher turnover, layoffs, and less career security. *Christian Science Monitor,* 1–2.

Shama, A. (2001, August 8). Separating dotcom winners from losers. *Christian Science Monitor,* 9.

Sieler, M., & King, P. H. (1986, January 28). Shuttle explodes: All seven die [Electronic version]. *Los Angeles Times.* Retrieved on February 11, 2000, from http://www.latimes.com

Stevenson, R. W., & Gerth, J. (2002, January 20). Multiple safeguards failed to detect problems at Enron [Electronic version]. *New York Times.* Retrieved on January 20, 2002, from http://nytimes.com

U.S. Census Bureau. (2003). *Historical income tables—Families.* Retrieved on March 31, 2003, from U.S. Census via AmeriStats Access: http://www.census.gov/hhes/income/histinc/f03.html

Chapter 3

Abrahamian, E. (1986). Structural causes of the Iranian evolution. In J. S. Goldstone (Ed.), *Revolutions: Theoretical, comparative, and historical studies* (pp. 111–154). New York: Harcourt Brace Jovanovich.

Aldrich, B. C., & Sandhu, R. S. (1995). *Housing the urban poor: Policy and practice in developing countries.* New Delhi, India: Vedams Books International.

Allbritton, C. (1999). It's a wired, wired world: Here's an atlas of digital hotspots. *Northwest Arkansas Times,* November 7, 1999, D9–011.

Baker, D., Epstein, G., & Pollin, R. (Eds.). (1998). *Globalization and progressive policy.* New York: Cambridge University Press.

Bendix, R. (1964). *Nation-building and citizenship.* Berkeley: University of California Press.

Berman, P. (2003, March 26). The philosopher of Islamic terror [Electronic version]. *New York Times.* Retrieved on March 26, 2003, from http://nytimes.com

Brandon, J. J. (2000). Raising the world's standard of living. *Christian Science Monitor,* January 6, 2000, 16.

Center for Global, International and Regional Studies (2003). *Atlas of Global Inequality: Income Inequality.* Retrieved April 14, 2003, from http://www2.ucsc.edu/atlas/income.html

Chirot, D. (1986). *Social change in the modern era.* New York: Harcourt Brace Jevanovich.

Cobban, H. (2000). No globalization without representation [Electronic version]. *Christian Science Monitor.* Retrieved on March 9, 2000, from http://www.csmonitor.com

Davis, K. (1945). The world demographic transition. *The Annals of the American Academy of Political and Social Science, 237,* 1–11.

Davis, K., & Golden, H. H. (1954). Urbanization and the development of pre-industrial areas. *Economic Development and Cultural Change, 3,* 6–26.

de la Barra, X. (1998). Poverty: The main cause of ill health in urban children. *Health Education and Behavior, 25*(1): 46–59.

Deshnukh, V. (2003). *Bangalore: India's hi-tech birthplace.* Retrieved March 7, 2003, from the Center for International Private Enterprise Web site: http://www.cipe.org/publications/fs/ert/e09/india-3.htm

Downey, T., & Williamson, J. (2000, February 11). Developing a world that works. *Christian Science Monitor,* 2000, 17.

Fernandes, E., & Varley, A. (Eds.). (1998). *Illegal cities: Law and urban change in developing countries.* New York: Zed Books.

Friedman, T. L. (1999). *The Lexus and the olive tree: Understanding globalization.* New York: Farrar, Straus, and Giroux.

Fukuyama, F. (1992). *The end of history and the last man.* New York: Free Press.

Gilbert, A., & Gugler, J. (1992). *Cities, poverty and development: Urbanization in the third world.* New York: Oxford University Press.

Goldscheider, C. (1971). *Population, modernization and social structure.* Boston: Little, Brown.

Gugler, J. (Ed.). (1990). *The urbanization of the third world.* Oxford, England: Oxford University Press.

Jefferson, M. (1939). The law of the primate city. *Geographic Review, 39,* 226–232.

Mander, J., & Goldsmith, E. (1996). *The case against the global economy.* San Francisco: Sierra Club.

Melchior, A., Telle, K., & Wiig, H. (2000, October). Globalisation and inequality: World income distribution and living standards, 1960–1998. Oslo: Royal Norwegian Ministry of Foreign Affairs Studies on Foreign Policy Issues, Report 6B.

Population Reference Bureau. (2000). *1999 world population data sheet* [Electronic version]. Retrieved on March 8, 2000, from http://www.prb.org/pubs/wpds99/wpds99_1.html

Schwab, W. A. (1992). *The sociology of cities.* Englewood Cliffs, NJ: Prentice Hall.

Shunnaq, M., & Schwab, W. (2000). Continuity and change in a Middle Eastern city: The social ecology of Irbid City, Jordan. *Cultural Anthropology, 26*(1):1–18.

Slambrouck, V. (1999, December 28). In world of high tech, everyone is an island. *Christian Science Monitor,* 2–3.

Smith, D. A. (1996). *Third world cities in global perspective: The politcal economy of uneven urbanization.* Boulder, CO: Westview Press.

Thinkquest. (2000). *Megacities: Mexico City* [Electronic version]. Retrieved on March 8, 2000, from http://library.thinkquest.org/20377/english/mxcity/home_engtext.htm

United Nations Commission on Human Security. (1999). *Best practice data base: Poverty alleviation through community participation.* New York: Author.

United Nations. (1996). United Nations development programme: Human development report. New York: Author.

United Nations Population Division. (1996). Urban agglomerations, 1950–2015. New York: United Nations.

United Nations Population Division. (1996). World urbanization prospects. New York: United Nations.

United Nations Population Division. (2003a). *World population prospects: The 2002 revision* [Electronic version]. Retrieved from United Nations Population Division Web site, http://www.un.org/popin/data.html

United Nations Population Division, Department of Economic and Social Affairs. (2003b). *World population prospects: The 2002 revision—Population growth in* [Electronic version]. Retrieved from United Nations Population Division Web site, http://www.un.org/esa/population/publications/wup2001/WUP2001report.html

Wallerstein, I. (1974). *The modern world system.* New York: Academic Press.

World Economic Forum. (2003, January 23). *Global competitiveness report 2002–2003.* Retrieved April 5, 2003, from http://www.weforum.org/gcr

World Resources Institute. (1999). *World resources 1997–98.* New York: Oxford University Press.

World Resources Institute. (2000). *Global trends: Population and human well-being—urban growth* [Electronic version]. Retrieved on March 8, 2000, from http://www.sri.org/wr-98–99/citygrow.htm

World Resources Institute. (2000). *Population and human well-being: Urban growth* [Electronic version]. Retrieved on March 3, 2000, from http://www.wri.org/wr-98–99/city-grow.htm

World Resources Institute. (2003). *World resources 2000–2001: Population, health and human well-being—Table HD.1: Demographic indicators, 2003* [Electronic version]. Retrieved from World Resources Web site, http://earthtrends.sri.org/databases/index.cfm

Chapter 4

Felson, M. (1997). Reconciling Hirschi's 1969 control theory with the general theory of crime. In S. P. Lab (Ed.), *Crime prevention at a crossroads.* Cincinnati, OH: Anderson.

Felson, M. (1998). *Crime and everyday life.* (2nd ed.). Thousand Oaks, CA: Pine Forge Press.

Fisher, B., Sloan, J., Cullen, F., & Lu, C. (1997). The on-campus victimization patterns of students: Implications for crime prevention by students in post-secondary institutions. In S. P. Lab (Ed.), *Crime prevention at a crossroads.* Cincinnati, OH: Anderson.

Garreau, J. (1992). *Edge cities: Life on the urban frontier.* New York: Anchor Books, Doubleday.

Jacobs, J. (1961). *The death and life of great American cities.* New York: Random House.

Katz, P. (1994). *The new urbanism: Toward an architecture of community.* New York: McGraw-Hill.

Kunstler, J. H. (1993). *The geography of nowhere: The rise and decline of America's man-made landscape.* New York: Simon & Schuster.

Kunstler, J. (1996). *Home from nowhere: Remaking our everyday world for the twenty-first century.* New York: Simon & Schuster.

Lofland, L. H. (1985). *A world of strangers: Order and action in urban public space.* Prospect Heights, IL: Waveland Press, Inc. [Original edition, 1973]

Lofland, L. H. (1998). *The public realm: Exploring the city's quintessential social territory.* New York: Aldine De. Gruyter.

Lynch, K. (1960). *The image of the city, publications of the joint center for urban studies.* Cambridge, MA: MIT Press.

Lynch, K. (1972). *What time is this place?* Cambridge, MA: MIT Press.

Putnam, R. D. (2000). *Bowling alone: The collapse and revival of American community.* New York: Simon & Schuster.

Remington, J. (2000). Classic crime prevention: Neighborhood watch. *Sheriff: The Magazine of the National Sheriffs Association,* 1–10.

Taylor, R. B. (1997). Crime, grime, and responses to crime: Relative impacts of neighborhood structure, crime, and physical deterioration on residents and business personnel in the Twin Cities. In S. P. Lab (Ed.), *Crime prevention at a crossroads.* Cincinnati, OH: Anderson.

U.S. Department of Justice, Bureau of Justice Statistics. (2000). *Criminal victimization in United States, 1998: Statistical tables* [Electronic version]. Retrieved on November 22, 2000, from http://www.ojp.usdoj.gov/bjs/pub/pdf/cvus9806.pdf

U.S. Department of Justice, Federal Bureau of Investigation. (2000). *Uniform crime report* [Electronic version]. Retrieved on November 22, 2000, from http://www.FBI.gov/ucr/Cius_99/99crime/99c2_01.pdf

Chapter 5

Axelrod, M. (1955). Urban structure and participation. In P. K. Hatt & A. J. Reiss (Eds.), *Cities and society.* Glencoe, IL: Free Press.

Bell, C., & Newby, H. (1972). *Community studies: An introduction to the sociology of local community.* New York: Praeger.

Coser, L. A. (1971). *Masters of sociological thought.* New York: Harcourt Brace Jovanovich.

Davie, M. R. (1938). The pattern of urban growth. In G. D. Murdock (Ed.), *Studies in the science of society.* New Haven, CT: Yale University Press.

Form, W. H., Smith, J., Stone, G. P., & Cowhig, J. (1954). The compatibility of alternative approaches to the delimitation of urban subareas. *American Sociological Review, 19*(2):176–187.

Gans, H. J. (1962). *The urban villagers: Group and class in the life of Italian Americans.* New York: Free Press.

Giddens, A. (1972). *Emile Durkheim: Selected writings.* Cambridge, England: Cambridge University Press.

Greer, S. (1962). *The emerging city: Myth and reality.* New York: Free Press.

Greer, S. (1970). The social structure of the political process of suburbia. In R. Gutman & D. Popenoe (Eds.), *Neighborhood, city, and metropolis: An integrated reader in urban sociology.* New York: Random House.

Greer, S., & Orleans, P. (1962). The mass society and the parapolitical structure. *American Sociological Review, 27*(4):634–646.

Hatt, P. K. (1946). The concept of natural area. *American Sociological Review, 11,* 423–428.

Hawley, A. (1950). *Human ecology: A theory of community structure.* New York: Ronald Press.

Hawley, A., & Zimmer, B. (1970). *The metropolitan community.* Beverly Hills, CA: Sage Publications.

Hillery, G. (1955). Definitions of community: Areas of agreement. *Rural Sociology, 20,* 111–123.

Hunter, A. (1974). *Symbolic communities: The persistence and change of Chicago's local communities.* Chicago: University of Chicago Press.

Janowitz, M. (1961). *The community press in an urban setting: The social elements of urbanism.* Chicgao: University of Chicago Press.

Karp, D., Stone, G. P., & Yoels, W. C. (1977). *Being urban: A social psychological view of city life.* Lexington, MA: D. C. Heath.

Kasarda, J. D., & Janowitz, M. (1974). Community attachments in mass society. *American Sociological Review, 39,* 328–339.

Keller, S. (1968). *The urban neighborhood: A sociological perspective.* New York: Random House.

Kitagawa, E. M., & Taeuber, K. E. (1963). *Local community fact book for Chicago metropolitan area, 1960.* Chicago: Chicago Community Inventory, University of Chicago.

Liebow, E. (1967). *Tally's corner.* Chicago: Dorsey Press.

Lyon, L. (1987). *The community in urban society.* Chicago: Dorsey Press.

Maine, H. S. (1870). *Ancient law.* London: John Murray.

Meier, R. L. (1968). The metropolis as a transaction-maximizing system. *Daedalus, 97,* 1293–1313.

Michelson, W. (1970). *Man and his urban environment.* Reading, MA: Addison-Wesley.

Morris, R. N., & Mogey, J. (1965). *The sociology of housing.* London: Cambridge University Press.

Nisbet, R. (1966). *The sociological tradition.* New York: Basic Books.

Park, R. (1952). *Human communities.* Glencoe, IL: Free Press.

Park, R., & Miller, H. (1921). *Old world traits transplanted.* New York: Harper.

Simmel, G. (1955). The web of group-affiliations. In E. Wolff & R. Bendix (Eds.), *Conflict and the web of group affiliations.* Glencoe, IL: Free Press.

Stein, M. (1972). *The eclipse of community: An interpretation of American studies.* Princeton, NJ: Princeton University Press.

Suttles, G. (1968). *The social order of the slums.* Chicago: University of Chicago Press.

Suttles, G. (1972). *The social construction of communities.* Chicago: University of Chicago Press.

Thrasher, F. (1926). *The gang.* Chicago: University of Chicago Press.

Tobin, G. A. (1976). Suburbanization and the development of motor transportation: Transportation technology and the suburbanization process. In B. Schwartz (Ed.), *The changing face of suburbs.*

Warren, R. L. (1978). *The community in America.* Chicago: Rand McNally.

Whythe, W. F. (1943). Social organization in the slums. *American Sociological Review, 8*(1):34–39.

Whythe, W. F. (1955). *Street corner society.* Chicago: University of Chicago Press.

Wirth, L. (1928). *The ghetto.* Chicago: University of Chicago Press.

Wirth, L. (1938). Urbanism as a way of life. *American Journal of Sociology, 44,* 1–24.

Zorbaugh, H. (1929). *The gold coast and the slum.* Chicago: University of Chicago Press.

Chapter 6

Fischer, C. (1982). *To dwell among friends: Personal networks in town and city.* Chicago: University of Chicago Press.

Harvey, D. (1989). *The condition of postmodernity: An enquiry into the origins of cultural change.* Oxford, England: Blackwell.

Pescosolido, B. A., & Rubin, B. A. (2000). The web of group affiliations revisited: social life, postmodernism and sociology. *American Sociological Review, 65*(1), 52–76.

Schwab, W. (1992). *The sociology of cities.* Englewood Cliffs, NJ: Prentice Hall.

Wellman, B. (1999). *Networks in the global village: Life in contemporary communities.* Boulder, CO: Westview Press.

Chapter 7

Anderson, T. R., & Egeland, J. A. (1961). Spatial aspects of social area analysis. *American Sociological Review* 26: 392–399.

Arvidson, E. (1999). Remapping Los Angeles, or taking the risk of class in postmodern urban theory. *Economic Geography, 75*(2), 134–156.

Dear, M. J. (2000). *The postmodern urban condition.* Malden, MA: Blackwell.

Dear, M. J., & Flusty, S. (1997, May). The iron lotus: Los Angeles and postmodern urbanism. *Annals of the American Academy of Political and Social Science, 551,* 151–163.

Dear, M. J., & Flusty, S. (1998). Postmodern urbanism. *Annals of the Association of American Geographers, 88*(1), 50–72.

Garreau, J. (1991). *Edge cities: Life on the new frontier.* New York: Doubleday.

Harris, C. D. (1998). Diffusion of urban models: A case study. *Urban Geography, 19*(1), 49–67.

Harris, C. D., & Ullman, E. L. (1945). The nature of cities. *Annals of the Academy of Political and Social Science,* 242: 105–117.

Harvey, D. (1985). *The urbanization of capital: Studies in the history and theory of capitalist urbanization.* Baltimore, Johns Hopkins University Press.

Harvey, D. (1990). *The condition of postmodernity.* Malden, MA: Blackwell.

Hoyt, H. (1939). *The structure and growth of residential neighborhoods in American cities.* Washington, D.C.: Federal Housing Authority.

Kaplan, R. D. (1998). *The empire wilderness: Travels into America's future.* New York: Random House.

Park, R. (1952). *Human communities.* Glencoe, IL: Free Press.

Park, R. E., Burgess, E., & McKenzie, R. (1925). *The city.* Chicago: University of Chicago Press.

Schwab, W. A. (1992). *The sociology of cities.* Englewood Cliffs, NJ: Prentice Hall.

Scott, A. J., & Soja, E. W. (1996). *The city: Los Angeles and urban theory at the end of the twentieth century.* Berkeley: University of California Press.

Scott, A. J., & Soja, E. W. (2000). *At home in the heteropolis: Understanding postmodern L.A.*

Soja, E. W. (1996). *Thirdspace : Journeys to Los Angeles and other real-and-imagined places.* Cambridge, MA: Blackwell.

Soja, E. W. (2000). *Postmetropolis: Critical studies of cities and regions.* Malden, MA: Blackwell.

Sorkin, M. (Ed.). (1992). *Variations on a theme park: The new American city and the end of public space.* New York: Hill and Wang.

White, M. J. (1987). *American neighborhoods and residential differentiation.* New York: Russell Sage Foundation.

Chapter 8

Bach, R. L., & Smith, J. (1977). Community satisfaction, expectations of moving and migration. *Demography,* 14: 147–167.

Clark, S. E., & Gaile, G. L. (1998). *The work of cities.* Minneapolis: University of Minnesota Press.

Clark, W. A. V. (1986). *Human migration.* Beverly Hills, CA: Sage Publications.

Gans, H. J. (1962a). *The urban villagers: Group and class in the life of Italian Americans.* New York: Free Press.

Gans, H. J. (1962b). Urbanism and suburbanism as ways of life: A re-evaluation of definitions. In A. Rose (Ed.), *Human behavior and social processes.* Boston: Houghton Mifflin.

Hoover, E. M., & Vernon, R. (1959). *Anatomy of metropolis.* Cambridge, MA: Harvard University Press.

Johnson, G. T. (1981). *Mobility, residential location, and urban change : A partially annotated bibliography, CPL bibliography. no. 48.* Chicago: CPL Bibliographies.

LaGory, M., & Pipkin, J. (1981). *Urban social space.* Belmont, CA: Wadsworth Publishing.

London, B., & Palen, J. (1984). *Gentrification, displacement, and neighborhood revitalization.* Albany: State University of New York Press.

Makimoto, T., & Manners, D. (1997). *Digital nomad.* New York: Wiley.

Munro, M. (1987). Residential mobility in the private housing sector. In M. Pacione (Ed.), *Social geography: Progress and prospect.* London: Croom Helm.

Rees, P. H. (1970). Concepts of social space: Toward an urban social geography. In B. J. L. Berry & F. E. Horton (Eds.), *Geographical perspectives in urban systems.* Englewood Cliffs, NJ: Prentice Hall.

Rossi, P. H. (1955). *Why families move.* (2nd ed.). Beverly Hills, CA: Sage Publications.

Schwab, W. A. (1982). *Urban sociology: A human ecological perspective.* Boston: Addison-Wesley.

Schwab, W. A. (1992). *The sociology of cities.* Englewood Cliffs, NJ: Prentice Hall.

Simmons, J. W. (1974). *Patterns of residential movement in metropolitan Toronto*. Toronto: University of Toronto Press.

U.S. Census Bureau. (2001). *Homeownership by citizenship and race* [Electronic version]. Retrieved on August 10, 1999, from http://www.census.gov/hhes/housing/ homeown/tab5.html

U.S. Department of Commerce. (1999, May 27). *STAT-USA: State of the Nation* [Electronic version]. Retrieved on May 27, 1999, from http://www.stat-usa.gov/econtest.nsf

U.S. Department of Housing and Urban Development. (1997). *Homebuyer education learning program guide: FHA, we'll get you home*. Washington, D.C.: Author.

U.S. Department of Commerce, Bureau of Economic Analysis. (2004). National income and product accounts tables. Downloaded on March 5, 2004 from Bureau of Economic Analysis website at http://www.bea.gov

U.S. Department of Housing and Urban Development. Office of Policy Development and Research. (2004). Housing investment. Downloaded on March 3, 2004 from HUD website at www.hud.gov/pdr/

Wolpert, J. (1965). Behavioral aspects of the decision to migrate. *Papers of the Regional Science Association, 15,* 159–169.

Chapter 9

Rossi, P. H. (1955). *Why families move*. Beverly Hills, CA: Sage Publications.

U.S. Department of Housing and Urban Development. (1997). *Buying your home: Settlement costs and helpful information*. Washington, D.C.: Author. Housing and Urban Development.

U.S. Department of Housing and Urban Development. (1989). *Home buyer's vocabulary*. Washington, D.C.: Author.

Chapter 10

Baumgartner, M. P. (1988). *The moral order of a suburb*. New York: Oxford University Press.

Belsie, L. (2001, July 5). Blacks leaving cities for suburbs. *Christian Science Monitor,* 1, 4.

Booth, A., & Choldin, H. (1985). Housing type and the residential experiences of middle-class mothers. *Sociological Focus, 18*(2), 97–107.

Brennan, J., & Hill, E. W. (1999). *Where are the jobs?: Cities, suburbs, and the competition for employment*. Washington, D.C.: The Brookings Institution, Center on Urban and Metropolitan Policy.

Cook, C. C. (1988). Components of neighborhood satisfaction: Responses from urban and suburban single-parent women. *Environment and Behavior, 20*(21), 115–149.

Douglas, P. H. (1925). *The suburban trend*. New York: Century Publishers.

Fischer, C. (1975). Toward a subcultural theory of urbanism. *American Journal of Sociology 80*(6): 1319–1351.

Fitzpatrick, K. M., & Logan, J. R. (1985, February). The aging of the suburbs, 1960–1980. *American Sociological Review, 50,* 106–117.

Frey, W. H. (2001). *Melting pot suburbs: A Census 2000 study of suburban diversity*. Washington, D.C.: The Brookings Institution, Center on Urban and Metropolitan Policy.

Fulton, W., Pendall, R., Nguyen, M., & Harrison, A. (2001). *Who sprawls most? How growth patterns differ across the U.S.* Washington, D.C.: The Brookings Institution Center on Urban and Metropolitan Policy.

Garreau, J. (1991). *Edge city: Life on the new frontier*. New York: Anchor.

Glaeser, E. L. (2001). *City growth and the 2000 census: Which places grew, and why*. Washington, D.C.: The Brookings Institution, Center on Urban and Metropolitan Policy.

Glaeser, E. L., Kahn, M., & Chu, C. (2001). *Job sprawl: Employment location in U.S. metropolitan areas*. Washington, DC: The Brookings Institution, Center on Urban and Metropolitan Policy.

Greer, S. (1962). *The emerging city: Myth and reality*. New York: The Free Press.

Harris, D. (1999). *All suburbs are not created equal: A new look at racial difference in suburban location*. Ann Arbor: University of Michigan, Population Studies Center.

Jackson, K. T. (1985). *Crabgrass frontier: The suburbanization of the United States*. New York: Oxford University Press.

Katz, B. (2001). *Smart growth and new urbanism*. Paper read at Congress for New Urbanism, Washington, D.C.

Lang, R. E. (2000). *Office sprawl: The evolving geography of business*. Washington, D.C.: The Brookings Institution, Center on Urban and Metropolitan Policy.

Lang, R. E., & Simmons, P. A. (2001). *"Boomburbs": The emergence of large, fast-growing suburban cities in the United States*. Washington, D.C.: Fannie Mae Foundation.

Logan, J. R. (2001). The new ethnic enclaves in America's suburbs. Albany, NY: University of Albany, Lewis Mumford Center for Comparative Urban and Regional Research.

Logan, J. R., & Schneider, M. (1981, April). The stratification of metropolitan suburbs. *American Sociological Review, 46*, 175–186.

Lopata, H. Z. (1980). The Chicago woman: A study of patterns of mobility and transportation. *Signs: Journal of Women in Culture and Society, 5*(3), 161–169.

McKelvey, B. (1963). *The urbanization of America, 1860–1915*. New Brunswick, NJ: Rutgers University Press.

Muller, P. O. (1981). *Contemporary suburban America*. Englewood Cliffs, NJ: Prentice Hall.

Reisman, D. (1958). The suburban sadness. In W. M. Dobriner (Ed.), *The suburban community*. New York: G. P. Putnam.

Rosenberg, C. E. (1962). *The cholera years: The disease in America, 1832, 1846, 1867*. Chicago: University of Chicago Press.

Rothblatt, D. N., Garr, D. F. J., & Sprague, J. (1979). *The suburban environment and women*. New York: Praeger Publishers.

Schwab, W. (1988). The predictive value of three ecological models. *Urban Affairs Quarterly, 23*(2), 295–308.

Schwartz, B. (1979). *The changing face of the suburbs*. Chicago: University of Chicago Press.

Sims, M. (1998). *A comparative analysis of high-status residential segregation and neighborhood concentration in five metro areas, 1980–90*. Ann Arbor: University of Michigan, Population Studies Center.

Sohmer, R. R., & Lang, R. E. (2001). *Downtown rebound*. Washington, D.C.: Fannie Mae Foundation and Brookings Institution on Urban and Metropolitan Policy.

Spain, D. (1988). An examination of residential preferences in the suburban era. *Sociological Focus, 21*(1), 1–8.

Stahura, J. M. (1987). Suburban socioeconomic status change: A comparison of models. *American Sociological Review, 52*(2), 268–277.

Tobin, M. (1976). Suburbanization and the development of motor transportation: Transportation technology and the suburbanization process. In B. Schwartz (Ed.), *The changing face of suburbs*. Chicago: University of Chicago Press.

U.S. Census Bureau. (2001). *Census 2000 brief: Population change and distribution, 1990–2000*. Washington, D.C.: U.S. Census Bureau.

Ward, D. (1964). A comparative historical geography of streetcar suburbs in Boston, Massachusetts and Leeds, England: 1850–1920. *Annals of the Association of American Geographers, 54*: 1477–1489.

Warner, S. B. (1962). *Streetcar suburbs: The process of growth of Boston*. Cambridge, MA: Harvard University Press.

Weber, A. F. (1963). *The growth of cities in the nineteenth century: A study of statistics*. Ithaca, NY: Cornell University Press.

Wekerle, G. R. (1980). Women in the urban environment. *Signs: Journal of Women in Culture and Society, 5*(3), 188–214.

Welfeld, I. H. (1985, Fall). Our graying suburbs: Solving an unusual housing problem. *The Public Interest, 85*, 50–57.

Yinger, J. (1995). *Closed doors*. New York: Russell Sage Foundation.

Chapter 11

Agocs, C. (1981). Ethnic settlement in a metropolitan area: A typology of communities. *Ethnicity, 8*: 127–148.

AmeriStat. (2001). *Occupational segregation.* Population Reference Bureau. Social Science Data Analysis Network, 2001. Retrieved on July 19, 2001, from http://www.ameristat.org/racethnic/job.htm

Armas, G. C. (2001, April 13). Segregation amid growing diversity. *Asian Week,* 1.

Asian American Federation. (2001). *New national demograhic profile shows increasing diversity of Asian Americans.* Retrieved on July 19, 2001, from http://www.aafny.org/proom/pr/pr200010515.asp

Bierstedt, R. (1974). *The social order.* New York: McGraw-Hill.

Bledea, S. E. (1979). Socioeconomic, demographic, and cultural bases of ethnic residential segregation. *Ethnicity, 6,* 147–167.

Boal, F. W. (1981). Ethnic residential segregation. In H. Johnston (Ed.), *The geography of housing.* London: Aldeln.

Burgess, E. W. (1925). The growth of the city: An introduction to a research project. In R. E. Park, E. W. Burgess, & R. D. McKenzie (Eds.), *The city.* Chicago: University of Chicago Press.

Burgess, E. W. (1928, November). Residential segregation in American cities. *Annals of the American Academy of Political and Social Sciences, 140,* 105–115.

Callaghan, S. J. (2001). *Comparative perspectives on housing segregation.* CAIN Web Service. Retrieved on July 3, 2001, from wysiwyg://2http://cain.ulst.ac.ur/issues/segregat/callaghan01.htm

Chrisman, N. J. (1981). Ethnic persistence in an urban setting. *Ethnicity, 8:* 256–292.

Clark, W. A. V. (1986). Residential segregation in American cities: A review and interpretation. *Population Research and Policy Review, 5,* 95–127.

Curry, L. P. (1981). *The free black in urban America: The shadow of a dream.* Chicago: University of Chicago Press.

Ellison, K. D. (2001). *Hispanic, Latino, person of color, what's the right label?* [Electronic version]. Retrieved on July 19, 2001, from the Global Center for Diversity Web Site, http://www.globaldiversity.org.uk

Farley, R., (1990). Blacks, Hispanics, and White ethnic groups: Are Blacks uniquely disadvantaged? *The American Economic Review, 80*(2), 237–241.

Farley, R., & Wilger, R. (1987). Recent changes in the residential segregation of blacks from whites: An analysis of 203 metropolises. Ann Arbor, MI: Population Studies Center.

Francis, D. R. (2004). U.S. moves—quietly—toward flat tax. *Christian Science Monitor,* downloaded on March 12, 2004 from www.csmonitor.com

Frey, W. H. (2001). Census 2000 shows large black return to the south, reinforcing the region's "white-black" demographic profile. Ann Arbor: University of Michigan, Population Studies Center.

Glaeser, E. L., & Vigdor, J. (2001). *Racial segregation in the 2000 census: Promising news.* Washington, D.C.: The Brookings Institution.

Glazer, N., & Moynihan, D. (1963). *Beyond the melting pot: The Negroes, Puerto Ricans, Jews, Italians, and Irish of New York City.* Cambridge, MA: MIT Press.

Hanlin, O. (1969). *Boston's immigrants: 1790–1880.* New York: Atheneum.

Hershberg, T., Burstein, A. N., Ericksen, E. P., Greenberg, S., & Yancey, W. L. (1979, January). A tale of three cities: Blacks and immigrants in Philadelphia: 1850–1880, 1930, and 1970. *The Annals of the American Academy of Political and Social Science, 441,* 55–81.

Hershberg, T., Cox, H., Light, D., & Greenfield, R. R. (1981). The journey to work: An empirical investigation of work, space, family, and transportation in Philadelphia, 1850–1880. In T. Hershberg (Ed.), *Work, space, family and group experience in the nineteenth century.* New York: Oxford University Press.

Houston, D., McConville, S., Rickles, J., & Ong, P. (2001). *Census 2000 fact sheet: Racial/ethnic isolation decline in the 1990s.* Los Angeles: University of California, School of Public Policy and Social Research, Ralph and Goldy Lewis Center for Regional Policy Studies.

Lee, S. M. (2001). *Census 2000: Using the new racial categories in the 2000 census.* Washington, D.C.: The Annie E. Casey Foundation and The Population Reference Bureau.

Lewin-Epstein, N. (1986). *Effects of residential segregation and neighborhood opportunity structure on the employment of black and white youth.* The Sociological Quarterly, 27(4), 559–570.

Logan, J. R. (2001a). *Immigrant enclaves in the American metropolis, 1990–2000.* Albany, NY: Lewis Mumford Center for Comparative Urban and Regional Research, University of Albany.

Logan, J. R. (2001b). *The new ethnic enclaves in America's suburbs.* Albany, NY: Lewis Mumford Center for Comparative Urban and Regional Research, University of Albany.

Logan, J. R., & Schneider, M. (1984). Racial segregation and racial change in American suburbs, 1970–1980. *American Journal of Sociology, 89*(4): 874–888.

Massey, D. S. (1981). Dimensions of the new immigration to the United States and the prospects for assimilation. *Annual Review of Sociology, 7*, 57–87.

Massey, D. S. (1985). Ethnic residential segregation: A theoretical synthesis and empirical review. *Sociology and Social Research, 69*(3), 315–350.

Massey, D. S. (1987, December). Understanding Mexican migration to the United States. *American Sociological Review, 52*, 802–825.

Massey, D. S. (1993). *American apartheid: Segregation and the making of the underclass.* Cambridge, MA: Harvard University Press.

Massey, D. S. (1996). The age of extremes: Concentrated affluence and poverty in the twenty-first century. *Demography, 33*, 395–412.

Neidert, L. J., & Farley, R. (1985, December). Assimilation in the United States: An analysis of ethnic and generation differences in status and achievement. *American Sociological Review, 50*, 840–850.

Nordell, J. (2001). U.S. schools have become more segregated during the past decade [Electronic version]. *Christian Science Monitor.* Retrieved on July 18, 2001, from http://www.csmonitor.com

Pinal, J., & Singe, A. (2001). Generations of diversity: Latinos in the United States. Washington, D.C.: Population Reference Bureau.

Population Reference Bureau. (2001a). *AmeriStat: The changing American pie, 1999 and 2025.* Retrieved on July 14, 2001, from http://www.ameristat.org/raceethnic/pie.htm

Population Reference Bureau. (2001b). *AmeriStat: The rich, the poor, and the in between.* Retrieved on July 14, 2001, from http://www.ameristat.org/incpov/hshlds.htm

Porter, E. (2001, March 2). The 2000 count: Even 126 sizes don't fit all. *New York Times*, 1.

Prandy, K. (1980). Residential segregation and ethnic distance in English cities. *Ethnicity, 7*(3), 367–389.

Riche, M. F. (2000). *America's diversity and growth: Signposts for the 21st century.* Washington, D.C.: Population Reference Bureau.

Schmitt, E. (2001, May 6). The new urban minority. *New York Times*, 3.

Seitles, M. (1996). The perpetuation of residential racial segregation in America: Historical discrimination, modern forms of exclusion, and inclusionary remedies. *Journal of Land Use & Environmental Law, 141*(1), 1–11.

Sims, M. (1998). *A comparative analysis of high-status residential segregation and neighborhood concentration in five metro areas, 1980–1990.* Ann Arbor: University of Michigan, Population Studies Center.

Smith, T. L., & Zopf, P. E. (1976). Demography: Principles and methods. Port Washington, NY: Alfred.

Stahura, J. M. (1988). Changing patterns of suburban racial composition, 1970–1980. *Urban Affairs Quarterly, 23*(3), 448–460.

Stearns, L. B., & Logan, J. R. (1986). The racial structuring of the housing market and segregation in suburban areas. *Social Forces, 65*(1): 28–42.

Taylor, H. L. (1986). Spatial organization and the residential experience: Black Cincinnati in 1850. *Social Science History, 10*(1), 45–69.

Techatraisak, B. (1978). *The changes in residential patterns of an ethno-religious group: The case of Greeks in Cincinnati, Ohio.* Cincinnati: University of Cincinnati.

Timms, D. W. G. (1971). *The urban mosaic: Towards a theory of residential differentiation.* Cambridge, England: Cambridge University Press.

U.S. Census Bureau. (2001). Census 2000: Population by race and Hispanic/Latino status. Washington, D.C.: Author.

U.S. Civil Rights Commission. (2001). *Voting irregularities in Florida during the 2000 presidential election.* Retrieved on March 16, 2004, from http://www.usccr.gov/ pubs/pubsndx.htm

U.S. Civil Rights Commission. (2001a). *U.S. civil rights commission finds evidence of Florida violations.* Retrieved on July 14, 2001, from http://www.usccr.gov/vote2000/flstrpt1.htm

U.S. Civil Rights Commission. (2001b). *Status report on probe of election practices in Florida during the 2000 presidential election.* Retrieved on July 16, 2001, from http://www.usccr.gov/vote2000/flstrpt1.htm

U.S. Commission on Civil Rights. (1975). *Twenty years after Brown: Equal opportunity in housing.* Washington, D.C.: U.S. Commission on Civil Rights.

U.S. Conference of Mayors. (2001). *U.S. metro economies: The engines of America's growth.* Washington, D.C.: U.S. Conference of Mayors.

Weeks, J. R. (1996). *Population: An introduction to concepts and issues.* Belmont, CA: Wadsworth.

Wilson, W. J. (1987). *The truly disadvantaged: The inner city, the underclass, and public policy.* Chicago: University of Chicago Press.

Chapter 12

AmeriStat. (2003). *Traditional families account for only 7 percent of U.S. households.* Retrieved on May 9, 2003, from http://www.ameristat.org

Banfield, E. C. (1970). *The unheavenly city.* Boston: Little, Brown.

Berube, A., & Frey, W. H. (2002). *A decade of mixed blessings: Urban and suburban poverty in census 2000.* Washington, D.C.: Brookings Institution; Center on Urban & Metropolitan Policy.

Best, J. (2001). *Damned lies and statistics: Untangling numbers from the media, politicians, and activists.* Berkeley, CA: University of California Press.

Burt, M. R. (2001). *What will it take to end homelessness?* Washington, D.C.: Urban Institute.

Caton, C. L. M. (1990). *Homeless in America.* New York: Oxford University Press.

Castells, M. (1977). *The urban question.* London: Edward Arnold.

Chapman, J., & Bernstein, J. (2003, April). *Falling through the safety net: Low-income single mothers in the jobless recovery.* Retrieved on May 9, 2003, from http://www.epinet.org

Conklin, J. E. (2003). *Why crime rates fell.* Boston: Pearson Education.

Employment Policy Foundation. (2000). *The American workplace 1998: Recent U.S. labor market trends.* Retrieved on May 9, 2003, from http://www.epf.org

Felson, M. (2002). *Crime and everyday life* (3rd ed.). Thousand Oaks, CA: Sage.

Fischer, C. S. (1975). Toward a subcultural theory of urbanism. *American Journal of Sociology, 80,* 1319–1341.

Gilbert, D. (1998). *The American class structure in an age of growing inequality.* Belmont, CA: Wadsworth.

Hoch, C. (1989). *A brief history of the homeless problem in the United States.* Philadelphia: Temple University Press.

Jargowsky, P. A. (1996). Take the money and run: Economic segregation in U.S. metropolitan areas. *American Sociological Review, 61,* 984–998.

Jargowsky, P. A. (1997). *Poverty and place: Ghettos, barrios, and the American city.* New York: Russell Sage Foundation.

Jargowsky, P. A. (2003). *Stunning progress, hidden problems: The dramatic decline of concentrated poverty in the 1990s.* Washington, D.C.: Brookings Institution, Center on Urban & Metropolitan Policy.

Jones, A. F., Jr., & Weinberg, D. H. (2002, June). *The changing shape of the nation's income distribution* (U.S. Census Bureau, Current Population Reports, P60–204). Washington, D.C.: U.S. Government Printing Office.

LaGory, M., Ritchey, F. J., O'Donoghue, T., & Mullins, J. (1989). Homelessness in Alabama: A variety of people and experiences. In J. A. Momeni (Ed.), *Homelessnes in the United States.* (pp. 1–20). New York: Greenwood Press.

Logan, J. R. (2002a). *Regional divisions dampen 90s prosperity: New census data show economic gains vary by region.* Albany, NY: University of Albany, Lewis Mumford Center for Comparative Urban and Regional Research.

Logan, J. R. (2002b). *The suburban advantage: New census data show unyielding city-suburban economic gap and surprising shifts in some places.* Albany, NY: University of Albany, Lewis Mumford Center for Comparative Urban and Regional Research.

Logan, J. R. (2002c) *Separate and unequal: The neighborhood gap for blacks and Hispanics in metropolitan America.* Albany, NY: University of Albany, Lewis Mumford Center for Comparative Urban and Regional Research.

Morris, M., & Western, B. (1999). Inequality in earnings at the close of the twentieth century. *Annual Review of Sociology, 25,* 623–657.

National Alliance to End Homelessness. (2003). *Facts and figures.* Retrieved on June 8, 2003, from http://www.endhomelessness.org/back/index.htm

National Coalition for the Homeless. (2002). *NCH fact sheet.* Retrieved on June 8, 2003, from http://www.nationalhomeless.org/who.html

Pastore, A. L., & Maguire, K. (Eds.). (2003, June). *Sourcebook of criminal justice statistics* [Electronic version]. Retrieved on June 18, 2003, from http://www.albany.edu/sourcebook

Proctor, B. D., & Dalaker, J. (2002). *Poverty in the United States: 2001.* (U.S. Census Bureau, Current Population Reports, P60–219). Washington, D.C.: U.S. Government Printing Office.

Reich, R. B. (1991). *The work of nations: Preparing ourselves for the 21st century.* New York: Knopf.

Rose, S. J. (2000). *Social stratification in the United States: The new American profile poster.* New York: New Press.

Sassen, S. (1990). Economic restructuring and the American city. *Annual Review of Sociology, 16,* 465–490.

Schmid, C. F. (1960a). Urban areas, part 1. *American Sociological Review, 25,* 527–542.

Schmid, C. F. (1960b). Urban areas, part 2. *American Sociological Review, 25,* 655–678.

Sernau, S. (2001). *Worlds apart: Social inequalities in a new century.* Thousand Oaks, CA: Pine Forge Press.

Shaw, C., Zorbaugh, H., McKay, H. D., & Cottrell, L. S. (1929). *Delinquency areas.* Chicago: University of Chicago Press.

Sherman, A. (1997). *Poverty matters: The cost of child poverty in America.* Washington, D.C.: Children's Defense Fund.

Short, K., & Shea, M. (1995, November). *Beyond poverty, extended measures of well-being: 1992.* (U.S. Census Bureau, Current Population Reports, P70–50rv). Washington, D.C.: U.S. Government Printing Office.

Smith, A. C., & Smith, D. I. (2001, October). *Emergency and transitional shelter population: 2000.* (U.S. Census Bureau, Census 2000 Special Reports CENSR/01–2). Washington, D.C.: U.S. Government Printing Office.

Snow, D. A., & Anderson, L. (1993). *Down of their luck: A study of homeless street people.* Berkeley, CA: University of California Press.

Thrasher. F. M. (1927). *The gang.* Chicago: University of Chicago Press.

U.S. Census Bureau, Statistical Research Division. (1976). *Bicentennial statistics.* (RR-26-102). Washington, D.C.: Government Printing Office.

U.S. Conference of Mayors. (2002, December). *A status report on hunger and homelessness in America's cities, 2002: A 25-city survey.* Retrieved on June 15, 2003, from http://www.usmayors.org/uscm/hungersurvey/2002/onlinereport/HungerAndHomel essReport2002.pdf

U.S. Conference of Mayors. (2003). *Nashville Mayor Purcell Celebrates Hunger Awareness Day June 5.* Retrieved on June 15, 2003, from http://www.usmayors.org/uscm/us_mayor_newspaper/documents/05_12_03/nashville.asp

U.S. Department of Housing and Urban Development (HUD). (2000). *A report on worst case housing needs in 1999: New opportunity amid continuing challenges.* Retrieved on June 15, 2003, from http://www.huduser.org/publications/afthsg/wc99.html

U.S. Department of Housing and Urban Development (2003). *Homelessness: Programs and the people they serve.* Retrieved on June 16, 2003, from http://www.huduser.org/publications/homeless/homelessness/highrpt.html

U.S. Department of Justice, Bureau of Justice Statistics. (2003). *National crime victimization study, 2001.* Retrieved on June 3, 2003, from http://www.ojp.usdoj.gov/bjs/pub/cv01.pdf

U.S. Department of Justice, Federal Bureau of Investigation. (2003). *Uniform crime report, 2001.* Retrieved on June 3, 2003, from http://www.fbi.gov/ucr/cius_01/01crime2.pdf

U.S. Department of Labor, Bureau of Labor Statistics. (1990). *Employment and Earning.* Washington, D.C. Government Printing Office.

U.S. Department of Labor, Bureau of Labor Statistics. (2003). *Tomorrow's jobs.* Retrieved on May 23, 2003, from http://stats.bls.gov/oco/oco2003.htm

Wilson, J. Q. (1983). *Thinking about crime.* New York:Vintage Books.

Wilson, W. J. (1987). *The truly disadvantaged: The inner city, the underclass, and public policy.* Chicago: University of Chicago Press.

Chapter 13

Atkin, R. (1998). *Suburbia revisited: Housing that promotes neighborliness through design.* Retrieved on June 3, 1998, from www.csmonitor.com

Berry, B. J. L. (1973). *The human consequences of urbanization: Divergent paths in the urban experience of the twentieth century.* New York: St. Martin's Press.

Brown, J. (2001, June 11). Where urban sprawl has some backers. *Christian Science Monitor, 3.*

Burchell, R. W. (Ed.). (1998). *The costs of sprawl: Revisited.* Washington, D.C.: National Academy Press.

Calthorpe, P. (2000). New urbanism and the apologists for sprawl. *Places 13*(2), 48–60.

Carson, R. (2000). Viewpoint: New urbanism. *Planning, 66*(8), 54–56.

Congress for the New Urbanism. (2001). *Charter for the new urbanism.* Retrieved on June 7, 2001, from http://www.cnu.org

Downs, A. (2001). What does 'smart growth' really mean. *Planning, 67*(4), 20–25.

Duany, A., Plater-Zyberk, E., & Speck, J. (2000). *Suburban nation: The rise of sprawl and the decline of the American dream.* New York: North Point Press.

El Nasser, H. (2001). Sprawl: Not what you'd expect. Retrieved on February 22, 2001, from http://www.usatoday.com

Glasser, J. (2001). *Boomtown, U.S.A.: In Arkansas, a new economy—and an unlikely Xanadu.* Retrieved on June 22, 2001, from http://www/usnews.com/usnews/issue/010625/usnews/arkansas.htm

Glendening, P. N. (2001). *2001 Legislative session: A solid record of success; a solid foundation for Maryland's future.* Retrieved on June 22, 2001, from http://www.gov.state.md.us/gov/legagenda/2001/html/legisaccom2001.html

Harvey, D. (1985). *The urbanization of capital: Studies in the history and theory of capitalist urbanization.* Baltimore, MD: The Johns Hopkins University Press.

Kim, J. (2000). Creating community: Does the Kentlands live up to its goals? *Places, 13*(2), 33–39.

Kunstler, J. H. (1993). *The geography of nowhere: The rise and decline of America's manmade landscape.* New York: Simon & Schuster.

Kunstler, J. (1996). *Home from nowhere: Remaking our everyday world for the twenty-first century.* New York: Simon & Schuster.

Langdon, P. (1997). Can design make community? *Responsive Community, 7*(2), 25–37.

Lehrer, U., & Milgrom, R. (1998). New (sub)urbanism: Countersprawl or repackaging the product. *Capitalism, Nature, Socialism, 7*(2(26)), 49–64.

Li, J., & Wachs, M. (2001, Spring). How federal subsidies shape local transit choices. *Access: Transportation Research at the University of California, 18,* 11–14.

Molotch, H. L., & Logan, J. R. (1987). *Urban fortunes: The political economy of place.* Berleley, CA: University of California Press.

Muto, S. (1999, August 4). Valuing new urbanism: The case of Kentlands. *Wall Street Journal,* 6.

Padgett, T. (August 16, 1999). *Saving suburbia. Time Magazine Online Edition.* Retrieved on July 11, 2001, from http:www/time.com

Paul, N. C. (April 5, 2001). *Putting people back into architecture* [Electronic version]. *Christian Science Monitor.* Retrieved on July 11, 2001, from www.csmonitor.com

Plater-Zyberk, E., Duany, A., & Speck, J. (2000, December). *Suburban nation: The rise of sprawl and the decline of the American dream.* New York: North Point Press.

Putnam, R. D. (2000, December). *Bowling alone: The collapse and revival of American community.* New York: Simon & Schuster.

Salisbury, D. F. (March 11, 1996). *Cities plan to build a sense of community* [Electronic version]. *Christian Science Monitor.* Retrieved on July 11, 2001, from http://www.csmonitor.com

Sands, E. (1998). New urbanism triumphs in Washington, D.C. *Architectural Record,* 32–33.

Schwab, W. A. (1992). *The sociology of cities.* Englewood Cliffs, NJ: Prentice Hall.

Smith, W. C. (2000, December). The brawl over sprawl. *American Bar Association Journal, 51,* 48–52.

Sneider, D. (April 17, 1996). *To halt sprawl, San Jose draws green line in sand* [Electronic version]. *Christian Science Monitor.* Retrieved on July 11, 2001, from http://www.csmonitor.com

Stein, C. S. (1966). *Toward new towns for America.* Cambridge, MA: MIT Press.

Steuteville, R. (1998). Sustainable development meets new urbanism. *In Business, 20*(4), 26–30.

Stevens, W. K. (December 7, 1999). Sprawl quickens its attack on forests. [Electronic version]. *New York Times.* Retrieved on September 16, 2000, from http://www.nytimes.com

Trumbull, M. (May 2, 1994). *Seattle fights urban sprawl with 'villages'* [Electronic version]. *Christian Science Monitor.* Retrieved on September 19, 2000, from http://www.csmonitor.com

Tu, C. C., & Eppli, M. J. (1999). Valuing new urbanism: The case of Kentlands. *Real Estate Economics, 27*(3), 425–451.

Tyler, A. F. (1944). *Freedom's ferment: Phases of American social history from the colonial period to the outbreak of the Civil War.* Minneapolis: University of Minnesota Press.

Tyson, A. S. (March 21, 1997). *Urban sprawl's appetite for rich farmland* [Electronic version]. *Christian Science Monitor.* Retrieved on September 16, 2000, from http://www.csmonitor.com

U.S. Department of Housing and Urban Development. (1999). Rebuilding communities: Hope VI and new urbanism. *Places, 12*(3), 72–75.

U.S. Department of Housing and Urban Development (2001). Hope VI: Community Building Makes a Difference. Retrieved on June 22, 2001, from http://www.huduser.org:80/periodicals/rrr/rrr_3_2000/0300_4.html

Von Hoffman, A. (1999). *Housing heats up: Home building patterns in metropolitan areas.* Washington, D.C.: The Brookings Institution, Center on Urban and Metropolitan Policy.

Wells, B. (2001). *Governors' smart growth initiatives.* Washington, D.C.: Northeast-Midwest Institute.

Wood, D. B. (September 11, 1997). *Suburbia consumes California's fruit basket to the world* [Electronic version]. *Christian Science Monitor.* Retrieved on September 16, 2000, from http://www.csmonitor.com

Author Index

Subject Index